BUILDINGS OF VIRGINIA
Tidewater and Piedmont

Buildings of the United States is a series of books on American architecture compiled and written on a state-by-state basis. The primary objective of the series is to identify and celebrate the rich cultural, economic, and geographical diversity of the United States as it is reflected in the architecture of each state. The series has been commissioned by the Society of Architectural Historians, an organization dedicated to the study, interpretation, and preservation of the built environment throughout the world.

Buildings of Alaska
Alison K. Hoagland (1993)

Buildings of Colorado
Thomas J. Noel (1997)

Buildings of the District of Columbia
Pamela Scott and Antoinette J. Lee (1993)

Buildings of Iowa
David Gebhard and Gerald Mansheim (1993)

Buildings of Michigan
Kathryn Bishop Eckert (1993)

Buildings of Nevada
Julie Nicoletta, with photographs by Bret Morgan (2000)

Buildings of
VIRGINIA

Tidewater and Piedmont

EDITED BY

RICHARD GUY WILSON

WITH CONTRIBUTIONS BY

Sara A. Butler, Edward Chappell

Sarah Shields Driggs, Hal Larsen

Debra A. McClane, Thomas Tyler Potterfield, Jr.

William M. S. Rasmussen, Selden Richardson

Edwin Slipek, Jr., Marc C. Wagner, Robert Wojtowicz

and Others

OXFORD
UNIVERSITY PRESS

2002

OXFORD
UNIVERSITY PRESS

Oxford   New York
Auckland   Bangkok   Buenos Aires   Cape Town   Chennai
Dar es Salaam   Delhi   Hong Kong   Istanbul   Karachi   Kolkata
Kuala Lumpur   Madrid   Melbourne   Mexico City   Mumbai   Nairobi
São Paulo   Shanghai   Singapore   Taipei   Tokyo   Toronto

and an associated company in Berlin

Copyright © 2002 by the Society of Architectural Historians
1365 North Astor Street, Chicago, Illinois, 60610-2144

Published by Oxford University Press, Inc.
198 Madison Avenue, New York, New York 10016

www.oup.com

Oxford is a registered trademark of Oxford University Press

Library of Congress Cataloging-in-Publication Data
Buildings of Virginia : Tidewater and Piedmont / edited by Richard Guy Wilson ;
with contributions by Sara A. Butler . . . [et al.].
p. cm. — (Buildings of the United States)
Includes bibliographical references and index.
ISBN 0-19-515206-9
1. Architecture—Virginia—Guidebooks. I. Wilson, Richard Guy, 1940–
II. Butler, Sara A., 1952– III. Series.
NA730.V8 B85 2002
720'.9755—dc21   2002001454

2 4 6 8 9 7 5 3 1

Printed in the United States of America
on acid-free paper

The Society of Architectural Historians gratefully acknowledges the support of the following donors whose generous gifts helped bring Buildings of Virginia: Tidewater and Piedmont *to publication:*

National Endowment for the Humanities,
an independent federal agency

Getty Grant Program

A private Richmond foundation

Mary Morton Parsons Foundation

Beirne Carter Foundation

Richard S. Reynolds Foundation

The late Paul Mellon

Dr. and Mrs. John L. McClenahan

University of Delaware

David Tennant Bryan

Edmund A. Rennolds, Jr.

A number of other Virginians throughout the state

Southeast and Latrobe chapters of the
Society of Architectural Historians

Many individual members of the SAH

*Initial and ongoing support for
the Buildings of the United States series has come from*

National Endowment for the Humanities

Graham Foundation for Advanced Studies in the Fine Arts

Pew Charitable Trusts

University of Delaware

College of Fellows of the American Institute of Architects

Contents

List of Maps

Foreword

Buildings of Virginia: Tidewater and Piedmont is the seventh of a projected fifty-eight volumes in the series Buildings of the United States, which is sponsored by the Society of Architectural Historians (SAH). The first volume for the South, it will also, together with the forthcoming *Buildings of Virginia: The Valley, South, and West,* form part of the first multi-volume set devoted to a single state. When the series is completed, it will provide a detailed survey and history of the architecture of the whole country, including both vernacular and high-style structures for a complete range of building types from skyscrapers to barns and everything in between.

The idea for such a series was in the minds of the founders of the SAH in the early 1940s, but it was not brought to fruition until Nikolaus Pevsner, the eminent British architectural historian who had conceived and carried out Buildings of England, originally published between 1951 and 1974, challenged SAH to do for this country what he had done for his. That was in 1976, and it was another ten years before we were able to organize the effort, commission authors for the initial group of volumes, and secure the first funding, a grant from the National Endowment for the Humanities. Matched by grants from the Pew Charitable Trusts, the Graham Foundation, and the Michigan Bicentennial Commission, this enabled us to produce the first four volumes, *Buildings of Michigan, Buildings of Iowa, Buildings of Alaska,* and *Buildings of the District of Columbia,* all of which were published in 1993. *Buildings of Colorado* followed in 1997 and *Buildings of Nevada* in 2000. Another thirteen volumes are expected in the next five years, with many more to follow.

Although Buildings of England provided the model, in both method and approach Buildings of the United States was to be as different as American architecture is from English. Pevsner was confronted by a coherent culture on a relatively small island, with an architectural history that spans more than two thousand years. Here we are dealing with a vast land of immense regional, geographic, climatic, and ethnic diversity, with most of its buildings—wide-ranging, exciting, and sometimes dramatic—essentially concentrated into the last four hundred years, although with significant Native American remains stretching back well beyond that. In contrast to the national integrity of English architecture, therefore, American architecture is marked by a dynamic heterogeneity, a heterogeneity woven of a thousand strands of originality, or, actually, a unity woven of a thousand strands of heterogeneity. It is this quality that Buildings of the United States reflects and records.

Unity born of heterogeneity was a condition of American architecture from the first European settlements of the sixteenth and seventeenth centuries. Not only did the buildings of the Russian, Spanish, French, Dutch, Swedish, and English colonies differ according to national origin (to say nothing of their differences from Native American structures), but in the translation to North America they also assumed a special scale and character, qualities that were largely determined by the aspirations and traditions of a people struggling to fashion a new world in an abundant but demanding land. Diversity marked even the English colonies of the Eastern Seaboard, though they shared a common architectural heritage. The brick mutations of English prototypes in the Virginia Colony, as exemplified in the present volume, were very different, for example, from the wooden architecture of the Massachusetts Bay Colony. They were different because Virginia was a farm and plantation society dominated by the Anglican church, whereas Massachusetts was a communal society nurtured entirely by Puritanism. But they were different also because of natural resources and the traditions of the parts of England from which the settlers had come. As the colonies became a nation and developed westward, similar radical contrasts became the way of America's growth. The infinite variety of physical environment, together with the complex origins and motivations of the settlers, made it inevitable that each new state would have a character uniquely its own.

The primary objective of each volume, therefore, is to record, analyze, and evaluate the architecture of the state. The authors are trained architectural historians who are thoroughly informed in the local aspects of their subjects. In each volume, special conditions that shaped the state or part of the state, together with the building types necessary to meet those conditions, are identified and discussed; barns, silos, mining buildings, factories, warehouses, bridges, and transportation buildings take their places alongside the familiar building types conventional to the nation as a whole—churches, courthouses, city halls, commercial structures, and the infinite variety of domestic architecture. Although the great national and international masters of American architecture receive proper attention, especially in the volumes for the states in which they did their greatest work, outstanding local architects, as well as the buildings of skilled but often anonymous carpenter-builders, are also brought prominently into the picture. Each volume is thus a detailed and precise portrait of the architecture of the state that it represents. At the same time, however, all of these local issues are examined as they relate to architectural developments in the country at large. Volumes will continue to appear state by state until every state is represented. When the overview and inventory are completed, the series will form a comprehensive history of the architecture of the United States.

These volumes deal with more than the highlights and the high points of architecture in this country. They deal with the very fabric of American architecture, with the context in time and in place of each specific building, with the entirety of urban and rural America, with the whole architectural patrimony. This fabric includes modern architecture, as, on the other end of the scale, it includes pre-Columbian and Native American remains. But it must be said, regretfully, that the series cannot cover every building of merit; practical considerations have dictated some difficult choices in the buildings that are represented in this as in other volumes. There are, unavoidably, omissions from the abundance of structures built across the land, the thousands of modest but lovely edifices and the vernacular attempts that merit a second look but which by their very multitude cannot be included in even the thickest volume.

Thus it must be stated in the strongest possible terms that omission of a building from this or any volume of the series does not constitute an invitation to the bulldozers and the wrecking ball. In every community there will be structures not included in Buildings of the United States that are clearly deserving of being preserved. Indeed, it is hoped that the publication of this series will help to stop at least the worst destruction of architecture across the land by fostering a deeper appreciation of its beauty and richness and of its historic and associative importance.

The volumes of Buildings of the United States are meant to be tools of serious research in the study of American architecture. But they are also intended as guidebooks for everyone interested in the buildings of this country and are designed to facilitate such use; they can and should be used on the spot, indeed, should lead the user to the spot. It is our earnest hope that they will be not only on the shelves of every library from major research centers to neighborhood public libraries, but that they will also be in a great many raincoat pockets, glove compartments, and backpacks.

During the long gestation process of the series, many have come forward with generous assistance. We are especially grateful, both for financial support for the series as a whole and for confidence in our efforts, to the National Endowment for the Humanities, the Graham Foundation for Advanced Studies in the Fine Arts, the Pew Charitable Trusts, and the College of Fellows of the American Institute of Architects. For this volume, we are also enormously indebted to the Getty Grant Program, the Mary Morton Parsons Foundation, a private Richmond foundation, the Beirne Carter Foundation, the Richard S. Reynolds Foundation, the late Paul Mellon, Dr. and Mrs. John L. McClenahan, the University of Delaware, the Southeast and Latrobe chapters of the Society of Architectural Historians, and many individual members of the SAH. We are thankful, too, to the members of the BUS Leadership Development Committee: J. Carter Brown, Madelyn Bell Ewing, Elizabeth Harris, Ada Louise Huxtable, Philip Johnson, Keith Morgan, Victoria Newhouse, and Robert Venturi.

We are very grateful to Dean Larry Clark of the University of Missouri and to Provost Mel Schiavelli and Deans Mary Richards, Margaret Andersen, and Thomas DiLorenzo of the College of Arts and Science at the University of Delaware for providing institutional support for two successive editors in chief of the series.

Our gratitude extends to many other individuals. These include a large number of presidents, executive committees, and boards of directors of the SAH, going back at least to the adoption of the project by the Society in 1979, and a series of executive directors covering that same span. All of these individuals have supported the series in words and deeds, and without them it would not have seen the light of day.

We would also like to express our appreciation to the current members of our editorial board, listed earlier in this volume, and the following former members: Adolf K. Placzek,

Richard Betts, Catherine Bishir, J. A. Chewning, S. Allen Chambers, Jr., Alex Cochran, John Freeman, David Gebhard, Alan Gowans, Alison K. Hoagland, William H. Jordy, Robert Kapsch, Henry Magaziner, Tom Martinson, Sally Kress Tompkins, and Robert J. Winter. Of this group, we would like especially to single out Dolf Placzek, founding editor in chief, who served in that capacity from the early 1980s to 1989 and continued to play a major role in the project until his death in the spring of 2000.

We have tried to establish as far as possible a consistent terminology of architectural history, and we are especially appreciative of the efforts of J. A. Chewning in the creation of the series glossary included in every volume. The *Art and Architecture Thesaurus*, a comprehensive publication and database compiled by The Getty Art History Information Program and published by Oxford University Press, has also become an invaluable resource.

In our fund-raising efforts we have benefited enormously from the services of our wonderful directors of development, first Anita Nowery Durel and then Barbara Reed, as well as associate director of development William Cosper, and of our administrative staff: first fiscal coordinator Hillary Stone and then comptroller William Tyre; and the current executive director of the SAH, Pauline Saliga, who is the fiscal officer for the project.

Editorial work for this volume was overseen by our excellent managing editor for the series, Cynthia Ware. Winfield Swanson provided assistance with copy editing, Inge Lockwood read the proof, and Jennifer Rushing-Schurr compiled the index. Maps were prepared by the Geographic Resources Center in the Department of Geography at the University of Missouri–Columbia, under the project management of Andrew Dolan. Research assistants at the University of Delaware were Jhennifer Amundson, Anna Andrzewjewski, Heather Campbell, Ellen Menefee, Martha Hagood, Nancy Holst, Amy Johnson, Sarah Killinger, and Louis Nelson.

Finally, there are our present and former colleagues in this enterprise at Oxford University Press in New York and Cary, North Carolina, especially Ed Barry, Laura Brown, Claude Conyers, Karen Casey, Karen Day, Ralph Carlson, Stephen Chasteen, Matt Giarratano, Nancy Hoagland, Mark Mones, Robert Oppedisano, Rebecca Seger, and Leslie Phillips.

To all of these we are enormously grateful.

Damie Stillman
Osmund Overby
William H. Pierson, Jr.

Acknowledgments

Buildings of Virginia: Tidewater and Piedmont began in the fall of 1992 when Damie Stillman, then coeditor in chief of the Buildings of the United States series, approached me about undertaking the project. I had just completed, in tandem with several colleagues, the exhibition and book *The Making of Virginia Architecture* and was well aware of the complexities of treating the varied riches of the commonwealth. I tentatively agreed, but with the conditions that I would work with collaborators and build on an earlier attempt at a BUS volume on Virginia undertaken by Hal Larsen. Other projects intervened, but by January 1996 we began to hold meetings and divide responsibilities for the project. With Anne Carter Lee, the editor of the BUS volume on western Virginia (*Buildings of Virginia: The Valley, South, and West*, forthcoming), we split the state between the two volumes.

Primary collaborators for the eastern section and their geographical areas of responsibility are as follows: Sara A. Butler, architectural historian, Roger Williams University (Charlottesville and Albemarle County and assistant editor for the volume); Edward Chappell, director, Architectural Research Department, Colonial Williamsburg Foundation (Williamsburg and area, Rosewell, and selected seventeenth- and eighteenth-century sites); Sarah Shields Driggs, architectural historian (Richmond); Debra A. McClane, architectural historian (southern Tidewater); Thomas Tyler Potterfield, Jr., senior planner for environmental and historic review, Department of Community Development, City of Richmond (Richmond; Loudoun County excluding Leesburg); William Rasmussen, curator, Virginia Historical Society (selected entries on eighteenth-century buildings); Selden Richardson, archivist for architectural records, The Library of Virginia (Richmond); Edwin Slipek, Jr., architecture critic, *Style* magazine, Richmond (Richmond); Marc C. Wagner, architectural historian, Virginia Department of Historic Resources, Richmond (Richmond and Henrico County); Robert Wojtowicz, Department of Art, Old Dominion University (Norfolk, Virginia Beach, Portsmouth, Hampton Roads). I was responsible for the Eastern Shore, northern Virginia, Alexandria, Peninsulas, Fredericksburg and metropolitan area, Piedmont, Charlottesville, portions of Hampton Roads, and, in the Northern Piedmont, Leesburg and Fauquier County. I have served as editor, attempting to ensure uniformity of material.

In addition to selecting sites and writing entries for their specific areas, all of these individuals have offered extensive advice on other areas and buildings and have contributed in many other ways. They are fully joint authors of this volume.

For financial support of all phases of manuscript development I and my coauthors are indebted to the Society of Architectural Historians and to the organizations and individuals whose contributions are acknowledged in the front of this volume. Thanks to Damie Stillman and C. Ford Peatross, who reviewed the manuscript on behalf of the Buildings of the United States editorial board and to Cynthia Ware, whose astute editing greatly helped this volume.

The many illustrations come from a variety of sources, which are credited preceding the index. New photography was supplied by William Sublette, Jason R. Waicunas, and Pierre Courtois. Sara Butler and Ann Hunter McLane researched archival photographs. I and my coauthors also gratefully acknowledge help in obtaining photographs from Suzanne Durham, Department of Historic Resources, Commonwealth of Virginia; Ginger Mauler, Picture Collection, Library of Virginia; Margaret D. Hraber, Special Collections, Alderman Library, University of Virginia; and Monica Rumsey, director of publications, Virginia Museum of Fine Arts.

The following individuals provided great assistance and in some cases entries: Stephen Bedford (John Russell Pope), Anne E. Bruder (Plains), David S. Cannon (Tysons Corner), Cary Carson (Jamestown), Kimble A. David (Thomas U. Walter in Norfolk), Kathryn A. Gettings (Hilton Village), Julia King (Peninsulas and Fredericksburg), Carl Lounsbury (eighteenth-century Virginia courthouses and churches), Bridget Maley (Mount Airy), Ann Miller (Montpelier), Susan E. Smead (Henrico County), Camille Wells (Menokin), Mark R. Wenger (Westover, Nelson House, Yorktown), Tony Wrenn (Fredericksburg).

The contributions of others were essential to realization of this volume. Calder Loth, senior architectural historian, Department of Historic Resources, one of the most knowledgeable authorities on Virginia architecture and author of *The Virginia Landmarks Register*, assisted in many ways. Marc Wagner, in addition to being an author, through his position as National Register coordinator, Department of Historic Resources, provided material, frequently on short notice. The files of the Department of Historic Resources and register nominations, representing the work of many people over the years, were critical to a number of entries. University and college students have contributed to this volume through their papers, National Register entries, and theses. John Wells and Robert E. Dalton's *Virginia Architects, 1835–1955* (1997), an indispensable tool for the study of Virginia architecture, appeared at a crucial time. Robert P. Winthrop's books on Richmond provided a basis for many of our entries. The late Betty Leake, secretary, Department of Architectural History, University of Virginia, helped in many ways. To all of them a heartfelt thank you.

This volume depended on the research and writing of a number of others who answered questions and provided information: William Bergen, on the Civil War; David Edwards, on Loudoun County; David W. Gaddy, on Tappahannock churches; Fred Lee George III, Fred Lee George, Jr., and Suzanne George, all on Loudoun County; Willie Graham, on early Virginia architecture; David L. Holmes, on churches; Greg Hunt, on Hollin Hills; Randall Jennings James, on Richmond; Asa Moore Janney, on Waterford; K. Edward Lay, on Albemarle County; Robert Legard, on Lovettsville; Joseph Dye Lehandro, on Pear Valley and other sites; John Lewis, on Loudoun County; Richard Longstreth, on northern Virginia housing; Vernon Mays, on recent architecture; Maura J. Meinhardt, on Oregon Hill and Hollywood Cemetery, Richmond; the late Floyd Nock, on the Eastern Shore; Nicholas Page, on railroad stations; Virginia Fisher and Denis Pogue, on Mount Vernon; Virginia Raguin, on stained glass; Peter Smith and Al Cox, on Alexandria; Craig Tuminaro, on Woodlawn; Edmund Tyler, on Warrenton; Joseph Senter White, on Richmond; Robert Wire, on Loudoun County. In addition, I and my coauthors thank T. Patrick Brennan, director of historic houses, Chrysler Museum of Art; Peggy Haile, Norfolk city historian; Doris R. McTague, historian, Old Donation Episcopal Church; James R. and Marilyn S. Melchor, architectural historians, Portsmouth Regional Office; Mark Reed, administrator, Francis Land House Historic Site and Garden; Patricia H. Spriggs, architectural historian; Fielding L. Tyler, executive director, Old Coast Guard Station; Mary Ruffin Viles, architectural historian, Department of Historic Resources.

Many libraries, museums, and historical societies not already mentioned also contributed, including the Association for the Preservation of Virginia Antiquities; Fiske Kimball Fine Arts Library, University of Virginia; Eastern Shore Library; Chrysler Museum; Manassas Museum; Purcellville Library; Culpeper Historical Museum; The Library of Virginia; Thomas Balch Library of Leesburg; and the Virginia Historical Society.

Richard Guy Wilson

Guide for Users of This Volume

This guide covers the eastern half of Virginia, specifically, the part of the state from the Atlantic coast and Chesapeake Bay to the area east of the Blue Ridge Mountains known as the Piedmont (see Eastern Virginia map, p. 6). It is broken down into fourteen geographical sections, each covering either a city, with its neighborhoods and outlying areas, or a group of several or more counties comprising urban centers, small towns, and dispersed rural sites. Within each section, sites are arranged in touring order. Overview maps of each region or city as well as many street-level maps, keyed to entries by site number, are included; commercially published state road atlases that provide a good supplement are easily available. Sites that are open to the public are so noted in entry headings. Some historic houses are open during Historic Garden Week, sponsored annually in late April by the Garden Club of Virginia in Richmond. In general, buildings that are not visible from a public road and whose exterior viewing would entail trespassing are excluded, though there are a few exceptions to this rule (noted as "not visible" in the entry heading).

In the 1,500 individual buildings, landscapes, and other entities selected, this volume attempts both to note the high points and to sketch out a built environment that is truly representative of Virginia's history and society. The traditional focus of much of Virginia studies has been on the English inheritance, typified by the mythic FFV (first family of Virginia), which has the name Lee, Byrd, Carter, or Randolph somewhere in its family tree, is Episcopalian, and owns a large eighteenth-century red brick Georgian plantation house on the James. Some of this aspect of Virginia history is represented here, since myths do reflect realities, but Virginia also has significant population groups of other origins (Scots-Irish, continental European, African American, and Asian) and religious affiliations (Baptists, Presbyterians, Jews, Catholics, Pentecostals, Buddhists, and members of other religious groups), whose buildings are included in this volume. Although the title of the series is Buildings of the United States, that is interpreted to include settings for buildings: landscapes (including agricultural, memorial, and recreational), roads, and, where appropriate, notable sculpture and other accessories.

Many important buildings are not mentioned in this book, and the noninclusion of a building should not imply that it has no value. Although this guide has drawn extensively from the listings on the Virginia Register and the National Register of Historic Places, the selective criteria of those two registers are very different from those applied here. The registers include buildings and places of historical, but not necessarily architectural, significance and exclude anything less than fifty years old, whereas this guide includes buildings recently completed and even still under construction. Sorting out the tremendous building activity of the twentieth century in Virginia has required being very selective, and certainly a guidebook compiled fifty years from now will criticize the omissions of this selection. In many cases the devices of group entries and walking and driving tours are employed in an attempt to cover more sites. Many small towns are treated, since they are an important part of Virginia, but frequently their treatment is very brief.

One guiding principle has been that what is included should help provide some sense of the history of the built environment. The emphasis is on buildings that provide and express identity and community; hence, this volume describes government structures, churches, and institutions that have served as centers of community life and in many cases have architectural features distinctive to their locales. A special characteristic of Virginia's built environment has been isolation: small county courthouses with subsidiary buildings in rural settings, churches in similarly lonely locations. In describing them, this guide tries to demonstrate how important they are to the texture of the built environment. Designs by nationally known architects and landscape architects are noted, along with what is judged to be the best-known work of important Virginia designers. At the same time structures that make up the everyday texture of cities, such as vernacular buildings and houses constructed from pattern books and kits, are represented. Many structures from the seventeenth century are included since survivors are so rare. But the vast number of structures from the eighteenth and early nineteenth centuries has meant selectivity, identifying and describing those buildings that are most easily seen and best display the characteristics of their particular idioms. Given the strong presence of the past in Virginia, various forms of the Colonial Revival are extensively represented here. In the same way that history is made not just by those who act in the event but by those who record it, architectural history is made not only by those who commission, design, build, and live in buildings, but by how buildings are interpreted and restored. Wherever possible, building information notes names of restorers, what is original, and what has been replaced.

BUILDINGS OF VIRGINIA
Tidewater and Piedmont

Introduction

F OR MOST VIRGINIANS THE LEGACY OF THEIR COMMONWEALTH, OR, AS IT IS nicknamed, the Old Dominion, is not simply local, but of paramount national significance. As an editorial cartoon from a 1939 number of the *Richmond News Leader* graphically asserted, the United States, as we traditionally conceive of it, began in Virginia when the English founded Jamestown in 1607. Sir Walter Raleigh named the colony for Elizabeth I, the Virgin Queen, and the name implies the promise the early settlers saw. At the very beginning, Captain John Smith proclaimed Virginia a "country that may have the prerogative over the most pleasant places of Europe, Asia, Africa, or America. . . . Here are mountains, hills, plains, valleys, rivers and brooks all running most pleasantly into a fair bay compassed, but for the mouth, with fruitful and delightsome land."[1]

The home of many of the founding fathers and early political leaders of the nation, Virginia was also the center of the Confederacy, and on its soil were fought some of the bloodiest battles of the Civil War. It has been the home of national heroes and heroines, from Pocahontas and George Washington to Bill "Bojangles" Robinson and Arthur Ashe. Until 1820 Virginia, as both colony and state, led the country in population. Richmond, the state capital from 1779 onward, conceived of itself as the first city of the South, and until the 1890s, when other regional cities surpassed it in population and manufacturing, it was the leading southern metropolis in finance, production of goods, and, many would claim, sophistication. Norfolk and the Tidewater cities were early commercial and shipping centers for the new country. Agriculturally, Virginia was and remains a major producer of livestock, corn, peanuts, and "green gold," as Captain Smith called tobacco. From the 1930s onward a new aspect of Virginia's legacy opened as the northern part of the state closest to Washington, D.C., became the locus for military bases, the Pentagon, massive suburbanization, and "Edge City."

Artistically and culturally, Virginia's greatest legacy is its architecture. Far more than through painting, literature, or any other traditional art form, it is through built form that

3

Fred O. Seibel, "Birthplace of America," *Richmond News Leader,* January 1, 1939

Virginia has been known and has influenced the nation. George Washington's Mount Vernon and Thomas Jefferson's Monticello easily rank as two of the most famous historic houses in the United States and among the most visited. Colonial Williamsburg is the touchstone for understanding eighteenth-century life in this country as well as the paramount example of restoration on a large scale. Most Americans know of it even if they have not visited it. Virginia's prototypical houses—the large red brick, white-trimmed manorial house and the small, one-and-one-half-story clapboard cottage—and architectural details such as the spindly posts of Mount Vernon's portico can be found all across the United States. Scarcely an American city lacks evidence of the Virginia heritage. Over the last century the study and preservation of Virginia's early architecture has been the state's most important contribution to the nation.

But the built environment of Virginia is far more than grand houses or restored colonial villages. It is, beginning with Jamestown in 1607, the nearly four-centuries-old accumulation of the traditional perspective of most American history. Eastern Virginia has been molded almost constantly by the hand of man for thousands of years—and much more intensely in the past four hundred. Scarcely a place, from cleared fields, now so overgrown that they appear natural, to the coastal area, has not been altered in some artificial manner. Before the English settled here, Native Americans tended and shaped the land and constructed buildings and villages, although very little remains of their culture. Moreover, many European-built buildings have also disappeared, leaving faint trace.

Nevertheless, the remaining built legacy of Virginia is vast, and, from a broad architectural point of view, every constructed element and every alteration or artificial mark on the landscape contains some level of significance and can be interpreted. Of course not everything can be included here. The purpose of a guide such as this, and of architectural history, is to select: to choose those buildings, cities, towns, and landscapes that tell both representative and unique stories.

Virginia contains an embarrassment of riches, from its well-known and high-profile buildings to its hidden treasures. Traditionally, most attention has focused on the colonial and the antebellum periods. There is an old saying: "In Virginia, history stops in 1826" (or 1840, or 1860). The date depends on who is talking, but the fact remains that the past is very present in Virginia, and especially in its historic architecture and the mania for reproducing it. However, in recent years interest in later architecture—for instance, Victorian and even early modern—has risen.

The amount of published material on Virginia architecture would make even the most compulsive bibliophile quake. More has probably been written about its buildings than those of any other state. Earlier than any other state, Virginia had a statewide historic preservation organization, the Association for the Preservation of Virginia Antiquities (APVA, founded 1889); its efforts, along with others, have staved off the destruction of some important elements of the past. Still, too much has been lost. The program in architectural history at the University of Virginia, established in 1958, was the first in the nation.

In 1965 the commonwealth's General Assembly began to consider what role the state should have in the preservation of the past. Its examination led in 1966—well before such measures in most other states—to the establishment of the Virginia Historic Landmarks Commission, now the Virginia Department of Historic Resources. By 2001 the Historic Resources staff had placed on either the Virginia Register or the National Register of Historic Places more than 2,100 buildings and places and more than 230 historic districts. It is estimated that more than 50,000 resources (buildings, landscapes, sites) are included. The staff maintains files on approximately 100,000 properties. A compilation of this listing, *The Virginia Landmarks Register*, is in its fourth edition (1999). Several cities, such as Richmond, Leesburg, and Alexandria, have architectural historians on their planning staffs. Virginia is probably the only state that has had two exhibitions devoted to architectural drawings of its buildings, the first in 1969 and another in 1992, and a guidebook to its architecture published as early as 1968.[2] All of these activities and publications and the many more noted later in this introduction and in the bibliography indicate the tremendous richness—and the problem of selection (see Guide for Users of This Volume, preceding this introduction).

The Contours of Eastern Virginia's Built Environment

During the colonial period and until 1784, Virginia claimed lands that stretched to the Mississippi River; indeed, it was the largest of the original thirteen states. Until 1863, the area that is now the state of West Virginia was part of the Commonwealth of Virginia. This volume

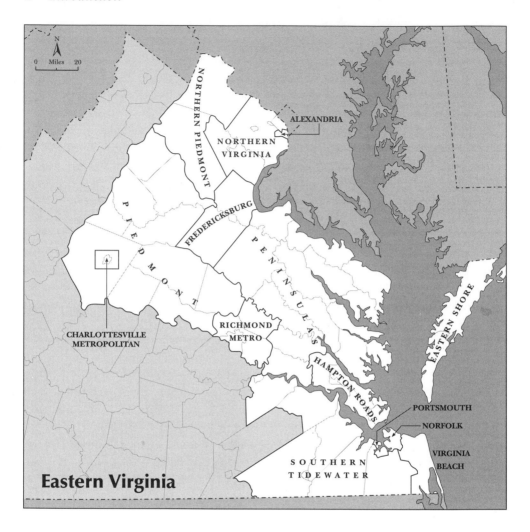

covers the eastern portion of present-day Virginia, defined as the area that lies between the Atlantic and the Blue Ridge Mountains. A companion volume will cover the western portion.[3] Eastern Virginia comprises three distinct geographical regions: at the east, the Eastern Shore and the Tidewater; to the west, the Piedmont; and, at the western edge, the Blue Ridge. At the eastern edge of the state, hanging down as a guillotine blade ready to shut the mouth of the Chesapeake, is the Eastern Shore, a large peninsula of land physically connected to Maryland, not Virginia. Topographically flat and hauntingly beautiful, it is dominated by agriculture and fishing. The vast region of the Tidewater incorporates both Atlantic seacoast and Chesapeake bayfront. The Tidewater is dominated by major rivers: the Potomac at the north, the Rappahannock and the York in the middle, and the James and a series of smaller estuaries—such as the Nansemond, the Elizabeth, the North Landing, and the man-made Atlantic Intracoastal Waterway at the southern edge—which create a series of large, almost flat peninsulas. Major cities—Norfolk, Portsmouth, Hampton, Newport News, and Virginia Beach—are located at critical junctures of land and water. Suburban fallout has spread adjacent to the cities and the water, whereas the remainder of the Tidewater is rural, open fields for crops, woodland, and small towns or villages. The boundary of the Tidewater at the west is an axis running almost straight north from Richmond to Washington, D.C. (95 miles and almost directly paralleled by I-95), known as the fall line, in reference to the small falls that occur as rivers flow out of the Piedmont onto the lower coastal, or Tidewater, plain. Traditionally (though not really), the fall line has marked the limits of navigation. Along the line from south to north are the major cities of Richmond, on the James River; Fredericksburg, on the Rappahannock River; and Alexandria, on the Potomac across from Washington, D.C. The Piedmont, which stretches to the west, grows in its uneven topography and crescendoes with the dramatic uplift of the Blue Ridge Mountains at the far edge. It is cut not only by the rivers noted above, but by smaller, though also navigable, rivers such as the Rapidan and the Rivanna. The Piedmont is largely agricultural, though with a growing light industrial and technological base. Along the western edge and skirting the base of the Blue Ridge Mountains are the population centers of Charlottesville in the south and, progressing north, Culpeper, Warrenton, and Leesburg. It is 165 miles from the western edge of the Piedmont at Charlottesville to the eastern edge of the Tidewater at Virginia Beach, and 100 miles from Charlottesville at the south to the northern edge in Loudoun County—a distance enhanced before railroads by the lack of north-south rivers.

These geographical distinctions and distances divide eastern Virginia into four very different parts, almost separate entities: the Tidewater, the Eastern Shore, the Piedmont, and northern Virginia. An additional division is the usual disjuncture between large metropolitan and rural areas. Eastern Virginia also represents many different settlement types: large metropolitan cities of about 200,000, such as Richmond and Norfolk; medium-sized cities (with populations of around 50,000), such as Charlottesville and Suffolk; smaller regional cities (under 25,000 in population), such as Warrenton, Leesburg, and Fredericksburg; increasingly vast suburban areas (such as those in northern Virginia, Virginia Beach, Hampton Roads, and around Richmond and Fredericksburg); small rural towns (under 10,000), such as Orange and Heathsville; and large agricultural areas.

Landscape both influences and reflects settlement patterns. The initial settlements of the seventeenth century followed the shoreline. Although many came to make their lives in Virginia permanently, the paramount objective was to extract as much as possible from the land as quickly as possible. Religion played a central role in the establishment of other colonies, such as Massachusetts Bay and Pennsylvania; in contrast, Virginians pursued money and commercial return on investment. The search for precious minerals gave way to agricultural exploitation and the formation of large landholdings, or plantations. Tobacco, which by 1650 had become the dominant crop, rapidly depleted the soil; the result was constant expansion to new land.

Towns were established at Jamestown and other places, such as Flowerdew Hundred, but the primary mode of settlement was isolated houses and accompanying farm buildings along the major waterways, or a short distance inland but with access to water transportation. Thomas Jefferson observed in his *Notes on the State of Virginia* (1786) that the colony "being much intersected with navigable waters, and trade brought to our doors . . . has probably been one of the causes why we have no towns of any consequence."[4] Until the mid-nineteenth century waterways remained the primary transportation routes for agriculture, timber, goods, and people. Hence, all the major settlements were on navigable rivers, or those that could be made accessible through locks and canals. Starting in the late eighteenth century, canals became an alternative to river transportation. They could provide a way to bypass falls, as did the Patowmack Canal at Great Falls in Fairfax County and the Rappahannock Navigation Company in Spotsylvania County. George Washington envisioned the future of Virginia as linked to long-distance canals. In the 1830s the Virginia legislature created the James River Company, which attempted to link the James and Kanawha rivers and the Ohio Valley by a canal over the Allegheny Mountains. Roads and turnpikes tended to follow the east-west direction of the major rivers; north-south routes entailed fords and bridges. In 1801, when Thomas Jefferson journeyed north from Charlottesville to Washington, D.C., to take office as president, he spent four days on horseback; today the same journey takes two hours by car (if there are no traffic jams). Railroads supplanted canals beginning in the 1840s and increasingly took over river traffic in the post–Civil War period. They also began to link, though not necessarily unite, the state from the south to the north.

Railroads still cross the state carrying heavy goods, but in the twentieth century the motorized vehicle has become the major means of personal transportation, and highways open areas heretofore inaccessible. Now one can live in the suburbs of Loudoun County and commute daily more than sixty miles into Washington. Thus in the late twentieth century a new, sprawling form of dense suburbanization developed throughout many portions of the state. Whereas initial settlement clustered on or near navigable rivers or bays, now suburbs, or edge cities composed of housing developments, malls, and office parks, are located on or near rivers of vehicles. At the same time, agriculture is still a major sector of the state's economy, and the early rural way of life, with its dispersed settlements and accompanying mindset, continues. Most observers agree that politically the state tilts toward agricultural interests, that rural counties and their representatives hold inordinate power compared with their urban counterparts. The county is still in most areas the primary political unit. Many buildings are known by location in a county rather than a town or a city. The myth of country living, even though it may be in a subdivision, still exerts a strong pull on the minds of Virginians.

Native American Habitation

When the English stepped ashore in 1607, they found a native culture with its own settlement patterns and buildings that had shaped the landscape in distinctive ways. Virginia was populated by tribes that included the Pamunkey, Mattaponi, Chickahominy, Powhatan, Iroquois, and Susquehannock; but almost all of this native culture has disappeared. The ancestors of the seventeenth-century Native Americans had been here for at least 10,000 years, and one of the earliest Paleo-Indian sites in the Western Hemisphere is located in Warren County in western Virginia. The buildings of the Native Americans recorded in European prints and other documents show light, wood-frame structures, earth fast (with the poles or framing se-

Tidewater Indian village, c. 1590, engraving by Theodor de Bry, in Thomas Harriot, *A Briefe and True Report of the New Found Land of Virginia* (1590)

cured directly in the ground), covered with mud, bark, woven mats, or hides, and shaped something like a beehive. Settlements were organized in a hierarchy, and apparently some were defended by timber palisades. The Native Americans farmed fields, hunted, and maintained the landscape. The trails became the foundations for later roads and turnpikes. Although the earliest colonists, such as Captain John Smith, had some interest in the natives and attempted to describe and depict them, and the story of the earliest American heroine, Pocahontas, results from this interaction, most of the colonists saw them only as impediments to exploitation of the land and decimated them. Apart from the odd visitor's chronicle, the Native Americans did not become objects of interest until nearly 180 years later, when Thomas Jefferson began a small archaeological excavation on the Rivanna River in Albemarle County. The state designated two Indian reservations, for the Pamunkey and Mattaponi in King William County, on the Middle Peninsula.

Early Settlement (1607–c. 1720)

Virginia building, like all American building, is a combination of many factors that may include outside influences (whether imported traditions, designers, or pattern books), local environmental conditions and available materials, the builder's competence and tradition, and a response to need. What remains of seventeenth-century building is very fragmentary and contested as to its authenticity and interpretation. When Virginia was a frontier, practicality and urgency dictated any type of rude structure; the consequence was—and would be for centuries—a tradition of fulfilling immediate needs with little sense of permanence. The impermanent architecture that resulted may have been influenced by the Native American post-hole building construction, although this method was also known in England. One difference from construction in England was Virginia's plenitude of timber, which allowed utilization and exploitation of wood on a scale unknown back home. Archaeological investigations at Jamestown and other early sites show a tremendous variety of construction techniques: wooden earth-fast posts, wooden block and sills, or brick foundations, on which an upper frame would be erected and then covered with a stucco type of wattle and daub, tar over straw, or some type of wood sheathing aligned either vertically or horizontally. Roofs could be wood, straw, or, less frequently, tile. Most of the population lived in one-room dwellings that lacked wood floors, plaster walls, or window glass; and earth-fast frame walls required frequent shoring up to survive a decade or two. This level of housing would continue through the eighteenth and well into the nineteenth century—and in some places into the twentieth. Life for a sizable group of people was, by twenty-first-century middle-class standards, not very pretty.

Brick did come into use very early, for both foundations and chimneys (though wooden chimneys existed into the early nineteenth century). Its use for an entire structure was much less common and indicated a building of importance or an occupant of wealth. Most of the initial building was for dwellings, and the plans initially followed those of the farmhouses of southwestern England, from which most of the early settlers came: either a one-room structure with a large end chimney or two rooms with a large central chimney. By the second half

Scale model of Cliffs Plantation, Westmoreland County (c. 1670)

of the seventeenth century the central chimney had moved to an outer wall, and some of the cooking may have been done in outbuildings, leaving a two-room house, named the hall-parlor (or hall-chamber), in which most activities took place. Given sufficient height, loft space could be created above. Bacon's Castle in Surry County is the best surviving example of this type.

Brick was occasionally used in Jamestown before 1650, but on plantations most of the houses were the post-hole type. No wooden houses from the seventeenth century survive in Virginia, and most historians have focused on the small number of brick buildings, such as Bacon's Castle, or, more contentious in date, the Adam Thoroughgood House in Virginia Beach. These are upscale dwellings, sometimes called "gentry houses," indicating the elite status of their occupants. Bacon's Castle, with its stepped and curving end gables and clustered chimney stacks, shows an awareness of high-style English buildings. The Thoroughgood House is more middle class, a typical hall-parlor house. Pear Valley, in Northampton County, on the Eastern Shore, although probably built early in the eighteenth century, is an excellent example of a wood-frame single-chamber house, once widespread in the Tidewater region.

In the boom economy of seventeenth-century Virginia, the population, which had been about 2,200 in 1620, surpassed 8,000 by 1640 and stood near 40,000 in 1680. Initially, the crown granted large tracts of land to favored courtiers, a practice that frequently caused conflicts with other Virginians. The large proprietary tracts, such as that of Thomas, Lord

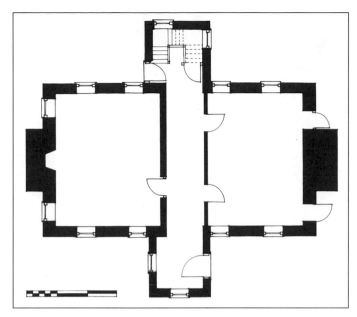

Plan of Bacon's Castle

Green Spring, house of Sir William Berkeley, James City County (c. 1645, destroyed), sketch by Benjamin Henry Latrobe, 1798

12

Culpeper, whose grant included much of the Northern Neck, remained in descendants' hands until the General Assembly abolished the inheritance of proprietorships in 1786. Tremendous profits were to be made from land speculation and especially from "green gold." John Rolfe, who married Pocahontas, brought tobacco seeds from Trinidad in either 1610 or 1611. This "pernicious weed" flourished in the soil of the Virginia peninsulas, and tobacco exports soared, from 20,000 pounds in 1619 to 60,000 pounds in 1622 and 1.5 million pounds by 1629. A pattern of economic disparity, of extremes of wealth and poverty, grew up. William Fitzhugh of Stafford County built a "very good" wood-frame residence c. 1680, and at his death owned 122 pieces of English silver. His house, which does not survive, was constructed on brick foundations and could be built only because he hired in London, as indentured servants, a bricklayer and a carpenter. Even larger was the house of a governor of Virginia, Sir William Berkeley, Green Spring, built near Jamestown. It survives in two drawings, made in 1683 and 1798. Sometimes called a "long house" because of its stretched-out form, and mammoth by Virginia standards, it was begun c. 1643 and then enlarged several times. Constructed on brick foundations with wooden framing, houses such as this underwent constant enlargement, which becomes a Virginia trait, as did the prominent entrance portico. Status in Virginia—as almost everywhere—came to be defined by size and by references—pedimented entry, clustered chimneys—to earlier elite buildings. The large porch—elevated at Green Spring—is an early instance of what became an identifying American feature.

The dispersed nature of Virginia settlement meant that only a few institutional buildings were constructed during the early period, and even fewer survive. Again, the post-hole, earth-fast type of impermanent construction was used. An act passed by the House of Burgesses in 1667 empowered the county courts (established in 1634 when eight shires, or counties, were created) to condemn "two acres of land and noe more for erecting churches and or court-houses."[5] The official religion was Anglican, and it was state-supported by taxes until disestablishment in 1786. St. Luke's Church, Isle of Wight County, is justly famous as the earliest survivor of Virginia's Anglican churches, though the exact date of certain elements of its fabric, such as the pediment on the tower and the crow-stepped gables, remains contentious.

The others, which might be called semi-survivors, are the reconstructions at Williamsburg of the College of William and Mary and the Capitol, or Statehouse. The design of the original building of 1695–1700 for the College of William and Mary (founded to train Anglican ministers) came from London and may have been the product—as tradition has always claimed—of Sir Christopher Wren's Office of Works. Accompanying the plans were a "surveyor" (or construction manager), three English bricklayers, and other "workmen [from] England."[6] The building burned in 1705, and the second building—on which the present reconstruction by Thomas Tileston Waterman and the Colonial Williamsburg Foundation architectural staff is based—was smaller and its proportions were more pinched, as seen in the squeezed entry pavilion. It was undoubtedly designed as a square building with an interior courtyard, but only half was constructed, leaving exposed a rear arcade, called a piazza, which significantly influenced later educational buildings (for example, the University of Virginia) and early courthouses.

Williamsburg became the capital of the colony in 1699 while the college building was un-

The Bodleian Plate (c. 1732–1747). In the upper row, College of William and Mary, showing the Brafferton Indian School on the left, the main building in the center, and the President's House to the right; in the middle row, the Capitol on the left, the rear (west) elevation of the main building of the College of William and Mary in the center, and the Governor's Palace to the right.

derway. Jamestown had proven to be subject to floods, the site was unhealthy, and the State-house—the second one—had burned. The governor of the colony, Sir Francis Nicholson, formerly of Maryland, moved the seat of government, and, as one of his contemporaries described him, he "flatter'd himself with the fond Imagination, of being the Founder of a new City. He mark's out the Streets in many Places, so as they might represent the Figure of a W, in Memory of his late Majesty King William. . . . There he provid'e a stately Fabrick to be erected, which he placed opposite to the College, and graced it with the magnificent Name of the Capitol." But only a few years later, Governor Spotswood altered "the streets of the Town . . . from the fanciful Forms of Ws. and Ms. to much more Conveniences."[7] Virginia's other towns had been planned before Williamsburg, and, although some of the earliest descriptions of Jamestown indicate a random disposition of elements, order and hierarchy existed. The ciphers of Nicholson's plan obscure the real importance of Williamsburg's layout, which was a grid dominated by a central main street—Duke of Gloucester Street—six poles (99 feet) wide, with areas set aside for major public structures such as the courthouse, the church, and the market. Not every town had these elements, and many were laid out on paper and remained unbuilt, but in Williamsburg's grid can be seen the form of most later Virginia towns.

The story and reconstruction of the Capitol (first built c. 1701–1705) and that of the Governor's Palace are explained in the Hampton Roads section of this volume. In a 1724 account of his travels, the Reverend Hugh Jones claimed that they—and the college—were "exceeded by few of their kind." Jones went on to describe Virginians: "They live in the same neat manner, dress after the same modes, and behave themselves exactly as the gentry in London. . . . The habits, life, customs, computations &c of the Virginians are much the same as about London, which they esteem their home."[8]

Eighteenth-Century Change (c. 1720–c. 1780)

The selection of a date such as 1720 to begin or end a period in architecture is for the most part arbitrary. Nothing completely stops or starts; instead, older forms, such as the single-room or the two-room hall-parlor plan, continue, and the roots of what appears as a new development usually go back long before. Traditionally, historians have asserted that around 1700, or 1720, or 1740, a change occurred, and Virginians adopted a new architectural idiom that is often labeled as Georgian, originally a political and dynastic term referring to the reigns of the four Georges. The Georgian era in England, which extended from 1714 to 1830, in fact encompassed styles that ranged from classical forms derived from Italy and France to experiments with the revival of Gothic. Idioms such as late Baroque, Rococo, neoclassical, and Adamesque all belong to English Georgian. Wealthy Virginians, as Hugh Jones remarked and as Rhys Isaac has pointed out in his seminal book *The Transformation of Virginia, 1740–1790* (1982), did attempt to emulate Londoners and English gentry through the importation of material goods and the imitation of English manners, furniture, and architecture. However, the buildings produced in Virginia, although derived from such English models as the smaller gentry houses of Sussex, were, in the end, thoroughly American in plan, materials, and usage.[9] Changes in English architectural fashions were reflected in Virginia, sometimes directly, as in the intricate woodwork at Gunston Hall, Fairfax County, and at other times more remotely, as at Mount Vernon.

The change that occurred can be called a classical revolution, and—although already apparent in the Governor's Palace at Williamsburg and, in a lesser way, at the Capitol and the College of William and Mary—it had arrived by 1720. But after that date it became more apparent, not just in the mini-metropolis of Williamsburg but in the countryside. The most dramatic change was at the elite level of wealthy landowners' plantation houses and of institutional buildings, in which more classical elements appeared in overall form (for instance, symmetry) and in details (for instance, correct orders.) This classicism slowly worked its way down to the growing middle class and its housing.

The shift in aesthetics had several sources. Primary, of course, was increasing wealth, not only of the elite, but also of the growing "middling" class of farmers, merchants, and those of other occupations who also profited from a boom economy. They all sought to emulate London and partake in a consumer society. An accompanying cause was the expansion of publishing and the new availability of pattern books. Classicism is essentially a "language" based upon books, written rules, patterns, and forms that can be transmitted on the printed page. William Byrd brought from London in 1729 a copy of Colen Campbell's important tome, *Vit-*

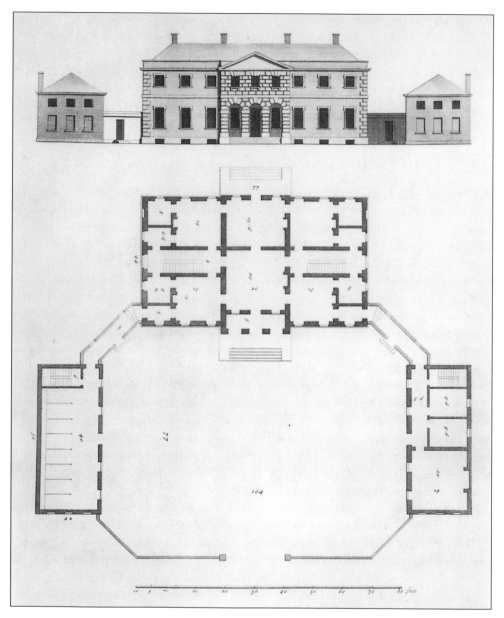

James Gibbs, *A Book of Architecture* (1728), plate 58

ruvius Britannicus (1715), which played a role in the design of Byrd's son's house, Westover, Charles City County. It is probable, though undocumented, that either Langdon Carter or a builder had a copy of Sebastiano Serlio's *L'Architettura* (Venice, 1600; London, 1611), or that plates or drawings derived from it were a source for the doorways of Sabine Hall; and similarly that either John Tayloe II or a person in his employ owned a copy of James Gibbs's popular *Book of Architecture* (1728), from which Tayloe's house, Mount Airy, was derived. Architecture books were plentiful enough so that the young Thomas Jefferson purchased a treatise on classical architecture from a cabinetmaker near the college gates in Williamsburg about 1762 while he was a student. In time Jefferson would amass the greatest collection of architecture books in the young country.

Another source of the change was growth in population and the corresponding increase in the number of skilled artisans and workers, slave and free, who could carry out substantial building projects. It is too little recognized that the building profession in all its variety of activities was one of the major occupations in pre- and post-Revolutionary Virginia. The importation of skilled craftsmen, either as freedmen or as indentured servants, which had begun in the seventeenth century, continued and became more common, bringing individuals such as William Buckland. This expertise made possible grandiloquent and ill-fated building projects such as Rosewell, or the more modest houses of tradesmen, such as Benjamin Powell and James Geddy, Jr., in Williamsburg. Virginia brickwork is justly renowned for its skill and became one of the standard images by which the state's architecture is known; however, only a few could afford it. Much more common were wooden houses, frequently plain on the exterior, but on the interior fitted with superb joinery drawn from a combination of pattern books, as at Tuckahoe Plantation, Goochland County. The question of who actually designed these buildings is contentious, and in spite of the determination of an earlier generation of scholars to assign them to one mastermind, the present consensus is that the design of houses and other buildings came from the interaction of the patron and the builders and a mixture of precedent, local conditions, and usage.

Slavery and the importation of Africans began in 1619 and grew. Slave labor took the place of indentured and independent white laborers. Africans and their descendants made up 9 percent of the population in 1700, 25 percent by 1715, and 40 percent by 1750. The flowering of Virginia in the eighteenth century was based upon black slave labor. Most Africans were agricultural workers, but some worked on construction projects and learned the skills of artisans. Slavery led to changes in the built environment, such as slave housing on plantations and the creation of small slave communities. It also led to a shift in room usage and increased subdivision of interior spaces in houses related to desire for privacy and to new models of decorum and behavior, but also intended to shield the owner from the presence of house servants.

Institutional buildings changed dramatically, at least from the evidence of those that have survived. More than fifty churches from the pre-Revolutionary period survive in Virginia, all Anglican originally and now mostly Episcopalian, though a few have changed denominations. Many are modest, but all are of brick, and the most opulent, such as Christ Church, Lancaster County, evidence the power and wealth of a primary patron (in the case of Christ Church, Robert "King" Carter). In churches such as this, and many others that have been altered, the local gentry would express their status by having their family pews raised higher than those of the lesser members of the congregation.

Eleven courthouses also survive—with the aid of restoration—from the pre-Revolutionary period. Originally most of them (except James County Courthouse in Williamsburg) stood in isolated settings—as did churches—located for convenience in the center of the county, often at a crossroads. In time a jail, a clerk's office, and other auxiliary structures would be added, and perhaps a tavern (necessary for court days). Some of these courthouses were modest rectangular structures (Essex, Northampton, and Middlesex), but the quintessential Virginia courthouse had an arcaded front, like that of the Old Isle of Wight County Courthouse in Smithfield. The origins of the arcade, sometimes locally called a piazza, may have been the Wren Building of the College of William and Mary and the Capitol in Williamsburg and, going back farther, town and market halls in London. The arcaded front became an identifying feature of Virginia in the twentieth century; the Virginia Department of Transportation even uses it for rest area facilities on major highways. The attempt at a temple front with the James City Courthouse, 1770, in Williamsburg, and its cupola indicate the beginning of a tradition that became national after the Revolution.

To think of Virginia as urban in this period would be incorrect; it was rural. A minor building boom in Williamsburg after the fire of 1747 that destroyed the Capitol resulted in some growth, and on the eve of the Revolution in 1775 its population stood at 1,880, of which 52 percent were black. Land speculation and the need for more ports or shipment points led to the laying out of Fredericksburg (1728), Richmond (1737), and Alexandria (1749); but they remained small, as did the Piedmont villages of Leesburg (1758) and Charlottesville (1762).

Nineteenth-Century Prosperity (c. 1780–c. 1840)

After the Revolution Virginia experienced tremendous prosperity, and, although business declined periodically, until around 1840 the state stood at the peak of its economic and political power. Its status was apparent in the decision to locate the national capital, Washington, D.C., on the Potomac and in the fact that seven of the first twelve presidents were Virginians. Settlement spread west, up through the Piedmont and beyond, and modest commercial cities developed. But about 1840, Virginia's position as the first among equals began to recede. Its soil was increasingly worn out, and although alternatives were sought by some enterprising businessmen, such as those involved in the establishment of the Tredegar Iron Works in Richmond, an increasingly defensive mentality ruled.

Richmond became the capital of Virginia in 1779 at the instigation of Thomas Jefferson, and the focus of power shifted. Williamsburg, which was Virginia's only real urban center, began to fade away, not to regain importance until the 1930s, as a museum. Other cities—Alexandria, Fredericksburg, Norfolk, and Portsmouth—emerged as major trading centers, and the smaller Piedmont towns gained slowly in size. Virginia's ethos remained in the countryside, in the Jeffersonian ideal of the farmer and the landed gentry as the bedrock of the new nation, but a new and very different environment developed.

The so-called Federal era in Virginia, c. 1780–1810, was typified by a "great rebuilding," common along much of the East Coast, as members of the newly risen middle class either extensively remodeled their houses or built completely new ones. Not just an architectural stylistic change, this rebuilding was accompanied by changes in manners, activities, and possessions. In Virginia—and elsewhere—a number of forms developed, but the most popular type was in many places the so-called I-house, a fusion of earlier vernacular and high styles into a dwelling with a single-pile plan for the front part—a central hall and a room to each side—

two stories in height, and a wing, or ell, to the rear. Constructed of wood or brick, the I-house could have, depending on the wealth and hubris of the owner, various degrees of ornamentation as well as size. The ornament and trim of these houses increasingly came from American pattern books, such as Asher Benjamin's and Minard Lafever's various publications, which were the most popular among Virginians. The I-house was a staple of the Virginia building economy well into the twentieth century. Houses built during the Federal period vastly outnumber everything built before the late eighteenth century, indicating the new prosperity. At a lesser scale was a one-story variant of the I-house with a main-floor plan of central hall and a room to either side, bedrooms or chambers under the sloping roof, and an ell to the rear. Along with new building, a change took place in modest older houses, in single-room shacks and hall-parlor houses, which received new furnishings and frequently subdivision of interior spaces. In Virginia some of this interior subdivision, as with the shift in room usage during the earlier part of the eighteenth century, was related to new concepts of privacy and etiquette and an attempt to create visual barriers and keep slaves from view.

In cities and towns a variety of house types developed. Although freestanding I-houses were common, the row house type, three bays wide, with an entrance-side passage and room across the front, was becoming the norm in Virginia and can still be found from Norfolk to Charlottesville. Size and materials depended on the owner's wealth. Frequently, the owner's workshop or store would occupy the ground floor. Surviving commercial structures are rare: a few late eighteenth-century warehouses along King Street in Alexandria; Hugh Mercer's apothecary shop (1780), Fredericksburg; and the restored and reconstructed buildings along Duke of Gloucester Street in Williamsburg.

Another major change in the Virginia landscape was the appearance, often in isolated locations, of a new church type, along with new denominations. The Anglican church, which became the Episcopal church after the Revolution, was disestablished in 1786, and glebe lands—which had helped support the Anglican clergy—were sold off. Competing for souls were new, or dissenter, sects—Baptists, Presbyterians, Lutherans, Quakers, Methodists—and in time Roman Catholics. All had been present before the Revolution but in small numbers. With religious freedom, they flourished at the expense of the Episcopal church. Many Episcopal churches completely disappeared, and others included in this guidebook fell out of use between the 1780s and the 1830s. In reaction to the popularity of the dissenter groups, the Episcopal church, under the leadership of bishops Richard Channing Moore and William Meade, became resolutely "low church" and de-emphasized liturgy. This anti–"high church" policy remained in effect well into the latter nineteenth century, and consequently, with few exceptions, such as Benjamin Henry Latrobe's St. Paul's, Alexandria—a nationally significant building—the Episcopal church in Virginia never took the stylistic lead in the Gothic Revival as it did in other parts of the country. Instead, it was the Presbyterians, with Minard Lafever's Second Church, Richmond (1848), and the Baptists, with Thomas U. Walter's Freemason Street Baptist Church, Norfolk (1849–1850), who established the Gothic Revival of the mid-nineteenth century in Virginia. Not until after the Civil War did Episcopalians begin to build in the Gothic Revival style.

However, the dominant Virginia church form of the period 1780–1840 and beyond was not Gothic; it was typically a rectangular box with twin entrance doors on a narrow end, and its interior was a single large preaching space with possibly a gallery, as at Emmaus Baptist Church, near Providence Forge, New Kent County, on the Lower Peninsula. Built of wood or brick, these twin-entrance-door churches could have Federal, Roman Revival, or Greek Revival details. The twin doors reflected an interior arrangement that responded to the shift in worship, the emphasis on the spoken word; hence, the pulpit, usually placed at the center of the back wall, became the focal point. Instead of the traditional central aisle, the middle of the nave was furnished with a block of seats with an aisle to either side and corresponding twin entrance doors or twin doors in the narthex. Additionally, some churches separated men in the congregation from women and children, and the doors were assigned by gender. Although this practice largely died out, a few Primitive Baptist congregations today continue to separate the sexes. The twin-entrance church became the archetype in Virginia after 1800, so popular that it was used for the few new Episcopal churches built, such as Christ Church, Glendower, Albemarle County (1831–1832), which could be mistaken for Baptist, were it not for its rich Jeffersonian details.

The development of Virginia's industrial landscape had begun early with a glassworks in Jamestown. Iron furnaces and ironworks were set up in rural areas, in the Chancellorsville vicinity in Spotsylvania County c. 1717, the Falmouth vicinity in Stafford County c. 1750, and other places; but only modest stone ruins remain. The Tredegar Iron Works was established in Richmond in 1837, and its rapid growth after 1841 helped bring Virginia industry into the big time. It was the source for iron fronts for commercial buildings and other goods, including weapons for the Civil War. Portsmouth and Norfolk prospered from shipbuilding, long established in the Tidewater area. Accompanying this activity was a dramatic increase in scale of government installations, such as Fort Monroe, guarding Hampton Roads, and the Portsmouth Naval Hospital, which stretches along the Elizabeth River.

Rural areas always had a mini-industrial landscape of grain mills and lumber mills. The most prominent survivors from this period are Colvin Run Mill, Fairfax County, and Aldie Mill, Loudoun County. Although increasingly the land was worn out, tobacco was a major crop until the 1840s. Tobacco barns, used for curing, were usually insubstantial wooden structures and have left few remains. Tobacco was shipped north to be processed for plug and chewing; not until the 1880s did cigarette production begin.

In 1831, the Chesterfield Railroad Company opened the first railroad, which hauled coal on tracks some twelve miles, the motive power supplied by mules and horses. Steam-powered rail transportation appeared by 1837, and the Richmond, Fredericksburg, and Potomac line had tracks between Richmond and Fredericksburg. Farther north, transportation was still by steamboat, and through rail connections to Washington waited until 1872. Instead of focusing on railroads, Virginians continued to build the great folly, the James River–Kanawha Canal, which would link the Potomac and the Ohio rivers. Millions of dollars and too much time were wasted on this unsuccessful venture, whereas by 1850 the Erie Canal had been open for twenty-five years, and by 1852 the Baltimore and Ohio Railroad had completed its line to Wheeling, funneling rail traffic to Baltimore, not to Richmond.

These events and resultant building contributed to the vernacular landscape of Virginia. Another transformation occurred as professional architects made an appearance and substantially changed the look of high-profile buildings. Certainly designers existed earlier, so-

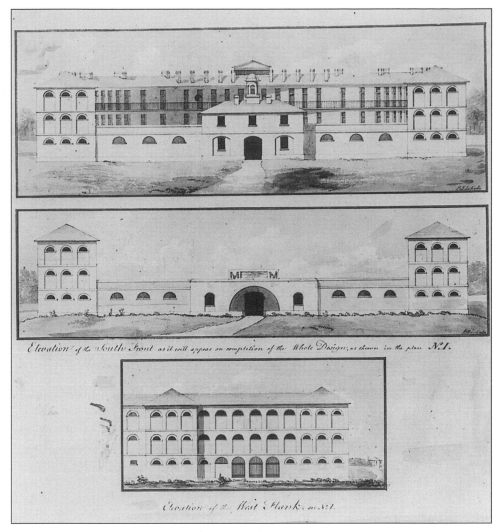

Benjamin Henry Latrobe, Virginia State Penitentiary, 1797

called gentleman architects such as Governor Francis Nicholson in Williamsburg and William Byrd III at Westover. Others were skilled craftsmen: John Ariss, a mason who contributed to several churches and possibly other buildings; James Wren, who designed several northern Virginia churches; and William Buckland, a talented joiner who was responsible for the interior at Gunston Hall and a few houses. With some exceptions, the designs of most of this latter group were a byproduct of their involvement in the process of construction. They were not hired specifically to design a structure that would be built by somebody else. Nor were they professionally trained, either through the apprentice system or schooling, to practice as architects. All of this changed in 1796 when Benjamin Henry Latrobe, an architect born and trained in England (though his mother had been born in America), landed in Nor-

Benjamin Henry Latrobe, watercolor view of Richmond from the south side of the James, showing the Virginia State Capitol

folk, and during the next three years (sometimes under the patronage of Jefferson), mainly in Richmond, designed houses, a prison, and a projected theater and traveled around the state making a series of drawings that remain one of the best records of Virginia buildings. Most of Latrobe's Virginia buildings are gone, but his architectural drawings survive. They illuminate the difference between the professional and the amateur or the builder. Latrobe ultimately traveled north to Philadelphia and trained some of the next generation of American architects, Robert Mills and William Strickland, both of whom made notable contributions to the state's building stock.

Although professional architects functioned primarily as designers, the split between architectural design and construction was not complete until much later in the century. Builders, or housewrights, or joiners, or masons frequently styled themselves as architects. In 1810 Alexander Parris came south to Richmond from Boston, where building activity was at a standstill because of British embargo, and in the next two years designed a house for John Wickham and a mansion for the governor in the most up-to-date neoclassical style. Similarly, the workmen Thomas Jefferson employed at the University of Virginia—John Neilson, James Dinsmore, William B. Phillips, Malcolm Crawford, and others—began in the building trade; learned about designing through books, observation, and construction; and went on to significant careers.

Thomas Jefferson's place in this changing role of the designer is ambiguous. In many ways he was a gentleman amateur, strictly self-trained from books, observation, and travel. Jefferson had more knowledge and experience of travel abroad than any architect in this country with the exception of the European émigrés, such as Latrobe and Maximilian Godefroy (who worked in Richmond during 1816); indeed, until the advent of the mid-nineteenth-century Beaux-Arts-trained generation represented first by Richard Morris Hunt, Jefferson, among native-born American architects, stands with Charles Bulfinch in firsthand knowledge of European architecture. Jefferson designed his own houses, Monticello and Poplar Forest, Bedford County (the latter in western Virginia), and he was involved in the construction process, which puts him in the categories of both gentleman architect and builder. However, the scale of his later projects, including directing the building of the University of Virginia, is mammoth; the university was one of the largest construction projects in the country at the time. Jefferson did depend on books, as Latrobe complained, but Jefferson also thought very much like a professional architect; his drawings reveal his consideration of alternatives and departure from "rules" when it suited him. When Jefferson's various designs are assembled and compared, it is obvious that he was among the major architects, not just of Virginia, but of the United States; he was both a form giver and a symbol maker.

Monticello remains the primarily personal touchstone for understanding both Jefferson's genius as an architect and limitations as a human being (for instance, the design of the wings to submerge services and keep slavery out of sight); but it was in the public realm, at the Virginia State Capitol, where his importance emerged. From a practical standpoint the design is folly, compressing all the functions of government into a rectangle, but from a symbolic standpoint it is sheer genius: American government symbolized by a religious temple in a classical form which became the official national architectural language. The centerpiece of the interior, Jean-Antoine Houdon's standing figure of George Washington (1788), the commission for which Houdon received through Jefferson's instigation, was not just the first of a long line of monuments to Washington, but the beginning of the national—and Virginia—mania for monuments and memorials. Jefferson also designed, or at least contributed to, three Virginia courthouses (Botetourt, Buckingham, and Charlotte counties, all in western Virginia), which helped create the American predilection for temple porticoes. His design for the University of Virginia, Charlottesville, is certainly his masterpiece and is a model not just for an "academical village" but for how American settlements and the landscape might be ordered.

Some historians have concluded that Jefferson exercised little influence outside the immediate Piedmont area, the location of structures designed and built by the brickmasons, carpenters, and undertakers who worked for him at Monticello and the university. But a larger heritage exists that includes college campuses, houses, and public buildings throughout Virginia and the South that show his influence. His involvement in developing the plan for Washington, D.C., and then the designs for the President's House and the U.S. Capitol was critical: without his participation the public image of the nation's capital would be very different. Moreover, although Jefferson tended to rely on Palladian and antique Roman forms, the Greek Revival, which began in earnest in the 1820s, was indebted to his popularization of the temple form. Indeed, the Greek Revival was not particularly Greek in many of its manifestations, and buildings such as Ammi B. Young's U.S. Customhouse in Norfolk are more Roman than Greek. The debate over Jefferson's architectural proclivities—whether he was a neo–English Palladianist or more committed to French architecture—misses the point that his eclecticism set the stage for the succession of rapidly changing styles that

Monticello (1769–1809)

dominated the nineteenth century. Around 1900 Jefferson rose again as a source for the Colonial Revival.

Eclecticism and deferent stylistic solutions that involved the personal taste and symbolism of the architect and client dominated Virginia architecture after the 1820s. Important Virginia buildings by such noted figures as Alexander Jackson Davis, Thomas U. Walter, Thomas Stewart, Minard Lafever, James Renwick, Thomas Tefft, Calvin Pollard, Robert Mills, and William Strickland date from this period.

Decline, Recovery, and the Revival of the Past (c. 1840–c. 1940)

Virginia buildings from the 1840s and 1850s do not look greatly different from those of the 1830s. Perhaps they incorporate a bit more ornament and strain for the picturesque silhouette, as is true of the Virginia Theological Seminary (1857–1860) in Alexandria, by Norris G. Starkwether, but no great shift in aesthetics occurred. A real difference appeared later in the nineteenth century and in the twentieth, in structures that are larger and more extremely picturesque, such as Richard Morris Hunt's Virginia Hall at Hampton Institute (1872–1879), in Hampton, and E. E. Myers's Richmond City Hall (1886–1894), or that represent a self-conscious turn to earlier traditions, as with McKim, Mead and White's red brick and white-columned structures at the University of Virginia (1896–1898 and 1906–1910), Charlottesville, or that reflect modern ideas from the Midwest, such as Frank Lloyd Wright's design for Loren Pope (1939) in northern Virginia. In the countryside, or in the growing suburban areas, one can see the influence of pattern books by A. J. Downing until the 1880s; then designs from books by George and Charles Palliser and George Barber; and, in the 1920s, the appearance of kit homes sold by Sears, Roebuck and by other companies. The regional character of Virginia's architecture began to disappear, and Virginia began to look more and more like everywhere else.

Equally important, the architects mentioned in the last paragraph were not Virginians, but outsiders brought in to design new buildings or authors of nationally published pattern books. Virginia lost its architectural leadership except in the retrospective view. With the emergence of the Colonial Revival, Virginia became a source for national architecture, but again it was outsiders who came to look and carry ideas away. Buildings designed by Virginians were seldom noted in the national press, and frequently the important commissions in the state went to high-profile architects from other places. Even in the case of Virginia's most important twentieth-century architectural contribution, Colonial Williamsburg, the architects were not Virginians, but Yankees.

This shift in architectural production was but one symptom of a change that began sometime around 1840: Virginians began to lose their self-confidence. The change was evolutionary, occurring over many years, and its causes are not totally apparent. One, however, was the economic decline resulting from overreliance on one crop, tobacco, and the resulting depletion of the soil. Many of the early families migrated farther south or to the West. For those who remained, the economic disparity noted earlier continued. Testifying to the declining fortunes of agriculture in the 1840s and 1850s is the near-total absence in Virginia of the large multi-columned antebellum plantation and city houses that can be found in other, more prosperous southern states such as Georgia, Alabama, and Mississippi. And yet the state held onto its outmoded plantation system and to slavery. Despite attempts to introduce modern manufacturing, of which the Tredegar Iron Works was a successful example, the Virginia ethos was still rural. The continuing reliance on slavery debilitated whatever new ideas might have been imported before the Civil War. After the war, racism and segregation ensured a highly stratified society, in which movement from one group or class to another was difficult if not nonexistent. And of course the new sources of wealth were in the cities, not the country. Although Virginia developed large urban centers, its self-created mythology looked in other directions.

Virginia's cities and towns grew in the hundred years between 1840 and 1940, and, although the rural areas still prevailed politically, new industries were created. The Tidewater grew as a major center for shipping and, in 1882, Newport News, which was only a small town, became the eastern terminus of the Chesapeake and Ohio Railroad. The Huntington railroad family subsequently established the Newport News Shipbuilding and Dry Dock Company there. Except for the development of some suburbs, from which the wealthy might commute, Virginia cities until the 1870s remained largely pedestrian in which almost any destination lay within an hour's walk. Richmond was the site of the world's first successful electric streetcar system, inaugurated in February 1888; it encouraged the city to spread out. Although the automobile has continued this trend, suburbs, even in the 1930s, were typically compact, with houses on small lots, and their distance from a commercial center was seldom more than five miles. Ginter Park and the West End in Richmond, Ghent in Norfolk, and Hilton Village in Newport News all illustrate this pattern. Economic and racial segregation became more the norm in cities than they had been earlier. Certain streets or areas, the so-called show streets or grand avenues, became preserves of the wealthy. In Norfolk, West Freemason Street was the prestigious address; in Richmond, it became West Franklin Street and its continuation as Monument Avenue.

As an antidote to the increasing urbanization, parks and open spaces were developed. Hollywood Cemetery in Richmond, designed by Philadelphia-based John Notman in 1848, remains the state's major example of a romantic cemetery. By 1851, Richmond had acquired park sites, though their major development came after the Civil War. In the early twentieth century the preeminent example of large-scale landscaping was a federal government initiative, the George Washington Memorial Parkway in northern Virginia, which initially linked Mount Vernon with Alexandria and was later extended west.

Many earlier building traditions continued throughout the nineteenth and well into the twentieth century. The I-house remained a staple of the Virginia countryside, though now frequently it had a front gable and porch, which reflected the impact of Downing and other pattern-book authors, and also of Mount Vernon. In cities the three-bay row house form was decked out in whatever were the current national fads in ornament and style. The same pattern can be followed in other building types. Virginia building in many ways mirrored well-known national trends. The history of architecture and building, however, is more than the recording of styles; buildings are more than physical shelter for activities.

Davis Circle, Hollywood Cemetery, Richmond, c. 1865

Buildings also represent mental shelters; they encompass values, beliefs, and views about the world. Behind buildings and landscapes lie ideas and beliefs that give distinction to Virginia's environment.

Some of what was distinctive about Virginia's landscape in the century 1840–1940 can be attributed to three interrelated factors or developments: the Civil War, the New South, and the quest for a historic past. The Civil War is, of course, primary, for it dramatically changed the state. But perhaps more important was the aftermath, the emotional reaction and the growth of a mythology that helped fuel several contradictory impulses: a celebration of defeat, the development of a "New South" mentality, and the search for a past, which resulted most prominently in the Colonial Revival and historic preservation.

The Civil War, the bloody conflict itself, and Reconstruction become ever present in Virginia, both as fact and as myth. Certainly the vast destruction caused by the war, such as the evacuation burning of Richmond, and the consequent economic deprivation immediately afterward must be factored into the loss of confidence. However, as cast iron buildings such as the Stearns Block (1869) attest, Richmond began rebuilding almost immediately. The belief that no recovery occurred between 1865 and the end of Reconstruction in 1876 is false, but rebuilding and growth came at a slower pace in Virginia than in the states and cities of the victorious North, where post–Civil War prosperity resulted almost immediately. Mam-

Richmond after the evacuation fire, April 1865

moth High Victorian structures with bulging mansard roofs, towers, and acres of ornament were not common in Virginia in the 1860s; instead they appeared in the 1870s and 1880s.

The Civil War gave freedom to African Americans, but the aftermath disenfranchised them as a group. It has only recently been recognized that a sizable free black population existed in the state, and particularly in Richmond, before the war. Knowledge of this community was obliterated for years; one of the few physical remains is the Third Street Bethel African Methodist Episcopal Church (1859) in Richmond, one of the rare surviving antebellum black churches in the country. After the war, prosperous black communities developed in Richmond, for instance, the Jackson Ward Historic District, and in Hampton in conjunction with the Hampton Institute. A black building and architectural community developed in the late nineteenth century. But just as blacks were segregated by Jim Crow laws in schools and residences, so was their architectural employment essentially restricted to the black community. Several black architects—John Lankford, Harvey Nathaniel Johnson, and Hilyard Robinson, to name a few—maintained successful practices.

Although inherently destructive, war leaves permanent remains. The cemeteries, battlefields, and monuments and memorials of the Civil War became a part of the Virginia landscape. Buildings actually constructed for the war are rare and only partially preserved, as in the case of Grant's headquarters in Hopewell. Some buildings sustained damage, and their subsequent rebuilding, like that of the Spotsylvania Courthouse, is part of their history. Not every Civil War cemetery is included in this book, but such notable ones as those in Arlington, Hopewell, Fredericksburg, and others contain small but important structures and monuments and evocative landscapes. Equally important are the battlefield remains, the various fortifications, earthworks, and open fields. The history of battlefield identification and preservation is complex, but some of the more significant activities took place around Richmond in the 1920s, when James Ambler Johnson and Douglas Southhall Freeman (the author of a biography of Robert E. Lee) "spent every Sunday for several years," according to Johnson's recollection, locating and verifying sites that are now marked with signs along Virginia 156, the "Battlefield Route," in eastern Henrico County. With assistance from the Richmond chapter of the Rotarians, a Battlefield Markers Association was formed, and about sixty stone-based markers with metal plaques were placed at various sites. Johnson and Freeman also developed a driving tour of the route.[10]

"The War" began to be commemorated, and with commemoration came the development of a very particular myth, the idea of the "Lost Cause," which began in earnest in the 1870s and rose to prominence from the 1880s to the 1920s.[11] At its most basic, the Lost Cause myth claimed that before the war a noble and genteel civilization had flourished in the South and in Virginia in particular—a culture based upon humanitarian and Christian motives and beliefs and states' rights and rooted in the soil and an agrarian life. This culture—the myth held—stood in contrast with the evil and profit-motivated industrial civilization that arose in the North and had unjustly subjugated the South through armed conflict. According to the Lost Cause adherents, the war was not about slavery, but about states' rights and the triumph of the mercantile capitalist system. According to this myth, African Americans were far better off under slavery than as freedmen. Although the idea of the Lost Cause began to wane in the 1920s, it never totally died out; and in addition to visible remains of antebellum society, it set the stage for *Gone with the Wind* and other examples of the plantation genre in literature and movies.

One of the most visible manifestations of the Lost Cause is the ambitious statuary program undertaken by a group of former Confederate officers, women, and ministers, which left its mark in Richmond, on Monument Avenue, and on the grounds of nearly every courthouse and public building in the state. The first monuments, installed in the 1870s and 1880s, were simple obelisks; in the 1890s they began to portray equestrian generals and enlisted foot soldiers. Many of the monuments were created in reaction to similar programs in the North, and the peak of activity was 1900–1920, with the United Daughters of the Confederacy, founded in 1895, as the driving force. The sculptors of the famous generals are known; some commissions, such as Monument Avenue's *Lee*, by Jean Antonin Mercie, of Paris, resulted from international competitions. The creators of the monuments to Johnny Reb remain as anonymous as their subject; some of these works came from the Roman Bronze Works of New York City and the McNeel Marble Company of Marietta, Georgia. Both companies of-

Richmond, Monument Avenue looking west, with the J. E. B. Stuart Monument, c. 1925

fered easy credit terms to clients. Also a legacy of the Lost Cause myth were various military historical markers; cannons scattered about the state; and "encampments," including Confederate veterans' homes, for example, in Richmond at the present-day site of the Virginia Museum of Fine Arts, where the Confederate Memorial Chapel (1887), by Marion J. Dimmock, and the Home for Needy Confederate Women (1930–1937), now the museum's education building, remain. Other elements of the Lost Cause landscape include Battle Abbey, originally the Confederate Memorial Institute (1911–1913), now the Virginia Historical Society in Richmond, the product of a national competition; the White House of the Confederacy, also in Richmond; the innumerable (historic) houses lived in by Lee and other Confederate leaders; Confederate grave markers; stained glass in churches (St. Luke's, Isle of Wight County; St. Paul's, Richmond); and the various flag-laying ceremonies that are still carried out as faint memories of the giant celebrations of Confederate veterans. A sacred landscape was thus created out of the war and its resultant myths. Of course, this was a white southern vision, not one shared by all segments of the population. The sacred landscape tells many tales, but the most evident is that the losers were really the victors, a type of historical reconstruction that has few parallels in the United States.

The counterpoint to the Lost Cause is the New South, which is a landscape of progressive business, factories, skyscrapers, and large Classical Revival banks and commercial buildings.[12] The term "New South" was the invention of the Atlanta *Constitution* editor Henry Grady, who advocated in his speeches, editorials, and other writings of the 1880s that the South abandon its fixation on the agrarian past and embrace modern industry and commerce. Instead of wallowing in a poverty-stricken past, the South should actively compete with the North, attract investment, and become part of the modern world. Many southern business leaders agreed and argued that the South's natural resources—waterpower, mineral deposits, timber—coupled with a low-income population and an antipathy toward organized labor could replace the textile mills of New England, the chemical factories of the Middle Atlantic, and the furniture manufacturers of the Midwest. To what degree advocacy of the New South was an organized movement is questionable, but the idea did resound, and the consequences could be seen in the metropolitan centers and new industrial landscape of Virginia. New wealth also resulted, apparent in luxury hotels such as the Jefferson Hotel, Richmond (1895, 1901), by the New York firm of Carrère and Hastings and later John Kevan Peebles of Norfolk; the various large bank buildings; and railroad terminals. Private wealth expressed itself in mansions along Monument Avenue, Richmond, or the homes of Major James H. Dooley and his wife, Sallie May, in Richmond at Maymont (1890), by Richmond architect Edgerton Rogers, and Swannanoa (1913), Nelson County (in western Virginia). A tremendous wave of church building also resulted, with sometimes impressive results, such as the Catholic Cathedral of the Sacred Heart (1901–1906), by New Jersey architect Joseph H. McGuire, and Beth Ahabah Synagogue (1903–1904), by Richmond designers Noland and Baskervill, both in Richmond.

The search for a historical past is part of both the Lost Cause landscape and the New South; many of the buildings associated with both are examples of the Colonial Revival. The roots of the Colonial Revival, however, go farther back than the 1870s and 1880s, and tracing them also brings to light the issue of the lack of self-confidence among Virginians that first appeared around 1840. One of the first architectural examples of consciously reviving the past is Bremo Recess (1834–1836), Fluvanna County, in the Piedmont. General John Hartwell Cocke, a former associate of Jefferson and owner of the very Jeffersonian Upper Bremo, explicitly duplicated two seventeenth-century Virginia buildings, one of which was Bacon's Castle, which he re-created in a Jacobean Revival structure with clustered chimneys and curved and stepped gables. In the 1850s, as the question of what was American and the possibility of a great conflict became more evident, interest in the past grew. Examples are Richmond's mammoth Washington Monument (1850–1869), begun by Thomas Crawford and completed by Randolph Rogers, in which an equestrian Washington is surrounded by a pantheon of Revolutionary worthies. In 1858 Ann Pamela Cunningham formed the Mount Vernon Ladies' Association and saved Washington's home, assisting in putting it in the public eye and establishing it as a venerable structure, worthy of emulation. However, it was in the 1870s, and especially around the time of the U.S. Centennial, that interest in the colonial period moved into a more public realm.

Virginia's role in the Colonial Revival in the 1870s and after was central and yet also demonstrated a lack of confidence; only after Yankees validated the Colonial Revival did Virginia become a full participant. Many of the discoverers of Virginia's architectural riches were northerners, one example being the firm of McKim, Mead and White, who first used the red brick southern plantation house image in Newport, Rhode Island, in the 1880s. The

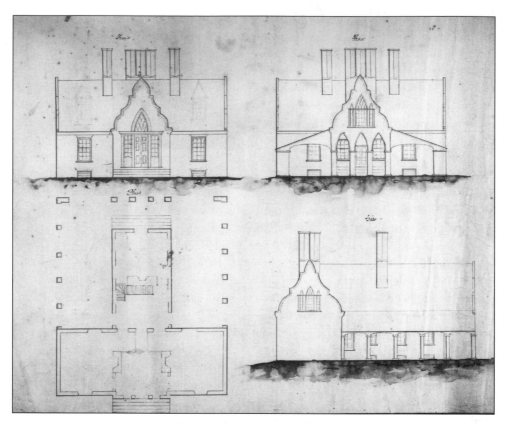

Bremo Recess, Fluvanna County (c. 1834)

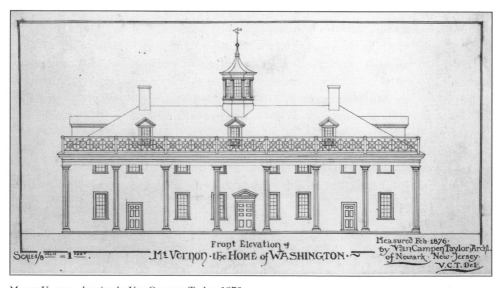

Mount Vernon, drawing by Van Campen Taylor, 1876

first measured drawings of Mount Vernon were made by the obscure New Jersey designer Van Campen Taylor in 1876.

Virginia's own participation in the Colonial Revival has many sides, which may be construed as the naive, the antiquarian, and the sophisticated. By naive is meant the continuation of earlier traditions, for instance, in the Culpeper County Courthouse (1870–1874), by a local builder, Samuel Proctor. Proctor probably was thinking not of a revival, but of continuing the Piedmont courthouse tradition begun by Jefferson. In 1889, dismayed at what seemed to be the neglect and decay of Virginia's colonial remains, such as the ruins at Williamsburg and the church tower at Jamestown, Cynthia Beverley Tucker and Mary Jeffery Galt founded the Association for the Preservation of Virginia Antiquities (APVA), the first such statewide association in the United States. Oriented toward the antiquarian, they were concerned with enshrining "interesting Colonial relics." The APVA acquired property, became involved in preservation battles, and—through its restoration activities, such as the John Marshall house in Richmond (1911–1913)—promoted the Colonial Revival ethic.[13]

In the sophisticated category were the professional architects, whose interest was exemplified by the drawings and brief descriptions of northern Virginia colonial houses that appeared in *American Architect and Building News* in the late 1880s. The work of Glenn Brown, an Alexandria native (though trained at the Massachusetts Institute of Technology) who would become a leading restorer and Colonial Revival architect, these contributions to *American Architect* mark a shift in Virginia architects' appreciation of Virginia's past.[14] The exploitation of Jefferson's architectural imagery began in 1893 with a design by John Kevan Peebles (in conjunction with James R. Carpenter) for a new gymnasium at the University of Virginia. Peebles wrote one of the first articles in the architectural press on Jefferson as an architect.[15] Also in 1893, the first full-scale replica of Mount Vernon was constructed as the Virginia pavilion at the World's Columbian Exposition in Chicago after designs by Richmond architect Edgerton Rogers.

The exploitation of Virginia's colonial architectural heritage on a national scale by architects from across the country, noted above, also helped Virginians appreciate its value. McKim, Mead and White's work at the University of Virginia helped establish the large columnar portico, derived from Jefferson, as part of the southern colonial image. In the 1920s and 1930s, William Lawrence Bottomley, a New York–based architect, became the designer of choice for Virginia's elite. Bottomley's connections came through the Garden Club of Virginia; he designed buildings for many of the club's presidents. The Garden Club of Virginia, founded in 1920 (the Garden Club of America was founded in 1913), grew into a considerable force through its annual tours and funding of restoration projects. To this list might be added those historians and restoration architects who focused on Virginia architecture, such as Fiske Kimball, a Bostonian who wrote *Thomas Jefferson Architect* (1916), and Thomas Tileston Waterman and John A. Barrows, who wrote *Domestic Colonial Architecture of Tidewater Virginia* (1932).

Native Virginia architects have designed in many idioms, as this book illustrates, but what became the most pervasive was the Colonial Revival in its several Virginia manifestations. Red brick and white trim, or the James River image, is one, along with the white clapboard house and the Jeffersonian Roman temple. The Virginia architects of the Colonial Revival seldom

Jamestown Ter-Centennial Exposition (Norfolk, 1907), Auditorium and Convention Hall, John Kevan Peebles and Parker and Thomas

appeared on the national stage; they remained quietly local. John Kevan Peebles was one of the leaders and helped to pro-ject the Virginia image through his work as chairman of the Board of Design and also main designer for the Jamestown Ter-Centennial Exposition, held in Norfolk in 1907, Virginia's entry in the series of Beaux-Arts extravaganzas mounted in a number of American cities in the wake of the Chicago World's Columbian Exposition. Many architectural images were represented at the Norfolk exposition, which included an early building by Frank Lloyd Wright, but the dominant style was gigantic-porticoed Colonial Revival. Large firms—such as Carneal and Johnston, Noland and Baskervill, and Marcellus Wright—as well as individual practitioners like W. Duncan Lee adopted the image.

If the Colonial Revival became the image of the new century, the most significant building type, at least from 1900 to 1940, was the school building. At the collegiate level a major building boom took place at both established institutions, such as the University of Virginia, and newly founded schools, such as Mary Washington College and Old Dominion University. More important, perhaps, in concretizing the colonial image were the tremendous number of primary and secondary schools erected. School consolidation in rural areas brought about the need for new educational plants, designs for which came both from individual architects, such as Charles M. Robinson, who designed several hundred buildings for school districts, and the state itself, through the School Buildings Service of the state Department of Education. Between 1920 and 1950 the School Buildings Service provided plans and specifications for many of the rural schools built during this period. Personnel in the School Buildings Service developed standardized plans, which were then modified to suit individual sites.[16]

The restoration, or more properly, the building, of Colonial Williamsburg, which began in the late 1920s, continued the interest in the colonial past. Initially in charge at Williamsburg was the Boston architecture firm of Perry, Shaw and Hepburn; they trained a group of native Virginians, including Milton L. Grigg and J. Everette Fauber, who became the new leaders. Colonial Williamsburg is the most famous design created in Virginia in the twentieth century, and its impact nationwide can scarcely be overestimated. From houses to corporate headquarters, from paint colors to interior decor, Williamsburg reproductions appear everywhere. The faux colonial Merchants Square at the end of Duke of Gloucester Street, designed and erected 1929–1935 as the tourist and commercial center for the town, became the model for innumerable shopping centers over the next sixty-five years.

Modernism, Tradition, and Large-Scale Growth (c. 1940–c. 2000)

"A local preference in general for the architectural styles of tradition" was how *Architectural Record* magazine summarized the results of a 1940 poll it conducted of Richmonders' opinions on the most admired recent architecture.[17] Modernized, or stripped, classicism led the way, with the Virginia Department of Transportation Building (1939, Carneal and Johnston) ranked first and the Library of Virginia and Supreme Court Building (1939–1940, Carneal, Johnston and Wright with Baskervill and Son) in second place. The only really modern structure ranked was the recently completed Model Tobacco Factory (1938–1940), a Streamline Moderne design by the Chicago firm of Schmidt, Garden and Erikson, which took fourth place. Since the poll Virginia has gained many notable examples of modern architecture; indeed, the state is home to one of the most acclaimed post–World War II buildings, the passenger terminal at Dulles International Airport (1958–1962, Eero Saarinen with Ammann and Whitney Engineers), Chantilly. The nation's leading corporate architecture firm, Skidmore, Owings and Merrill, has produced a number of designs for Virginia clients, including the Reynolds Aluminum Building (1953–1956) and the new Library of Virginia (1993–1997), both in Richmond, as well as buildings in Norfolk. One could go on with the list, for especially in Virginia's cities and in the new rings of industrial parks are many fine modern works designed by Virginians and by outsiders. But if a poll similar to that of 1940 took place today, most Richmonders and Virginians would rank as most admired those buildings with a historical image, especially that of the Colonial Revival.

Virginia has remained architecturally conservative (paralleling its political stance). During the three decades after World War II, when the American architectural press seemed to ban any consideration of the Colonial Revival or other traditional architectural idioms and aggressive modernism was the reigning orthodoxy in architecture schools (including Virginia's), many Virginia firms remained with the traditional styles. With the appearance of postmodernism in the mid-1970s and then, in the 1980s and 1990s, the highly promoted return to traditional architectural sources, Virginians eagerly commissioned new buildings. College and university campuses nationally became showplaces for new architecture, but Virginia was slightly different. Both the College of William and Mary and the University of Virginia continued to build traditional red brick, white-trimmed buildings until the 1960s. Then, for a brief period, modernism made an appearance, sometimes with some success, as with Carlton Abbott's Muscarelle Museum of Art (1982–1983) at the College of William and Mary or with Pietro Belluschi and Sasaki, Dawson, DeMay's Campbell Hall for the School of Architecture (1969) at the University of Virginia, Charlottesville. Less successful were Hugh Stubbins's buildings for the School of Law and the Darden School of Business at the University of Virginia, which were drastically remodeled in 1998. The University of Virginia commissioned designs by leading modernists, like Louis Kahn and Marcel Breuer, which never left the drawing boards. Certainly, other modern buildings exist at both universities, but one almost senses a sigh of relief when, with the reappearance of the Colonial Revival and Jeffersonian Revival as legitimate solutions, architects like Hartman-Cox, Robert A. M. Stern, and Allan Greenberg could be commissioned to design new—and stylistically safe—buildings.

So on one level, Virginia's built environment at the beginning of the twenty-first century still exhibits many of the features of earlier periods. But to note only those is to ignore vast changes in the larger landscape, especially in eastern Virginia. One set of figures will tell the story: in 1900, Virginia had no motorized vehicles; in 1940, the number of registered cars was 422,591; in 1997, registered cars and trucks totaled 5,709,000. Eastern Virginia became suburban—like much of the rest of the eastern seaboard—in the post–World War II years. Mobility became the key for almost all development. As late as the 1930s many rural Virginians had traveled no farther than twenty miles from where they were born, but now everybody could visit the big city. Suburbs; the commercial strip with its diners, motels, and fast food outlets; local and regional shopping centers; and industrial and office parks became the new dominant elements of the landscape. Joel Garreau's much-discussed book of the early 1990s, *Edge City*, took its cue from the rampant development of northern Virginia and of Fairfax County and Tyson's Corner in particular.

As the highway became the locus of development, the older U.S. highways (1, 15, 29, 60, 250) were widened and routed around cities and small towns, preserving some, killing others. Then, beginning in the early 1960s, the interstates (64, 66, 95, and 495) were built. Marvels of engineering in some ways—the multilevel interchange of I-95 in Richmond is one example—they are well landscaped for the most part, deadly boring, and frequently insensitive as they plow through cities and farmlands.

The larger Virginia cities—Richmond, Norfolk, Newport News, and Virginia Beach—dramatically show the impact of the new mobility: a spreading suburban ring, a downtown filled with large post–World War II office buildings and empty of much street activity, and large sections of the inner city filled with the disadvantaged. Many attempts to sustain downtowns through programs such as urban renewal seem to hurt them further. Northern Virginia— and the counties of Fairfax, Arlington, Prince William, and portions of Loudoun and Stafford—have become one vast area of suburban sprawl. Some of the same pattern of strip development and sprawl can be seen around smaller towns; however, as of this date, Charlottesville, Culpeper, Tappahannock, Warrenton, Leesburg, and Fredericksburg appear to have retained semi-vital downtowns. Charlottesville's Main Street is worth examining as one of the few successful examples of an urban mall. Great portions of eastern Virginia remain rural, and small towns, such as Onancock, Heathsville, and Louisa, survive. However, some small villages (population under 1,000), such as Madison and Stanardsville, are almost gone; only the presence of a county courthouse in some cases allows them to survive. But in the countryside another change has occurred, a form of development known as "plops." Larger farms are divided into 5-, 10-, or 40-acre sites, on which single houses, typically outfitted with satellite dishes, are built. The occupants emulate the life of independent landowners of earlier times. But they derive their income from jobs to which they commute and relate to no immediate community.

Virginia's intense development since 1940 is not unique, but aspects of it may be cited as significant and defining. These include historic preservation planning, a large national government presence, and innovations in housing.

Perhaps ironically, given Virginia's reigning agrarian myth, the state is noteworthy for the development of historic towns and districts. Certainly Colonial Williamsburg has served as a model, though it is a museum and only partially a town where the company employees live. More important as an example is Old Town Alexandria, which began to develop a historic consciousness early in the twentieth century. In the late 1920s the Alexandria Chamber of Commerce promoted the use of the "colonial style" for new construction, at a time when ordinances were already in place in Santa Barbara, California, and Palm Beach, Florida. However, Santa Barbara and Palm Beach were really new creations, whereas Alexandria was building on preexisting stock. Alexandria passed a historic district ordinance in 1946, and, although some urban renewal took place in the 1970s, Old Town retained a vital mix of building types, periods, and uses, and the city has on its planning staff an architectural historian and an architect sensitive to historical values and preservation. The historic districts created in Richmond—Monument Avenue (designated 1969), Shockoe Slip (designated 1971), Jackson Ward (designated 1976), and the Fan (designated 1985)—and Norfolk's Ghent (designated 1979) all illustrate in various ways how preservation planning can affect cities.

Helping to define Virginia since 1940 has been the increasing presence of a burgeoning federal government. Again, a sense of irony dominates, for, despite Virginia's prevailing conservative political stance in favor of small government, which derives from Thomas Jefferson's anti-big-government rhetoric, the prosperity the commonwealth has enjoyed is directly related to the expansion of the federal government in Washington and the presence of large military bases in the eastern part of the state. Of course, Jefferson and his cohorts eagerly sought the location of the national capital on the Potomac River, and originally a portion of northern Virginia, including Alexandria and what is now Arlington, was part of the District of Columbia. (It was ceded back to Virginia in 1846.) Before the late 1930s the federal government's Washington facilities remained largely within the boundaries of the District of Columbia. A few wealthy politicians had country estates in northern Virginia, such as Oatlands in Loudoun County and Woodlawn in Fairfax County, and small commuter suburbs grew up in Arlington, but they were minor. But around 1940 the situation changed; the federal government built the Fourteenth Street Bridge between Washington and Arlington and constructed National Airport (1938–1941) and the Pentagon (1941–1942). These heralded later expansions, which included the Central Intelligence Agency at Langley (1955), Dulles Airport at Chantilly (1958–1962), and many more too numerous to mention.

With these projects and the growth of government in Washington itself came the intense development of the last sixty years in northern Virginia and the creation of centers such as Rosslyn, Crystal City, Pentagon City, and Tyson's Corner and of the vast suburban wilderness stretching through Fairfax, Arlington, Loudoun, and Prince William counties. Architecturally, most of it is eminently forgettable, and it is difficult to believe that much of it, especially the commercial construction, will ever inspire the efforts of historic preservationists. Among commercial retail developments, Arlington's Pentagon City (1985–1989, RTKL) is worthy of a look as a demonstration of current mall design practices. Relentless development has meant that the few roadside delights the state possessed in the form of diners and motels are rapidly disappearing, although a few can still be found around Fairfax and in other areas.

Large military installations have helped to define Virginia since 1940. The military presence goes back many years. Fort Monroe (1836) in Hampton has been noted, and the U.S. Navy purchased the site of the Jamestown Ter-Centennial and established a base in Norfolk in 1917. The critical shortage of housing for workers at the Newport News Shipbuilding and Dry Dock Company during World War I led the government's U.S. Housing Corporation to construct Hilton Village (1917–1919). Similarly, World War I brought about the establishment of Fort Belvoir and Quantico Marine Corps Base in northern Virginia. Although they became permanent posts and some building was done, it was through the massive buildup for World War II and the subsequent Cold War that these bases made an impact on their surroundings. Other installations—for example, Fort Robert E. Lee near Richmond, Langley Air Force Base, and naval weapons depots in the Tidewater—contributed to the intense suburbanization of Virginia. Architecturally, most of the bases are undistinguished. The exceptions and worthy of examination are, for the navy, the remains of the Jamestown Exposition at Norfolk Naval Base in Norfolk; for the army, the central group of classroom buildings and spaces and the extraordinary officers' housing in (what else?) a Colonial Revival mode, at Fort Belvoir; and, for the Marines, the Lustron enamel steel housing at Quantico—a fitting contrast to housing built by the army.

A few exceptions relieve the undistinguished character of the suburban housing that has sprung up in northern Virginia and around Richmond and the Tidewater cities. Much of it reflects national trends, including the dominance of large building consortiums, which purchase land, then design, build, and sell a total package. Prefabricated and factory-made modular homes are everywhere, and, as is common nationwide, the architect has largely disappeared from the process, except for high-profile, wealthy clients. Red brick, white-trimmed colonial rules for the most part, though in every post–World War II house, the brick is simply a veneer over a wooden stud frame.

Virginia's distinction in twentieth-century housing is apparent in several forms: the apartment complex, the subdivision, and the new town. In Arlington County, Colonial Village (1935–1940, Harvey Warwick) was the first project insured by the Federal Housing Administration (FHA). Inspired by the greenbelt town concept of Henry Wright and Clarence Stein, as promoted by Lewis Mumford, Colonial Village was built on sloping ground with two-story units arranged around landscaped courtyards.[18] Buckingham Village, a short distance away

Reston, Lake Anne

from Colonial Village, and also in Arlington, was started a year later, in 1936, and construction continued until 1953. More extensive and advertised as a "community of the future," Buckingham Village was planned by Henry Wright and embodied a more coherent social philosophy. The layout of Buckingham is more varied than that of Colonial Village, but it represents the same garden city principles. Working for the FHA was Chloethiel Woodward Smith, who became an important Washington and northern Virginia architect; she was responsible for codifying the Wright-Stein principles for FHA projects. The impact of Colonial Village and Buckingham was immediate, in Washington and, in northern Virginia, at Arlington Village, Parkfairfax, and Fairlington, and nationwide; they served as prototypes for many town house developments.

Amid the morass of suburban subdivisions, several, such as Pine Springs in Fairfax County, might be noted, but the single most important, not just for Virginia, but nationally, is Hollin Hills (1946–1971, Charles Goodman, architect; Lou Bernard Voight, Dan Kiley, and Eric Paepcke, landscape architects), in Fairfax County. Goodman, working for the developer Robert Davenport, created a variety of houses in a modernist idiom. They became the basis for designs Goodman provided in the early 1950s for the National Homes Corporation, one of the country's largest merchant builders. The recipient of numerous awards and citations, Hollin Hills was covered in *Life* magazine and cited by the American Institute of Architects on its 100th anniversary as one of the "Ten Buildings in America's Future."[19] In siting, style, interior planning, and overall layout, it is a critically important example of one direction Virginia's and America's suburbs could have taken but did not.

A similar observation could be made of Reston, Virginia's other major contribution to the problem of postwar suburban sprawl. Accounts of Reston appeared in nearly every major periodical in the early 1960s. It was the first, the best known, and, in most ways, the most successful of American new towns.[20] Sited around a lake with an integrated commercial-residential area and aggressively modern in style, it was designed by the New York firm of Whittlesey, Conklin, and Rossant; Charles Goodman and Chloethiel Woodward Smith also participated. The initial scheme imposed strong design restrictions; however, the original developer, Robert Simon, lost financial control of the project, and subsequent owners, including corporate giant Mobil, allowed anything to be built. The small scale of the commercial area built as part of the first scheme proved to be a problem, especially with the emergence of large-square-footage franchise stores. The next stage can be seen at Reston Town Square (1986–1990, RTKL and Sasaki Associates), which is postmodern and reasserts "the old main street," though devoid of traffic, as the new image; parking is in the acres of asphalt that surround the center.

Significant examples of modern architecture have been built in Virginia since 1940 with, perhaps, Eero Saarinen's Dulles Airport leading the way. Postmodernism and the variants under that vague label have also been constructed by architects as diverse as Michael Graves, Robert A. M. Stern, Hardy Holzman Pfeiffer Associates, and Cesar Pelli, all of national stature; and by such regional firms as Marcellus Wright, Cox and Smith; The Glave Firm; and Baskervill and Son. But, as noted at the opening of this section, and indeed throughout this introduction, Virginians have shown a preference for the architectural styles of tradition, and the various revival styles still ride high. The past is always very present in Virginia.

Notes

1. John Smith, *The Complete Works of Captain John Smith (1580–1631)*, ed. Philip L. Barbour (Chapel Hill: Published for the Institute of Early American History and Culture, Williamsburg, Va., by the University of North Carolina Press, 1986), 1: 144.

2. William Bainter O'Neal, *Architectural Drawing in Virginia, 1819–1969*, exh. cat. (Charlottesville: University of Virginia, School of Architecture, and Richmond: Virginia Museum of Fine Arts, 1969); Charles Brownell, Calder Loth, William M. S. Rasmussen, and Richard Guy Wilson, *The Making of Virginia Architecture* (Richmond: Virginia Museum of Fine Arts, and Charlottesville: University Press of Virginia, 1992), and William Bainter O'Neal, *Architecture in Virginia: An Official Guide to the Old Dominion* (New York: Walker and Co., for the Virginia Museum of Fine Arts, 1968).

3. Anne Carter Lee et al., *Buildings of Virginia: The Valley, South, and West*, Buildings of the United States (Society of Architectural Historians and Oxford University Press, forthcoming).

4. Thomas Jefferson, *Notes on the State of Virginia*, ed. William Peden (Chapel Hill: University of North Carolina Press, 1955), 108.

5. William Waller Hening, comp., *The Statutes at Large: Being a Collection of All the Laws of Virginia, From the First Session of the Legislature, in the Year 1619*, 13 vols. (Richmond, 1809–1823), 2: 261. See also John O. and Margaret T. Peters, *Virginia's Historic Courthouses* (Charlottesville: University Press of Virginia, 1995).

6. James Kornwolf, *"So Good A Design," The Colonial Campus of William and Mary: Its History, Background, and Legacy*, exh. cat. (Williamsburg: The College of William and Mary, Joseph and Margaret Muscarelle Museum of Art, 1989).

7. Robert Beverly, *The History and Present State of Virginia* [London, 1705], ed. L. B. Wright (Chapel Hill: University of North Carolina Press, 1947), 105.

8. Hugh Jones, *The Present State of Virginia*, ed. Richard L. Morton (Chapel Hill: University of North Carolina Press, 1966), 70.

9. Daniel D. Reiff, *Small Georgian Houses in England and Virginia: Origins and Development through the 1750s* (Newark, Del.: University of Delaware Press, 1986).

10. Ambler Johnson, "Echoes of 1861–1961," *Automobile Tour of Principal Battlefields near Richmond* (Richmond: Chamber of Commerce, 1970), n.p.

11. For background, see Gaines M. Foster, *Ghosts of the Confederacy: Defeat, The Lost Cause, and the Emergence of the New South, 1865 to 1913* (New York: Oxford University Press, 1987).

12. The classic treatment is C. Vann Woodward, *Origins of the New South* (Baton Rouge: Louisiana State University, 1951); see also Edward L. Ayers, *The Promise of the New South: Life After Reconstruction* (New York: Oxford University Press, 1992).

13. James Michael Lindgren, *Preserving the Old Dominion: Historic Preservation and Virginia Traditionalism* (Charlottesville: University Press of Virginia, 1993).

14. Glenn Brown, "Old Colonial Work in Virginia and Maryland," *American Architect and Building News* 22 (22 October; 19, 26 November 1887), 198–199, 242–243, 254. Reprinted in *The Georgian Period*, parts 1–2 (New York: American Architect and Building News, 1898–1901).

15. John Kevan Peebles, "Thos. Jefferson, Architect," *Alumni Bulletin [University of Virginia]* 1 (November 1894), 68–74; reprinted as "Thomas Jefferson, Architect," *American Architect and Building News* 47 (January 19, 1895), 29–30.

16. Selden Richardson of the State Library and Archives, Richmond, kindly provided this information; the School Buildings Service archive is housed there.

17. "The Record Poll," *Architectural Record* 88 (December 1940), 16–18.

18. See Clarence S. Stein, *Toward New Towns for America*, rev. ed. (New York: Reinhold, 1957).

19. "Best House under $15,000 . . ," *Life*, September 10, 1951, 123–127; "Notable Modern Buildings," *Life*, June 3, 1957, 72–73; Paul Rudolph, "Frank Adding up of Assets" and "New Homes: Wacky and Staid," *Life*, November 24, 1961, 111–116; and Frederick Gutheim, *1857–1957: One Hundred Years of Architecture in America* (New York: Reinhold, 1957), 16.

20. "Reston: An Answer to Suburban Sprawl," *Architectural Record* 136 (July 1963): 119–134; John Morris Dixon, "Progress in Planning: A New Town Brings Urban Living Patterns to the Countryside," *Architectural Forum* 123 (July–August, 1965), 84–89; Ada Louise Huxtable, "Fully Planned Town Opens in Virginia," *New York Times*, December 5, 1965, 1, 85; "New Towns," *Time*, May 21, 1965, 77; "Reston: First of the New Satellite Cities," *Life*, December 24, 1965, 144–145; Wolf von Eckardt, "The Community: Could This Be Our Town?" *The New Republic*, November 7, 1964, 17–24; Tom Grubisich and Peter McCandless, *Reston: The First Twenty Years* (Reston: Reston Publishing Co., 1985).

Northern Virginia (NV)

THIS SECTION COVERS ARLINGTON MUNICIPAL COUNTY AND THE COUN-
ties of Fairfax and Prince William. Treated under a separate section is the city of
Alexandria. Adjacent to Washington, D.C., these three counties (and Alexandria)
are the most populous area of Virginia with more than 1.5 million residents.

Before European settlement, present-day northern Virginia was the home of various Algo-
nquin tribes. Captain John Smith stopped at an Indian village on the Potomac somewhere in
the area in July 1608. For the next century, competing land claims and the resistance of Native American inhabitants prevented settlement. Finally, proprietorship passed to the Fairfax
family, and in 1722 the Iroquois ceded their rights. The eighteenth century saw some settlement. Alexandria, the principal port, was established in 1749, and several large land holdings
emerged, such as those of the Washingtons (see Mount Vernon), the Masons (see Gunston
Hall), and others. Other than a few churches and the large estates, very little eighteenth-
century building remains. From 1791 to 1846 portions of present-day Arlington County and
the city of Alexandria were part of Washington, D.C. During the Civil War the Union army
built forts in the area to guard Washington, and major battles, such as those at Manassas,
were fought nearby.

Alexandria became an independent city in 1870, and the ensuing confusion over a county
and a city with the same name led in 1920 to the renaming of the county for Arlington, the
Custis-Lee House and the cemetery. (Arlington is a municipal county, not a city.) Alexandria
remained the only urban area of any size in northern Virginia well into the twentieth century.
The remaining area was largely agricultural, with a few small farming villages. Until World
War II, the northernmost counties—Arlington and Fairfax—remained rural, but then
changes started. In 1940 Arlington's population was 57,040; by 1948 it had grown to 123,832.
Fairfax in 1950 had about 1,500 farmers and was the greatest milk-producing county in the
commonwealth; by 1970 it had only twelve farmers left. Similarly, Prince William County had
a population of 144,703 in 1980 and 286,813 by 2000.

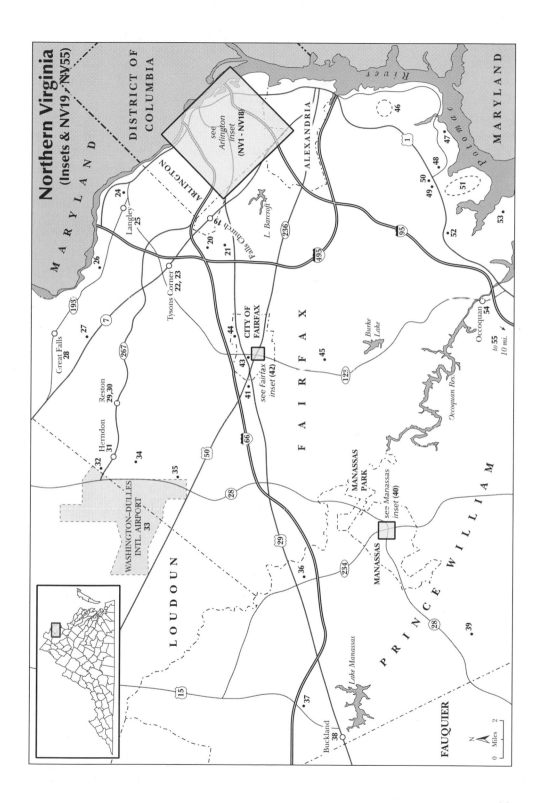

Northern Virginia
(Insets & NV19, NV55)

DISTRICT OF COLUMBIA

MARYLAND

MARYLAND

Potomac River

ALEXANDRIA

• 46

1

• 47

• 48

• 50

• 49

• 51

• 53

95

• 52

495

236

see Arlington inset (NV1 - NV18)

ARLINGTON

• 24 Langley
• 25

L. Barcroft

• 26

Falls Church 19
• 20
• 21

193

7

Great Falls 28
• 27

Tysons Corner 22, 23

• 44
43 • 41
CITY OF FAIRFAX

45 •

Burke Lake

12

Occoquan 54

to 55
10 mi.

267

Reston 29,30

see Fairfax inset (42)

FAIRFAX

66

Occoquan Res.

Herndon 31
32 •
• 34

50

WASHINGTON-DULLES INTL. AIRPORT 33

35 •

28

MANASSAS PARK

see Manassas inset (40)

29

36 •

234

MANASSAS

LOUDOUN

PRINCE WILLIAM

28

• 39

15

• 37

Lake Manassas

Buckland
38

FAUQUIER

N

0   Miles   2

These changes resulted from the growth of the federal government; the relocation of major businesses to the area, frequently at the invitation of either local or state governments; and the resultant construction of major highways and public transportation. Metrorail for Washington, D.C., reaches into northern Virginia on two major lines. The state has set up a public rail system for commuters on the I-95 corridor and is considering expansion in other areas.

The consequence is a vast suburban wilderness of undistinguished housing tracts, shopping malls, and strip developments. Traffic tie-ups on the various interstate highways have become legendary, perhaps the worst in the country. The western reaches of Fairfax County, McLean and beyond, are "McMansion heaven"; thousands of houses of 7,000 square feet and larger, with three-car garages, have been built on small plots. Closer to Washington, in and around Rosslyn and Crystal City, a forest of high rises has appeared, almost all devoid of architectural interest. The high-rise boom along the Potomac River waterfront at Crystal City and Rosslyn resulted from height restrictions in downtown Washington, D.C., and a major exodus of many businesses following the 1968 riots in Washington. The result is not just architectural mediocrity and banality, but the creation, in these places and in the office parks around Tysons Corner, of environments in which the pedestrian is banned. Gems of importance do appear, and some important urban models as well, but overall, northern Virginia illustrates the ills of uncontrolled development and the need for coordinated plans and environmental considerations for future growth.

Because of the complexity and the geographical configuration of northern Virginia, the sequence of entries begins with the area closest to the Potomac River across from Washington and spirals up to the north, and then swings back around to the south.

Arlington County (NV1–NV18)

NV1 George Washington Memorial Parkway (Mount Vernon Memorial Highway)

1928–1932, 1930–1965, Gilmore Clarke, landscape architect; Jay Downer, engineer. From I-495 (north) to U.S. 1 (south)

Skirting the west bank of the Potomac from north of Washington, D.C., south to Mount Vernon, a length of approximately 25 miles, the parkway provides scenic views of the river, landscape, and Washington, as well as access to various memorials and institutions. The concept of a "great road" linking Mount Vernon and Washington was envisioned as early as 1872 and then revived with the McMillan Commission study of 1901–1902. The sesquicentennial fervor of 1926 and the vision of recreational uses in the new motor age brought a new study in 1927 by Charles W. Eliot, who served as director of planning for the National Capital Park and Planning Commission. The Capper-Cramton Act of 1930 provided the initial funds, and construction began under the aegis of the Bureau of Public Roads. Opened to traffic in 1932 as part of the bicentennial celebration of Washington's birth, the initial section ran from the Virginia terminus of Memorial Bridge at the north, south through downtown Alexandria to Mount Vernon, a length of 15.5 miles. Highly praised at the time, it was considered by an engineering publication to be "America's Most Modern Motorway." Initially named the Mount Vernon Memorial Highway, it was renamed the George Washington Memorial Parkway. The 9.7-mile section to the north, from Memorial Bridge to I-495 (the Capital Beltway), was planned almost immediately, but took until the 1960s for completion. The initial designers, Clarke and Downer, and the arborist, Henry

NV1 George Washington Memorial Parkway (Mount Vernon Memorial Highway)

Nye, had all worked for the Westchester, New York, County Parkway Commission and had designed a series of path-breaking parkways in the years after World War I. Clarke defined the parkway as a "strip of public land dedicated to recreation, over which abutting owners have no right of light, air, or access." Enjoyment of nature on a pleasure drive is the essential concept of a parkway, but unfortunately in recent years that idea has been lost as parkways have come to be viewed simply as transportation corridors. The GWPK still retains many of the virtues of the parkway concept with a carefully scripted sequence of nature and the glories of architecture, along with notable design features such as stone-faced arched bridges, concrete slab base, and beveled curbing. The views across to Washington, D.C., are spectacular.

NV2 Arlington Memorial Bridge

1923–1932, McKim, Mead and White. Potomac River between Lincoln Memorial, Washington, D.C., and entrance to Arlington National Cemetery, VA 400

The idea of a bridge symbolically linking the North and the South and providing a grand entranceway into Washington and Arlington National Cemetery came forward several times in the latter nineteenth century. Under the McMillan Commission of 1901–1902 (Daniel F. Burnham, Charles Follen McKim, Frederick Law Olmsted, Jr., and Augustus Saint-Gaudens) a low, Roman-arched bridge linking the projected Lincoln Memorial and Arlington House was proposed as part of the embellishments for

parks. The proposal languished for many years, until the dedication of the Tomb of the Unknown Soldier at Arlington Cemetery on Armistice Day, November 11, 1921. A monstrous traffic jam caused the presidential party to be an hour and a half late for the ceremony, and shortly thereafter the bridge received approval. The firm of McKim, Mead and White was selected. The designer was William Mitchell Kendall, a senior partner who had worked with McKim on the McMillan Commission and was a member of the National Commission of Fine Arts. Part of the proposal was to extend the bridge's forecourts and create monumental entrances to the Lincoln Memorial and Arlington National Cemetery. The bridge is a reinforced concrete structure of nine low arches, the central arch operating as a drawbridge. It is faced with North Carolina granite. The keystones are carved with bison heads, by Alexander Proctor, and eagles, the work of C. Paul Jennewein, decorate the piers.

NV3 Arlington National Cemetery

NV3.1 Arlington House (Custis-Lee House, Robert E. Lee Memorial)

1802–1804. 1818, George Hadfield. Arlington National Cemetery. Open to the public

The site is imposing, and the architect took full advantage, drawing upon several Greek models (the Temple of Poseidon, c. 460 B.C. at Paestum

Arlington County
(NV1 - NV18)

and the Temple of Hephaestus, c. 449 B.C. in Athens) to create one of the most sublime and dominant porticoes in the United States. The overscaled Doric columns (brick covered by stucco) became a landmark and influenced the future planning of Washington, D.C., particularly the placement of Memorial Bridge. The site was originally the center of a 1,000-acre plantation owned by George Washington Parke Custis, Washington's stepson, and his wife, Mary Lee Fitzhugh. Arlington House began as two small buildings completed between 1802 and 1804, which served as their home and a treasury of Washington memorabilia. The central section, uniting the two wings and creating a 100-foot-long facade (with wings it measures 140 feet) was designed by Hadfield, a British-born architect who had worked on the U.S.

Capitol in 1795–1798. Hadfield's intention, following Custis's instructions, was to create a memorial for George Washington: a frontispiece for the display of Custis's collection of objects associated with the first president. At the house in 1831 Robert E. Lee married the Custises' daughter, Mary Anna Randolph, and subsequently the house became his property. During the Civil War the Union army occupied the house, and the federal government assumed title. Union dead were buried on the grounds, and an office of the Freedmen's Bureau for former slaves operated there. In 1873 Lee heirs sued for the return of the house, and after a Supreme Court decision, the federal government purchased the estate and used it for various purposes, including headquarters for the National Cemetery. Illustrating the changing

NV3.1 Arlington House (Custis-Lee House, Robert E. Lee Memorial) with entrance to Arlington National Cemetery

nature of reputations, by 1925 Lee had become a national (rather than a southern) hero, and the mansion became a federal memorial dedicated to him. Restoration began under the war department and was transferred in 1933 to the National Park Service, which has continued to restore and maintain the property. The original floor plan remains. The interior decoration is a mixture of periods, though the focus is on the time of the Lee occupancy and especially the 1850s. In the south wing, elements of G. W. P. Custis's Washington "treasury" remain. To the west of the house are the former servant or slave quarters.

NV3.2 Arlington National Cemetery Grounds

1864–present

Union dead were buried on the grounds of Arlington House in 1864. Shortly thereafter, on June 15 of that year, Quartermaster General of the Army Montgomery C. Meigs petitioned Secretary of War Edwin Stanton to establish a national cemetery on the site. Meigs, although born in Georgia, viewed Confederates as traitors and had a deep-seated vindictiveness toward the South and toward Lee in particular. Meigs assigned his assistant, Edward Clark (later Architect of the Capitol), to lay out the grounds. Clark's design—since extended—follows the topography with the curvilinear roads popularized by the rural cemetery movement. By the end of 1864 more than 7,000 Union dead had been interred, and by the end of the

war, more than 16,000. In April 1866, in Mrs. Lee's former rose garden, Meigs had erected the Tomb for the Unknown Dead from the war, which contained the remains of 2,111 soldiers. Nearby he erected a Temple of Fame, a colonnaded gazebo dedicated to the memory of George Washington and eleven Union generals. This was removed in the 1960s during restoration of Arlington House. Meigs's own memorial (and his family's) is 100 yards east of the former rose garden. In 1868, the first Memorial Day, then called Decoration Day, was declared at Arlington Cemetery.

The initial government cemetery encompassed 200 acres immediately surrounding Arlington House; in 1897 it took in 408 acres, and then in 1981 an area of Fort Myer was added, making the total 612 acres. The formal entrance at the Virginia terminus of Memorial Bridge was part of William Kendall's bridge scheme (1923–1932, McKim, Mead and White) and follows the stock classicism of that firm. Immediately behind it is the United States Women's War Memorial (1995–1998, Manfriedo and Weiss), which consists of glass shafts and lights, especially effective at night. Among the notable monuments are Major Pierre Charles L'Enfant's tomb, directly in front of the mansion; the John F. Kennedy grave (1965–1967, John Carl Warnecke); the Confederate Monument (1906–1914, Moses Ezekiel, sculptor), a 30-foot-tall shaft crowned by *Vindicatrix*; the Canadian Cross (1927, Sir Reginald Blomfield); the General George B. McClellan Arch (c. 1875, Lot Flannery), also 30 feet tall; and the United States Coast Guard Memorial

(1928, George Howe; Gaston Lachaise, sculptor). Also on the grounds is the Memorial Amphitheater (1913–1920, Frederick B. Owens of Carrère and Hastings), an elliptical structure of white Danby, Vermont, marble with a colonnade in the Doric order. Owens's sources included the Theater of Dionysus at Athens and the Roman Theater at Orange in France. The entablature is inscribed with quotations and names of battle sites. The amphitheater is a typical early twentieth-century example of ritualistic military commemoration. Note the seat for the presiding officer. Adjacent is the Tomb of the Unknown Soldier (1931, Lorimer Rich; Thomas Hudson Jones, sculptor), a place of great solemnity and pageantry. Adjacent to the immediate north of the cemetery, at Arlington Boulevard and Ridge Road, is the United States Marine Corps War Memorial, the Iwo Jima monument (1954, Felix de Weldon, sculptor), which is reputedly the largest bronze sculpture in the world. De Weldon based his design on journalist Joe Rosenthal's photograph of the flag raising on Mt. Suribachi, February 23, 1945.

NV4 Arlington National Cemetery Buildings

1996, KressCox Associates (Maintenance Facility); Kerns Group (Marine Corps Multipurpose Building and Navy Mutual Aid Society). Southern edge of Arlington Cemetery, Fort Myer, off Columbia Pk.

This group of largely utilitarian structures is united by the use of fieldstone walls, brick, and repeated elemental forms, such as low pyramidal shapes. The strategy of breaking up the mass of the buildings helps to minimize their visual intrusion. The result is above the level of most current armed forces design.

NV5 The Pentagon

1941–1942, George Edwin Bergstrom and David Julius Witmer, and Office of the Quartermaster General, Construction Division. Later modifications. Jefferson Davis Hwy. between Boundary Rd. and Shirley Memorial Hwy.

Perhaps best known as a symbol or a mind set, the Pentagon is among Virginia's famous buildings, and, at 6,240,000 square feet, one of the world's largest office structures. Intended to house under one roof all federal defense headquarters operations (approximately 25,000 workers), it was designed as war clouds gathered in mid-1941. Bergstrom and Witmer were from Los Angeles and got the commission through positions they held in the American Institute of Architects (AIA). The pentagonal form was a vague reference to traditional fortifications. Bergstrom and Witmer's original plan contained internal barrackslike fingers, but personnel in the quartermaster general's office changed the floor plan to concentric interior rings of office spaces, an arrangement which appealed to the efficient military mind. The 4,600-foot limestone exterior has squared piers in the "stripped" or "modernized" classical idiom common to the 1930s. The most remarkable feature of the building, though, was its construction time: only sixteen months, from September 1941 to December 1942.

The Pentagon assumed a new role as a symbol after the terrorist attack of September 11, 2001, when a hijacked airliner crashed into the west side, penetrating three office rings and killing 125 office and military personnel in the building and 64 passengers and crew on the plane. The section is being rebuilt and a memorial is planned for the grounds in front.

NV6 Pentagon City

1985–1989, RTKL. Bounded by Hayes St., Joyce St., and 15th St., Arlington (Pentagon City Metro stop)

Relentlessly glitzy, this is probably the best of the various northern Virginia indoor shopping malls. Designed by the large Baltimore firm that specializes in bringing the latest architectural fashions to the populace, it must be visited. Its 116-acre site includes an 11-acre park turned back to the county of Arlington. The development has 1.5 million square feet of mixed use, including an office tower, a hotel, and several major retailers, and the 809,000-square-foot Fashion Centre, or the actual mall. The exterior skin is a mix of forms and modernist and postmodern idioms: mock Georgian, cut-rate classical, and tinted glass curtain walls surround the interior activity. The Fashion Centre is a series of three- and four-story atria, each in a different architectural idiom, expressed in columns and trim, to provide "character" and "orientation." Department stores anchor either end. Carefully planned so that the visitor must traverse great sections of each level to escape, Pentagon City displays "architecture until you drop."

NV7 Arlington Historical Museum (Hume School)

1895, B. Stanley Simmons. 1805 S. Arlington Ridge Rd. Open to the public

From Pentagon City, the former Hume School is a step back in time. Brick, two stories with a three-story tower, and Queen Anne in style, the school was designed by a Washington, D.C., architect. It now serves as the museum of the Arlington Historical Society.

NV8 Ronald Reagan National Airport (National Airport)

1938–1941, Howard L. Cheney, with Charles M. Goodman. Later additions. 1994–1997, extension, Cesar Pelli. George Washington Memorial Pkwy., Arlington (National Airport Metro stop)

Intended as the gateway to the national capital, National Airport sits on the Potomac River across from Washington. The Army Corps of Engineers built up the site, known as "Gravelly Point," from deposits of sand and gravel during a dredging operation on the Potomac. The runways are actually in the District of Columbia, while the terminals and hangars are in Virginia. The airport resulted from the 1938 Civil Aeronautics Act, which created the Civil Aviation Authority, later known as the Federal Aviation Administration (FAA), and allowed the federal government to build and operate an airport. The architect of record was Howard L. Cheney, originally of Chicago, who worked in the Washington office of the Public Buildings Administration. Cheney in turn engaged Charles M. Goodman, recently arrived from Chicago, who designed a streamlined terminal with extensive glass facades. President Franklin D. Roosevelt, who reviewed the design, suggested that the main facades incorporate a national image and suggested Mount Vernon. The design was substantially modified to incorporate eight square piers that articulate the curving entrance facade and cylindrical columns in antis on the runway facade. The main waiting room has a large picture window overlooking the runways and retains some original decorative features in the lighting, balusters, and etched glass.

Cesar Pelli's major addition of a series of domed pavilions forming a new concourse is openly reminiscent of nineteenth-century iron and glass structures such as Joseph Paxton's Crystal Palace in London and Henri Labrouste's Bibliothèque Nationale in Paris (Pelli has written in admiring terms about these prototypes). The web joists, low saucer domes, and great glass walls are compelling. Of particular note is the use of contemporary art in the form of murals, sculptures, and other decoration, by Frank Stella, Joyce Kozloff, Kent Bloomer, Al Held, and William Jacklin, among others. The art is extensive and impressive and rises above the usual governmental "percentage for art" or "airport art." The concourse doubles as a shopping mall, though the shops are on the exterior side of the security check and apparently not very successful.

The nearby Terminal A Parking Garage (1991, HNTB with Hartman-Cox) is a welcome relief from the boring appearance of most parking structures. Hartman-Cox, the design architects, used glass block to create a striking replay of 1930s Streamline Moderne.

NV9 Fairlington

1942–1944, Kenneth Franzheim and Alan Balch Mills. I-395 (Shirley Hwy.), S. Abingdon St., S. 28th St., Quaker Ln., and VA 7 (King St.), Arlington

Encompassing 322 acres and containing 3,449 apartment and town house units, two community center buildings, a maintenance building, a real estate office, and outdoor recreation areas, Fairlington is the largest of the Defense Homes Corporation's World War II housing projects for defense workers and their families. Many of Fairlington's original residents worked at the Pentagon and the Navy Annex, about two and one-half miles northwest. Straddling both sides of the Shirley Highway, Fairlington's layout follows the already developing northern

Virginia tradition, seen at nearby Colonial and Buckingham villages, of garden apartments in a generic Colonial Revival idiom set within ample green space and trees, accessible by curving roads. A variety of housing forms with different-shaped roofs give some individual distinction. Kenneth Franzheim, the architect in charge, had designed large commercial buildings in Houston and New York before working on defense housing. Alan B. Mills, the local associate, had worked in the Office of the Supervising Architect of the Treasury, and then for the Public Buildings Administration. Construction, by the Thompson-Starrett Company of New York, took a little over eighteen months. Sold to a private developer in 1947, the complex was turned into condominiums in 1972–1977. Today the generic names of Village, Mews, Arbor, Meadows, Glen, Green, and Common have been added to the name of Fairlington to distinguish the different parts.

NV10 Arlington Village

1939, Harvey Warwick. Columbia Pk. (entrance), S. Barton St., S. Cleveland St., 13th Rd. S., 16th St. S., and S. Edgewood St.

Gustave Ring, who had built Colonial Village, developed this 53-acre site as a further modification of the Stein-Wright garden city scheme used at Chatham Village, Pittsburgh. Warwick created five superblock groupings, containing

655 garden apartments, on about 12 percent of the space, leaving about 47 acres for green space, parks, recreation, roads, and parking. A shopping center was located on Columbia Pike. As usual, Colonial Revival forms and details were the architectural idiom.

NV11 John Ball House (Ball-Sellers House)

c. 1745. 1885, addition. 5620 S. 3rd St. Open to the public

Tucked into a subdivision, the John Ball House includes an original one-and-one-half-story section, constructed of logs and with a rare surviving clapboard roof. Consisting of one room on the ground floor, it exemplifies the unpretentious dwellings of many of the early settlers. The two-story wing dates from 1885. The house is maintained by the Arlington Historical Society.

NV12 Unitarian Church of Arlington

1964, Charles M. Goodman. 4444 Arlington Blvd. (near the southwest corner of Arlington Blvd. and George Mason Dr.)

Goodman's design stresses structural features with its strong piers and dominant flat roof plane. The interior, essentially a great meeting room with high walls and narrow clerestory, shows the influence of Goodman's Chicago

NV12 Unitarian Church of Arlington

NV14.2 Dan Kain Trophies, Inc. (Sheff Store Building)

background and of Frank Lloyd Wright's Unity Temple.

NV13 **Buckingham Village**

1936–1953, Henry Wright, Albert Lueders, and Allan Foeke Kamstra, architects; H. E. Van Gelder, landscape architect. 4319 N. Pershing Dr. (intersection of N. Glebe Rd. and Pershing Dr.); North George Mason Dr. (Ballston Metro stop)

Another attempt to bring the utopian theories of the garden city movement into American suburbia, Buckingham Village was a "community of the future." Built on 100 acres, it contains 183 apartment blocks and a neighborhood center for shopping, theater, and other activities around the intersection of Glebe Road and Pershing Drive as well as other assorted structures, including two gatehouses on George Mason Drive near U.S. 50. These are set in substantial green space and a network of roads, with pedestrian paths separate from the streets. Behind the project was the Committee for Economic Recovery (later named the Committee for Economic and Social Progress), a group of businessmen committed to the ideals of Roosevelt's New Deal who insisted that private industry had a role to play in economic recovery. The head was Allie Freed, a New York businessman who became convinced that highly capitalized home-building companies and socially conscious design could help alleviate the housing crisis of the 1930s. He purchased 100 acres of farmland in Arlington County and obtained the necessary mortgages. Governmental involvement was limited to FHA mortgage insurance. Developed in six phases from 1937 to 1953, the complex displays a consistent use of the Colonial Revival style in brick. The one exception is an apartment house at the corner of North 4th and North Piedmont streets, an experiment in nontraditional design with a flat roof and cantilevered balconies reminiscent of 1920s German apartment buildings. Henry Wright, who, along with his sometime partner Clarence Stein, led the garden city movement in the United States, worked on the initial layout before his death in 1936; Lueders and Kamstra, who had worked for Stein and Wright, continued with the project. Widely publicized at the time, Buckingham Village became a model for many other developments. Portions of Buckingham Village have been turned into condominiums and in the process painted different colors.

NV14 **Clarendon**

Clarendon Metro stop

For years the traditional center of Arlington, Clarendon is formed by a hub of roads known as Five Points. Around the various intersections of Clarendon Boulevard, Washington Boulevard, Wilson Boulevard, and Fairfax Drive have grown up a group of buildings that span six decades of development.

NV14.1 **3100 Clarendon Boulevard** (Office Tower)

1987, Martin and Jones

Clarendon's centerpiece and most prominent vertical landmark is an office tower designed by a local postmodernist firm. They chose Michael Graves's Portland (Oregon) Public Services building (1979–1983) as their model. The design has the typical squat form, pyramidal top, and overscaled simplified details; unfortunately, neither the detailing nor the wit match the richness of Graves's original.

NV14.2 **Dan Kain Trophies, Inc.** (Sheff Store Building)

1945–1946, Donald Hudson Drayer. 3100 Washington Blvd. (southwest corner of Washington Blvd. and N. Highland St.)

Originally an appliance store, the building is a surviving remnant of post–World War II streamlined design, with a long, horizontal form and a cylinder serving as a corner marker and entrance. The original interior is completely gone.

NV14.3 **U.S. Post Office**

1937, Louis A. Simon, Supervising Architect, U.S. Treasury Department. 3118 Washington Blvd. (southeast corner of Washington Blvd. and N. Hudson St.)

Jeffersonian Deco might be the term for this wonderful post office with a splayed plan and a domed entrance that skillfully turns the corner at this intersection. In keeping with other federal designs for post offices in Virginia, it is red brick with light-colored stone trim, but as a departure from strait-laced Colonial Revival, details such as the piers are abstracted. The interior furnishings are largely original. The public lobby also contains six small murals by Auriel

Bessener (1940) that depict local history in subjects ranging from Native Americans to activities of the halcyon days of pre–World War II, apple picking and polo playing.

NV14.4 Silver Diner

1997, Cato Gobe. 3200 Wilson Blvd.

This is one of a chain of new diners, vastly larger than their prototypes, that have been built in the Washington area in the past few years. The original design (by a New York firm, though based upon an earlier model by Richard Gutman) dates from 1989 and draws on the Mountain View (New Jersey) Company's designs of the 1950s. The marquee is perhaps a little too cute and the overall design too nostalgic, but they are a welcome change from standard fast-food outlets. Other Virginia locations for Silver Diners are Springfield, Reston, Fair Oaks, Tysons Corner, and Potomac Mills.

NV14.5 Al's Motors

c. 1948, J. Raymond Mims. 3910 Wilson Blvd.

A rare survivor, this auto dealership—which has changed names and owners several times—illustrates post–World War II strip commercial development with its large plate glass windows right on the street. The concrete cornice has two speed lines, and the entrance incorporates glass block. In contrast to the formal front, the service wing to the rear is built of less expensive multicolored brick. The front showroom still has splayed neon tubes in the ceiling.

NV14.6 Atilla's Restaurant (Little Tavern)

c. 1940, George E. V. Stone. 3125 Wilson Blvd. (corner of N. Herndon St. and Wilson Blvd.)

Little Taverns abounded in the Washington–northern Virginia area in the 1930s, 1940s, and 1950s. Predecessors to the vast chains of fast-food outlets, they offered five-cent hamburgers as their staple. The company tried a comeback in the 1980s but failed. Still visible in this survivor is the imagery of the small, humble tavern with tall roofs, incongruously carried out in white porcelain panels for the walls and green Texaco service-station-style trim. The Little Tavern was produced primarily by Luther Reason Ray's Structural Porcelain Enamel Company from a prototype design created by George E. V. Stone in 1931.

NV14.3 U.S. Post Office, Arlington

NV14.7 Whole Foods Company Supermarket (Bread and Circus)

1996, MR+A/Mushinsky; interior, Tom Hatch. 2700 Wilson Blvd.

A yuppie grazer's nirvana, and certainly a shift from the standard boring box of most supermarkets, the building partakes of certain late 1990s environmental design fads, such as a large roof canopy with exposed trusses. However, in this case the canopy may recall nineteenth-century food markets and tent-covered stalls. It is exquisitely detailed for a supermarket; the lower orange- and cream-colored brick walls sport quoins, and the entrance recalls older main street buildings. The interior, well worth a visit, shows two systems in conflict: the exposed ducts, pipes, and guts of environmental brutalism, and then, at the aisle level, a series of marquees for the different departments, each of which is treated as a separate shop. Don't miss the uplifting quotes on the walls, even one by John La Farge! The fresh produce is the star of the show.

NV15 Calvert Manor

1948, Mihran Mesrobian. 1925–1927 N. Calvert St.

The designer and owner, Mesrobian (born in Turkey to Armenian parents), was known for his large Washington, D.C., apartment blocks and elegant hotels of the 1920s and 1930s. Following the migration of Washington to the suburbs he designed a number of apartments and shopping centers in northern Virginia. For this

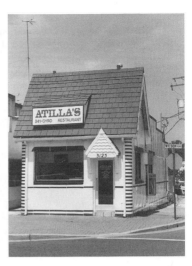

NV14.4 Silver Diner   NV14.6 Atilla's Restaurant (Little Tavern)

NV15 Calvert Manor (left)   NV17 Colonial Village

three-story apartment building Mesrobian used red brick over concrete block bearing walls, but the details—raised brick quoins, belt courses, and strip windows—might be called Moderne.

NV16 Key Boulevard Apartments

1941–1942, Albert D. Lueders. 1537–1545 N. Key Blvd.

The modest Art Deco style of this three-building group of forty-one garden apartments stands out against the prevailing Colonial Re-

vival idiom. Constructed of brick, they incorporate glass block, raised speed lines, and porthole windows.

NV17 Colonial Village

1935–1940, Harvey Warwick, Frances Koening. Bounded by Lee Hwy., Queens Ln., N. Veitch St., and Wilson Blvd. (Courthouse Metro stop)

The oldest of the northern Virginia garden apartment complexes was also the first Federal Housing Authority project in the nation. The FHA worked closely with Washington developer Gustave Ring to create a model apartment village. Colonial Village was built in four phases, the first three designed by Harvey Warwick and the fourth by Frances Koening. In keeping with some of the most advanced garden city ideas of Clarence Stein and others, which were readily observable at Greenbelt, Maryland, the two-story apartment units cluster around courtyards, a substantial greenbelt runs through the center, and the staggering and setback of the units increase variety, ventilation, and light. Pedestrian and vehicular traffic are rigorously separated. Differentiating this project from other modernist schemes was the Colonial Revival idiom of red brick, light trim, and small sculptural embellishments.

NV18 Rosslyn

(Rosslyn Metro stop)

Surreal is perhaps the best description for Rosslyn, which is Arlington's major high-rise center: it resembles a set in a bad science fiction movie. Benjamin Forgey, the *Washington Post*'s architecture critic, claimed that it was "dramatically transformed from a backwater to boomtown at a bad architectural moment." Here and there a fragment of a pre–World War II low-rise city can be spied, but the explosive growth of the 1960s to the 1990s has transformed the area into the world's worst collection of (about sixty) mid-level high rises and a stunning example of anti-civility. Only a few buildings are worth noting.

NV18.1, NV18.2 USA Today Building and Gannett Building

1982, 1985, Hellmuth, Obata and Kassabaum. 1000 and 1100 Wilson Blvd.

The twin silver towers in a minimalist sculptural form that play off each other with identical sleek aluminum skins are eye catchers. Although the Gannett Building has the easier entrance to find, the interior mall is undistinguished. The entrance to the USA Today Building is memorable. Escalators and water cascade down, and the view toward Washington from the stairs and the third- and fourth-floor malls is impressive. In September 1999 the Gannett Corporation announced it would relo-

NV18.1, NV18.2 USA Today Building and Gannett Building

cate to Tysons Corner in 2001; hence the buildings will receive new names.

NV18.3 Freedom Park

1996, Philip Tefft of Ralph Appelbaum Associates. 1997, addition. Kent St. to N. 17th St.

An illustration of what might be done with unused freeway ramps in the future, this is an adaptation of a 1,000-foot-long freeway ramp so poorly constructed that it could not be used. It was ingeniously transformed into an urban park by the owners of the Newseum (Gannett, USA Today, and Westfield Realty), which sits at its center (see next entry). The park, which can be accessed from a number of points, is a series of terraces inscribed with quotations. It serves as a setting for "icons of freedom" such as a door from a jail cell that held Martin Luther King, segments of the Berlin Wall, stones from the Warsaw ghetto, and a memorial to journalists who have died on duty.

NV18.4 The Newseum (former)

1997, Thomas Bantel with Ralph Appelbaum Associates. 1101 Wilson Blvd. Closed 2002

An unconventional museum occupied the lower two stories of this building, originally designed as a shopping mall. The prominent dome projects a civic air, although the museum's ownership (see preceding entry) is very much private enterprise. Bantel and Appelbaum squeezed a spectacular multimedia display inside with a "video news wall" and, in a 36-foot-high lobby, a geodesic globe festooned with the mastheads of more than 1,800 newspapers.

At the end of 2001 the Freedom Forum announced that it would close the Newseum in March 2002 in preparation for a move to a new site and a much larger, purpose-built facility on Pennsylvania Avenue in downtown Washington, D.C. As of this writing, the Rosslyn site awaits yet another reuse.

NV18.5 Commonwealth Tower

1971. 1995, renovation, Skidmore, Owings and Merrill. 1300 Wilson Blvd.

The tower was originally a formidably ugly structure with large brown brick piers that articulated the facades and terminated in a weighty crown, a perfect example, as Benjamin Forgey observed, of a "surpassingly unlovable urban fortress." The Washington office of SOM redesigned the facades as a bright, crisp grid of glass and added three floors. Part of the "modernist revival" of recent years, it suggests what might be done to improve some of the other monsters in the area.

Fairfax and Prince William Counties (NV19–NV55)
Map, p. 43

NV19 The Falls Church (Episcopal)

1767–1769, James Wren. 1838–1839, renovation. 1865, 1906–1907, rebuilding. 1959, addition. 1992, parish hall. 115 E. Fairfax St. (corner of E. Fairfax and N. Washington sts.), Falls Church

The original wooden church was built 1723–1734 in what was then an isolated country setting near the falls of the Potomac River, which provided the name for this part of present-day Arlington. The "new" two-story brick church bears a resemblance to Wren's other northern Virginia churches, Christ Church, Alexandria, and Pohick. George Washington served as a churchwarden but left the parish before the new building was constructed. A stone doorway, now replaced, once gave the south facade greater distinction. Most of the rest of the exterior, including the molded brick west door, is original. The vestry record notes: "the Quoins and arches to be rubbed brick in the Tuscan Order," which describes the present exterior. For the interior the vestry book mentioned "alter piece, pulpit and canopy . . . completed in Ionic Order." Very little of the original interior remains. The church suffered during the post-Revolutionary disestablishment and was abandoned. When it returned to service in 1839, the pulpit that originally stood on the north wall, opposite the south entrance, began to migrate toward the east end. Union forces damaged the church during the Civil War, and some rebuilding occurred. Then in 1908 a substantial rebuilding took place, followed in 1959 by the addition of the unfortunate chancel to the east. This rebuilding included new pews and the addition of the galleries (apparently called for in Wren's plans). The church still serves as the focal point of the Falls Church community.

NV20 National Memorial Park

1934. Walter Marlowe. 7400 Lee Hwy. (U.S. 29), west of Falls Church, Fairfax County

Marlowe, the owner of this cemetery, apparently designed the scheme of a grand central axis and cross axes, creating, as he explained it, a "living cross." Surrounding the central axis are curvilinear roads. The cemetery has a number of sculptural embellishments, including the Fountain of Faith (1952, Carl Milles), a composition of varied figures and jets of water; the Sunsinger sculpture (c. 1952, Carl Milles); and the Four Chaplains Memorial Fountain (1955, Constantino Nivola, sculptor, and Walter Marlowe, architect), which is more abstract than the others.

NV21 Pine Spring Housing Development

1952–1954, Keyes, Smith, Satterlee and Lethbridge. Cedar Hill Rd, Woodberry Ln., Pine Spring Rd. (across from National Memorial Park, adjacent to Lee Hwy. [U.S. 29], or Arlington Blvd. [U.S. 50]), Fairfax County

Indicative of Washington-area architects' fascination with "California contemporary" or modern houses, the Pine Spring development would look more at home on the West Coast than among the red brick colonials that make up the Washington suburbs. The design was also influenced by Hollin Hills (see below), on which Francis Lethbridge, who was the principal designer for this project, had worked. The developers, Gerald and Eli Luria, directed the architects to lay out a community that would respect the terrain. The result was a 130-unit development with no through roads, a series of cul-de-sacs, and houses sited to take advantage of the rolling terrain and tall trees. The houses are largely one story, of post-and-beam construction, with large floor-to-ceiling windows and cathedral ceilings. As Lethbridge explained: "It was almost a fetish with us, the conviction that superficial decoration should be abolished. And it did save money, as well as making a clean, honest, if rustic, structure." Although some of the houses have been altered and the carports enclosed, the original concept is still visible.

NV22 Tysons Corner

1962–1968, Lathrop Douglass. 1986–1988, RTKL. I-495, exit 10 to Leesburg Pk. (VA 7) and exit 11 to Chain Bridge Rd. (VA 123)

A name and a place, rather than memorable architecture, Tysons Corner is virtually synonymous with sprawl. The convergence of several highways and new interstates and the Dulles Toll Road gave this triangular site an almost perfect location for one of the largest East Coast shopping centers. The initial phase, built by local developers Gudelsky, Lerner and Ammermann, was the first covered mall in the Washington area and supposedly the largest single-level mall in the country. Designed as a "triple-pull" mall with three large department stores as anchors, it actually had two levels: an upper main retail area and a below-grade area for truck tunnel, delivery, storage, and utilities. In 1985 the mall was sold, and the new developers, Lehndorf-Babson, expanded it into two levels by opening up the underground truck tunnel as the new retail space. Covering an area of about 95 acres, containing five major department stores, more than 250 smaller shops, 2.2 million square feet of retail space, and parking for 10,500 automobiles, it is mammoth. In 1986–1988 Tysons II, or the Galleria, opened across the road, and subsequently other malls, hotels, and speculative office buildings gathered in the area. The traffic pattern is confusing. In 1999 it was estimated that Tysons Corner was home to 80,000 jobs and 12,000 residents. Malls undergo renovation about every ten years, and a new one is in the offing. In 1999 it was announced that a new town center, intended to put a "heart in Tysons," would be built following the style of Reston Town Center (see below), to a design by the same architects, RTKL of Baltimore. Also in late 1999 the Gannett Corporation announced it would construct a new corporate complex and move the USA Today operation from Rosslyn. The projected completion date for the complex of buildings, designed by Kohn Pedersen Fox of New York with William Pedersen as design architect, is 2001.

NV23 Tycon Towers

1986, Johnson/Burgee. 8000 Towers Crescent Dr. (I-495, exit 11, off Chain Bridge Rd. [VA 123], Tysons Corner

Designed by New York superstar Philip Johnson, this strange, overgrown neo-Palladian "spec" office tower building can't be missed from I-495, and it may well be the most egregious example in the region of the excesses of postmodernism. From a distance the tower's frankly false columns and pediment look silly, though a closer view reveals a few redeeming qualities in the raised moldings at the entrance and the usual splashy lobby.

NV24 Immanuel Presbyterian Church

1978–1980, Hartman-Cox. 1995–1996, addition, McCartney-Lewis. 1125 Savile Ln. (off Chain Bridge Rd. [VA 123] to the east of the CIA entrance), McLean

The original east section of the church, the sanctuary, was designed by Hartman-Cox to appear as a large, barnlike structure behind a preexisting house, which became the church offices. The sanctuary openly invokes nineteenth-century Carpenter's Gothic, though what appears to be board-and-batten siding is actually plywood sheets with battens added. The various forms appear additive, though the piled-up dormers on the side elevation are actually drawn from the Sisters' House at Ephrata, a German sectarian community in Pennsylvania. The design was one of the first in Virginia that might be called historical postmodern, and it was widely hailed at the time. The most recent addition, a parish house by Jack McCartney, picks up on Hartman-Cox's large gable form but without its clarity. Although its details relate to the house, the addition's overall shape resembles a stable.

NV25 Langley Fork Historic District

Intersection of Georgetown Pk. (VA 193) and Chain Bridge Rd. (VA 123), Langley

The small historic district around Langley Fork retains some of the character of late nineteenth-century northern Virginia. It includes the Langley Ordinary (c. 1850), a two-story wooden I-house; the Langley Toll House (c. 1870), modest and much altered; Gunnels Chapel (c. 1870), a small wooden African American chapel; the Langley Friends Meeting House (1893), originally built for a Methodist congregation, wooden with decorative bargeboards and a bell tower; and Hickory Hill (c. 1868, 1931, 1964), a substantially remodeled house, actually part of an estate, and for a time the residence of Senator Robert F. Kennedy.

NV26 Madeira School

1929, Waldron Faulkner; later additions. 8328 Georgetown Pk. (VA 193), McLean

Lucy Madeira (married in 1917 to David L. Wing) founded a private girls' secondary school along progressive lines in Washington, D.C., in 1906. In 1927 she decided to remove the school to a site along the Potomac called Greenway. After initially contacting the Boston firm of Strickland, Blodget and Law, the school commissioned Washington, D.C., architect Waldron Faulkner. Faulkner's wife, Elizabeth Coonley Faulkner, was president of the alumnae association and the daughter of a trustee, Mrs. Avery (Queene Ferry) Coonley, who had commissioned several buildings from Frank Lloyd Wright and was interested in progressive education. The eight interconnected buildings of the initial complex (1929–1931, Faulkner with Alexander Trowbridge, consulting architect) are in the red brick Colonial Revival mode and are carefully arranged around courts similar to those of the nearly contemporary colleges at Yale and Harvard, though more modest in scale. Faulkner graduated the height, mass, and roof shape to indicate the hierarchy of the buildings. Later additions to the campus include the brick Chapel and Auditorium (1969–1970, David N. Yerkes), which displays the angles and planes of minimalist design of the period. The lobby and auditorium take advantage of the site with spectacular views of the Potomac. The Science Building (1974–1975, Arthur Cotton Moore) resembles an overgrown piece of minimalist sculpture. The vast roof originally was a solar panel, but it never worked, and the surface is now a sea of asphalt shingles. Faulkner's original gymnasium has been converted into the Huffington Library (1993, Bowie Gridley), which has a squat postmodernist clock tower; the interior is a tremendous trussed space with balconies. The Hurd Gymnasium (1992, Bowie Gridley), on the entrance road, is in a similar postmodernist mode, a sort of squashed Colonial Revival idiom.

NV27 Colvin Run Mill

c. 1820, attributed to Philip Carper. 1969, restoration, E. Blaine Cliver. 10017 Colvin Run Rd. (intersection of Leesburg Pk. [U.S. 7] and Colvin Run Rd.), Great Falls. Open to the public

Although local tradition holds that a mill was established here in 1794, the present mill dates

NV27 Colvin Run Mill

from c. 1820 and was related to the construction of the Alexandria-Leesburg Pike. The mill—which has gone under several names— was a custom or merchant's mill which ground grain commercially and stored both grain and flour. It was in operation through the 1930s. The exterior walls are laid up in common or American bond; however, the brick is smaller than average, so replacement bricks must be made by hand. On the interior are corner fireplaces on the first and second levels. The restored machinery, based on the mechanized process invented by Oliver Evans, uses three pairs of stones for the grinding. Also on the property is the mill owner's house, a two-story brick I-house (c. 1820), and a general store (c. 1900). The complex also includes a former ironworks that houses displays of early technology. Farther up Colvin Run Road is a vast subdivision of tract "McMansions."

NV28 Great Falls Grange No. 738 and Schoolhouse

1929 (grange), c. 1890 (schoolhouse). 9812 Georgetown Pk. (VA 193), Great Falls. Open to the public (schoolhouse only)

Indicative of the original agricultural nature of Fairfax County is this quiet Craftsman structure, erected on the eve of the Depression. Tapestry brick walls sit on a high concrete basement; simple wooden brackets articulate the overhanging eaves. The large hall on the main floor was used for social gatherings and political causes such as lobbying for better roads. The Grange stayed active into the late 1950s. It

is now operated by Fairfax Parks Authority. Also on the property is a former one-room schoolhouse, of wood in a late Greek Revival mode, with gingerbread trim.

NV29 Reston–Lake Anne Village Center

1963–1972. Village Rd., off Baron Cameron Ave. (VA 606), Reston

When Reston opened in 1965 it was immediately and widely hailed as the most highly visible "new town" of the period, pictured and described in *Life* and other publications. As a planned community 18 miles west of Washington, D.C., and near Dulles Airport, it appeared to be the solution to both inner-city ills and the banality of suburbia. The creation of Robert E. Simon, Jr. (his initials provided the name), a former New York developer and owner of Carnegie Hall, the initial development occupied 6,750 acres. Projected were seven village centers, each with a population of 10,000, and substantial open and green spaces. Simon envisioned a density and population mix of age and race similar to those of New York. Since Fairfax County's zoning regulations called for two acres per dwelling unit, major variations had to be obtained. Only the Lake Anne Village Center, planned by the New York firm of Whittlesey, Conklin and Rossant, was fully carried out before Simon lost financial control of the project in 1969 to Gulf Oil Company. (Subsequently, Gulf sold it to a Mobil Oil subsidiary, Reston Land Corporation.) Julian Whittlesey had worked with Clarence Stein, one of the designers of greenbelt towns of the 1920s and 1930s, and Simon's father had been involved in Radburn, New Jersey, designed by Stein and Henry Wright. The subsequent history of the other parts of Reston follows only too sadly the undistinguished example of other northern Virginia suburbs.

The Lake Anne Village Center preserves remarkably well the vision of Simon and his architects. The overall scheme, including the man-made lake, is by Whittlesey and especially William Conklin and James Rossant, who took over after Whittlesey retired. They and Simon envisioned the lake as a community focus with water sports as the theme; quays were provided in front the town houses for tying up boats. Conklin and Rossant designed combined shops and town houses, a fifteen-story apartment tower, and the so-called Chimney House cluster, along the east side of the lake, in a modestly abstract idiom with exposed concrete frames inspired to some degree by the work of Le Corbusier and Paul Rudolph. Rossant designed the plaza fountain. The Washington Plaza Baptist Church, on the west side of the plaza (1967–1969, Ward Hall), fits in seamlessly with the Conklin-Rossant buildings. Signage, lighting, and street furniture were designed by Chermayeff and Geismar of New York, and the various abstract concrete sculptures were by Gonzalo Fonseca, formerly of Uruguay.

The Waterview cluster of more conventional town houses around the lake to the southeast were designed by Washington, D.C., architect Chloethiel Woodward Smith. For the ninety-unit development, Smith used pastel hues which suggested to Simon a "French fishing village." To the immediate northwest of the Lake Anne center, Charles M. Goodman designed the Hickory cluster, also ninety units, more aggressively abstract, with bold-colored concrete panels. In spite of good intentions, construction costs mounted, and the buildings were initially overpriced for the local housing market. Also, the supposedly casy commute to Washington proved difficult, and in the 1960s there was little local employment in this western section of Fairfax County. Thirty years later the employment situation is different, but commuting by car, either locally or into Washington, is an even more difficult proposition. The small scale of the shops at the Lake Anne center bespeaks an earlier concept of retail development, in contrast to the larger square footage of most mall stores of today, making the center a period piece and a utopian vision of American suburbia.

NV30 Reston Town Center

NV30 Reston Town Center

1986–1990, RTKL and Sasaki Associates. Reston Pkwy. (VA 602), Reston

Graphically evident is the contrast between 1960s ideals in the Lake Anne Village and 1980s consumerism in this suburban town center built by the Reston Land Corporation. Here a re-created main street is a pedestrian mall and community plaza located in the center of a large-scale shopping, restaurant, entertainment, and hotel development. Cars are excluded from the center; drivers must park either in large lots on several sides or in one of the various garages. Stylistically, the architecture is the Disneyesque postmodernist variety, a sort of theme park with vague elements of Art Deco and classicism. The movie theater has pylons topped by large globes. A substantial addition with supposedly "softer, more American town squares," by the Sasaki firm, is in the planning stages.

NV31 Herndon Historic District

VA 657 at VA 606

Now overrun by intense development and automobile traffic, the center of Herndon tries to maintain its earlier farming community atmosphere. Virginia 657 and 606 (Centerville Road, then Elden Street, and then Washington Street) bisect the center of town.

Herndon traces its development to the Alexandria, Loudoun and Hampshire Railroad, which passed through in the mid-nineteenth century. At the center are the Herndon Depot (1857) and the town green. The depot is one of the earliest surviving Virginia board-and-batten stations; well maintained, it now serves as the Herndon Historical Society Museum and other offices. Around the depot grew up a commercial and residential core that still contains some buildings of interest. Across is the Town Hall (1939; 730 Elden Street), an unassuming Colonial Revival brick structure that originally housed the post office on the first floor. Adjacent is the recent Herndon Municipal Center (master plan, 1993–1995, Cooper-Lecky), a group of buildings clustered around an extension to the town green. Underneath the complex and town green is a parking garage reached from the glazed gazebo on the south side. The site was a brownfield, or polluted tract of land, reclaimed for the new municipal use. The Herndon Council Chambers (1993–1995, Cooper-Lecky) is one of the region's finer examples of postmodern civic-image design, exemplified by the abstraction of historical forms in the overall massing and the cylindrical cupola. Across this new town green is Herndon Fortnightly Library (1996, Hughes Group) with a prominent copper-sheeted dome. The exposed steel trusswork on the interior is especially worth notice. More buildings are envisioned for the municipal center. The Paul Brothers automotive dealership (c. 1920; 770 Elden Street), is a nice surviving example of a stepped concrete commercial structure. A Sears, Roebuck bungalow with elaborate brackets (c. 1913; 652 Jefferson Street) is one of the finest examples of the Craftsman style in northern Virginia.

NV32 Center for Innovative Technology (CIT)

1985–1989, Arquitectonica with Ward/Hall Associates. 2214 Rock Hill Rd., Herndon. Inquire at desk for admission.

Visible from Dulles Airport and surrounding roads, CIT is an entry in the "airport sweepstakes," the competition to create eye-catching advertising forms in the vast wastelands that surround airports. It is a controversial building with a controversial purpose: to provide space for high-technology companies that the commonwealth of Virginia wished to attract to the area. Cost-conscious governments, however, have cut most of the support funds and turned it into rental spaces. The building's design resulted from a "national ideas" architectural competition, from which one of the finalists,

Jennifer Luce, was subsequently hired by the Arquitectonica firm of Miami. One of Arquitectonica's partners, Bernardo Fort-Brescia, pursued the commission in a joint venture with Ward/Hall of Fairfax. The final design reflects the impact of the deconstructivist movement in architecture with its upside-down truncated pyramid rising out of a back podium base, angled planes, semicircular forms, and contrasting colored glass curtain walls. Each of the parts originally contained a specific function: the pyramid for offices, the horizontal parallelogram for software production, and the wedge for an auditorium. The interior, with its juxtaposed grids, is equally unsettling. But this is an extremely impressive example of "Decon."

NV33 Dulles International Airport

1958–1962, Eero Saarinen and Ammann and Whitney Engineers; Dan Kiley, landscape architect. 1980, addition, Hellmuth, Obata and Kassabaum. 1989, international arrivals addition, Skidmore, Owings and Merrill. 1995–1997, expansion, SOM. 1996–1998, Concourse B expansion, HOK. Washington-Dulles Toll Road (VA 267), Chantilly

Eero Saarinen described the design for the Dulles terminal as "a strong form between earth and sky that seems both to rise from the plain and hover over it," and "a huge, continuous hammock suspended between concrete trees." The dramatic form with huge piers and sloping roof captured the *Zeitgeist.* Saarinen, who died ten months before its completion, created a new monumental gateway to the capital of the United States and, from the perspec-

NV33 Dulles International Airport

tive of the time, the "free" (i.e., non-Communist) West. Its naming for Eisenhower's secretary of state, John Foster Dulles, one of the hardiest of the Cold War warriors, was thus entirely appropriate. The site was gigantic (9,600 acres), and Saarinen conceived of the terminal as indeterminately expandable, a rigorous critique of existing terminals. The thrusting suspended roof, with piers 65 feet high on the approach side and 43 feet on the field side, sits on top of a podium that contains in its basement all the messy activities of baggage handling and services. The main floor was designed as an open, porous space with ticket counters along the middle, from which passengers would proceed to mobile lounges that would convey them to planes waiting at mid-field. Saarinen wanted to avoid the long walks and finger terminals common to most American airports and to enhance the aesthetic of flight. Seating was designed by the Office of Charles and Ray Eames, both of whom had been Saarinen's colleagues at Cranbrook in the 1930s. Dan Kiley, who collaborated with Saarinen on many projects, designed the graceful approach from which the terminal rises out of the Piedmont plain and the close-in parking lot.

Unfortunately, Saarinen could not foresee the many changes that would come in the late twentieth century: security check-in; "hubbing"; the proliferation of commuter airlines, which require means of access other than mobile lounges; mammoth jetliners; waiting areas; and, indeed, the vast expansion of air travel. Along the rear of the terminal SOM designed a 50-foot-wide corridor and an ungainly box at mid-field that became the terminal for long-distance jets, with mobile lounges to ferry passengers back and forth. Saarinen's concept of the terminal itself as expandable has been achieved with a 600-foot addition by SOM (1995–1997) that doubles the original length. The extension—or, really, extrusion—of the original actually makes the building more commanding against the backdrop of the Blue Ridge Mountains. A new mid-field terminal by HOK has an appropriately subservient exterior and a bright and airy interior. Slated for obsolescence are the mobile lounges. Hailed at its completion and ever since as one of the great modern buildings, the terminal itself remains a thrilling architectural space and an aesthetic delight.

The area surrounding Dulles Airport is booming as a corporate center. New buildings are announced with amazing frequency, and a few are of interest. In addition to CIT (preceding entry), see also the National Reconnaissance Office (1988–1993, Dewberry and Davis; 14765 Lee Road), observable from Virginia 28 (Sully Road), adjacent to Dulles. The striking blue glass and metal structures do not hide very well this supposedly "secret" governmental agency.

NV34 Frying Pan Meetinghouse

c. 1783–1791. 2615 Centerville Rd. (VA 657), Floris

A lonely survivor along a busy road, this gabled, one-room Baptist meetinghouse originally served a mixed white and black congregation. On the interior, four large, hand-hewn posts with chamfered edges march down the center.

NV35 Sully Plantation

c. 1794. VA 28 (5 miles south of Dulles Toll Road, .5 mile north of U.S. 50, 4 miles north of I-66). Identified with a sign and open to the public

Overrestored and too pretty, still Sully, built for Richard Bland Lee, younger brother of Henry (Light Horse Harry) Lee, provides a glimpse of less pretentious homes of the late eighteenth century. It is not a mansion but a rambling farmhouse, fronted by a wide (original) piazza decorated with scalloped eaves. The interior woodwork is particularly fine. The farmstead includes numerous outbuildings of interest, among them a stone dairy and servants' structure covered with pargeting, or stucco set with small stones, which is rare in Virginia. It is operated by the Fairfax County Parks Authority.

NV36 Manassas National Battlefield Park

6511 Sudley Rd. (VA 234)

The Union and Confederate armies met twice in this area, known variously as Manassas and Bull Run, July 18–21, 1861, and August 25–28, 1862. The major portion of the battlefield park, formed in the 1930s, encompasses nearly 5,000 acres of open fields and woods, which, from a landscape and protected-open-space point of view, is significant. From an architectural point of view, the major interest is fourfold. The Visitors Center (1941–1942, later additions, National Park Service Design Staff) has a massive and primitive Doric-columned portico that recalls Arlington House. Nearby is a statue depicting Stonewall Jackson (1938, J. P. Polla); the base is inscribed, "There stands Jackson, like a

NV35 Sully Plantation (right)

NV37 St. Paul's Episcopal Church (Virginia Courts) (below, left)

NV38 Buckland (below, right)

stonewall." The statue amply demonstrates that the heavy WPA sculptural idiom does not work for all subjects. Jackson, who was small, slouched in his saddle, and was known for his tattered uniforms, looks like Batman. It is certainly one of the more ludicrous interpretations of the subject. Also nearby is the Henry Hill Monument (dedicated June 13, 1865), one of the first Civil War memorials: a stumpy central obelisk with four short piers at the corners, each topped by a howitzer shell. On the corner of U.S. 20 and Virginia 234 is the four-bay fieldstone Stone House (c. 1828), a former tavern that served a number of other purposes during the battles.

NV37   **St. Paul's Episcopal Church (Virginia Courts)**

1801, attributed to James Wren. Later additions. 6760 Fayette St., .2 mile south of VA 55, Haymarket

Haymarket is a small crossroads village at the intersection of Virginia 55 and 625. It jumped into the national spotlight in the early 1990s when the Disney Company proposed building a history theme park on the surrounding farmland. Although Disney withdrew the proposal, the area still is threatened with overdevelopment.

St. Paul's origins as a Virginia district court building for the northern Virginia counties can be seen in its red brick, two-story, town hall form, similar to that of Fairfax Courthouse, which it probably closely resembled. However, the disbanding of the district court system within a few years after the building's completion sent it into limbo. Eventually, in 1822, it became an Episcopal church. Haymarket was the site of a Civil War battle, and Union troops severely damaged the structure. During the subsequent rebuilding the arcade was closed in, the upper windows received a Palladian treatment, and a steeple was added.

NV38 **Buckland**

1798 and later. Lee Hwy. (U.S. 29) at Buckland Mill Rd. (VA 684)

Once an industrial site on the Broad Run River, a tributary of the Occoquan River, this is a small and pretty enclave of about a dozen structures tucked along busy U.S. 29. Chartered in 1798 as "Buck Land," the town, according to local tradition, was named in honor of the architect-builder William Buckland. Buckland, who died in 1774, had designed a house for Samuel Love, the father of John Love, who established the town. Important as a transportation stop along the turnpike that ran west from Washington, it also had several mills, including a woolen mill. In 1869 a local newspaper claimed it was "the

'Lowell' of Prince William County." Today, only the remains of an 1899 gristmill survive, along with several former taverns and houses, a few of which have been restored. The houses, in a variety of sizes and materials, all date from c. 1800–c. 1840.

NV39 **Nokesville Truss Bridge**

1882, Keystone Bridge Company. Aden Rd., off VA 28, Nokesville

Examples of this type of single-span Pratt wrought iron truss bridge used to dot the countryside. The manufacturer, the Keystone Bridge Company of Pittsburgh, was a pioneer in metal truss technology.

Manassas

Best known for the Civil War battles fought nearby, Manassas began in 1852 as a junction stop on two local railroads, the Manassas Gap and the Orange and Alexandria. The railroad brought the two armies together in 1861 and 1862, and great portions of the town were destroyed. The present-day Southern Railway (and Amtrak) still helps to define the town. Manassas experienced significant growth after the Civil War and became the county seat in 1892. In 1905 fire destroyed a portion of downtown Manassas. Albert Speiden, a Manassas architect with an office in Washington, and the builders John, Frank, and Ira Cannon designed and built much of the town in the late nineteenth and early twentieth centuries. After 1920 the town languished until the 1960s, when the explosive growth of northern Virginia began to reach this far west. Manassas and the surrounding communities of Manassas Park and Yorkshire exhibit the undistinguished results.

NV40.1 Southern Railway Station–Visitor Center

NV40 **Manassas Downtown**

Although some erosion of the downtown has taken place and "boutiquization" is all too evident, much remains. The following tour through the older section can be walked or driven.

NV40.1 **Southern Railway Station–Visitor Center**

1914, Southern Railway Engineers Office. 9457 West St. Open to the public

The Manassas Visitor Center is housed in a well-preserved passenger depot constructed of red-painted brick, with pebble dash upper walls, a high hipped roof with overhanging eaves supported on long brackets, and a signalman's turret. Amtrak still uses the depot. Stylistically, the building is closest to an Arts and Crafts idiom.

NV40.2 Manassas Museum

1990–1991, Carlton Abbott. 9101 Prince William St. Open to the public

Brick and concrete with a square center, which acts as a rotunda, and two wings, the museum is an awkward concoction. The attempt to escape from the Colonial Revival syndrome is laudable, but the abstraction of classical motifs in overscaled concrete forms appears forced. The exhibits focus on the history of the Northern Piedmont.

NV40.3 Hopkins Candy Factory

1908–1909, Albert Speiden. 9415 Battle St.

North, and just across the tracks from the station, stands this large brick factory and warehouse, which was the largest industrial structure in Manassas for many years. The building is of a straightforward mill type, with one ornamental feature, the oddly crenellated trim around the entrance.

NV40.4 Heritage Bar and Grill (People's National Bank)

1904. 9110–9112 Center St. (northwest corner of Center and Battle sts.)

A bank always occupies one of the major corners in an older downtown. Here an angle entrance scoops up depositors from all directions. The quoins and dentils give a Renais-

sance Revival air to the structure, though the cornice with its battlements projects a medieval image.

NV40.5 Things I Love (Hazen Building)

c. 1875. 9406 Battle St.

A wooden commercial structure such as this is a rare survivor in a downtown. The two-story building has details in an Italianate commercial idiom.

NV40.6 Hibbs and Giddings Building

1911–1912, Albert Speiden; Ira Cannon, builder. 9129 Center St. (southwest corner of Center and West sts.)

The most interesting commercial building in town is topped by a heavy classical cornice and has twin glass cages, originally for the display of men's clothing, at street level. The interior has a pressed metal ceiling.

NV40.7 U.S. Post Office

1931, Louis A. Simon, Supervising Architect, U.S. Treasury Department. Church St. (northeast corner of Church and West sts.)

The post office is a well-executed government-issue Federal Revival design. The single-story building is modest in form, but the details incorporate an in antis portico with capitals derived from the Temple of the Winds in Athens and Homewood in Baltimore.

NV40.8 Offices (Prince William County Courthouse)

1892–1894, Teague and Marye. c. 1985, conversion. 9248 Lee Ave. (northwest corner of Lee Ave. and Grant St.)

The county seat was moved to Manassas in 1892. The county commissioners rejected a Colonial Revival design and instead selected a vaguely Romanesque Revival–Second Empire confection that in more cosmopolitan centers would have been considered very out of date. The architects, James C. Teague and Philip Thornton Marye, of Norfolk and Newport News, used the *parti* of Brooks Hall at the University of Virginia but slightly changed the exterior, adding some red sandstone details to a tall, painted red brick box. In front is a Civil

War monument commemorating a "Love Feast of the Blues and Grays" that took place in 1911. The county government departed in the mid-1980s, and the building is currently commercial office space.

NV40.9 Bennett School

1908–1909, attributed to Virginia Department of Education Design Staff. 9250 Lee Ave.

Built as one of ten agricultural high schools authorized by the state legislature, the Bennett School never served that purpose because of space limitations. Instead it was used as a primary school for years. The daunting portico with six giant-order Corinthian columns gives it the usual "Southern Colonial" appearance, but the red sandstone base is more Richardsonian. The structure has stood empty for a number of years and its future is uncertain.

NV40.10 Grant Avenue Houses

Grant Avenue was the upper-middle-class housing area of Manassas at the turn of the twentieth century. The Hobbs house (c. 1910, Ira Cannon; 9139 Grant Avenue), is Colonial Revival, though Cannon's preference was for more picturesque styles. The Ira Cannon house (1904, Ira Cannon; 9138 Grant Avenue), shows his personal preference—the Queen Anne style—with a few Colonial Revival touches such

as Palladian windows and a one-story Ionic-columned porch. The Ratcliffe House (1904, Ira Cannon; 9136 Grant Avenue), is also Queen Anne, with a corner tower and slender Tuscan columns that sit on shingled piers. The Payne house (c. 1915, Waddy B. Wood; 9134 Grant Avenue), is by a Washington, D.C.–based architect, better known for his Colonial Revival designs. Here Wood appears to have adopted some elements of the Craftsman style, though the entrance portico is nominally Colonial Revival. The Manassas Institute (1896, Albert Speiden; 9132 Grant Avenue), a large Italianate structure, was built by John Cannon as a school and is now a residence.

NV40.11 Libeau Row

1905, Donation Libeau. 9300 West St. and 9227, 9229, 9231 Portner St.

This group of four houses, vaguely Italianate (though some obvious remodeling has taken place, as on number 9227), was constructed by the local brickyard owner, a native of New Zealand, who built them as speculation. Row house duplications like this are unusual for northern Virginia at the turn of the twentieth century.

NV40.12 Annaburg Nursing Home (Annaburg)

1892–1894, Gustav Friebus. Many later additions. 9201 Maple St.

Commissioned by Robert Portner, an Alexandria beer baron, the central portion of this building was one of northern Virginia's showplaces: the main house of a 2,500-acre estate that stretched to the Manassas battlefields. The gatehouse still stands nearby at 9218 Portner, though it has been modified. The estate also included a model farm, all of which is subdivided and gone. The main house cost in excess of $50,000, which was a very large sum for the 1890s. Designed in the Italian Renaissance idiom with a large front porch, the house was embellished on the interior with murals and other works of art. The architect is a shadowy figure who was active in Washington in the 1880s and 1890s and then turned up in Norfolk as a supplier of building materials. Since Germans dominated the American beer industry, Friebus's Germanic background probably recommended him to Portner.

NV40.10 Grant Avenue Houses: Ratcliffe House

NV40.13 House

c. 1921, Sears, Roebuck and Co. 9306 Main St.

Sears's Kilbourne model, which was in the catalogue from 1921 to 1929, was probably the source for this example of the so-called California bungalow erected on the East Coast.

NV40.14 New Redemption Christian Church (Grace Methodist Church)

1926–1931, Albert Speiden. 9400 Main St.

A somewhat tame brick Gothic Revival structure, this church has a big crenellated tower that holds down the corner.

NV40.15 Fishscale and Mousetooth (National Bank of Manassas)

1896, Albert Speiden; John Cannon, builder. 9406 Main St.

Speiden here drew upon Richardsonian Romanesque examples for the red sandstone details, though overall the building is really Queen Anne in feeling.

NV40.16 Manassas Town Hall

1915, Albert Speiden. 9025 Center St.

The town hall is a sophisticated Colonial Revival building in which the fire company originally occupied the ground floor, with the town offices and council chambers above. A cupola has disappeared, the arcades for the fire equipment have been enclosed, and the town offices now occupy all of the building.

NV40.17 Hynson's Department Store

c. 1906. 9101 Center St.

Even though this building dates from after the devastating 1905 fire, and cast iron was known to be vulnerable to fire, the material was used in the first floor of this structure. The upper floors are plain. The original metal ceiling remains.

NV40.18 Masonic Hall

1906, Jon Tillett. 9107 Center St.

Tillett was apparently in the building trades, but although he designed this structure, John Cannon constructed it. One of the more architecturally conscious buildings in downtown Manassas, the building is heavily rusticated. The upper-floor arcades of this brick structure have been enclosed; the Masonic emblem remains in the parapet.

NV40.19 Innovation Park

University Blvd. (off Wellington Rd.)

This 124-acre research industrial park a short distance outside Manassas has some of the best recent office buildings in northern Virginia. The centerpiece is the George Mason Prince William County Campus buildings. George Mason University has three northern Virginia campuses, but this is the only one with any architectural distinction. It is, of course, campus as office park. Prince William Building Number 1 (1997, The Architects Collaborative [TAC] and Dewberry and Davis) is the least prepossessing, a large four-story office building with vague postmodern details. It indicates why TAC went out of business. Prince William Building Number 2 (1998, Polshek Partnership and Tobey and Davis) is far more interesting; its varicolored brick skin and pieced-together composition enliven its facades. The varied forms, and especially the ventilation shafts, have a deconstructivist air. The Fitness Center (1999, Bohlin Cywinski Jackson and Burt Hill Kosar Rittelmann Associates) is a vast white box at the end of a vast parking lot. The long bands of translucent clerestory windows help unify the huge structure. Across the street from the George Mason campus, at 10801 University Boulevard, is the ATCC Building (1998, Tobey and Davis), a sleek series of large white and light gray boxes, very well carried out.

NV41 Fairfax County Government Center Complex

1991–1992, RTKL. 12000 Government Center Pkwy.

A 100-acre suburban office park, this is the latest in a series of solutions to the problem of housing the county government: first, the original courthouse in the city of Fairfax, then various additions, then buildings in the immediate area, and finally complete removal from the town. The site offers hiking trails and provides parking for 2,800 vehicles. RTKL of Baltimore designed the Government Center, a vast, horseshoe-shaped structure focused on an atrium that looks out on a sunken garden and woods beyond. The governmental enterprise is abstractly recalled in the classical pediment shape that forms the massive glazed entrance opening. The remainder of the exterior from the entrance side looks like a fortress. In contrast, the courtyard facade is open and surrounds an amphitheater. The wings also contain atria that recall Frank Lloyd Wright's Marin County Center.

City of Fairfax

Originally a tavern stood at this crossroads, then known as Providence. The Virginia General Assembly moved the county seat here in 1798, when it became apparent that Alexandria would be incorporated into the District of Columbia. The town retained the name of Providence until 1875. It grew slowly until the twentieth century and did not become a city until 1961. Today it sprawls in all directions; indeed, the name Fairfax is synonymous with rampant development.

NV42 Fairfax Center

The historic center of the town contains several structures of interest, and numerous other buildings have identifying plaques with dates.

NV42.1 Fairfax County Courthouse

1799–1800, James Wren; James Bogue and Mungo Dykes, builders. 1928, addition, William I. Deming. 1953, addition, Robert A. Willgoos and Dwight Chase. 1964–1967, restoration of original courthouse, James Macomber. 4000 Chain Bridge Rd.

Fairfax County's third courthouse, a two-story building designed in a temple-front format with an arcade at ground level, can be read in a number of ways. Wren may have been combining the arcade common to pre-Revolutionary Virginia courthouses with the new interest in temples evidenced in the Virginia State Capitol. Of importance is that the courthouse predates Jefferson's employment of the format for some of the pavilions at the University of Virginia (Jefferson's workmen would use this form for their own courthouse projects). But the form may also relate to the English town hall, a model that was certainly available to Wren through publications. Any resemblance to the English town hall, however, stops at the front door, for instead of the arrangement of a great room on the upper floor with market stalls beneath, the courtroom takes up the entire ground floor and the jury rooms are over the piazza.

Military action in the area during the Civil War destroyed the interior, and as the *Alexandria Gazette* reported, "Nothing remains . . . but the walls and roof." Repairs were made. William J. Deming, a noted Washington Colonial Revival architect, expanded the courthouse in 1928 by adding a wing and duplicating the original structure on the exterior. The next addition, in the 1950s, followed this format, though with a longer wing that contained

NV42.1 Fairfax County Courthouse

a new main entrance, so that four identical pavilions are lined up. On the interior of the last addition is a mural (1954, Esther L. Stewart) that depicts the county's heroes and architectural treasures. James Macomber, of the Colonial Williamsburg staff, using evidence from other period courthouses, restored the original courthouse section in the 1960s.

NV42.2 Fairfax County Massey Building

1969, Vosbeck, Vosbeck, Kendrick and Redinger. 4100 Chain Bridge Rd. (actually on Courthouse Rd. behind the courthouse)

Symbolizing the growth of Fairfax is this incongruous precast concrete high rise of twelve stories stuck in a two-story downtown. The only feature that identifies it as a government structure is the plaza. The building's tripartite composition of base, middle section, and top and its inclined, bronze-sashed windows are typical of its period.

NV42.3 Fairfax County Judicial Center

1982, Hellmuth, Obata and Kassabaum. 4110 Chain Bridge Rd. (actually on Courthouse Rd. behind the courthouse)

The massive L-shaped, vaguely Brutalist structure of reinforced concrete has an atrium en-

trance at the center. The overall monotony gives it an oppressive air, perhaps appropriate for a judicial center.

NV42.4 Old Jail

1886–1891. 10459 Main St. (behind original courthouse)

Illuminating an earlier and perhaps more genial time, this former jail is essentially a T-shaped house. The front porch, with its elaborate Italianate details, actually welcomes the visitor.

NV42.5 Truro Episcopal Church

1933–1934, Delos Smith. 1953, parish hall, Milton Grigg. 1958–1959, William Heyl Thompson. 1984, Henry Browne. 10520 Main St.

The name Truro is venerable in Virginia history, since it was the original northern Virginia parish and encompassed the entire area. This church traces its lineage back to Payne's Church (1766), nearby on Ox Road, disestablished in the 1780s and destroyed. The present complex began in 1934 with the chapel, by Delos Smith, supposedly designed in imitation of the old Payne's Church but displaying more affinity with the contemporary Williamsburg restoration. The chapel's excellent brickwork recalls Carter's Grove as well as Wren's various northern Virginia churches. Milton Grigg added the parish hall in 1953. William Heyl Thompson, of Philadelphia, designed the main church building in 1957; construction followed

in 1958–1959. The entrance, though over-scaled, recalls Jefferson's niche entrance at Pavilion IX at the University of Virginia. Grigg was called back in the early 1980s to add transepts, but he died, and his partner, Henry Browne, completed the work. Jefferson's dramatic forms are easily mixed with the more modest ones of the eighteenth century. The church complex offers a mini-survey of changing interpretations of colonial architecture over the past sixty years.

NV42.6 NationsBank (National Bank of Fairfax)

1930–1931, Arthur B. Heaton; later additions. 10440 Main St. (northeast corner of Main St. and Chain Bridge Rd.)

This brick building, on a prominent corner across from the courthouse and on the site of an earlier ordinary, was designed by a well-known Washington, D.C., architect. Flemish bond brickwork and overscaled round-arched, multipaned windows set off the elaborately detailed entrance. The main banking room recalls a period when banking was a genteel activity: it is wonderfully detailed, with a balcony such as those seen on the exteriors of colonial buildings surmounting the safe.

NV42.7 Fairfax Arts Center (Town Hall)

1900; later renovations. 3995 University Dr. (southeast corner of University Dr. at Main St.). Open to the public

The temple front on the wood-frame town hall has a Tuscan column portico that reflects the rediscovery of Jefferson's architecture around the turn of the twentieth century. The structure was donated to the town by Joseph E. Willard, the son of the builder of the Willard Hotel in Washington, D.C., whose mother was a well-known resident of Fairfax and a Confederate sympathizer. The interior is essentially two large rooms, the second story lighted by dormers in the temple's roof. The building is now a center for the arts.

NV42.8 Ratcliff-Allison House (Earp's Ordinary)

c. 1813. Later additions; restoration. 200 E. Main St. Open to the public

In scale and plan, this structure is typical of small houses of the area in the early nineteenth century. Although those were normally built of wood, this house is constructed of brick, which perhaps accounts for its survival. Each floor has two rooms.

NV43 Tastee 29 Diner

1947, Mountain View Diner Co., Singac, N.J. 10536 Lee Hwy. (U.S. 29), Fairfax

Originally five diners were located on this stretch of U.S. 29. The Tastee is the only one that survives in its nearly original high-style Moderne form with porcelain enamel siding, stainless steel prows, glass block, blue and white awnings, and multicolored neon. The exterior red steel and neon sign is original except for the 1973 addition of the word "Tastee." The interior is nearly intact with blue Naugahyde seats, Formica, tile, and continuous back bar of stainless steel panels in radiating and diamond patterns. The original owner, Delmas T. Glascock, splurged on a gray-veined marble counter (instead of Formica) and a terrazzo floor. The best seats are the corner booths, where the glass block wall is lit by vertical fluorescent tubes.

NV44 Anchorage Motel

c. 1960. 9865 Lee Hwy. (U.S. 29), Fairfax

A roadside delight and rare survivor from the time when U.S. 29 was the major transportation corridor for Fairfax County, the Anchorage shows the hand of an exuberant designer, entranced with nautical imagery. Prows, a lighthouse, and portholes dominate the facade. How much longer it will exist before development takes it over is unknown.

NV45 Burke Presbyterian Church

1981–1983, 1988–1989, Lawrence Cook Associates. 5690 Oak Leather Dr., Burke

One of the most celebrated recent churches in Virginia, this structure is designed to take advantage of natural lighting and to be energy efficient. It is constructed of concrete block covered with stained cedar shiplap siding. The main meetinghouse is articulated by the stepped trombe (heat-absorbing) wall on the south and the tower on the north. To this composition is attached a low education wing and another, later wing for more offices and services.

NV46 Hollin Hills

1946–1971, Charles M. Goodman, architect; Lou Bernard Voight, Dan Kiley, and Eric Paepcke, landscape architects. Entrance at 1223 Fort Hunt Rd. (VA 629), Fairfax County (U.S. 1 south from Alexandria to Fort Hunt Rd. 2 miles, turn on Paul Spring Rd.)

This development of 463 contemporary houses on 300 acres of heavily wooded, uneven terrain is one of Virginia's most noteworthy contributions to modern architecture. Highly praised in the 1950s and 1960s and recipient of numerous awards, it seemed to many people the design solution to the standardized tract house. Robert Davenport, the developer, hired Charles M. Goodman, at that point beginning his practice in the Washington, D.C., area, to develop a site plan that avoided the usual bulldozed, flattened landscape, devoid of all vegetation and character. Goodman developed a master plan that emphasized natural contours and saved trees where possible. Park areas and open spaces were set aside, and Goodman utilized cul-de-sacs to reduce through traffic and laid out roads to follow the terrain. A variety of plan types for different sites and sizes of houses were developed. Costs were kept down through the use of standard parts, prefabricated millwork, simplified carpentry, the avoidance of intricate details, and such elements of advanced building technology as concrete slab floors, steel sash windows, and grouping all utilities into a central core. Houses were sited with regard to orientation, trees, long views, and relationships between neighboring houses. Houses are seldom exactly parallel to the street, but are set at an angle. A landscaping plan could be purchased with each house; initially these were by Voight, later by Kiley and Paepcke. Fencing individual property was discouraged, as Voight summarized it, to "make the community look as if there were no individual lots but a beautiful park." Davenport arranged financing so that the residents could purchase contemporary furniture and housewares from Knoll, Kurt Versen, and other companies known for modern design. Goodman and Davenport wanted to avoid the usual developer's vocabulary of model names, such as "Jefferson" or "Oak Park," and instead used numbers and letters. It

NV46 Hollin Hills

is easy to drive through Hollin Hills and identify the house types and dates. Variations crept in, and many houses have been modified. The following tour, which begins at Paul Spring Road, picks out many basic models. There are a few custom designs by Goodman and about eight non-Goodman houses.

Numbers 7300–7318 Rippon Lane are examples of house type 1 (split level, 1,600 square feet); they sold for $16,920, including the lot, in 1949. Numbers 1800, 1809, 1813, 1814, 1815, 1816, and 1820 Drury Lane (a cul-de-sac off Rippon Lane) are house type 2, the most common in this first section of Hollin Hills, a one-story, 1,150-square-foot, oblong box with a massive chimney that sold at $12,000. A two-story variant type, 2B42LB (two levels, four bedrooms, with a walk-out basement level) can be found on sloping sites; examples are at 1808 and 1812 Drury Lane; 7200 and 7201 Rebecca Drive; and 2106, 2108, 2110, 2112, 2114 Popkins Lane, among others. Back on Paul Spring Road, numbers 1805, 1809, and 1813 are type 2, but with 4- and 8-foot enlargements that added an extra belt of space for storage, dining, kitchen, or bedrooms. (Goodman's lingo gets complicated; "2B4K4" means a type 2 with an extra four feet for bedroom and kitchen). Numbers 7315, 7317, and 7319 Stafford Road (left off Paul Spring Road) are type 4, a three-bedroom, two-story shorter version of the 2B42LB type. Martha's Lane (which intersects Stafford) is filled with examples of type 3, which looks like a longer and wider version of type 2 but contains three bedrooms, a study, and two baths and originally sold for $20,000. Number 7213 Beechwood (left onto Pickwick from Paul Spring Road, then right) is a type 5A, with a flat roof lacking any overhangs and a central interior utility core. Number 2105 Paul Spring Road is a type 2 with a butterfly roof across the short dimension of the house. Numbers 2217, 2219, and 2121 Paul Spring Road are type 6, a two-level unit with a butterfly roof along the long dimension.

On Rebecca Drive (left from the end of Paul Spring Road), in the 7100 block (righthand side) are several houses of type 5B, a slightly enlarged type 5A, set on an unfinished basement plinth. Numbers 7202 and 7204 are examples of type 5CS, similar to type 5B, but with a mono-pitched roof. In the 2300 block of Glasgow Road (right off Rebecca Drive near the top of the hill) are nearly a dozen examples of type 7, a one-level three-bedroom house that was almost totally prefabricated, with 12-foot-by-8-foot exterior wall panels. On either side of the 7400 block of Rebecca Drive are a number of custom-designed houses by a variety of architects. Numbers 7413 and 7417 Rebecca are type 8, a large, T-shaped four-bedroom, two-level unit with double side porches. At the bottom of Rebecca Road, turn right on Range Road, and then left on Elba Road. In 1956 a new tract of land to the southwest (Elba Road, Brentwood Road) was added to Hollin Hills, and many of the earlier housing types were used along with new ones. The 7700 block of Elba had a number of the new Mainline type, a longer one-

story variant of the type 7, but with glazed upper gable ends and vertically scored Texture XI plywood siding. The Customline type, a four-bedroom, elongated type 7, can be found at numbers 7519 and 7618 Elba Road and at numbers 2402, 2404, and 2406 Daphne Lane. Type 260, a later variant of type 3 but with a splayed chimney mass and "bay" window, is at numbers 7527, 7528, 7601, and 7615 Elba Road. At number 7801 Elba Road is an all-aluminum house, a design which Goodman developed in 1957 for the Aluminum Corporation of America as the Alcoa 1957 House. Prototypes were built in fifteen states. Goodman ended his involvement with Hollin Hills c. 1962, but Robert Davenport (the developer) continued to construct his designs with subtle modifications. In addition Davenport designed two of his own models, the Decca, an economy version which is at 2101 Mason Hill Drive, and the Atrium, a large two-story at 7422 Saville Court and 2104 White Oaks Drive.

NV47 **Mount Vernon**

c. 1735. 1758–1763, 1774–1787, George Washington; many later additions and restorations. Terminus of George Washington Memorial Pkwy. (VA 400) and Mount Vernon Memorial Hwy. (VA 235)

Arguably the most famous house in America and certainly the most imitated, George Washington's home is also among the most visited. It not only provides insights into the man and his visions, but also gives a view of late eighteenth-

NV47 Mount Vernon

century plantation life and of American popular perceptions of it. In 1754 Washington inherited the house, built c. 1735, one and one-half stories with four small rooms and a central hall. Just before his marriage in 1759 he launched a building campaign that raised the house to two stories with an attic and replanned the garden near the house as a series of geometrical elements. Then, in 1774 and continuing intermittently during the Revolutionary War, Washington completely updated the house to conform to what he thought a British gentleman or lord would desire, as seen in various editions of *Vitruvius Britannicus* in his library. He doubled the length; raised the house again, to three stories; redecorated substantial parts of the interior; and added the grand banquet hall, the east piazza, a cupola, and arcades to the east and west to link the new outbuildings. He also replanned major portions of the grounds near the house, including the approach from the west, which he landscaped in the English picturesque manner. Throughout the 1790s Washington continued to make changes to the grounds and outbuildings and refurbish the house. In spite of all this work, the house remained a thoroughly American adaptation: wood siding, albeit rusticated to resemble stone; frame rather than masonry; asymmetrical fenestration on the west facade instead of strict symmetry; and a tall, wide piazza for viewing the landscape—all features basically unknown to or modified from the Old World.

Although the house continued to be a point of pilgrimage and a shrine after his death in 1799, it gradually fell into disrepair and was threatened by development. In spite of numerous proposals for a tomb in Washington, D.C., Washington remained interred at the site. The enclosure of the tomb was designed by William Strickland and built in 1837–1838 but has since been modified. Strickland also designed the sarcophagus, which was carved by John Struthers, a Philadelphia sculptor. In 1858 Ann Pamela Cunningham and the national group she formed, the Mount Vernon Ladies' Association, purchased the house and 200 of its original 8,000 acres and began restoration in what is frequently described as the beginning of the preservation movement in America. They later added more acreage. The subsequent history of the house and the succession of tastes and interpretations it has represented, from the Chinese Chippendale railing on the piazza, in-

stalled by 1876 and subsequently removed, to color schemes and ground treatments, is a virtual textbook of American preservation. In the 1930s Morely Williams and Charles Killam directed extensive restoration. In the 1950s Morley Walter Macomber, earlier at Colonial Williamsburg, directed restoration of the outbuildings. Over the years the site has been the subject of archaeological, landscape, and other studies.

Mount Vernon shows the aesthetic and personal side of Washington, and, although it is not as intimate as Jefferson's Monticello and Washington remains a somewhat distant figure, still his involvement in every aspect indicates the importance of architecture and decorative arts for the Virginia gentry of the period. The problem of turning a small house into a mansion is amply shown in the plan and the contrast of low, narrow spaces, with rooms of great proportion. Washington's taste for grandeur is amply demonstrated in the banquet hall with its cove ceiling and grand Palladian window, though he did object to the mantel sent from England by one Samuel Vaughn as "too elegant and costly by far." Washington's architectural aesthetics was complicated; the room is frequently described as neoclassical because of the Adamesque decoration, but its form, a double cube, undoubtedly lies with the earlier Palladians, Inigo Jones and Colen Campbell, while the great window is derived from Batty Langley's *Treasury of Designs* (London, 1751). Abraham Swan's *British Architect* (London, 1745) provided inspiration for the chimneypieces in the small dining room and the front (west) parlor.

Washington's interest in landscape is amply shown by the house and the gardens. The great piazza, or veranda, along the north side, two stories in height and carried on thin, spindly posts, was intended for viewing the Potomac and as an escape from summer heat. It has become one of the great iconic features of American architecture. The picturesque treatment of the grounds and the incorporation of a view shed show a side of the man seldom recognized.

The current emphasis of Mount Vernon's interpretation on the many other individuals—white and black—who made the place run helps show the entire estate as a large and profitable plantation. Worthy of close inspection are the numerous outbuildings. The most recent major work is the reconstruction (1995–

1997, Quinn Evans) of Washington's sixteen-sided grain-treading barn (1790s), which stood until the 1870s. It reveals Washington as a pioneer in advanced farming techniques.

Also worthy of note are the gatekeepers' lodges at the entrance, which apparently date from 1899 but were reconstructed (1931–1932) by Edward W. Donn, Jr., and more recently (1987–1988) by Lewis/Wisnewski. Donn also designed the concession stand and restaurant (1931–1932), to the right of the entrance, in a vernacular Colonial Revival idiom as part of the Mount Vernon Memorial Highway project. Also on the grounds are the West Gates, apparently designed by Bushrod Washington (c. 1820) and then modified by Samuel Bootes in 1875.

NV48 George Washington's Gristmill

1932–1934. Mount Vernon Memorial Hwy. (VA 235), 3 miles west of Mount Vernon,.3 mile east of U.S. 1. Open seasonally to the public

An excellent example of the 1930s interest in reviving vernacular forms, this three-and-one-half-story structure of semidressed stone was erected by the Virginia Department of Conservation and Economic Development on Dogue Run, across from the actual site of Washington's gristmill. Washington's father, Augustine Washington, constructed a mill c. 1730 on the opposite side of the creek; in 1770 its dilapidated state caused Washington to build a new one. In 1791 he contracted with Oliver Evans, a millwright and inventor, to remodel and upgrade the mill. In 1932, as part of the George Washington Birthday Bicentennial, the commonwealth of Virginia decided to recreate the mill. Henry Ford donated the stone, which came from his factory in Alexandria, and the waterwheel and gears came from a mill near Front Royal, Virginia, which Evans had constructed. The designer of the reconstructed mill was apparently R. E. Burson, a landscape engineer; Carl A. Ries drew up the plans and supervised the construction using a local workforce. The Civilian Conservation Corps cleared some of the property. On the exterior the restoration is fairly accurate; the interior framing is obviously modern. The "miller's cottage" stands on its original foundations, but it is more generically 1930s Colonial Revival than the mill. The complex originally contained a distillery, cooper's shop, and other buildings, but their reconstruction was never carried out.

NV49 Woodlawn Plantation

1800–1806, attributed to William Thornton. c. 1893, enlargement. 1915–1916, restoration and enlargement, Edward W. Donn, Jr. 1925, restoration, Waddy B. Wood; Alden Hopkins, landscape architect. 9000 Richmond Hwy. (U.S. 1), Fairfax County. Open to the public

This five-part brick house on a hill within sight of Mount Vernon and property of 2,030 acres (the present site contains 137 acres) was a gift from George Washington to Eleanor ("Nelly") Parke Custis and her husband, Lawrence Lewis, respectively his ward and his nephew. They were married at Mount Vernon on Washington's last birthday. William Thornton's wife, Anna Maria, refers to the house, but no other related correspondence or drawings survive. Although the attribution to Thornton is fairly certain, Woodlawn is conventional and shows little of Thornton's sparky originality. Its form, though—five bays and a central pediment—has proven exceedingly popular, and it is one of the most imitated of early Virginia houses. The pedimented five-bay central block has a standard plan with a central hall that allows the visitor a panoramic view of the countryside toward Mount Vernon. Originally the south hyphen was a well room, with kitchen beyond. The major interior space is the high-ceilinged music room, which causes interesting floor-level changes upstairs. The house passed out of the Lewis family in 1846 and had a number of owners—including a Quaker community—and deteriorated until Paul Kester, a New York playwright, purchased it in 1902 and raised the hyphens and wings. The architect is unknown, and the work lacks sympathy with the original. The house then passed in 1905 to Elizabeth M. Sharpe of Pennsylvania, who hired Edward W. Donn, Jr., who also worked on Thornton's Octagon House in Washington, D.C., to rebuild the wings in a more sympathetic manner. Later Waddy B. Wood, who had been Donn's partner, restored the dining room and made other alterations. Senator and Mrs. Oscar Underwood of Alabama acquired the property in 1925 and made further changes. It subsequently passed to the National Trust for Historic Preservation as the trust's first property. The interior is restored to c. 1805, and about a third of the interior furnishings are original. The various gardens are a mixture of restorations and conjectures. In 1958–1960 Alden Hopkins, landscape architect, with funding from the Garden Club of Virginia, designed the approach and formal gardens.

NV50 Pope-Leighey House

1939–1940, Frank Lloyd Wright; moved and restored. 1995–1996, reconstruction. Woodlawn Plantation, 9000 Richmond Hwy. (U.S. 1), Fairfax County. Open to the public

The most accessible of Wright's three surviving Virginia buildings, the Pope-Leighey House is one of his best-known Usonian houses. It was designed and built for Loren and Charlotte Pope and for a site in Falls Church; they sold it in 1947 to Robert and Marjorie Leighey. The construction of I-66 threatened the house, and the National Trust for Historic Preservation acquired it and moved it to Woodlawn Plantation. Unstable foundations brought about a reconstruction in 1995–1996. The new Woodlawn site, while similar to the Falls Church location in being wooded, has differences; the original orientation was east-west, not the present north-south. The recent restoration, however, allows the house to be approached as it was originally, from below. The original interior cypress has been maintained along with most fixtures and furniture. The brick is a replacement, and although the house still has a radiant-heated floor (not the original concrete pad!), it also has 1990s heating, ventilation, and air conditioning.

Loren Pope read Wright's *An Autobiography* (1932) and became a true believer. He wrote asking for a house design, explaining that his reporter's salary at the *Washington Evening Star* permitted a budget of only $5,500. Wright replied, "Of course I am ready to give you a house," and, without ever visiting the site but working with a contour map, presented the Popes with a version of his Usonian house similar to the Herbert Jacobs house in Madison, Wisconsin (1936). The cost was nearly double Pope's budget. The house, as constructed under the supervision of Wright's apprentice Gordon Chadwick, reflects Wright's belief that simplicity and elimination of nonessentials solved the problem of the middle-income American house. The garage is replaced by a carport, the basement disappears for a radiant heated concrete slab, all unnecessary hardware and ornament (downspouts, etc.) vanish, the roof is flat, prefabricated wood wall panels eliminate costly on-site labor, wood is left unfinished (or natural) inside and out to avoid painting, interior and exterior become a continuum, rooms are kept small except for the combined living-dining area, and where possible furniture is built in or integral to the structure. The plan is L-shaped, with bedrooms along a single-loaded corridor in a low wing and the major living space and narrow, cramped kitchen in the higher wing. Loren Pope described the house as "like living with a great and quiet soul."

NV51 Fort Belvoir

1917–1941, Washington District, U.S. Army Corps of Engineers and William I. Deming. Entrance off U.S. 1 at Belvoir Rd. or Gunston Rd. (1 mile south of Woodlawn Plantation). Open to visitors

Belvoir was originally the grand eighteenth-century mansion of Colonel William Fairfax, which stood on this spit of land overlooking the Potomac. The present Fort Belvoir sprawls over several thousand acres on both sides of U.S. 1, but the most interesting part is the Post Headquarters, grouped around the Long Parade Ground, and the adjacent Senior and Non-Commissioned Officers' (NCO) housing. These can be reached from either of the entrances noted above.

The home of the U.S. Army Corps of Engineers since World War I, the post saw its most intense development in the 1930s with the addition of large classroom buildings and housing, all in the Colonial Revival style. Lieutenant H. B. Nurse laid out the central section (c. 1928) following his design philosophy or "laws" that included "Unity," "Consonance in Design," "Natural Beauty," and "Balance." Nurse believed that army posts should "radiate from or otherwise refer back to common centers." At Fort Belvoir, which in many ways resembles college campuses of the period, the center is the rectangular parade ground, which is surrounded by structures of red brick and light-colored trim of stone or wood. The most imposing is the neo-Palladian composition of Abbot Hall (Post Headquarters, Building 269) and its two flankers, Williams and Thayer halls (buildings 268 and 270), designed by William I. Deming and erected in 1935. The Post Chapel, on the south side of the parade ground, is standard government issue, replicated at other

NV51 Fort Belvoir

posts but here placed in a commanding position. The other Colonial Revival buildings in this area, all dating from the late 1920s and early 1930s, were designed by the corps architecture staff. Immediately adjacent to the west, along 18th, 19th, 20th, and 21st streets and Gunston Road, is the NCO housing (buildings 101–112, 114–153, 155, 157, 159, 161–165) (1930–1931, 1934), composed of sixty identical one-and-one-half-story units, again in colonial garb, with enriched entries, latticework, and columnar supports.

The Senior Officers' housing (buildings 2–19, 21–60) (1934–1935), which stretches to the south of the Parade Ground along Belvoir Drive and branches off onto Woodlawn, Mason, and Fairfax drives, is in a winding, wooded parklike area that respects the terrain with central green spaces and generous grounds and vistas. It is a stunning composition resembling garden suburbs of the 1920s and 1930s, though here carried out with appropriate precision and order. The basic model for the fifty-nine identical units is a two-and-one-half-story red brick Colonial Revival dwelling that allowed for small variations in entrances and wings. Appropriately, the two departures from this uniformity are the Commandant's Quarters (building 1) and the Officers' Club (building 20), though both follow the same basic brick and trim palette of the Colonial Revival idiom.

As evidence of what officers had to live in before all this richness, six low, one-story, bungalow-like "temporary" houses (buildings T436–441) (1921), designed by Captain A. A. Hockman, survive along Mount Vernon Road.

NV52 Pohick Episcopal Church

1769–1774, attributed to James Wren and William West. 1901–1916, restoration, Glenn Brown. 1931, restoration, Edward W. Donn, Jr. 9301 Richmond Hwy. (U.S. 1) (12 miles south of Alexandria), Lorton

One of the most sophisticated (and famous) of Virginia's colonial churches, Pohick has a complicated history. It is traditionally associated with George Washington (Mount Vernon is 6 miles distant), who served on the vestry from 1762 to 1784, and George Mason (Gunston Hall is five miles distant), who also served on the vestry for thirty-five years. They have frequently been named as designers, Washington credited with drawing an elevation and plan and selecting the site and Mason with taking a hand in the construction. Recent research tends to support an attribution of the design to James Wren and William West, though, as with many buildings of the time, the design was probably a group effort. In March 1769, Wren and West were paid for building plans "furnished the Vestry." Pohick does resemble Wren's other northern Virginia work, the Falls Church in Falls Church and Christ Church in Alexandria. The original undertaker was William French, and the mason was William Copein. The carver for the interior, of which only the cornice and a baluster survive, was William Bernard Sears, who also worked at Gunston Hall. The stonework on the exterior of the two-story brick box is some of the most lavish in Virginia, with quoins and door surrounds of carved Aquia Creek sandstone. (It is also covered with nineteenth-century graffiti, some of it from the Union army's occupation during 1862–1863, when the church was used as a stable and partially destroyed.) Copein also created a stone font, with the directions that it be "according to a draught in the 150th Plate in Langley's Designs—for the price of six pounds, he finding for himself, everything," and that the font should be appropriate for "dipping the Infant in the water discreetly and warily." Also in the church is a large font, which reputedly is medieval and was brought from England; the carved date A.D. 1773 is a later insertion. The church received a new roof and ceiling in 1840. Union troops stripped most of the interior during the Civil War. A partial restoration occurred in 1874, and then, between 1901 and 1916, Glenn Brown created the present Georgian Revival interior, closely following what he found as evidence. The interior is white and bright and contains features reminiscent of English Dis-

NV53 Gunston Hall
NV53 Gunston Hall, dining room

senter chapels of the eighteenth century. The entrance is on the long south side, and on its axis on the north wall is the pulpit. The altar is on the east and a balcony on the west. Box pews are on either side of the aisles. In 1772 the vestry "Ordered that a Vestry House be built at this Church of Brick . . . " but canceled the project two years later. In honor of the bicentennials of Washington's birth and the establishment of Truro Parish, in 1931 Edward W. Donn, Jr., designed the vestry house following the original specifications. Donn also designed the brick walls for the churchyard, copying Ware Church in Gloucester County.

NV53 **Gunston Hall**

1755–1758, George Mason and William Buckland. 1912–1915, restoration, Glenn Brown, Bedford Brown IV, and others; Charles Gillette, landscape architect. 10709 Gunston Rd. (VA 242; I-95 or U.S. 1 south), Mason Neck

Deceptively, Gunston Hall appears modest, only a story and a half, though, on approach, the dramatic site overlooking the Potomac, the Aquia stone quoins, and the lavishly carved entrance porch indicate the possibility of great display. Probably George Mason (statesman, author of the Virginia Declaration of Rights [1776], and principal contributor to the U.S. Constitution [1787]) is responsible for the basic house. The elaborate design of the porches—including pointed arches on the garden, or river, side—and the interior are principally the work of William Buckland, who was indentured to Mason for several years. Buckland was a joiner, carver, and later a full-fledged architect who worked in Annapolis. Buckland or Mason or friends (Washington and others) had access to various English and possibly French pattern books; and the interior, downstairs as well as up, is perhaps the greatest surviving display of architectural elements from the colonial period. The intent may have been a hierar-

NV55 Quantico Marine Corps Base, Lustron house

chy of orders, from the more formal Doric for the most public parlor, through the Ionic in the little parlor, and then the more festive Corinthian and Chinese for the dining rooms. However, the interior also displays the combination of different orders in decidedly unorthodox ways and with tremendous inventiveness. Buckland was partially responsible for the carving, but he also assembled a team, one of whom was William Bernard Sears.

The house was given to the Commonwealth of Virginia in 1932, and since 1949 it has been administered by the National Society of Colonial Dames of America. Restoration, begun in 1912–1915 by Glenn Brown and Bedford Brown IV, has continued with a variety of other approaches. Only some of the furniture is original to Mason's time. The garden supposedly follows Mason's design but is essentially the work of Charles Gillette. The outbuildings—kitchen, laundry, dairy, and smokehouse—are all reconstructions.

NV54 Occoquan Historic District

Bounded by the Occoquan River and Mill St. on the north, Rockledge St. on the west, Commerce St. on the south, and Washington St. on the east

Its site on the Potomac River allowed Occoquan to become a center for iron smelting, gristmills and sawmills, and shipping. These industries declined after Occoquan Creek silted up. Fire and floods have destroyed many of the older buildings, but some survive. Occoquan's location along I-95 has made it a bedroom community for northern Virginia and a small boat center, and it has developed an "olde towne" atmosphere of faux Victorian and Colonial Revival. Among the buildings of note are Rockledge (1759; 412 Mill Street), attributed to

William Buckland, a six-bay, two-story stone house, originally the home of William Ballendien, who established the iron furnace. It has burned and been restored several times. Ellicott's Mill (1759; Mill Street, west end) is a three-and-one-half-story gristmill in ruins. The former Mill House (c. 1755; 413 Mill Street), is of stone and brick. The remainder of the town has a variety of nineteenth-century structures, some with identifying plaques and dates.

NV55 Quantico Marine Corps Base, Lustron District

1948–1949, Lustron Co. Mainside area, 35 units in Argonne Hills, and 26 in Geiger Ridge, Quantico

Quantico began as a temporary Marine training camp during World War I and became permanent in 1918. Early officers' housing consisted of bungalows and Colonial Revival houses, some supplied by the Turton Company in 1920. Glenn Brown designed a master plan for the base in 1926, but most of the building is undistinguished. In 1948 the corps contracted with the Lustron Company of Columbus, Ohio, for sixty-one units of prefabricated housing. The so-called Lustron house was the brain child of Carl G. Strandland, who hired Roy Blass of Blass and Beckman architects, Wilmette, Illinois, to design a small ranch house— "a modern rambler"—built of enamel-coated steel panels similar to those used in service station construction. The Lustron Company was funded by the Reconstruction Finance Corporation and was never profitable. It went into receivership in 1950. Of the nearly 2,500 units the Lustron Company produced, Quantico has the largest concentration. The concept involved mass producing the 2,334 exterior and interior components needed for each house and then trucking them to the site, where they could be assembled quickly, in nine to twenty-one days. The basic Lustron house was a single-story ranch house with an attached carport, two or three bedrooms, a single bath, a living room with a dining area, and a utility room. Enameled steel was used for all interior and exterior surfaces. All were built on concrete pads. The houses supposedly never need painting, and all of the Quantico units retain their 1940s pastel colors, though slightly faded. Thirty-five two-bedroom units for enlisted personnel were built in Argonne Hill, and twenty-six two-bedroom units for officers were constructed in Geiger Ridge.

Alexandria (AL)

ALEXANDRIA WAS NAMED FOR SCOTSMAN JOHN ALEXANDER, WHO IN 1669 purchased a site on the Potomac River for "Six thousand punds [*sic*] of Tobacco and Cask." The Virginia Assembly established a town there in 1749, and John West, Jr., surveyed the site and laid out the gridiron plan. Tradition holds that seventeen-year-old George Washington assisted him; local legend asserts that Washington planned the town. In July 1749, building lots were auctioned off from the town square. Streets carry the names of various English and Virginia worthies. Soon Alexandria became a major and prosperous center of pre- and post-Revolutionary commerce. George Washington owned a town house, and, depending on the source, he appears to have dined in almost every house in Old Town. In 1791, the District of Columbia absorbed Alexandria; the federal government ceded it back to Virginia in 1846. During the Civil War, Union troops occupied the town and used it as a base of operations.

In the twentieth century, during two world wars the city was a major munitions manufactory site, and on the waterfront large factories were constructed, of which only portions of one, the Torpedo Factory, remain. A selective historic preservation conscience began to develop as early as 1903, as the town began to identify itself as a home of George Washington and Robert E. Lee. As a result of a 1920s study, in September 1929 the Chamber of Commerce passed a recommendation that "the colonial style be adhered to wherever possible." Additional studies through the 1930s and early 1940s led to the passage of a 1946 historic district preservation ordinance establishing an area in the heart of downtown, and an architectural review board—both of which proved to be controversial. The ordinance has been amended thirty-three times and threatened with repeal but although significant buildings have been lost, especially along King Street, overall the legislation has been effective in preserving an important legacy. In the late 1950s an urban renewal project envisioned demolishing sixty-four square blocks of Old Town. After preservationists opposed the plan the targeted area was scaled back to six blocks along King Street.

The city is the eleventh most dense in the United States, and significant new construction continues. Its 2000 population stood at 128,283. Although the mania for faux colonial may grate on some visitors, a respect for later nineteenth-century architecture has developed since the mid-1970s and, more recently, even for the late nineteenth- and early twentieth-century Colonial Revival. Alexandria maintains an overall cohesiveness along with a wealth of identified and researched eighteenth- and nineteenth-century buildings, of which only a representative sample can be included in this guide. Some of the buildings in the Old Town section display plaques or signs with dates; however, this information is not always accurate.

Old Town   (AL1–AL41)

This walking tour of King Street and environs makes a large circle through the commercial and residential section of downtown. The appropriate beginning—and conclusion—is Market Square, which since 1749 has been the civic, if not the physical, center of the city.

AL1 Alexandria City Hall

1871–1873, Adolph Cluss and Benjamin F. Price. 1960–1962, additions, Robert A. Willgoos and Dwight G. Chase. 1967, plaza, Neer and Graef. 1982–1984, interior renovations, Neer and Graef. Entire block bounded by King, Royal, Cameron, and Fairfax sts.

This structure replaced Benjamin Henry Latrobe's City Hall of 1817, which occupied the site set aside for the market and city hall and burned in 1871. The complex illustrates Americans' changing tastes. Cluss, German émigré architect and founder of the American Communist Party, designed a notable building which fronts on three streets. The facade on Cameron Street, in the French Second Empire mode common to American city halls in the post–Civil War years, was intended as the main entrance. The facade on North Fairfax Street originally housed the police department. It is fewer stories and more in an Italianate vein.

The tall steeple mass on North Royal Street is not by Cluss, but a design by the local architect Benjamin F. Price. It is supposedly a replica of Latrobe's original 1817 design, but one that he would only faintly recognize. The Alexandria-Washington Masonic Lodge financed the project under a separate contract with the builder, Edward H. Dulahay. Market sheds and commercial buildings on the south half of the block were torn down during urban renewal and replaced with the plaza. In the early 1960s a Colonial Revival structure that vaguely recalls the Governor's Palace in Williamsburg filled in the courtyard on the south side of City Hall. City Hall's interior has been gutted and refitted several times.

AL2 Carlyle House

1751–1753. 1976, restoration, J. Everett Fauber, Jr. 121 N. Fairfax St. Open to the public

Perhaps the most ambitious and finest city house for its date in Virginia outside Williamsburg, this would not be out of place in Salisbury Close in England. Constructed by a Scottish tobacco trader, John Carlyle, who married a daughter of Colonel William Fairfax in 1748, the house was placed far back on the lot with dependencies to either side and a garden facing Fairfax Street. Even before the house was completed the town authorities adopted a law requiring all new houses to grip the front property line. Subsequently, a large hotel filled the front garden; it was removed for the 1970s restoration.

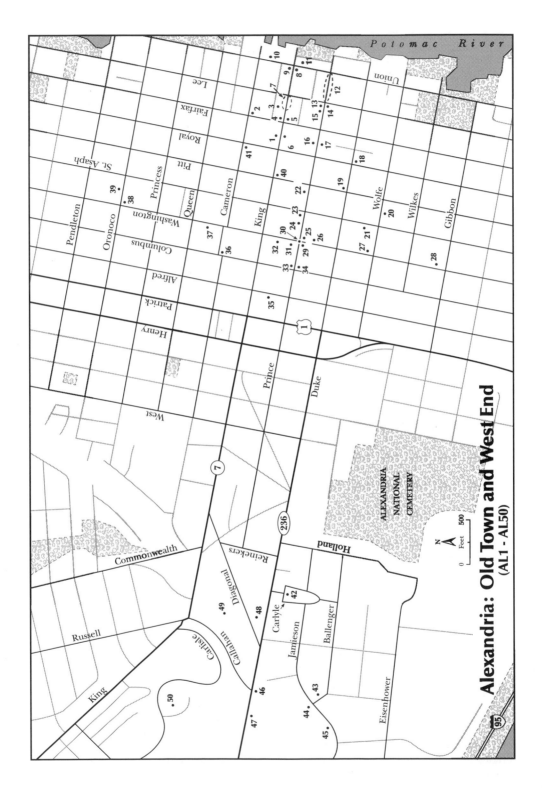

Alexandria: Old Town and West End
(AL1 - AL50)

AL2 Carlyle House

AL6 Stabler-Leadbeater Apothecary Museum

The exterior also displays an affinity to William Adam's Craigiehall, Midlothian, Scotland. The rich exterior details draw on a variety of English pattern books, especially the work of James Gibbs. Although John Ariss has been credited with the design, no evidence exists to support the attribution. Originally the house was built of random sandstone rubble covered with scored stucco on three sides and then clad with dressed Aquia sandstone on the primary facade. The 1976 restoration substituted limestone. The same rich quality continues on the interior. The interior organization is conventional: a two-story, double-pile, central-hall plan. Although portions of the restoration are conjectural, especially the east Palladian window on the staircase, it contains much original

trim, including an overdoor broken pediment and a fine modillion cornice in the northeast parlor.

AL3 House

c. 1799. 207 Ramsay Alley

In the alley south of Carlyle House stands an example of a "flounder house," a simple row house with a shed roof sloping to one side, lacking windows on the higher side wall. Although local lore holds that the "flounder" was unique to Alexandria, it actually can be found in many urban areas throughout the northeast. Easy to construct, the house type was a result of Alexandria's early laws, which mandated that a lot had to be improved within two years or be forfeited. In many cases flounders became ells to larger houses erected in front. Most have disappeared, but the form was revived in the late twentieth century for both residential and commercial construction.

AL4 Alexandria Convention and Visitors Bureau (Ramsay House)

c. 1724. 1946–1955, restoration, Milton L. Grigg. 221 King St.

The city visitor center is a reconstruction, containing a few original fragments, of a house thought to have been built in 1724 and moved to the site c. 1748. The house is an excellent example, based upon photographs and archaeology, of the highly detailed work for which Grigg, a Charlottesville-based architect and Alexandria native, became known. Maps and information can be obtained here.

AL5 Burke and Herbert Bank

1904, Wood, Donn and Deming. 1941, renovation. 1947, extension, Edgar T. Jenkinson. 100 S. Fairfax St.

This sophisticated design in the usual bankers' formula of classicism which illustrates the nexus of power of banks and government is, of course, across the street from City Hall.

AL6 Stabler-Leadbeater Apothecary Museum

c. 1775. 1938, restoration, Thomas Tileston Waterman. 105–107 S. Fairfax St. Open to the public

This building housed an apothecary from 1792 to 1933. The "colonial" look of the exterior, designed by one of Virginia's leading restoration architects, is not very accurate, for it covers an essentially Victorian interior, which contains wonderful Gothic-inspired shelves and counters.

AL7 Commercial Buildings

200 block of King St.

Lower King Street contains a group of early commercial buildings and warehouses not as important individually as they are for their unity as a group. Most are three stories high and three bays wide. On the north side, they date from c. 1803 (numbers 217 and 215), c. 1810 (number 207, built by William Bartleman, and number 205), and 1851 (no. 201, built by William Bayne). On the south side, they date from c. 1800 (number 210, built by John Ramose), 1798 (numbers 208 and 206, built by George Gilpin, and numbers 204 and 202, built by Bernard Chequire), and c. 1802–1810 (number 200, built by Jacob Hoffman).

AL8 Corn Exchange

1871, Benjamin F. Price. 100 King St.

The former Corn Exchange, now a restaurant, marks an important corner. The imposing Renaissance Revival structure owes a small debt to the Palazzo Farnese, as well as pointing back to the earlier tradition of a market hall with trading area at street level and hall and offices above. The ground floor has always been enclosed. The second-floor hall was 25 feet high and had a gallery, but this atrium space was filled in some years ago. Price's employment of the Renaissance idiom indicates its continuing applicability, even during the 1870s, at the height of the Gothic Revival. Originally, the exterior was stucco.

AL9 Fitzgerald's Warehouses

1789. 6 King St.

Standing at the corner of Union and King streets and originally fronting on the river, this large, imposing structure is really three buildings. Constructed on a swampy area that was filled in by Colonel John Fitzgerald, it was described in an 1801 advertisement as "three brick warehouses, twenty-four feet four inches in front, and three stores high . . . a Sail Loft above the upper story seventy-three feet in length, and forty-two feet wide upon the floor . . . all under one roof."

AL10 The Torpedo Factory

1918, attributed to Construction Division, U.S. Navy. 1976–1980, renovation and adaptation, Metcalf and Associates, Keyes Condon Florance, Arthur Keyes in charge. 105 S. Union St.

The factory displays its reinforced concrete construction forthrightly. It is the lone survivor of several large factories that used to line the Potomac River in this area. Perhaps as important is its renovation in the 1970s for reuse as craftspeople's and artists' studios and display spaces. The postmodern addition on the south is part of the 1978 renovation.

AL11 Dean Witter and Company

1991, Rust, Orling and Neale. 110 S. Union St.

This postmodern Colonial Revival structure fits into the streetscape context with its scale, massing, and facade of brick. Of course in this case the brick is nonstructural.

AL12 Captains' Row

1827 and later. 100 block of Prince St. (from Union St. to Lee St.)

The 100 block of Prince Street evokes eighteenth-century Alexandria, especially with its cobblestone paving. A portion of the lower end, known as Captains' Row, occupies land filled in before the Revolutionary War. Although many of the buildings display dates that go back to the 1780s, the entire block and many of the surroundings were destroyed by fire on January 18, 1827. The block was rebuilt almost immediately, but many of the houses have subsequently been "colonialized."

AL13 The Athenaeum

1851–1852, B. H. Jenkins, carpenter; E. Francis, bricklayer. 201 Prince St. Open to the public

The Athenaeum is a stout, Doric-porticoed structure described in 1851 in the *Alexandria Gazette* as "of the Grecian order of architecture, plain in its exterior and of ample accommodations for the business of the bank." Following

AL12 Captains' Row

its life as a bank, the building served as a warehouse and a church. It became an arts center in 1925 and was named the Athenaeum in 1964. The Northern Virginia Fine Arts Association now owns it. Nothing of the original interior decoration remains.

AL14 Robert Hooe House

c. 1780. 200 Prince St. and 201 S. Lee St.

The entire 200 block of Prince Street is collectively known as Gentry Row because of the eminence of the early residents. This large brick double house on the corner of Prince and Lee streets was originally a single dwelling owned by Robert Hooe, Alexandria's first mayor. Washington "dined at Colo. Hooe's" on several occasions. The original dining-room woodwork—Georgian in style—is on display in the St. Louis Art Museum. It was converted into a double house c. 1910.

AL15 William Fairfax House

1752, later alterations. 207 Prince St.

Originally built as the Fairfax family town residence, this house of three stories plus attic and basement was one of the most impressive in town. George Washington witnessed its sale in 1771 when the Fairfaxes decided to move to England. Their land holdings, the most extensive in northern Virginia, included the large plantation Belvoir (now a U.S. Army base). The house has been extensively altered over the

years, especially c. 1800, so its appearance is more Federal than colonial.

AL16 Relief Truck and Engine Company No. 1

c. 1915, attributed to Emmett C. Dunn, Alexandria City architect-engineer. 317 Prince St.

The impressive three-bay arcade of this brick and limestone-trimmed firehouse may refer to a house at 211 North Fairfax Street that has been attributed to Latrobe and has a similar loggia in the rear. It has been converted into apartments.

AL17 Prince Street Club (Elks' Lodge)

1909, William R. Hamilton, of Wagner and Hamilton. 1985, addition and renovation, Brown, Donald, Lemay and Page. 314–318 Prince St.

The great elk's head sculpture on the upper facade displays the building's former function as a men's club. The imposing bulk of the structure helps to maintain the wall of buildings on this side of the block.

AL18 St. Mary's Roman Catholic Church

1827, 1881. 1894–1895, Philip N. Dwyer. 301 Royal St.

St. Mary's serves the oldest Catholic parish in Virginia, founded in 1788. George Washington contributed to the building fund for an earlier church located elsewhere. The present building began as a Greek Revival structure, but in 1881, Dwyer, a local architect only twenty-one years old, began making alterations that culminated in the stone Gothic Revival western front, *tourelle*, and tower. Two German glass firms, Franz Mayer and F. X. Zettler, made most of the stained glass.

AL19 St. Paul's Episcopal Church

1817–1818, Benjamin Henry Latrobe. 1867, remodeling, Benjamin F. Price. 1878, stained glass, W. W. Vaughan. 1897–1899, 1906, additions, Emmett C. Dunn. 1958, additions, H. Delos Smith. 1996–1997, restoration, C. Richard Bierce. 222 Pitt St. (Duke and Pitt sts.)

Although much modified, St. Paul's is one of the most significant "Gothick" buildings in the

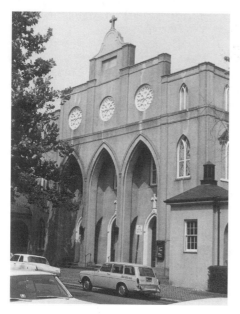

AL19 St. Paul's Episcopal Church
AL22 Patrick Murray House

country and an important example of Latrobe's work. Its history is complicated. Latrobe produced drawings for the structure,
but, much to his distress, the design was altered
during construction. Essentially it is a rectangular building with high entrance arches.
Some historians have traced the arches to Pe-
terborough Cathedral; inspiration may also
have come from a book Latrobe owned, Batty
Langley's *Gothic Architecture* (1742), and a
sketch he made of Kirkstall Abbey. Latrobe's
original interior, a large box, was very much in
the meetinghouse tradition of the period. The
chancel was remodeled in 1867 by Benjamin
F. Price and then in 1906 was extended about
40 feet by Emmett C. Dunn, who also added
the north building, Norton Hall, 1897–1899.
These interior changes made it more "high"
Episcopalian than it was originally. In 1878, the
original clear glass windows were replaced with
Victorian patterned stained glass, made by W.
W. Vaughan, of Washington, D.C. Vaughan's
windows remain at the gallery level and in the
chancel, but at ground level some opalescent
glass and medievalist revival windows from c.
1900 have been substituted. Two windows in
the north aisle, which date from c. 1950, are by
Philadelphia's Willet Studios. In 1923, the original scored stucco exterior was replaced. H.
Delos Smith made further additions to the
south in 1958 and again stuccoed the exterior,

this time with the present exposed aggregate.
In 1996–1997 the exterior and interior were
extensively refurbished and restored by C.
Richard Bierce. The interior retains some
sense of the meetinghouse character of Latrobe's design, though Latrobe objected to the
side balconies. The woodwork of the balconies,
including the clustered columns, is original;
Dunn imitated the columns in his chancel of
1906.

AL20 Francis L. Smith House

1854. 510 Wolfe St.

This large Italianate house bears a strong resemblance to "Design Twenty-First: A Suburban
Residence," published in Samuel Sloan's *The
Model Architect* (1852). Sloan, a Philadelphia architect, found in Virginia a ready following for
his bombastic designs. In the 1850s Wolfe
Street marked the southern edge of Alexandria; beyond lay open fields.

AL21 Houses

c 1800. 317 and 321 S. St. Asaph St.

John Roberts was the probable builder of these
two flounder houses, which dramatically show

the shed roof form. That they have survived in this often-rebuilt area is amazing.

AL22 Patrick Murray House

c. 1775, 517 Prince St.

This small house typifies the alternative to the flounder house. It is perhaps the least altered of pre-Revolutionary Alexandria houses. The high exposed basement of Potomac River granite was originally below grade, but a regrading of the street and most of Old Town in 1790 lowered the elevation.

AL23 EDAW (Second Presbyterian Church)

1840. 1889–1895, remodeling, Glenn Brown. 1980, remodeling, EDAW. 601 Prince St.

Brown covered the earlier Greek Revival structure with Richardsonian forms carried out in brick but with none of Richardson's force and drama. The record is unclear as to whether Brown, who went on to a significant career as a colonial revivalist and preservationist, actually worked for the "great mogul." Stamped sheet metal is used for the entrance capitals and the colonnettes above. The building is now the home of an environmental and landscape design firm.

AL26 Downtown Baptist Church (First Baptist Church)

AL24 Society of Military Engineers

c. 1790?. 1869, rebuilt or remodeled, James Graham. 605–607 Prince St.

This ornate row of buildings may have at their core an earlier structure. William B. Klipstein purchased them in 1853 and 1858 and hired Graham to rebuild them. Graham installed cast iron lintels, window hoods, and cornices on top of the brick facade.

AL25 U.S. Customhouse, Courthouse, and Post Office (former)

1930, James A. Wetmore, Supervising Architect, U.S. Treasury Department; Warren Noll, associate. 200 S. Washington St. (corner of Prince and S. Washington sts).

The imperial piano nobile and columnar Federal–Colonial Revival mode favored by the federal government in the 1920s and early 1930s are shown in this well-detailed structure. Ironically, the historical reference is more to New England and Charles Bulfinch than to the South. The design was contemporaneous with that of the reconstructed Governor's Palace in Colonial Williamsburg, which would soon influence the appearance of federal buildings.

AL26 Downtown Baptist Church (First Baptist Church)

1854, Thomas A. Tefft, with later alterations. 212 S. Washington St.

This fine example of the Providence, Rhode Island–based architect's Lombard Romanesque style lacks the heaviness of later Richardsonian interpretations such as Glenn Brown's work around the corner. The northern steeple is a later addition, though Tefft's drawings show spires. The light tan color is different from Tefft's original ocher stucco.

AL27 Alexandria Academy

c. 1785. 1996–1997, restoration, C. Richard Bierce. 300 block S. Washington St., at the rear (near corner of Wolfe St.). Open by appointment

Public education in Alexandria began in this small, unpretentious three-bay brick I-house form. George Washington contributed to the subscription campaign. The restoration emphasizes early construction techniques.

AL28 Suburban Drive-In Cleaners and Laundry

1957, Daumit and Sargent. 630 S. Washington St.

Every city needs some humor in its architecture. This essentially modernist box has brick walls and large plate glass windows. As a bow to local tradition, the architects inserted a broken pediment door frame into the glazing, creating instant "colonialism."

AL29 Lyceum Hall

1839, attributed to Benjamin Hallowell. 1974, restoration, Carroll Curtice. 201 S. Washington St. Open to the public

One of Virginia's preeminent Greek Revival structures, the Lyceum, with a library and museum on the ground floor and a lecture hall upstairs, served as the intellectual center of antebellum Alexandria. Hallowell, the head of the group that organized the Lyceum Company in 1838, described the building as having "four fluted columns, with a triglyph cornice . . . surrounded with an iron railing and a beautiful yard of flowers." Converted into a residence after the Civil War, it was restored as a museum for the city of Alexandria in connection with the U.S. Bicentennial, and a lecture hall was reinstalled upstairs. It contains exhibits on the history of Alexandria.

AL30 Confederate Monument

1889, M. Casper Buberl, sculptor. S. Washington and Prince sts.

For some time, May 24 was celebrated as the Southern Memorial Day (in contrast to the North's May 30), and on that day in 1889, this statue was dedicated. Buberl's "Johnny Reb" is a bronze soldier standing with arms folded and looking off toward the South. Its location in the middle of the original main north-south road through Alexandria was appropriately symbolic. When, in the 1930s, South Washington Street became part of Mount Vernon Memorial Parkway, all efforts to relocate the sculpture failed.

AL31 Pier 1 (Virginia Public Service Company Building)

1930, Frank D. Chase, Inc. 117 S. Washington St.

The Public Service Company, which supplied electricity and sold electric appliances, needed a building with large ground-level windows to show off its merchandise. This well-detailed classical Art Deco commercial structure resembles, in its restrained ornament, buildings in Chicago, the architect's home.

AL32 Washington Street Methodist Church

1876 remodeling, John Lambdin. 109 S. Washington St.

Originally Greek Revival in appearance, the church was transformed into an Italianate design in the mid-1870s. Lambdin based his new facade upon that of a Venetian church, San Zaccaria (c. 1458 and c. 1490), which incorporates a lower story by Antonio Gambello and an upper story, with curvilinear pediments, added by Marco Codussi. Lambdin, who came to Alexandria from Baltimore, chose to reproduce this unique and disjunctive Venetian facade with its brackets and arches.

AL33 Swann-Daingerfield House

c. 1803. c. 1850, c. 1870, and c. 1905, remodeling and enlargement. 706 Prince St.

When Thomas Swann owned it, this house was a Federal structure at the east end of the property. Swann, the original owner, sold it to Henry Daingerfield in 1832. Daingerfield added a Greek Revival wing and in the 1870s severely remodeled the exterior and interior. A massive Second Empire mansard, including arched dormers, and an arcaded porch completely changed the appearance. The property passed to the Sisters of the Holy Cross, who added a massive wing but maintained the mansard and details.

AL34 Patton-Fowle House

1797, c. 1820, c. 1900. 711 Prince St.

A fitting contrast with the Swann-Daingerfield House across the street and an earlier era's symbol of prosperity is this very substantial

AL29 Lyceum Hall

AL36 Christ Church exterior (above) and interior (left)

three-story brick Federal house. Originally built in 1797 by James Patton, it was purchased in 1819 by William Fowle, who owned a substantial portion of the Alexandria Canal Company and a local bank. His enlargements of c. 1820 have been attributed to Charles Bulfinch because of the Palladian window and the fanlighted entrance. Other evidence, though, points to these features as part of a later, Federal–Colonial Revival remodeling.

AL35 Friendship Fire Company

1855. 1871, remodeling. 107 S. Alfred St.

The odd-shaped belfry and tower date the company—as the inscription indicates—to 1774; George Washington was a member. Constructed in 1855 after the first firehouse, on Royal Street at Market Square, burned, the building was altered in 1871 when the belfry was replaced and a pressed brick front was erected. The cornice and cast iron lintels may date from the 1855 structure; the pilaster capitals flanking the entrance bear a remote resemblance to those of the Tower of the Winds in Athens.

AL36 Christ Church

1767–1773, James Wren. Additions and restorations, including 1891, Glenn Brown, and c. 1946–1955, Milton L. Grigg. 137 N. Columbus St. (southeast corner of Cameron and Columbus sts.)

One of Virginia's best-known churches, Christ Church is still surrounded by an old churchyard. The original building is a two-story brick box very much in the London mode and similar to Wren's design at nearby Pohick. The stone trim is from the Aquia Creek quarry. James Parsons began construction, and John Carlyle took over from him and completed the church. It was accepted by the vestry as "finished in workmanlike order" on February 27, 1773. The awkward tower and steeple date from 1785–1799 but were apparently altered c. 1818. The interior gallery was added sometime between 1785 and 1818. By the 1870s the ecclesiology movement, which called for a return to medieval forms in Anglican church design and worship, had reached Virginia, and the interior received a Gothic treatment. But by 1891, Glenn Brown, an Alexandria native, had passed out of his Richardsonian period (in addition to EDAW, see 219 and 228 North Columbus Street, two Queen Anne houses by Brown from c. 1887) and, under the influence of Charles F. McKim, discovered the "colonial." Brown "restored" the interior, painting it white, and designed the wineglass pulpit and other modifications. Milton L. Grigg further restored the church after World War II and in 1948 designed the parish hall, which was erected in 1950. Hence, the church as we see it is a combination of many different periods and a textbook of attitudes toward church design. The exterior, especially the tower, is impressive, and the interior is a light-filled box.

AL37 John Lloyd House

1798, John Wise, builder. 220 N. Washington St. Open to the public

The lack of a water table and belt courses betrays the date of this elegant five-bay late Georgian house. The brickwork in the splayed lintels and modillioned cornice is of the highest order. Refurbished in 1974 in connection with the national bicentennial, it is owned by the Alexandria Preservation and Restoration Commission.

AL38 Lee-Fendall House

1785. 1850, addition. 429 N. Washington St. (southeast corner of Washington and Oronoco sts.). Open to the public

The original building was a three-bay, two-and-one-half-story town house built as the residence of Philip and Elizabeth Lee Fendall. In the

1850s it received some additions and new Greek Revival trim. As indicated, the house has many associations with the Lees, and then, incongruously, with John L. Lewis, the labor leader, who occupied it 1937–1969.

AL39 Wilson-Potts Houses

1795. 609–607 Oronoco St.

These large twin five-bay houses were built as a pair by William Wilson and John Potts, Jr., respectively, and originally each had half a city block. Washington, of course, dined at both, and 607, long open to the public as "The Boyhood Home of Robert E. Lee," has other important associations. Constructed of brick laid up in Flemish bond with splayed lintels and prominent water tables, the houses feature pedimented center pavilions which project slightly and have typically restrained pedimented entrances. At press time, number 607 was under purchase agreement for possible conversion to private use.

AL40 Holiday I11nn

1975, Vosbeck, Vosbeck, Kendrick and Redinger. 480 King St.

At one time it seemed that every city needed a Holiday Inn. An urban renewal program placed this one right in downtown rather than out along the highway. The original urban renewal scheme was far larger, but ultimately it was scaled back to a few blocks; this was the

AL38 Lee-Fendall House

AL41 Gadsby's Tavern Museum

AL41 Gadsby's Tavern Museum

c. 1770, 1782, 1792. 1878, ell. Restorations: 1932–1934, Milton Grigg; 1936, Thomas T. Waterman; 1976, J. Everett Fauber, Jr. 134 N. Royal St. Open to the public

Gadsby's Tavern Museum consists of two buildings, the smaller of which was originally Wise's Coffee House and Tavern (c. 1770). In 1782 Wise remodeled and enlarged the tavern, creating a symmetrical two-story brick structure with delicate detailing. Next door is the three-story City Tavern and Hotel (1792), asymmetrical and awkward. John Gadsby operated a tavern and hotel in the buildings from 1796 to 1808. The Metropolitan Museum of Art installed the ballroom from the City Tavern in its American Wing (c. 1924), but otherwise the buildings survive largely intact. Saved by the American Legion in 1929, they were presented to the city, which restored them as a museum and eighteenth century–style restaurant, as part of the fashion for Williamsburg-iana that swept Virginia in those years. A replica of the original ballroom has been installed on the second floor of the City Tavern. More restoration was done for the U.S. Bicentennial.

penultimate project. The architects incongruously chose the large warehouses that flank Faneuil Hall Market in Boston as the model for Alexandria. Why not the local Alexandria warehouses? Why a maritime structure a good five blocks from the waterfront? These questions were never addressed.

West End (AL42–AL50)
(Map, p. 80)

Buildings in this part of Alexandria date largely from the 1920s through the 1990s. Much of the recent development has been directed by the City of Alexandria Department of Planning and Zoning, which has attempted to maintain the density and architectural quality common to the adjacent Old Town area. To a significant degree the effort has succeeded.

AL42 Carlyle

1989–present, master plan, Cooper, Robertson and Partners; landscape, EDAW. Duke St.

The Carlyle, an 82-acre, 16-square-block office-apartment park, was developed on the former railyards of the Southern Railway Company by the Oliver Carr Company and Norfolk Southern Corporation. The neotraditional design makes references to English residential squares and baroque planning, for example, in the two pretentious lions marking the entrance on Duke Street.

AL43 Albert V. Bryan United States Court House

1992–1995, Spillis Candela/Warnecke. Courthouse Sq.

The centerpiece of the Carlyle development is this ten-story postmodern courthouse recalling 1930s skyscrapers with Public Works Administration–inspired Colonial Revival detailing. Varied setbacks lend interest to the overall form. The detailing is rather bland, except for the 12-foot-tall statue *Justice Delayed, Justice Denied*, by Raymond Kaskey, atop the entrance, and the bas-relief frieze immediately below depicting the race between the tortoise and the hare. The two-story entrance space is impressive, and a park opens to the rear.

AL44 Carlyle Towers

1992–1999, Holle and Lin, with Wayne Williams as designer. Jamieson Ave. and Dulany St.

Across from the courthouse stands this hapless, excruciatingly awful group of apartments and condominiums, which well illustrates that the colonial idiom cannot be expanded to fit all situations. One wonders whether it is intended as parody. More towers are planned.

AL45 Burke and Herbert Bank Building

1996–1998, Rust, Orling and Neale. 220 Jamieson Ave.

More modest than its nearby neighbor, the bank bows demurely with its red-brick, white-trim idiom.

AL46 Time-Life Building

1993–1997, FEEK. 1900 Duke St.

More successful than many postmodern compositions, this building is abstract in form and detailing rather than cutesy. The tower successfully holds and turns the corner. The architects are the successors to the older Keyes Condon Florance firm, which was prominent in the northern Virginia–Washington, D.C. area during the 1950s–1980s.

AL47 Society for Human Resource Management

1996–1998, Joe Boggs. 1800 Duke St.

The problem of designing large office blocks so that they relate to the surroundings is apparent in this rather schizophrenic building. A pretentious cast stone window wall articulates the west facade, but a quieter brick wall on the east relates somewhat better to Old Town.

AL48 King Street Station Complex

1984–1992, Keyes Condon Florance. 1904 Diagonal Rd., 1725–1775 Duke St., and 225 Reineker Ln. (occupies entire block)

The station complex, designed to fill a wedge-shaped site, contains a variety of uses, including offices, a Metro station, retail space, and a hotel. A crescent form recalling examples in Bath, England, helps define the street front on both sides and is an interesting example of urbanistic models well employed.

AL49 Alexandria Union Station

1905, Architecture Department, Pennsylvania Railroad Company; 1997, restoration, VITETTA Group. 110 Calahan Dr.

Now used by Amtrak and Virginia Rail Express, the station is a result of the Senate Parks Commission, or McMillan, Plan of 1901–1902. As it also did for Washington, D.C., the Parks Commission suggested a single station unifying the various rail services to Alexandria. It is carried out in a vaguely Federal Revival idiom with red brick and white trim (what else?). The Pennsylvania Railroad architects employed similar designs at other locations and apparently passed the design on to other railroads, since the Fredericksburg Station, put up by the Richmond, Fredericksburg, and Potomac Railroad, looks the same.

AL50 George Washington Masonic National Memorial

1917–1932, Helmle and Corbett. 101 Calahan Dr.

The memorial, looming over the town, is impossible to miss and is perhaps the largest example of architectural kitsch in the United States. It was the work of the well-known New York firm that later participated in the design of Rockefeller Center. Helmle chose as his model one of the seven wonders of the ancient world, the lighthouse of c. 280 B.C. which stood in the harbor at Alexandria, Egypt. Reconstructions of the Alexandria Lighthouse were a common feature of Beaux-Arts programs, and both Frank J. Helmle, the initial designer, and Harvey Wiley Corbett, who took over c. 1920, were products of the Ecole. The original design of 1917 was modified in 1920 by the addition of the pyramidal crest. Symbolically, the ancient model links Washington, a Mason, not only to the founding of the country but also to the cradle of civilization and suggests a guiding light into the future. Construction began in 1922, and the building was dedicated in 1932, even though many features were incomplete (eleva-

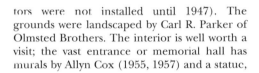

AL49 Alexandria Union Station

AL50 George Washington Masonic National Memorial

tors were not installed until 1947). The grounds were landscaped by Carl R. Parker of Olmsted Brothers. The interior is well worth a visit; the vast entrance or memorial hall has murals by Allyn Cox (1955, 1957) and a statue,

by Bryant Baker, of Washington wearing a Masonic apron. Other spaces, such as the auditorium and the various meeting rooms, display elements of Masonic and architectural exotica and should not be missed.

Alexandria Suburbs (AL51–AL56)

AL51 St. Agnes and St. Stephen's School (Richard Lloyd House)

c. 1866–1879, Benjamin F. Price. 400 Fontaine St. (Russell Rd., turn west on Windsor Ave. and Small St. to Fontaine St.)

Whether the three stacked Palladian windows in the four-story mansard-roofed tower are a reference to colonial precedent is unknown, but this is probably northern Virginia's most exuberant High Victorian house. Benjamin F. Price, the local builder-architect, designed the house for Richard Lloyd, who came from Illinois, began to purchase property in 1865, and became the owner and operator of one of the area's largest farms. The midwestern heritage may have something to do with the aggressive and public character of the house, similar to that of contemporary courthouses. Certainly it lacks the common Virginian restraint. Its location along a bluff overlooking downtown Alexan-

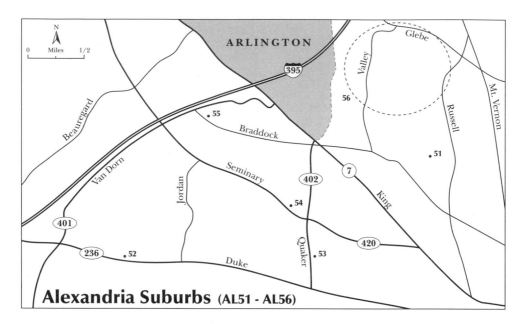

N

0   Miles   1/2

ARLINGTON

395

Glebe

Valley

56

Russell

Mt. Vernon

Beauregard

•55

Braddock

•51

Van Dorn

Seminary

402

7

Jordan

•54

King

401

236   •52

Quaker

•53

420

Duke

Alexandria Suburbs (AL51 - AL56)

dria proclaimed Lloyd's arrival. Now it is in the middle of a private school campus.

AL52 Charles E. Beatley, Jr., Central Library

1996–1999, P.G.A.L. with Michael Graves, design architect. 5005 Duke St.

In this building, Graves, one of postmodernism's superstars, has created one of his typical cluster of building forms and pavilions around a courtyard remindful of his San Juan Capistrano (California) library. Characteristic Gravesian features of large gables, abstract pediments, bay windows, and a circular form, as well as his usual color palette, are intended to relate to a "traditional" neighborhood development across Duke Street on the site of a recently closed army depot. A series of differently shaped interior spaces provide an enlivening experience and also rooms for actually reading a book.

AL53 Charles M. Goodman House

c. 1900. 1952–1954, Charles Goodman. 514 North Quaker Ln. Private

Goodman, Virginia's most prominent post–World War II modern architect, purchased the property in 1949 and spent several years design-

ing and modifying a Victorian farmhouse and adding a living room. He removed the front porch and gutted portions of the interior, though he reused some of the elements, such as the exterior doors, banister, and porch ceiling. The exterior of the house he encased in black prefabricated plywood, known as Texture 1–11, in one of its first uses of the material anywhere in the country. He outlined the frames of the house and the addition in white paint. His glazed living-room addition recalls the work of Mies van der Rohe (Goodman studied architecture at the Armour Institute in Chicago, which, after he left, became IIT) and the contemporary Case Study Houses of southern California. Measuring 21 feet by 34 feet, it is a glazed box. The room has a flagstone floor, large chimney mass, and extensive built-ins; it was a showplace for 1950s furniture. Each elevation is related to a season and is designed so that from both the interior and the exterior the space extends through landscaping, the flagstone terrace, stone walls, and pergolas.

AL54 Virginia Theological Seminary

1827–present. 3737 Seminary Rd.

This major complex of High Victorian and later structures on the ridge west of downtown Alexandria contains two houses, Maywood and

AL54 Virginia Theological Seminary

Oakwood, c. 1810, Federal in style and altered. They predate the building of the Episcopal church on the grounds in 1827. In the 1850s major growth ensued, and Andrew Jackson Downing, just before his death, laid out several roads and specified some ornamental plantings. In 1855 J. W. Johns designed a library, now Key Hall, currently serving as a preaching chapel. The main feature is the large building complex of Aspinwall Hall (1857–1858), in the center; Meade Hall (1859), to the north; and Bohlen Hall (1860), to the south, all designed by Norris G. Starkwether, probably the most accomplished pre–Civil War architect in northern Virginia. The south porch of Aspinwall Hall has been removed, and the roofline is missing a few of the original crenellations and pinnacles, but the remainder of the exterior, including the vibrantly molded brick details and the three-stage cupola, is original. Although much of the interior is altered, the basic spaces remain where Phillips Brooks, later rector of Trinity Church, Boston, attended school. Immanuel Chapel (1879–1881) was designed by Baltimore architect Charles E. Cassell in a muscular Ruskinian Gothic mode and constructed of red brick at a cost of $11,000. The chancel, to the south (Virginia Episcopalians were low church and hence did not follow the normal orientations), is a 1916 addition. The white presently used for the interior is inaccurate, but many of the details, including the pews and gallery, are original; in the south wall is a signed Tiffany window. To the south and flanking the drive are the former

Packard-Laird Hall (originally a library) (1921, Joseph Evans Sperry) and Sparrow Hall (1923, Frederick H. Brooks), both in a refined colonial mode. The present Seminary Library (1956–1957, J. Russell Bailey, and addition, 1980, also by Bailey), is, as would be expected, in a modern idiom, as is the Addison Academic Center (1992, Walton, Madden, Cooper).

AL55 Fort Ward Museum and Historic Site

4301 West Braddock Rd. Open to the public

The centerpiece of this 40-acre park is an important example of Civil War—Union side—military engineering. Fort Ward was a link in the Union defenses of sixty-eight forts that surrounded Washington, D.C. The northwest bastion, constructed and modified between 1861 and 1865, was part of fortifications equipped with thirty-six guns and manned by 1,200 troops. The city of Alexandria restored the bastion in 1961–1964 and reconstructed some faux Victorian structures and the ceremonial gate.

AL56 Parkfairfax

1941–1943, Leonard Schultze and Associates. I-395 (Shirley Hwy.), Quaker Ln., Beverly Dr., Wellington Rd., Gunston Rd., Valley Dr., Glebe Rd., and Four-Mile Run

Responding to President Franklin D. Roosevelt's request for middle-class rental housing near the Pentagon, Frederick Ecker, chairman of the board of Metropolitan Life and already the owner of large apartment complexes in New York, had his company build 285 separate two- and three-story buildings with 1,684 units. The layout followed a modified Radburn or garden city plan already in place at nearby Colonial and Buckingham villages in Arlington. Ample internal green space, curving roads, cul-de-sacs, the preservation of trees where possible, and provision for outdoor recreation were common features. Leonard Schultze of New York, who was known for the design of high-rise buildings, was the architect. Starrett Brothers, one of the largest firms in the United States, carried out the construction in two years. Stylistically, the buildings wear generic Colonial Revival garb; some have spindly-legged porches derived from Mount Vernon, others are more reticent. After the war, Parkfairfax attracted individuals on their way up, including young politicians such as Richard M. Nixon and Gerald Ford. In the late 1970s it became a condominium.

Northern Piedmont (NP)

FOR MUCH OF THEIR HISTORY THE NORTHERN PIEDMONT COUNTIES OF Loudoun and Fauquier were largely rural and agricultural, a gentle, rolling landscape of fertile fields, riverine valleys, and small hills that rise to the Blue Ridge Mountains. The English settled there in the early eighteenth century, but a substantial German settlement also grew up in the western sections. Despite the odd attempt at manufacturing, through the nineteenth century the area focused on agriculture, large estates sharply contrasting with smaller farms. Beginning in the late nineteenth century small summer resort colonies began to appear; in the twentieth century an influx of wealthy northerners either purchased the large estates or built new ones. Horses and fox hunting followed, and the area today is best known in the popular mind for the large estates in the Middleburg, Plains, and Warrenton areas. Vineyards have also made an appearance.

Beginning in the 1960s, Washington, D.C.–northern Virginia suburban sprawl began to spread, and it has intensified in recent years. Fauquier County has tried to stave off sprawl with a tough zoning requirement, the so-called eighty-five-percent rule, which requires developers to leave untouched 85 percent of any rural property on which they build and to focus large developments in towns and villages. In contrast, Loudoun County, which lies closer to Washington, has more "McMansions." Its population grew an estimated 55 percent between 1990 and 2000. How long this charming landscape will last is open to question.

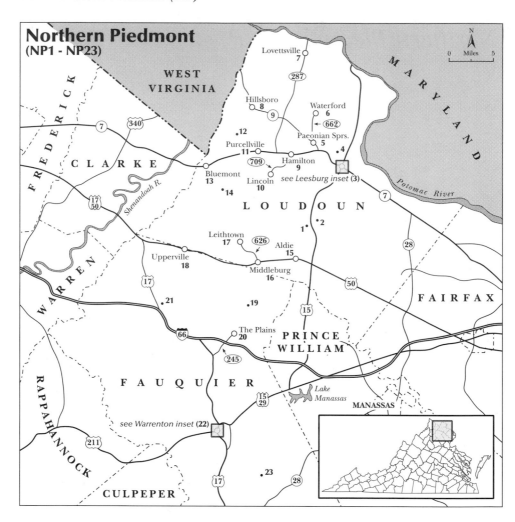

Northern Piedmont
(NP1 - NP23)

WEST
VIRGINIA

N

0   Miles   5

Lovettsville
7

287

Hillsboro
8

Waterford
6

9

662

FREDERICK

7   340

.12

Paeonian Sprs.
5

Purcellville
11

.4

C L A R K E

709   Hamilton
9

Bluemont
13

Lincoln   *see Leesburg inset (3)*
10

Potomac River

7

.14

17
50

Shenandoah R.

L O U D O U N

1 .   .2

28

Leithtown
17   626   Aldie
15

Upperville
18

Middleburg
16

50

W A R R E N

17

F A I R F A X

.21   .19

15

66   The Plains
20   P R I N C E
W I L L I A M

245

RAPPAHANNOCK

F A U Q U I E R

Lake
Manassas

211

15
29

MANASSAS

see Warrenton inset (22)

17   .23   28

CULPEPER

Loudoun County   (NP1–NP17)

NP1 Oak Hill (James Monroe House)

1820–1823, 1870s, 1922, 1949. U.S. 15 (west side, 8.2 miles south of Leesburg)

Easily observable from the road, Oak Hill dominates the landscape with its two-story Roman Doric pentastyle portico. James Monroe began construction of the house while he was president and then retired here to live until 1830, a year before his death. Both Monroe's close association with Jefferson and the similarity of the portico to Jefferson's work have given rise to speculation that Jefferson played a role, but there is little evidence. Similarly, William Thornton and James Hoban knew Monroe, but again the evidence of involvement is inconclusive. Benjamin Henry Latrobe has also been associated with the design, but that is even more doubtful. William Benton, a local builder, constructed the house of red brick with white stucco and wood trim. It was modified in 1870 and greatly enlarged in 1922, and the interior was modified in 1949. A large formal garden is in front of the portico.

NP1 Oak Hill (James Monroe House)

NP2 Oatlands

NP2 **Oatlands**

1804, 1827, 1910. 1904, gardens. 1980–1998, restoration, Alfredo Siani. VA 15 (6.7 miles south of Leesburg). Open to the public

Commanding a hilltop and oriented to the south, Oatlands projects authority and also a lightness uncommon for the period. The stucco-covered brick structure was originally constructed by a George Carter, who took years to build it. The original scheme appears to have been derived from Sir William Chambers's *Treatise on Civil Architecture* (1768 edition), but much of overall form and interior details are Federal. The large main hall has extraordinary moldings, especially the Indian-feathers motif over the doors. The portico, with columns and capitals made by Henry Farnham of New York, was added in 1827. In spite of the date, their slender proportions are those of c. 1800. Oatlands remained in the Carter family until 1897; in the early twentieth century Mr. and Mrs. William Corcoran Eustis of Washington, D.C., purchased the house and began restoration and additions, such as the rear porch (1910). The National Trust for Historic Preservation acquired it in 1965, and many of the furnishings reflect the early twentieth-century glory years of the house as a center for Washington society and politics. To the east is a substantial terraced garden, originally laid out by Carter, with original brick and stone walls. Mrs. Eustis restored the gardens following Carter's scheme and made some additions, such as the stone balustrades, which she drew from Chambers's book. They fell into decay in the 1960s, and the recent restoration follows her scheme. The grounds contain a variety of outbuildings, including a smokehouse, a granary, and a brick greenhouse.

The house was the center of a large estate, to the south of which, along Goose Creek, stood a large mill complex, also built by George Carter. The small village of Oatlands on Virginia 15 has, as a survivor, the Episcopal Church of Our Savior (1878), a simple red brick building. Farther north on Virginia 15 is Mountain Gap School (c. 1880), a one-room schoolhouse now operating as a museum.

Leesburg

The principal city of the Northern Piedmont, Leesburg, is also one of the most cohesive and best preserved. It was established in 1757 as a courthouse town, about three miles southeast of the Potomac River. Laid out on a gridiron plan, it is intersected east-west by Market Street (Virginia 7, beyond the town proper the Harry Byrd Highway), and north-south by King Street (U.S. 15, beyond the town James Monroe Highway, which follows a Native American trail). A recent bypass also carries these highways around the town.

NP3 Leesburg Downtown

This walking tour of "Old Town" Leesburg makes a large circle through the commercial and residential section of downtown, beginning with Courthouse Square at King and Market streets, the physical center of the city since the 1760s.

NP3.1 Loudoun County Courthouse

1894–1895, William C. West. 10 N. King St.

The third courthouse on this site follows Virginia's temple courthouse tradition: red brick, a tetrastyle portico, and on the interior a small vestibule and a large courtroom. However, in contrast to similar courthouses of this date (Fauquier, Culpeper), the building is not raised on a high podium but sits on a low basement. John Norris and Sons of Leesburg, who built much of the town between the Civil War and World War I, acted as contractors. An unusual feature of the exterior of the building is the shift from the Corinthian order of the portico and Market Street facades to the Doric for the rear and north facades. West may have changed the order so as to harmonize with the Doric pilasters on the Boys' Academy (1844), which stands to the east or rear; the academy's Ionic portico was added later. This structure now contains courtrooms, as does its next-door twin (c. 1950). In front stands a Civil War memorial, a Confederate soldier (1907, F. William Sievers).

NP3.2 County Office Building

1976, Kamstra, Dickerson and Associates. 10 N. King St.

Just to the north of the courthouse stands this modernist structure, which, although in the minimalist idiom of the period, fits well with the historic surroundings because of its scale, materials, and texture.

NP3.3 People's National Bank of Leesburg (former)

c. 1885, Smithmeyer and Pelz. 1905, remodeling, Paul J. Pelz. 13 N. King St.

On King Street across from the courthouse are five commercial brick structures from c. 1800 (at numbers 1, 3, 5, 7, and 11) and then this

NP3.3 People's National Bank of Leesburg (former)

former bank, an aggressive Richardsonian Romanesque structure by the architects of the Library of Congress. The original red sandstone base and brick upper floors have been painted white, but the various carved heads and foliage are still visible; it is being rehabilitated as a restaurant.

NP3.4 Henry Tazewell Harrison House

1848. 205 N. King St.

North King Street contains a number of substantial Federal, Greek Revival, Gothic Revival, and Italianate houses, the Harrison house easily being the most impressive with its giant Italianate brackets. Its symmetry and the portico indicate a lingering classicism.

NP3.5 John Janney House

1780. 1800, c. 1825, additions. 10 Cornwall St., N.E.

The house began as the small structure to the east and then received two additions, which make up the larger Federal house. Janney's Law Office (c. 1800, 4 Cornwall Street, N.E.) is the two-story brick structure closer to the street.

NP3.6 St. James Episcopal Church

1891–1897, Leon E. Dessez. 1931 and later, additions. 14 Cornwall St., N.W.

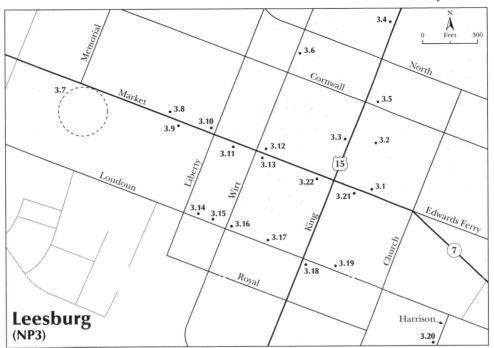

Leesburg
(NP3)

The design for this massive Richardsonian Romanesque structure with a substantial corner tower was published in *American Architect and Building News* in 1892. Dessez came from Washington, where he had apprenticed with the Hornblower firm, and the building resembles several churches in the District of Columbia. The wide interior space and hammerbeam roof are impressive, as is the glass, which consists of two signed Tiffany windows and several from England by the Heaton firm. Farther west on Cornwall Street at the corner of Liberty is a small park which commemorates the site of the Old Stone Church (1766), the first Methodist-owned property in the United States.

NP3.7 **Bungalow Court**

c. 1930, Claude Honicon, builder. 221–233 W. Market St.

Constructed of local fieldstone with Colonial Revival details, this group is composed of seven buildings. The plan draws upon southern California bungalow courts and possibly the Lawn at the University of Virginia.

NP3.8 **Thomas Balch Library**

1922, Waddy B. Wood. 208 W. Market St. Open to the public

Wood was one of the leading colonial revivalist architects of northern Virginia and Washington, D.C., in the early twentieth century, and this building offers a good chance to inspect his work. Although nominally Jeffersonian–Federal Revival, the design, with its thin, attenuated details, has a Regency delicacy. A square central block on the exterior becomes a cube on the interior. Designed as a subscription library, today it is operated by the city as a local history and genealogy library.

NP3.9 **Leesburg Presbyterian Church**

1804, W. Wright. 1975, remodeling. 207 W. Market St.

This austere meetinghouse with asymmetrical dual entrances resulted from a contract that called for a church "of brick [Flemish bond] 40 feet by 30 feet, in the clear [i.e., overall]." The belfry dates from c. 1905. The interior, although remodeled, follows the original plan with a balcony to the rear.

NP3.9 Leesburg Presbyterian Church

NP3.14 Norris House

NP3.10 **Cottage**

c. 1800. 3 Liberty St., N.W. (northwest corner of Liberty and Market sts.)

This one-room house of wood with a gable roof is typical of Leesburg's more modest housing of the late eighteenth and early nineteenth centuries. Two more examples are on Liberty Street.

NP3.11 **Leesburg Methodist Church**

1853, 1879, 1890s, 1951, 1986. 107 Market St.

This structure indicates mid-nineteenth-century prosperity in the Northern Piedmont with its elaborate pilasters, stone Ionic capitals, and molded brick trim. The tall windows of the piano nobile create a raised, light-filled nave; the basement story contains a vestibule and parish hall. The interior has been remodeled and smoothed over, but the papyrus-leaf columns supporting the balcony are original. The pews and tin ceiling date from the 1890s.

NP3.12 **Laurel Brigade Inn**

c. 1770, 1795, 1825, 1834. 20 W. Market St.

The inn has a five-bay facade of local fieldstone and a side-entrance-hall plan. The structure typifies tavern construction in its growth over time.

NP3.13 **Leesburg Government Center**

1987–1992, Hanno Weber. Corner of Market and Wirt sts.

A highlight of recent Virginia architecture, Leesburg's government center resulted from a well-publicized competition of the late 1980s. Weber, a Chicago-based architect, conceived of a contextual fit in which an octagonal form—derived from work by Aldo Rossi—stands out as an object and a symbol of the city but the exterior walls blend into the streetscape. Parking for 320 cars is integrated into the scheme, and the familiar Lawn scheme from the University of Virginia makes an appearance as the courtyard. The rear of the complex, accessible from the parking lot on Wirt and Loudoun streets, is equally impressive. The focus is on the octagon and the council chambers on the upper floor, which are worth a visit, though the interior detailing is neither as strong nor as inventive as the exterior.

NP3.14 **Norris House**

1806. 1885, remodeling, John Norris. 108 Loudoun St., S.W.

John Norris, who was the principal later-nineteenth century builder in Leesburg, owned this house and remodeled it, illustrating how to dress up, or make a Queen Anne showplace of, a five-bay symmetrical I-house.

NP3.15 **Stone House Tea Room**

c. 1755. 106 Loudoun St., S.W.

Every town needs one: a "colonial" tearoom. In this case it is a one-room stone house, possibly the oldest in town (and possibly Washington slept here).

NP3.16 **Loudoun Museum**

1877. 1969, renovation. 16 Loudoun St., S.W.

Originally Birby's House Furnishing Goods and Undertaking Shop, this building served a variety of commercial purposes until its conversion to a museum in 1969.

NP3.17 **Loudoun Museum Gift Shop**

1767. 1978, restoration, KDA Architects. 14 Loudoun St., S.W.

A fictional re-creation that illustrates the log-cabin myth, this structure was originally built by Stephen Donaldson as a silversmith's shop. He covered it in weatherboards, which were removed to display the unusual diamond-shaped notched logs. Unusual also is the center stone chimney.

NP3.18 **Thompson-Plaster House**

1899, Lemuel Norris. 102 S. King St. (southeast corner of King and Loudoun sts.)

In this red brick Georgian Revival structure, one of John Norris's sons who practiced architecture in Washington, D.C., created a wonderful confection that solved the problem of locating a large house on a prominent downtown corner by breaking up the mass into three distinct sections.

NP3.19 **Patterson House**

c. 1759. 4 Loudoun St., S.E.

This area west of King Street was in the eighteenth century the elite housing section of Leesburg, as illustrated by this impressive five-bay stone structure and its neighbor. Several other similar houses that used to stand nearby have vanished.

NP3.20 **Mighty Midget**

1946, F. W. Corbett Science Laboratories. Market Square at the corner of Loudoun and Harrison sts.

One of Virginia's best-known roadside delights, this walk-up restaurant, which measures 6 by 8 feet, used to stand a short distance away on Virginia 7. Designed and constructed in Glendale, a suburb of Los Angeles, of aluminum B-29 bomber fuselage parts and riveted in the same manner as an aircraft, these structures were

NP3.20 Mighty Midget

similar, albeit at a smaller scale, to diners. An identical structure in Middleburg was demolished in 1956; the original Leesburg model was totaled by a sports car crash in 1959, and a replacement was found in Alexandria. Operated by the Castello family until 1989, it is currently undergoing restoration.

NP3.21 **U.S. Post Office**

1923, James A. Wetmore, Supervising Architect, U.S. Treasury Department. 15 E. Market St.

Post offices used to be downtown near the center of power, as is this fine yet modest Georgian Revival structure. Of interest is its contextual fit with the former Dodge Motors building (1916, Leon Fry) next door at 9 East Market Street.

NP3.22 **Farmers' and Merchants' Bank**

c. 1870. 7 W. Market St.

South King Street and Market Street contain a variety of late nineteenth- and early twentieth-century structures, of which this small, one-story brick bank with an elaborate cornice is the best preserved.

NP4 **Morven Park**

c. 1780. c. 1830, 1858, c. 1908. 17638 Old Waterford Rd. Open to the public

This sprawling house began as a fieldstone farmhouse constructed by Wilson Cary Seldon, which is contained in one wing of the present structure. In 1808 Judge Thomas Swann purchased the property and in the 1830s made additions, including the massive Greek Revival portico and a wing. The architect for this relatively sophisticated essay remains unknown. In 1858 Thomas Swann, Jr., a Baltimore banker and later governor of Maryland, hired the firm of Edmund G. Lind and William Turnbull Murdoch to design further additions, which included a series of Italianate towers that resembled Osborne, Queen Victoria's house on the Isle of Wight. A rendering of the proposed fantasy is on view in the house. A portion of the additions was carried out by the successor firm of Murdoch and his new partner, William T. Richards. The Civil War intervened, and the project was dropped with only one smaller tower completed. Westmoreland Davis purchased the property in 1903 and with his wife carried out remodelings; it is essentially their interiors one views today on tours. Davis became a political powerhouse in Virginia, serving as governor in 1918–1922, and the house became an entertainment center on a grand scale. The interiors are in the usual period vein of the turn of the twentieth century, with elements—fireplaces, moldings—of the earlier house showing through. The hall is loosely described as "Renaissance," the dining room as "Jacobean," and the drawing room as "French." The house also contains a "foxhound collection"—a museum of hounds and hunting—as well as a collection of horse-drawn carriages. A large boxwood garden carried out in the 1930s adjoins the house. The estate encompasses about 1,200 acres and illustrates some of the ambience of Upper Piedmont "hunt country" mansions. Although the house is ungainly, the great portico helps to unify it and dominate the landscape.

NP5 Paeonian Springs

1890, John Milton, planner. VA 9

The Washington and Ohio (later Washington and Old Dominion) Railroad crossed this property, originally a farm, in 1871, and in the late 1880s a group of Loudoun County investors acquired the land and set out to create a spa and associated real estate development around the natural springs. To give the community some cachet they gave their development the euphemistic name of Paeonian (derived from the Greek for "healer of the gods") and hired a surveyor from the nearby town of Hamilton to lay out an impressive plat. The plan for the community attempted to fuse the radial streets of Washington, D.C., with the curving lines of a park by Frederick Law Olmsted. Lots were sold, and a hotel, bottling plant, dance hall, and boardinghouses were constructed. The community, however, never reached the scale envisioned in the plan. Today many of the lots are vacant and the features of the plan are obscured to a large degree by vegetation.

NP6 Waterford

VA 9

Waterford is almost too perfect, a "state of mind," as one observer commented. A tightly laid-out town of urban character set within a steep valley, it is a model of preservation and foresight. It was settled c. 1733 by members of the Society of Friends (from Bucks and Chester counties in Pennsylvania). By 1741 Amos Janney had constructed a gristmill across the creek from the present mill building and a log meetinghouse. In 1750 Mahlon Janney laid out Main Street and building lots along it from the site of the present mill building to present 2nd Street. Scots-Irish joined the founding Quakers, and the village of Waterford grew along the street and on the hill above the mill. In the 1780s and 1790s the executors of Mahlon Janney extended Main Street up the hill at the eastern edge of the village, and residential development quickly expanded into this part of town. Waterford was incorporated in 1811, and the Janney executors laid out New Town along 2nd and High streets in 1812. This expansion created deep quarter-acre house lots. The New Town section developed slowly over the course of the nineteenth century and less densely than the older sections of the town.

By 1834 Waterford possessed a population of 400 and seventy houses. The town boasted six stores, four taverns, a merchant flour mill, a gristmill, a sawmill, a plaster mill, two small cotton mills, and a woolen mill. But by the early twentieth century the community was in decline; the Fairfax Friends meeting closed in 1927 for lack of members, and in 1936 the state revoked the town charter. By this time, many buildings had substantially deteriorated.

Restoration began in the 1930s with renovations by several individuals, notably brothers Edward and Roy Chamberlain. The Waterford Foundation was formed in 1943 to "re-create the town of Waterford as it existed in previous times," to promote crafts, and to "restore as many buildings as possible" in "a like manner in which they were originally constructed." The preservation movement emphasized the pristine pastoral setting of Waterford. Promotional literature even went so far as to refer to Waterford as an architectural "Brigadoon." To raise money for preservation, in 1944 the foundation started a craft fair, which has been a community mainstay ever since. In 1970 the town became a National Historic Landmark, and in 1972 the Waterford Foundation completed a conservation plan and developed the Waterford Compact. The compact agreed to preserve the community through private means; its primary tool of implementation was voluntary preservation easements. By 1995, more than sixty easements had been purchased by or donated to various preservation agencies. Great attention was paid to preserving the open space view lines around the village and minimizing the amount of new construction. The majority of the building stock today dates from the first half of the nineteenth century.

At the center of town and the primary street junction, originally known as Market Square, the Country Store (c. 1900; 40183 Main Street, at the intersection of 2nd Street) is the most prominent central landmark. The frame country store has a false mansard or "French" roof. Its facade handles the intersection of several streets.

The Loudoun Mutual Fire Insurance Company Building (1872; 15479 2nd Street) displays the type of solid brick construction its original owner no doubt sought to encourage customers to use in their buildings. The corbeled brick cornice and parapet wall hide an angled roof.

The Pink House (c. 1816–c. 1825; c. 1945, renovations, additions, and landscaping; c. 1990, porch reconstruction; 40174 Main Street, northwest corner at Water Street) is the large town house in the center of town. Erected by Lewis Klein as a "house of entertainment," or tavern, it represents a pattern used all along the north side of Main Street with shops or stores on the first floor and living quarters upstairs. The restored balcony provided exterior access to the upper floors. As a part of this early Waterford preservation project, boxed gardens were created on earlier foundations.

Main Street Row (c. 1810–1830; 40158–40176 Main Street) is a block of attached houses, each constructed in brick, wood, stone, or some combination thereof. The architectural opening in the Arch House, in the center

of the block, provided access to a public well. The first floors usually accommodated stores or workshops and were often covered with balconies and canopies. Some have been removed or fancifully replaced. The Isaac Steer Hough House (c. 1820; porch and additions, c. 1880; 40142 Main Street) is a detached frame town house. In the late nineteenth century, the owner added an upper floor and a large rambling porch. The Janney-Moore-Means house (c. 1762; c. 1803, c. 1940, addition and renovation; 40128 Bond Street) occupies the western terminus of Main Street. The stone section is the original portion of the house, the narrow brick section the later addition. Mahlon Janney constructed the house on axis with the portion of Main Street he laid out in 1760.

The John Wesley Church (1891; 40125 Bond Street, at Ligget Street) has Carpenter's Gothic details. It is one of the larger churches in western Loudoun County expressly built for an African American congregation. It is no longer active.

Mill End (1817; 40090 1st Street) is an example of the center-hall houses scattered around Waterford. They show the prosperity of Waterford during the Federal era. All of them have decorative brick or wooden cornices and fanlights over the entranceways. Mill End, with its lofty perch at the western edge of town, is the most spectacularly sited of this group of buildings.

The Thomas Phillips Mill (c. 1830; 40105 Main Street, at Bond Street) was a merchant flour mill that ground flour for export to a larger market. A millrace that extended the length of Waterford and an undershot wheel provided waterpower for the mill. The original Janney Mill sat across Catoctin Creek from the structure, and in the nineteenth century a sawmill was located on the opposite side of the millrace. The mill shut down in the early twentieth century, and the machinery was gutted for scrap. As one of its first projects the Waterford Foundation restored the mill as a craft center for the Waterford Festival.

The Log House (c. 1760; relocation, c. 1870; 40125 Main Street), moved from another site in Waterford by Marshall Claggett c. 1870, was the home of several African American families. It was whitewashed to give an appearance of clapboard, a common treatment of log structures in Loudoun County. Wisteria Cottage (NP6.1) (c. 1810; 40129 Main Street) is a well-preserved and unaltered example of an early nineteenth-century brick cottage. Mahlon Jan-

NP6.1 Wisteria Cottage (left)
NP6.2 Schooley House (above)

ney deeded the Town Green to the new town of Waterford in 1812. The town jail (1812, intersection of Main and Water streets) was constructed on it, with the public well shortly thereafter. At the same time, the town constructed a market house, the foundations of which are visible.

The Asa Moore House (1803; addition, 1880; 40195 Main Street) is a good example of a raised cottage that dates from before the 1804 town expansion. The original section of the house is juxtaposed with a boxy two-story addition. The Schooley House (NP6.2) (c. 1815; 40210 Main Street) is an interesting example of a telescoping house. It appears that the buildings began as a one-and-one-half-story cottage and the two-story and one-story wings were added later. The shallow structure expanded parallel to the street instead of perpendicular because of the steep drop at the rear.

The Waterford School (1910; auditorium, 1930; 40222 Fairfax Street) has wide, overhanging eaves typical of the turn-of-the-twentieth-century Arts and Crafts movement, but the major effect of the pediment and the Roman Doric portico is Georgian Revival.

A substantial Greek Revival brick structure, the Waterford Baptist Church (Baptist Meetinghouse) (1853; 15545 High Street, at Patrick Street) boasts an unusual entrance treatment with a distyle-in-antis-muris portico. Proportionally, the portico appears diminutive against the scale of the cornice and the implied corner pilasters.

The Catoctin Presbyterian Church (1880–1882; education wing, c. 1950; 15565 High Street) replaced an earlier structure on the site. Such elaborate brickwork, with raised moldings and strip buttresses, is unusual both for the town and for Presbyterian churches in Virginia. Although the designer is unknown, the overall quality suggests an out-of-town hand.

The Loudoun County Fire Insurance Company (1949, Albert D. Leuders; addition, c. 1990; 15609 High Street) was inspired by Gunston Hall but expands on the model with substantial side and rear additions. The choice of a Tidewater plantation house for a compact town like Waterford seems incongruous.

The Second Street School (1867; 15611 2nd Street) is a modest one-room frame building that served as a school and chapel for African Americans in Waterford after the Civil War. Sunnyside (c. 1850; porch, 1997; 15570 2nd Street), a raised-basement, one-and-one-half-story Greek Revival cottage, illuminates the progress of preservation. In the 1930s it received a Colonial Revival treatment involving removal of the Doric porch; by the 1990s the porch had been reconstructed.

NP7 Lovettsville

VA 287

German immigrants came to northwestern Loudoun County via Pennsylvania and Maryland beginning in 1733, and this immigration continued over the course of the eighteenth century. The ethnic enclave in and around Lovettsville was known simply as the German Settlement. Throughout much of its early history the settlement was characterized by dispersed farmsteads. In the early nineteenth century the village of Lovettsville (originally Thrasher's Corner) developed around the post office, and the town became the center of far northwestern Loudoun. In the late nineteenth and early twentieth centuries, Lovettsville became something of a suburb for Brunswick, Maryland. Many residents of the community worked in the massive railroad yards across the Potomac River, and many of the frame residences in town are from this era. In more recent years, Washington, D.C.–area commuters have made their homes in the community. The result is that new subdivisions are rapidly replacing farms within the expanded town limits.

The Lovettsville Museum (Potterfield Meat Shop) (1890; Pennsylvania Avenue at Church Street) is a frame structure that once served as a meat processing facility for a retail outlet in Brunswick, Maryland. The Lovettsville Historical Society converted the building into an impressive local history museum.

Willard Hall (1820; Pennsylvania Avenue at Light Street), a brick structure, has the distinction of being one of the oldest residences in town and is similar to Federal-era brick residences in Waterford. The Wenner House (c. 1820; Pennsylvania Avenue) is characteristic of many of the early log buildings in the German Settlement. It received a weatherboard exterior early in its history, but its original configuration is still apparent: a double-pen (two log boxes side by side), one-and-one-half-story log house with a porch. St. James' United Church of Christ (Reformed Church) (c. 1901; Broad Way at Church Street) is a modest Gothic Revival church. In relocating from the 1733 church site south of town, the congregation took the economical as well as commemorative step of reusing bricks from its early nineteenth-century church for this new in-town building.

South of town off Virginia 287 is New Jerusalem Lutheran Church and Cemetery (church, 1868; tower, 1904; Church Lane), the fourth church on the site, which was settled in 1765. The present building, raised on a high basement, is nominally Greek Revival. A large, round-arched Venetian Gothic tower was added to change the appearance of the church from a "dingy colored barn to a beautiful and churchly edifice," as recorded by the pastor of that era. Adjacent is the Lovettsville Union Cemetery, created when the church cemeteries filled up. The highlights of the cemetery are the cast iron gate and fence facing Church Lane and the gazebo with stamped metal ornamental panels, wire brackets, and built-in seats.

NP8 Hillsboro

The defining characteristic of Hillsboro, a remarkable community in a fine state of preservation, is the extensive use of locally quarried stone. Located in the gap of the Short Hill Mountain range, it became a major center on the road to Keyes Gap in the Blue Ridge Mountains and the Shenandoah Valley beyond. The first settlers, Quakers who came in the eighteenth century from Bucks County, Pennsylvania, were followed by Germans and other non-Quakers. In the first half of the nineteenth century, Hillsboro developed into a bustling commercial center serving a large portion of western Loudoun County. Most of the town dates from this period. Local artisans lived and worked in a number of the houses. The town boasted three gristmills, a woolen mill, and a furniture factory. The agriculturist and mapmaker Yardley Taylor noted in the 1850s that on Short Hill "rock rises in towering peaks above the forest trees. This sandstone rock makes an excellent building stone, and is much sought after for that purpose." The stonework can be classified as random ashlar, rubble, or a combination of the two. An early traveler noted that the community was "a town made of stone even to the pig sties." Although stone is used extensively throughout western Loudoun County, Hillsboro is the only community that is nearly completely built of stone. The community is in a remarkable state of preservation, retaining roughly the same number of buildings and people it had in the early nineteenth century.

At the eastern end of Gap Road (Virginia 9) stands the Hillsboro Old Stone School (Locust Grove Academy) (1874; wings, 1917; auditorium, 1929), one of the first public school buildings in Loudoun County. The center section with its distinctive cupola was built first; the front porch and gabled wings are highly compatible additions in random ashlar similar to the original. The brick gymnasium, however, ignored the stone building tradition of Hillsboro. The large stone house at 37004 Gap Road (1833; additions, c. 1850) is an example of an

artisan's house with first-floor workshop, originally for a wagon maker and later for a blacksmith. The building began as a raised cottage
and was expanded with a two-story addition. As
is typical of Hillsboro, a large veranda faces the
road. The Brown-Fritts Tavern (NP8.1) (1810;
36982 Gap Road) is a simple, gabled stone
structure. The English basement area beneath
the porch served as a shoe shop. The Taylor
House (c. 1780; renovations, 1866; 36974 Gap
Road) predates the other buildings and breaks
the close setbacks of the street. The building
began as a log house which later owners expanded and remodeled with a new porch,
bracketed cornice, and coat of stucco. The
stone Tribbey House (c. 1800; 36956 Gap
Road) aspires to a certain grandeur with a stuccoed end wall and a three-tiered porch which
has square piers on the ground level and primitive Roman Doric columns above.

The Gaver Woolen Factory and Truss Bridge
(1844; c. 1890, bridge; Catoctin Creek and Virginia 719) are remnants of the several water-
powered industries in the vicinity of Hillsboro.
The woolen factory operated between 1844
and 1888. Largely gutted in the 1930s, the
stone mill has undergone partial reconstruction. The stone miller's house is situated in the
woods above the structure.

The Methodist Church (1858; brackets and
bell tower, c. 1880; Gap Road) is of stone and
was one of two Methodist churches in town in
the mid-nineteenth century, reflecting the sec-
tional crisis of the period. The several structures that make up the building at 36959 Gap
Road (east wing, c. 1780; center section, c.
1825; west wing, c. 1840) illustrate the remarkable continuity of the town's buildings. The
east wing of the building began as a stone cottage and received a large addition. The final,
west wing served as an office and store at various times.

also developed as a summer community for
Washington, D.C., and many of the larger
homes along its main street, the Colonial Highway (Virginia 7) reflect this background. Today
it is being rapidly suburbanized. The major period of architectural interest is the post–Civil
War boom.

The Gothic Revival–Shingle Style Harmony
Methodist Church (1893; education wing, c.
1920; East Colonial Highway, southwest corner
of Harmony Road) replaces an earlier structure
on the site. Dark rubble fieldstone is combined
with light-colored ashlar for the quoins, while
shingles appear in the gable ends. The bell
tower incongruously contains a small rose window.

The Hamilton Baptist Church (1889, Richard Ruse, builder; East Colonial Highway)
owes a debt to Richard Upjohn's *Upjohn's
Rural Architecture* (1852). Ruse, a builder in
Waterford, significantly reduced the windows
in Upjohn's design, creating diminutive
Gothic-arched openings.

Representing the architectural conservatism
of the area, the Farmers and Merchants Bank
(c. 1890; 1 East Colonial Highway) has a late example of a Second Empire mansard roof,
which gives the one-and-one-half-story building
a commanding appearance at the town's original center.

The combination Hamilton School and Masonic lodge (NP9.1) (1872; Richard Ruse,
builder; 45 Rodgers Street) is an interesting
anomaly that illustrates compliance with the
Public School Act, passed in 1872. The Masonic
lodge used the top of the building; the school
occupied the lowest floor. It is one of the oldest
school buildings in the county. A large date
stone bears the name of the officers of the
lodge presiding at the dedication. The Italianate brackets are the primary ornamentation
on this otherwise severe building.

NP9 Hamilton

VA 7

A long, linear town, Hamilton originated in a
Society of Friends settlement of the 1740s
known as Harmony. The Snickers Gap Turnpike came through in the early nineteenth century, but the real period of growth came after
the Civil War, when, with the arrival of the
Washington and Old Dominion Railroad,
Hamilton developed into an important agricultural trading center. From the 1870s onward it

NP10 Lincoln

Intersection of VA 722, 709, 723

A Friends' community since the 1740s, Lincoln
still centers on the meetinghouse. The Goose
Creek Friends were leaders in education, agricultural reform, and the abolition, temperance, and pacifist movements. The (Goose
Creek) Old Stone Meeting House (1765, west
side of the intersection of routes 709 and 722),
with its stone structure, is one of the earliest
and most pristine houses of worship in the

NP8.1 Brown-Fritts Tavern (below, left)

NP9.1 Hamilton School and Masonic Lodge (right)

NP10.1 Lincoln High School (bottom)

Northern Piedmont. Unlike the Fairfax Friends Meeting, which expanded its original building, the Goose Creek Meeting opted to build anew across the road. That building still stands, though greatly altered by the removal of the original second story. The Friends converted the original Old Stone Meeting House to a caretaker's residence.

The Oakdale School (1815; center of intersection of Virginia 722 and 709) is a simple brick structure that replaced an earlier log school building. Education was of great importance to the Goose Creek Quakers, who opened the first school in the county for African Americans in 1866 and the first public school in 1870.

The Lincoln High School (NP10.1) (1926, Division of School Buildings, State Department of Education) is the second high school on this site; the first, which was largely funded by the Goose Creek Friends, was constructed in 1908. A fire destroyed it, and the Commonwealth of Virginia provided the plans for the present one-story building. Classrooms surround a central gymnasium-auditorium lighted and ventilated by a clerestory window. The ornate polychrome brickwork on the exterior is particularly noteworthy.

Just outside the village is the Hatcher-Brown Farm (1813, Virginia 709 at the intersection with Virginia 726), which illuminates the history of the prosperous yeomen farmer Friends of the area, known for tidy farms and abundant wheat harvests. The latter were made possible by crop rotation and the use of fertilizers. The Hatcher-Brown Farm is one of the few early farms that can readily be viewed from the road. The early farmhouses of the area were predominantly log houses and small stone cottages. As the area matured larger brick and stone houses using what has been called the Loudoun-Stuga floor plan became common. The Stuga plan—a large hall with the cooking hearth on one side of the house and two smaller rooms on the opposite side—was introduced to the Delaware Valley in the seventeenth century. William Penn promoted it in his *Instructions*, written for early colonists, and later generations of Pennsylvanians brought it to Loudoun County. The Hatcher farmhouse uses one front entrance into the hall. (Variations sometimes have two front entrances.) Additions on this and many other Loudoun-Stuga houses are placed to the side to allow cross ventilation. The Hatcher farm has a complete collection of outbuildings typical of the Goose Creek area. The stone bank barn reflects Pennsylvania origins.

NP11 Purcellville

VA 7

Although the origins of Purcellville go back to an ordinary on the "Great Road" (later the Snickers Gap Turnpike) from Alexandria to the Shenandoah Valley, the community remained small until the Washington and Ohio Railroad (later the Washington and Old Dominion) came though in the 1870s. The area prospered as a summer resort (as did Round Hill, five miles west), and also through large-scale agricultural businesses. Mills, apple-packing houses, slaughterhouses, a stockyard, creameries, and stores sprang up in this strategically located commercial center. The city grew rapidly and incorporated in 1908. Portions of the downtown area were rebuilt after a 1914 fire. The closing of the Washington and Old Dominion Railroad in 1939 diminished the importance of the agricultural trade, but in more recent years the town has become a bedroom community for the metropolitan Washington area.

NP11.1 Loudoun Valley Milling Company

1905. Depot St. at the Washington and Old Dominion Railroad Trail

This large mill structure was clad with pressed metal to "fireproof" it from the sparks of passing railroad locomotives. The steam-powered operation was located in the center of what was Purcellville's agricultural service and industrial district. The adjoining depot, warehouse, and shop buildings reflect the prosperity of Purcellville during its sixty-four-year railroad era.

NP11.2 Nichols Hardware Complex

1914, brick building. c. 1900, frame structure. 135 Depot St.

The Nichols complex is an important example of a retail business which has retained its original character. The false-front frame building was a livery stable built in close proximity to the rail depot. The brick building was constructed for the hardware store and reflects the requirement for brick and stone exteriors passed by the town council after the 1914 fire.

NP11.3 White Palace (Purcellville Post Office and Town Hall)

1908, J. E. Hampton, builder. Northwest corner of Loudoun and Depot sts.

Strategically occupying the central corner in town, this rusticated concrete block structure gains its civic presence from crow-stepped gables topped by round finals and simulated stonework. The building originally housed the post office and other commercial operations. The second-floor hall served as the town hall and a general-purpose community auditorium. The White Palace restaurant is a largely unaltered eatery that has served the community since 1908.

NP11.4 West Main Street (Virginia 7)

c. 1890–1930

West Main Street is one of the more attractive residential streets in Loudoun County. The diverse collection of Queen Anne, Georgian Revival, and Arts and Crafts houses on spacious lots reflects the affluence of the community during its heyday as an agricultural and railroad center and a resort. The huge false front and segmental pediment of the Samuel L. Case Galleries (1921; 100 West Main Street) give a

NP12 Ketoctin Baptist Church

civic presence to a former automobile dealership, while below, the show and shop windows revealed the activities within.

NP11.5 Bethany Methodist Church

1922, Wilmer Baker, builder. 120 E. Main St.

This Collegiate Gothic church is one of the few early twentieth-century churches in western Loudoun County. The stone structure was built by Wilmer Baker, of a family of noted Morrisonville stonemasons.

NP11.7 Purcellville Fireman's Community Center (Bush Meeting Tabernacle)

1889, Arch Simpson, builder. c. 1930, enclosure. Dillon's Woods between South and Nursery sts.

The Prohibition and Evangelical Society of Loudoun County started a summer revival in Lincoln during 1876. The meeting, named for the place where it was originally held, which was known as the Bush Arbor, relocated to Dillon's Wood shortly after it was established. The Tabernacle replaced tents which accommodated large crowds from Loudoun County and beyond.

The Chautauqua-like gathering was "an intellectual feast of music, art, and literature" with a "moral and spiritual atmosphere pure and inspiring," as one visitor described it. The structure witnessed countless lectures, revivals, and concerts before closing in 1930. The subsequent enclosure of the building changed the open-air nature of the structure.

NP12 Ketoctin Baptist Church

1853–1854. Intersection of VA 716 and 711, Round Hill vicinity

The setting of the Ketoctin Baptist Church is particularly pastoral, down a county lane in a grove of large trees. This temple-form building displays the simple and straightforward architecture nineteenth-century Baptists preferred. The inactivity of the congregation has eliminated any need to alter the facility, and the interior, with galleries, is largely unchanged. The structure has also benefited from an active maintenance program. The cemetery possesses a fine collection of mid-to-late nineteenth-century funerary art.

NP13 Bluemont

VA 7 and VA 34

This village, originally named Snickersville after a local ferryman, grew when two turnpikes converged in the 1830s. Snickersville was a link connecting the commerce of the Shenandoah Valley and western Loudoun County with Alexandria. Railroads stalemated the town's development after the Civil War, and to spur tourist traffic it was renamed Bluemont, because Snickersville was the "ugliest name on the most beautiful of spots." The town has a number of stone buildings dating from the pre–Civil War years and a few remains of late nineteenth-century boardinghouses.

NP14 Ebenezer Church and Cemetery Complex

c. 1769–1804, Old Ebenezer Church. 1855, New Ebenezer Church. c. 1800 and 1888, cemeteries. VA 719 at intersection with VA 779

The original meetinghouse of this important Baptist church complex was constructed during the late eighteenth century. The entrance and interior have been reconfigured several times. In the early nineteenth century a theological rift divided the membership into so-called Old School and New School congregations. Both groups used the Old Ebenezer

NP15.1 Aldie Mill Complex (left)

NP16.1 Red Fox Inn (above)

Church for worship. Damage to the building from a fire in 1855 prompted the New School congregation to construct the New Ebenezer Church. Its full classical portico is unusual for rural Baptist churches. Another significant element of the building is the trompe l'oeil painting at the pulpit end of the sanctuary, an extraordinary image of a large apse flanked by engaged columns. This work was completed in the late nineteenth century by Loudoun County artist Lucien Whiting Powell. By the 1930s the congregation had diminished and possession passed to the Ebenezer Cemetery Company, which has maintained and restored the structures. The complex is used occasionally for services and other events.

NP15 Aldie

U.S. 50 and VA 734

Located at an important gap in the Bull Run Mountains and on a flat site at a bend in the Little River, Aldie reflects improvements in agriculture and transportation in the early nineteenth century. Turnpikes converged here, and General Charles Fenton Mercer of Leesburg both helped fund them and built a mill. Mercer also founded a village west of his mill complex in 1810 and named it Aldie after his ancestral seat in Perthshire, Scotland. Aldie developed as a small but prosperous village of artisans, stores, taverns, and churches over the course of the nineteenth century. The village

retains a variety of buildings from this long history as a trade, transportation, and industrial center.

NP15.1 Aldie Mill Complex

1807–1808, William Cooke, builder, and Matthew Adam, millwright. c. 1900, improvements. c. 1980, restoration, William Davis, engineer. c. 1810–1816, granary. U.S. 50 at the Little River Turnpike

The largest structure and centerpiece of the mill complex was and remains the large merchant mill. At the time of construction the building was a state-of-the-art structure on the cutting edge of the Industrial Revolution. Mercer obtained licenses from the noted Delaware mill designer and theorist Oliver Evans. In 1795 Evans had obtained patents on his equipment, which mechanized what had been a labor-intensive process. The Scots millwright Matthew Adam installed Evans's equipment, which was powered by three overshot waterwheels. The mill ground wheat and corn using imported French burrstones. Around 1900 two iron waterwheels replaced the wooden wheels, and updated milling equipment was added to the building's interior.

To the east of the main mill building is an auxiliary mill structure and warehouse, which may have been an earlier mill. Constructed in conjunction with the mill was the miller's house, south of the millrace. To the west of the mill is a granary and beyond that a store building, also contemporary with the main mill. The complex originally included a distillery, sawmill, wheelwright shop, and blacksmith shop. The mill was in continuous operation, using the original equipment, until 1971. The current owners, the Virginia Outdoors Foundation, undertook a major renovation of the complex and restored the mill to working condition.

Adjacent to the complex is the Little River Turnpike Bridge (1810; Little River Turnpike at the Little River) a graceful double-arch structure. Across the road is the Bodmer Wheelwrights shop (c. 1870; north side of the Little River Turnpike on the east side of the Little River), a stone and frame structure from Aldie's industrial heyday.

NP15.2 Charles Fenton Mercer House
(Aldie Manor)

1810. North side of U.S. 50 at the intersection with Tailrace Rd.

The mill owner's house had a commanding view of the mill complex and the Little River Turnpike. It is typical of the large brick homes constructed in Loudoun County during the Federal period. The income from the mill allowed Mercer to pursue other interests, and he spent much of his time away from his village. His career included eleven terms in the U.S. House of Representatives and service as a general in the War of 1812. He was an advocate of internal improvements and a proponent of liberal causes of his day: public education and African American recolonization.

NP16 Middleburg

U.S. 50

Literally the middle burg (town) on the turnpike between Alexandria and Winchester (though closer to the latter city), Middleburg was probably settled c. 1731. It was laid out on a small grid plan in 1787 by Leven Powell as a coach stop on the turnpike and is still dominated by that route, now U.S. 50, or Washington Street. It prospered and became one of the largest towns in the Northern Piedmont and the center of fierce Confederate loyalty during the Civil War. It declined after the war until the 1900s, when it became the center for the horse and country house set of the area. Today it is the main shopping center for the hunt country,

and consequently Washington and its major cross street, Madison, have received an extensive boutique treatment. The town contains an impressive number of early buildings that cluster along Washington Street.

The Red Fox Inn (NP16.1) (c. 1750, c. 1790, many later alterations; 2 East Washington Street), also known by other names, may contain the remains of the early coach inn, but the large three-and-one-half-story stone structure one sees from the street dates from c. 1790. A large two-story porch originally dominated its front. The most interesting exterior feature is the tall single chimney on the east end (as compared to twin chimneys on the west wall). Across Madison Street is the Noble Beverage house (1824; 2 West Washington Street), a thoughtfully designed structure in which, although it is of brick, the builder matched the scale of the Red Fox Inn and duplicated the twin end chimneys. Farther west on Washington, at the southeast corner of Pendelton Street, is the United Methodist Church (1858, later interior remodeling), a robust Italianate structure with very large exterior brackets. Farther west, on the south side of Washington Street with an entrance from Plains Road, is Vine Hill, or the National Sporting Library and Chronicle of the Horse (1804, later enlargements; 1998, restoration and conversion, Earth Design Associates), a large brick house in the Federal style with three irregular bays in the main structure. Across Washington Street is the Middleburg Community Center (1948, William Bland Dew), a big Colonial Revival building that cries out for some energy in its design. Back east on Washington Street at the center of town is the former Middleburg National Bank Building (1937, Will Hall; 1 East Washington Street, southeast corner of Washington at Madison streets), an unusual design that employs fieldstone for the structure, though the details are the usual banker's dress of classical ornament, in this case including a heavy Doric portico. Farther east is Emmanuel Episcopal Church (1842, altered 1927 and later; 105 East Washington Street), which, with its plain brick front and Gothic arches, recalls Maximilian Godefroy's St. Mary's Chapel (1806–1808) in Baltimore and may indicate the origin of its unknown architect. The awkward stepped cornice from which the finials have obviously been removed is replayed in several Virginia churches. Two bays were added to create the chancel.

NP17 **Leithtown**

VA 745 and 626, 6 miles north of Middleburg

A modest crossroads village reinvented to reflect the country life aspirations of its twentieth-century property owners, Leithtown was originally known as Pot House because of the brick and pot factory located there. William Benton, a builder from Leesburg, constructed two houses, New Lisbon and Leith House, in the 1830s. In the second decade of the twentieth century two notable enthusiasts of the country life movement, Joseph B. Thomas and Charlotte Haxall Noland, remade New Lisbon and the Leith farm. Writing in *Country Life* magazine about 1906, Walter A. Dyer exclaimed: "Loudoun County exemplifies country life in about purest and pleasantest form that I have yet found in the United States. . . . The ideals there are practically identical with those that have made country life in English counties world famous." This bucolic image of the county inspired Thomas and Noland to undertake their respective projects.

Huntlands (1837, William Benton, builder; renovation, 1913; northwest corner of Virginia 745 and 626) as it exists today is the creation of Joseph Thomas of New York, who married Clara Fargo, a Wells Fargo heiress, and aspired to become the lion of the local fox-hunting scene. He remade New Lisbon to serve this end, adding a portico and wings and redecorating the interior. Site improvements included a massive stone wall pargeted with stucco and equipped with brick coping and the porter's lodge at the entrance. Thomas became master of the Piedmont Hunt and, on the basis of study in Europe, wrote the landmark work *Hounds and Hunting through the Ages.* His enthusiasm for the hunt is reflected in the symmetrically placed stables and kennels behind the main house. Each of the large structures consists of arcaded ranges around a courtyard. The kennels were equipped with a trophy room and hound hospital.

Down the road a few hundred yards is Foxcroft School (1837, William Benton, builder; renovation and additions, 1914–1947; southeast corner of Virginia 745 and 626), created by Charlotte Haxall Noland, a native of the Middleburg area. She was a teacher who had begun her career at private schools in the Northeast. She acquired the Leith farm in 1914 and over the next fifty years rebuilt it to replicate the schools where she had taught. The daughters of the eastern elite were and are schooled in the virtues of the country life at the school. Horsemanship has always been a major part of the school's regimen, as reflected in the equestrian facilities and country setting. The original farmhouse was expanded and several additional buildings were constructed during the first ten years of the school's history. The campus has evolved since in a fairly random manner.

Fauquier County   (NP18–NP23)
(Map, p. 96)

NP18 **Upperville**

A linear village strung along U.S. 50, which runs though it, Upperville was laid out in 1797 by Joseph Carr along the Alexandria-Winchester Turnpike. The physical center of the Virginia hunt country, the town retains a quiet, reserved air, with a small commercial section at one end. Houses in a variety of styles are visible along the tree-lined road and beyond the neatly tended fields of the large estates, all of which are private, guarded, and protected by alarms. The major architectural interest is provided by Trinity Episcopal Church (NP39.1) (1951–1960, Howard Page Cross), an amazing adaptation, constructed of sandstone from nearby Warrenton, of the twelfth- and thirteenth-century rural churches of the Champagne region of France. It was paid for by the town's best-known residents, Mr. and Mrs. Paul Mellon, who moved to the town in 1940. The New York architect designed several houses for the Mellons and other society figures. At a time when modernism rode high, Cross continued to design in traditional idioms. The highlight of the complex is the church interior, with its hammerbeam roof and fittings. Its quality demonstrates that ecclesiastical arts and crafts survived into the 1950s. Heinz Warnaco, who worked on the National Cathedral in Washington, carved the column capitals; the pew ends, each of which contains portrayals of plants native to the countryside; and the pulpit. The wrought ironwork came from the shop of P. A.

Fiebiger, of New York. The windows in the nave and choir were made by Joe Nicholas in Amsterdam, Holland; those in the north transept are by Willet of Philadelphia; and those in the south transept came from an earlier church that occupied the site. Cross also designed the adjoining parish house and rectory, which are appropriately vernacular forms of Georgian idioms mixed with a little of rural France. The entire ensemble is remarkable and deserves to be better known.

NP19 **Piedmont Vineyards** (Waverly)

c. 1780, c. 1840. 1945, remodeling, David Adler. VA 245, 4.2 miles north of The Plains and VA 55

A landmark on the road between The Plains and Middleburg, this ocher-colored house has a long and complex history beginning with its inner core, which is a stone cottage, and continuing with the addition of the front and the Greek Revival portico and still later the Gothic Revival rear wing. David Adler, the Chicago society and country house architect, made some additions for Mr. and Mrs. Thomas W. Furness, who were personal friends and whom he visited often. He created the entrance garden, arbor, and gazebo and decorated the porch with stencils. Now owned by Piedmont Vineyards, the house can be visited.

NP20 **The Plains**

VA 245 and 55

Originally a small agricultural crossroads town, now in the heart of horse country, The Plains has been "boutique-ized" in recent years. It boasts a number of large houses along Virginia 245, as well as a substantial former school building (c. 1900) of concrete block at the west end of town. The major focus of architectural interest is Grace Episcopal Church (1916–1918, William H. Irwin Fleming; Virginia 55 west of intersection with Virginia 245), an impressive design by a Washington, D.C., architect trained at George Washington and Cornell universities who was described by a contemporary as "shy and introverted." Fleming never employed a draftsman and was known for controlling all aspects of his designs. Here Fleming created a masterpiece, nominally Neo-Gothic in style, in which the only orthodox revival element is the tower. Otherwise the building is "modern," with its long, huge sloping roof and tall, abstract lancet windows. The random rubble stonework, which, according to local legend, was supplied by nearby farmers, is masterful. The interior is a wide expanse with king-post trusses, purlins, and rafters. Moravian tile from Henry Mercer's works near Doylestown, Pennsylvania, is used in the sanctuary. The original glass was by Century Stained Glass of Philadelphia, but it has been replaced. The chancel window (1920) is by Henry Wynd Young of New York. William Burnham of Boston supplied new pictorial nave windows in the 1970s.

NP21 **Ashleigh**

c. 1840. U.S. 17, 1.2 miles south of Delaplane

Sited prominently with a superb view to the south (and now to I-66), this large, pedimented Greek Revival dwelling with a white-painted stucco exterior recalls the single-story raised-basement houses of the deep South, such as those in Alabama, rather than Virginia houses. Local tradition holds that its original owner, Margaret Marshall, granddaughter of Chief Justice John Marshall, designed it after a trip through the deep South.

Warrenton

A town of major architectural interest, Warrenton is a farming center for the region, a crossroads town, and a social center for a number of large equestrian estates in the region. The county seat of Fauquier County (formed 1759), it was known as Fauquier Courthouse before its incorporation in 1810. In 1811 the town was laid out in a gridiron pattern imposed on the hilly slopes. Main Street follows the top of the ridge, and cross streets run downhill. Since the 1960s the town has fallen into the northern Virginia–Washington, D.C., orbit, and sprawl has developed. Attempts to bypass and preserve the old town have been semisuccessful. Warrenton has a tremendous stock of nineteenth-century houses, of which only a few can be covered here. Much of the downtown tour should be walked.

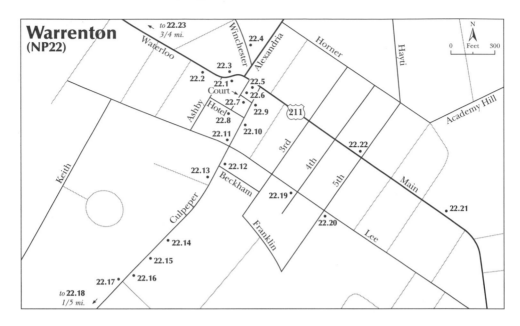

Warrenton
(NP22)

to **22.23**
3/4 mi.

Waterloo

Winchester

22.4

Alexandria

Horner

Hayti

N

0　Feet　300

22.3

22.2
22.1
Court

22.5
22.6

Ashby

Hotel
22.7
22.8

22.9

(211)

Academy Hill

22.11

22.10

3rd

22.22

Keith

22.13

22.12

Beckham

4th

5th

Main

22.19

22.21

Culpeper

Franklin

22.20

Lee

22.14

22.15

22.17　**22.16**

to **22.18**
1/5 mi.

NP22　Warrentown Downtown

NP22.1　Old Fauquier County Courthouse

1890, John R. Spilman, builder. Courthouse Sq., Main St. (south side) at Court St.

Perched on a hill at the north end of Main Street where five streets converge, the courthouse dominates the town. This structure bears an extremely close resemblance to the courthouse constructed in 1853, probably designed by William H. Baldwin. It was destroyed by fire in 1889, and Spilman, as indicated by newspaper accounts and surviving illustrations, essentially duplicated the 1853 building and its Ionic tetrastyle portico, steeple, and high basement. What differs undoubtedly is the yellow brick, more common in the 1890s than in the 1850s. The courthouse has such an ecclesiastical air that when president-elect Bill Clinton stopped in Warrenton on his way from Monticello to Washington for his inauguration, he mistook it for a church. Other buildings in the square bow to the dominant courthouse, but make their own statements.

NP22.2　Old Jail Museum

1808, 1823. 10 Waterloo St. Open to the public

Two parallel structures consisting of the earlier brick jailer's quarters and a later fieldstone jail and yard have been remodeled as the Fauquier Historical Society's museum.

NP22.3　Payne Community Hall (County Library)

1923, Donn and Deming. Waterloo St. at Courthouse Sq.

A very handsome Colonial Revival structure by Washington masters of the idiom, the former library has a tetrastyle Doric portico flanked by arches.

NP22.4 Fauquier County Library

1923, 1992, Lukemire Partners. 11 Winchester St.

Originally an automobile dealership and then a van lines storage building, this has been remodeled as a library in (what else?) colonial garb.

NP22.5 Fauquier County Administration Building

1928, William H. Irwin Fleming. 8 Main St.

Colonial Revival with a Doric portico, this building replaced an earlier clerk's office. In front is a statue of John Marshall (1955, Benjamin Baker).

NP22.6 Warrenton Municipal Building (Fauquier National Bank)

1925, Stuart H. Edmonds. 18 Court St.

Tan brick with limestone trim in the standard bankers' classical idiom of its period, the former bank bows appropriately to the courthouse next door.

NP22.7 California Building

c. 1850. 1 Wall St.

William "Extra Billy" Smith, who went on to be a Confederate general and twice governor of Virginia, paid for this building with profits he made in California during the Gold Rush. It is a five-bay brick house with Greek Revival trim and a Gothic cornice. Its wrought iron fence is a good example.

NP22.8 Warren Green Hotel

1876, John R. Spilman. Hotel St.

Terminating the Court Street vista is this imposing, three-story brick building, with a central gable and two-story porch supported by Doric columns. This magnificent hostelry has served travelers, doubled as a resort hotel, and acted as the town's social center. It is now used as county offices.

NP22.9 Masonic Building

1876. 9 Culpeper St.

One of the most robust Victorian-era commercial structures in the Piedmont area, the Masonic Building has wide windows, needed because its northern exposure. The pediments on the upper floors are cast iron.

NP22.10 Fauquier Club

c. 1847. 37 Culpeper St.

A three-bay town house that was formerly a residence, this modest brick structure is typical of buildings that once lined Culpeper Street.

NP22.11 Fauquier County Building

1971–1974, Johnson, Craven and Gibson. 40 Culpeper St.

That these Charlottesville-based architects were always more comfortable with the Colonial Revival than with contemporary design is evident in this very awkward structure, which was designed to ease the overload on the old courthouse.

NP22.12 St. James Episcopal Church

1912, William H. Irwin Fleming. Later alterations. 81 Culpeper St.

Building on the foundations of a church destroyed by fire, Fleming employed the Gothic Revival style, but kept the scale suitably residential in character. The architect specified a pebble dash stucco on the exterior, but recent renewal makes it appear as if covered with caramel candy.

NP22.13 John Wise House

1905. 100 Culpeper St.

Beginning with this house, Culpeper Street becomes one of Warrenton's "power streets," whose nineteenth-century inhabitants demonstrated Thorstein Veblen's theory of conspicuous consumption. In this case, a fully developed, weatherboarded example of the Colonial Revival, with several Palladian windows, proudly shows off its plumage. However, the architect or builder must have been thinking of New England, since the house would be more appropriate there than in Virginia.

NP22.14 Emily M. Fair House (Fauquier Institute)

c. 1871. 139 Culpeper St.

Imposing with its bulging mansard roof, this was originally built as an educational institution and had grounds of ten acres. The institute's catalogue for 1877 claimed it "stands on an eminence commanding on the one hand, a fine view of the town, and on the other, a rural prospect extending to the top of the Blue Ridge, twenty five miles off, so that every day there is spread out before its inmates . . . a varied landscape of unsurpassed richness and beauty."

NP22.15 Callie and A. Ullman House

c. 1876. 157 Culpeper St.

The architectural competition intensifies with this house, which is larger than its neighbor, its mansard roof even more prominent, and its porch more impressive.

NP22.16 Thomas J. Semmes House

1885. 191 Culpeper St.

The date is extremely late for the Second Empire style, but obviously the Semmeses had no choice but to construct an even larger house than the Ullmans had, also with a bulging mansard roof.

NP22.17 Colonel Rice W. Payne House (Mecca)

1858. 194 Culpeper St.

This is the house that set the sweepstakes going along Culpeper Street. It is one of the outstanding Italianate houses in Virginia and certainly one of the best preserved. That Samuel Sloan was doing work in Warrenton (see the Warrenton Baptist Church, below) raises the interesting possibility that he or his book had a hand. Note the finely molded shells above the tall windows and the delicate iron porch.

NP22.18 Monte Rosa–Neptune Lodge (Smith-Maddux house)

c. 1847, c. 1856, c. 1908–1921. 343 Culpeper St.

"Extra Billy" Smith purchased a house built c. 1847 and greatly enlarged it with Italianate detailing. Then it was radically "colonialized" in the early twentieth century and now sports a two-story Doric portico. More significant is its Italianate stable block (c. 1856 and later additions), 100 yards southeast (easily visible from the road). It is possibly the best surviving example of such stables in Virginia. Built in four sections, it is of brick, measures 164 feet in length, and has a central three-bay section with a pyramidal-roofed cupola.

NP22.19 Brent-Payne House

c. 1830. c. 1880, remodeling. 114 Lee St.

Built in the Federal style for Robert Brent, this was later the home of General William Payne, a prominent Confederate cavalryman, who remodeled it, adding the Italianate porch and Eastlake brackets and bargeboards: a real confection and a standout!

NP22.20 Sunrise Retirement Home (Fauquier Female Seminary)

1857. 194 Lee St.

As did many towns, nineteenth-century Warrenton had a number of educational institu-

NP22.18 Monte Rosa–Neptune Lodge (Smith-Maddux house) (below)

NP22.22 Warrenton Baptist Church (right)

tions that served various constituencies. Originally located on a large lot, this Italianate building was a major structure for the town when built.

NP22.21 **Brentmoor** (Spilman-Mosby House)

c. 1859–1861. 173 Main St.

The other "power street" in Warrenton was this section of Main Street, which runs along the top of a ridge. Brentmoor is an imposing Italianate design with scored stucco over brick. The form is essentially rectangular, enlivened with projecting bays, a deep overhanging and bracketed cornice, and paired, chamfered porch posts. It is similar to a design in A. J. Downing's *Country Houses* (1850) recommended for "the southern part of the Union." The house was built for John Spilman, a prominent Warrenton builder, and was later the home of the Confederate general and "raider" John Singleton Mosby.

NP22.22 **Warrenton Baptist Church**

1857, Samuel Sloan; John Spilman, builder. Later additions. 109 Main St.

An Italianate design with vertical proportions, Warrenton Baptist Church has recessed brick panels, giant paired pilasters, and round arches. The Philadelphia architect Samuel Sloan was active in Virginia before the Civil War.

NP22.23 **Frost Diner**

1955, Jerry O'Mahony Diner Co. U.S. Business 29 (west of downtown)

Stainless steel by day and neon by night, the Frost is an excellent example of the Bayonne, New Jersey, diner company's motto: "In our line we lead the world." Originally outfitted with its own postcards and matching menus, the diner features an interior with a full stainless steel back bar with diamond flourishes and a salmon-pink Formica counter.

NP23 **Melrose**

1856–1860, George Washington Holtzclaw. VA 602 (Rogues Rd.; 1.4 miles north of Casanova). Not visible

A stunning castle that well illustrates the impact of Sir Walter Scott's romantic novels in the South before the Civil War, Melrose was constructed for Dr. James H. Murray and Edward Murray. Although Holtzclaw, a Fauquier County builder, is given credit for the house, the designs probably came from a big-city architect. In the twentieth century the house inspired Mary Roberts Rinehart's *The Circular Staircase*.

Piedmont (PI)

THE WORD "PIEDMONT" DERIVES FROM THE ITALIAN FOR "FOOT OF THE mountain." In the case of Virginia it is a rather broad foot, of about sixty miles, from the Blue Ridge Mountains on the west to the fall line on the east. For the purposes of this guide, the Piedmont area is defined as the counties of Albemarle (the county seat of Charlottesville is treated in a separate section), Culpeper, Fluvanna, Goochland, Greene, Louisa, Madison, Orange, Rappahannock, and parts of Hanover. County lines do not necessarily follow geography; thus Hanover County, which lies on both sides of the fall line, is partially treated in the Richmond section.

The landscape changes from relatively flat in the east to low, rolling hills and valleys and finally the upward surge of the mountains in the west. Native American remains are, with a few minor exceptions, completely gone. The English penetrated the area in the seventeenth century, but the earliest permanent remains are from the eighteenth century. Traditionally an agricultural and rural area, the Piedmont still retains this character for the most part, though in the twentieth century highways have allowed for the inevitable sprawl.

The entries in this section are arranged roughly in tiers across the region, beginning in the northwest and progressing east, and then returning across the southern portion to the west. The order, by county, is Rappahannock, Culpeper, Madison, Orange, Hanover (partial), Goochland, Louisa, Fluvanna, Albemarle, and Greene.

Rappahannock County   (PI1–PI4)

PI1 Ben Venue

1844–1846, attributed to James Leake Powers. Intersection of U.S. 211 and VA 729 (north .2 mile for better view)

Commanding tremendous views to the west, the main house, a five-bay brick composition with a parapet gable roof and a one-story, three-bay Doric portico, is one of the most elaborate houses of its decade in Virginia. The owner, William V. Fletcher, obviously had a strong ego. Across Virginia 729 stand three identical slave houses, unusual in that they survive, in their brick construction (most slave housing was of wood), and in their detailing, with their parapet gable roofs and exterior end chimneys. The arrangement of the slave houses in such a prominent position, rather than to the rear or hidden, as was the common practice, indicates their role as part of the landscape composition: picturesque foreground elements with a broad view beyond.

PI2 Washington

U.S. 522 and 211

George Washington, in company with John Lonem and Edward Corder, platted the town in 1749 on a grid plan with two main north-south streets—present-day Main and Gay—and five cross streets—present-day Wheeler, Calvert, Middle, Jett, and Porter. The town was incorporated in 1796, at which time it received its present name. It became the county seat in 1833 when Rappahannock County was partitioned off from Culpeper. U.S. 522 and U.S. 211 bypass the town. It still retains its nineteenth-century rural character, with numerous wooden dwellings in a regional vernacular and several more pretentious structures. In recent years it has become a tourist and gourmet destination and has suffered the usual boutique-ization. Important buildings include the Rappahannock County Courthouse (PI2.1) (1834, Malcolm Crawford; Gay Street), located near the highest point in the town, designed in the Jeffersonian courthouse tradition by one of the workmen, or "undertakers," from the University of Virginia project. The low budget of $4,500 precluded the typical portico, and Crawford provided white-painted brick Tuscan pilasters, a lunette window, a full wooden entablature, and a belfry. On the Court Green is a cluster of mid-nineteenth-century county government buildings, including the jail (c. 1850) and offices for lawyers, the clerk, and the treasurer. The treasurer's office has a raised end parapet similar to that at Ben Venue nearby. The courthouse is the nucleus of the small business district on Gay Street, which includes the substantial brick Italianate Washington Baptist Church and Masonic Hall (1873; Gay Street) and the Greek Revival Town Hall (originally the Presbyterian Church) (1858, attributed to James Leake Powers; Gay Street), a single-story brick structure with pilasters. Another notable building is the Italianate Trinity Episcopal Church (1852, attributed to James Leake Powers; Gay Street), which has been altered and stuccoed. Powers may have worked for Jefferson at the university and come to town with Crawford. On Main Street is the Washington House Tavern (originally Coxes Hotel) (c. 1820, later additions; 411 Main Street). It is a rambling affair with the typical two-story front porch. The Henry Johnson House (Heritage House) (1837; 291 Main Street) is a single-pile, two-story house, large for its time, with a columnar front added later.

PI2.1 Rappahannock County Courthouse

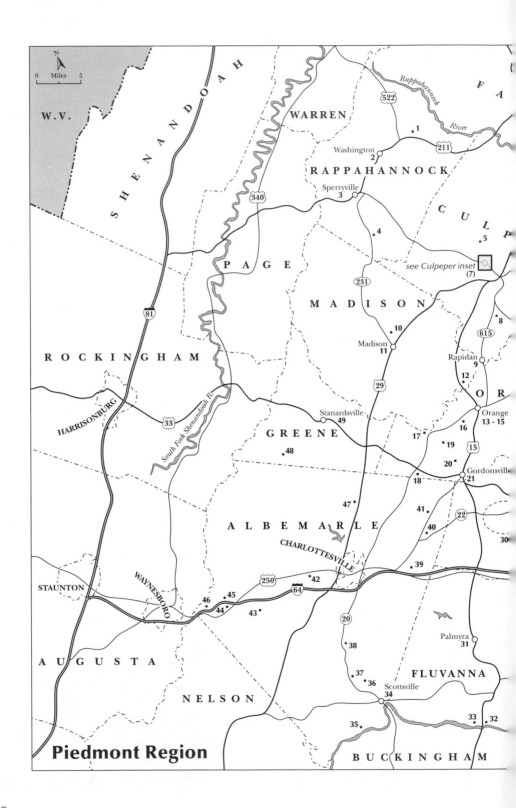

Piedmont Region

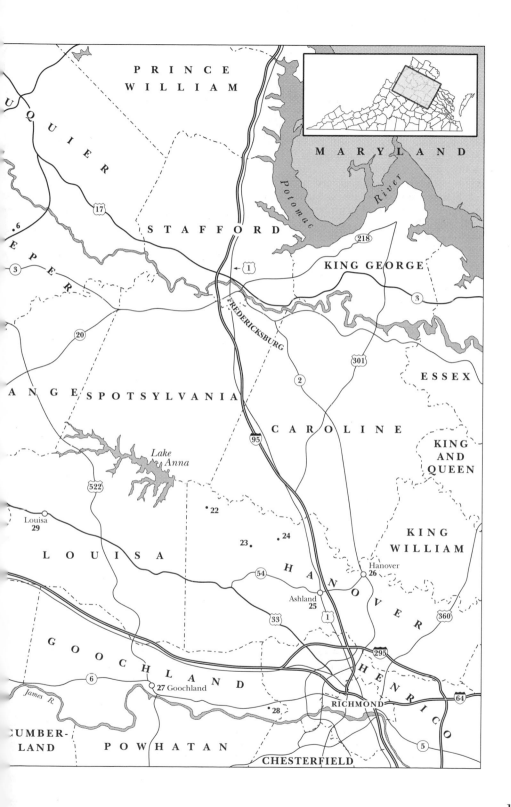

PI3 Sperryville Historic District

U.S. 522, U.S. 211, and VA 1001 (Main St.)

In 1820 Francis Thornton, Jr., laid out Sperryville, a small crossroads town now serving the apple-growing economy and the tourist trade. A few houses were built, which survive along Virginia 1001, but little happened until 1867, when the Smoot Tannery Works located here and built mills on the Thornton River. The mills, which do not survive, employed forty to fifty workers. Simple wooden residences built for them still line the east end of Main Street (Virginia 1001) and the Thornton River. The workers' housing is intermingled with the houses of the more prosperous citizens and factory managers. At the intersection of U.S. 211 and Main Street is the former tavern (c. 1825), a substantial brick structure, much altered, but still retaining its two-story front porch.

PI4 Montpelier

c. 1780. c. 1790, c. 1850, additions and renovations. VA 231 (south from Sperryville 4.5 miles, east side of road near VA 618)

An eye-catching composition of provincial grandeur, this house (not to be confused with the identically named home of James Madison; see entry below) crowns the top of a hill with

PI4 Montpelier

views in all directions. The core of the house dates from c. 1780, when Francis Thornton built the structure for his son William (unrelated to the physician-architect). The front facade has a Palladian window. In the mid-nineteenth century end wings were added, and the whole was united at the rear by a huge Tuscan colonnade raised on a basement and crowned by an Italianate cornice and pediment. Aggressively unacademic, it dominates the surroundings.

Culpeper County   (PI5–PI9)

PI5 Little Fork Church

1774–1776, attributed to John Ariss. 1974, restoration, Milton L. Grigg. Rixeyville vicinity (8 miles north of Culpeper on VA 229; .3 mile on VA 726)

Standing dramatically alone on its windswept site, Little Fork is a surviving example, rare in the Piedmont, of a nearly intact colonial house of worship. It has been attributed to Ariss because of its similarity to Lamb's Creek Church in King George County. John Voss, a local brickmason, built it and may have had a hand in the design. The church is a long, low structure of Flemish bond brick with its principal entrance in the south wall. The interior is intact and contains box pews and an elaborate carved reredos with a broken pediment and Doric pilasters.

PI6 Farley

c. 1805. 1980, restoration, Don A. Swofford. Brandy Station vicinity (VA 663 to VA 679; 2 miles). Not visible from the road

One of the most impressive frame and weatherboard houses in the state, Farley boasts a 96-foot-long facade, marked by three pedimented pavilions. On the first floor are a suite of four reception rooms connected by a T-plan hall and two staircases. Built by William Champe Carter, of the Albemarle County branch of the ubiquitous Carter family, it was named Farley in honor of his wife, Maria Farley Carter. During the Civil War, Union General John Sedgwick used it as his headquarters during the battle of Brandy Station, the largest cavalry engagement in the history of the western hemisphere.

Brandy Station is also the projected site for a neotraditional village, Clevengers Corner, designed by Quinn Evans Architects of Washington, D.C. Intended to draw on Piedmont Virginia small-town vernacular forms, it is awaiting final county approvals.

Culpeper

Culpeper County was formed from part of Orange County in 1749. The county seat, originally named Fairfax but changed to Culpeper in 1870 to avoid the obvious confusion with the Northern Virginia town and county, was established and platted in a gridiron pattern in 1759. The site was a major turnpike crossroads, and the railroad arrived in 1854. The area was heavily fought over during the Civil War. Because U.S. 29 bypassed Culpeper to the east, it has retained the feeling of a small, agriculturally based town. Commercial downtown Culpeper reflects the impact of the city's 1888 Fire Code—enacted following a disastrous fire—which required brick- or stone-faced facades and slate or metal roofs.

PI7 **Culpeper Downtown**

The following tour begins at the courthouse and moves through the commercial and civic section and concludes with a principal residential street.

The Culpeper County Courthouse (PI7.1) (1870–1874, Samuel Proctor; West Davis Street at the northeast corner of West Street) is the third courthouse to occupy the site. Proctor, a local builder who apparently acted as the architect, constructed the red brick, white-trimmed edifice for $18,700, which was the highest cost for a building in Culpeper until well into the twentieth century. Proctor's design illustrates

Culpeper (PI7)

the continuing attraction of the Roman temple form for rural Virginians even after the Civil War and foreshadows the easy acceptance of Colonial Revival and American Renaissance idioms at the turn of the twentieth century. With its tower and cupola, the building could be mistaken for a church. Proctor's design also contains elements of mid-nineteenth-century French-influenced design, such as stacked arched windows and heavy moldings, in a manner like that of Brooks Hall at the University of Virginia. Remains of frescoes by Joseph Oddenino are on the interior.

The A. P. Hill Boyhood Home (PI7.2) (c. 1770; remodeling, 1889; c. 1970; 102 North Main Street, northwest corner of Davis Street) helps to define the town's crossroads. The large, bulky, Italianate structure is the most prominent historic site in downtown. Both Civil War General Ambrose P. Hill and Revolutionary War General Edward Stevens lived here. Across, on the southwest corner, is the former Second National Bank (PI7.3) (1913, Holmboe and Lafferty; 102 South Main Street), banker's style, with massive Doric columns and a truncated corner entrance. The southwest corner is held down by Gayheart's Drugs (Booton Building) (PI7.4) (1898, 101 East Davis Street), an Italianate commercial block with a giant fascia-like finial at the top. Farther north on Main Street are the County of Culpeper Offices (U.S. Post Office) (PI7.5) (1932, Louis A. Simon, Supervising Architect, U.S. Treasury Department; 302 North Main Street), an elegant Colonial Revival structure in red brick with white trim.

Among the buildings on East Davis Street, several are especially noteworthy. The Martin Furniture Building (Farmers and Merchants

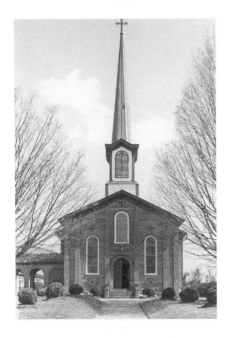

PI7.8 St. Stephen's Episcopal Church

PI7.10 Fairfax Masonic Building

Bank Block) (PI7.6) (c. 1900; 125 East Davis) is faced in dressed ashlar block. The shed roof with three rounded pediments recalls the three original tenants, the post office, the bank, and a grocery store. The Free Gospel Church of Christ (Culpeper Baptist Church) (PI7.7) (1894; 176 Main Street) is red brick Romanesque Revival and provides the focal point to the north side of the block. North on East Street, St. Stephen's Episcopal Church (PI7.8) (1821, 1861, 1916; 115 North East Street) began as a typical 1820s brick church but underwent a vast rebuilding in 1861 with the addition of a vestibule, western front, and Italianate steeple. In 1916 the interior galleries were removed and the chapel and an arcade were added. The glass includes three Tiffany Studio windows from 1888.

The Columns apartments (formerly the Ann Wingfield School) (PI7.9) (1929, School Buildings Service, State Department of Education; 1985, remodeling; 201 North East Street), so named because of its colossal Ionic portico, is typically Colonial Revival. Back on Davis Street, the Fairfax Masonic Building (PI7.10) (1902; 201 East Davis Street) is the visual triumph of downtown with its ornamented parapet, finials, and rusticated Composite columns. The James Hotel (PI7.11) (1890; 302 East Davis Street) is decayed but representative of the several hotels that used to stand in this area adjacent to the station. The Southern Railway Station (PI7.12)

(1904, Southern Railway Architects Office; 109 South Commerce Street) anchors one end of the district. Its design is standard, with a dominant, overhanging, double-hipped roof supported by massive carved brackets. Restoration is planned. One block south is the Culpeper Grocery Company Warehouse (PI7.13) (1919, William S. Plager; 301 Culpeper Street), a steel-frame structure encased with glass and brick walls and a battlement parapet with terra-cotta caps. The architect, who came from Washington, D.C., specialized in this type of structure.

PI8 Mitchell's Presbyterian Church

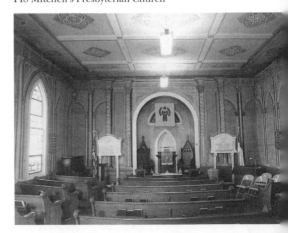

PI9.1 Rapidan, schoolhouse and library

South East Street was Culpeper's elite residential street in the nineteenth century. The Edward B. Hill House (PI7.14) (1855; 501 South East Street) is a large Italianate villa with scored and painted stucco, cast iron and wooden porches, and bracketed cornices. Bearing some resemblance to houses pictured in Samuel Sloan's *The Model Architect* (1852), it is unusual in its four bays and off-center entrance. The Lawrence-Payne-Chelf House (PI7.15) (1852; 605 South East Street), a good example of the cottage orné popularized by A. J. Downing, has lots of wood trim. The Crimora Waite House (PI7.16) (1885; 602 South East Street) is also Downingesque, but from much later, and indicates how long his idiom remained popular. On Main Street is the Burgandine House (PI7.17) (c. 1749; restored 1997; South Main Street), of log covered by clapboards, which is reputedly Culpeper's earliest house. It is open to the public.

PI8 Mitchell's Presbyterian Church

1879. 1892–1899, interior, Joseph Dominick Phillip Oddenino, decorative painter. VA 665 (Mitchell Rd.) (.2 mile east from Virginia 615), Mitchell's Station

Although from the exterior this recently restored, small wooden Gothic Revival structure seems tame, the interior is extraordinary. A complex series of trompe l'oeil frescoes transform it into a masonry Gothic/Renaissance structure with clustered and twisted columns, arches, cornices, coffered ceiling, quatrefoils, and other architectural details, seemingly straight from Italy. It remains the best surviving work of an Italian immigrant—sometimes

termed the "hobo painter"—who was born in Chieri, Torino, Italy, in 1831 and died in Madison County in 1913.

PI9 Rapidan

VA 615

Rapidan, a small farming community on the Rapidan River, contains the ruin of a large concrete flour mill (c. 1910). Across from the mill ruins are a vernacular mill house (c. 1774) and a one-room schoolhouse and library (PI9.1) (1887), a pretty Queen Anne/Gothic structure. North, across the river and in Culpeper County, is "Lower" Rapidan, which contains several Victorian structures including the former Southern Railway Depot and Freight House (c. 1893 and c. 1853). On the small cross street are two structures of note: a foursquare brick post office (c. 1905) and one of the best-preserved country stores in the Piedmont, Rapidan Trading Post (PI9.2) (c. 1880), a two-story wooden structure with cast iron columns for the single-story porch. The major feature of the town is the Waddell Memorial Presbyterian Church (PI9.3) (1872–1874, John Buchanan Danforth; later additions; 7133 Rapidan Road [Virginia 615, 6.3 miles north from Orange]). The architect signed the drawings (owned by the church) "J B Danforth, Amateur," and his obituary, from 1875, claimed that he "often drew plans for public and private edifices." For many years Danforth was chief clerk for Richmond's Mutual Assurance Society. He also served as an elder in that city's prominent Grace Street Presbyterian Church, which undoubtedly played a role in his obtaining the commission for this

PI9.2 Rapidan Trading Post
PI9.3 Waddell Memorial Presbyterian Church

church, erected in memory of James Waddell, the "Blind Preacher" of Orange. The structure as erected was a slightly subdued and reduced version of Danforth's design but still is an exuberant example of Carpenter's Gothic with board-and-batten siding. A virtual forest of spires sprouts from the exterior. On the interior, cast iron columns support the clerestory. That Presbyterians could by the 1870s accept the Gothic indicates how much the taint of "Romanism" had fallen away from the style. A parish house addition (c. 1930) is to the rear.

Madison County (PI10–PI12)

PI10 Hebron Lutheran Church

1740. 1885, ceiling, Joseph Dominick Phillip Oddenino, decorative painter. c. 1980, restoration. VA 638 (1 mile north from Madison on VA 231, right on VA 638 for .8 mile)

Isolated in open countryside, this simple T-shaped building—the cruciform shape the result of an addition—is the oldest structure in continuous use by the Lutherans in the United States. The congregation was formed by Germans working at Governor Spotswood's nearby mining community of Germanna (destroyed, now an archaeological site). The original framing remains; it has been re-clapboarded and new foundations have been installed. The interior contains galleries at the entrance and in the transept arms. The Italian muralist Oddenino decorated the ceilings with fresco in 1885. The pipe organ, dated 1800, came from Lititz, Pennsylvania.

PI11 Madison

Main St., U.S. Business 29, and VA 231

PI11.1 Madison County Courthouse

PI12.1 William Madison House, Woodberry Forest School

Madison County broke away from Culpeper County in 1792 and is named for Congressman and later President James Madison, who practiced law in the small county seat. The town retains its rural feeling principally because U.S. 29 bypasses it about half a mile to the east. The Madison County Courthouse (PI11.1) (1828, William B. Phillips and Malcolm Crawford; 1979, addition, Bailey and Gardner), which replaced a log cabin courthouse, occupies the center of the town. Phillips, a brickmason, and Crawford, a carpenter, had worked for Jefferson at the university. In the contract, the county commissioners agreed to pay a total of $3,600 and stipulated that the roof was "to have a pediment pitch with a Tuscan cornice drawn in proportion to the height of the building." Although very much in Jefferson's Roman Revival mode and bearing a strong similarity to Pavilion VII at the University of Virginia, it also fits into the tradition of earlier Virginia town halls and arcade-fronted courthouses. The cupola is of a later date. The interior of the courthouse, essentially one large space with the judge's podium terminating the entrance axis, is well preserved and contains original woodwork. The stairs on the entrance side lead up to a gallery level that contains the jury rooms, lighted by the upper windows of the facade. The office annex is to the north. Adjacent are the clerk's office (c. 1829) and the jail (c. 1892). Across from the courthouse to the south is Eagle House (William Carpenter's Tavern) (c. 1832), a substantial, symmetrical five-bay brick structure that indicates how earlier building traditions remained in use well into the nineteenth century. Attached to Eagle House and fronting on Main Street is the Old Masonic Hall (1834), a three-bay Italianate structure with pilasters on the second floor and the Masonic "eye" and name still in place. To the east 200 yards from the intersection of Church Street and Main Street is the Piedmont Episcopal Church (1832–1834; Church Street), a pedimented brick structure that looks more Baptist than Episcopalian. The twin doors are united in an unusual manner by a common architrave.

PI12 Woodberry Forest School

U.S. 15 to VA 622, Woodberry Forest (Madison Mills vicinity)

At the heart of this private boys' school is The Residence, or the William Madison House (PI12.1) (1793, Thomas Jefferson; later additions), the home of President James Madison's brother, a local politician and owner of the site in the 1790s. Correspondence between Thomas Jefferson and James Madison discusses a house that apparently was constructed for the plantation at Woodberry Forest. No drawings have been identified. The symmetrical single-story villa with a Doric portico is Jeffersonian in appearance, although executed in wood. In the late nineteenth century Robert Walker purchased the house, greatly enlarged and remodeled it, and in 1884 established a boys' preparatory school bearing the same name. After serving as the headmaster's house, the William Madison House is now used as the guest house for the school. Also on the grounds is the Walker Building (1899, John Minor Botts), which for years served as the school's main building, a tall and awkward Georgian Revival structure built from bricks fired in a kiln on the property. The Georgian Revival mode has been followed for most of the school's later buildings, including the impressive Dick Gymnasium (1939, Turner and Fisher), designed by architects from nearby Culpeper, and for the White Library (1958, White and Wilkerson), by architects from Richmond. More contemporary, with shed roofs and obviously veneered brick walls, but fitting in well, is the Dowd-Finch Dormitory (PI12.5) (1978, VMDO), designed by Robert Vickery of Charlottesville.

Orange County   (PI13–PI21)

PI13 **Orange**

U.S. 15 and VA 20

Orange retains the ambience of a small agricultural county seat. Not located on a major river, it has always been a "road town"—first turnpikes, then the railroad, which still rumbles through downtown, and then the automobile. The domination of the railroad is still evident, and the auto orientation can be seen along U.S. 15 north and south of downtown. A fire in 1908 destroyed much of downtown's business district; hence most buildings date from 1909 to 1918. Along Main Street (Virginia 20), and especially on the hill to the east, are large houses. The Orange County Courthouse (PI13.1) (1858–1859, Haskins and Alexander; later alterations; Main Street at Madison Road [U.S. 15], northwest corner) is the only Virginia example of the Italian Villa style—complete with tower, or campanile—applied to a courthouse. The building is marked by the economic growth of Orange in the mid-nineteenth century and the decision of the Orange and Alexandria Railroad to run straight through town and to cut off a piece of the existing courthouse, which had been built in 1804. The town fathers acceded to the request. The design, by

PI13.1 Orange County Courthouse

Washington architect Charles Haskins, recalled stylistically, especially in the tower, the station that the Baltimore and Ohio Railroad built in 1851 on the Mall in Washington. The large loggia across the front (unfortunately partially enclosed in 1949), originally topped by a balustrade, was Italianate in style but also linked the building to the earlier arcade porches used in Virginia courthouses. Originally red brick, the structure is currently painted. A restoration plan is under consideration. To the rear stand the clerk's office (1894) and jail (1891); in front stands a Confederate monument (1900).

The Southern Railway Depot (1909–1910, Southern Railway Chief Engineer's Office, Washington, D.C.; later alterations; 122 East Main Street) is typical of the high quality of the Southern Railway's architecture. Including a passenger and freight section, it is constructed of tan brick with Colonial Revival details and has a deep, overhanging, bracketed roof. The station was very much the center of Orange. Built immediately after the 1908 fire destroyed the earlier station, it is now used as the tourist and town center. Immediately to the west stands the Billiard Building (c. 1909; Railroad Avenue), composed of three storefronts that open directly onto the tracks. They contained at different times a soft drinks emporium; a sash, door, and blinds factory; a restaurant; a barbershop; and the Sherman Pool Room.

The NationsBank Building (Citizens National Bank) (1925, A. Stanley Miller; 113 West Main Street) is monumental and slightly Moderne, or what might be called Banker's Deco. Miller, who came from Brooklyn and designed many banks, obviously played his design against the more staid neoclassical Wachovia Bank (Jefferson National Bank) (1892; remodeling; 102 East Main Street), which stands diagonally across the street. Farther west is the Holladay House (c. 1830; 155 West Main Street), originally a mercantile building, a five-bay brick structure that is one of the earliest surviving in town. St. Thomas's Episcopal Church (1833–1834, attributed to William B. Phillips; 1853 and later, additions; 119 Caroline Street) is an impressive design; Phillips had worked on the University of Virginia and built throughout the area. The fine brickwork matches his hand. The facade, with a Tuscan distyle in antis por-

PI15 Mayhurst Inn (Mayhurst)
PI16 Montpelier

tico, is magnificent. The church was enlarged in 1853 and, probably at that date, received its Gothic windows. Although many sources claim that St. Thomas and its portico are based on Christ Church in Charlottesville (the original of which was demolished and in which Thomas Jefferson may have played a role), the facts are that St. Thomas's portico was built in 1833–1834 and a similar portico was added to Christ Church c. 1850.

PI14 Berry Hill

1824, attributed to William B. Phillips and Malcolm F. Crawford. 12261 Old Gordonsville Rd. (VA 647) (.2 mile south of Orange)

Berry Hill was constructed for Reynolds Chapman, who knew both Phillips and Crawford; at the time they were working for Jefferson at the University of Virginia. Berry Hill resembles Pavilion VII, with the addition of a service wing. The main structure is a pedimented block with a single-story arcade supporting a portico that was originally open but later enclosed.

PI15 Mayhurst Inn (Mayhurst)

1859, attributed to Norris G. Starkwether. 12460 Mayhurst Ln. (U.S. 15 south 0.6 mile from town, west side), Orange

Now operated as a bed-and-breakfast, this is one of Virginia's finest antebellum Victorian structures. No architect is recorded, but the similarity to Starkwether's Camden in Caroline County makes him a likely candidate. Built for Colonel John Willis, as the head house of a 1,500-acre plantation, the house is exuberant and wild, with possibly the largest cornice brackets in existence. Constructed of wood rusticated to look like masonry, with a scroll-ornamented finial, the cupola alone is worth the trip.

PI16 Montpelier

c. 1755. c. 1797–1800, 1809–1812, 1902–1939. 1995–present, restoration. VA 20 (4 miles east of Orange), Montpelier Station. Open to the public

The home of James Madison, Jr., the fourth U.S. president, and owned from 1902 onward by du Ponts from Delaware, Montpelier became a property of the National Trust for Historic Preservation in 1984. Madison is buried in the family plot adjacent to the estate. James Madison, Sr., built the two-room core of the present house c. 1755. Madison, Jr., and wife, Dolley, enlarged it considerably in 1797–1800, adding a wing for their residence and a Tuscan portico mounted on a high basement that was removed c. 1850. Jefferson advised on the portico and then in 1809–1812 again gave advice and loaned his two workmen, James Dinsmore and John Neilson, to make further additions. During this period the small, domed garden temple north of the house was constructed. On its completion Montpelier, with its 6,000 acres, was one of the largest country estates in Virginia, though a visiting Frenchman, the baron de Montlezun, remarked that it "is not at all pretentious, nor in consonance with what the high position of the owner would lead one to expect."

Dolley Madison sold Montpelier in 1844, and, after it had passed through numerous hands, William du Pont of Delaware purchased the estate in 1901. Highly enamored of the English country life that he had lived for several years, du Pont set about creating a country estate, purchasing adjoining acreage, restoring and constructing farm and workers' buildings, and tripling the size of the mansion from fifteen to fifty-one rooms. The additions, to the sides and rear, are nondescript and blend in. The interior, however, was completely altered and fitted out in the neo–Adam Style then favored by the wealthy. Montpelier became a self-contained fiefdom with its own passenger and freight train station (next to the entrance; c. 1910, Southern Railway Chief Engineer's Office, Washington, D.C.); power plant; sawmill; electrical, water, and sewage systems; school for the tenants, who resided in some thirty houses; fourteen barns and stables; and other assorted buildings. The designer for most of this work was a local contractor, George E. Ficklin, who also handled the construction. Du Pont's wife, Annie Rogers Zinn du Pont, reworked the ornamental gardens behind the house, which have been inaccurately attributed to Pierre Charles L'Enfant. She may have followed an earlier garden layout, but the brick wall and most of the planting pattern are hers.

Daughter Marion du Pont Scott (for a time the wife of movie actor Randolph Scott) inherited the estate in 1928, built the racecourse and steeplechase track, and instituted the Montpe-lier Stakes, which still run each fall. She also continued to build on the estate. The gambrel-roofed, three-barn racehorse complex to the east of the track came from Sears, Roebuck and Company of Chicago, and the two barns west of the track and the two workers' houses were supplied by Montgomery Ward. A 1937 Colonial Revival house for her equestrian trainer and longtime companion, Carroll Bassett, was a modular design supplied by the Hogdson Company of Massachusetts; Charles Gillette designed the grounds and aviary. In the main mansion her principal addition was an Art Deco lounge and bar, decorated with portraits of her winning horses. This room is being preserved, but the National Trust has removed and is restoring the central section to the period of Madison's tenancy. The entire complex of 2,700 acres is one of the best extant examples of a Virginia country estate open to the public.

PI17 Somerset Christian Church

c. 1855, Virginia 668 (off of VA 20), Somerset

The small village of Old Somerset has been by-passed by Virginia 20 and sits isolated. The Christian Church, virtually intact, is a small Italianate structure of wood, very different from most Virginia churches of its date. Well maintained, the interior has a rear gallery, original pews decorated with wood graining, and a shallow, triple-arched chancel.

PI18 Barboursville

c. 1817–1822, Thomas Jefferson. VA 678 (.5 mile east from VA 20). Access via the main office of the winery

The house burned on Christmas Day, 1884, leaving one of the most romantic and evocative ruins in the country. The visitor, however, can appreciate Jefferson's original scheme for the main house of a large plantation for James Barbour (1775–1842), governor, senator, and minister to the Court of St. James. The drawings, now in the Massachusetts Historical Society, called for an octagonal dome and balustrade that were never built. The north side, which is the approach, has a turf ramp that helps to create the appearance a single-story villa, even though the structure is a large three-story dwelling. The Roman Doric portico (duplicated on the south) gave access to an impressive two-story hexagonal reception room and an octagonal drawing room. University of Virginia students, led by Professor Mario di Val-marana, stabilized the ruins in 1976. To the north of the house the outlines of Barbour's racetrack can be seen. To the west of the house and built into the hillside are a pair of large brick dependencies with two-story brick columns that support galleries on the south elevations. They underscore the importance of service buildings to the main house and farm. Barboursville is now part of a winery.

PI19 Frascati

1821–1823, attributed to John M. Perry. 9281 Blue Ridge Turnpike (VA 231) (2.2 miles south of intersection with Virginia 20), Somerset vicinity

John Perry had worked for Jefferson at Monticello and the university. He built—and no doubt designed—Frascati for Philip Pendelton Barbour, a Speaker of the U.S. House of Representatives, U.S. Supreme Court justice, and brother of James Barbour, whose Barboursville lies only four miles away as the crow flies. Visible from the road are the monumental pedimented Tuscan portico and the blocky, more conventional house. The grounds contain an impressive array of outbuildings.

PI20 Lochiel

1916–1918, Griffin and Wynkoop. c. 1930, entry court and gardens, Charles Gillette, landscape architect. 18285 Blue Ridge Turnpike (VA 231) (2.5 miles north of intersection with U.S. 33)

Visible from the road is the seven-bay brick facade of this extraordinary single-pile Georgian Revival mansion. Griffin and Wynkoop of New York, well known in suburban mansion circles, designed the house for Flora Zinn, whose father owned nearby Cameron Lodge (now burned), one of the state's most impressive houses. Gillette added the granite-paved entry court, gardens, and associated features.

PI21 Gordonsville

U.S. 15 and U.S. 33

A perfect example of a railroad junction town, Gordonsville grew from a crossroads tavern in the decades before the Civil War, when two railroads and two turnpikes crossed here. The town prospered, though in recent years decline has set in. The Chesapeake and Ohio Railroad (now CSX) overpass still runs through town and helps to define it. Along the railroad tracks are a water tower, a freight shed, and a C&O signal tower (c. 1904), designed in a Colonial Revival mode. Many of the houses on both sides of the tracks have large rear porches that overlook the tracks. The Magnolia House (c. 1873, 109 North Commerce Street) was a hotel that sat within twenty feet of the tracks. The passenger station was torn down in the 1970s, but the former C&O Freight Depot (c. 1850; 201 Depot Street) is a classic example of early railroad building.

Main Street (U.S. 15 and 33) bisects the town and is divided into north and south portions by the railroad overpass. Along Main Street are several structures of interest. The Gordonsville Methodist Church (1873; 407 North Main Street) is a wild, vibrant Italianate structure, with projecting eaves, large dentils, and brackets and the original distyle in antis portico surmounted by a Palladian arch motif. Such exuberance is rare in small-town churches of the Piedmont. The former E. J. Faulconer House (c. 1856; 304 North Main Street) exhibits Italianate characteristics.

South Main Street is more commercial. The L. M. Acree Building (c. 1920; 102 South Main Street) retains its original glazed shopfront and sheet metal cornice. The building is executed in yellow brick on the front and red brick on the side. The Allman Building (c. 1920; 103 South Main Street) is also largely original and has paired brick recesses that articulate the upper story. The Virginia ABC Store (c. 1936; 201 South Main Street) is streamlined Art Deco with glass block. Terminating the axis of South Main is the Exchange Hotel (1860; 400 South Main Street), now a library and museum run by Historic Gordonsville, Inc., and open to the public. Greek Revival in style, it has two large gallery-type porches that overlook the original railroad junction.

Hanover County (Western)   (PI22–PI26)

PI22 Beaverdam Railroad Depot

1866. Beaverdam

This is the fourth depot to occupy the site. The three earlier stations were destroyed by Union forces during the Civil War. The line was originally the Virginia Central Railroad Company, purchased a few years later by the Chesapeake and Ohio Railroad Company. The long, low brick structure housed waiting rooms, an office, and freight and baggage rooms. It is one of the earliest surviving depots in the state and, although no longer in use, is well preserved. The interior is remarkably intact, with original beaded-board walls and ceilings as well as shelving and switching mechanisms.

PI23 Scotchtown

c. 1717. 1958, restoration. 1970, gardens, Griswold, Winters and Swain. Scotchtown Rd. (VA 685). Open to the public

Scotchtown is important historically because Patrick Henry, the fiery Revolutionary orator, lived at this plantation between 1771 and 1778 and during this period gave some of his most impassioned addresses. It is important in architectural terms as the largest surviving one-story colonial house in Virginia. It dates to some time after 1717, when Charles Chiswell of Williamsburg purchased the property. With nine bays, it resembles a barn. Eight rooms and a central passage occupy the main floor, and

more space is provided under the clipped or jerkinhead gable roof. Several outbuildings have been restored along with the gardens. The property is owned by the APVA.

PI24 Fork Episcopal Church (St. Martin's Parish Church)

c. 1736. VA 738 (4 miles west of Gum Tree and the junction of U.S. 1; 4.5 miles north of Ashland)

One of nearly three dozen surviving eighteenth-century Anglican parish churches in Virginia, this structure has a simple rectangular plan, 34 feet by 74 feet, and eleven segmental-arched windows. The brick walls are 22 inches thick, with English bond below the water table and Flemish bond with regular glazed headers above. The bricks of the segmental arches and window jambs are rubbed a uniform red color in a manner characteristic of Virginia brickwork of the mid-eighteenth century. The modillion cornice and window sash and jambs were originally painted Spanish brown. The porches for the front and side entrances are from 1804. The church interior is one of the few not vandalized during disestablishment or by northern troops during the Civil War. Although much has been altered and moved around, a significant amount of the early fabric remains, including fragments of pews, doors, and locks, as well as the framing, flooring, staircase, and the balustrade of the west gallery. The pulpit originally stood on the north wall and was moved c. 1830 and again in 1913 to its present position. The pews are original, although cut down. The west gallery and stairway date to the original construction, but the lower partition is later.

PI25 Ashland Historic District

Center Street (along the railroad tracks and streets off it)

Ashland, about twelve miles north of Richmond, was formed around the railroad; the double tracks of the Richmond, Fredericksburg and Potomac Railroad (RF&P) run through the center of town, with Center Street on either side of the tracks. The railroad laid tracks through the area in 1836 and purchased a tract of land. Initially developed in the 1850s as a resort and as a passenger rest stop, the town had hotels, a racecourse, and a few cottages. It was incorporated as a city in 1858, named for the Kentucky estate of a native son, Henry Clay. The Civil War brought widespread destruction to the town. Recovery was aided by the arrival of Randolph-Macon College, but not until the late nineteenth century did the town became a commuter suburb for Richmond. It contains at its core a group of important buildings.

The Visitors Center and Richmond, Fredericksburg and Potomac Railroad Depot (1922, W. Duncan Lee; 110 North Center Street) is in the center of the road and tracks. Modest in size with a prominent roof, it is in the Colonial Revival idiom. Across from it is the Henry Clay Inn (1992), a re-creation of a hotel of the same name that had burned. Adjacent is the former and modified Hanover Bank Building (1919, Albert F. Huntt; 104 North Center Street), with its four engaged Doric columns.

On the opposite (east) side of Center Street is the campus of Randolph-Macon College. Chartered in 1830, this Methodist men's college invested heavily in Confederate bonds and found itself in financial difficulties after the war. The RF&P Railroad offered land as an inducement if the college would move from Boydton, Virginia. In 1868 the college trustees accepted a former hotel at the northern end of town and moved. By 1871 the college had prospered and had erected, facing the railroad tracks, Washington-Franklin Hall (PI25.1) (1871–1872, Benjamin F. Price), a large brick Italianate structure. Impressive, with large,

round-arched pediments on its two major facades, the structure served as a literary society for the college. This was followed by the adjacent Italianate structure, Pace Lecture Hall (1876, Albert Lawrence West), a much tamer design, and then, between the two, a joint town-gown chapel, formerly the Duncan Memorial Chapel, now the Old Chapel Theater (1879, Albert Lawrence West), a red brick Gothic Revival structure. These made an impressive High Victorian array along the tracks for all who were traveling either north or south. Twentieth-century additions to the campus have followed, not too surprisingly, in the Colonial Revival mode, with the most important being the former Carnegie Library, now the Peele Administration Building (1922, Edward L. Tilton), designed by a former McKim, Mead and White employee who specialized in libraries.

The former Ashland Theater (c. 1950; 207 England Street) possesses a striking Art Deco tower. Across is the Randolph-Macon College Fine Arts Center (formerly St. Ann's Catholic Church) (1892; alterations, 1925, Luther P. Hartsook; northwest corner of England and Henry Streets), which has half timbering characteristic of the Arts and Crafts movement.

Back on Center Street is the Richard S. Gilles Jr. Public Library (1997, DePasquale Gentil Homme Group and Luckmire Associates; 200 South Center Street), which attempts to pick up the commercial scale of the surrounding context with its strange configuration of a small tower and long horizontal form: a gentle sort of postmodernism.

PI25.1 Washington-Franklin Hall, Randolph-Macon College

PI26 **Hanover Courthouse**

U.S. 301, VA 2, and VA 54

A quintessential rural Virginia courthouse settlement, Hanover Courthouse was located on a crossroads and near river transportation. The county was formed in 1720. Although it has experienced some growth at the margins, the town retains a nineteenth-century feel.

PI26.1 **Hanover County Courthouse**

c. 1737–1741. Courthouse green, east side of U.S. 301

Situated on a spacious green, the Hanover County Courthouse is very similar to other arcade courthouses, especially that in contiguous

King William County. T-shaped with a hipped roof, five-bay arcade, and fine brickwork, the building is imposing though diminutive. It has been renovated several times, and nothing remains of the original interior. The courtroom was expanded in the nineteenth century, first with a small extension to the rear or east end, which was replaced by a larger, 10-foot bay in the late nineteenth century. Unfortunately, the common bond (every fifth course composed of headers) used for the brick of the extension was replaced with Flemish bond with glazed headers to match the original section. This replacement was part of a very thorough restoration of the building in the 1950s, which obliterated evidence of earlier alterations and decorative features.

Patrick Henry argued several cases here and in 1774 gave an important address. Until the Virginia legislature passed a law in the early 1790s requiring the construction of fireproof clerk's offices, many court clerks kept the county records in their personal possession, often miles from the courthouse. Such was the case in Hanover County, where only in the second quarter of the nineteenth century was the first purpose-built clerk's office built just northwest of the colonial courthouse. The building has more than tripled in size over the last 150 years from the original three-bay, one-story brick portion measuring 35 by 22 feet. Also on the grounds is the jail (c. 1840), built of locally quarried sandstone.

PI26.2 Hanover Tavern

c. 1790. West of courthouse grounds, west side of U.S. 301

The Hanover Tavern is a rambling, two-story frame structure that served as the local tavern in the nineteenth and early twentieth centuries. Through much of the twentieth century, the building was thought to be the original courthouse tavern, but apparently the present structure replaced an earlier wooden building located across the road, perhaps just south of the jail. The present tavern took shape over several major building campaigns. The original section to the north consisted of five bays, with two rooms on either side of a broad central stair passage. The detailing of the staircase, chimney, and other features suggests that this part was built at the very end of the eighteenth century. Some two or three decades later, an L-shaped addition was constructed to the south and linked to the older section by a one-bay section, which probably served as a bar. This new addition provided a large entertaining room on the ground floor and more than doubled the number of sleeping chambers on the second floor. A number of modifications were made through the end of the nineteenth century. In the early 1950s the cellar was enlarged and converted into a dinner theater. Also in the complex is the Pamunkey Regional Library (1942), in the Colonial Revival mode, a gift from David K. E. Bruce, the diplomat.

Goochland County   (PI27)

PI27 Goochland County Courthouse

1826, Dabney Cosby and Valentine Parrish. 1955, addition. 1989–1990, renovation and restoration, Wood Sweet Swofford. U.S. 522 and VA 6, Goochland Court House

Although the cornerstone refers to Cosby, who worked for Jefferson on the university, and Parrish, a Cumberland builder, as the architects for the building, in actuality the five county building commissioners furnished detailed specifications and drawings. These documents included those of the Buckingham County Courthouse, designed by Jefferson four years earlier and destroyed by fire in 1869. Hence this building is probably very close to what Jefferson would have wanted, a full Roman temple form with widely spaced Tuscan columns and entablature. The courthouse meets the ground and is not elevated. The Flemish bond brickwork on the entrance is of high quality with very tight joints. The interior is one large two-story space. The presiding authority is seated on the axis. Originally there was an apsidal end. A gallery across the entrance end of the space contains two jury rooms lighted by the windows under the portico. A 1955 addition is to the rear. In 1989–1990, Wood Sweet Swofford Architects of Charlottesville renovated and restored the building and put another addition to the rear. Also on the grassy courthouse grounds are the former jail (1848) in stone, a brick clerk's office (1826), and several minor structures. A brick wall was erected to keep out wandering cattle.

Louisa County (PI28–PI29)

PI28 **Tuckahoe**

c. 1723 and later. River Rd. (VA 650) (.6 mile east of intersection of VA 650 and VA 647). Not visible from the road; open by appointment and during Garden Week

Standing on a bluff above the James River, Tuckahoe is extremely complex. It is basically an H-shaped house covered in weatherboard, the north wing of which was begun by Thomas Randolph. The south wing, with its brick end, and the connecting salon were constructed by his son, William Randolph, after his marriage in 1734 to Judith Page, daughter of Mann Page I, of Rosewell. The north stair, presumably installed after this date, displays some of the finest carving of its period, a virtuoso display of rococo vines and leaves. On the northwest side of the house is a row of slave cabins for the house servants, a kitchen, and other outbuildings arranged in a formal pattern. East of the house is a schoolhouse (c. 1750), where Thomas Jefferson attended classes while his father, Peter Jefferson, lived at the plantation.

PI29 **Louisa**

In this small farming county seat, the Louisa County Courthouse (PI29.1) (1904–1905, D. Wiley Anderson; Main Street, intersection of U.S. 33, Virginia 22, and Virginia 208) domi-

PI29.1 Louisa County Courthouse

nates the center. D. Wiley Anderson, a prominent Richmond architect, received the commission when the county supervisors decided the 1818 building, the county's third courthouse, was beyond repair. Anderson, who delighted in overscaled elements, created a giant Ionic portico and an octagonal dome that engulfs the brick building. Certainly, Anderson had in mind Jeffersonian precedents, but as with many of his designs, he inflated the details. On the interior, the ground floor is given over to offices and the second floor, under the dome, to a large courtroom. The dome has only a plain cornice and no decoration. To the rear is a three-story jail addition. On the grounds of the courthouse are the typical outbuildings. To the southeast is the red brick old jail (1818, rebuilt in 1868 after a fire), which now serves as the Louisa County Historical Society Museum. On the northwest is the one-story brick Crank Building (c. 1850), which originally housed law offices. The Confederate monument (1904, Roman Bronze Works, New York) stands on the entrance approach to the courthouse. Also on the Courthouse Square at the corner of Elm Avenue and Main Street is the Ogg Building, now a courthouse annex (formerly First National Bank of Louisa) (1917–1918, Eugene R. Bradbury), a brick structure with a distyle in antis portico and Tuscan columns.

The rest of downtown maintains a rural, unprettified quality and is worthy of inspection. See in particular the former Louisa Railroad Depot (c. 1870, Church Street), board-and-batten with Eastlake, or Stick Style, brackets in the extended eaves of the gabled roof. It is a rare surviving depot. Now part of the Maddox Feed Store complex, the Freight Depot (c. 1880) next door is appropriately simpler.

PI30 **Green Springs National Historic Landmark District**

Bounded by U.S. 15 and U.S. 22 (between Boswell's Tavern and Zion Crossroads)

A 14,000-acre bowl of extremely fertile pastures and fields stands in contrast to the thin soil and scrub pine of the surrounding hills. The area was settled in 1722 and today still retains much of the agricultural feel of the mid-nineteenth century. The name comes from a spring near the center that became a spa in the late eighteenth century. In the early 1970s the area became the site of a major preservation battle as the state attempted to build a high-security prison, and other interests attempted to secure the land for strip mining of vermiculite for kitty litter. After a protracted battle, it became a National Historic Landmark. The area has a number of significant buildings, not visible from the road, such as Hawkwood (1851–1854, Alexander Jackson Davis).

Fluvanna County　(PI31–PI33)

PI31　Fluvanna County Courthouse

1829–1831, John Hartwell Cocke. U.S. 15 (15 miles south from I-64), Palmyra

Standing on the Rivanna River is the building that Talbot Hamlin described as the "Acropolis" of Palmyra. Cocke's architectural adventurousness (see entry for Bremo, below) is obvious in his departure from the Roman idiom favored by his mentor Jefferson and found in other Piedmont courthouses. Cocke, one of the county's building commissioners, obtained the building specifications for the Goochland courthouse and adapted them, perhaps using Asher Benjamin's *The Practical House Carpenter* (1830) for the Greek Doric order. As was typical of Virginia building practices, the columns are unfluted. Cocke and Walter Timberlake, a Methodist minister, were the building's undertakers. Although constructed of brick, the courthouse made extensive use of stone for the column and pilaster capitals, the steps, water table, windowsills, and lintels. The stone lintel over the door reads: *The maxim held sacred by every free people / Obey the laws.* With two levels of windows, the interior is bright and airy. Most of the interior woodwork is original, with heavy balustrades and lecterns on the

staircases. The stairs lead to the jury rooms above. The courthouse is unusual in having no additions. The problems of expansion led to an ill-fated attempt to abandon the courthouse in 1996 and move to a new site. The proposal met defeat at the polls. Under consideration is a courthouse annex on adjacent property. The usual auxiliary buildings surround the courthouse, the most significant being the former jail (1829), constructed of stone by John G. Hughes and similar to outbuildings at nearby Bremo. A small commercial area grew up around the courthouse, but a fire in the early twentieth century destroyed it. Strip development has sucked away most other business so that today Palmyra really is just a courthouse town.

PI32　Bremo Slave Chapel

1835. U.S. 15, Bremo Bluff

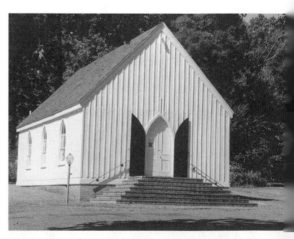

In the small James River village of Bremo Bluff, which sprang up around a ferry service and the James River and Kanawha Canal, the most important landmark is the former Bremo Slave Chapel, which used to stand on Bremo Planta-

PI33.1 Upper Bremo, drawing by John Neilson

tion, a short distance away, and is the only known surviving slave chapel in Virginia. Perhaps designed by John Hartwell Cocke, the building is a board-and-batten, pointed-arched structure. Cocke was an outspoken opponent of slavery and served as vice president of the American Colonization Society. He kept slaves but believed that they should be prepared for freedom. He illegally taught his slaves to read and provided them with religious instruction, often conducting services in this chapel. After the Civil War, the chapel fell into disuse and was moved c. 1883 to Bremo Bluff to serve as the Episcopal Church. Today it is the parish house for Grace Episcopal Church (1926), a Colonial-Jeffersonian Revival structure.

PI33 Bremo

Not open to the public and not visible from the road

Despite its inaccessibility, the Bremo complex is so important it must be noted. The major architectural elements were created under the direction of General John Hartwell Cocke, a planter who was a noted reformer and an associate of Jefferson. Upper Bremo (PI33.1) (1817–1820, John Neilson and others) is very much in the Jeffersonian villa idiom. Consist-

ing of a central pavilion, hyphens, and two end pavilions, it stretches along the bluff overlooking the James River. Neilson, who had worked for Jefferson at Monticello and the University of Virginia, prepared the drawings and drew together several schemes developed over the years by Cocke and others. Cocke, however, provided ideas. Neilson's drawings, located at the University of Virginia, were misplaced for years, and consequently some scholars have attributed the house to Jefferson. That attribution has been disproved by recent scholarship.

Below the house are farm buildings and a porticoed stone barn, reminiscent of Palladio's work. Bremo Recess (1807–1808; 1834–1836, renovation, John Hartwell Cocke) is located on another part of the plantation and was originally a wooden house that Cocke lived in while Upper Bremo was being constructed. Later, when he had turned the management of the plantation over to his son, he encased the house in a brick Jacobean Revival facade, with gables and clustered chimneys. In a letter of 1844 Cocke stated, "the stile is copied from the only two specimens of the like buildings I ever saw—the well remembered old Six-chimney House in Wmsburg . . . and Bacons Castle." An early example of American Colonial Revival, the design also owes a debt to the contemporary English cottage orné and perhaps to the work of Alexander Jackson Davis. Lower Bremo (1839–1840, Cocke; 1917, renovation, Robert E. Lee Taylor), on still another part of the plantation, is a further essay in the Jacobean Revival. Here Cocke added a wing to a preexisting house for another son, and Taylor later completed the house in the same idiom. Also on the estate is Temperance Spring (1845, Alexander Jackson Davis), a small Doric temple that stood near the James River and Kanawha Canal and was intended to influence riverboat men to give up the evils of drink: the Temperance Movement was another passion of Cocke's. The building has been moved to Upper Bremo.

Albemarle County (PI34–PI47)

PI34 Scottsville

Located at a large bend on the James River, this small town served as the original county seat of Albemarle County, from 1744 to 1762. The community prospered in the late eighteenth

and nineteenth centuries as a major trading center. Its ferry served the various turnpikes that passed through, and the James River and Kanawha Canal once passed through the town. When the Richmond and Allegheny Railroad (now CSX) arrived in the 1880s, the town was already in decline, for in 1865 Union cavalry pillaged the place. The town's location, partially on the river's floodplain, has resulted in flood damage, and a series of fires have destroyed much of the original fabric. However, a few buildings of interest remain. The town plan is L-shaped. Main Street parallels the river. Perpendicular to Main Street, Valley Road (Virginia 20) climbs the hill. Parallel to Valley Road is Harrison Street.

On Main Street, all on the north side, are the James Turner Barclay House (c. 1825; Main Street), an elegant three-bay brick town house with fine corbeled cornice and Federal details around the door and windows. Next door is the Scottsville Museum (Disciples of Christ Church) (1846; Main Street; open to the public), a brick building with double entrances, in a Greco-Roman classical revival style that illustrates lingering Jeffersonian influence. The west end of Main Street is terminated by the Scottsville Apartments (Scottsville School) (1939, Department of Education, School Buildings Service; Main Street). The building has a large Colonial Revival portico that masks the standard single-story school plan. On Harrison Street is St. John's Episcopal Church (1875; Harrison Street), a board-and-batten structure with pointed-arched openings that shows the influence of Richard Upjohn and of *Upjohn's Rural Architecture* (1852). The interior has been altered. Valley Street has a variety of structures, some worthy of note. Two miles north on Virginia 20 is the Scottsville Elementary School (c. 1960; 1979, addition, VMDO), which is a noteworthy rejuvenation of an older school building with a new entrance and a large, diagonally cut cylinder serving as the library, rather Corbusian in form. Clad in glazed red brick, the building is an eye-catching civic presence.

PI35   William Walker House

c. 1803, James Walker. 9727 Warren Ferry Rd. (VA 627), Warren

A particularly well-preserved example of small-scale domestic architecture in the Jeffersonian manner, this single-story house, elevated on a high basement, is reminiscent of the central cores of the Palladian villas that Jefferson admired. Although the red brick and pedimented wood portico with a tympanum lunette are characteristic of Jefferson's work, there is no evidence of his direct involvement in the design.

A former Jefferson workman, James Walker, built the house for his brother, William. Like many of Palladio's patrons, William Walker was a prominent merchant. The elegant house suited his position in the small village, which was a trading port on the James River. Modifications, added later in the nineteenth century, have been removed. The small brick service wing on the east is a twentieth-century addition.

PI36   Christ Episcopal Church, Glendower

1831–1832, William B. Phillips. 900 Glendower Rd., Scottsville-Glendower vicinity

Phillips, a mason recruited from Richmond to work on the University of Virginia, created a delightful play on the Roman idiom favored by Jefferson. Phillips's church is a simple brick temple, without the portico often found in his mentor's work. A full Doric entablature, a familiar element from Jefferson's work at the University of Virginia, encircles the building below the eaves. The pediment above the double entry contains a very Jeffersonian lunette window. In Phillips's hands the familiar lunette window form, borrowed from the work of his former employer, becomes the dominant motif of the exterior. At the consecration, future bishop William Meade, a key figure in the revival of the Episcopal Church in Virginia, described Phillips's work as "a neat and excellent brick church."

PI37   Estouteville

1827–1830, James Dinsmore. Intersection of Estouteville Farm and Plank rds. (VA 712), Keene

Dinsmore, another of Jefferson's "workmen," replays many of the Jefferson themes—a symmetrical three-part composition, carefully executed proportions, academically correct classical details, and monumental tetrastyle, pedimented Tuscan porticoes— in this large county house for a Jefferson relative, John Coles III. The design of the residence demonstrates the sustained power of Jefferson's classical Roman vocabulary, disseminated through his former employees. In the ornate central hall, the carved wooden Doric entablature, with bucrania in the metopes, is identical to that at the university's Pavilion II, on which Dinsmore had worked.

PI38 **Redlands**

c. 1798–1808. Intersection of Redlands Farm and Secretarys rds. (VA 708) Not visible

The unknown designer of Redlands looked to the colonial mansions of eastern Virginia to create an imposing house in the Piedmont for an owner with an equally notable pedigree. Begun c. 1798 for Robert Carter, great-grandson of Robert "King" Carter, the house was not finished until a year before his death in 1809. Martin Thacker was the builder. The architect is unknown. Redlands, a two-story brick structure with a hipped roof and modillioned cornice, is reminiscent of such well-known Tidewater Georgian mansions as Westover. The addition of dormers in the twentieth century reinforced the connection. By contrast, the porch, modified in the twentieth century, is a departure from the model. The Georgian shell of the Federal-period mansion encloses elaborate Adamesque interiors. The carefully selected elevated situation of Redlands heightens the dramatic impact of the house.

PI39 **Keswick Hall** (Villa Crawford)

c. 1910, Eugene Bradbury. 1990, additions and renovation, Dalgliesh, Eichman, Gilpin and Paxton. Keswick Rd. (VA 731)

Relentlessly pretentious with its evocation of Old World status, this hotel is the center of a large gated community and golf course. Bradbury, a Charlottesville architect, designed an eighteen-room Georgian-Italianate structure for the A. E. Crawfords of New York City. Subsequently, the property passed through several incarnations before Sir Bernard Ashley, of Laura Ashley fabrics, purchased it and converted it

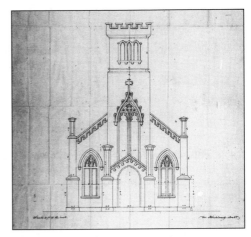

PI40 Grace Episcopal Church, drawing by William Strickland

into a hotel. Robert Paxton, the lead architect, more than doubled the size of the original structure (now the north wing) and enhanced the Italian character of the exterior. The well-designed terrace along the east front offers great views. The interior is overloaded comfy English, faux country house, but without the tatters and wear. In 1999 the house was sold to Orient-Express Hotels.

PI40 **Grace Episcopal Church**

1847–1855, William Strickland. 1895, rebuilding. VA 231, Cismont vicinity, Keswick

Better known for his Greek Revival buildings in Philadelphia and Nashville, Strickland designed only a few Gothic Revival structures, of which this is the best surviving example. The drawings are at the University of Virginia. Construction was funded by Mrs. William Cabell Rives of nearby Castle Hill, and the cornerstone was laid in 1848, but the church was not completed until 1855. The interior and roof were rebuilt after a fire in 1895. Stylistically, Strickland appears unaware of the Gothic revolution sparked by Pugin and Ruskin in England and looks back to the earlier "Gothick" mode. He may have owed a debt to his fellow Philadelphian Thomas Ustick Walter, and his 1843 design for the Baptist Mariner's Church, unbuilt but intended for Norfolk. Grace Episcopal resembles Walter's design in style and massing and in the large window in the tower. However, Strickland's window is placed higher and is essentially nonfunctional, shedding light only in the cramped tower space. Of particular note are the "stovepipe" finials, wonderfully oversized forms.

PI41 Castle Hill

1764. 1823–1824, John M. Perry. 1844, William B. Phillips. c. 1940, renovations, Marshall Swain Wells. VA 231, Cismont vicinity, Keswick. Not visible from the road; open occasionally

Castle Hill is a well-known landmark. It was built in two sections, the first a story-and-a-half frame dwelling with seven bays constructed for Dr. Thomas Walker. Traditional in plan, it typifies the houses of the upper Piedmont gentry. Connected by an ell to the south is a two-story Jeffersonian block, built—and presumably designed—by a university workman, John M. Perry. The owner was William Cabell Rives, minister to France, U.S. senator, and Confederate congressman. In the 1840s another Jefferson workman, William B. Phillips, added rooms at either end of the 1820s block. In the 1940s Charlottesville architect Marshall Swain Wells "colonialized" parts of the interior. Also notable are the landscaped grounds and several outbuildings, some of which date to the eighteenth century.

PI42 D. S. Tavern

c. 1750. c. 1790, addition. 3449 Ivy Rd. (U.S. 250), Charlottesville vicinity

The tavern, a survivor of the commercial activity spawned by the transportation routes through the Piedmont, was named for a well-known landmark on the site. The D. S. Tree marked the intersection of the Three Notched Road and the Dick Woods Road, two important routes to the west. The one-room log portion of the structure, built in the mid-eighteenth century, is thought to have been a claims house. In the late eighteenth century, a frame addition converted the small log structure into a two-story, two-room central-hall plan ordinary. A single-story hyphen connects the tavern to an early nineteenth-century kitchen on the east. The ordinary continued to serve travelers along the much-traveled road until the mid-nineteenth century, when the railroad and new roads provided alternate routes to the west. The most famous of the tavern's numerous owners was Chief Justice John Marshall, who held the title to the property from 1810 to 1813.

PI43 Miller School of Albemarle

1874 and later, Albert Lybrock and D. Wiley Anderson. VA 635, Batesville vicinity

One of central Virginia's few examples of Ruskinian Venetian Gothic, the Miller School, with its polychrome brick and weighty scale, recalls English "redbrick" universities. The will of Samuel Miller (1792–1869), who was born nearby and who amassed a considerable fortune in tobacco and agricultural commodities, provided for the establishment of an institution for the education and maintenance of the orphaned and poor children of Albemarle County. The result was a school devoted to industrial arts and manual labor. Construction began on a 1,000-acre farm in 1874 and continued for the next twenty years. The first students entered in 1877. The school became coeducational in 1884. It remains a thriving institution, and its student body is no longer restricted to the disadvantaged. The central block is enormous and richly detailed. The interior still retains many details.

PI44 Blue Ridge Farm

c. 1860. 1923–1927, William Lawrence Bottomley. 1920–early 1930s, Charles F. Gillette, landscape architect. Intersection of Blue Ridge Farm and Ortman rds. (VA 691), Yancy Mills vicinity

Blue Ridge Farm is an exemplary product of the frequent collaboration between New York architect Bottomley and Richmond landscape architect Gillette. At Blue Ridge Farm between 1923 and 1927, Bottomley transformed a mid-nineteenth-century Albemarle County farmhouse into an elegant country house for Randolph and Blanche Ortman. The two-story brick mansard-roofed farmhouse became the two-and-one-half-story central block, flanked by Bottomley's asymmetrical one-story wings. The extensively remodeled interiors are also largely his work. The fine workmanship and materials and the imaginative interpretation of Georgian details are typical of Bottomley's work. Gillette's planting plan—now somewhat altered—complemented the work of his collaborator. Gillette held the formal and compact planting patterns to locations near the buildings and major circulation paths. Outside these areas, large sweeps of turf, reminiscent of the work of the English landscape school, connect, apparently seamlessly, to the sweeping vistas beyond.

PI43 Miller School of Albemarle

PI46 Mirador

PI45 Emmanuel Episcopal Church

1862–1863. 1911–1914, renovation, Waddy B.
Wood. U.S. 250, Greenwood-Crozet vicinity

The original structure of Emmanuel closely followed the standard mid-nineteenth-century
rural church, a gable-fronted brick box. The reworking began with a gift in 1905 and then continued with a major building campaign in
1911–1914, led by Nancy Langhorne of nearby
Mirador (see next entry), who married Waldorf
Astor in 1906 and later became Viscountess
Astor of Cliveden. The Washington, D.C., architect Waddy B. Wood transformed the modest
structure into a substantial building, drawing
upon details of several colonial churches, including Christ Church, Alexandria.

PI46 Mirador

c. 1832. c. 1920, William Adams Delano; gardens,
Charles Gillette. U.S. 250 (2 miles west of VA 690)

Originally built for James Bowen as a substantial Federal house, Mirador was purchased by
the Langhorne family in 1892. In the 1920s
Nancy Langhorne Astor's niece, Nancy Perkins,

and her husband, Ronald Tree, hired the New
York architect William Adams Delano. What
was already a large house received wings to either side, and the interiors were upgraded with
Georgian motifs. The house became one of the
showplaces of the Piedmont, especially during
the frequent visits of Nancy Astor and her sister,
Irene Langhorne Gibson, the prototype for the
Gibson Girl.

PI47 University of Virginia Research Park at North Fork

1996–present, Duany Plater-Zyberk, planners;
Mitchell/Matthews, architects; Gregg Bleam, landscape architect. Lewis and Clark Dr. (U.S. 29, 1.2
miles north of VA 649)

An attempt to create a neotraditional office/re-
search park, this 532-acre site has been laid out
by the nationally known firm that designed Seaside in Florida. The intention was a pedestrian-
conscious grouping of buildings that harmonize in style, materials, and form and that
imitate the downtowns of an earlier day. The
project's renderings show tree-lined streets with
awnings and shops on the ground floors of

buildings and even a steeple. Stylistically the buildings are postmodern Georgian or Jeffersonian Revival. Abundant architectural controls specify the size of brick, the type of bond (Flem- ish), the size of posts, the thickness of garden walls, and other items. To date only one building has been constructed. Whether this bold vision will be carried out remains to be seen.

Greene County (PI48–PI49)

PI48 Blue Ridge School

1910. VA 627, Dyke

Founded as the Blue Ridge Industrial School in 1910, this institution was a pioneering effort of the Episcopal Church to provide education to isolated communities in the Blue Ridge Mountains. Mountain children would be trained in the agricultural and industrial arts while receiving Christian education. Girls were the initial students. In 1915 boys were also admitted. Later, as the isolated character of the area receded, Blue Ridge became a private school. Its major buildings include the Bishop Robert A. Gibson Memorial Chapel (PI48.1) (1929–1932, Cram and Ferguson, with Stanislaw Makielski), constructed from uncut and uncoursed local fieldstone in a nominally Gothic idiom, with rose windows in the east and west facades and lancet windows along the sides. Ralph Adams Cram donated the design and Makielski, a Charlottesville architect and teacher at the university, supervised the construction. Much of the labor came from local workmen and from the students. Simplicity is the keynote of the Cram design. The building has been slowly decorated over the years. Immediately adjacent to the north of the chapel is the Martha Bagby Battle (formerly Headmaster's) House (PI48.2) (1931–1934, Stanislaw Makielski), constructed of native fieldstone and in an English Gothic Revival mode. Again, student and local workmen built the structure.

PI49 Stanardsville

U.S. 33

Stanardsville is a small rural village that gained minor prominence as the county seat when, in 1838, Greene County split off from Orange County. The major attraction is the Greene County Courthouse (1838, William B. Phillips and William Donoho; 1928, addition; 1979, restoration, Thomas R. Wyant, Jr.; Courthouse Square), presumably designed by Phillips, who did the brickwork for the builder of record, Donoho. The courthouse is a simple rectangular one-room Roman Revival structure with rather primitive woodwork of the Doric order. The contract price of $6,832 meant applied pilasters and no portico. In the 1920s, as part of the wave of Jeffersonian and "Old South" nostalgia that swept over the state, it received the four-column Tuscan portico, which improved its appearance. A gas explosion in 1979 badly damaged the structure, and it was restored and brought up to date. The other prominent landmark in town is the Lafayette Hotel (c. 1840; U.S. 30), prominently located on the village's major road and retaining its tiered porches. Of particular interest are the wide floor-to-ceiling doors that opened into the bar, on the ground floor at the west end. Those seeking a drink had ample access.

Charlottesville Metropolitan Area (CH)

C HARLOTTESVILLE, NAMED FOR QUEEN CHARLOTTE SOPHIA OF MECKLEN-
burg-Strelitz, wife of George III, is sited on a low plateau in central Albemarle
County. The Rivanna River, a major transportation route, lies to the southeast. The
city was platted in 1762 when the county seat of Albemarle County was moved from
Scottsville, a port along the James River. The site selected for the new county seat was along
the Three Notched Road, a colonial highway that connected Richmond to the Shenandoah
Valley. The courthouse, originally located outside the town, was the administrative center of
the county. The University of Virginia, established nearby in 1817, has had a profound impact on the development of the city. The railroad arrived in Charlottesville during the mid-
nineteenth century. Eventually two rail lines intersected near the center of the town and
spurred additional growth. The initial grid has been expanded many times, and the uneven
terrain has made for a confusing city plan. Over the years, contiguous but different centers
for government, commerce, residence, and education have developed.

Downtown Area (CH1–CH27)

Court Square

CH1 Albemarle County Courthouse

1803; many additions. 501 E. Jefferson St.

The square is dominated by the courthouse,
which began as a two-story Flemish bond brick
structure (now the north wing) with modillioned cornice and perhaps an arcaded porch
to the south, which has disappeared. The court-

house served several purposes, including a
place of worship for four religious denominations. Thomas Jefferson in 1822 described it as
a "common temple" where "all mix in society in
perfect harmony." William M. Pratt, an engineer who was the University of Virginia's first
superintendent of buildings and grounds, designed a new entrance wing (1859–1860) incor-

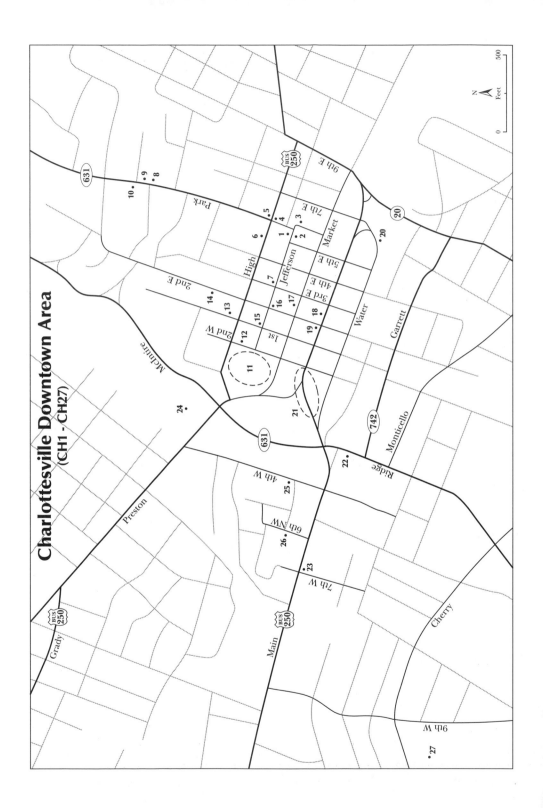

Charlottesville Downtown Area
(CH1 - CH27)

porating Gothic Revival details. Pratt placed his addition across the south end of the existing courthouse and stuccoed the entire structure. In 1875–1880 George W. Spooner, a local builder who sometimes acted as an architect, removed most of the Gothic touches and added the present Ionic portico. His work is evidence both of the incipient Colonial Revival and of the strong undercurrent of continuity with earlier Virginia architecture. In 1938 Milton Grigg with Floyd Johnson "restored" the courthouse and removed the yellow stucco finish and the remainder of Pratt's Gothic work. In front stands a Confederate monument, a statue of an infantryman (1909, American Bronze Co.) and, to the west, a mounted Stonewall Jackson (1921, Charles Keck). The Courthouse Annex (1939, Elmer Burrus), attached to the northwest, was a PWA project that fits in seamlessly.

CH2 **500 Court Square** (Hotel Monticello)

1924–1926, Stanhope Johnson of Johnson and Brannan

Now a condominium, the Hotel Monticello was one of Charlottesville's entries in the skyscraper-building mania of the age, and at twelve stories it dominated the city's skyline when it was completed. On the roof was what was reputed to be the world's largest skylight. The hotel's red brick exterior skin, limestone base, and white-painted wood trim paid homage to its namesake on the nearby hilltop. Intended as a luxury hotel, it had a particularly impressive lobby, and some of that original glamour can

still be spied through the doors. A regionally prominent architect based in nearby Lynchburg, Johnson was a versatile designer who worked in a variety of styles from Colonial Revival to Art Deco. He designed a number of important commissions in the Charlottesville area.

CH3 **Number 00 Court Square**

c. 1823

Along the east side of Court Square is a row of early nineteenth-century brick town houses, taverns, and law offices. The most notable, numbered 00, is a two-story, four-bay Flemish bond structure with pedimented end gables. It is typical of the mercantile duplexes once common in the area.

CH4 **Levy Opera House**

1851, 1857, 1888, 1980. 350 Park St. (corner of E. High St.)

A bold Greek Revival structure with four massive pilasters supporting the entablature of the facade, the Levy Opera House was built as the town hall, then converted into a theater in the 1880s by Jefferson Monroe Levy, who owned Monticello at the time. It is now an apartment building.

CH5 **Suntrust Bank**

1970, Jack M. Rinehart. 402 Park St.

The design is a nice contextual fit of a contemporary shed-roofed, abstract building. It maintains the street wall of buildings but opens into a pleasant interior courtyard.

CH6 City Courthouse

1962, Johnson, Craven and Gibson. 315–317 E. High St.

This two-story brick structure with a three-bay arcade and pediment is in these architects' usual Jeffersonian Revival mode.

CH7 Beth Israel Synagogue

1882, attributed to George W. Spooner. 1995–1996, addition, Bruce R. Wardell. 301 East Jefferson St.

The synagogue is a brick building in the Gothic Revival style, unusual for Charlottesville. The recent addition is handled with sympathetic care.

Park Street

Running north from Court Square is Park Street, which in the late nineteenth century was Charlottesville's lone "great street," or center of conspicuous consumption. Charlottesville was not a particularly wealthy community until the twentieth century and hence it lacks large, impressive Victorian houses.

CH8 Duke House

c. 1884. 616 Park St.

The Duke House is an asymmetrical frame Queen Anne house with complex massing. The front veranda, which is supported by turned columns, terminates at a small gazebo at the south end.

CH9 Marshall-Rocker House

1894, William T. Vandergrift. 1930, addition. 620 Park St.

The grandest house on Park Street blends a Romanesque Revival arcade, Queen Anne massing, and a Colonial Revival porch into a harmonious composition. Vandergrift ran a construction company in town and probably got the plans from George Barber or another plan company.

Built for Carrie and James Marshall, the house was sold in 1913 to wealthy philanthropist William J. Rucker, who added the south wing in 1930.

CH10 Hulfish Residence

1902, Thomas A. Mullett. 625 Park St.

The Hulfish residence is of interest not only for its delicate combination of Renaissance and Colonial Revival motifs and its light tan brick facade, but also because of its architect. Thomas Mullett of Washington, D.C., was the son and the successor in practice of Alfred B. Mullett, who had designed the State, War and Navy Building (now the old Executive Office Building) in Washington and many federal courthouses, customhouses, and post offices throughout the nation.

Market Street Area

Although the market for which it is named is long departed, Market Street and its immediate area contain some of downtown's most impressive buildings.

CH11 McGuffey Art Center (McGuffey School)

1915–1916, Ferguson, Calrow, and Taylor. 201 2nd St. NW (corner of Market St.)

This suitably impressive Colonial Revival school building is named for the famous author of the series of school readers, who taught at the university. The lead designer of the building, R. E. Lee Taylor, practiced in Norfolk but did a great deal of work in Charlottesville. In the early 1970s it was converted into artists' studios and galleries, which are open to the public.

The group of linked, pitched-roofed contemporary town houses on the hill behind are the McGuffey Hill Condominiums (1981, Frank Folsom Smith), 203–311 2nd Street NW, designed by one of the members of the Sarasota (Florida) School who was a former partner of Paul Rudolph.

CH12 Christ Episcopal Church

1895–1898, McDonald Brothers. 120 W. High St.

Christ Episcopal Church is on the site of an earlier brick church (c. 1824), sometimes attributed to Jefferson, although his authorship remains unclear. Remains of the earlier foundations are in the present church's basement. A Greek Revival portico (similar to that of St. Thomas, Orange) was added to Christ Church in the 1850s. The portico is known only through photographs taken c. 1870. By the 1890s the congregation wanted a new building. The present structure was designed by the Louisville (Kentucky) architect Harry P. McDonald, who had an association with the local builder, Spooner Construction Company. It is an unscholarly Gothic Revival structure, awkwardly massed, of forbidding gray granite. The interior, with its hammer-beam roof and several Tiffany Studio windows (c. 1904), is impressive.

CH13 Vickery House

1995, Robert Vickery. 430 N. 1st St.

This excellent example of a modern infill house blends in seamlessly. It is designed on a square plan and has sculptural side elevations.

CH14 Van Groll House

CH14 Van Groll House

1990, James Tulley. 517 2nd Street NE

The very modern Van Groll House is International Style, or, more specifically, De Stijl, in its massing. The owner has a significant collection of De Stijl furniture. Tulley, who taught at the university from 1968 to 1994, was perhaps the most accomplished modernist to practice in central Virginia. He designed a number of important houses, most of which are inaccessible; hence this is a chance to view a real masterpiece.

CH15 First United Methodist Church

1923–1924, Joseph Hudnut. 101 E. Jefferson St. (northeast corner of 1st St.)

First United Methodist illuminates the early work of one of American modernism's greatest apostles. Joseph Hudnut briefly headed the architecture school at the University of Virginia, before assuming academic posts at Columbia and then Harvard. As dean at Harvard, he brought Walter Gropius to this country; the rest is history. But before his conversion to modernism, Hudnut was a competent academic architect who drew upon James Gibbs, as shown in this masterful composition, which hugs the street corner with its broad flight of steps.

CH16 Albemarle Historical Society
(McIntire Public Library)

1919–1922, Walter Dabney Blair. 200 2nd St. NE

This elegant brick building on the east side of Lee Park is marked by a semicircular portico carried on columns with monolithic marble shafts. Flanking niches with urns honoring Homer and Dante give a clue to the building's original function. It was the gift of wealthy Charlottesville native and philanthropist Paul McIntire, who funded numerous projects throughout the city, including the equestrian statue of Robert E. Lee (1924, Henry M. Shrady, finished by Leo Lentelli) across the way in Lee Park. Walter Dabney Blair, who designed the structure and participated in buildings at the university, studied architecture at the University of Pennsylvania and the Ecole des Beaux-Arts.

CH17 Jefferson-Madison Regional Library
(U.S. Post Office and Courthouse)

1904, 1908, James Knox Taylor, Supervising Architect, U.S. Treasury Department. 1936, Louis A. Simon, Supervising Architect, U.S. Treasury Department. 1979–1981, conversion, Jack M. Rinehart and Williams and Tazewell. 201 E. Market St.

Exemplifying the classicism that Taylor endorsed, the former Charlottesville post office was originally a seven-bay building with a trabeated Ionic portico. In 1936 Simon's office expanded the structure to the present fifteen bays and relocated the portico, topped by a new pediment, to the center of the structure, creating a daunting facade that takes up one side of a city block. In the mid-1970s the post office and courts relocated, and the building was converted into a library. The new library retains nothing of the original interior.

Main Street (Mall) and Water Street

A portion of Main Street is the Mall (1972–1975, Lawrence Halprin), a concept which has proven successful in Charlottesville, in spite of problems with it elsewhere. The large department stores have departed for the greener pastures of suburban malls and shopping centers, but smaller stores have survived and prospered. Halprin worked in cooperation with local officials. Most of the older buildings lining Main Street are appropriate background structures and have extensively remodeled ground floors.

  Water Street, which parallels Main Street to the south, was the more industrial side of town and contains a series of large mid- and late-nineteenth-century warehouses. The 200 and 300 blocks are taken up by an impressive parking garage (1991, VMDO Architects).

CH18 Paramount Theater

1931, Rapp and Rapp. 215 E. Main St.

The Paramount, designed by well-known Chicago theater architects, has classical detailing on its high, partially false facade, an indication that, here in the land of Jefferson and the Colonial Revival, Art Deco was a hard sell, even for theaters. The murals inside the octagonal auditorium continue the "colonial" theme. Competition from less expensive theaters at shopping malls, beginning in the 1960s, forced its closure, and it awaits restoration.

CH19 Wachovia Bank (National Bank of Charlottesville)

1919–1920, Marsh and Peter; 1998–2000, remodeling and restoration, Train and Spencer. 123 E. Main St.

Washington, D.C., architects who specialized in banks designed one of the earliest high rises in town. The classical dress on the two-story base is a familiar formula for banks of the period. Classical detailing on a building of a decidedly non-antique type was meant to draw a connection between the stability of the government, whose contemporary buildings often came clad in similar garb, and that of the institution. The neoclassical limestone base supports a brick shaft, originally crowned by an elaborate Italian Renaissance cornice that was removed but has been restored.

CH20 C&O Railway Station

1904–1905, Wilson, Harris and Richards. 1990, renovations and addition, Randorn, Wildman, Krause, and Brezinski. 600 E. Water St.

The station served one of the two railroad lines that cross at Charlottesville, the east-west car-

Main Street Mall

rier, the Chesapeake & Ohio. It replaced a c. 1880 wooden Stick Style building; it succeeded two earlier stations, one built c. 1865 and the first one, from c. 1850, which was burned under Union general Sheridan's occupation of Charlottesville during the Civil War. Initially, the C&O intended to build a Richardsonian Romanesque station in Charlottesville, but then, to give a new look to an important station, decided to go outside the company and hired the prolific Philadelphia firm of Wilson, Harris and Richards, which specialized in railroad stations. The Charlottesville station was the progenitor of eight Colonial Revival C&O stations built over the next twenty years.

The two-story brick building with its large Ionic-columned portico was intended as the gateway to Charlottesville, the classical detailing foreshadowing for the traveler the dominant architectural idiom of the city and the university beyond. The interior spaces were divided into white men's and women's sections, and then a smaller room for black passengers. Rail passenger traffic declined after World War I, and the passenger station finally closed in 1982. The renovated structure reopened in 1990 as an office building. To the west of the main block of the structure, new bay windows step around the cast iron columns of the former station canopy.

West Main Street from Ridge Street to 7th Street and Surrounding Area

This part of Charlottesville has seen major changes in recent years. Originally, it was the city's prominent African American residential area; however, urban renewal in the 1960s wiped out a significant portion of the housing on Vinegar Hill, northeast of the current intersection of Main and Ridge. The area does retain some significant African American landmarks.

CH21 200 Block of West Main Street

A group of undistinguished modern buildings that replaced houses in the former Vinegar Hill neighborhood illustrates the problem of civic design. At the east end sits the minimalist and atrocious Omni Hotel (c. 1980, Smallwood, Reynolds, Stewart, and Stewart), 235 West Main Street, designed by a firm from Atlanta. Next door is the U.S. Courthouse and Federal Building (1982, Romweber Bornhorst), 255 West Main Street, which amply demonstrates the low level to which federal design sank in the 1980s. Designed by a Cleveland firm, it was developed as a speculative office building, which the government leases. The building has no redeeming qualities. Across from the courthouse is the awkward postmodern Lewis Clark Apartments (1990, VMDO), 250 West Main Street. Near the center of the intersection is the Lewis and Clark Monument (1919, Charles Keck), a sculptural grouping in which Sacajawea appears to crouch behind the explorers.

CH22 Mount Zion Baptist Church

1883–1884, attributed to George W. Spooner and/or George A. Sinclair, builder. Later alterations. 105 Ridge St.

Mount Zion Baptist Church played a central role in the formation of Charlottesville's African American community in the period after the Civil War. A group of former slaves established the congregation in 1867. The 1883–1884 brick structure replaced an earlier (c. 1875) frame church on the same site. Local lore holds that Spooner, a Charlottesville architect, designed the structure. In the Italianate idiom popular with Baptists after the Civil War, the church is relatively plain on the exterior with a dominant entrance tower and steeple and corbeled brick detailing at the eaves and in recessed panels on the tower. The interior is a large three-aisle space with galleries on three sides and some stock colored glass windows.

CH23 First Baptist Church (Delevan and First Colored Baptist Church)

1877–c. 1883, attributed to George A. Sinclair. 632 W. Main St. (southeast corner of 7th St.)

First Baptist traces its lineage back to an 1863 petition by members of the African American community to separate from the white-run First Baptist Church. The petition was granted, and by 1877 they had a building underway at this site. Sinclair apparently built the structure, but his role in the design is controversial. His ethnicity is unknown, but he is associated with all three African American Baptist churches in this area. The appearance of First Baptist is so similar to Mount Zion Baptist Church as to suggest the same hand. Also a large Italianate brick structure with a prominent entrance tower, First Baptist has a different cupola and finial-capped pier buttresses at the front. The interior is divided into two aisles rather than three, but it has a similar gallery arrangement. The colored glass windows appear to be from the same supplier as those of Mount Zion.

CH24 Albemarle County Office Building (Lane High School)

1939–1940, Pendleton Scott Clark. 401 McIntire Rd.

Lynchburg architect Clark designed Lane High School for the white student population. The large Georgian Revival building with the colossal pedimented portico was funded in part by a Public Works Administration grant. This imposing structure, sited at a prominent crossroads and across from the black Vinegar Hill housing area, certainly underlined the dominance of whites in segregated Virginia in those years. After the opening of Charlottesville High School in 1974, the high school was reworked to become the Albemarle County Office Building, which opened in 1981.

CH25 Charlottesville Public School Building (Thomas Jefferson High School, renamed George Washington Carver School)

1926, Calrow and Wrenn. 1938, addition, Stainback and Brown. Later additions. 201 4th Street NW

Originally the "colored" high school for the city, this red brick, white-trimmed building tucked away on a side street is more modest than the nearby white high school and follows the standard form set by the Division of School Buildings, Virginia State Department of Education.

CH26 Ebenezer Baptist Church

1908, John Anderson Lankford. 113 6th Street NW

The congregation split off from Mount Zion and c. 1884 constructed a building on this site to which Sinclair's name has been attached.

CH26 Ebenezer Baptist Church

That structure burned in 1907. The present church is a red brick Gothic Revival structure with a wide nave, pointed-arched windows, strip buttresses, and an attached tower on the south side. The interior follows the Baptist format of a large space with focus upon the pulpit. Lankford, one of the first professional black architects in the United States, was considered the dean of African American architects at the time of his death. Although the Washington, D.C.–based designer's work covered a wide range of building types, most of his projects were ecclesiastical. In 1908, Lankford was named supervising architect for the A.M.E. Church and, in that capacity, designed churches in a number of cities in the United States, including Virginia, and even abroad.

CH27 Oak Lawn (Bramham-Fife House)

1824. 501 9th St.

Although no specific builder has been tied to the house, William Phillips, James Dinsmore, and John Neilson have each been suggested as the individual responsible for design and construction. The house is a three-part Neo-Palladian Jeffersonian structure. The pedimented central section, with a Tuscan portico, is flanked by lower symmetrical wings. Built for Nimrod Bramham, who served in the Virginia House of Delegates, it passed to the Reverend James Fife, an important figure in the Baptist General Convention.

University of Virginia Campus   (CH28–CH32)

Thomas Jefferson proposed a state-supported university during his term as governor in 1779 and repeatedly returned to the subject over the following decades. Not until after his presidency (1801–1809) did he accomplish the goal. Beginning with a scheme for an Albemarle Academy in 1814, Jefferson and his political cohorts maneuvered the state legislature into establishing Central College in 1817. In 1819 the college was renamed the University of Virginia. Jefferson's design was constructed between 1817 and 1826. What began as a small school for several hundred young men on 196 acres is now a sprawling campus for 18,000 students on about 1,065 acres. The development of the university displays evolving American attitudes toward space, planning, and architecture. In addition to Jefferson, many others, including McKim, Mead and White, Robert A. M. Stern, Pietro Belluschi, and regionally important figures, have designed for the university. The tour is divided into five parts.

CH28 University of Virginia: Academical Village and Central Grounds

Jefferson's original campus, the Academical Village (CH28.1; 1817–1826; many later additions, remodelings, and restorations), surrounds the space known as the Lawn and comprises the Rotunda, the pavilions, dormitories, and ranges. Ground was broken on "a poor old turned out field" west of the small town of Charlottesville on October 6, 1817. Jefferson selected the site atop a small ridge, which was subsequently leveled into terraces. The site caused Jefferson to modify an earlier (1814) scheme (a vast U-shaped plan nearly 300 yards across with three pavilions to a side) into a plan with two parallel rows 250 feet apart consisting of five pavilions on each side. From the begin-

ning Jefferson intended that professors would live on the upper floors of the pavilions and give instruction on the ground floor. Between the pavilions, fronted by a Tuscan colonnade, lay dormitory rooms for the students, who were originally housed two in a room. The concept of a large central building serving as a library was added in 1817. Jefferson wanted to create an "academical village" where the students would live near their professors and their classes and would be shielded from worldly temptations. Although the concept was largely Jefferson's, he requested advice from William Thornton and Benjamin Henry Latrobe. Thornton's hand is discernible in the facade of Pavilion VII, and Latrobe influenced the Rotunda and several of the pavilions. He recommended the giant orders, and the facades of

CH28 University of Virginia, the Lawn

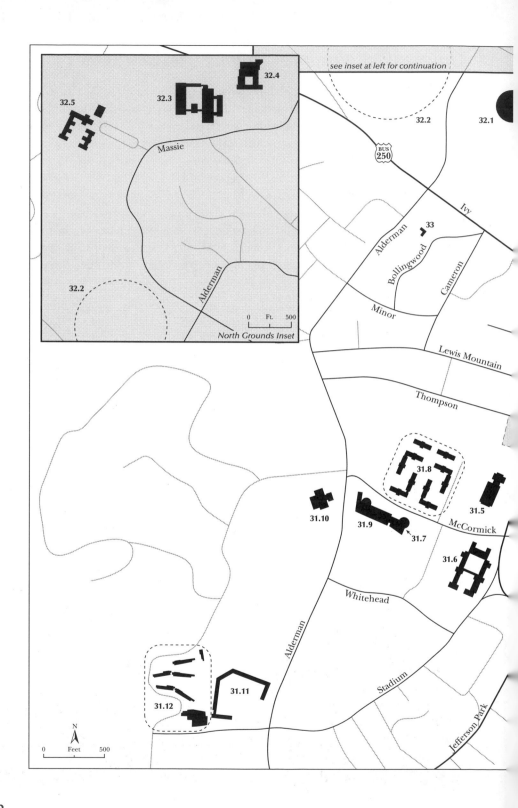

see inset at left for continuation

32.4

32.3

32.5

32.2

32.1

Massie

BUS 250

Ivy

Alderman

Bollingwood

Cameron

33

Minor

Lewis Mountain

Thompson

Alderman

32.2

0   Ft.   500

North Grounds Inset

31.8

31.5

31.10

31.9

31.7

McCormick

31.6

Whitehead

Alderman

Stadium

Jefferson Park

31.11

31.12

N

0   Feet   500

Massie

BUS 29

Emmet

35

Rugby

34

Grady

BUS 250

30.13

30.12

31.3

Carr's Hill

30.11

Sprigg

30.9

University

30.6

30.10

30.8

30.7

30.5

30.4

30.2

30.3

31.1

14th

Newcomb

30.1

28.18

28.17

28.19

28.3

29.1

31.4

31.2

28.16

28.2

28.15

28.14

28.12

29.2

28.1

28.13

Hospital

29.5

28.7

Main

28.9

28.10

28.5

29.6

29.3

29.7

29.4

28.11

28.4

28.8

28.6

Jefferson Park

BUS 250

11th

BUS 29

Lee

Lane

29.8

University of Virginia
(CH28 - CH35)

pavilions III and V closely follow his concepts. Pavilion IX is apparently his design—or at least Jefferson so noted it on his drawing.

The details of the facade of each pavilion represent different antique models found in two books Jefferson consulted, Giacomo Le-oni's *The Architecture of A. Palladio* (1742) and Roland Fréart de Chambray and Charles-Edouard Errard's *Parallèle de l'Architecture Antique avec la Moderne* (1766). Jefferson explained that the pavilions should "be models of good taste and good architecture, & of a variety of appearance, no two alike, so as to serve as specimens for the architectural lectures." The pavilions' orders and sources are: (I) Doric of Diocletian's Baths, Rome, from Chambray; (II) Ionic of the Temple of Fortuna Virilis, Rome, from Palladio; (III) Corinthian from Palladio; (IV) Doric of Albano, from Chambray (though Jefferson added a base); (V) Ionic from Palladio; (VI) Ionic of the Theater of Marcellus, Rome, from Chambray; (VII) Doric from Palladio; (VIII) Corinthian of Diocletian's Baths, Rome, from Chambray; (IX) Ionic of the Temple of Fortuna Virilis, Rome, from Palladio (originally Jefferson intended Tuscan, but altered it in construction); (X) Doric of the Theater of Marcellus, Rome, from Chambray. For the Rotunda (inspired by Latrobe's suggestion and by drawings that have been lost), Jefferson turned to the Pantheon in Rome as shown in Palladio, and, as he explained, changed the scale: "The diameter of the building 77 feet, being ½ of the Pantheon, consequently ¼A, area, H ⅛ volume." Jefferson specified a wooden truss for the dome, derived from Philibert Delorme's book *Nouvelles Inventions* (1561). The upper floor was the library, and the lower floors were for classes. Jefferson also noted that chapel services could be accommodated in the Rotunda.

Additional student housing was provided in the outer ranges, which were articulated by arcades and had larger structures—called hotels—at the ends to serve as centers for eating. Gardens separated the pavilions and ranges and were enclosed by curving—or serpentine—brick walls. In 1952 and 1965, with funds provided by the Garden Club of Virginia, the west garden walls were restored and "colonial"-type gardens created after designs by Alden Hopkins. In 1965 the Garden Club paid for the east garden walls and gardens designed by Donald E. Parker and Ralph E. Griswold.

Jefferson produced most of the drawings for the project, though John Neilson assisted him in an attempt to produce prints that could be sold to raise funds. Neilson drew the widely reproduced "Maverick Plan" (named for the engraver), c. 1822, and many of the drawings that for years were attributed to Jefferson's granddaughter, Cornelia Jefferson Randolph. Recent research indicates that Neilson was the author. The university was one of the largest single projects undertaken up to that point in the United States, under construction from 1817 to 1826. Jefferson supervised the initial stages of construction, but he found the task too much for his age, and ultimately a "proctor" was hired to oversee the project. Jefferson also designed the curriculum and selected the library and the faculty.

Jefferson intended that the entrance to the complex be at the south, or open, end, with an approach up the central space toward the Rotunda. The trees that line the space were initially planted c. 1830 and have been replaced many times. Whether Jefferson intended the trees is hotly debated; several of his early schemes indicate grass and trees, and the university did purchase live trees before his death. Since the early 1980s the university has embarked on an ambitious restoration program for the Lawn (J. Murray Howard, restoration architect). Pavilions VIII and X display Jefferson's original tin roofing.

Robert Mills designed the Annex, constructed on the north side of the Rotunda in 1853; it was destroyed in the fire of 1895. Brooks Hall (CH28.2) (1876–1877, John R. Thomas), to the east of the Rotunda, is a Second Empire structure with carved animal heads (including a tapir!), which originally housed a natural history museum. The names and heads on the building represent a theory of natural history, a radical concept for a southern school in the 1870s and probably not understood. (Thomas came from Rochester, New York.)

Brooks Hall is balanced to the west of the Rotunda by the Gothic Revival University Chapel (CH28.3) (1884–1890, Charles E. Cassell). J. & R. Lamb and Sons provided most of the opalescent window glass for the chapel, except for the mandorla in the east transept, which is by Tiffany Studios (c. 1905). The chapel attempted to answer the charge of heathenism at the university, since Jefferson had specified no chapel. The location of the chapel and Brooks Hall along the sides of the Rotunda and adjacent to the major east-west road indicate that most people approached the university from

CH28.1 Academical Village, Pavilion IX

CH28.2 Brooks Hall, drawing by John R. Thomas

the north end and not from the south as Jefferson had envisioned.

The Rotunda and Mills's Annex were consumed by fire in 1895, and the subsequent rebuilding, under the direction of Stanford White, of McKim, Mead and White of New York, reoriented the campus. Directed by the university's Board of Visitors, Stanford White added a new entrance portico and terrace to the north front of the Rotunda, along with additional wings duplicating Jefferson's original on the south side. Although White otherwise respected Jefferson's form on the exterior, his Rotunda interior differed markedly from Jefferson's. White created a vast, two-story central library space that looked back to Jefferson's original model of the Pantheon. The intention was that the visitor enter at the north portico into the library and then exit by the south portico onto the Lawn. The library was removed in 1939, and what to do with the building, the campus's major architectural element and symbol, has remained a problem since. A Jefferson-inspired interior, designed by Ballou and Justice of Richmond with Frederick Doveton Nichols, architectural history professor at the university as advisor, was installed in 1973–1976.

White designed the buildings closing the south end of the Lawn: Cabell, Rouse, and Cocke halls (CH28.4–CH28.6; 1896–1898). The controversial siting of the buildings, which closed off the vista, was directed by the Board of Visitors. These structures buffered the campus from an African American neighborhood

below and were part of White's plan for future expansion. Cabell Hall, with its pediment sculpture by George Zolnay, occupies the center of the new group, and its semicircular auditorium, with a large mural by George W. Breck after Raphael's *School of Athens*, echoes the shape of the Rotunda at the head of the Lawn. White initially participated in the design of Garrett Hall (University Commons) (CH28.7) (1906–1908), but after his death in 1906, his New York office redesigned it. All of the sculptures in the Lawn area were installed in 1919 during a wave of campus beautification. They include Moses Ezekiel's Homer (1907); Karl Bitter's seated Jefferson (1916), which is a reduced version of a larger one in St. Louis; a copy of Jean Antoine Houdon's Washington (1913); and, on the Rotunda's north terrace, Ezekiel's Jefferson (1910), showing him perched on top of the Liberty Bell.

Subsequent buildings on the central grounds in general respect the palette of red brick with white trim and the neo-Jeffersonian Roman classicism, which is more popularly called Colonial Revival, even though Jefferson was hardly colonial. Randall Hall (CH28.8) (1898–1899, Paul J. Pelz), originally a dormitory and now the history department, by the architect of the Library of Congress, and Minor Hall (CH28.9) (1908–1911, John Kevan Peebles), on opposite sides of White's south Lawn buildings, follow his scheme for expansion, with lateral extensions to the east and west. Boston landscape architect Warren Manning worked at the university between 1908

CH28.9 Minor Hall

CH28.14 Monroe Hall, extension

CH28.18 Special Collections Library,
Drawing by Hartman-Cox Architects

and 1913 and provided a new plan in 1913. Peebles, a Norfolk architect and University of Virginia alumnus, became the favored architect for the first three decades of the twentieth century, serving as a member of an "architectural advisory board." The board designed many university structures, such as Clark Hall (CH28.9) (1930–1932, Peebles with Walter Dabney Blair, Edmund S. Campbell, and R. E. Lee Taylor), which contains murals by Allyn Cox. Now the Environmental Sciences Department, it features a mammoth portico that announces that the building originally housed the law school. Fiske Kimball, who had a reputation as a Jefferson scholar, came to the university in 1919 to head the new department of fine arts, which principally included an architecture school. Kimball, following an earlier suggestion of Manning, designed the McIntire Amphitheater (CH28.10) (1920–1921), which is an expression of an American mania of the 1910s and 1920s for outdoor theaters of the ancient Greek type.

To the south, looming over the amphitheater, is a recent interpretation of Jefferson, the postmodernist Bryan Hall (CH28.11) (1987–1995, Michael Graves). Graves's building provided an important cross-campus link. The columns of his Tuscan colonnade resemble milk bottles. Edmund S. Campbell, the head of the architecture department from 1928 to 1950, took the lead after Kimball's departure as the university architect and, in association with Peebles and others, guided the university's development in the 1930s and 1940s, maintaining the red brick and white trim imagery. The Monroe Hill Dormitories (CH28.12) (1928–1929, Campbell, Peebles, Blair, and Taylor) form a series of small courtyards. Next door is the oldest building on the campus, Monroe Hill House (CH28.13) (c. 1790 and c. 1840), which James Monroe owned before Jefferson selected the site for the university. The arcaded wing was added to provide additional housing for students.

To the immediate north stands Monroe Hall (CH28.14) (1929–1930, Peebles, Blair, Campbell and Taylor; 1984–1987, extension, Hartman-Cox). Originally Monroe Hall's main entrance was to the south, but Hartman-Cox of Washington, D.C., was employed to extend the building to the north and provide a fitting facade to join the other grand porticoes on a large "secondary lawn" that had grown up in the twentieth century. The Hartman-Cox addition is one of the best recent works at the university. Next to Monroe Hall to the north is the giant portico of Peabody Hall (CH28.15) (1912–1914, Ferguson, Calrow, and Taylor), which originally served as the School of Education. Behind Peabody is the student union, Newcomb Hall (CH28.16) (1952–1958, Eggers and Higgins; later renovations), a surprisingly awkward structure by this well-known New York firm.

The inherent problems of adding to a circular library and the university's expansion brought about a new structure, Alderman Library (CH28.17) (1936–1938, R. E. Lee Taylor and D. K. Este Fisher, Jr.; later additions), to the west of the Rotunda and north of Peabody Hall. Designed to be the new centerpiece to the university, it had the appropriate grand colonnade and great entry space. Alderman Library's construction led to the demolition of Jefferson's last design for the university, the Anatomical Theater, 1826, which originally stood in front.

Plans call for construction of a new Special Collections Library (CH28.18) (2001, Hartman-Cox) next to Alderman on the site of Miller Hall (to be demolished). The entrance pavilion draws upon Jefferson's Anatomical Theater and Charles McKim's Pierpont Morgan Library, New York (1906). Most of the library, however, will be underground. Behind is the undergraduate Clemons Library (CH28.19) (1979–1982, TAC), for which Norman Fletcher acted as lead architect. This is the only modernist intrusion on the central grounds, rendered in red brick and hidden in the hillside.

The university's central grounds encompass over 180 years of architecture and many diverse trends. The use of open space and landscaping has also changed dramatically over that time. Jefferson's original design for the Lawn still remains the central focus, and the various additions illuminate both its genius and the problems of adding to such a dominant design. Although it is fashionable to diminish all the subsequent work, the fact remains that Jefferson designed for a select community of about ten professors and several hundred students. The subsequent additions respect the original but also, in their own way, create a number of wonderful spaces.

CH29 University of Virginia: The Corner and Health Sciences Center Complex

"The Corner," or the area where present-day U.S. Business 250, or West Main Street, turns into University Avenue, was very early a commercial center for the university community. The road has always been a major east-west highway. James Dinsmore, one of Jefferson's builders, was one of its first developers. Along the north side at The Corner stands Saint Paul's Episcopal Church (CH29.1) (1925–1927, Eugene Bradbury), 1700 University Avenue), whose giant portico rather pompously relates to Jefferson and White across the street. Bradbury submitted a more humble design loosely based on Bruton Parish Church in Williamsburg, with a small entrance tower, but Saint Paul's vestry demanded grandeur. The luminous box of the interior recalls the work of Charles Bulfinch. Farther east, the Anderson Brothers' Bookstore (CH29.2) (1891, J. K. Mesker Co. of St. Louis), 1419 University Avenue, with its pressed metal facade, is the most distinguished commercial building. Several blocks to the east is the University Baptist Church (CH29.3) (1928, Herbert Levi Cain),

1223 West Main Street, whose vestry were not to be outdone by the Episcopalians up the street: they created their own giant portico, which in this case marks another important intersection. Still farther east, Stacey Hall and the MRI Facility (originally Sears, Roebuck) (CH29.4) (1957, Stevens and Wilkinson; later alterations), 1105 West Main Street, represent the decade of the 1950s, when shopping centers were still located inside towns. Designed by Atlanta architects who adopted Ludwig Mies van der Rohe's IIT idiom, it is Charlottesville's only example, and one of the few in Virginia, of Miesian architecture. The university has carefully enhanced the complex's Miesian character.

Back to the west and across from the Corner, on the south side stand the Senff Entrance Gates (CH29.5) (1914–1915, Henry Bacon), by the designer of the Lincoln Memorial, which provide a terminus to West Main Street. Although such gating and enclosing fencing was a common collegiate feature of those years, Bacon's gates indicate a continuing problem with entrance to the university. To the south of the gates (and east of the Jefferson precinct) lies the Health Sciences or Medical School–Hospital Center, a vast, labyrinthine maze created by many building campaigns and architects. Notable buildings include the Entrance Building (CH29.6) (1912–1914, Eugene Bradbury), in, of course, a very refined colonial-Jeffersonian idiom. But the dominant element is the Medical School Building (CH29.7) (1929, Coolidge, Shepley, Bulfinch and Abbott), its vast portico entrance looming over everything. The original hospital wing (1899–1901, Paul J. Pelz and many others) is around the corner to the west, but it is hidden by later additions. Behind this giant complex is an even larger one to the east, on Lee Street, visible from all over town, the high-rise University Hospital (CH29.8) (1987–1991, Metcalf, Davis, Brody and Partners with Russo and Sonder; later additions) and associated buildings. The main hospital building, with its simple form and sleek skin of white enamel panels and glazing, resembling minimalist sculpture, is an alien intruder from New York.

CH30 University of Virginia: North of University Avenue and along Rugby Road

Rugby Road runs north from the Jefferson precinct. This area contained boardinghouses in the nineteenth century and began to be de-

CH29.4 Stacey Hall and MRI Facility

veloped by the university and associated activities in the 1890s. North, directly across University Avenue from the Rotunda and obsequiously bowing with its portico, is Madison Hall (originally the YMCA) (CH30.1) (1904–1905, Parish and Schroeder), now the hall of power, the main administration building. The architects were from New York and specialized in education buildings. The university had the first campus YMCA in the country, built in 1858. The building is refined Jefferson Revival. On the hill west along Rugby Road sits Carr's Hill (CH30.2) (1906–1909, McKim, Mead and White), or the President's House, on which Stanford White began work before his death. His firm substantially redesigned it following some suggestions by the wife of the university's first president, Edwin A. Alderman. (Until 1904 the university was run by a chair of the faculty and the rector of the Board of Visitors; however, the chaos resulting from rebuilding after the fire of 1895 brought about the concept of a "strong" university president.) Its giant portico became one of the paradigms for the distinctively southern version of the Colonial Revival. Next on Rugby Road comes Fayerweather Hall (CH30.3) (1892–1893, Carpenter and Peebles), which was originally a gymnasium and now serves the art department. This building, largely designed by Peebles, a university alumnus who practiced in Norfolk, reintroduced Jeffersonian Roman classicism to the university with its Corinthian columned portico. This is an early essay by Peebles and tentative. The overall articulated form is more Victorian, but it helped set the stage for McKim, Mead and White's work, since, reputedly, Peebles urged the university administration to hire them after the great fire of 1895. The Bayly Museum (CH30.4) (1933–1935, Edmund S. Campbell and R. E. Lee Taylor), next on Rugby Road, has a gigantic Palladian/Serliana motif as the entrance. The Bayly collection contains some notable art. Rugby Road is also fraternity house heaven; the houses can be seen along it and on Madison Lane, across the large depression of athletic playing fields known as "Mad (Madison) Bowl." The most important fraternities architecturally are the harmonious group of Colonial Revival houses that create the quadrangle just north of the Bayly Museum: Chi Phi (CH30.5) (1922, Eugene Bradbury), 161 Rugby Road; Delta Tau Delta (CH30.6) (1911, Ludlow and Peabody), 163 Rugby Road; and Kappa Sigma (CH30.7) (1908–1911, James L. Burley), 165 Rugby Road. Warren Manning planned the layout.

Accessible off Rugby Road on Bayly Drive, behind the fraternity group and the Bayly Museum, is the so-called Fine Arts Center. A product of the intense growth of the university in the 1960s, the concept, not fully realized at the time, was to locate all the fine arts facilities in one precinct. A 1999 proposal would add more buildings and relocate the music department to the area. The siting of the complex resulted from a master plan (1965), by Sasaki, Dawson, DeMay of Cambridge, Massachusetts, that tried to envision the university's growth. Components actually built include the School of Architecture (Campbell Hall) and the Fiske Kimball Fine Arts Library (CH30.8) (1965–1970, Sasaki, Dawson, DeMay with Pietro Belluschi and Rawlings and Wilson). Kenneth DeMay acted as the principal designer, and Belluschi (then architecture dean at MIT) was the design consultant. Rawlings and Wilson, of Richmond, was the local firm (required by all state contracts at that time). Belluschi and DeMay's design is an attempt to abstract some of the modular elements of Jefferson's Lawn—hence the large suspended glass bays—and to use the red and white palette, here translated into red brick and white concrete. Very Bauhaus with a bridge linking the two buildings, the "A school" has on its upper floors the loft spaces loved by architects. The major problem with the building is . . . Where is the entrance? An addition to the complex is currently under consideration. The drama building, Culbreth and Helms Theatres (CH30.9) (1970–1974, Rawlings, Wilson and Fraher) down the hill picks up on the Belluschi and DeMay palette of materials.

The Zeta Psi Fraternity (CH30.10) (1926, Louis F. Voorhees), 169 Rugby Road, reproduces the entrance front of Monticello. Voorhees taught briefly at the architecture school before setting up practice in High Point, North Carolina. Just past the bridge, at 190 Rugby Road, is Westminster Presbyterian Church (CH30.11) (1939, Marshall Wells), which draws upon the venerable Abingdon Church, Gloucester County, for its sanctuary and carries it off quite convincingly. Across the street are the Rugby Faculty Apartments (CH30.12) (1919–1922, Fiske Kimball), 203 Rugby Road which were built on top of foundations intended for an athletic clubhouse. Kimball was hampered by the preexisting footprint, and the result is rather bland. Immediately behind the apartments are the extraordinary colonnades of Lambeth Field (CH30.13) (1911–1913, R. E. Lee Taylor), which marked the university's entry into big-time athletics. Now in very sad shape, they still resonate with a Greco-Roman grandeur, a perfect setting for an Alma-Tadema painting.

CH31 University of Virginia: Emmett Street, McCormick Road, Alderman Road, and Western Expansion

Hindered by the residential area that grew up to the north along Rugby Road and by the city of Charlottesville to the east, since the 1920s the university has expanded mostly to the west. Jefferson had originally purchased portions of this land, and over the years it served as the site of professors' gardens, an experimental farm, a golf course, and other uses. Along present-day Emmett Street flowed a creek that had to be controlled to enable any major building. By 1920 the creek was tamed by a culvert and building could begin. The major structure of interest along Emmet Street is the vast, Roman-baths-inspired Memorial Gymnasium (CH31.1) (1921–1924, Kimball, Blair, Taylor, Peebles, and Lambeth), on which Kimball reputedly took the lead as supervising architect. Kimball's favorite contemporary architects were McKim, Mead and White. Obviously the scale of their work and their use of historical references influenced the design. Still, Kimball lacked their skill at integration, and although the central section with the great Roman bath windows is impressive, the end sections appear tacked on. Next to Memorial Gymnasium is the extremely misguided Parking Garage and Bookstore

(CH31.2) (1989–1994, Walker Parking Consultants and Engineers with Mariani and Associates), known locally as "the Monster." Parking engineers acted as the primary designers, leading to the unfortunate results. The Colonial Revival idiom simply cannot cover up the scale. Across is the short street of Sprigg Lane, site of the Sprigg Lane Dormitories (CH31.3) (1982–1984, Robert A. M. Stern with Marcellus Wright, Cox, and Smith). The product of a "design-build" contract that attempted to lower costs, they appear pale and anemic in comparison to the older Colonial Revival buildings. Indeed, they resemble speculative office parks. Back on Emmet Street is the delightful Dell (CH31.4) (c. 1916, attributed to William Lambeth), a small park area, sadly neglected, which was originally a formal Italian-style garden laid out by a university professor whose house still stands nearby. Originally, statues stood in the gardens; ruins of his twin casinos remain. Next to the Dell and connected by a bridge to the central grounds is Ruffner Hall (CH31.5) (1970–1973, Caudill Rowlett Scott [CRS] with Rawlings, Wilson, and Fraher), a large brick, blank minimalist box, common to the modernism of the period. CRS of Houston built a national reputation as pioneers in architectural programming and as architects of school buildings coast to coast, including several in Charlottesville. They were natural choices for Ruffner Hall, which houses the Curry School of Education. The shifting relationship of university buildings to site is obvious, since surface parking lots dominate on two sides.

Along McCormick Road and to the west, the university becomes more suburban in scale, with an almost office-park atmosphere of separate and unrelated buildings. Worthy of comment is Thornton Hall, the School of Engineering and Applied Sciences (CH31.6) (1930–1935, Peebles, Blair, Campbell and Taylor) in the usual colonial–Jefferson Revival idiom. To diminish the scale of the structure, the architects designed it around a court. Farther on is the Gilmore Hall Addition (CH31.7) (1984–1987, R. M. Kliment and Frances Halsband), an attempt to relate urbanistically to the street, designed by a leading New York postmodernist firm. The bold curving front and Palladian window make reference to the campus architecture and terminate the axis of the McCormick Road Dormitories (CH31.8) (1946–1951, Eggers and Higgins) across the street. (Kliment and Halsband used an almost identical facade at Princeton University in

CH31.1 Memorial Gymnasium

1980.) Next door is Gilmore Hall (CH31.9) (1961–1963, Ballou and Justice, and Stainback and Scribner), with a pierced concrete-block screen, derived from Edward Durrell Stone's work of the 1950s. (The university seems to have gotten one of each style from those years.)

On the southwest corner of McCormick and Alderman roads sits Observatory Hill Dining Hall (CH31.10) (1972–1974, Williams and Tazewell; 1984 remodeling, Robert A. M. Stern, Marcellus Wright, Cox, and Smith). Originally designed in the "shed-roof modern" idiom, the building was so unloved that Stern was engaged to camouflage the earlier building. Stern shows much more confidence and wit with this design than in the contemporary Sprigg Lane Dormitories. The arches are low and segmental rather than round, and the glazed pavilion-like elements and the pyramidal roof play on Jefferson, but with a modernist twist: At night they glow. The interiors are worthy of a visit. South on Alderman Road from Observatory Hill Dining Hall lies Scott Stadium (1929–1931, Architectural Commission; many later additions)— the less said about it the better—and a series of dormitories and residential colleges. Gooch-Dillard Dormitory (CH31.11) (1980–1984, Edward Larrabee Barnes) fits into the hillside with its many terraces and balconies. Barnes, well known for his respectful and low-key designs, appears indecisive. The buildings have no impact. West on Stadium Road is Hereford College (CH31.12) (1990–1992, Tod Williams, Billie Tsien with VMDO), one of the most recent additions to the campus by high-profile New York architects. This project can also be approached by retracing steps to McCormick

CH32.5 Colgate Darden School of Business Administration

Road, turning west, and following the signs. Totally, and fortunately, unrelated to the reigning Jeffersonian idiom, Hereford is a thoughtful rethinking of the serialism implicit in the original siting of the Academical Village. The individual dormitory units march up the hillside, affording vistas through the complex while remaining focused on the dining hall with its canopy entrance. The entrance cutouts and the brickwork and wraparound corner windows recall Dutch housing of the 1920s and 1930s.

CH32 **University of Virginia: North Grounds**

In common with many other universities during the growth decades of the 1960s and 1970s, the University of Virginia developed a satellite campus, or an office park, in which buildings were spaced far apart and buses, or more realistically, the automobile, became the major means of transportation. It started innocently enough with a new sports complex, University ("U") Hall (CH32.1) (1960–1965, Baskervill and Son, and Anderson, Beckwith, and Haible) and its associated buildings, intended for basketball and other indoor spectator sports, and for which much parking was required. Lawrence Anderson, a former dean of MIT's School of Architecture and Planning and a leading designer of university sports facilities, provided the basic form of a lightweight, scalloped concrete shell that obliquely looked back to the Rotunda's dome and also to the recent work of Pier Luigi Nervi in Rome. Seating 9,000 spectators, U Hall marked the university's entry

into the Atlantic Coast Conference. The U Hall complex sat alone; indeed, the 1965 master plan by Sasaki, Dawson, DeMay envisioned nothing more for the area and called for new development closer to the central grounds. But by 1969 plans had changed, and a full satellite campus was underway. Across Alderman Road from U Hall is Klockner Soccer Stadium and Field (CH32.2) (1988–1992, VMDO), an elegant minimalist design, strikingly classical at its heart.

Other than student housing, the major use of the North Grounds involved relocating two professional schools, law and business, deep into the site, a good two miles from the Academical Village. The School of Law (and originally also the Darden School of Business) (CH32.3) (1970–1975, Hugh Stubbins with Stainback and Scribner; 1994–1997, remodeling, Ayers Saint Gross) is very much in a modernist idiom, a late International Style mode, for which Stubbins, from Boston, was known. In an abstraction of Jefferson's Lawn, two parallel buildings are treated as flat, floating planes, completely devoid of ornament. The complex's palette of materials, white concrete and red brick, again recalls the work of the founder. Against the reductivist exteriors the interiors, although modern, gain in character through the extensive use of wood. Originally, the schools of law and business each occupied a wing, but when the business school departed in 1996 for its new quarters, the law school bought its wing and remodeled, adding an entrance pavilion, which ties together the two buildings and creates a courtyard. The entrance unit, which contains the Caplin Pavilion (1994–

1997) by Ayers, Saint, Gross of Baltimore, is an astute piece of postmodernism, a sort of neo-1930s classicism with its flat planar walls, and recalling Jefferson in the roof and cupola. Adjacent is the Judge Advocate General School (CH32.4) (1968–1975, Hugh Stubbins, and Rawlings, Wilson, and Fraher), which is a continuation of Stubbins's original idiom.

There is no mistaking the intention of the Colgate Darden School of Business Administration (CH32.5) (1992–1996, Robert A. M. Stern with Ayers Saint Gross); this is full-bore neo-Jeffersonian Revival and a direct refutation of the business school's former home. Although in many ways the forms and details do recall Jefferson—the south side courtyard with pavilions reminiscent of Pavilion IX on the Lawn is particularly well done—the overall effect is of a too-loud pretentiousness. The entrance portico is far overscaled and leads to a pompous lobby and sequence of rooms that recall upscale hotels. They are not very comfortable; the visitor is dwarfed and sounds echo, making conversation difficult. The complex resembles an office park—large, anonymous, and dropped from outer space. An addition by Ayers, Saint, Gross is planned.

University Area

CH33 Nannie M. Cole Residence

1933–1935, Kenneth Day. 135 Bollingwood Rd.

Designed by a Philadelphia architect, this house is a strange intruder into the genteel Colonial Revival atmosphere of Charlottesville. The earliest example of the International Style in the city, the asymmetrically balanced composition of simple volumes, flat roof, bands of ribbon windows, and lack of historical ornament embody the principles set forth by Henry-Russell Hitchcock and Philip Johnson in their 1932 manifesto. At the same time, the rounded corners nod to American streamlining of the 1930s.

CH34 Thomas Jefferson Unitarian Church

1947–1950, Stanislaw Makielski. 717 Rugby Rd.

An elegant tapered steeple of interlocking spirals tops the large concave entrance portico of the church. The portico is an enlarged version of Pavilion IX at the university. The complex, intricate geometry of the steeple is reminiscent of the work of seventeenth-century Italian Baroque architects Francesco Borromini and Guarino Guarini. The familiar presented with an eccentric twist is a theme in the work of Makielski, an early graduate of the university's architecture program, later a faculty member, and an area architect.

CH35 Rugby Road Houses

Farther down Rugby Road are several houses of interest: the Dulaney House (1929, Stanislaw Makielski), 931 Rugby Road, is a large bear of a Colonial Revival design with an enormous entrance portico. Next door, at 933, is the Aldermann House (1931–1932, Marshall Swain Wells), which is more refined. At the bend of Rugby Road is Belvoir, the Twyman House (1928, Stanhope Johnson), 1007 Rugby Road, by a Lynchburg architect, which is an expanded version of Gunston Hall with wings. Across the street is the Randolph House (1910, Eugene Bradbury), 936 Rugby Road, which takes its clue from the plaster houses of English architect C. F. A. Voysey.

Charlottesville Area   (CH36–CH50)

CH36 **Ednam**

c. 1905, D. Wiley Anderson. 1100 Dryden Ln.

Ednam, prominently sited on a bluff west of Charlottesville, is a notable early example of the Southern Colonial Revival house in Virginia, a precocious interpretation of an imagined past. The prolific Richmond architect designed the country seat for a wealthy transported northerner, Edwin O. Meyer. His work at Ednam gave built form to a contemporary popular and romantic vision of a glorious southern past. Ednam's stately Ionic portico, elaborate classical detailing, and sumptuous interiors presented an image, woven from a mythical local context, that suited the aspirations of the patron. Like other examples of the Colonial Revival, popularized throughout the country at the turn of the century by prominent firms such as McKim, Mead and White, Ednam is hardly colonial. Although the materials and construction are traditional—wood frame sheathed with weatherboards—the colossal portico and enormous size of the house aggrandize the view of the past to announce the prestige and prominence of the new resident.

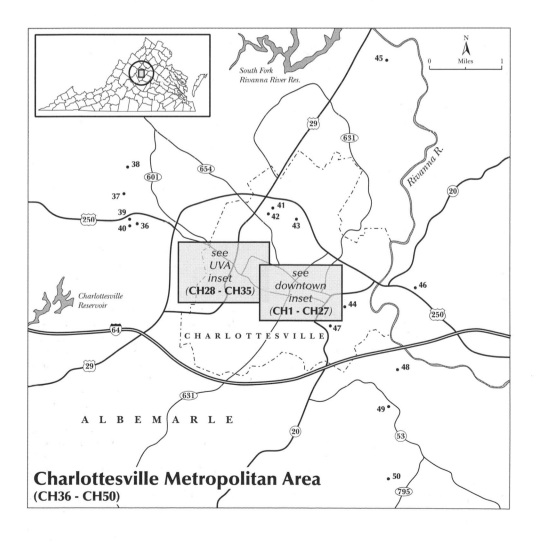

Charlottesville Metropolitan Area
(CH36 - CH50)

A major renovation around 1937 reordered the interior and relocated the entry from the stately portico on the north to the porte-cochere. The grand southern image embodied in Ednam has been a potent symbol. The building was purchased in the 1980s to accommodate a new function. The country house became the nucleus of a colony of homeowners seeking a prestigious address and image, which had been aptly captured in the design of Ednam a half-century before.

CH37 Farmington

c. 1760–1780, 1802, Thomas Jefferson. Later additions. Farmington Dr. (north of U.S. 250, about 2 miles west of Charlottesville). Private; check at desk for interior viewing

Farmington is the clubhouse of a country club that also includes adjacent housing. The clubhouse was erected c. 1760–1780 for Francis Jerdone and was a substantial brick side-passage-plan building with the principal entrance to the north. In about 1802, while occupying the White House, Thomas Jefferson designed for its new owner, George Divers, a distinctive octagon-ended wing, fronted by a massive Tuscan portico and nine round windows, for the east side. The original drawings at the Massachusetts Historical Society indicate that the wing was subdivided into two tall spaces with triple-sash windows. When the Jefferson interior burned in the mid-nineteenth century, the wing was converted into a single large space with two fireplaces. Subsequently other additions were made to the houses. Around 1927 the property and extensive outbuildings were converted into a clubhouse for a new country club and more additions made. The Jefferson section was restored by Frederick Doveton Nichols (c. 1970), but it still retains the mid-nineteenth-century single space.

CH38 Gallison Hall

1931–1933, Stanhope Johnson; landscape design, Charles Gillette. c. 1996, renovations. 24 Farmington Dr.

Gallison Hall, an outstanding example of the so-called James River Georgian style, is an eclectic collage of quotations from venerable Virginia mansions. The two-and-one-half-story block, capped by a steeply pitched slate roof with dormers, recalls Westover. The clustered, square chimney stacks, diagonally set, are reminiscent of Bacon's Castle. The elaborate interiors reference such well-known colonial sources as Westover, Shirley, and Stratford Hall. Mr. and Mrs. Julio Suarez-Galban commissioned Lynchburg architect Johnson to design their country estate, near the Farmington Country Club. The formal but restrained gardens by Richmond landscape architect Gillette complemented the complexity of the architecture. Built for a member of the aspiring twentieth-century gentry, Gallison Hall is an imaginative product of the scholarly, professional, and popular interest in Virginia's architectural heritage, prompted in part by the contemporary restoration of Colonial Williamsburg.

CH39 Boar's Head Inn and Development

1960 and later, Johnson, Craven and Gibson. South side of U.S. 250 West (2.2 miles west of Charlottesville)

The Boar's Head development is dominated by the Boar's Head Inn, designed by Charlottesville architects Floyd Johnson, Thomas Craven, and David Gibson. A Colonial Revival confection that far exceeds in scale anything from the eighteenth century, the main lodge is an overscaled one-and-one-half-story Virginia house. The interiors, such as the main dining room and taproom, possess fine detailing. Many of the immediately surrounding buildings that house shops and offices, designed by the same firm, are re-creations of various eighteenth- and early nineteenth-century Virginia vernacular structures. Once sneered at by critics and historians as out of date with regard to

CH38 Gallison Hall

mid-twentieth-century modernism, this complex shows how the Colonial Revival survived.

CH40 **Amvest Corporate Headquarters**

1984–1986, Jacquelin Taylor Robinson. 1 Boar's Head Pl.

This corporate headquarters adjacent to Boar's Head overlooks a pond. The siting is reminiscent of Eero Saarinen's John Deere Headquarters, East Moline, Illinois (1956). But in Virginia in the 1980s the style chosen was good-taste postmodern: a giant portico and lots of glass. The tripartite massing recalls Jefferson, whereas the copper roof relates to the colors of the landscape and to Virginia vernacular traditions. The well-detailed interior can be visited through the lunchroom.

CH41 **W. G. Clark House**

1995, Clark and Menefee. 2313 Pine Top Rd.

Clark and Menefee are frequently listed among the leading architects in the United States. Known for their uncompromising modernist stance, they are especially known for their work in the Charleston, South Carolina, area. However, both have taught at the University of Virginia for years. For his own house, Clark drew upon both his earlier work and several Piedmont examples, including one-room central-chimney houses and Jefferson's first building at Monticello, the so-called honeymoon cabin. The 1,400-square-foot structure on a steep site is essentially two large rooms. Constructed of poured-in-place concrete and structural con-

crete block, the house expands through the use of both opaque and transparent openings. Detailing, while minimal, is crisp and straightforward, as is the house, with its large entrance opening that splits the facade.

CH42 **Charles Frankel House**

1952, Edward Durrell Stone. 2020 Spotswood Rd.

In the 1930s Stone explored the International Style idiom, producing a series of landmark designs, such as the original building of the Museum of Modern Art (1939), New York. In the 1950s he rediscovered the power of ornament with his pierced block walls and columns. This house, with its flat roof, large areas of glazing, and open plan, is very much in the International Style, but the brick screen predicts the coming return to ornament.

CH43 **Walker Middle School**

1965–1966, Caudill Rowlett Scott. Later modifications. 1564 Dairy Rd.

Caudill Rowlett Scott (CRS), of Houston, Texas, emerged in the 1950s as one of the nation's leading designers of schools. Designing in a thoroughly modernist idiom, they pioneered the concepts of dispersed buildings in a campuslike setting, the open classroom, and programming. For Charlottesville, they provided two similar middle schools. Walker Middle School and Buford Middle School (1965–1966), 9th Street SW, are similar in the use of a Miesian IIT idiom: exposed steel columns and beams, brick wall infill, and ele-

CH44 The Farm (Davis-Bednar House)

gant minimalist detailing. The interiors were originally open plan, but that scheme has vanished with new concepts of schooling.

CH44　**The Farm** (Davis-Bednar House)

c. 1826, attributed to William B. Phillips. 1993–1995, restoration, Bednar-Lawson. 1201 East Jefferson St.

Constructed shortly after Jefferson's death, this house reflects the influence of his architecture and in particular the pavilions at the University of Virginia. The probable designer and builder had done substantial work at the Lawn and was a master brickmason. The form of the house is really an enlarged pavilion from the university, though with one-story Tuscan porticoes in keeping with its domestic scale. The original owner, John A. B. Davis, a professor of law at the university, was murdered by a student in 1840. The incident contributed to the introduction of the university's famed honor code. After years of neglect and abandonment the house was purchased and restored by (Michael) Bednar and (Elizabeth) Lawson Architects.

CH45　**Carrs-Brook**

1780s. 313 Gloucester Rd. (VA 1424)

The hierarchically ordered composition of masses at Carrs-Brook is a provincial interpretation of the five-part Palladian formula, known in the United States in the eighteenth century through publications such as Robert Morris's *Select Architecture* (1757). The frame structure consists of a two-and-one-half-story central block with pedimented gable ends, connected by hyphens to flanking one-and-one-half-story wings, also with pedimented gable ends. Carrs-Brook was built for Captain Thomas Carr between 1780 and 1790. From 1798 to 1815, Jefferson's ward and nephew, Peter Carr, used the structure as his residence and as a school. Jefferson has been suggested as the architect, due both to his close relationship with the Carr family and to his familiarity with Morris's work. However, his influence may have been indirect, since the emphatic verticality of the central mass and the steep roof pitches are decidedly un-Jeffersonian and suggest another hand.

CH46　**Aloha Chinese Gourmet Restaurant** (Town and Country Restaurant)

1955, Stanislaw Makielski. 1382 Richmond Rd. (U.S. 250 East)

About the only "roadside delight" in Charlottesville, this Monticello rip-off was a totally serious design by Makielski, who was trying to modernize Jefferson. When built, this and the adjacent Town and Country Motel (1956, Stanislaw Makielski), 1344 Richmond Road, were upscale tourist destinations. The restaurant dates from the days when Albemarle County was dry; a "bottle club" was located in the basement. Since then, this area, known as Pan Tops Mountain, has changed considerably, and the building's life is probably limited.

CH47　**George Rogers Clark Elementary School**

1930–1931, David Fitz-Gibbon. Later alterations and additions. 1000 Belmont Ave.

Of the several elementary schools constructed in Charlottesville between the world wars, Clark, named for the Albemarle County native, Revolutionary War general, and conqueror of the Northwest Territory, is the most interesting. The architect made an interesting concession to incipient modernism. The plan and form are standard for the period, two stories plus basement, double-loaded corridors, and staircases at either end; but the red brick elevations with steel sash windows appear almost factorylike. The entrance portico is the only embellishment, a flat roof with giant columns derived from the Temple of the Winds.

CH48 Monticello

1769–1809, Thomas Jefferson. 1926–present, restoration. Virginia 53, 3 miles southwest of Charlottesville. Second and third stories of the house not open to the public

Jefferson was born about four miles east at Shadwell (across the Rivanna River) in 1743. He began contemplating a house on "Little Mountain" in c. 1760, and leveling of the mountaintop began c. 1769. First constructed was the small east pavilion known as the honeymoon cabin. As historians have pointed out, it takes its form and plan from Virginia vernacular buildings. The initial house (how much was built is disputed) was based upon a Palladian formula of a two-story central section, one-story wings, and a basement section (or wings) built into the hillside and then terminated by two small pavilions. In 1793, after his time in France, where he admired the Hotel de Salm, and in England, where he visited Chiswick, Jefferson embarked upon a substantial rebuilding. Although the house was largely complete about 1809, he continued to make alterations until his death in 1826. In a sense Monticello remained under construction throughout Jefferson's lifetime. The problem of incorporating the earlier building can be seen in the second-floor windows, which interrupt the impression of a single-story building that Jefferson wanted to create. Although many specific sources can be pointed out for Monticello, ultimately Jefferson's design far transcends them. It became a personal statement of his taste and its evolution—and an ideal of what Jefferson believed was the appropriate architecture for the young nation. Although its true function is that of a plantation house, architecturally it is much more a villa.

The interior is composed around two large central rooms, the entrance hall, or museum, where Jefferson displayed relics, and the sitting room, or music room. Jefferson's taste in furniture favored a combination of simpler French (Louis XVI) designs, which he imported, and American pieces, some made in Monticello's cabinet shop by slaves. For art, Jefferson collected many copies of Old Masters, a few American works, and busts of famous individuals. In a sense the house was a didactic tool. At the same time, not to be ignored is the submerging of all the servant spaces and, from a post-Freudian point of view, the masking or obliteration of the black slaves who made the running of the house possible. The most memorable interior spaces are his bedroom-library, which takes up most of the first-floor east wing, and the dining room, which, through the use of a dumbwaiter and a turning shelf, made servants invisible.

Jefferson died deeply in debt, and the house passed through several hands before the Thomas Jefferson Memorial Foundation acquired it in 1923. The foundation has carried out an ambitious program of preservation, restoration, reconstruction, and interpretation. The initial campaign, under the direction of Fiske Kimball and largely executed by Milton Grigg, involved the reconstruction of the west wing, which had fallen in. Internally the house received a Colonial Revival treatment with much white paint on the wood surfaces. Grigg and Kimball remained connected with work at Monticello for the rest of their lives, but in the 1960s and 1970s Floyd Johnson and Frederick Doveton Nichols became involved. Since the 1980s and 1990s John Messick has been the architect and William L. Beiswanger of the staff has been in charge of the restoration. In the 1980s Jefferson's original graining on the doors was restored. In the early 1990s a tin-shingled roof copying Jefferson's original was installed. In 1998 two shuttered verandas opening off his wing were reinstalled, altering the symmetry of the house. Internally much attention has been directed to Jefferson's original furnishing plan, and many of the furnishings are original.

Monticello was the main house of an extensive plantation and home to over 100 people, including slaves, who lived on the mountaintop. In the immediate vicinity of the house Jefferson tried a number of landscaping schemes over the years, in a series of different styles. The meandering path of the garden to the immediate southwest of the house indicates his interest in the English picturesque garden. In recent years attention has been paid to the sites of the various other buildings Jefferson erected on the hilltop. Along Mulberry Row are outlined the foundations for shops, slave housing, and a nailery. On the hillside below, some of Jefferson's original orchards and vegetable gardens have been restored. A gazebo Jefferson designed to view the landscape was reconstructed in 1990 with Floyd Johnson, of Johnson, Craven and Gibson, as the architect.

CH49 International Center for Jefferson Studies (Kenwood)

1939, William Adams Delano. VA 53, 1 mile south of Monticello. Inquire at office for access

Well known for his Long Island estates of the 1910s and 1920s and public work in Washington, D.C., designed in partnership with Chester Holmes Aldrich, Delano designed several country houses in Virginia and the Charlottesville area. Kenwood, for General and Mrs. Edwin Watson, is the most accessible of these and has some historical significance as well, since General Watson was Franklin D. Roosevelt's military attaché, and, from 1940 onward, his secretary. President Roosevelt visited the house during World War II. Delano's preference for English classical forms is well demonstrated. An interesting variation on the traditional plan is the entrance through what is essentially the service wing into a long hall that terminates in a double cube sitting room–music salon designed to display a set of antique Belgian tapestries and containing original furnishings. The music salon overlooks the boxwood garden. The other public spaces are to either side.

The cornerstone was laid in 2000 for a 15,000-square-foot research library building (Hartman-Cox of Washington, D.C.) sited adjacent to the house and designed to harmonize with it.

CH50 Ashlawn (Highland)

1799 and later. VA 795, 5 miles south of Monticello, Simeon vicinity. Open to the public

Described by its owner, James Monroe (the fifth U.S. president), as his "castle cabin," Ashlawn contrasts strikingly with nearby Monticello. A small cottage, with five rooms on the main floor, it is more representative of the common building stock of the period than of a design concept. Monroe was deeply in debt at the time of its construction. He made some additions during 1816–1818 and converted the slave quarters into guest quarters. Jefferson, Monroe's mentor, selected the site, reputedly with a view line to Monticello. Jefferson, who wanted to create a "society to our taste," composed of friends and political allies, urged Monroe to move to the area. Monroe occupied the property intermittently until 1823. In 1882 a large two-story porticoed house that overwhelmed the modest cottage was added by the Massey family. In 1930 Jay Winston Johns purchased the house, and with his family collected many of Monroe's original furnishings and opened it to the public. The College of William and Mary has operated the property as a museum since 1975. They have embarked on an ambitious restoration program initially led by Milton Grigg. The slave quarters were reconstructed (1985–1988, Douglas Gilpin, Jr.) according to best evidence. Later work and restoration, including significant portions of the Monroe house, have been undertaken by Don A. Swofford and John Waite.

Richmond Metropolitan Area (RI)

THIS SECTION INCLUDES THE CITY OF RICHMOND AND THE ADJACENT metropolitan area of Henrico County as well as a portion of Hanover County. The 2000 census recorded 197,790 residents for the city and about 1 million in the metropolitan area.

Europeans discovered the future site of Richmond, at the falls of the James River, when Captains John Smith and Christopher Newport landed somewhere near what is now Great Shiplock Park, at the eastern end of the falls, in May 1607. Not until the 1730s, however, did major English settlement take place, when the James River falls site became by law a location for the grading of tobacco exports. William Byrd II recorded on September 19, 1733: "When we got home we laid the foundation of two large Citys. One at Shacco's [Shockoe Creek], to be called Richmond." The name apparently came from the similarity of the site on the James with that of Richmond on the Thames in England. In 1737 he commissioned Colonel William Mayo to lay out the new city in series of "squares," or city blocks. Mayo's neat rectangular grid, oriented northwest-southeast to align with the riverbank, fronted the James River with a town common. The original town incorporated the area bounded by the James River to the south, present-day 15th Street to the west, Broad Street to the north, and 25th Street to the east. Mayo's grid plan set the standard for future city expansion. A small settlement grew up in the 1740s, and in 1752 the General Assembly moved the Henrico County seat to Richmond. On the eve of the American Revolution, about 600 persons lived in the tobacco-trading port.

The big shift came in 1779, when, under the leadership of Governor Thomas Jefferson, the state capital was moved from Williamsburg to Richmond; the General Assembly first met there in a rented frame building in May 1780. The assembly decreed that the Richmond plan would be expanded by 200 "squares" and that six blocks of the new seat of Virginia government were to be reserved for state government. In 1780 Governor Jefferson, after surveying the expansion, selected the six blocks that would make up present-day Capitol Square. The

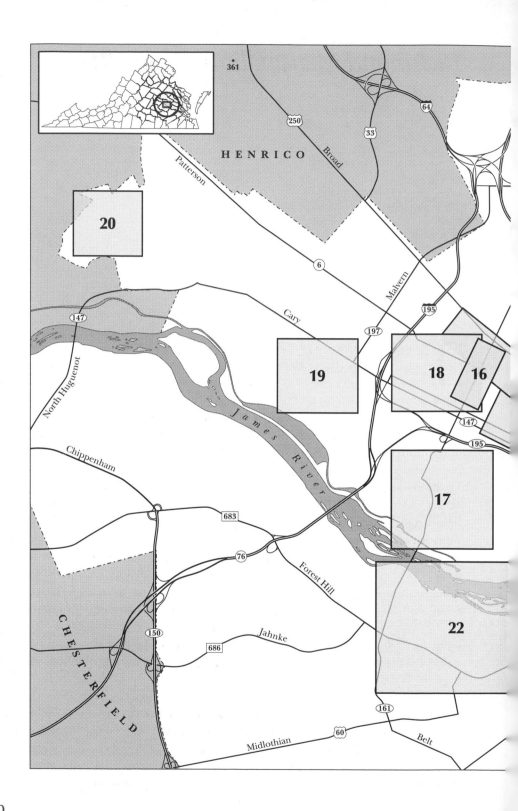

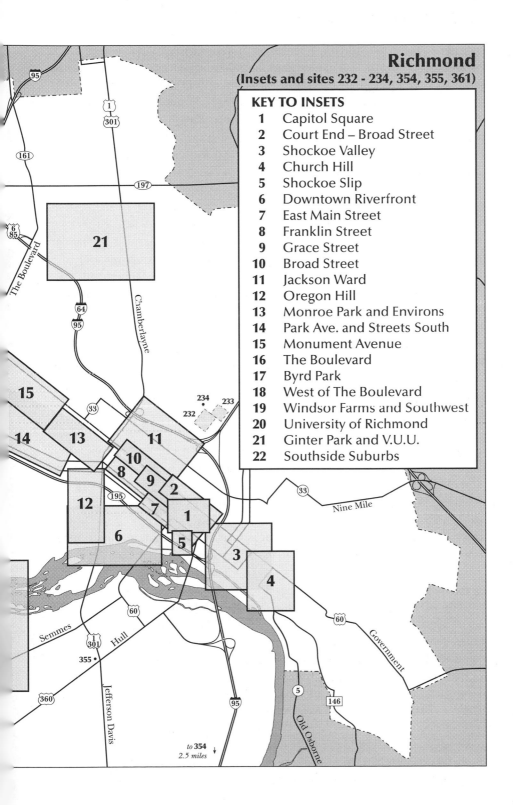

Richmond
(Insets and sites 232 - 234, 354, 355, 361)

KEY TO INSETS

1 Capitol Square
2 Court End – Broad Street
3 Shockoe Valley
4 Church Hill
5 Shockoe Slip
6 Downtown Riverfront
7 East Main Street
8 Franklin Street
9 Grace Street
10 Broad Street
11 Jackson Ward
12 Oregon Hill
13 Monroe Park and Environs
14 Park Ave. and Streets South
15 Monument Avenue
16 The Boulevard
17 Byrd Park
18 West of The Boulevard
19 Windsor Farms and Southwest
20 University of Richmond
21 Ginter Park and V.U.U.
22 Southside Suburbs

to **354**
2.5 miles

small tobacco port became overnight the capital of the largest and most populous state of the new United States. The provincial community became a cosmopolitan city, attracting a varied and talented population that included lawyers, actors, artisans, and architects. Although Virginia retained for only a few decades the distinction of being "first among equals," Richmonders never lost that feeling of self-importance. Until well after the Civil War Richmond considered itself the first city of the South and a leader in finance, commerce, industry, and culture. The result is a remarkable series of buildings and a cityscape that can be easily glimpsed downtown, out Franklin Street, along Monument Avenue, and in western suburbs such as Windsor Farms.

The major expansion of Richmond in the nineteenth century and for the greater portion of the twentieth has been to the west. The James River on the south and Shockoe Creek on the east provided natural barriers; and even though Church Hill, across the creek, was part of the original Byrd-Mayo plan, its location meant its initial development was relatively dispersed. West of the creek or in Richmond proper the result is a series of neighborhoods that, with some exceptions, flow out to the west and north. Periods of intense real estate speculation and development occurred nearly every decade, followed by the inevitable downturn. Architects of national stature, following the money, came to the city: Benjamin Henry Latrobe in the 1790s, Robert Mills and Alexander Parris in the 1810s, Thomas U. Walter and Thomas S. Stewart in the 1840s, Carrère and Hastings in the 1890s, John Russell Pope in the 1910s, and William Lawrence Bottomley in the 1920s. They were supplemented by local talent: Albert West, D. Wiley Anderson, William Noland, Henry Baskervill, Marcellus Wright, Charles M. Robinson, and others, and their successor firms, who helped create the fabric of the city.

From the early nineteenth century until the mid-twentieth, the riverfront, Shockoe Valley, and the James River and Kanawha Canal (Richmond's attempt to secure a western transportation route) served as a commerce and transportation center. Along it grew up large tobacco warehouses, processing plants for various products, and ironworks. In the three decades before 1860 Richmond became the tobacco manufacturing center of the United States. It also became known as the city of cast iron porches, which began to appear in the 1850s and increased in usage until about 1900. Remnants of these industries, such as the Tredegar Iron Works complex or the tobacco warehouses, can still be found, although the character of the riverfront, especially along the James River, has changed considerably. Adjacent to the industrial waterfront, the commercial sector developed, initially along Main Street and in the Shockoe Slip area, and then leapfrogged over Capitol Square to Broad Street in the 1860s and spread west. In the late 1840s John Notman of Philadelphia laid out Hollywood, a rural cemetery, and in 1851 the city of Richmond acquired three park sites.

By 1861, at the outbreak of the Civil War, Richmond had an area of two-and-one-half square miles and a population of 38,000, of whom 14,275 were slaves and free blacks. Among American cities it ranked twenty-fifth in size but thirteenth in manufactures. Home of four banks, fifty-two tobacco factories, the largest flour mill in the world, and the largest iron foundry in the South, and served by five railroad lines, Richmond was essential to the Confederate cause. Between May 29, 1861, when Jefferson Davis arrived, and April 3, 1865, when he hastily departed, Richmond, the capital of the Confederate States of America, was the prize the North sought. As the Confederates left, they planted explosives, set fires, and destroyed much of the city's industrial base along with twenty blocks of the commercial sector to keep these resources out of the hands of the Union army.

Nevertheless, post–Civil War Richmond recovered with amazing speed. The idea of Reconstruction hardships that applies to areas of the rural South in Richmond's case has been overblown. The commercial section along Main Street was rebuilt rapidly—ironically, with significant northern investment—in new, larger brick and cast-iron-front buildings. The population grew rapidly, and the city's industries—the Tredegar Iron Works, Albemarle Paper Company, Old Dominion Nail Works, and Belle Isle granite quarries—recovered. Tensions between whites and newly freed blacks and problems of political representation were constant. The politics of race remains an ongoing problem for the city. Richmond felt the effects of national economic depressions; the big slump of 1873 halted growth for the rest of the decade. Until the 1870s Richmond was a walking city, but this changed as horse trolleys began tentatively to push development to the west. In 1888 Richmond introduced the world's first successful electric streetcar system, and the urban center exploded, creating areas such as Ginter Park and and the West End. Almost no building activity occurred in Richmond between 1893 and 1900 because of the depression triggered by the panic of 1893. Afterward, the city grew geographically, annexing the areas just mentioned, as well as Manchester, or South Richmond, in 1910 and Barton Heights and others in 1914.

Architecturally, Richmond followed national trends; some important commissions, such as the Jefferson Hotel, went to Yankee firms. Locally, a major innovation gave built form to the myth of earlier Virginia. The creation of the giant-columned Southern colonial style by architects such as William Noland and nostalgia for the "Lost Cause," played out on Monument Avenue and elsewhere through the area, pointed to a proud past. The Colonial Revival and especially its James River variant remain very strong in Richmond today.

Richmond in the early twentieth century appeared to be, especially from an architectural point of view, a supremely confident city. The infrastructure created up to World War II is overwhelming. Although there was none of the radical innovation that took place in Chicago or Los Angeles, the overall quality and consistency were certainly equal, if not better. Richmond entered the twentieth century believing that its position was intact, but in reality it was no longer the first city of the South. Indeed, even within the region its stature would be diminished. The conditions for this change had been established much earlier, even before the Civil War, when Richmond remained focused on the Kanawha Canal rather than fully embracing the railroad as the primary form of transportation. Instead of thinking on a national scale, Richmonders remained provincial. Hence today a walk down Broad and Grace streets tells part of the story. The former large department stores, Thalhimer's and Miller and Rhoads, are closed. In part this is a national trend. The building of I-95 a few blocks away was a contributing factor. The unresolved problems of race continue to plague the city, and the population is declining. This is not to say that significant post–World War II buildings and landmarks do not exist in Richmond. The Virginia Museum of Fine Arts addition, the Federal Reserve Building, and, in Henrico County, the Reynolds Metals Building, Best Products, and others date from this period.

The major highway projects of the 1960s such as Interstates 95, 64, and 195 created a controversial splitting of the city, cutting off sections and causing major destruction in portions of Jackson Ward (a large African American community) and Oregon Hill. At the same time it linked Richmond with the major cities of the North. Richmond became the southern end of the East Coast megalopolis. The consequence is that many Americans see Richmond only by highway as they speed past the old Main Street Station, sitting now in lonely splendor.

Part of the importance of Richmond is its past and the preservation of that heritage. Beginning in 1935, the local chapter of the Association for the Preservation of Virginia Antiquities, the William Byrd Branch, led by Mary Wingfield Scott, Richmond's first architectural historian and preservationist, pioneered preservation techniques such as revolving funds. Scott held a doctorate in French art but devoted herself to her native city's imperiled historic buildings, saying modestly, late in life, "You try to do the right thing at the right time." Members of the William Byrd Branch founded the Historic Richmond Foundation in 1956 to focus on the St. John's Church area as a decaying urban neighborhood with significant historic building fabric. The block just west of the church, bounded by Broad, Grace, 23rd, and 24th streets, was selected as Carrington Square, popularly known as the Pilot Block. The block—rejuvenated through the cooperative efforts of individuals, government, and nonprofit organizations—was intended to serve as a springboard for restoring the entire neighborhood. Historic Richmond has continued in its efforts and been joined by other organizations, such as the Monument Avenue Preservation Society. Also underway is a revitalization of the James River waterfront in a San Antonio–type River Walk.

Capitol Square Area   (RI1–RI15)

Capitol Square has been the government center of Richmond since Thomas Jefferson selected the site and laid out the square in 1780. Initially the square was occupied by Jefferson's capitol building and the Virginia Executive Mansion. Over time the Commonwealth of Virginia has constructed a number of buildings on the square proper. Originally, residential neighborhoods adjoined the square to the north, east, and west, and the commercial-financial area was to the south. Throughout the nineteenth century the Virginia State Capitol dominated the skyline of the city. Twentieth-century encroachments by state high rises and the buildings of the financial district have blocked the Jefferson "Acropolis" and diminished the visual prominence of the square to the rest of the city.

RI1 Capitol Square

1780, layout, Thomas Jefferson and Directors of Public Works. 1816, first landscaping plan, Maximilian Godefroy. 1850–1860, second landscaping plan, John Notman. 1906–1922, landscaping

In 1779 the Commonwealth of Virginia decreed that the Richmond plan would be expanded by 200 "squares" or city blocks and that six blocks on Shockoe Hill were to be reserved

for state government. In 1780 Governor Thomas Jefferson selected the six blocks that would make up present-day Capitol Square. To center the square on the promontory intended for the future capitol building, Jefferson took half blocks on the north and south. This offset arrangement terminated Franklin Street and Grace Street at the square and created Bank and Capitol streets to the north and south. Through most of its early history the square re-

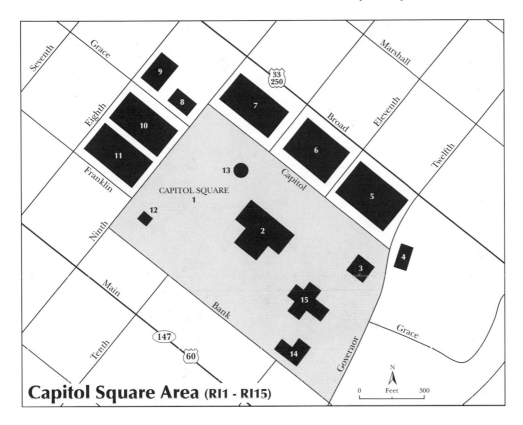

Capitol Square Area (RI1 - RI15)

mained as Jefferson found it: a rough, hilly site with two large ravines. The first attempt to landscape the square came with Maximilian Godefroy's neoclassical plan of 1816. This plan proved unsuccessful because the workmen could not implement its rigid formality in the untamed gullies of the square. The only remaining element is the cast iron fence that surrounds the square. The landscape as it appears today reflects the improvements made by John Notman in the 1850s. The picturesque system of walks and fountains shows the influence of his work at Hollywood Cemetery. A number of other improvements followed the expansion of the capitol in 1906, the most significant being the widening of Bank Street. In 1980, Capitol Street to the north succumbed to the plaza mania and was closed.

RI2 Virginia State Capitol

1785–1798, Thomas Jefferson, with Charles-Louis Clérisseau; modifications by Samuel Dobie, contractor. 1816, redesign of exterior stairs and other minor alterations, Maximilian Godefroy. 1840, interior reorganization, Otis Manson and Samuel Freeman. 1846, alteration of exterior stairs, George Brown, mason. 1904–1906, gutting and rebuilding of original building and addition of wings, John Kevan Peebles, Noland and Baskervill, Frye and Chesterman. 1926, restoration of old House of Delegates chamber, A. G. Lambert of Baskervill and Lambert. 1954, restoration of old Senate chamber, J. Ambler Johnston. 1962–1964, widening of hyphens, major repairs, and modernization, Ballou and Justice, and E. Tucker Carlton. 100 Bank St. (Capitol Sq.). Open to the public

Jefferson designed the Virginia State Capitol in 1785 and 1786 while minister to France. He was aided by Clérisseau, a distinguished French architect, who persuaded Jefferson to use the Maison Carrée, a Roman temple in Nîmes, France, as his model. The capitol's construction marked the first use anywhere in modern history of the temple form in a public building. Its awe-inspiring position on a hill overlooking the growing city and the untamed James River began a wave of temple-style public buildings that was to spread across the nation.

The first capital of the colony had been

RI1 Virginia State Capitol and Capitol Square
RI2 Virginia State Capitol, Central Hall

Jamestown, where the General Assembly first met in the settlement's church in 1619. In 1699 the government moved to Williamsburg. Jefferson's desire for a new capitol for Virginia, and perhaps even his preference for the temple form, can be traced to 1776, when, as a member of the House of Delegates, he presented one of a number of bills proposing the removal of the capital to Richmond, which was better protected from attack by British forces and more centrally located than Williamsburg. Jefferson's earliest plan for a capitol, now thought to have been drawn in 1776, shows a temple with a portico at either end. In 1779, during Jefferson's term as governor, the House of Delegates selected Richmond as the new capital. By the time the assembly was in a position to set funds aside for construction, Jefferson had been appointed minister to France.

A plan was drawn and the cornerstone laid, and construction began on a rectangular building in August 1785. Friends of Jefferson who disliked the proposed plan, possibly led by Richard Randolph, had written to him in France in March. He responded by sending plans drawn by Clérisseau in January 1786. Clérisseau, having published measured drawings of Roman buildings, was an authority on antiquities whom Jefferson sought out to help articulate his ideas. Later in 1786 Jefferson sent sections and a model, which were commonly used for presentation in France and proved very persuasive in Virginia.

The plan of Jefferson's capitol is very similar to that of the earlier H-shaped capitol in Williamsburg. Chambers for the court and the burgesses, or delegates, were at either end of the lower floor; the senate chamber and meeting rooms were located above. In Richmond, the spaces on either side of the hyphen would be used as stair halls and vestibules. In the central hall, Jefferson designed a two-story space, with a balcony supported by enormous columns. He planned for a large skylight over the space and, below, a marble sculpture of Washington, which the assembly had already commissioned.

Jean Antoine Houdon, a French sculptor who had made a bust of Lafayette for the General Assembly and a bust of Benjamin Franklin, had been commissioned in the spring of 1785 to sculpt Washington from life. He traveled to America early that fall and spent more than two weeks at Mount Vernon, sketching, modeling, and taking a life mask of Washington. Houdon returned to France and worked for two years on the life-sized marble sculpture, which was not delivered until after the French Revolution. There is no record that Washington saw it before his death in 1799, but his acquaintances thought it an impressive likeness. Lafayette noted that the appearance was so lifelike that he expected it to move. Houdon depicted Washington as the Roman citizen-soldier Cincinnatus, with his plow and walking stick. He wears his uniform, and his gun is hung from the fasces on which he leans. It has been pointed out that this placement in the central hall of a public building of the sculpture of Washington, in an antique style, though not antique clothing, is similar to that of the placement of statues of gods in temples.

Jefferson probably invested great symbolic significance in his choice of the temple form, as have numerous scholars since then. The tremendous momentum of the desire for independence during the American Revolution inspired patriots to believe that they were taking steps that would change the world. The Enlightenment mind revered rightness, logic, and geometry, as well as Athenian democracy and the Roman Republic. The hill on which the capitol sat, overlooking the rugged beauty of the James River, provided a perfect setting for a temple to goodness, intellect, the morality of the American spirit, and independence. Jefferson deliberately chose ancient, authoritative forms to inspire a new American art and architecture.

As initially completed in Jeffferson's absence, the building differed from the one planned. Samuel Dobie, the contractor, had to adjust the building to fit the foundation already laid. Because of this and other adjustments Dobie made, Jefferson found the building disappointing, though many others thought it spectacular. Dobie raised the basement and placed offices there rather than in the attic, as the plans had directed. He then designed a smaller, curved staircase on each side of the structure, rather than the imposing staircase in the front, presumably so that he could provide windows for the lower offices. He continued the Ionic pilasters along the sides of the building rather than ending them at the junction of the portico and the body of the temple. Inside, Dobie made one spectacular change. In the central hall—Jefferson's cubical room with columns supporting a balcony and with a large skylight overhead—Dobie placed the balcony on brackets and inserted a dome with an oculus that is covered by the skylight. The dome is completely concealed on the exterior of the building but creates a space within referred to as the rotunda.

The building was occupied in 1798, and, with the completion of the stucco covering in 1800, it was considered finished. A series of repairs and alterations began almost immediately. The roof, in particular, was a problem throughout the nineteenth century. In 1816 the French emigré architect Maximilian Godefroy, while engaged with landscaping Capitol Square, redesigned the exterior stairs so that they came directly out from the building, rather than curving. He also altered some of the woodwork and finished some of the exterior work. Cycles of neglect and care continued for decades with enlargements and shifts of quarters. Governors repeatedly called for the addition of a staircase to the front portico. In 1857 plans were drawn for a major renovation, but the cost was deemed too high, and repairs sufficed.

During most of the Civil War, the state legislature shared its space with the Confederate Congress. The building bore much wear with little attention. During the evacuation fire of 1865, federal troops surrounded the capitol, protecting it from fire and looters. On April 27, 1870, while the third-floor courtroom was packed during an important trial, the balcony pulled away from the wall, collapsing on the room below, which in turn fell through the floor into the chamber of the House of Delegates below. Sixty-two people were killed and

251 were injured. Though necessary repairs were made, the state's economy had not recovered completely from the Civil War, so complete renovation was not possible.

By the turn of the century the building was in an embarrassing state of disrepair. Questions about fireproofing the building had been raised many times. At this time, the American Renaissance mentality generated nationwide interest in civic redesign and the creation of grand public spaces, a movement accompanied by enthusiastic interest in the nation's past. The same period saw a growth in government bureaucracy. Thus state capitols were being renovated and enlarged, or new ones built, all over the country. The governor of Virginia was worried about protecting and preserving a structure whose historic value was growing by the year. The courts had moved out, as had other functions, but the capitol building was still too small.

In 1902 a competition was announced, and five firms from around the country, including such luminaries as McKim, Mead and White, along with every Virginia firm, were invited to submit drawings for the repair and enlargement of the building. The committee received no out-of-state entries, having allowed entrants only one month for study. It interviewed six Virginia firms about their plans. Two—Noland and Baskervill of Richmond and Frye and Chesterman of Lynchburg—were asked to submit a joint plan for a second stage. Their entry did not succeed, but one of the others continued to draw attention—that of John Kevan Peebles of Norfolk, who proposed two wings attached by hyphens to the sides of the existing capitol. The proposed wings had ornament that was subdued but similar to that of the historic building. After redesign and negotiation, Peebles was hired along with the other two firms. The project was started in August 1904 and completed by January 1906.

The stairs were finally added to the front portico, stretching the full width. Hyphens connected the wings to the capitol, as planned. The wings were smaller, lower, and set back to respect the importance of the central structure, and each boasted an Ionic portico. Stairs also led into the first floor of the hyphens. Two of the main reasons for the renovation—fireproofing and improving the structural integrity to preserve the historic structure for the ages—ironically resulted in gutting the building. Though some select decorative features, such as pilasters, cornices, and door frames, were re-tained and reused, only the exterior masonry walls and columns were left standing. The Senate moved into a new chamber in the west wing and the House of Delegates into theirs in the east wing.

Interest in the building's history led the assembly to restore the chamber of the House of Delegates to its nineteenth-century configuration in 1926. The old Senate chamber followed in 1954. The most recent refurbishment took place from 1962 to 1964 under the direction of the Richmond firm of Ballou and Justice. The building was enlarged by widening the hyphens and removing their exterior stairs. The attic was finished for use as offices and committee rooms. Modernization included the installation of an elevator and updating all wiring and plumbing.

RI3 Virginia Executive Mansion

1813, Alexander Parris. 1906–1908, rear addition and alterations, W. Duncan Lee. 1992, exterior restoration, Browne, Eichman, Dagliesh, and Gilpin. 2000, interior restoration, Hanbury Evans Newill Vlattas. Capitol Sq. Open to the public

The governor's house is a neoclassical building inspired by the work of British architect Robert Adam and Bostonian Charles Bulfinch. It is the oldest continuously occupied executive mansion in the United States. The building was one of three in Richmond designed by Boston architect Parris (see entry for the Wickham House, below). The brick facade is five bays with the central bay pulled slightly forward. Exterior detail is restrained to the point of austerity. In contrast, the interior is lavish, though with typically delicate Federal-era detailing. After a major fire, W. Duncan Lee, a prolific Richmond-based architect who specialized in the Colonial Revival, began his career when he undertook interior renovations and added a substantial rear wing. More recently, the original paint colors and balustrade were restored on the exterior, and an interior restoration was completed in 2000.

RI4 Morson's Row

1853, Alfred Lybrock. 219–223 Governor St.

These stepped and bow-fronted buildings, the last of a number of fashionable residences that once adjoined Capitol Square, compose one of the outstanding groups of Italianate town houses in the city. They are stuccoed brick with door surrounds and window hoods of cast iron. The removal of ornate cast iron fencing and rails and the obliteration of much of the stucco scoring have somewhat diminished the impact of German emigré Alfred Lybrock's design. Lybrock studied architecture in Karlsruhe before coming to New York after the revolutions of 1848. He arrived in Richmond in 1852, and this is one of his earliest designs.

RI5 Library of Virginia and Supreme Court Building (former)

1939–1940, Carneal, Johnston and Wright, architects; Baskervill and Son, associated architects; Alfred M. Githens and Francis Keally, consulting architects. c. 1970, addition, Carneal and Johnston. Broad, 11th, and Governors sts. at Capitol Sq.

The building is one of Virginia's best examples of Moderne classicism. The austerity of the lower floors is reminiscent of a Masonic temple. At the same time the massing recalls John Russell Pope's contemporaneous National Archives (1936) in Washington, D.C. The Supreme Court of Virginia entrance was on Broad Street, whereas the main lobby and library reading rooms were entered off Capitol Street (now Capitol Square). The exterior is a curtain of Indiana limestone on a pink granite base pierced by tall rectangular windows that illuminate the reading rooms of the first floor. Minnesota granite is used for the entrances, with restrained bronze screens above the doorways. Entrance is through ornamental bronze gates and grillwork depicting stylized papyrus leaves. The lobby at the south (Capitol Square) doorway is a dramatic space with indirect lighting, accentuating the richness of the paneling and large mural facing the doors. The mural (1951), by Julien Binford, is an allegory of George Mason's Virginia Declaration of Rights. Both the library and the Virginia Supreme Court have vacated the building, and at the time of writing the Commonwealth of Virginia was determining a use for the structure.

RI6 Old City Hall (Richmond City Hall)

1887–1893, Elijah E. Myers. 1983, renovation, Landmark Design Associates. 1001 E. Broad St.

The lively facade of Old City Hall breaks through the ranks of the more demure structures that line the north side of Capitol Square, its clock tower and spire demanding attention for the grandest municipal project of Richmond's Victorian age. A city promotional publication stated in glowing terms in 1893: "A tenement, this, for the body corporate, which . . . evinces to the stranger not a little of Richmond's civic aspirations and pride." This important location had been vacant for fourteen years following the demolition in 1873 of Robert Mills's city hall (1816–1818), which had stood on the site. After a long and confused process of selection, a design by Detroit architect Elijah E. Myers was chosen. Myers had a well-deserved reputation for misjudging construction costs, and the city of Richmond took control of the construction of the building. The completed and furnished city hall cost 400 percent of the original estimate. Rather than expressing outrage at the cost overruns, the citizens of Richmond reacted with delight to the new building.

The very fabric of the walls of City Hall reflects the city's natural and industrial resources. Almost 2 million cubic feet of James River granite were removed from quarries along the river at Richmond and used in construction of the building. The astonishing cast iron interior, the most splendid interior space in Richmond, is also the product of local materials and artisans. Stretching up three stories to a skylight, the courtyard, surrounded by ranges of heavily ornamented Gothic arches, complements the exterior in complexity and richness of decoration. The ironwork, made to fireproof standards, was cast in Richmond by the firm of Asa Snyder. The interior public spaces still contain their original lighting fixtures and hardware, whose quality offers further testimony to the materials lavished on the building.

Happily City Hall survived several proposals of demolition in the 1960s and 1970s. After

RI6 Old City Hall (Richmond City Hall) exterior (left) and interior court (above)

construction in 1971 of a twenty-eight-story replacement across Broad Street, the city of Richmond declared the grimy edifice surplus. After a spirited preservation campaign, City Hall was purchased by the Commonwealth of Virginia and leased as office space with covenants that will ensure the preservation of its appearance. During a 1983 restoration the interior received appropriate polychrome decoration recalling its original appearance. In addition to interior repainting, the exterior was cleaned.

RI7 Virginia General Assembly Building (Life of Virginia Insurance Building)

1906, Clinton and Russell. 1922, addition, Clinton and Russell. 1964, addition, Marcellus Wright and Associates. Colgate Darden Park (formerly Capitol St.) at 9th St. and Broad St. at 9th St.

The General Assembly Building reflects the long evolution of a private office complex recently adapted for government use. The original portion of the building facing Capitol Square is in scale with and provides a classical counterpoint to Old City Hall. With ornate layered Corinthian pilasters incorporating Pegasus figures and a large entablature and attic story, it is one of Richmond's most lavish classical buildings. Architects Clinton and Russell designed a number of commercial buildings in Richmond. The 1922 addition is more re-

strained and built to a larger scale that reflects the character of Broad Street. The 1964 Brutalist addition successfully maintains the rhythm of the earlier structures.

RI8 Ninth Street Office Building (Hotel Richmond)

1904, Carrère and Hastings. 1911, addition, John Kevan Peebles. 9th and E. Grace sts.

Throughout the history of Capitol Square, hotels accounted for the principal commercial activity in the area. The firm of Carrère and Hastings followed its success with the Jefferson Hotel with the more modest Hotel Richmond. The yellow brick and limestone exterior is notably reticent, perhaps a bow to the state capitol across the way. The same year he designed the two-story addition, Peebles designed the Hotel Murphy at 807 East Broad Street. Charles Robinson designed the Commonwealth Suites (formerly Hotel Rueger) at 9th and Bank in 1912.

RI9 St. Peter's Catholic Church (Cathedral)

1834. 1855, transept. 800 E. Grace St. (at N. 8th St.)

In the year of its construction, a Richmond newspaper viewed this building as inaugurating a new architectural era for the city. It would be more accurate to describe it as a bridge between two architectural eras. Within and without, the building is executed in a simple, restrained classicism. The Doric portico clearly foreshadowed the Greek Revival architecture of subsequent decades, while the attenuated form of the colums and simple cupola show the influence of neoclassicism of the 1810s and 1820s. The essence of the original design, supposedly based on the Parisian model of the Church of St.-Philippe-du-Roule, is intact and well preserved.

The building was the second Catholic church constructed in Richmond. In 1840, when the Diocese of Richmond was created, it became the first cathedral of that diocese. The 1855 transept, while somewhat boxy from the exterior, creates an elegant cruciform interior. There was considerable discussion in the 1880s about demolishing the building for a grander edifice, but the size of the site and a lack of funding precluded new construction. The consecration of the new Cathedral of the Sacred Heart on Monroe Park in 1906 relegated the building to parish status.

RI10 St. Paul's Episcopal Church

1845, Thomas Stewart. 1890, alterations. 1959, parish house and parking garage, Baskervill and Son. 1992, renovation. 815 E. Grace St.

A group of members of Monumental Episcopal Church began planning St. Paul's in 1845. The new congregation appears to have been architecturally conscious and went on a tour of the Northeast to seek ideas. They especially admired St. Luke's Episcopal Church in Philadel- phia and commissioned the designer of that church, Stewart, to provide a Richmond version. Many of the features of the Stewart design remain intact, including the Corinthian portico and the steeple. The cast iron capitals that top the stuccoed brick columns are one of the first uses of cast iron ornament in Richmond. The Gibbs-influenced steeple originally supported a Gothic-like octagonal needle spire. Along the sides of the buildings are large Corinthian pilasters and a continuation of the full entablature of the pedimented portico.

In the 1890s the large central pulpit was removed and the shallow apse expanded to its present configuration. The gallery, supported by slender cast iron columns, is original. Ornament in the Corinthian order is used throughout the sanctuary, including pilasters, columns, and coffered panels along the gallery and in the plaster ceiling. The most spectacular feature of the ceiling is the large sunburst panel in the center. The prominence of the church in the history of the Confederacy (President Jefferson Davis, General Robert E. Lee, and other notables worshiped here) resulted in a large number of memorials in the sanctuary, including a window and an altar mosaic by Tiffany Studios.

To the east of the sanctuary is a parish house complex which includes a courtyard, an atrium, and parking garages on 8th Street. The complex is one of Richmond's most sophisticated examples of classicism from the second half of the twentieth century. Significantly, the congregation rejected the original modernist proposal in favor of the current design. The 1992 renovation created an atrium and remodeled the undercroft.

RI11 Virginia Supreme Court (Federal Reserve Bank)

1919, Sill, Buckler and Fehagen. 1922, annex, Carneal and Johnston. 110 N. 9th St.

The 1919 section of the building that now serves as the Virginia Supreme Court, at Franklin and 8th streets, was designed by an obscure Baltimore firm that won the design competition for the Federal Reserve Bank. The construction of the annex extended the building and relocated the entrance to Capitol Square. The building represents the reserved monumental classicism of the American Renaissance popularized by McKim, Mead and White, in contrast to Virginia's preferred image of a re-

RI13 Washington Monument

helped to generate a national wave of representational memorial sculptures. Sculptor Thomas Crawford won a major competition for the monument and undertook the work in 1849. Crawford's design, including the figure of Washington and those of Jefferson, Mason, and Henry, was partially erected in 1858. The Civil War disrupted completion, and Crawford died. Rogers, a northerner, undertook the remaining work in 1869. The completed monument occupies the important terminus of Grace Street. The design consists of three tiers of pedestals: Washington on top, Virginia patriots in the middle tier, and trophies representing Revolutionary battlefields on the lower tier. Nearby on the square are smaller subsequent monuments to Virginians: Edgar Allan Poe, Harry Flood Byrd, Governor William "Extra Billy" Smith, General Thomas J. "Stonewall" Jackson, and Hunter Holmes McGuire.

vived colonial-Jeffersonian idiom. With its impressive Ionic colonnades the building would not seem out of place in the Federal Triangle in Washington, D.C.

RI12 Bell Tower

1824, Levi Swain. 1911, renovation, Carneal and Johnston. Franklin St. at Capitol Sq.

The Bell Tower, which replaced an earlier structure on the site, provides a significant visual terminus to Franklin Street. The bell was used to rally the local citizenry and military units in times of emergency. Swain hailed from Boston and came to Richmond at about the same time as Alexander Parris.

RI13 Washington Monument

1850, design and initial sculpture, Thomas Crawford. 1869, completed sculpture, Randolph Rogers. Grace St. at capitol grounds

In a city known for its outdoor monuments, this was the first. It was also the first equestrian Washington to be erected nationally and

RI14 Virginia State Washington Office Building

1922, Carneal and Johnston. 1100 Bank St.

The first high-rise building constructed by the Commonwealth of Virginia, this began the process of closing off vistas of the capitol. The Renaissance Revival skyscraper has two major facades, one facing the financial district and the other Capitol Square. On Capitol Square the building is U-shaped and blocks the view of the southeast corner of the square. The major entrance to the building, facing the square, consists of an Ionic portico topped by a notable sculptural group.

RI15 Treasury Building (Library of Virginia)

1895, William Poindexter. c. 1920, addition, W. Duncan Lee. 1102 Bank St.

Constructed as the Library of Virginia, this was originally an asymmetrical structure consisting of the present portico and north wing. Later renovations added the south wing and removed a large Palladian window. The Ionic portico reflects the influence of Jefferson's capitol.

Court End–East Broad Street from 14th Street to 3rd Street   (RI16–RI37)

Court End originally referred to a residential neighborhood on Shockoe Hill, chiefly north of the capitol, which included churches along Broad Street. Today it includes only the area bounded by East Broad Street on the south, I-95 on the east, and Leigh Street on the north and reaches as far west as 8th Street. After Shockoe Hill was established as the site of the capitol in 1780, many leading citizens began to build their houses nearby. These "plantations-in-town," as Richmond historian Mary Wingfield Scott called them, included several outbuildings and sometimes large gardens. Only one eighteenth-century dwelling (the Marshall House) remains, but several prominent residences and churches have survived from the nineteenth century. Both city and state government began to intrude on the area after the Civil War. The growth of the Medical College of Virginia (MCV) over the past 150 years has provided a modern use for many important buildings. Unfortunately, it has also dramatically transformed the scale, density, and character of the neighborhood. Some of Court End's leafy residential streets are now Richmond's worst specimens of urban wind tunnels. MCV has contributed some hulking, unfriendly boxes to the streetscape, and its use of historic structures seems less an endorsement of historic preservation than utilization of the neighborhood's available building stock. The city's unrealized dream of a civic center north of City Hall has contributed to the neighborhood's planning challenges, but the new Library of Virginia and the city's Social Services Building have improved the western portion of Court End in recent years.

RI16 Virginia Department of Transportation (VDOT) Building

1939, Carneal and Johnston. 1401 E. Broad St.

The VDOT building lords it over East Broad Street and contributes to making this district of

RI17 Medical College of Virginia, Virginia Commonwealth University (First African Church)

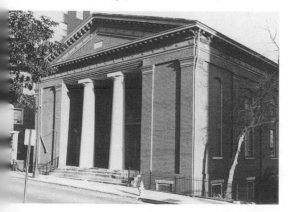

state government and other institutional buildings as dignified and impressive as any in the city. The four-story building, set on a raised base, melds classicism and modernism with moderate success. On the front facade, each of the eighteen three-story stone piers is topped by a stylized Composite capital. They support an entablature whose frieze is emblazoned: "Dedicated to the comfort and safety of those who travel the highways of the Commonwealth of Virginia." A slightly recessed attic, with large, carved eagles serving as sentries at the east and west ends, provides another office level.

RI17 Medical College of Virginia (MCV), Virginia Commonwealth University (First African Church)

1876. 301 College St. (northeast corner of College and Broad sts.)

When the white members of the original First Baptist Church congregation moved up the hill in 1841 to their new edifice, designed by

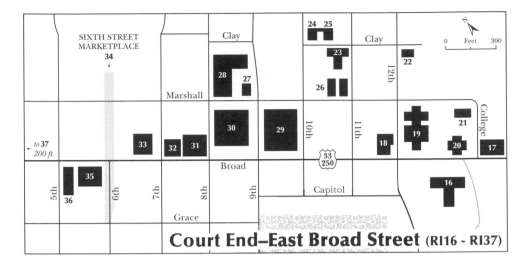

SIXTH STREET MARKETPLACE
34

Clay

24 25

Clay

0   Feet   300

23

22

12th

28   27

26

Marshall

30

29

10th

11th

21

19

18

College

to 37
200 ft.

33

32   31

33
250

20

17

Broad

35

Capitol

16

5th

6th

7th

8th

9th

36

Grace

Court End–East Broad Street (RI16 - RI37)

Thomas U. Walter (see next entry), the African American members stayed in the old church, on this site. They replaced it with this building, obviously influenced by Walter's design, in 1876. Originally the building was stuccoed and had a cupola, which has been removed. Other detailing, such as the rich moldings and rounded arches at the former window openings, is decidedly more Italianate than Greek Revival. The congregation moved to the north side of the city in the 1960s. The interior has been unattractively altered for use as classrooms and offices.

RI18 Hunton Hall (First Baptist Church)

1841, Thomas U. Walter. 1982, renovation, SWA Partnership. 302 N. 11th St. (northwest corner of Broad and 12th sts.)

Walter, a student of William Strickland and a rival of Robert Mills, designed a careful, somber Greek temple for this prominent corner. The distyle in antis porch provided inspiration for other Baptist churches in Richmond for years. The steeple was removed early in the twentieth century. The congregation moved to Monument Avenue in 1938, and MCV has owned this building since then.

RI19 Medical College of Virginia (MCV) West Hospital

1936–1941, Baskervill and Son. 1200 E. Broad St.

This was MCV's main hospital for decades. It faces the old Memorial Hospital across Broad Street, providing a contrast in style, planning, and height. The cruciform plan was the most modern footprint for hospitals in the 1930s, with nurses' stations in the center and wards radiating out. The straightforward Moderne styling in brick reflects its Depression-era construction. A fine metal grille depicting notable medical scientists is suspended over the Broad Street entrance. The tiny garden at the corner contributes a wonderful urban oasis to a concrete stretch of Broad Street. A marker on the lower rear wing on 12th Street commemorates the site of the building where Virginia ratified the U.S. Constitution in 1788.

RI20 Monumental Church

1812–1814, Robert Mills. 1976–1981, restoration, Glave, Newman, Anderson. 1200 block of E. Broad St. Open on request

On December 26, 1811, a stagehand hurriedly raised a lit chandelier into the rafters of the Richmond Theater and ignited one of the worst theater fires in American history. Within minutes seventy-two people were dead, including the governor of Virginia. When the ashes cooled, a brick vault was constructed to hold the remains of the dead, and the city began a campaign to raise a memorial on the site. Robert Mills, who had studied with both Latrobe and Jefferson, won the commission—beating out Latrobe—with this design for an octagonal auditorium church fronted by a monumental porch. An enormous tower based on the Lighthouse of Alexandria was planned

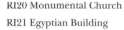
RI20 Monumental Church
RI21 Egyptian Building

to rise behind the auditorium, but it was never built.

The ornament expresses the building's somber program, inside and out. A monument on the porch lists the names of the dead; overhead is a ceiling medallion by Daniel Raynerd, coauthor, with Asher Benjamin, of *The American Builder's Companion* (1806). The interior is a brilliant space, flooded with light from the triple windows and cupola. A graceful balcony curves around seven sides of the interior. The apse is set back behind the pulpit, which is accentuated in the all-white space by its dark green marbling. A window out of sight at the top of the apse provides mysterious light from above. Two oval stairwells flank the auditorium. Their cantilevered stairs elegantly rise to the balcony, and their banisters trace a dark curve against the white ceiling. John Marshall, the marquis de Lafayette, and Edgar Allan Poe's family all worshiped here. The original congregation moved to St. Paul's in 1845, but Monumental remained in use as a church until 1965. The Medical College of Virginia Foundation donated the building to the Historic Richmond Foundation, and it was restored between 1976 and 1981. No viable current use has been found for it, so few visitors get a glimpse of the interior. An overwhelming, emotional space, Monumental Church is both simple and complex—a city's heart-wrenching memorial to deceased friends and relatives.

RI21 **Egyptian Building**

1845, Thomas S. Stewart. 1938–1939, renovation, Baskervill and Son. Southwest corner of College and Marshall sts.

The oldest medical college building in the South housed the forerunner of the Medical College of Virginia. Hampden-Sydney College opened a medical department in the old Union Hotel in Richmond in 1837 and soon needed more space. Designed by Stewart within a year of St. Paul's, this building demonstrates the significance of iconography to nineteenth-century architects and patrons; the medical expertise of the ancient Egyptians evidently suggested the use of the style. A five-story building was effectively disguised in temple form, with giant-order columns, battered walls, and a cove cornice. The exotic detail continues even to the cast iron fence, with herm posts that are often mistaken for mummy cases. (Be sure to count the toes!) The interior renovation carried out in 1938–1939 created a fabulous Art Deco, Egyptian Revival auditorium. This twentieth-century enhancement makes the Egyptian Building probably the only building in America with contributions from two major Egyptian revival periods.

Also worth noting is the base of the unbuilt tower of Monumental Church, only yards away from the Egyptian Building. The level of Richmond's patronage in the nineteenth century on this block alone is evidence of a city at the leading edge of both academic and stylish architecture.

RI22 White House of the Confederacy
(Brockenbrough House)

1818, attributed to Robert Mills. c. 1820s, 1857, alterations. 1895, fireproofing, Henry Baskervill. 1978–1988, restoration, Paul Buchanan and Charles Phillips; Torrence Dreelin Farthing and Buford, historical consultants and associated architects. 1201 E. Clay St.

Now restored to its Civil War–era appearance, the White House of the Confederacy has a complex architectural heritage and a compelling historical site that challenges visitors to confront the human side of a national tragedy. Formerly known as the Brockenbrough House for the prominent banker who commissioned it, the two-story neoclassical house originally boasted a parapet and a shallow hipped roof like the nearby Wickham House. Outbuildings, including a two-story kitchen, were erected over the next few decades. Gardens cascaded over the slope of the hill at the end of Clay Street, and the site commanded views across Shockoe Valley. In 1857 the fourth owner added a third floor, transforming the horizontal neoclassical house into an Italianate mansion with vertical proportions but leaving the spectacular two-story portico facing the garden.

In 1861 the city of Richmond purchased the house and then leased it to serve as the White House of the Confederacy. President Jefferson Davis not only lived here with his family and some staff but also entertained state visitors and worked much of the time from an office on the second floor next to his bedroom. Fewer than thirty-six hours after Davis's departure in April 1865, and only eleven days before he was assassinated, Abraham Lincoln visited the house. Federal troops occupied the house until 1870. For the next twenty years the building served as a public school. As the cult of the Lost Cause intensified, the house acquired a hallowed air of tragedy associated with the fall of the Confederacy and with the Davis family's anguish. When the city declared it unfit to serve as a school in 1890, a movement to save it from demolition grew. The house was purchased by the Confederate Memorial Literary Society in 1894. After fireproofing, it opened as the Confederate Museum in 1896 and remained furnished with artifacts and memorabilia of the Civil War until the 1960s, when enough of the household furnishings had been collected to open a number of rooms. An adjacent museum building was erected in 1975, allowing study and fund raising, which culminated in 1988 with the opening of the scholarly re-creation of the interior spaces in the White House of the Confederacy.

RI23 Wickham House, Valentine Museum

1811–1813, Alexander Parris. 1990, restoration. 1015 E. Clay St. Open to the public

A three-way collaboration produced this exceptional neoclassical house, one of three houses that make up the Valentine Museum complex. The designer, a young builder from New England named Alexander Parris, traveled through the mid-Atlantic region in search of architectural education and experience. John Wickham, a wealthy and sophisticated Richmond attorney who wished to display his taste and fortune, hired him to design a new mansion in Court End. During the design process Wickham sent a draft of Parris's plans to his acquaintance, the architect Benjamin Henry Latrobe, whose advice was incorporated into the final scheme. Parris also designed the Executive Mansion (RI3) and at least one other house during his stay in Richmond. He returned in 1812 to Massachusetts, where he established himself as a leading architect.

Parris eventually provided Wickham with this restrained, three-bay design, with a small entrance porch and a circular central stair hall. The three rear rooms offer egress through triple-hung windows onto a single-story portico that overlooks the garden. The central bay of the rear of the house bows out, enlivening the flow between the interior and the exterior. Wickham owned the entire block, and his correspondence indicates that he gardened enthusiastically. Elements from this house and others influenced by Latrobe reappeared in Richmond for several decades. After architectural investigations by Charles Phillips and Paul Buchanan, the high-style building was recently restored and appropriately furnished. Of special interest are neoclassical wall paintings in the parlor and the dining room.

The Wickham House and an eclectic collection of artifacts were willed to the city in 1892 by a later resident, Mann S. Valentine II. The studio of Valentine's brother, the sculptor Edward Virginius Valentine, was moved from a nearby site to the garden in the 1930s, and its

cluttered interior provides a haunting view of an artist's life at the turn of the twentieth century. The studio is currently under restoration.

In addition to the Wickham House, the Valentine Museum includes the Italianate Granville Valentine House (1869; 1978, rear addition, Glave, Newman, Anderson) and the Greek Revival Bransford-Cecil House (1840; moved to site in 1954). The museum has exhibitions, a library, and archives devoted to the history of Richmond.

RI24 Benjamin Watkins Leigh House

1812–1816. c. 1850, addition. 1000 E. Clay St.

John Wickham built the Leigh House for his daughter and her husband, a United States senator. A third story and Italianate trim and front porch were added to the original Federal house in the 1850s. Little of its original interior remains.

RI25 William H. Grant House

1857. 1908, conversion to a hospital. 1008 E. Clay St.

The Grant House appears fortresslike with its ornate cast iron window caps and Italianate detailing. One of the largest houses built in the city before the Civil War, it has a massive red brick facade that appears to swallow up the openings. The heavy cornice is of wood. Converted into a hospital in 1908, the building now houses administrative offices for the Medical College of Virginia.

RI26 Putney Houses

1861 and 1859. 1010 and 1012 E. Marshall St.

These two dignified town houses blend well together but have decorative elements that compete. The Samuel Putney House, at number 1010, is richly Italianate, with an ornate cast iron porch and wonderful wall painting in the parlors. The Stephen Putney House next door has a simpler facade with a two-story cast iron veranda manufactured by the Phoenix Iron Foundry of Richmond.

RI27 John Marshall House

1788–1790. 818 E. Marshall St.

The oldest surviving brick house in the city contains on the interior the type of handsome

RI22 White House of the Confederacy (Brockenbrough House)

RI23 Wickham House, Valentine Museum

RI27 John Marshall House

paneling and woodwork that ornamented many eighteenth-century Virginia houses. John Marshall, chief justice of the United States Supreme Court, lived here from the time the house was completed until his death in 1835. Marshall was a dignified, unassuming man, and his simple, handsome house expresses the owner's character. In 1907 Marshall's descendants sold the house to the city, whose intention was to demolish it and build a school on the lot. Women's groups banned together to save the house in an effort characteristic of the burgeoning historic preservation movement. The house was deeded to the APVA in 1911, and the new John Marshall High School was built in an L shape around it. Ironically, the high school was later demolished, and now the house is engulfed by the John Marshall Courts Building.

RI28 John Marshall Courts Building

1978, C. F. Murphy and Associates; Helmut Jahn, project architect. 1993, alterations, Hening-Vest-Covey. 800 E. Marshall St.

Designed to respect the Marshall House next door, the sleek, black glass box of the John Marshall Courts Building sets off the house, emphasizing its iconic, welcoming facade. This is perhaps its only success, because the court building has been plagued with criticism for its dysfunction. Recent alterations have attempted to correct traffic and security issues.

RI29 Richmond City Hall

1971, Ballou and Justice. 900 E. Broad St. Observation deck open weekdays

Conceived as the centerpiece of an ambitious civic center plan that also saw construction of the nearby Safety, Health and Welfare Building and the Richmond Coliseum, this clumsy nineteen-story exercise in modernism sorely lacks any contextual fit. By the mid-1990s its stark white marble cladding posed a significant safety hazard when it began to fall onto the surrounding sidewalks. The sheathing is now secured by a semipermanent system of nylon straps, which serve as Band-Aids for a larger problem. The building occupies an entire block and manages to address all four street fronts adequately. Although the entrance is on Broad Street, the ceremonial front, with an impressive relief seal of the city embedded over the entrance, faces Marshall Street. Spindly antennae and other communications equipment projecting from the roof give the building a cartoonlike, Buck Rogers look. A top-floor observation deck provides a marvelous bird's-eye view of downtown.

RI30 Library of Virginia

1993–1997, Skidmore, Owings and Merrill, and Glave, Newman, Anderson. 800 E. Broad St.

The impressive procession of state government and other institutional buildings reaches its apex at this bold, modernistic statement in limestone, glass, and aluminum. Craig Hartman of the San Francisco office of SOM was the design partner. Despite its nod to urbanism—battered granite walls at the ground level, three sweeping canopies marking the main entrance, and even display windows to entice would-be patrons inside—the building is unsatisfactorily sited. It is aligned neither with the setback of City Hall, to the east, nor with Theater Row to its west. Thus the bulky building seems oddly in limbo. But the library's central atrium is an impressive, light-filled space and serves to orient the visitor visually to the library's offerings. A gently tapering flight of granite steps entices patrons from the lobby to the reading rooms and research spaces on the second level. Taken as a whole, the interior lifts the spirits and inspires—something that powerful architecture should do.

RI31 Theater Row

1919, Colonial Theatre. 1993, office tower, Glave, Newman, Anderson. 718 E. Broad St.

Throughout most of twentieth century this block was part of a theater district that included both playhouses and cinemas. Richmond has an abundance of elaborate old movie palaces, and apparently (and unfortunately) civic leaders thought that the auditorium of the Colonial, the oldest standing movie theater in Richmond, could be sacrificed for an office building. The resulting "facade-ectomy" retains the Renaissance Revival facade with its lavish ornaments by Richmond sculptor Ferruccio Legnaioli. While the boxy office tower that rises behind the facade makes an attempt at context, it is overly fussy and looks like a giant 1920s floor-model radio.

was designed to incorporate mixed uses on Richmond's traditional main commercial thoroughfare. Shops at the sidewalk level and office spaces on upper levels encase a spectacular Adamesque auditorium that awaits a new use. The front is ornately detailed with a frieze of dancing nymphs, festive balconies, and ornate medallions. The refined decoration, inside and out, was designed by Richmonder Ferruccio Legnaioli. During the late 1990s the exterior of this spectacular Italian Renaissance Revival building was restored to its original sheen.

RI33 **The Elder Building**

1982, Skidmore, Owings and Merrill. 600 E. Broad St.

Although this simple brick modernist office structure is one of the architecturally more successful aspects of Project One (a public-private effort to reinvigorate parts of Broad Street downtown), it fails in an ironic way: it has few shopfronts to enhance the vitality of Broad Street.

RI34 **Sixth Street Marketplace**

1982, Marcellus Wright, Cox and Smith. 1984. Pedestrian bridge crossing Broad St. at 6th St. and continuing along former 6th St. two blocks north and one block south

RI28 John Marshall Courts Building

RI30 Library of Virginia

RI31 Theater Row

RI32 **The National Theater**

1922, Claude K. Howell. 1997, restoration. 704 E. Broad St.

This solidly massed building, with a central four-story block and flanking two-story wings,

This downtown shopping mall crosses Broad Street dramatically via a steel bridge that evokes the Victorian fascination with construction materials. From this dramatic point, however, the downtown mall then disappears as it is wedged into the path of former 6th Street. The interior of the three-block-long mall is handsomely detailed (as late twentieth-century shopping malls go) with tile flooring and exposed ductwork near the ceiling. Immediately north of Marshall Street, in an airy, soaring conservatory-like structure, is the mall's food court. The structure is attached to, but does not diminish, the former Blues Armory building. Problems with retaining tenants may lead to the market's demise.

RI35 Miller and Rhoads Department Store (former)

1915, Charles M. Robinson. 1933, alterations, Carneal, Johnston and Wright. 1922, Grace St. elevation, Starrett and Van Vleck. c. 1950, additional floors, Grace St., Carneal and Johnston. 517 E. Broad St.

The 1933 sandstone "Syrian" Art Deco facade of this Richmond-based former department store was a stylish update of an earlier building: "Naturally, we wish to keep up to the forefront and to be as modern as possible," said the store's president at the dedication. The Broad Street facade and its more sedate but no less handsome classical fronts facing 5th and Grace streets are part of the fabric of downtown's fading retail district. The wealth of Art Deco fronts waits to be rediscovered and cleaned. As of this writing the building stands empty, as the city of Richmond considers razing the landmark to establish a large public plaza on the site.

RI36 F. W. Woolworth Co.

1954, Carneal and Johnston. 509 E. Broad St.

It is obvious that when the architects who designed the Miller and Rhoads Broad Street facade received the commission for this midtown Woolworth, they would seek a sympathetic if not contextual solution. Shifting stylistic gears dramatically from the department store's Art Deco facade, Carneal and Johnston designed a building of sleek 1950s modernism. The horizontality of three levels of ribbon windows contrasts strongly with the verticality of the large Woolworth sign.

RI37 W. T. Grant and Company

1939, Baskervill and Son. 323 E. Broad St.

This Classical Deco facade provides an architectural lesson in adept handling of an urban street corner. The curved glass shop windows, capped with a steel canopy, direct the pedestrian's attention in two directions, to the Broad Street and 4th Street entrances. A display window on the second-level corner was designed to catch the attention of approaching drivers and pedestrian traffic.

Shockoe Valley   (RI38–RI63)

The Shockoe Valley (or Shockoe Bottom) area is the oldest section of Richmond. The name of the area comes from Shockoe (sometimes spelled Shacco, from a Native American word referring to a large flat rock) Creek, which flowed into the James River at the uppermost point of navigation. Until it was enclosed as a culvert in 1877, the creek, which ran between present-day 15th and 16th streets, divided Richmond in two. Shockoe Valley was laid out in a grid as part of William Mayo's plan, with a town common fronting the James River. Throughout the eighteenth century the valley was the center of the thriving but small settlement of Richmond. During this time the area developed slowly with construction of a few modest residences, commercial structures, and tobacco warehouses. The establishment of a market in 1796 at what is presently the intersection of 17th and Main streets caused a thriving retail district to develop. A wave of commercial development during the flush times after the War of 1812 resulted in the construction of the Richmond Navigation Canal along the James River. Commercial development continued in the 1840s and 1850s with the arrival of the first railroads and the growth of Richmond as a major tobacco manufacturing center. The develop-

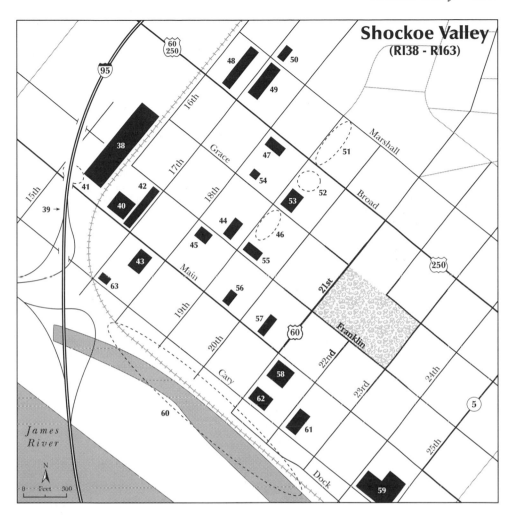

ment of the area as a major transportation, warehousing, and manufacturing hub continued well into the twentieth century.

Throughout the history of Shockoe Valley, the area was also a center of immigration into the city. Successive waves of northerners and rural African Americans as well as Scots, Irish, Germans, and German, Eastern European, and Sephardic Jews tended to settle here on arrival. These and other immigrant groups opened businesses, worked as laborers, and often lived above the commercial structures in the neighborhood.

Development came to an abrupt halt with the Great Depression. Shockoe Valley went into a fifty-year period of decline. Many of the businesses in the area closed or relocated. A considerable number of buildings fell into neglect or to the wrecking ball. Richmond preservationists worked to save some of the more historic structures. However, substantial revitalization did not occur until the late 1980s. Since then, a considerable number of industrial buildings have been converted to residential use, and the area has become the center of the city's night life. It has developed a popular identity as Shockoe Bottom or simply "the Bottom."

RI38 Main Street Station

1899–1901, Wilson, Harris, and Richards. 1983–1985, renovation, SWA Architects, Inc. 1520 E. Main St.

Located in the center of what was then one of Richmond's principal business districts, Main Street Station was designed as the gateway to a flourishing downtown. It was built to serve as both depot and offices for the Chesapeake and Ohio and the Seaboard Air Line railroads, whose elevated tracks stretch out on viaducts and trestles in three directions from this former transportation hub. The designers, the architectural partnership of Wilson, Harris, and Richards of Philadelphia, specialized in railroad architecture. Earlier known as Wilson Brothers, it was for years headed by Joseph Wilson, an engineer as well as an architect.

The metal shed, more than 400 feet long, is itself a rare and noteworthy survivor of this type of station design. The station head house is a five-story brick building that rises from a rock-faced ashlar base. The predominant French Renaissance style of the building is enlivened by the distinctive steep red terra-cotta tile roof, pierced by ranks of dormers of varied size and decoration. Corinthian columns and terra-cotta details frame the clock faces on four sides of the tower and support a tiled roof crowned by a large finial 110 feet above the ground. In comparison to the richness of the exterior decoration, the interior emphasized functionality for the accommodation of passengers, freight,

and the railroad administrators, housed in offices on the upper floors.

Flood damage and the decline of railroad travel led to the closing of Main Street Station as a passenger depot in 1975. A devastating fire in 1983 destroyed the entire tile roof of the main station and heavily damaged the upper floors and the clock tower. The conversion in 1985 of the station into a shopping mall entailed both the careful reconstruction of the damaged roof and the enclosure of the rail shed. The shopping mall subsequently failed, and in 1988 the Commonwealth of Virginia purchased Main Street Station for use as office space for the Department of Health. Funding is being secured to return the facility to service as a transportation center by 2003.

RI39 Richmond Petersburg Turnpike Viaduct

1958, Virginia Department of Transportation. 15th and Main sts.

The massive elevated freeway that looms over Shockoe Bottom neatly detours around Main Street Station. The viaduct nearly follows the bed of Shockoe Creek and serves as a divider between Shockoe Valley and downtown Richmond.

RI40 Railroad YMCA (former)

1907, Wilson, Harris, and Richards. 1552 E. Main St.

This nearly ruined structure is a smaller but notable exercise in the French Renaissance style, similar to its elder neighbor, Main Street Station. The building possesses a significant array of ornamental brickwork and terra-cotta. It was constructed to serve railroad workers from the numerous rail facilities in the area.

RI41 1553–1561 East Main Street

1900. 1996, renovation, SWA Architects

This block is one of the best groups of late nineteenth- and early twentieth-century commercial architecture in the Shockoe Valley area. The entire block has been recently gutted, new storefronts have been inserted, and a parking deck has been constructed at the rear.

RI42 Richmond Farmers Market

1976, Glave, Newman, Anderson. 1600 E. Main St.

This open shed stands on the site of an earlier enclosed market and successive buildings of 1796, 1858, and 1913. It was the center of the meat and produce business in the city. The terra-cotta bull's heads are relics from a demolished market building on 6th Street.

RI43 McCurdy Building

c. 1845. 1731 E. Main St.

Antebellum commercial buildings like this once characterized Main Street, from Shockoe Bottom to the financial district. This structure is one of the last of its kind in the city. The granite storefront and stepped gable are characteristic of the building type.

RI44 None-Such Place Restaurant

1828. c. 1870 and later, alterations and additions. E. Franklin St.

This commercial building is credited with being the oldest surviving commercial building in the city. Constructed during the flush times following the War of 1812, it received several additions. The upper floors, with segmental-arched windows and parapet gables, date from the 1970s.

RI45 Masons' Hall

1785–1787. c. 1850, renovations. 1809 E. Franklin St.

Built for Richmond Lodge Number 12, this hall is reputed to be the oldest Masonic building in the United States. The frame structure on a raised brick basement is Anglo-Palladian in style. The pediment, cupola, and other details appear to have been influenced by an English pattern book, possibly Robert Morris's *Select Architecture* (1757). The Greek Revival portico is a later addition, possibly from the 1850s.

RI46 Belle Boisseaux Block

1878. 101–109 N. 18th St.

One of the best surviving examples of an Italianate business block in Shockoe Bottom, this three-story, multibay building has cast iron balconies, normally used only on houses, on both its 18th Street and its Franklin Street facades. In this case, the ground floors served commerical establishments and the offices on the upper two floors were provided with balconies.

RI47 Richmond Public Baths

1908, Allen and Archer. 1801 E. Broad St.

Designed by a Baltimore firm, this building reveals the immigrant and working-class character of the area at the turn of the twentieth century. The cornice is typical of the Mediterranean Revival style, while the brickwork and windows have an Arts and Crafts orientation.

RI48 Chesapeake and Ohio Freight Depot and Warehouse

c. 1890. 1600 E. Broad St.

A largely intact freight depot, the building, with its long clerestory roof, extends back from Broad Street for nearly two blocks. Along the sides of the depot are sheds and loading bays. Behind the depot is a plain two-story warehouse.

RI49 Spence-Nunnamaker Warehouse

1909, Albert T. Huntt. 317 N. 17th St.

Huntt, born in Richmond and the grandson of one of Richmond's earliest architects, Otis Manson, practiced in town from 1892 to 1920, designing a host of buildings of every type and in every style. This is his finest surviving commercial design. The fireproof reinforced concrete building has exterior details reminiscent of the Arts and Crafts movement. The facade has massive piers topped by round corbeled arches. Beneath the arches are steel casement

RI49 Spence-Nunnamaker Warehouse

windows. The exterior cladding alternates between green and white tile and dark brick.

RI50 Richmond Cold Storage Warehouses

1911. 401 N. 17th St.

The reinforced concrete structure of this complex of refrigerated warehouses is hidden by brick cladding. This portion of Shockoe Bottom is largely taken up by food processing and cold storage facilities which clustered here in the nineteenth century because of the railroads and are evidence of major commerce in produce and meat.

RI51 Elmtree Row

1853–1854. 301–307 N. 19th St.

Simple Greek Revival residences such as these once filled Shockoe Valley. The gable-roofed, three-bay row houses are two-story structures with English basements. Several of the Doric entrance porticoes are intact or are being restored.

RI52 Hebrew Sheltering Aid Society and Temple Keneseth Israel

c. 1870. c. 1910, addition. c. 1890, synagogue. 211–219 N. 19th St.

This complex of buildings represents the immigrant history of Shockoe Bottom. The Temple Keneseth Israel was built by Eastern European Jewish immigrants. To assist those who arrived to Richmond by train, the Hebrew Sheltering Aid Society purchased the Second Empire house and around 1910 added a large Renaissance Revival wing. The long history of the Jewish community in Shockoe Bottom also survives in the old Hebrew Cemetery at North 20th and East Franklin streets.

RI53 Pace King House

1860. 205 N. 19th St.

A brick three-bay Italianate mansion, this has one of the most lavish cast iron porches ever built in the city. Of particular interest are the building's two-story slave quarters at the rear, some of the last left in Richmond.

RI54 Adam Craig House

1784. 1820, dependency. c. 1850, alterations. 1812 E. Grace St.

The house is one of the few surviving examples of what Mary Wingfield Scott termed a "plantation-in-town." Building complexes such as this one commonly occupied one or more of the large lots that characterize the 1737 Mayo plan and later additions. This building occupies an entire original city lot. The builder followed the practice of some early Richmond builders of siting the house askew to the city grid on a true east-west axis. The house itself is an I-house with a long rear wing. Portions of the addition and the porch were added in the mid-nineteenth century. A brick dependency was added at the rear of the structure. The original owner, Adam Craig, the clerk of the Richmond court, maintained a small office at the corner of 19th and Grace.

RI55 Grant Tobacco Factory

1853, Samuel Freeman. 1900 E. Franklin St.

In large, warehouselike buildings such as the Grant factory, slave laborers stemmed, flavored, and pressed plug tobacco. Scottish-born architect-builder Samuel Freeman built a number of these factories. The Yarborough Factory at 25th and Franklin streets is another example.

RI56 Old Stone House and Edgar Allan Poe Museum

c. 1737. 1928, museum addition. 1916–1918 E. Main St.

This museum complex serves a dual purpose of preserving Richmond's oldest building and memorializing famous son Edgar Allan Poe. The stone house was reputedly constructed the year Richmond was laid out and is credited to German immigrant Joseph Ege (though some claim it dates from 1754). The cottage is typical of the design and scale of the city's colonial architecture, but the use of granite is unusual for the period. Even though Poe never had any association with the structure, Richmond antiquarians created a memorial to him here in the 1920s, a memorial garden and museum built of bricks from the Southern Literary Messenger building, where Poe worked as an editor.

RI57 Engine Company No. 2

1899, Wilfred Emory Cutshaw, Richmond City Engineer. 2016 E. Main St.

Cutsaw, as the city engineer, designed a significant number of buildings in Richmond in a variety of styles. In this case he picked the currently popular Dutch Colonial Revival and created a flamboyant example with a stepped gable roof in front, gambrel roof in rear, and vibrant limestone trim.

RI58 Henrico County Government Complex and Courthouse

1896, Carl Ruehrmund. c. 1920, addition. 1893, jail. 2117–2127 E. Main St.

The Henrico County government was located in the city of Richmond from 1752 until 1974, when it moved to the suburbs. The county moved to this site in 1843, and by 1895 the building was outmoded. Not desiring to repeat the cost overruns of Richmond City Hall, the county commissioners specified that the cost was not to exceed $20,000. They accepted the designs of the German-born and -trained architect Ruehrmund, who came to the United States in 1881 and shortly thereafter settled in Richmond. His career was long and profitable. The twin-towered facility is in the popular Richardsonian Romanesque style, with round arches and thick brick walls. The penury of the commissioners led to a rather tame design, lacking the vibrancy of other courthouses of the period.

RI59 Tobacco Row Apartment Complex

c. 1900. 1987, rehabilitation, Eisenman/Robertson Architects–Glave, Newman, Anderson. 25th and Main sts.

One of the largest rehabilitation projects ever conducted in the country, this one successfully adapted large portions of the American Tobacco Company (Lucky Strike) Factory for apartment use. The development incorporates many of the amenities of suburban apartment complexes, including a clubhouse, parking, and swimming pool. The complex extends to Cary Street, where a mile-long row of industrial buildings and warehouses creates a solid wall of industrial buildings. With largely open space on the south side of Cary Street, the Tobacco Row district offers one of the most striking architectural vistas in the city of Richmond.

RI60 Richmond Dock and Chesapeake and Ohio Elevated Railway

1816, Robert Mills, engineer for dock. c. 1900, railway. Between Dock St. and the James River

These engineering works can easily be viewed from Cary Street. The Richmond Dock was a major development of the Richmond Canal System, which allowed ships to pass upriver from Richmond's port, at the point known as Rocketts, all the way to 14th Street. It was eventually connected to the James River and Kanawha Canal. The elevated railway was a later improvement that allowed through trains literally to rise above the congested rail areas in Shockoe Valley and downtown Richmond.

RI61 Carolina Warehouse

1899, Albert T. Huntt. 2200 E. Cary St.

Typical of nineteenth-century industrial design, the Carolina Warehouse is characterized by massive masonry walls, small openings, and a lack of adornment. A twin to this building can be found in the Climax Warehouse at 2000 East Cary Street.

RI62 Larus Brothers Tobacco Factory

1923, 1925. 2100 E. Cary St.

With its finished concrete walls and steel casement windows, this building incorporated the
most up-to-date "fireproof" industrial design of
the 1920s. Such buildings are typically constructed of reinforced concrete with brick or
finished concrete exteriors, have large, expansive casement windows, and are taller than earlier industrial buildings.

RI63 Virginia Bonded Warehouse

1911, Scarborough and Howell. 1700 E. Cary St.

The building uses traditional "mill" construction (brick walls and wood framing). The large
brick piers create a handsome, articulated facade that sets it apart from the boxy warehouses of the nineteenth century.

Church Hill (RI64–RI96)

The western part of this area, named for St. John's Church and known by that name and as
Richmond Hill, dates from the original layout of Richmond in 1737. William Byrd donated
two lots for Henrico Parish Church, but their initially inaccessible location on the highest
point in the new town delayed construction of a church until 1741. The area was annexed by
Richmond in 1780, but substantial building began only after 1800. Each block or square was
divided into four large lots. Architectural historian Mary Wingfield Scott dubbed the few
early dwellings on these lots "plantations-in-town" because they had that appearance—a
brick or frame house surrounded by a rambling group of outbuildings and gardens. Development of the area was largely impeded because the grid plan did not consider the rough,
hilly topography. Until the 1840s the only means of access to the neighborhood was 25th
Street, a steep, ungraded hill. The neighborhood began to develop substantially in the 1840s,
as tobacconists whose factories or business concerns were located in the valley sought the
more healthful air of the hill. After 1850 the suburban landscape began to disappear as the
large lots were subdivided and detached town houses, semidetached double houses, and
rows of three or more houses were built. By 1900 the area had been filled in and decline set
in.

   By the 1950s the neighborhood directly around the church was threatened by such neglect
that the William Byrd Branch of APVA bought two significant houses with the intention of
restoring them for later sale with protective covenants. This led to the founding in 1956 of
the Historic Richmond Foundation, which initially focused on a pilot block, just west of the
church, known as Carrington Square. A collaboration of individuals with government and
nonprofit organizations succeeded in restoring it, and, in time, the entire neighborhood.

RI64 St. John's Church

1741, Richard Randolph, builder (current transept).
1772, northern nave addition. 1829, nave extension.
1833, tower. 1866, rebuilding of tower. 1874, additional entrances. 1877, apse. 1904–1905, rebuilding
of tower, replacement of apse with sanctuary and side
rooms. 1970–present, restoration, James Scott Rawlings, restoration architect; Vernon Perdue Davis, consultant. 2400 block E. Broad St.

St. John's Church is a frequently visited site and
one of the city's most famous buildings. Here
on March 23, 1775, Patrick Henry stirred patriots' souls with his "Give me liberty or give me
death!" The original section was built in 1741
as a small parish church in what was then Henrico County. In its earliest years it was known as
the Upper Church, or the church on Richmond Hill. It was the largest public building in

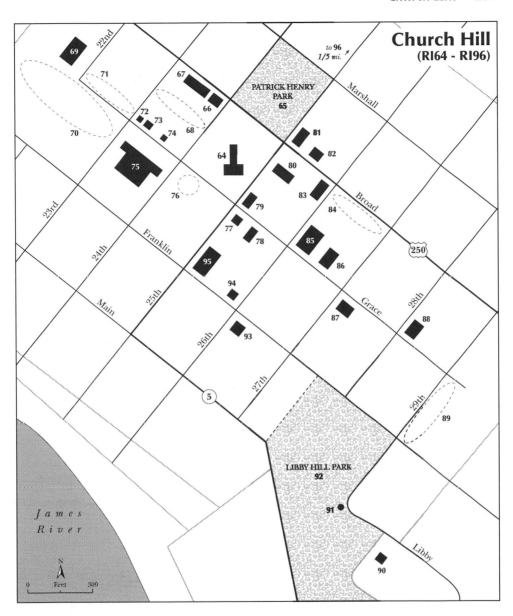

town for many years and had the only public burial ground until the city opened Shockoe Cemetery in 1826.

The building has grown in every direction, including up. The original structure is now the transept. Like many other Virginia country churches, it was a simple frame rectangular building with a double-pitched roof, built with the traditional east-west orientation. By 1772 more space was needed to serve the growing town. A nave was added to the north side of the

church, transforming it to a T-shaped plan. This was the configuration when Virginia's second Revolutionary convention met here to avoid conflict with the British colonial government in Williamsburg and Patrick Henry gave his famous address. Surprisingly, Henry's words were not recorded until 1835 when his biographer, William Wirt, interviewed witnesses.

Since then, the church has expanded into the building we see today. The nave was extended, a tower built and then rebuilt, an apse

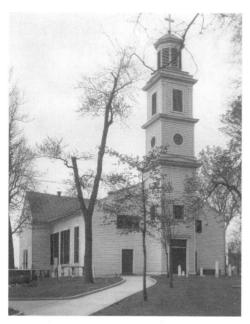

RI64 St. John's Church

added and then replaced with a sanctuary. Beginning in 1970, restoration has refined the changes, and research has clarified the metamorphosis of this historic site.

The churchyard is a fascinating history lesson, boasting the graves of two governors as well as those of John Marshall, George Wythe (a signer of the Declaration of Independence and Thomas Jefferson's law professor), and Elizabeth Arnold Poe (Edgar Allan Poe's actress mother). In 1799 the city purchased two lots on the north side of the block to augment the public burial ground and has maintained the churchyard ever since. Several other buildings populate the churchyard, including a frame parish hall (1876), a brick schoolhouse (1835), a brick furnace house (1929), and one of Richmond's most charming small buildings, the keeper's lodge (c. 1885), now used as a gift shop. It is a white-painted frame Carpenter's Gothic miniature with exuberant windows and buttresses that belie its size.

RI65　Patrick Henry Park

1961, 1964, 1966, partial implementation. 1992, redesign and planting, Higgins Associates, landscape architects. 2400 block of E. Broad St. (north side)

Planned as a setting to frame St. John's Church, the park across the street was an eyesore for years, with a deteriorating modern reflecting pool, painted light blue, at the center. The park was replanned and refurbished in the early 1990s.

RI66　Carrington Row

1818, attributed to Otis Manson; later additions. 2307–2311 E. Broad St.

These three handsome row houses have contributed to Richmond's architectural fabric in two important ways. First, they display the early nineteenth-century popularity of a handsome, muscular neoclassicism imported to Richmond through the work of Benjamin Latrobe and Robert Mills. Their design is attributed to Otis Manson, a builder and architect who had come from Boston. Second, they form an important part of the Pilot Block, which spurred preservation efforts in Richmond. The different entrance treatments were retained to record the stylistic changes rendered by generations of owners. The central doorway, with a simple fanlight and no covering, is the original. The Greek Revival porch at 2311 would have been added about three decades later. The pedimented Italianate hood at 2307 would have come last, in the late nineteenth century.

RI67　Houses

c. 1900. 2300 block of E. Broad St. (south side)

These buildings exhibit some of the typical nineteenth-century styles for which Church Hill is admired. They finish off the Broad Street face of the Pilot Block. Examples are 2305 East Broad Street (1854; c. 1916, alterations) and 2315 East Broad Street (1888).

RI68　The Mews

1965, landscaping restoration, Garden Club of Virginia; design by Ralph E. Griswold, Griswold, Winters and Swain of Pittsburgh, landscape architects

Between the 2300 block of East Broad and East Grace streets is the east-west alley called the Mews. It is an important component of the Pilot Block restoration project. This civilized urban space promotes the amenities of city liv-

RI66 Carrington Row

RI69 WRVA/WRVQ Radio Station

ing. On display are salvaged fragments exhibiting the city's ironwork.

RI69 **WRVA/WRVQ Radio Station**

1968, Philip Johnson with Budina and Freeman, associate architects. 200 N. 22nd St.

When WRVA radio built this studio and office, the revitalization of Church Hill was gathering momentum. Johnson, an internationally known architect, was commissioned because of the prominence of the site and the sensitivity needed to accommodate the historic neighborhood adjacent. This unobtrusive building may seem out of place, but it is a fascinating and quirky artifact that provides interest on the skyline. It is currently empty, its future uncertain.

RI70 **Richmond Hill** (Monte Maria)

c. 1810–c. 1920. 2100 and 2200 blocks of E. Grace St. (south side). Open to the public

These lots at the edge of the hill overlooking the river were the site of prominent early residences in the neighborhood. Richard Adams, who owned much of the hill, built his house here around 1790. About twenty years later, William Palmer built a house nearby, which was sold to William Taylor in 1859. Taylor added a second floor, a cupola, and double porches overlooking the river, creating a much grander house. In 1866 the houses were purchased by the Catholic Diocese of Richmond, and the Order of the Visitation of Mary opened a school named Monte Maria in the Adams House. The Romanesque Revival chapel was erected east of the Palmer-Taylor House in 1894–1895. After the nuns received a large donation, they closed the school in 1927 to devote themselves to prayer. The next year the Adams House was demolished to make way for a new dormitory. The nuns maintained a cloistered convent on the site until 1987, when they moved to a smaller, more isolated location. The complex was purchased by a religious organization founded to preserve the site as a place of prayer and worship in the city.

RI71 **Houses**

1870–c. 1890. 2200 block of E. Grace St. (north side)

This block boasts a number of fine Italianate and Queen Anne houses. Four row houses at the east end of the block are occupied by the 2300 Club, a small private club originally housed in the 2300 block of East Broad Street. It was founded in 1964 to encourage restoration of the area.

RI72 **Hardgrove House**

1849. Later alterations and restoration. 2300 E. Grace St.

This substantial three-bay brick Greek Revival house with a low but powerful portico served for years as the state headquarters of the APVA. Originally a parapet at the cornice line made the house even more impressive. On the grounds are a one-story dependency that was used for tobacco processing experiments and a two-story slave dependency.

RI73 Hilary Baker House

1813–1816. c. 1860, addition. 1955, restoration. 2302 E. Grace St.

The Baker House is important both for its architecture and for its role in Richmond's historic preservation efforts. It began as an austere Federal-period house with enormous chimneys. The addition of a large, elaborate veranda c. 1860 required the lengthening of the first-floor windows. The veranda was subsequently removed and, as part of a restoration of the house by the William Byrd Branch of the APVA, Mary Wingfield Scott designed an entrance porch. The original two-story servants' quarters, clearly visible from the Mews, is a rare survival.

RI74 Ann Carrington House

c. 1813, attributed to Otis Manson. 2306 E. Grace St.

The first house built on the Pilot Block, the neoclassical Carrington House is more sophisticated than the later Baker House, though it is not as elegant as Manson's later houses. Its bow front, exaggerated flat arches, and triple windows distinguish it. The remainder of this block exhibits elaborate porches, many of cast iron. The ironwork on 2312–2314 was saved from other demolished buildings and placed here in 1965.

RI75 Bellevue School

1911, Carneal and Johnston. 2301 E. Grace St.

The city of Richmond built this elementary school on the former site of a prominent residence, the Van Lew House, an enormous, architecturally sophisticated structure. The house was the home of Elizabeth Van Lew and the birthplace of Maggie Lena Walker. Van Lew's image has engaged the imagination of generations of Richmonders. A Union sympathizer, she supposedly was a spy who housed Union troops, trained housekeepers to infiltrate the White House of the Confederacy, and passed information to Union generals. Maggie Walker, daughter of the Van Lews' cook and born at the Van Lew House, was the first female bank president in the United States. Her house is preserved in Jackson Ward and is a National Historic Site. The red brick and limestone school building is nominally Collegiate Gothic in its pointed-arched entry but has Jacobean Revival parapet details.

RI76 Van Lew Twin Houses

1844. 2403 and 2407 E. Grace St.

These two brick Greek Revival houses, both two and one-half stories and three bays with side entrances and porticoes, were the only houses on the block for several decades. Both have two-story rear porches. Eliza Van Lew, mother of Elizabeth (see preceding entry), had them built as rental properties. From 1846 to 1852 Elmira Royster Shelton rented number 2407. Shelton, a widow, was a savvy businesswoman, but she is known today as Edgar Allan Poe's sweetheart. When they were both teenagers, she and Poe fell in love and secretly promised that they would marry. When Poe left Richmond to attend the University of Virginia, he wrote many letters to Elmira, but her father, who disapproved of the relationship, intercepted them. Each assumed that the other had lost interest and went on to marry someone else. In the 1840s, when Poe returned to Richmond, Poe and Shelton discovered that their attraction was still strong. Both had been widowed, and in 1849 they again decided to marry. After visiting Shelton here at 2407, Poe left for a business trip to New York, but died on the way in Baltimore. The Shelton House was restored in 1957–1958 and served as the headquarters for the Historic Richmond Foundation.

RI77 Adams Double House

c. 1810; later alterations. 2501–2503 E. Grace St.

Probably the oldest double house standing in Richmond, this two-and-one-half-story, four-bay brick block has raised side-bay entrances with porticoes. Stylistically, the house is Federal, with Flemish bond brickwork and keystone lintels. It was built as investment property by the heirs of Dr. Richard Adams. The double house would later become a predominant housing form in the city. The storefront on the 25th Street side of the building was an alteration promoted by extensive regrading of 25th Street as well as other streets in Church Hill.

RI78 2515 East Grace St.

1848. 1972, relocation and renovation. 2515 E. Grace St.

This two-bay brick house with an arched doorway and iron balcony originally stood downtown at 2nd Street. Threatened with demoli-

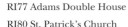
RI77 Adams Double House
RI80 St. Patrick's Church

tion, it was enlisted in the effort to make the St. John's Church neighborhood a showplace of antebellum buildings. Elisabeth Scott Bocock acquired it and had it dismantled and moved to this site.

RI79 Morris Cottages

1830, 1835, John Morris. 2500 E. Grace St. and 201 N. 25th St.

One-and-one-half-story gabled cottages such as these were a common sight in Richmond in the eighteenth and nineteenth centuries. The owner, John Morris, was a carpenter and built one structure as his home and the other as a rental property. The raised basements are not elements of the original design but rather a result of the regrading of 25th Street.

RI80 St. Patrick's Church

1858. 1885–1890, alterations. 217 N. 22nd St.

St. Patrick's is the second oldest Catholic church building in Richmond and one of the oldest in Virginia. Irish immigrants in the eastern section of the city founded the congregation and built the simple structure, reminiscent of A. W. N. Pugin's work. The buttressed and corbeled brick facade is one of the most ornate examples of antebellum brickwork in Rich-

mond. The original interior treatment consisted of wooden paneling and simple Gothic bosses. Renovations added a choir loft, an apse, a French tracker organ, and an Italian marble altar.

RI81 Crestar Bank (Church Hill Bank)

1923, Bascom Rowlett. 2500 E. Broad St.

This building is one of a number of substantial neighborhood banks constructed in the city during the first decades of the century. It is a fine example of a lavishly decorated Beaux-Arts classical facade built on a small scale. The three loggia arches are separated by fluted Ionic columns with rare and curiously formed capitals inspired by those discovered in 1765 at the Temple of Apollo at Bassae (fifth century B.C.). The columns serve as pedestals for two bold carved eagles.

RI82 Nolde Bakery Building

c. 1926, John Edwin Hopkins. 1950–1953. 2510 E. Broad St.

The Nolde Bakery was a Virginia institution for years. The original bakery is a straightforward, two-story warehouse-type structure. The Art Deco office block was added by a New York architect who specialized in bakeries.

RI83 **Belfry Condominiums** (Third Presbyterian Church Complex)

1876. 1890, manse. 1929, Sunday school buildings. 1979, condominium renovation, Glave, Newman, Anderson. 2519 E. Broad St.

This brick Gothic Revival Presbyterian church had become redundant by the mid-1970s and was scheduled to be demolished. Instead, it and the attached buildings were transformed into a housing complex in an excellent example of adaptive reuse that preserved both housing stock and an important local landmark.

RI84 **Mann-Netherwood Block**

1886 (2601–2611 East Broad St.), 1895 (2613 and 2615 East Broad St.), 1901 (2617–2621 East Broad St.). 1975, renovation

The scale of this block is typical of much of the post–Civil War architecture seen on Broad Street and elsewhere in the district. The brick and stone contractors John Mann and James Netherwood built these turreted row houses over a fifteen-year period. The fine brick and stone houses with their iron fences set an impressive rhythm along the street. The iron cresting and the original front and rear porches remain intact. The Historic Richmond Foundation saved the block, developed a common garden area in the rear of the properties, and founded an association to maintain the gardens and the facades in a unified manner.

RI85 **St. Patrick School**

1914, Marcellus Wright, Sr. 2600 E. Grace St.

The Doric portico is the only ornate component of an otherwise simple Georgian Revival structure and one that makes an important statement on the street. The building is one of the few schools the senior Wright designed.

RI86 **James Netherwood House**

1894, James Netherwood, contractor. 2612 E. Grace St.

This two-story, three-bay brick structure is a late example of a town house in the Italianate style, though some Georgian Revival elements are also apparent. The sandstone quoins and incised ornament display the skill of the building's contractor-occupant. Similar cast iron

porches can be found throughout the St. John's Church area, as well as in Jackson Ward, the Fan, and on Grace Street.

RI87 **2700 Block of East Grace Street**

This block represents the greatest architectural diversity to be found on Church Hill. The houses on the north (even-numbered) side are, with two exceptions, from c. 1900. The odd-looking number 2706 (1859) was originally five bays, but a central stair tower was added to the front (c. 1970) to facilitate conversion into a duplex. Cast iron is used for the front window cornices. The house at 2702 (1920) is is a three-bay house with an intact surviving porch. On the south side of the street is a similar mix of mid- and late-nineteenth-century houses. The frame house at number 2703 (1840) is an unusual survivor for Church Hill; frame houses are more typically found in the Jackson Ward and Oregon Hill areas of Richmond. The house has a full-width front porch and Greek Revival details. In 1852 a wing was added to the east side by the owner, Elmira Shelton. The White-Taylor House, number 2717 (1839, 1878–1882), is frequently pictured in books on Richmond and on historic preservation. It began as a two-and-one-half-story brick town house. Then in the late 1870s a new owner added a full third floor and installed decorative window heads. The first-floor windows were lengthened, and an elaborate cast iron porch was installed on the 28th Street side.

RI88 **Double Houses**

c. 1850. 2800–2802 E. Grace St.

Illustrating the conservatism of Richmond's architecture, these two-story, three-bay Greek Revival double houses with raised basements and side-hall entrances follow a formula that once dominated the city. The houses have entry porches with square columns and full entablatures, stepped gables, and two-story rear porches.

RI89 **Residences**

c. 1857–c. 1891. 100 and 200 block of N. 29th St.

Buildings on these two blocks are constructed of wood, unlike those in most of the rest of the district. They are Greek Revival and Italianate in style and also include one of the few Rich-

RI88 Double House

RI93 Walker House

mond examples of a "shotgun" house, at 119 West 29th Street.

RI90 Residence

c. 1868. 3005–3007 Libby Terrace

An important example of immediate post–Civil War construction, the building has the raised English basement and stepped gable of an antebellum town house. The bracketed cornice and cast iron porch with latticework and grapevines typify the architecture of the new era.

RI91 Soldiers and Sailors Monument

1894, Wilfred Emory Cutshaw, designer; William Ludwell Sheppard, sculptor. 29th St. and Libby Terrace

This project took form in 1888 when the Confederate Soldiers and Sailors Monument Association was formed. Cutshaw, the city engineer, selected Trajan's Column in Rome as the inspiration for the new monument, although he departed significantly from the model in his details. Employing a Roman victory column to memorialize a vanquished army seems an ironic choice. Cutshaw's alignment of the great Corinthian column with the axis of Main Street at the foot of Libby Hill was a gesture typical of the City Beautiful movement. Sheppard picked a local Confederate veteran as his model for

the quintessential Confederate soldier perched on the top of the column.

RI92 Libby Hill Park and Park Keeper's House

1873, c. 1890, Wilfred Emory Cutshaw. 1906, keeper's house attachment. 1995, park and building renovation, Higgins and Associates. 29th and E. Franklin sts.

The city of Richmond acquired a portion of the site for this park in 1851, but not until 1873, after the acquisition of additional lots on East Franklin Street and Libby Terrace, did it undertake construction, which included the gazebo, the park keeper's house, and most of the present paths and roadways. The completed project is one of the most dramatic urban spaces in Richmond. The recent renovation of the park provided additional paths, seating, and lighting.

RI93 Walker House

1857. 1861, east wing. 2605 E. Franklin St.

One of the finest Greek Revival houses in Richmond, the building began as a side-hall town house. The addition of the east wing converted it to a center-hall mansion. Particularly noteworthy are the classical cast iron balconies and full-length windows on the front facade and the two-story porch overlooking the James River on the rear. Next door, at 2601 East Franklin Street, is the Ligon-Cowardin House (c. 1860, 1872), a three-story brick house that originally began as two stories. It also has an addition to its east with a delicate cast iron entry.

RI94 Anthony Turner House

c. 1810. 1963, restoration. 2520 E. Franklin St.

One of the oldest dwellings in the neighborhood and a good example of a surviving plantation-in-town, this property still consists of the two original lots that extended from Grace to Franklin Street. The brick retaining walls mark the extensive regrading of Franklin Street. The brick house was built by its original owner, Anthony Turner, who was a master brickmason and a Richmond magistrate. He showed off his skills in the massive chimneys, rusticated jack arches, and segmental arches over windows.

RI95 Charity Square Condominiums

1988, Edwin H. Winks. 2500 E. Franklin St.

The new town houses on this site replaced a gas station. The buildings were loosely modeled on the Adams Double House at 2501–2503 East Grace Street (see entry above). The repetition of the two-bay rhythm and textural pattern of the brickwork give this group a unity unusual for Church Hill and for Richmond.

RI96 Leigh Street Baptist Church

1854–1857, Samuel Sloan. 1870, addition. 1880–1885, addition, attributed to Asa Snyder. 1911 and 1930, additions. 517 N. 25th St. (at Leigh St.)

The church, with its hexastyle pedimented Doric portico, is a fine example of Samuel Sloan's ability with the Greek Revival style. Sloan, from Philadelphia, is perhaps better known for his Italianate designs. The missionary Reuben Ford organized the congregation. Under the auspices of the Leigh Street Baptist Church, seven other Baptist churches in Richmond were started. Additions have diminished some of its effect, and the interior is completely changed. The iron fencing, believed to be by Asa Snyder, is some of the best in the city.

Shockoe Slip   (RI97–RI105)

Richmond's past prominence as a port is still apparent in the name of one of its historic warehouse districts, Shockoe Slip. The actual slip no longer exists, but the handsome brick warehouses with iron details and storefronts remain. The area between East Main Street and Canal and between 12th and 14th streets has been a commercial hub for more than 200 years. After the Virginia government arrived in Richmond in 1780, a commercial building at 14th and Cary streets served as the capitol, an indicator of the neighborhood's significance in the late eighteenth century. The entire area burned during the evacuation fire in 1865; rebuilding began immediately. The area thrived again for several decades as a center of of manufacturing, warehousing, and the rowdy hospitality industry supported by them. By the mid-twentieth century traffic in the Slip had slowed to a trickle. A new life for the Slip came when the state legislature in the early 1970s overturned the prohibition statute that forbade the sale of liquor by the drink. A rush ensued to initiate night life in downtown Richmond, and several businessmen who recognized that the real estate of the Slip was undervalued bought and began rehabilitating buildings along East Cary and South 13th streets. The product is a small but thriving retail and entertainment district. In 1978 the Bowers Building was adapted as apartments, the start of an ongoing trend to provide upscale housing in downtown Richmond.

RI97 The Tobacco Company

1866. 1978, renovation. 1201 E. Cary St.

The Tobacco Company was one of the pioneer restaurants in the revived Shockoe Slip area. It occupies a former tobacco warehouse, an impressive three-story brick building that announces entry into the neighborhood. The original slow-burning timber construction, of the type used for mills, can still be seen in the restaurant interior.

RI98 Berkeley Hotel

1988, Richard Stoffer. 1200 E. Cary St.

The Berkeley Hotel, across the street from the Tobacco Company, is a good example of infill architecture. With elements like the Berkeley's simple tower and understated entrance, architects and planners have enhanced the lively streetscape and skyline of the Slip without detracting from the historic character. The varying heights of the cornices and storefronts of the 1200 and 1300 blocks of East Cary Street articulate the slope of the street and create a stac-

Shockoe Slip (RI97 - RI105)

cato visual rhythm. With one exception, these buildings were rebuilt within about eleven years of the 1865 fire.

RI99 Storefronts

1865. 1983, renovation, Eisenman/Robertson Architects. 1211–1217 E. Cary St.

A row of storefronts, articulated by an elegant cast iron Doric colonnade-pilastrade, forms the base of the block. The wide, corbeled brick above enriches the upper body. One section above the storefronts was replaced after a fire.

RI100 Columbian Block

1871. 1973, renovation, James Glave. 1301 E. Cary St.

The trapezoidal, stone-paved plaza that is now called Shockoe Slip opens southward from the corner of 13th Street. One side is defined by a wonderful Italianate commercial structure that curves around the corner. Now offices, it was originally built as a corn and flour exchange. The second and third visible floors of the exchange were constructed of brick but covered in stucco, which was scored to resemble stone. The window caps and cornice are cast iron, as are the risers of the interior staircase. The exchange room on the third floor retains its square cupola, market boards used to tally the prices of goods, and attenuated, cast iron Corinthian columns that punctuate the interior space. This was the first building on this part of East Cary Street to be renovated in the 1970s and is now used for stores and offices. The stone fountain in the plaza is a 1909 replacement of an earlier one used for watering horses.

RI101 Bowers Building

1880. 1978, renovation, Glave, Newman, Anderson. 104 Shockoe Slip

The Bowers Building, originally a warehouse, was the first building in this area renovated for use as offices and upscale apartments. The adaptive reuse initiated a trend among young professionals who bought or rented apartments over storefronts in the Slip. The spectacular Italianate tobacco exchange building that once formed the south wall of the plaza was unfortunately demolished long ago, and the plaza has remained incomplete for decades.

RI102 One Shockoe Plaza

1995–1997, CMSS Architects, Burrell Saunders, principal designer

The success of Shockoe Slip's revitalization brought its by-product: too many professionals wanted to locate here. In the absence of strong design controls, buildings like this, which are primarily offices, have begun to appear. Designed by a Virginia Beach firm, this large brick office building makes a tenuous and unsuccessful attempt at relating to the nineteenth-century surroundings.

RI103 Peking Restaurant (Edmonds and Davenport)

1869. 1300–1302 E. Cary St.

This urbane building at the corner complements the former corn and flour exchange across the street. Its arched windows, brick pilasters, and deep cornice make it one of the most architecturally ambitious buildings in the area and a standout in this neighborhood of simpler utilitarian vocabularies.

RI104 Virginia Housing Authority

c. 1890. 1911, addition, Marcellus Wright. c. 1985, renovation. 13 S. 13th St.

Originally built for commercial and office use, this building has been renovated by the state government. The first floor is a cast iron front manufactured by Richmond's famous Tredegar Iron Works. The front has a small pediment in the middle of each bay. The upper floors are brick. Marcellus Wright's top-floor addition has arched windows.

RI105 Dransfield Jewelers (J. Murphy Building)

1866. 1308 E. Cary St.

This building, dating from soon after the Evacuation Fire, has all-wood exterior ornament, unusual in a city known for its cast iron and in a district that had just burned.

Downtown Riverfront   (RI106–RI115)

The north bank of the James River, from the Mayo (14th Street) Bridge to the Robert E. Lee Bridge at Belvidere Street, is traditionally considered to be the area where the English first came ashore at the falls in 1607. Today a monumental bronze cross, mounted on a base of river stones near the corner of 12th and Canal streets commemorates this party of explorers, which included Christopher Newport and John Smith. From the early nineteenth century until after the Civil War, the riverfront and the James River and Kanawha Canal (Richmond's attempt to secure a western transportation route) served as a commercial and transportation center linking the navigable waters of the James with areas west of the fall line. Today the riverfront area is defined on the north by a massive flood wall, a skeleton of a railroad trestle, and the Downtown Expressway (which was completed in 1977 atop parts of the former canal system). A generation after the loss of much of the canal, however, remaining segments are being reworked into a new canal system. This newly configured waterway is the centerpiece of a plan for additional office and retail and entertainment spaces near the riverfront. Its development should help meld the district's interesting mix of distinctly urban nineteenth-century industrial and warehouse buildings and late twentieth-century high rises, office buildings, and green spaces of a more suburban character.

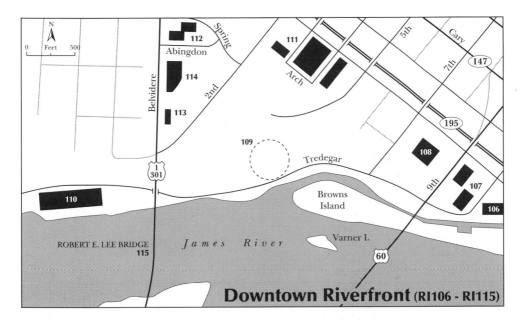

Downtown Riverfront (RI106 - RI115)

RI106 Virginia Electric and Power Company Hydroelectric Plant

1901. 1923, steam plant (south of 12th and Byrd sts.)

This monumental assemblage of structures is the latest in a series of industrial buildings that have stood at this critical spot on the falls since the eighteenth century. Four towering adjacent smokestacks make this structure a highly dramatic monument to waterpower and provide a visual highlight of the riverfront's ongoing development. The rectangular hydroelectric plant is built of concrete and brick faced with

RI106 Virginia Electric and Power Company Hydroelectric Plant

stucco. While the strong Doric entablature and continuous paired windows give the structure a Greek Revival appearance, the interest here is not just architectural, but also hydraulic, as gushing water from the Haxall Millrace (at the eastern end of the complex) plunges some fifty feet into the rushing James below. The former Union Envelope Company Building (1901) faces the millrace and adds immeasurably to this assemblage of faded industrial buildings. The solid, four-story brick Italianate confection, with a central stair tower that projects above the roofline, is flanked by two seven-bay wings.

RI107 Riverfront Plaza

1991, HKS Architects. 951 E. Byrd St.

The rosy brown–colored twin towers of Riverfront Plaza rise twenty-two stories to frame the gateway to downtown from south Richmond via the Manchester Bridge. While this 1.85-million-square-foot complex, designed by HKS of Dallas, is one of the most prominent features of the Richmond skyline, the two poorly articulated office towers, capped by massive mansard roofs punctuated with large, rounded arches, are more pretentious than handsome. Although the entrance court fronting Byrd Street and the elevated and fenced plaza overlooking the river are well-appointed and pleasant urban spaces, they are clearly intended only for those doing business here.

RI108 Federal Reserve Bank of Richmond

1978, Minoru Yamasaki and Associates. 701 E. Byrd St.

The headquarters for the Federal Reserve Bank's Twelfth District sits confidently like a gleaming, vertical silver radiator at river's edge. Yamasaki, who designed the Space Needle for the 1962 Seattle World's Fair and the World Trade Center in New York, created a sleek and decorative modern style very popular with corporate clients but less so with critics, who frequently panned his work. For Richmond he was perfect, and this is arguably one of Richmond's few truly impressive late twentieth-century buildings. Materials, craftsmanship, and the building's isolated parklike setting combine to create a sense of icy elegance. A pool in the front entrance court is the setting for a delicate sculpture by artist Harry Bertoia, which "hums" like soothing wind chimes.

RI109 Tredegar Iron Works

1861 and later. c. 1980, c. 1990, renovations. Tredegar St. (at the foot of 5th St.)

Founded in 1838 and later known as the "Arsenal of the Confederacy," the Tredegar Iron

Works was an impressive, if crowded, complex of dozens of mostly brick industrial structures. After it fell into disrepair, for many years the impressive brick arches recalled ancient Roman ruins. Very little of the original machinery remains. Some stabilization and restoration took place in the 1980s. In 1994 the complex served as Valentine Riverside, a short-lived attempt by the Valentine Museum to establish an industrial history theme park here. Today the brick foundry building serves the Ethyl Corporation, which owns the complex, as a multi-use conference center. In 1998 the National Park Service developed a visitor center at the site for Richmond-area Civil War battlefields.

RI110 Fort James Corporation Office Building

1992, Bond Comet Westmoreland. 120 Tredegar St.

Originally the James River Corporation built this structure as the flagship of its corporate campus in a parklike setting, wedged between the James River rapids and the canal bed at the foot of a steep cliff behind Hollywood Cemetery. In creating new office space on a challenging site, the architect designed a contemporary, highly contextual four-story building of 50,000 square feet directly on the site of an old city pumping station, which dated from 1832. Generous window openings and a series of balconies overlooking the rushing water make the experience from inside the building not unlike being aboard a riverboat.

RI109 Tredegar Iron Works

RI111 Ethyl Corporation Corporate Office Building

RI111 **Ethyl Corporation Corporate Office Building**

1954–1956, 1985, Carneal and Johnston. 1989, pavilion addition, Vincent Kling and Associates. 330 S. 4th St.

Amid the sleek and soaring glass and metal high rises of downtown Richmond, the Palladian and pristine Ethyl building so commands the area once known as Gamble's Hill that many visitors to Richmond mistake it for the Virginia Capitol. Ironically, the corporation specializes in high technology and chemicals. At the request of Floyd T. Gottwald, founder of the Ethyl Corporation, the architects looked closely at the Williamsburg Inn in Colonial Williamsburg as a design source. The entrance portico, an arcade that carries a colonnade of Ionic columns, has multiple sources, but for Virginians it recalls Pavilion VII at the University of Virginia. In 1985 Carneal and Johnston added a new cupola, inspired by the double-tiered cupola on the Governor's Palace in Williamsburg. The 1989 pavilion addition included a conference center and fitness complex. It maintains the scale and "classicism" of the original building while incorporating decidedly postmodern features such as a stylized broken pediment on the riverfront side. During the course of forty years Ethyl has leveled most of the surrounding Gamble's Hill neighborhood, eliminating many historic structures to create a grassy, corporate parklike setting. Any of the fine old homes that remained were torn down in the early 1970s for the Downtown Expressway. In addition, several landmarks, including Pratt's Castle (a Gothic Revival residence), the Virginia State Penitentiary (with

foundations from an eighteenth-century prison designed by Benjamin Henry Latrobe), a Depression-era reinforced concrete bridge constructed by the Works Progress Administration, and the triangular Binswanger Building, have been demolished.

RI112 **Ethyl Corporation Research Center**

1994, Albert Kahn and Associates. Southeast corner of Belvidere and Spring sts.

This six-story, 215,000-square-foot complex, designed by the great factory designer's successor firm, which is still in business in Detroit, houses petroleum-additive research facilities and engine-testing cells. Landscaping disguises many of the building's functions. A two story, gold domed lobby structure that gestures toward the company's headquarters buildings marks the building's entrance on Spring Street.

RI113 **Virginia War Memorial**

1955–1956, Samuel J. Collins, with Richard E. Collins, associate; Leo Friedlander, sculptor. 621 S. Belvidere St.

Designers for the war memorial were selected in a competition. The architects maintained a small regional practice in Staunton, Virginia, in the Shenandoah Valley. This limestone open-air pavilion on a commanding bluff overlooking the river honors Virginians who died during World War II, the Korean War, the Vietnam War, and the Persian Gulf War. Especially moving is the sweeping glass wall, on which are etched the names of those killed in the wars. It anticipates by more than thirty years a similar design solution at the Vietnam Veterans Memorial in Washington, D.C. At one end of the structure, a soaring statue of a grieving female figure looms above an eternal flame.

RI114 Virginia Housing Development Authority Building

1988, Odell Associates. 601 S. Belvidere St.

This four-story office building defers to the neighboring war memorial and helps establish an urban wall along Belvidere. At the entrance is a glass cylinder-like form injected into the otherwise boxy glass and precast concrete structure. Sheer glass walls on the river facade are stepped and curved to reflect the dramatically sloping site.

RI115 Robert E. Lee Bridge

1990, Hayes, Seay, Mattern and Mattern Inc., engineers

This sweeping stretch of reinforced concrete carries U.S. 1 across the James River and historic Belle Isle. Welcome features are the bicycle lanes flanking the six-lane span.

East Main Street   (RI116–RI149)

Since the late eighteenth century, East Main Street, which slopes gently uphill and westward from Shockoe Bottom, has been a continuously prosperous commercial and financial center. After being mostly destroyed by the devastating evacuation fire in April 1865 (when fleeing Richmonders burned Confederate munitions rather than have them fall into Union hands), the area was rebuilt rapidly—ironically, with significant northern investment—in brick and iron-fronted buildings. After the turn of the twentieth century, several Beaux-Arts banks, and later skyscrapers, gave Richmond a new skyline.

RI116 Cohen Building

1866. 1325 E. Main St.

Important for its urban design qualities, this building adeptly fills the obtuse angle formed at the southwest corner of 14th and Main streets. Built soon after the close of the Civil War by one of Richmond's oldest Jewish families, the three-story brick structure had an elaborate rusticated base with segmental-arched openings in which goods were displayed. The upper two floors are relatively plain with sharp-edged window openings.

RI117 Oppenheimer Building

1873. 1323 E. Main St.

Erected by a Mrs. Oppenheimer, who ran a millinery shop, each of this building's three stories is superbly proportioned and detailed. The design source for this Italianate structure was Venetian architecture. The glass-fronted shopfront at street level is highlighted by a recessed center door, which is flanked by curved glass display windows. The first floor is a cast iron structure, while the upper floors are brick with cast iron caps on the window heads. The bracketed cornice is galvanized iron.

RI118 Gardner Building

1873. 1321 ½ E. Main St.

A fascinating curiosity, this narrow facade, only 7½ feet wide, is one of Richmond's architectural oddities. It was built on a sliver of land to serve as a passageway and provide a Main Street address for a larger structure on the interior of the block. The windows on the second and third stories have handsome ornamental surrounds and are capped by segmental and triangular pediments, respectively.

RI119 Carpenter Building

c. 1869, c. 1890. 1317 E. Main St.

Although refaced around 1890, this four-story brick building with cast iron detailing at street level retains some reminders of its original Venetian Revival ornament. The stripping away

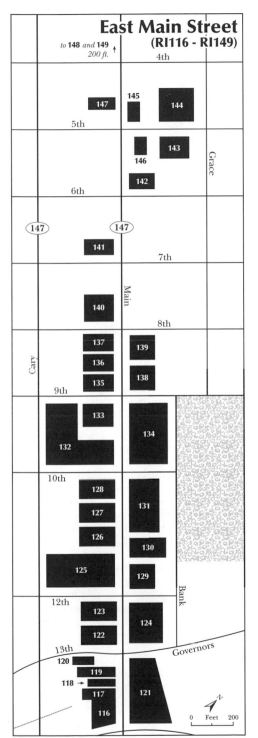

of ornamental upper floors and their replacement with a more bland brick facade indicates the new academic correctness of the turn of the twentieth century.

RI120 Exchange Place

c. 1870–1872. 1987, renovation, Richard L. Ford. 1315 (originally 1315–1309) E. Main St.

Five formerly independent two- and three-story commercial buildings from the early 1870s now constitute this modern office complex. They were constructed within two years of each other and occupied by different businesses, from an auction house to a real estate office. Each had a cast iron first floor and brick upper floors, some with cast iron details. In poor shape by the early 1980s, they were carefully preserved and rehabilitated.

RI121 State Corporation Commission Building

1992, Odell Associates. 1300 E. Main St.

In its evocation of a huge glacier, this granite and glass office complex, occupying an entire irregularly shaped city block, possesses an undeniable icy elegance. The primary entrance, at 13th and Main streets, is through the base of a soaring cylindrical structure that rises to an almost comical, Buck Rogers–like spire. The tower makes the view up 13th (from Shockoe Slip) or down Main Street a visual treat.

RI122 Donnan Block

1866, attributed to George H. Johnson. 1207–1213 E. Main St.

Although down at the heels, this is one of downtown Richmond's special architectural treasures. The block contains three attached four-story buildings with exuberantly decorated Italianate iron-front facades. The facing was probably cast in Baltimore by Bartlett Hayward, and Company. This is one of Richmond's earliest examples of prefabricated building construction. The dramatic street front is a tour de force of twelve Venetian-style window bays, each defined by engaged Corinthian columns. Engaged balustrades separate the third and fourth floors. The shopfronts at street level have been largely defaced.

RI122 Donnan Block (left)

RI124 Virginia Retirement System Building (above)

RI123 1203–1205 East Main St.

c. 1870

This pair of sturdy brick four-story buildings with cast iron window caps and a heavy cornice lacks its triplet, which unfortunately was demolished in the 1970s to make way for the stumpy two-story building on the corner. Some of the elements of the demolished building were incorporated in the new structure, a gesture which only draws attention to the senselessness of demolishing a good structure and replacing it with a poor example of infill design.

RI124 Virginia Retirement System Building

1893, Charles H. Read, Jr. 1984, renovation, Glave, Newman, Anderson. 1200 E. Main St.

Built initially for State Planters Bank (a forerunner of Crestar Bank), this is the oldest surviving major banking structure in the city. The three-story brick and stone building, with gabled attic level and English basement, is a theatrical but symmetrical play of masonry arches in a range of sizes, all very much in the so-called Richardsonian Romanesque idiom. The sensitively detailed 1984 addition, one of Richmond's best examples of infill construction, continues the building's mass and scale to the east corner. The addition also complements the nineteenth-century buildings across the street. Read, the architect of the original

building, also designed Watts Hall, a focal point of Union Theological Seminary in Ginter Park.

RI125 NationsBank Center

1973, Welton Becket Associates. 1996, Odell Associates. Southwest corner of 12th and Main sts.

This crisply detailed precast-concrete-clad office and retail complex was constructed following the controversial demolition of a handsome block of iron-front buildings that stood here. In response, the roofline and setback of the pavilion wing along Main were designed to maintain continuity with the remaining adjacent nineteenth-century iron fronts. Following a 1990s renovation, the twenty-three-story tower is now set back from Main Street beyond a paved and grass-planted plaza that includes a fountain and a mosaic mural. James Rosati's large red metal sculpture *Richmond Tripodal* (1974) has been placed on the grassy knoll to humanize the space. It begs the question, Why can't architects design more buildings that don't need humanizing?

RI126 Branch-Cabell and Company Building

1866, George H. Johnson. c. 1976, renovation. 1015 E. Main St.

The lower two levels of this Italianate structure, considered one of the finest and best preserved of the street's iron-front buildings, are set back behind a graceful arcade. Within the setback, an innovative split-level plan allows two stories to have convenient access and street presence. The structure was originally built for the Virginia Fire and Marine Insurance Company. The iron foundry was Baltimore's Hayward, Bartlett. The architect, Johnson, was an Englishman who came to New York and originally worked for Daniel Badger, a prominent manufacturer of cast iron building components. Johnson then moved to Baltimore, where he designed this building.

RI127 **Stearns Block** (The Ironfronts)

1866, George H. Johnson. 1976, Glave, Newman, Anderson. 1011 E. Main St.

Franklin Stearns, a Richmond businessman, built this imposing procession of iron-front buildings, with engaged Corinthian columns separating arched windows, immediately after the Civil War. Today the building represents the finest in mixed-use urban building design, with retail operations that open directly onto the sidewalk, service businesses on the basement level, and offices on the upper floors. Three of the buildings' fourteen bays open directly into an open-air lobby space. New wall openings on the interior create more marketable expanses of square footage.

RI128 **1005 East Main Street** (American Trust Company)

1919, Mobray and Uffinger

A wonderful insert into the Main Street line of buildings is this exquisitely detailed building. The facade is an elaborately articulated three-story Beaux-Arts triumphal arch with engaged, rusticated Ionic columns. The building was designed for a local bank by a firm of New York City architects which specialized in banks. The large banking room is behind the arch.

RI129 **Plantation House** (Travelers' Building)

1910, Clinton & Russell, W. Duncan Lee, associated architect. 1108 E. Main St.

This high rise of thirteen stories plus terraced penthouse is one of the city's oldest skyscrapers. Its New York City architects, who specialized in tall buildings, chose as their associate an unlikely local architect, W. Duncan Lee. Lee specialized in residential work and apparently never capitalized on this experience, never designing another high-rise building. Like many early skyscrapers, it has a clearly delineated division of base, shaft, and crown. The peculiar and clumsily detailed portico that extends over the Main Street sidewalk is a later addition.

RI130 **Courthouse Annex** (Parcel Post Building)

1929, Marcellus Wright, Sr., and Lee, and Smith and Van Dervoort. Later renovations. 1100 E. Main St.

Although this building was intended to complement the courthouse to its immediate west, it incorporates its own modernistic classical vocabulary with a restrained application of Art Deco reliefs.

RI131 **Lewis F. Powell, Jr., U.S. Courthouse** (U.S. Customhouse)

1855–1858, Ammi B. Young (architect), Albert Lybrock (construction supervision), Alexander H. Brown (engineer), Office of the Supervising Architect, U.S. Treasury Department. 1889, expansion. 1909–1910, expansion, James Knox Taylor, Supervising Architect, U.S. Treasury Department. 1918 and 1930, expansion, James A. Wetmore, Acting Supervising Architect, U.S. Treasury Department. 1000 E. Main St.

This heroic five-part building has grown over time. The first three floors of the center block constitute the original building. Young was the first Supervising Architect of the Treasury and

RI129 Plantation House (Travelers' Building) (right)

RI132 Crestar Bank (United Virginia Bank) Headquarters (far right)

RI135 First National Bank Building (below, left)

RI136 Virginia Trust Company (below, right)

designed federal buildings across the country during the 1850s. In Virginia he also designed the customhouses in Norfolk and Petersburg. His style varied, but for Richmond he chose as a model the solid Renaissance palazzo, or, as one historian has termed it, "Tuscan palazzo," instead of a Roman temple. The tight urban site helped determine the style, since the blocky form allowed Young to build to the street line. Young described the site, which bordered Capital Square at the rear, as the "very best in the city." Albert Lybrock, a young German immigrant who, after the Civil War, would become a leading architect in Richmond, acted as the local supervisor. During the Civil War, the building provided offices for the president and treasury of the Confederate States of America. Symbolically, it survived the 1865 evacuation fire and subsequently was expanded sympathetically several times by government architects. In 1991 it became a U.S. District Court of Appeals building. When sun hits the warm granite and deeply recessed Italianate arches of the south-facing facade on Main Street, it creates a dramatic interplay of light and shadow. Recently, two WPA murals, one painted by Paul Cadmus (*Pocahontas Rescuing John Smith*) and the other by Jared French (*Stuart's Raiders at the Swollen Fort*) (both 1939), originally next door in the former Parcel Post Building, were installed on the interior.

RI132 Crestar Bank Headquarters (United Virginia Bank)

1983, Lee, King and Poole. 920 E. Main St.

Bold and angular (but not unpleasant), this modern tower of granite is set back on a plaza of granite, not unlike the siting of the Nations-Bank Center to the east. The building's design employs hard-edged, sharply geometric angles right down to such details as the steps that lead to and from the front plaza and follow the sloping terrain. While hardly welcoming, the building does a better job of addressing its Cary Street front than do other buildings that face this major financial district thoroughfare. Although somewhat stark and Brutalist compared with neighboring buildings on Main, the Crestar complex possesses a sense of permanence that is lacking in many of Richmond's late twentieth-century office buildings. The sculpture on the plaza is *Quadrature* (1985), by Robert Engman.

RI133 Mutual Building

1904, 1912, Clinton and Russell. 909 E. Main St.

Clinton and Russell were the favorite high-rise architects for Richmond's banking and real estate community from 1904 to the 1920s. This especially fine example of their work has a sophisticated composition that allows for multiple levels. A two-story Roman Doric base supports an intermediate story or attic, which in turn carries a five-story shaft, and then another single-story attic. Clinton and Russell returned a few years later to top off the composition with a three-story capital composed of united windows. The building is U-shaped with a narrow courtyard facing 9th Street to provide air and light as well as a secondary entrance. The building is surrounded by a cast iron fence, unique in the financial district.

RI134 State Office Building (State Planters Bank)

1923, Clinton and Russell. 1962, Lee, King and Poole. 900 E. Main St.

This skyscraper was originally built as a bank headquarters. Above the heroic entrance portal framed by four massive in antis Ionic columns, the mass of the building diminishes slightly as it rises, accentuating its height. A comparison of its relative simplicity with Clinton and Russell's nearby Mutual Building (see preceding entry) illuminates the tastes of different decades. The 1962 addition is clumsily joined to its parent, although some attempt was made to maintain the horizontal lines of the original building's windows.

RI135 First National Bank Building

1912, Alfred C. Bossom, associated with Clinton and Russell. 823 E. Main St.

Also built for a bank, this impressive Beaux-Arts skyscraper is one of Richmond's landmark buildings. The limestone base is formed by deeply recessed, engaged Corinthian columns and projecting piers that carry an elaborate cornice and a small attic story. The building's nine-story shaft has deep-set paired windows broken by balconies near the top, an unusual feature for Richmond buildings. The shaft in turn supports an attic story and an extremely ornate, four-story terra-cotta crown. Unfortunately, the imposing projecting cornice was removed a number of years ago. Alfred C. Bossom, who teamed up with Clinton and Russell for this building and designed a number of other structures in Richmond, was an English-born architect who worked in New York. He designed high-rise buildings for locations throughout the South and West. He later returned to England and wrote an important book, *Building to the Skies: The Romance of the Skyscraper* (1934).

RI136 Virginia Trust Company

1919, Alfred C. Bossom. 821 E. Main St.

This magnificent Beaux-Arts building essentially takes the form of a Roman triumphal arch. The coffers of its deep, four-story barrel-vaulted entrance are decorated with roundels that incorporate Labrador retrievers—making this perhaps Richmond's only building with a canine motif in granite. The interior contains a spectacular coffered ceiling that frames an octagonal glass dome.

RI137 Ross Building

1965, Vlastimil Koubek. 801 E. Main St.

Designed by a Washington, D.C., architect, this modern skyscraper is a monument to Mies van der Rohe's axiom, "Less is more." Mies's Seagram Building in New York (1956) provided the basic motif for the base and curtain wall. Remarkably, the Ross Building has escaped exterior alterations and is as fresh today as the day it was built. Its glass curtain wall provides a refreshing contrast to many of the bombastic or clumsily detailed office buildings later built in Richmond.

RI138 One Capitol Square (The Fidelity Building)

1971, Marcellus Wright, Jr. 1996, renovation, Scribner Messer Brady Wade. 830 E. Main St.

A rather boring black and white box, this building originally had a lobby setback and an escalator to an open-air main lobby on the second level. The ground-floor facade was recently reworked into a deconstructivist statement that is more elaborate than the original facing.

RI139 Bank of Virginia Building (Morris Plan Bank)

1931, Hoggson Brothers. 1970, addition, Ballou and Justice. 800 E. Main St.

The Depression was well underway by the time this last of Richmond's large classical banks was completed. The limestone building includes an in antis colonnade of massive engaged Greek Doric columns that wraps around the block and continues up 8th Street. The entrance is at the corner, set within a handsome rusticated base. This is perhaps one of Richmond's best downtown structures in urbanistic terms and a high point of early twentieth-century architectural classicism.

RI140 Eighth and Main Building

1976, Skidmore, Owings and Merrill. 707 E. Main St. (at 8th St.)

Cleanly articulated but fairly bland, this office tower appears to splay near the roofline because the window openings become taller rather than shorter toward the top.

RI141 Main Street Center (Richmond Trust Company)

1922, Starrett and Van Vleck. c. 1990, renovation. 627 E. Main St.

This self-assured building with a limestone base and brick upper floors is restrained in comparison to other buildings of the early 1920s. Although the base, an in antis colonnade of four Greek Doric columns, is ornate, the upper reaches are surprisingly simple for a Richmond high rise of this era.

RI142 Eskimo Pie Building (Richmond Chamber of Commerce)

1912, Carneal and Johnston. 530 E. Main St.

Originally built for the Richmond Chamber of Commerce, which was promoting the city as progressive, up to date, and hospitable to new businesses, this building was intended to be an advertisement. Instead of out-of-town architects, a local firm was chosen. Carneal and Johnston designed a building with a splendid base of piers and columns in the Roman Doric order and handsome arches marking the portals on Main and 6th streets. The top two floors were covered in ornate, multicolored terracotta, providing a celebratory touch. Unfortunately, the cornice has been removed.

RI143 Second Presbyterian Church

1845–1848, Minard Lafever. c. 1905, chapel, Noland and Baskervill. Later additions. 13 N. 5th St.

Richmond's major entry into the mid-nineteenth-century Gothic Revival mode came not from Episcopalians, as was common in many other cities, but from Presbyterians. Virginia Episcopalians remained resolutely "low church," and hence the introduction of the style fell to a group of Richmond Presbyterians who wanted a building that would be "the most symmetrical and pleasing to an educated eye." The vestry committee traveled north to Brooklyn and asked Lafever to design a church. He complied with this brick English Decorated Gothic edifice. Lafever is best known for his

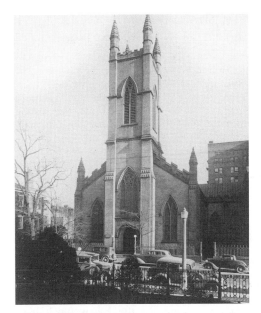

RI143 Second Presbyterian Church

RI144 YWCA

variously titled Greek Revival pattern books. Personally he favored the Gothic; the Greek sold books. The exterior, with its finials and crenellations, is relatively simple, but the wide meetinghouse space inside is overwhelming. It is probably the most impressive church interior in the city. Galleries surround three sides, and on the central axis is a dais for preaching and scripture reading. The wooden Gothic detailing is superb, and the hammerbeam roof that spans the vast space is a knockout. Transepts were added, and then Noland and Baskervill designed a small chapel at the east end, which

is a more intimate space. The glass is by various makers, including Tiffany Studios, which provided the window in the chapel.

RI144 YWCA

1913, Noland and Baskervill. 6 N. 5th St.

An extremely impressive work by Richmond's leading turn-of-the-century firm, the YWCA building is so elegant that one might think it was a private club. The basic form is a Renaissance palazzo of five bays. It is built of brick with limestone trim. The detailing—for example, the entrance porch—is a mixture of Italian and Federal Revival motifs.

RI145 Hancock-Wirt-Caskie House

1808–1809. c. 1988, restoration. 2 N. 5th St. (corner of 5th and Main sts.)

The plan and form of this house, one of the city's finest surviving examples of the Federal style, were undoubtedly inspired by a scheme for a house in Richmond with semioctagonal bays, designed by Benjamin Henry Latrobe. The two-story loggia is rare in Federal domestic architecture. With its fine Flemish bond brickwork and marble trim, this was a local showpiece. The original owner, Michael Hancock, lost the house almost immediately after it was built because of gambling debts to William Wirt. Wirt gained local fame as the author of a biography of Patrick Henry and attorney general of the United States under James Monroe and John Quincy Adams. After belonging to a mayor of Richmond, the house passed into the hands of the Caskie family, who owned it until the 1940s and preserved it. More recently it has served as attorneys' offices and has been restored. The interior woodwork is very fine.

RI146 Barret House

1844. 1980–present, restoration. 15 S. 5th St. Open upon request

Now the headquarters of the Virginia chapter of the American Institute of Architects, this house is one of the finest Greek Revival dwellings in the city. Similar to its neighbor, the Scott-Clark House (1841; 9 South 5th Street), but larger, the house was built for William Barret, a tobacconist who at his death in 1870 was considered the richest citizen in town. The demure Ionic portico leads to a central hall, a curved and cantilevered stair, and a series of high-ceilinged rooms. Originally some of the rooms were frescoed. However, the major feature is the triple-tiered rear portico, which once afforded a panoramic view of downtown Richmond and the James River. The house was threatened with destruction in 1936, and Mary Wingfield Scott and her cousin, Elisabeth Scott Bocock, purchased it. They in turn passed it to the local AIA, which has carried out an extensive restoration program. Also on the lot is a carriage house that contained servants' quarters.

RI147 American Red Cross

1951, Baskervill and Son. 409 E. Main St.

After Main crosses 5th Street, the tight urbanity of the financial district vanishes and surface parking lots dominate, along with a suburban feeling. The headquarters for the Red Cross is set back from the sidewalk behind a patch of grass and shrubs. The two-story structure, clad in red brick with limestone trim, is a good example of the parched neoclassical–Colonial Revival style of the 1950s. The two-story entrance portico leads to a circular entrance hall.

RI148 St. Alban's Hall

1869. 1982, renovation. 300–302 E. Main St.

One of the largest buildings constructed in Richmond immediately after the Civil War, St. Alban's Hall has a rare public presence. It was intended as a Masonic temple and became a focus of Richmond's social life for several decades. The three-story, tripartite Italianate building, of brick covered by stucco, has elongated windows that diminish in size from the first floor to the third. The second-floor windows, as appropriate for the piano nobile, are more ornate than those on the third, and the central bay is crowned by a pediment. The building was converted in 1982 for office use.

RI149 Third Street Diner

1875. c. 1915, storefronts. 218 W. Main St.

Although the three attached Italianate houses that once composed the Harris Block have been all but been obscured by storefronts, the one on the corner, which houses the Third Street Diner, is a twenty-four-hour-a-day landmark. Its exterior neon signage and interior detailing in pressed aluminum evoke American diners of the 1930s and 1940s.

Franklin Street from Capitol Square to Monroe Park   (RI150–RI170)

During most of the nineteenth century, Franklin Street was the axis of power in Richmond. Beginning at Capitol Square, it terminates two miles west at Monument Avenue. Large, impressive town houses originally lined the street, and although the character has changed in the twentieth century, it is still a significant street.

RI150 Stewart-Lee House

1844. 707 E. Franklin St.

The last remaining dwelling in what was once a fashionable residential district, this three-story brick house has a side-hall plan, a sedate Greek Doric entrance porch, and a three-tiered porch on the rear. The house, which served as the home of the Robert E. Lee family during and immediately following the Civil War, was one of a row of similar structures in the block. Although this historic house is overwhelmed in scale by the office tower to the immediate west,

it has hardly been diminished in street presence.

RI151 Richmond Centre (Virginia Electric and Power Building)

1913, Alfred C. Bossom. 702 E. Franklin St.

This exuberant early high-rise tower has a fine three-story base of Corinthian pilasters and seven-story shaft finished with a two-story crown entablature that has a frieze of giant Palladian windows. Originally, the top of the building

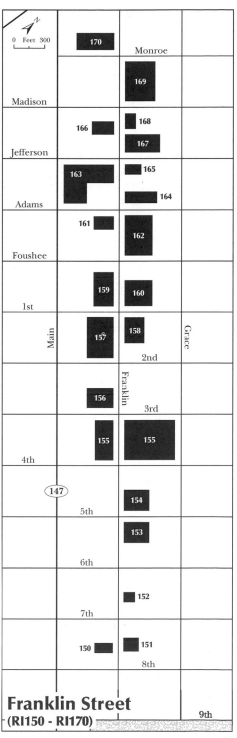

RI150 Stewart-Lee House

RI152 Office Building (Franklin Federal Savings and Loan Company)

boasted a roof garden encircled by large electric lanterns that were lit nightly. Altogether, this tour de force of architecture and special effects was one of Richmond's earliest attempts at real estate as marketing tool.

RI152 **Office Building** (Franklin Federal Savings and Loan Company)

1940, Edward F. Sinnott. 616 E. Franklin St.

This small building is classical in its symmetry and stoic restraint yet displays festive Art Deco touches such as glass block windows and the stylized eagles that serve as stanchions for the flagpoles.

RI153 Hotel John Marshall

1927, Marcellus Wright. Northeast corner of Franklin and 5th sts.

Long one of Richmond's premier hotels, the high-rise John Marshall has a sleek, urbane muscularity. A massive, three-story limestone base supports a U-shaped tower that rises to a cornice decorated in vividly colored terra-cotta panels. One of the city's finest buildings, it suffered the fate of many older inner-city hotels and was closed in the late 1970s. At the time of writing, its future looks brighter, since it is undergoing a slow renovation to return it to hotel use.

RI154 Imperial Building

1923, Neff and Thompson, Architects and Engineers. 422 E. Franklin St.

In many medium-sized American cities this dignified study in neoclassicism would be an architectural landmark serving as a courthouse, post office, or city hall. Constructed with a steel frame and limestone exterior, it displays a restraint that recalls the nearly contemporary work of Philadephia architect Paul P. Cret. On this Richmond street corner it is merely part of the "glue" that is so important to maintaining the city's fabric. The clumsy renovations of the portals have not detracted from its street presence.

RI155 Media General Building

1998, Burrell Saunders. 333 E. Franklin St.

This first phase of an envisioned corporate complex for Media General/Richmond Newspapers Inc. is a decidedly late-1990s twist on the popular Richmond stylistic scheme of melding classicism with modernism. Here, a semi-engaged portico of heroic columns on the second story is sheathed in aluminum. A modernist canopy (probably inspired by the much more refined Library of Virginia) announces the entry.

RI156 Woman's Club (Bolling Haxall House)

1858. 1915, auditorium addition, Carneal and Johnston. 1984, renovation, Wright, Cox and Smith. 1999, interior, C. Dudley Brown. 211 E. Franklin St. Open on request

RI153 Hotel John Marshall

RI158 Linden Row Inn (Linden Row)

Who designed this sophisticated Italianate building for Bolling Haxall, one of Richmond's leading businessmen just before the Civil War, remains a puzzle. Obviously it was someone very up to date, possibly an out-of-town architect, though the local builders George and John Gibson have been credited with the design. The central bay projects slightly from the main facade and is set off by a one-story entrance portico with Roman Doric columns. The central bay rises to an ebullient arch at the roofline. A cupola tops the roof. Highly ornate cast ironwork adorns the small balconies that accentuate the main floor and the window caps, and is used in the elegantly patterned fence that runs along the sidewalk. Inside, the rear ballroom, built in 1915 for the Woman's Club, is furnished in a highly decorative, Greek-inspired Beaux-Arts classical style. Much of the interior has been restored.

RI157 Richmond Public Library

1930, 1972, Baskervill and Son. 101 E. Franklin St.

In a renovation reputedly inspired by the modernism of Edward Durrell Stone, architect of the Kennedy Center for the Performing Arts in Washington, D.C., the Baskervill firm entombed Richmond's handsome Art Deco library inside a behemoth of glass and cast stone. What could they have been thinking of? The blocky, two-story exterior columns are short on gracefulness, but they do pick up the delightful rhythm of attached town houses of Linden Row across the street. Penetrate this forbidding exterior to find encased the original library building, a Greco-Deco structure. The original entrance hall, now the lobby of the art and music section, retains travertine walls and a plaster ceiling, testimony to a better time for architecture.

RI158 Linden Row Inn (Linden Row)

1847, 1853, Otis Manson. c. 1980, renovation. 100–114 E. Franklin St.

This procession of attached three-story town houses set in small, raised front yards behind granite and cast iron fencing is a highlight of East Franklin Street. Pristine Greek Doric porticoes relieve the somber appearance of the red brick buildings, which appear to glow in the afternoon sun. Mary Wingfield Scott, Richmond's doyenne of historic preservation, saved the houses, and they were given to the Historic Richmond Foundation, which in turn passed them on with covenants. They are now cleverly converted into a small hotel. The triple-tier porches along the rear have been cleverly widened to accommodate service functions but still retain their original flavor. Two houses at the east end of the block were demolished in the 1920s for construction of the Medical Arts

Building, which is now being renovated as apartments.

RI159 Town Houses

1837 (number 15), 1847 (number 13), 1840 (number 11), 1879 (number 9), 1894 (number 7), c. 1895 (number 5). 5–15. E. Franklin St.

With the exception of numbers 5 and 7, the houses in this eclectic collection have been altered for other uses without significantly damaging the visual effect of this human-scaled ensemble or the overall spirit and ambience of Franklin Street.

RI160 Garden Club of Virginia (Kent-Valentine House)

1845, Isaiah Rogers. 1910, renovation, Noland and Baskervill. Later renovations and restoration. 1998, interior renovation, C. Dudley Brown. 12 E. Franklin St. Open to the public

This once-narrow stucco-covered brick town house was widened and reworked in the Colonial Revival style in 1910 to become an imposing presence on Franklin Street. Essentially, Noland and Baskervill doubled Rogers's original design and added a giant portico with four Ionic columns to the front. The original house had an iron veranda, which has been incorporated as railings in the new structure. A rear carriage house, converted to offices, sits like a folly on the beautifully maintained grounds. The interior combines Greek Revival and

Beaux-Arts decoration. The Garden Club of Virginia, a major presence in the restoration of Virginia gardens, is slowly restoring the interior.

RI161 Jefferson Hotel Parking Facility
(Second Baptist Church)

1906, Noland and Baskervill. 9 W. Franklin St.

If Thomas Jefferson used the Maison Carrée in Nîmes, France, as his model for the capitol, just a few blocks away, the architects of this Baptist church were perhaps more faithful to the ancients in their handling of the fluted Corinthian columns and the overall proportions and detailing. Now part of the Jefferson Hotel complex and used for parking, this building is a significant city landmark that awaits a new use.

RI162 YMCA

1940, Baskervill and Son. 2 W. Franklin St.

Designed by the successors to the architecture firm responsible for the pedimented Second Baptist building across the street and the YWCA on North 5th Street, this three-part building has a central tetrastyle in antis portico on its second floor. The colonnade not only connects the two wings but lines up with the portico across the street. Stylistically, the "Y" is in the Colonial Revival–Georian Revival mode of Colonial Williamsburg, with wonderfully precise Flemish bond brickwork.

RI163 Jefferson Hotel

1893–1895, Carrère and Hastings. 1901–1907, John Kevan Peebles. c. 1985, renovation. 1996–2000, entrance court, pool house, and restaurant addition, Marcellus Wright, Cox and Smith. 101 block of W. Franklin St. (entire block, bounded by Franklin, Jefferson, West Main, and Adams sts.)

The grand hotel of Richmond for over a century, the Jefferson Hotel was commissioned by Major Lewis Ginter to be the showplace for the city. Carrère and Hastings, fresh from their triumphs at St. Augustine, Florida, created a Beaux-Arts confection that drew upon the Villa Medici in Rome for the West Franklin Street facade and Spanish buildings for the towers. The steel frame is covered in a pearly white brick with white terra-cotta decoration from the Perth Amboy Terra Cotta Company. When it opened the Jefferson had 342 guest rooms,

RI163 Jefferson Hotel, 1965

electric lighting, central heating, and hot and cold water in each room, and a grand lobby reached from West Franklin Street. The hotel was completed a few weeks ahead of schedule so that the wedding reception of Charles Dana Gibson and Irene Langhorne (his model for the "Gibson Girl") could be held there. A fire in 1901 destroyed portions of the central and south wings, and Norfolk architect John Kevan Peebles rebuilt those sections and created the present interior with its grand staircase and lobby. This spatial sequence became one of the best-known interiors in the city, the scene of many parties, grand entrances (and exits), and the set for several movies. After World War II, the hotel declined and in the 1970s was closed and slated for demolition. R. W. S. Partners purchased the hotel and renovated it, changing the entrance to the side to better accommodate the automobile.

RI164 Chesterman Place (Pace House)

1876. 1908, expansion, Aubrey Chesterman. 100–102 W. Franklin St.

Built for a local tobacconist and philanthropist, this imposing Italianate residence with its distinctive three-story window bays is, for Richmond, unique in that the major building material is sandstone, of the type commonly known as brownstone, such as that used in New York.

The tendency of brownstone to scale is amply apparent in the present building. Aubrey Chesterman, a leading Lynchburg, Virginia, architect, later converted the building to apartments, and more recently it has been used as an office building.

RI165 **Episcopal Diocese of Virginia** (Mayo Memorial House)

1845; later additions and renovations. 110 W. Franklin St.

This temple-form Greek Revival house, with four heroic Ionic columns carrying a pedimented portico, was built for William Taylor, a Richmond banker. Across the street stood an almost identical house that was destroyed to make way for the Hotel Jefferson. Originally this house had single-story wings flanking the central block, but c. 1870 they were enlarged to two stories.

RI166 **Junior League of Richmond** (Mayo-Carter House)

1895, Carrère and Hastings. 205 W. Franklin St.

This composition in limestone and brick evokes the French Renaissance style with its elaborate detailing, steep roof, and tall chimneys. In the same year, the architects also designed the Jefferson Hotel.

RI167 **Schoolcraft House**

1875. 200 W. Franklin St.

By the mid-1870s the French, or mansard, roof was passé in New York and Boston. But Richmond had not participated in the elaborate building of the decade after the Civil War, and hence this house was considered very up to date and evocative of Second Empire France. The house was a showpiece, especially with its elongated first-floor windows that allowed passersby to peer inside. These tall windows give the building a verticality different from

many of the other town houses on this rare intact block of nineteenth-century mansions.

RI168 **Association for the Preservation of Virginia Antiquities** (Cole-Diggs House)

c. 1800. 1910, remodeling, Noland and Baskervill. 204 W. Franklin St.

The two-tiered front porch is unusual on Franklin Street and probably was moved from another part of the house, perhaps the rear. This house, much altered over the years, predates others on the block and was part of very early real estate development.

RI169 **Berkshire Apartments**

1965, Marcellus Wright, Jr. 300 W. Franklin St.

An entire block of historic West Franklin Street was demolished to make room for this ungraceful apartment building. It was one of a number of high rises built in the 1960s and 1970s that threatened to change the character of the old avenue. Today, however, the historic structures and the high rises coexist and give the street a vitality it would not otherwise possess.

RI170 **Commonwealth Club**

1891, Carrère and Hastings. Later renovations and additions. 401 W. Franklin St.

Set atop a grassy rise, the Commonwealth Club has long been a bastion of social tradition in Richmond. Its clubhouse, however, is a surprisingly inventive piece of architecture that shows off Beaux-Arts design at its best by combining Italian and French Renaissance and colonial American elements to create a totally fresh design. The central two-story block, which contains a Palladian arch on the first floor, is topped by a triple-arched loggia on the second floor. At first glance, the two flanking wings appear to be symmetrical, but the roof treatments differ radically. A two-tiered side porch on the east end provides a wonderful transitional zone between the building and its grounds.

Grace Street　(RI171–RI183)

Once referred to as Richmond's "Fifth Avenue," Grace Street in the nineteenth century was a quiet residential area that started at Capitol Square and extended west to the edge of the city. A few Victorian houses survive behind shopfront additions, but the predominant character of the street is that of boisterous 1920s–1950s commercial growth. Grace Street from east to west presents a cross section of commercial architecture.

RI171　Sydnor and Hundley Furniture Store

1911, Charles K. Bryant. 700 E. Grace St.

This is one of the first large commercial structures erected on the formerly residential street. The building's wide window bays, made possible by structural steel, and the straightforward treatment of the elevations, which generally lack ornament except at the cornice, betray the influence of the Chicago Commercial Style.

RI172　Verizon (Bell Atlantic, Chesapeake and Potomac Telephone Company)

1929, Voorhees, Gmelin and Walker; later additions. 703 E. Grace St.

Designed by the New York firm that captured most of the East Coast telephone building market in the 1920s and 1930s, this building is a nice example of their work in the Art Deco style. Ralph Walker, the main designer for the firm, liked to create dramatic profiles against the skyline. A light-colored limestone base sets off brick upper walls that have a pier-buttress articulation with recessed windows. One end of the building has a pyramidal roof sheathed in decorative lead. Limestone, carved with rich floral decoration, also appears at the cornice level. Unfortunately, later additions have masked some of the drama of the original building.

RI173　Carpenter Center of the Virginia Center for the Performing Arts (Loew's Theater)

1927–1928, John Eberson. 1982, conversion, Marcellus Wright, Cox and Smith. 600 Grace St.

This is Virginia's premier example of the "atmospheric theater," designed by an architect nationally known in the 1920s and 1930s as the

RI173 Carpenter Center of the Virginia Center for the Performing Arts (Loew's Theater)

creator of elaborate movie palaces. The experience of going to the movies and the theater itself equaled, if not surpassed, what was on the screen. In this case the exterior is a blend of Spanish Baroque and Moorish styles, while the interior defies traditional description: a fantasy of sculpture, terra-cotta, and plaster, giving the sense of a Spanish plaza. The structure has been sympathetically adapted as a performing arts center.

RI174　Thalhimers Department Store

c. 1890. 1939, Tausig and Fleich. 1955, Copland, Novack, and Israel. 600 E. Grace St. (north side)

RI175　Miller and Rhoads Department Store

1922, Starrett and Van Vleck. Later additions. 500 E. Grace St. (north side)

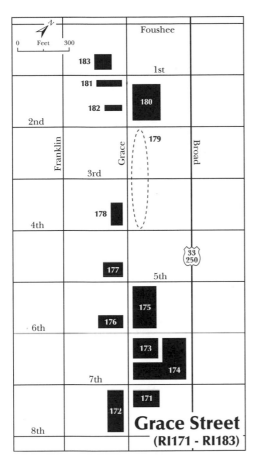

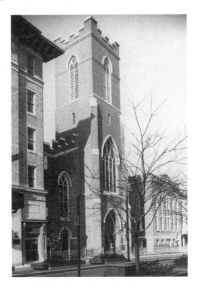

Built by a high-end clothing store, the building proclaims its purpose at the entrance with sculptures of mythological creatures and a shield carried by a man in a top hat. Essentially the building's form is that of an Italian Renaissance palazzo. The top floor and cornice are covered in colored terra-cotta ornament. The original bulb-lit steel sign still projects from the rooftop.

RI177 **Centenary Methodist Church**

1843, John and Samuel Freeman. 1874, alterations, Albert L. West. Later alterations. 1929, Sunday school wing, Charles M. Robinson. 411 E. Grace St.

This church began life as a Greek Revival structure. A Gothic facelift was planned about 1860, in an attempt to keep up with the nearby Second Presbyterian Church (see above), but the Civil War intervened, and not until 1874 did Albert L. West accomplish the remodeling. The relationship to Second Presbyterian is clear, even though West used darker brick and more vivid limestone trim. The interior was also remodeled with a hammerbeam and truss roof but lacks the spatial amplitude of Second Presbyterian Church. The focal point is the choir, with the organ behind, set apart from the nave by three tall pointed arches. The window glass is geometric except for one figural window. The baptismal font is by Tiffany Studios. Albert L. West had one of the largest architectural practices in Richmond in the mid-nineteenth

Grace Street owed its reputation as the shopping mecca for the upper South to these two department stores, now closed. Thalhimers was for nearly 100 years one of the best-known department stores in the South. Unified by an aluminum screen, the structure is actually a series of smaller buildings. At the corner of 6th Street is another portion of Thalhimers, built in 1939, with a restrained classical Art Deco facade that would be at home in New York. Next door is the former Miller and Rhoads Department Store (1922, Starrett and Van Vleck; later additions), which was the other big-name department store in Richmond. Closed as well, the Miller and Rhodes building, in a restrained red brick colonial idiom, was designed by a well-known New York firm.

RI176 **Berry-Burk Building**

1928, Baskervill and Lambert. 525–529 E. Grace St.

RI178 Media General (Richmond News-Leader Building, Richmond Times-Dispatch Building)

RI181, RI182 Richmond Art Company (right) and Joseph P. Winston House

century. His Methodist background brought him several other church commissions in addition to this one.

RI178 Media General (Richmond News-Leader Building, Richmond Times-Dispatch Building)

1922, Baskervill and Lambert. 1953, addition, Carneal and Johnston. Later additions. 333 E. Grace St.

Newspapers of various names have been edited (and for a time printed) on this site since the early 1920s. On the 4th Street facade can be seen remnants of the original Renaissance Revival structure. By the early 1950s the International Style had arrived in Richmond, and Carneal and Johnston added to and encased most of the original building with long, horizontal strips of industrial-sash metal windows and a thin veneer. They also created a plaza in front, the first example in Richmond of this post–World War II urban phenomenon.

RI179 Stores

300–200 blocks of E. Grace St.

The city's best examples of small-scale Art Deco are located in the 300 and 200 blocks of East Grace Street. Number 306 (1928, Carl Linder) and number 304 (1930, W. H. Pringle) were originally designed as women's clothing stores, and they look like it—direct from the 1925 Paris Exposition des Arts Décoratifs. Number

306, with its tall piers and incised ornament, is probably the wildest Art Deco building in the city. Drawings for numbers 308–312 (1927–1932, Carl Linder) were published in *American Commercial Buildings of Today* (1927), but by the time they were built, the ornament was considerably reduced. The Broad and Grace Street Arcade (1929, John Eberson; 216 East Grace Street, at the corner of 3rd Street) is a very restrained and delicately detailed part of Eberson's Art Deco tower that faces on Broad Street. It was designed to connect the two streets and contained some of the most exclusive shops in Richmond. It narrowly escaped demolition in the 1970s, but fortunately Central Fidelity Bank renovated it, and it is now used as offices. Number 208 East Grace Street (1930, Henry Carl Messerschmidt) is a lavishly decorated Art Deco jewel. Three vertical piers and recessed panels and balconies carry a wealth of vines and grapes.

RI180 Sydnor and Hundley Building

1931, Carneal and Johnston. 106–108 E. Grace St.

As its second store, this large furniture company built an Art Deco building with unusual yellow and black brick and carved floral ornament. At four stories the building almost looks like a section of a skyscraper.

RI181 Richmond Art Company

1919, W. Duncan Lee. 101 E. Grace St.

The increasing eclecticism of American architecture in the 1910s and 1920s is well illustrated by this spectacular Mediterranean Revival composition with tile roof, a third-floor loggia, iron railings, lions, and urns. Lee was much better known for Colonial Revival design, but, in a sense, this building would be Colonial Revival if it were located in California.

RI182 Joseph P. Winston House

1874. 103 E. Grace St.

Among the Art Deco and revivalist splendor of East Grace Street is this surprising survivor, a Second Empire house. It has a high, double-curved mansard roof, unique for Richmond, and a spectacular cast iron porch and fence. Winston was in real estate and developed several commercial properties after the Civil War.

RI183 Ragland Row

1858. 13–17 E. Grace St.

Another survivor from the past, this row of brick Greek Revival town houses is usual in Richmond. These buildings exhibit a subdued version of the style, demure entrances, and a small bracketed cornice. Now used as apartments, the original carriage and servants' house is at the rear.

Broad Street from West of 3rd Street to Belvidere Street   (RI184–RI203)

The origins of Broad Street lie in Thomas Jefferson's 1780 expansion plan for Richmond, in which the street was laid out to the present Foushee Street (the original western boundary of the city). Subsequently, the city grid expanded to the west, and the street became part of the Richmond Turnpike. Beginning in 1839, the Richmond, Fredericksburg and Potomac Railroad extended down the center of the street. In 1888 the first successful electric streetcar system in the world replaced it. Commercial activity on Broad Street before the Civil War was minimal, but following the great evacuation fire of 1865, retail activity began to move up Shockoe Hill. By the twentieth century, Broad Street had become one of the great retail and entertainment districts in the South. Department stores as well as theaters, saloons, furniture showrooms, jewelry stores, groceries, dry goods emporiums, and other establishments lined the street. The area remained a vibrant retail district until suburban flight took its toll in the 1970s. The last department store closed in 1992. The City of Richmond Master Plan, adopted in 1997, calls for the removal of most of the remaining vestiges of commercial architecture east of 4th Street to accommodate a convention center and government uses. Civic leaders view the loss of commercial activity and prestige on this part of Broad Street as a failure that must be swept away. The surviving area to the west is emerging as a mixed-use district of shopping, apartments, offices, and galleries. The city of Richmond's historic designation protects most of the area west of 3rd Street. This tour includes the surviving commercial corridor from 3rd Street to its western boundary at Belvidere.

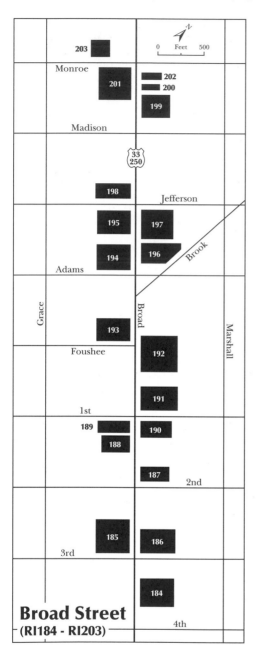

Broad Street
(RI184 - RI203)

RI184 Sears, Roebuck Building

1925. 312 E. Broad St.

The expansive Chicago windows of this straightforward steel-frame, brick-veneered building are not surprising given the Chicago origins of the Sears firm. Richmond architects may have

designed it, but the plans may also have come from a Chicago firm.

RI185 Central Fidelity Bank (Central National Bank)

1929, John Eberson. 219 E. Broad St.

Broad Street merchants created the Central National Bank to serve the retail district. The Broad Street financial concern specifically conceived of the Art Deco tower as a challenge to the skyscraper monopoly of the Main Street financial district. This building and the Medical College of Virginia West Hospital (see entry above) are the only stepped-back skyscrapers in the city. The building is one of the great twentieth-century landmarks of Virginia architecture. The exterior is composed in two parts with a tower toward Broad Street (which recalls Eliel Saarinen's entry in the Chicago Tribune competition of 1922) and a shorter tail to the rear. The large vaulted banking lobby is a lavish Art Deco exercise in nearly pristine condition.

RI186 United Way Offices–Virginia Federal Savings and Loan Company

1964, Cuneen Company. 224 E. Broad St.

This is a period piece, very much in what Philip Johnson and others bave called the "modern ballet school" mode, characterized by grilles of metal or brick, which was popularized by Minoru Yamasaki and Edward Durrell Stone in the 1950s. Robert Winthrop, in his *Architecture in Downtown Richmond* (1982), praises it as retaining "its sharp crispness."

RI189 Commercial Building   RI190 Harvey's Progressive Barbershop

RI187 **Shop**

1913, Albert F. Huntt. 118 E. Broad St.

A remarkably "modern" design for its date, this building is ornamented with Art Deco–like brickwork and cast stone ornament. Huntt, a progressive and gifted Richmond architect, used his skills to great effect on this project, as well as on other commercial buildings in the city.

RI188 **1708 Gallery** (Walter D. Moses and Company)

1895. 1950, renovation. 1994, renovation. 103 E. Broad St.

The Walter D. Moses music store occupied this brick Romanesque Revival building during most of its history. The firm commissioned an attractive but seemingly incongruous modernist storefront and interior renovation in the 1950s. The 1708 Gallery undertook a sophisticated adaptation of the first-floor space for its purposes in 1994.

RI189 **Commercial Building**

1890, Marion J. Dimmock. 1985, rehabilitation. 101 E. Broad St.

The ever-prolific Dimmock here adopts the Beaux-Arts idiom of New York designers, such as McKim, Mead and White, in this sophisti-

cated Renaissance Revival structure. It is a diminutive Italian palazzo, but Dimmock employed a heavy rustication on the piers that recalls H. H. Richardson. Dimmock designed many buildings in Richmond and the surrounding area between the Civil War and his death in 1908. He was born in Portsmouth in 1842 and served in the Confederate army. Nothing is known about his architectural training; his knowledge probably came through the building trade.

RI190 **Harvey's Progressive Barbershop**

1873, storefront. c. 1930, sign. 100 E. Broad St.

The illuminated Coca-Cola sign dominates the two-story brick structure. The sign faces two streets and has long been a downtown landmark. It was recently repainted but unfortunately has been without power for a number of years. Only a few of these impressive early twentieth-century illuminated signs survive in the city.

RI191 **Commercial Building**

1873. 8 E. Broad St.

The oldest surviving building on this block of Broad Street is this four-story brick structure. It has granite window dressings, but its major feature is the mansard roof. Richmond never took to the mansard mode for commercial buildings. Hence this structure is unusual for its pretense to the glamour associated with the Second Empire style.

RI192 Commercial Buildings

1881. 2–6 E. Broad St.

Arched windows, round medallions, and common stringcourses and cornices unify this impressive row of three buildings. Each is differentiated by a distinct parapet treatment that gives it its own identity.

RI193 Pemberton, Lordes and Mosby Drygoods Company

1898. 11–17 W. Broad St.

One of the few granite facades on a commercial building in Richmond incongruously combines Romanesque Revival upper floors with a classical pressed metal cornice.

RI194 The Cornerstone (Masonic Temple)

1888, Jackson Gott. 1990–1996, renovation, Henry Tenser. 101 W. Broad St.

The building now known as the Cornerstone is one of the few large Romanesque Revival commercial buildings to survive in the city. The facade is an ornate composition in brick and brownstone. The first floor and mezzanine, which originally but briefly housed a Woodward and Lothrop department store, have been adapted to offices. The large tower placed away from the corner on the interior of the block denotes a separate entrance to the upper floors. Recent research suggests that the entrance (an arch flanked by clustered columns topped by spheres) symbolizes the entrance to Solomon's Temple, an important Masonic architectural metaphor. This entrance led to the ballroom and Masonic meeting rooms, which are indicated by the large arched openings on the exterior of the structure and have now been renovated as meeting spaces. The ballroom is of particular interest as a grand space where Richmonders feted the rich and famous. The third and fourth floors accommodated offices. In the renovation they were converted to apartments.

RI195 Popkin Furniture Building

1909, Bergdoll and Paulding. 121 W. Broad St.

Erected by a Philadelphia-based design and contracting firm, this structure is safely conservative, with a tame, classic cast iron storefront, brick upper floors, and an ornate pressed metal cornice.

RI196 Regency Theater

1912, Charles K. Bryant. 1977, renovation, Bond, Comet, Westmorland. 116 W. Broad St.

Modest in size but with suave neoclassical details, including tall, fluted pilasters capped by urns, this theater building was constructed for African Americans during the height of segregation in Richmond. It has been appended by the Theater IV Company as a smaller theater to the adjoining Empire Theater.

RI197 Empire Theater

1912, Scarborough and Howell. 1977, renovation, Bond Comet Westmoreland. 118 W. Broad St.

The Empire is the oldest surviving theater building in Richmond. The exterior has been purged of its ornament, leaving only the coffered arch to suggest its original grandeur. Fortunately, the lavish neoclassical ornament on the interior of the theater escaped obliteration. Claude K. Howell, one of the partners of the designing firm, would later become one of the most prolific theater designers in the South.

RI198 Mosby Dry Goods Building

1916, Starrett and Van Vleck and Carneal and Johnston, associates. 1997, renovation, Scribner Messer Brady Wade. 201–205 W. Broad St.

A pioneering building for Richmond, this was the first entirely fireproof structure erected in the city. Built for a leading department store, the structure is Richmond's version of McKim, Mead and White's Gorham Building in New York. The classical detailing of the cornice and the arcaded first floor contrast with the sleek, unornamented upper floors. Carneal and Johnston reused this format for several of their buildings around Richmond.

RI199 Moore and Hardy Building

1916, Albert Huntt. 310 W. Broad St.

In contrast to his more austere project at 118 East Broad, Huntt was exuberant in this design for a Studebaker auto dealership: garland panels flank a massive Palladian window in the center pavilion.

RI200 Church Hill (C. G. Ekerts Building)

c. 1875. 316 W. Broad St.

This pristine example of a two-story Italianate commercial building has a wooden storefront on the first floor, a unique survivor. The ornate front consists of four arches separated by pilasters and decorative trim.

RI201 Miller and Rhoads Buildings

1913, Charles M. Robinson. 315–317 and 319–323 W. Broad St.

Robinson, primarily known for his schools, designed these two buildings, constructed side by side for the large Richmond-based department store. The Chicago School influence is evident in 319–323, with its expansive windows, riveted spandrel panels, and plain cornice broken by sleek paired brackets. Robinson initially practiced architecture in Pennsylvania and, perhaps as a result, was open to progressive designs from the Midwest.

RI202 Duggan Building

1858. 320 W. Broad St.

When constructed, this diminutive frame building was one of the few on Broad Street; that it has survived is surprising. It is probably one of the oldest commercial buildings in Richmond.

RI203 Moore's Auto Body (Standard Gas and Oil Supply)

1925, Smith and Van Dervoort. 401 W. Broad St.

Designed and built at a time when driving was romantic, this unusual Neo-Mediterranean survivor is one of the most ornate gas station buildings ever constructed in the Richmond area. Although the pumps are gone, the glamour remains.

Jackson Ward (RI204–RI231)

Jackson Ward is one of the oldest neighborhoods in Richmond and the only one of the large downtown residential neighborhoods to survive. It is bounded on the south by Marshall Street, on the west by Belvidere Street, on the east by 4th Street, and on the north by the Gilpin Court public housing project, which is just north of I-95. In the late eighteenth and early nineteenth centuries the area north of Leigh Street developed as a neighborhood of free blacks known as Little Africa. After the Civil War, freed slaves came to Jackson Ward in large numbers, creating one of the leading African American business centers in the United States. This concentration resulted in a considerable amount of building activity, undertaken by a strong community of African American builders and eventually by African American architects. After World War II the area suffered as property was condemned and demolished for governmental projects such as the convention center, parking lots, public housing, and the Richmond-Petersburg Turnpike. This is balanced somewhat by a substantial amount of rehabilitation in the district. The churches of Jackson Ward are important architectural and cultural landmarks that remain vital parts of the community. Efforts are underway to revitalize the business district as part of the Virginia Main Street program.

RI204 House

1853. 401 W. Marshall St.

The well-preserved frame Greek Revival house is one of a number of such buildings that once stood in the neighborhood. Of importance are the full-width Doric portico and rear ell, both original.

RI205 F. T. Idbell Houses

1848. 302–306 W. Marshall St.

These modest brick Greek Revival row houses, with their porches of square Doric piers, are typical of antebellum Jackson Ward buildings.

RI206 House

1850, 1880. 312 W. Marshall St.

Built as a raised cottage, this house received a Second Empire makeover with a second story, dormer windows, a mansard roof, and a lavish cast iron porch.

RI207 Richmond Dairy Company Building

1913, Carneal and Johnston. 1988, renovation. 201 W. Marshall St.

A "duck," in Robert Venturi's terminology, the Richmond Dairy has huge milk-bottle turrets that explicitly announce its original purpose. The structure is a vital reminder of the former commercial and industrial character of this part of the city. It has been renovated as apartments.

RI208 Richmond Fire Museum (Steamer Company No. 5)

1884, Wilfred Emory Cutshaw, city engineer. 200 W. Marshall St. Open to the public

Occupying a triangular site, this bracketed Italianate structure is one of several schools and markets in this style by Cutshaw, who designed a number of buildings in his position as city engineer. A cupola that once graced the roof housed a warning bell for the police and fire stations that shared the building. It now houses firefighting equipment on exhibit.

RI209 Jackson Center

1992, Freeman-Morgan. Clay and 2nd sts.

The center is a postmodern building effort aimed at community revitalization. The construction required the demolition of a number of commercial buildings on 2nd Street, including the office of the man for whom it is named, the noted African American attorney Giles B. Jackson.

RI210 Elks Club (R. W. Taylor House)

1904, John Anderson Lankford. 526 N. 2nd St.

This twenty-six-room Queen Anne mansion was the residence of Reverend R. W. Taylor, president of a Richmond-based African American fraternal organization, the Grand Fountain United Order of True Reformers. Taylor and his organization proved to be major patrons of Lankford, a Washington, D.C.–based African American architect who published a book of his designs in 1916. Much of the dec-

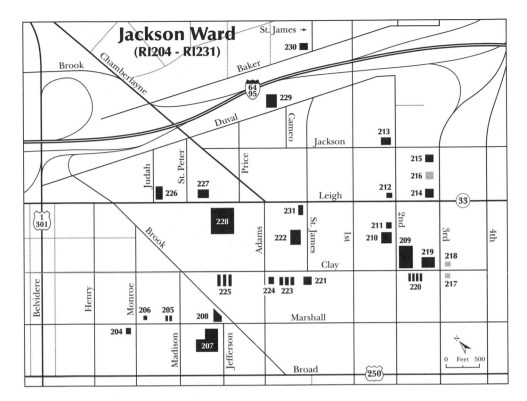

orative detail has been lost from this structure, but Lankford's boldly modeled forms, including a dominant tower and projecting bay window, remain.

RI211 **Hippodrome Theater**

1913. 1945, remodeling, attributed to John J. Zink. 528 N. 2nd St.

A fire gutted the original Hippodrome to the walls, and the present Moderne structure with cylindrical towers and vertical grille is the result of the rebuilding. In the early twentieth century, 2nd Street was a major African American entertainment district with a number of clubs and several theaters.

RI212 **Maggie Walker House**

1889, George Boyd, builder. 1918 and later alterations, Charles T. Russell. 110 ½ E. Leigh St. Open to the public

African American builder George Boyd constructed this originally Italianate building as

part of the Quality Row section of East Leigh Street, a group of fine town houses occupied and in many cases owned by African American professionals. Under the ownership of Maggie

RI212 Maggie Walker House

Walker, Grand Secretary of the Independent Order of St. Luke, this house was substantially modified with Colonial Revival details, a library, and a porch.

RI213 Richmond Beneficial Insurance Company Building

1911 Charles T. Russell. 700 N. 2nd St.

An important design by the first African American to maintain an architectural practice in Virginia, Charles T. Russell, this structure is similar in a number of ways to the St. Luke Penny Savings Bank (1910; demolished), Russell's first commission. The polychrome brick, three-story Renaissance Revival building originally housed offices on the upper floors and two storefront spaces on the first floor.

RI213 Richmond Beneficial Insurance Company Building

RI214 Price Funeral Home

1902; later alterations. 212 E. Leigh St.

A. D. Price and Company, one of the largest African American funeral and livery establishments in Richmond, built this three-story brick structure, originally part of a row of commercial buildings that lined the street. The idiom is standard early twentieth-century commercial with large upper-floor windows. The second-floor windows are rectangular, and those on the third floor are vaguely round-arched and vaguely Italianate. The lower floor has been "colonialized."

RI215 Third Street Bethel African Methodist Episcopal Church

c. 1857. 1875, addition. 1914, addition, Carl Ruehrmund. 614 N. 3rd St.

This rare pre–Civil War African American church has a twin-towered Gothic Revival facade. In 1875 spires were added to the towers, but they were later removed. The pedimented entrance was added in the early twentieth century.

RI216 Tucker Cottage

c. 1795. 612 N. 3rd St.

Gambrel-roofed frame cottages such as this were extremely common in late eighteenth- and early nineteenth-century Richmond, but most have been demolished. (Demolished, 2001)

RI217 House

1880. 319 E. Clay St.

Buildings in the Second Empire style are unusual in Richmond, and this handsome brick house was one of the better examples. The main block had arched windows, a cast iron porch, patterned slate mansard roof, and iron roof cresting. (Demolished, 2001)

RI218 House

1857, 1900. 308 E. Clay St.

This house began as a restrained Italianate structure with an elaborate cast iron porch that dated to the pre–Civil War period. The porch, one of the finest and most lavish in Richmond, is frequently pictured in books. In 1900 the house received a Colonial Revival update that included a gambrel dormer and fanlight windows. (Demolished, 2001)

RI219 Southern Aid Society (Mechanics Savings Bank)

1908, Carl Ruehrmund. 1931, additions, Carneal and Johnston. 212–214 E. Clay St.

This brick and stone Renaissance Revival building is an interesting example of a design by prominent white architects for African American clients. Ruehrmund designed the corner portion of the building for the Mechanics Savings Bank, and Carneal and Johnston added the western and rear additions.

RI220 Row Houses

c. 1890. 201–209 E. Clay St.

This outstanding set of Queen Anne row houses has stone facades. The projecting bay of the center house is gabled. The flanking bays alternate in form between three-sided and round towers. Each house has a false mansard roof.

RI221 The Black History Museum and Cultural Center of Central Virginia (Bowser Library; Dill House)

1830, 1918. 1991, renovations, Fry and Welch. 00 E. Clay St.

German immigrant Adolf Dill built this neoclassical structure as a suburban villa. When African Americans moved into this portion of Jackson Ward in the early twentieth century, it was adapted to become an African American women's club and circulating library. Most recently it has been transformed into a museum.

RI222 Hughes House

1915, Charles T. Russell. 508 St. James St.

RI225 Row Houses

This large Georgian Revival structure was the home of a prominent African American physician. Since segregation restricted African Americans to Jackson Ward and a few other neighborhoods, the secluded St. James site must have been one of the few lots in Jackson Ward large enough for this house.

RI223 Row Houses

c. 1885. 1, 3, and 5 W. Clay St.

Italianate row houses like these created the streetscape of Jackson Ward. The wooden porches are Eastlake in inspiration.

RI224 Dill House

c. 1846. 15 W. Clay St.

This excellent example of an unaltered Greek Revival house has a raised basement. Constructed of brick with stepped gables and three bays wide, it has a side entrance and a Doric portico. The house at 21 West Clay Street is similar.

RI225 Row Houses

c. 1880. 107–111 W. Clay St.

The reason Richmond is known as the city of cast iron porches is apparent here, for this is an amazing collection of slender columns, vine motifs, and fanciful elements across the fronts of three three-bay brick houses.

RI226 Ebenezer Baptist Church

c. 1875. 1915, renovation, Charles T. Russell. 214 W. Leigh St.

This began as a Victorian Gothic church which replaced an earlier church on the site. As part of a renovation it lost a spire from the top of the tower and acquired a pedimented neoclassical portico.

RI227 First Battalion Armory

1895, Wilfred Emory Cutshaw. 122 W. Leigh St.

Armories were a product of the 1870–1900 period, serving as men's clubs and as institutions for enforcing order at a time of strife in the American city. Nearly every American city of

RI227 First Battalion Armory (left)

RI228 Richmond Career Development Center (Armstrong High School) (below)

any size had at least one. Richmond had five armories, but only two survive. This martial Gothic fantasy in castellated brick and terracotta is a landmark and one of the very few armories in the country built for an African American population. The design is similar to that of two other armories by Cutshaw, the city engineer, which have been demolished. Built to serve four companies of soldiers, it was a point of pride and became a civic symbol for the Jackson Ward neighborhood. Unfortunately the white military units in the city refused to recognize the African American officers' authority, and by 1899 the companies had been disbanded. The building then became the Monroe School, the public elementary school for the ward, and during World War II it served as a recreation center for African American troops. Subsequently, it again became a school, then served other uses until a fire damaged the roof and upper stories. At present, it awaits a new use.

RI228 Richmond Career Development Center (Armstrong High School)

1922, Charles M. Robinson. 120 W. Leigh St.

This neoclassical brick structure was built as the single high school for African American students during the segregation era. Robinson was Richmond's school architect. The building

lacks the ornamental details of Robinson's other schools.

RI229 Sixth Mount Zion Baptist Church

1884, George Boyd, builder. 1925, additions, Charles T. Russell. 100 Duval St.

This brick church began as a Gothic Revival structure with a central crenellated tower. The growing congregation needed room for expansion, and Russell added a new front and rear and an education wing. The planned route of the Richmond-Petersburg Turnpike would have come right through the building. After a considerable campaign, the decision was made in 1957 to divert the turnpike and save the church, one of the first examples of preservation of an African American landmark in Richmond.

RI230 St. Luke's Building

1902, Peter J. White. 1918, renovation, Charles T. Russell. 902 St. James St.

This building is a testament to the architectural patronage of Maggie Walker, Grand Secretary of the humanitarian society known as the Independent Order of St. Luke. The building began as a three-story assembly hall for the local St. Luke chapters. The building served as the impetus for relocating the national headquarters to Richmond in 1903. Russell added an additional bay and fourth floor to the building. The building housed assembly rooms, print shop, and offices for the order.

RI231 St. Philip's Episcopal Church

c. 1870. c. 1890, remodeling. 1 W. Leigh St.

The only African American Episcopal congregation in the city constructed this building about 1870. When it was remodeled about twenty years later, the architect chose as the basis of the design H. H. Richardson's Allegheny Episcopal Church, Pittsburgh (1886). Essentially a rectangular box with a steep roof, the building has round-arched openings in light-colored sandstone set off by red brick.

Shockoe Hill Cemetery Environs (RI232–RI234)
(Map, pp. 170–171)

The Shockoe Hill Cemetery area is at the northern terminus of Shockoe Hill, which drops precipitously to Bacons Quarter Branch Valley. For many years this formed the northern boundary of Richmond. Away from the commercial and residential development along the James River, the area was well suited for secondary and what were considered undesirable uses. The city acquired most of the Shockoe Cemetery area for the establishment of a poorhouse in 1799, deeded a plot of land for the establishment of a Hebrew cemetery in 1816, and in 1825 surveyed the public land for a municipal cemetery.

RI232 Shockoe Hill Cemetery

1825, Richard Young, City Surveyor. Later additions. Hospital St. entrance

In 1825 the Richmond Common Council instructed the city surveyor to plat twelve acres of land for a public cemetery. The cemetery was created in response to overcrowding at St. John's Churchyard and a number of other private cemeteries. Young planned four-plot squares across the site with a network of small paths connecting the plots. When this system of circulation proved inadequate, a large oval avenue was added to connect the different portions of the cemetery. Within Shockoe Hill Cemetery is an outstanding and diverse array of primarily antebellum funerary art and architecture, including sarcophagi, columns, obelisks, figurative sculptures, and headstones. The monuments, many of Neo-Gothic design, are the handiwork of Richmond and northern artists.

RI233 Hebrew Cemetery

Hospital St.

Throughout most of the nineteenth century, Hebrew Cemetery served as the final resting place for much of Richmond's Jewish community. The monuments, which are oriented to the east in accordance with tradition, are generally restrained in ornamentation. Of interest is the Neo-Gothic chapel of 1916. The Confederate section is fenced by stacked arms is one of the most fascinating examples of cast iron design in Richmond.

RI234 Richmond Alms House

1860, Washington Gill. 1984–1985, renovation. 210 Hospital St.

Built on the site of the city's first almshouse (1804), this newer building is an interesting transitional structure. The brick Greek Revival facade shows the change from the more modest public buildings of the early nineteenth century to the larger Victorian institutional buildings of midcentury. The pedimented center section and wings are massive and in their form look forward to modern apartment blocks. After the the building ceased to be used for institutional purposes, it was renovated for elderly housing.

Oregon Hill   (RI235–RI251)

Oregon Hill is a nineteenth-century working-class neighborhood that retains its original character and all of its component parts: residential streetscapes, churches, commercial buildings, and schools. The origins of Oregon Hill go back to c. 1750, when William Byrd III built Belvedere (destroyed), a grand country house, on a site at the southern end of the present neighborhood, with a majestic view of the James River as it cascades and winds through Richmond. A deep ravine to the east and northeast of the community effectively cut the neighborhood off from Richmond proper, and Oregon Hill remained isolated.

In 1795 the James River and Kanawha Canal was completed around the falls of the James. The canal eventually brought industries to the foot of Oregon Hill and provided a path into the city for neighborhood residences. In 1798 the Commonwealth of Virginia constructed a penitentiary (demolished c. 1922), based on the designs of Benjamin Henry Latrobe, just to the east of the present neighborhood. In 1816 a group of developers laid out Sydney, an ambitious suburb west of the city, which incorporated most of Oregon Hill and the Fan. After the burning of Belvedere in 1851, the southern portion of the neighborhood was divided into lots. At this time Oregon Hill, because it was within walking distance of major industries, began to develop as a working-class suburb. After the Civil War, construction by real estate developers and residents created a dense streetscape. To serve this growing community, Grace Evelyn Arents, heiress to the fortune of Richmond tobacco magnate Lewis Ginter, took on Oregon Hill as her cause. She financed and sometimes oversaw the construction of a large collection of community buildings, some of which are described here. The recent history of Oregon Hill has included the intrusion of I-195 and demolition of many houses.

RI235 St. Andrew's Episcopal Church

1900–1903, A. H. Ellwood. 1904, parish hall, Noland and Baskervill. Laurel St. at Idlewood Ave.

The twin towers of this ashlar-trimmed, rock-faced masonry structure make it the dominant neighborhood landmark. Oregon Hill's great benefactor endowed this project to replace an earlier frame chapel in Oregon Hill. Grace Arents was a sophisticated architectural patron who selected an Elkhart, Indiana, architect because of his reputation as a designer of Episcopal churches. Arents was deeply involved with the project, to the point of serving as the contractor. Within and without, from the hammerbeams in the sanctuary to the exterior stonework, the building is imbued with the ideals of honest Gothic architecture advocated by A. W. N. Pugin and Ralph Adams Cram. The building was a substantial departure from the less academic interpretation that had characterized a number of earlier Gothic Revival

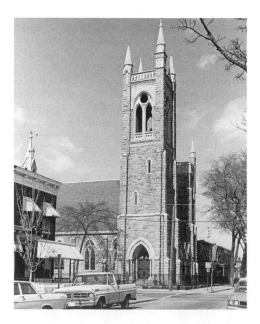

structures in Richmond (many of which have been demolished).

RI236 Houses

c. 1880–1900. 500–516 S. Laurel St.

In the building boom of the final decades of the nineteenth century, semidetached and detached Italianate frame town houses such as these—three bays wide and two stories in height, with full-width porches and relatively uniform setback—became the dominant form of building in the neighborhood. Most of the houses follow this pattern or some slight variation of it.

RI237 Houses

c. 1910. 614–618 S. Laurel St.

These detached buildings are an interesting variant on one of the Oregon Hill forms, the town house with two-story porches. There are several other examples in the neighborhood of this variant. In some cases the porches provided outdoor access for flats that occupied each floor; in others they were simply an amenity for single-family residences.

RI238 Riverside Park

1889. 1910, park house. Pine St. at Belvidere St.

The five-acre park on a strip of land overlooking the river is one of several dramatic hilltop parks with important views of the river and city. The octagonal park house is similar to a number of such structures built for the Richmond park system. The recent demolition of blocks of buildings to the north has increased the park's apparent size.

RI239 Grace Arents Public School

1911, Carneal and Johnston. 600 S. Pine St.

This foursquare, blocky Georgian Revival public school building was built with donations from and named in honor of Oregon Hill's great architectural patron, Grace Arents. Carneal and Johnston designed a number of school buildings in Richmond. In most cases the site was more suburban, and here the architects must have felt constrained. The stone-based brick structure has elaborate detailing around the entrance and in the window panels.

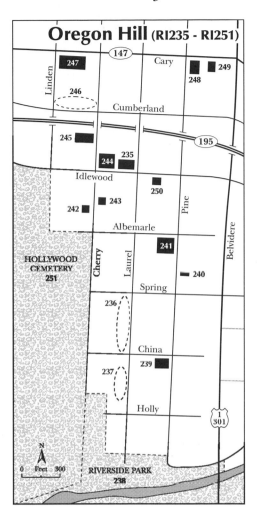

Oregon Hill (RI235 - RI251)

RI240 417 South Pine St.

1856

Although clearly influenced by the picturesque houses published by A. J. Downing, this frame residence lacks the ornamented bargeboards shown in his books.

RI241 Pine Street Baptist Church

1885, Baylor S. Martin, builder. 1927, Herbert Levi Cain, Sunday School annex. 400 S. Pine St.

The central tower, buttresses, and finials define this church as a pristine example of the Gothic Revival from the late nineteenth century. The builder of the church was an Oregon Hill resident and a member of the congregation.

RI242 J. G. Andrews House

c. 1850. 314–316 S. Cherry St.

This frame double house is an early example of an Italianate house in Richmond. The building exhibits the interesting possibilities of even modest Italianate architecture. Projecting bays define the ends, and a porch extends between the bays. It is dramatically different from the flat-fronted Italianate houses of the post–Civil War period.

RI243 307 South Cherry St.

c. 1840

This simple frame house is one of the oldest in Oregon Hill. When constructed it was probably the only building on the block. The house incorporates a deep setback that reflects its then-suburban location. Gabled cottages of this type were the dominant building type of the neighborhood in the antebellum period, and examples can be found interspersed among the later buildings.

RI244 St. Andrew's School

1900, D. Wiley Anderson. S. Cherry and Idlewood sts.

For this parochial school, Anderson picked up on the Gothic detailing and colored brickwork of the adjacent church. A noteworthy feature is the sign for the school, which is decorated with a T square and other symbols of the kind of practical education provided in the building.

RI245 William Byrd Community House
(Grace Arents Free Library)

1908–1914, Noland and Baskervill. 1947, conversion. 224 S. Cherry St.

Built by Grace Arents as a library for the community, this is now also a community center for inner-city Richmond. Instead of simply following the cue of the St. Andrew's complex across the street, the building is an important essay in Collegiate Gothic, which was gaining popularity at educational institutions in the North. The basic block of the building is simple, with large, clustered windows. The major element is the entrance, distinguished by its stylized Gothic ornament. Some of the curves in the carving are reminiscent of those found in Art Nouveau design. In 1947 a portion of the building was

RI245 William Byrd Community House (Grace Arents Free Library)

converted into a community house; a library for children is maintained in one wing. The brick structure next door, at 223 South Cherry (1903, Noland and Baskervill), is the former house for the teachers and administrators at St. Andrew's School.

RI246 Grace Arents Housing

1904. 912–924 Cumberland St. and 200–202 S. Linden St.

Constructed under the direction of Grace Arents to provide affordable housing, this is probably one of the earliest examples of subsidized housing in Virginia. The brick double houses with turned porch details, reminiscent of houses of the same period in the Fan District, replaced older wooden houses that were in poor shape. Many of the Grace Arents houses were demolished for the construction of the Downtown Expressway, and only nine still survive. Unfortunately, the future of the buildings is uncertain.

RI247 Virginia Commonwealth University Gymnasium (City Auditorium, Clay Ward Market)

1891, Wilfred Emory Cutshaw, city engineer. 1906, auditorium renovation, Noland and Baskervill. Later additions and renovations. W. Cary St. at Linden St.

This large building was constructed as a public market for the rapidly developing west end of Richmond but never succeeded economically. Subsequently it served as the city auditorium and as a warehouse. It currently functions as a gymnasium. The building is a remarkably well-preserved example of a late nineteenth-century public works project. Its most significant features are the detailed brickwork and the metal truss roof with clerestory windows, which apparently were inspired by the Pension Building in Washington, D.C. (1881–1887), designed and built under the direction of engineer Montgomery C. Meigs.

RI248 Winston-Jacobs House

1818. 1996, relocated. 601 W. Cary St.

George Winston, the original owner of this house, was a builder who trained free blacks as masons and carpenters. The building was relocated to the present site by Virginia Commonwealth University over the objections of members of the Oregon Hill and Richmond African American communities.

RI249 R. A. Siewers House

1890, attributed to R. A. Siewers. 609 W. Cary St.

Siewers, one of the leading contractors and millwrights of late nineteenth-century Richmond, presumably designed and built his own home. He employed a mansard roof and Italianate details on this three-story brick structure.

RI250 Norman T. Carter Dry Goods

c. 1890. 707 Idlewood Ave.

This modest corrugated metal structure is one of the most interesting commercial buildings in Richmond. A dry-goods business operated here for more than 100 years. Carter family members maintain the structure with window displays as an informal community museum.

RI251 Hollywood Cemetery

1847, John Notman. Later additions. Cherry St.

An important example of a rural cemetery, Hollywood originated in 1847 when a group of Richmonders sought to create a picturesque cemetery on a narrow tract of rugged terrain with spectacular vistas of Richmond. They commissioned John Notman of Philadelphia, a Scottish-born and -educated architect, who had designed Mount Laurel Cemetery in Philadelphia and Spring Grove Cemetery in Cincinnati. After overcoming opposition in the Virginia General Assembly to granting a charter, the Hollywood Company began work on the project in 1848. The chapel marks the original entrance to Hollywood and the beginning of the area planned by Notman. Basically the plan encompassed a ravine running north-south and four hills on its west side. Although Laurel Hill was decidedly classical in plan, here Notman chose to work with the natural lay of the land, and Hollywood is more picturesque. Notman laid out the cemetery by walking the site and employing a topographical survey; he suggested the name because of the site's many holly trees. Notman's plan served as a template the Hollywood Company used for later expansions to the cemetery.

Initially Richmonders were skeptical, and few lots were sold in the early 1850s. However, the re-interment there of President James Monroe in 1858 firmly established the popularity of the cemetery in the community. The parklike setting made Hollywood a popular destination for Richmonders throughout the nineteenth century. During the Civil War the cemetery became the burying ground for Confederate soldiers who had died on battlefields and in hospitals in the Richmond area. After the war, the re-interment and burial of Confederate soldiers and notables, combined with the erection of a number of significant monuments, made Hollywood Cemetery a focal point of the cult of the Lost Cause. Mary Mitchell, author of the definitive history of Hollywood, has aptly referred to it as a "southern shrine." The Hollywood Company successfully expanded the cemetery over the course of the nineteenth and early twentieth centuries, acquiring additional property to the west. The cemetery still admits burials.

The tour of the cemetery can be driven or undertaken as a fairly vigorous walk by following the blue line on the pavement. Visitors are cautioned to observe the rules of the cemetery posted at the gates.

The Superintendent's House (1894, George P. Barber; W. A. Chesterman, builder), a rambling Queen Anne dwelling, replaced an earlier structure for the superintendent. Chesterman owned a small planing mill in Richmond and also built houses. Apparently he ordered plans from Knoxville architect Barber, who had recently published *The Cottage Souvenir* (1888). The house built at Hollywood Cemetery has all the Barber trademarks of several different roof forms, including a clipped gable; a tower topped by a cupola; and a wide porch. The Hollywood Cemetery Chapel (1877, Henry Exall; 1897, Marion J. Dimmock), designed by an English-born and -trained architect, began as a Gothic "ruin" straddling the original entrance; the southern portion is still visible. The practical needs of the cemetery eventually outweighed the aesthetics of a ruin. Dimmock employed the northern portion of the ruin as the base of the tower and attached a chapel. The original entrance to the cemetery is marked by the ornamental iron gates. The present cemetery gates were constructed in the early twentieth century.

The Confederate Section and Confederate Monument (1863, burial lots; 1867–1868, monument, Charles H. Dimmock) was acquired and laid out in an impromptu manner to accommodate the war dead. In 1866 the federal government decided not to allow the burial of Confederate soldiers in national cemeteries. In response, the Hollywood Ladies' Memorial As-

RI251.1 Hollywood Cemetery, James Monroe Tomb, drawing by Oswald J. Heinrich

sociation organized what is credited with being the first Memorial Day celebration. The association commissioned the monument, one of the earliest Confederate monuments in the South. The rough granite pyramid perfectly captures the picturesque aesthetic of early Hollywood and met the financial limitations of the immediate postwar era. In 1869 the Ladies' Memorial Association reburied the majority of southern dead from the Battle of Gettysburg, Pennsylvania. Over the course of the late nineteenth century the Confederate Section was the setting for a number of events to memorialize the Lost Cause. The speaker's stand (1876) and the Pickett Monument are other noteworthy features.

Ellis Avenue (c. 1850–c. 1870) affords some of the best vantage points for viewing funerary art and architecture. Included in the area is an impressive array of statuary, columns, ironwork, obelisks, and Gothic Revival monuments. Ellis Avenue also provides a central point for viewing Notman's plan. The Weddell Monument (1950, Charles Gillette, landscape architect) was designed for Ambassador Alexander and Virginia Weddell's landscape architect, who worked on their Virginia House (see entry, below).

The Monroe Monument and Circle (RI251.1) (1858, Alfred Lybrock) resulted from an effort to gain popularity and respectability for the cemetery. The Hollywood Company donated this circle at the southwest corner of the Notman plan for the reburial of James Monroe. With considerable fanfare Monroe's body was returned to his native state from New York City in 1858. The fifth president's final resting place is distinguished by a cast iron crypt that might be described as a Gothic temple. The German-born and -trained architect Lybrock conceived of the monument as painted to resemble stone. Davis Circle (1877, C. P. E. Burgwyn, planner; 1899, 1906, George J. Zolnay, sculptor) marks the northwest terminus of the 1877 expansion of the cemetery. In a manner similar to its donation of land for the Monroe monument, the Hollywood Company gave the circle in 1877 for the interment of Jefferson Davis, president of the Confederacy. Davis was re-interred on the site in 1893. In 1899 the Hungarian-born and -trained sculptor Zolnay erected three monuments to the Davis family on the site: the bronze figure of Davis

himself, a broken column for his wife, Varina, and a grieving angel for daughter Varina Anne "Winnie" Davis. In 1909 another Davis daughter, Margaret Davis Hayes, died and received a monument, also by Zolnay, a draped figure standing within the oversized pages of a Bible. The Ellipse (1893, plan) is on a plateau with spectacular views of the James River. The Hollywood Company planned this section and permitted only one headstone per plot. The resulting severity contrasts sharply with the plots crowded with monuments in the older sections of the cemetery. To the north of the Ellipse are a number of outstanding mausoleums set into the hillside. The Lewis Ginter Mausoleum (1897), the resting place of Richmond's greatest architectural patron of the nineteenth century, is a splendid Beaux-Arts tempietto in the Corinthian order. Tiffany Studios provided the bronze doors and the stained glass.

Monroe Park and Environs (RI252–RI271)

Monroe Park, bounded by West Franklin, Laurel, West Main, and Belvidere streets, is a handsome urban oasis with a leafy canopy of huge trees. It is surrounded by some of the city's most eclectic buildings and serves as green space for landlocked Virginia Commonwealth University, which shares its upkeep with the city of Richmond.

The current configuration of the park dates from 1871, when nearby property owners prevailed upon the city to grade the site, pave pathways, and plant trees. The following year, a fountain was erected, which has subsequently been replaced by a four-tier cast iron fountain (c. 1903, J. W. Fiske Casting Company). The area surrounding the park became one of the most stylish addresses as Richmond's residential neighborhoods developed westward past

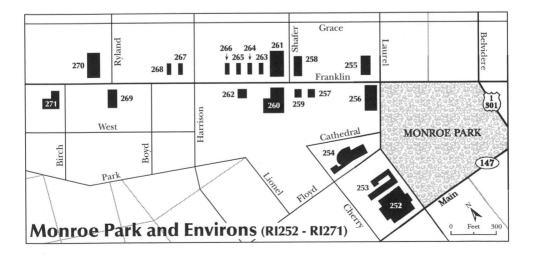

Monroe Park and Environs (RI252 - RI271)

Belvidere. The history of Monroe Park, however, dates back to 1851, when the city established a number of green spaces at the city's four edges to ensure "invigorating air" for its citizens. At first, this park was called Western Square, but it was soon renamed Monroe Square because it abutted Monroe Ward. By 1853, the space was being used for cattle shows and, by decade's end, full-fledged agricultural fairs. During the Civil War the square was used as a Confederate drill ground and eventually as space for barracks and hospital facilities. By the 1870s, the site was forlorn and ready for renewal as a public park. In addition to the fountain and a bandstand, the square contains a number of monuments commemorating leading citizens and historic events, including those for the Confederate William Carter Wickham (1891, Edward Valentine, sculptor) and the Richmond industrialist Joseph Bryan (1911, William Couper, sculptor).

RI252 **Richmond Landmark Theater** (The Mosque)

1926–1927, Marcellus Wright, Sr., and Charles M. Robinson; interior, J. Frank Jones, Raumbusch and Co.. 1966–1970, renovation, William Briggs. 1994–1995, renovation, Marcellus Wright Cox and Smith. 6 N. Laurel St.

The Mosque is an example of a national phenomenon, Egyptian- and Saracenic-inspired auditorium buildings built by the Masonic Nobles of the Mystic Shrine (or Shriners), who drew upon Middle Eastern forms for their costumes and rituals as well as their buildings. A tall Saracenic arch flanked by minarets defines the center, and tiles from the United States and Europe provide ornamental emphasis. The lobby of the building, including a fountain, makes lavish use of tilework. The 4,600-seat auditorium is extensively decorated with Islamic motifs and murals of Middle Eastern scenes. The Shriners conceived of the building as a great auditorium for Richmonders and a playground for themselves. Unfortunately, the building went into bankruptcy and closed during the Depression. It became a municipal auditorium in 1940 and was continually in use until 1994. The 1994 renovation restored the original decoration and provided additional public art, including a mural in the grand tiered lobby and metal grilles for the box office. The building spaces outside the lobby and auditorium generally are either unrestored or have been put to other uses. In addition to the auditorium, the Shriners equipped the building with forty-two hotel rooms, a restaurant, a bowling alley, a swimming pool, a banquet hall, a billiard room, and four lounges. In the basement is a large ballroom decorated with Egyptian-inspired Art Deco tiles. When Richmond Muslims objected to the name, the building was officially renamed, but most Richmonders continue to identify the building by its old name.

RI253 **Grace and Holy Trinity Church**

1895, William C. Noland, architect. 1926, parish hall, Baskervill and Lambert. 1980, addition, Glave, Newman, Anderson. 8 N. Laurel St.

A picturesque edifice with cragged gray stone walls soaring above Laurel Street like a granite cliff, this church is one of the earliest surviving designs by Noland, the so-called dean of Virginia architects. Born in Virginia, Noland trained with New York and Philadelphia architects and traveled for two years in Europe before opening his office in Richmond in 1895. A designer, he asked Henry Baskervill, an engineer, to join him in practice. The firm, Noland and Baskervill, designed many buildings throughout Virginia. This design, an exuberant meshing of Gothic and Romanesque forms, illustrates the transition in the 1890s from the older Richardsonian Romanesque to the academic Gothic of Ralph Adams Cram. The tower anchoring the southeastern corner of the sanctuary lost its steeple in a 1951 tornado but remains a muscular statement. The interior is appropriately dark and mystical, befitting the "high church" preferences of the congregation.

RI254 Cathedral of the Sacred Heart

1901–1906, Joseph H. McGuire. 1995, restoration, Robert P. Winthrop. Monroe Park between Floyd Ave. and Park Ave.

The architect of this spectacular building was Joseph H. McGuire, a Beaux-Arts-trained New York architect who specialized in buildings for Catholic organizations. He found patrons in Ida and Thomas Fortune Ryan of New York. Thomas Ryan was a Virginia-born industrialist and financier who, along with his wife, had a keen interest in buildings that served the Catholic church. The Richmond cathedral is constructed of limestone and has a dome, twin towers, and a monumental portico of six Corinthian columns supporting a pediment fronting Monroe Park. The building defies strict architectural classification, however, with its impressive synthesis of classical, Gothic, Renaissance, and baroque forms. The interior is a spectacular space with well-articulated ornamentation and finishes and a nave arcade that leads to a crossing capped by a magnificent dome.

West Franklin Street from Monroe Park to Monument Avenue (RI255–RI271)

From Monroe Park westward to where it becomes Monument Avenue, Franklin Street provides a timeline of fashionable Richmond's houses and churches in an array of styles—from Italianate and Second Empire to Richardsonian Romanesque, Colonial Revival, and classical and Spanish Colonial revivals. Virginia Commonwealth University's stewardship of many of these buildings has been a mixed blessing. Utilitarian modifications have changed the interiors. In a few instances, bland modern university structures have intruded onto the street. Nevertheless, much of this area of West Franklin retains a coherent streetscape.

Monroe Park is the point from which the radiating streets in this part of Richmond give name to the Fan District. After the Civil War this former drill field and fairground was graded and planted for use as a public park. The establishment of Monroe Park ensured that this area would become the neighborhood to which wealthy Richmonders would flee from the confines of downtown and express their wealth and social status in new homes. Here, wrote a commentator in 1893, "the opulence and taste and artistic ideals of this prosperous and progressive city are externally manifest most."

RI255 Williams House

1890–1891, Marion J. Dimmock. 800 W. Franklin St

This massive Romanesque Revival building with a rock-faced ashlar facade of James River granite provides an appropriate introduction to the neighborhood. As is typical of West Franklin Street patronage, it was designed by one of the premier Richmond architects of the day for a wealthy Richmond tobacco merchant.

RI256 Johnson Hall, Virginia Commonwealth University (Monroe Terrace Apartments)

1912–1915, Alfred C. Bossom. 801 W. Franklin St.

This apartment block is similar to Bossom's nearby Prestwould Apartments (1927; 612 W. Franklin Street). The use of brick and limestone Gothic details in an apartment building is unusual, but they enliven its tall silhouette against the sky. Many of the more delicate elements along the parapet have been lost, as was the interior decoration in the conversion to a university dormitory.

RI256 Johnson Hall, Virginia Commonwealth University (Monroe Terrace Apartments)

RI257 Ritter-Hickock House

RI260 Lewis Ginter House

RI257 Riter-Hickock House

c. 1870, 1903–1910. 821 W. Franklin St.

The earliest surviving building along West Franklin Street, this was built originally as a suburban Italianate villa. The house underwent a thorough Georgian Revival renovation in the early part of the century to make it harmonize with its stylish neighbors. The brick facade has a Federal Revival portico with paired Ionic columns.

RI258 Strause-Blanton House

1892, Charles H. Read, Jr. 826–828 W. Franklin St.

This house, carried out in the Romanesque Revival idiom, exhibits an unusual brownstone belt course contrasting with golden brick and a second-story arcade. The architect was born in Richmond and had good family connections, since his father was the noted minister of the Second Presbyterian Church. Read served in the Confederate army and then worked for the Supervising Architect of the Treasury. His favorite architectural style was Romanesque Revival, and he designed numerous buildings in Richmond up to his death in 1904.

RI259 Founder's Hall, Virginia Commonwealth University (Saunders House)

1883–1885. 827 W. Franklin St.

Nominally Second Empire in style, this house has a complex facade that also incorporates Gothic Revival elements. Note the three dissimilar dormers in the mansard roof and the cast iron porch.

RI260 Lewis Ginter House

1888–1892, Harvey L. Page. 901 W. Franklin St.

Critical to the movement of wealthy patrons to this area of West Franklin Street was the construction of this elaborate house by tobacco magnate Lewis Ginter. Ginter was a northern entrepreneur who came to Richmond after the Civil War and, through real estate development, became one of the wealthiest men in Virginia.

RI262 Frederic W. Scott–Bocock House, Virginia Commomwealth University

The opulent Jefferson Hotel was one of his projects. His investment in this richly appointed home demonstrates both the exclusive character of this neighborhood and Ginter's boundless enthusiasm for his adopted hometown. The house set the standard for the neighborhood, and evidence suggests that it was the most expensive home built in the state until that time. From the rough-finished brownstone base to the Spanish tile roof, Washington architect Harvey L. Page spared no expense in carrying out this important commission, with a result described in 1892 as "free and imposing in its architecture." There are distinctively Richardsonian influences in the dark brownstone and brick used in the construction, as well as in the round arch at the carriage entrance on the east side of the house. A handsomely detailed porch decorates the front of the building between the square and polygonal bays. Remarkably, much of the lavish original decoration of the house still exists, despite its use for university offices for more than sixty years.

RI261 Chesterfield Apartments

1902, Muhlenburg Brothers in collaboration with Noland and Baskervill. 900 W. Franklin St.

Termed the residential equivalent of the deluxe Jefferson Hotel, this apartment block provided an apartment address for Richmonders who wanted to experience the exclusive West Franklin Street ambiance. Stylistically, it utilizes elements of the Chicago School in projecting oriel windows and a cornice that recall

some of Louis Sullivan's work. And yet many of the details, such as the entrance portico, are Colonial Revival. The building is now primarily student housing.

RI262 Frederic W. Scott–Bocock House, Virginia Commonwealth University

1908–1911, Noland and Baskervill. 909 W. Franklin St.

A grand gesture in monumental classicism, this is Richmond's equivalent to Richard Morris Hunt's Marble House in Newport, Rhode Island (1892), which is sometimes cited as a design source. The facade, faced with Indiana limestone and terra-cotta, and the two-story Corinthian portico contrast sharply with the medieval-inspired designs along the street. The building, now owned by Virginia Commonwealth University, houses the architectural history program.

RI263 Allison House

1894–1896, Perry T. Griffin and T. Henry Randall. 910 W. Franklin St.

This red brick house is an early example of the use of the James River Georgian Revival style in a Richmond house. The semicircular portico, however, is Federal Revival. The house is now the offices of the president of Virginia Commonwealth University.

RI264 Stagg House

1891, Albert L. West. 912 W. Franklin St.

RI265 McAdams House

1891, Albert L. West. 914 W. Franklin St.

Albert L. West, one of the most prolific turn-of-the-twentieth-century architects in Richmond, designed these neighboring houses. At 912, a large, gabled bay dominates a rock-faced granite facade. Undercutting the symmetry of the gable are the offset entrance and the curving stair. Next door, at 914, the design is more complex, enlivened with belt courses, granite lintels and parapets, and brick planes set back from the street. Both houses were typical West Franklin Street commissions from newly successful businessmen of the period: Stagg rose from a simple carpenter to become a manufacturer, while McAdams was one of the principals of a premier Richmond clothier.

RI266 Millhiser House

1891–1894, attributed to Benjamin W. Poindexter. 916 W. Franklin St.

The most exotic survivor of the varied streetscape of West Franklin is this Moorish-inspired brick and brownstone house, with its arcaded third-story loggia, curvilinear parapet, and polygonal tower. Standing on a single corner column base, it is a breathtaking example of American eclecticism at its most vibrant. The complex, asymmetrical facade features a delightful array of molded brick, brownstone, and copper details.

RI267 W. J. Anderson House

1899. 1000–1002 W. Franklin St.

RI268 Henrietta Beale House

1899. 1010 W. Franklin St.

These two substantial rock-faced Romanesque Revival houses well illustrate the continuing attraction of the mode in Richmond long after its heyday in the Northeast. The Anderson house has two wide, pulvinated belt courses with allegorical carving of Adam and Eve.

RI269 Congregation Beth Ahabah Synagogue

1903–1904, Noland and Baskervill. 1957–1958, renovation, Edward N. Calish; educational building wing, Merrill C. Lee. 1111 W. Franklin St.

This synagogue on fashionable West Franklin Street indicates the prosperity and importance of Richmond's Jewish community. Built during a period of immigration and assimilation, the temple also affirms, in its use of classical references, the adoption of American ideals and aspirations by this, the oldest Jewish congregation in the city. The giant columnar portico rises above a broad flight of steps to form an impressive visual terminus for Ryland Street, which provides the approach to Beth Ahabah (literally, "house of love") from Broad Street. The dramatic site emphasizes the monumental scale of the temple and its Roman Doric portico and frieze, while the domed design recalls the Pantheon in Rome and the Rotunda at the University of Virginia. Inside the domed sanctuary, a richly painted proscenium arch rises above the bema, or dais. The tall reredos contrasts with the organ pipes above a columnar screen that frames the ark containing the Torah.

RI270 Parking Facility

1996, Marcellus Wright, Cox and Smith. 1100 W. Franklin St.

Built jointly by St. James Episcopal Church and Congregation Beth Ahabah, this parking facility demonstrates that the constant challenge of parking in urban areas can be overcome in a sensitive manner. The basis for the design of the shared parking deck was a conventional early 1900s town house on the corner of Ryland and West Franklin streets, which was gutted, leaving the side and front facades. The cornices, columns, and brickwork of the original building are echoed in the walls that conceal the massive concrete members of the multilevel parking deck while neatly fitting in with the streetscape.

RI271 St. James Episcopal Church

1911–1913, Noland and Baskervill. 1994–1997, restoration, Marcellus Wright, Cox and Smith. 1888, parish house, Marion J. Dimmock. 1205 W. Franklin St.

The congregation moved to this location from an earlier church downtown. The new Episcopal church marked the terminus of the axis of Franklin Street. (The other terminus is the Virginia State Capitol in Capitol Square.) The architects drew upon James Gibbs's St. Martin-in-the-Fields in London as a prototype. The tower recalls the churches of Sir Christopher Wren. The tall spire was struck by lightning July 13, 1994, and sparked a fire that destroyed the roof and heavily damaged the interior. During the restoration of St. James's, original working drawings were used to reproduce the elaborate neoclassical plaster decoration of the sanctuary. Among the furnishings saved through the efforts of Richmond firefighters were a brass pulpit, made in 1895, from the first church building and ten stained glass windows, four of which were made by the studio of Louis Comfort Tiffany. In a remarkable instance of architectural inheritance, three sets of nineteenth-century stained glass windows from Monumental Church were donated when it was decided to return Robert Mills's 1814 structure on Broad Street to its original appearance, which incorporated clear panes. The parish house was designed by Dimmock for Robert U. Powers in 1888.

The Fan District   (RI272–RI313)

The Fan District (bounded by Broad Street to the north, the Boulevard to west, Belvidere Street to the east, and Cary Street to the south) is one of Richmond's most famous neighborhoods. Historian Drew St. J. Carneal points out that the name dates from the mid-twentieth century. Earlier it was known as Sydney or simply the West End. Containing more than 2,500 properties, the Fan is one of the largest urban neighborhoods in Virginia. The area developed along with roads into Richmond in the eighteenth century. The Westham Road, the primary route, traversed what is now the Fan, generally following the route of the present Park Avenue. Over time additional roads were built, including the present Cary Street and the Richmond Turnpike, the present Broad Street. During the late eighteenth and early nineteenth centuries a small number of Richmond-ers built country homes in the area. In 1769 William Byrd III held a lottery for large development lots along the Westham Road, and a small community, known as Scuffletown, developed. Intense land speculation following the War of 1812 produced in 1816 a proposal for a community named Sydney, which encompassed most of the present-day Fan and provided its street pattern. The Sydney plan was presumably laid out by the developers Jacquelin B. Harvie, George Winston, and Benjamin Harris, Jr., who had consolidated property holdings between the Westham Plank Road (present Cary Street) on the south and the Westham Road (present Park Avenue) on the north. These streets diverge from the center of Richmond in a manner analogous to the struts of a fan. The 536 one-acre lots of the Sydney plan were laid out in four-block squares (to use the parlance of the times) that extended several blocks west of the present Boulevard. The squares east of Morris Street are on a due north-south axis. West of Morris Street the east-west streets bend slightly to the northwest. Unfortunately, the speculative bubble burst in 1819, and until the Civil War only a modest number of suburban homes and country villas were constructed.

After the Civil War, the area began to change from a suburban enclave to an urban neighborhood. In 1867 the city annexed the neighborhood west to Lombardy Street, and by 1900 it had annexed most of the remaining area. In 1869 a horse-drawn streetcar line connected the neighborhood to the center of Richmond. Starting in 1888, electric streetcar service extended out Broad and Main streets. This public transit enhanced the development of the neighborhood. By the 1880s large numbers of row houses and town houses had been constructed. Although the panic of 1893 halted development, by the turn of the twentieth century the neighborhood saw the construction of housing at a fever pitch. Churches, apartments, and commericial and institutional buildings followed. By 1920 the neighborhood essentially had been built. The Fan has remained a largely intact and popular neighborhood throughout the twentieth century.

The growth of the Virginia Commonwealth University (VCU) Academic Campus (1950–present; bounded by Grace, Cary, Harrison, and Cherry streets) has resulted in the large-scale clearance of much of the eastern tip of the Fan District for a haphazardly planned group of forgettable buildings. Notable exceptions are the Franklin Street buildings (see the following section, covering West Franklin Street), which predate most of the other structures on campus.

The sheer number of important buildings in the Fan makes it impossible to note every one. Emphasis here is on the contextual variety that makes up the Fan.

Park Avenue and Streets South   (RI272–RI295)

The heart of the Fan is the area south of Monument Avenue between Monroe Park and the Boulevard. The shape of this section—comparatively narrow at the east end and widening toward the west—gave the Fan its name in the 1950s. The streets are lined with long blocks of town houses and row houses constructed in the late nineteenth and early twentieth centuries. The neighborhood is perhaps the largest concentration of these building types in the state of Virginia.

RI272 Howitzer Place

1890. Park Ave. and Grove and Harrison sts.

This is one of three wedge-shaped parks in the Fan along Park Avenue. The shape of these parks is created by the convergence of east-west streets with Park Avenue. The Confederate monument in the center of the park is dedicated to the Richmond Howitzers artillery battery (1892, William Ludwell Sheppard). The monument, which faces east, consists of a Doric base supporting a Confederate artilleryman with his hat removed and a rammer at his feet.

RI273 Virginia Commonwealth University Music Building (Calvary Baptist Church)

1893, Marion J. Dimmock; later renovations. 1010 Grove St.

This is one of the few surviving nineteenth-century church buildings in the Fan, most having been replaced by other structures or simply torn down as the congregations relocated to the suburbs. The brick church was erected with the main body perpendicular to Grove Avenue and a disproportionately large (85-foot) tower at the juncture of the nave and transept. Although the building is nominally Gothic Revival in style, Dimmock, as always, departed from strict imitation by inflating elements and creating odd twists such as the exuberant top of the tower, which recalls H. H. Richardson's far squatter tower for Trinity Church, Boston. Each side of the tower is articulated by a pair of extremely elongated pointed arches. The entrance consists of a large archway ornamented with wrought iron and flanked by Gothic arches.

RI274 Store

1897, Noland and Baskervill. 200 N. Harrison St.

Throughout the Fan are a number of neighborhood stores. The buildings are of three basic types: converted town houses, stores with apartments above, and stores with the proprietor's residence to the side. This former pharmacy and residence is of particular interest as one of the early commissions of Noland and Baskervill, who would become one of Richmond's largest and most important architecture firms. Next to the commercial storefront is a fully developed single-bay row house facade that gave the proprietor access to a residence

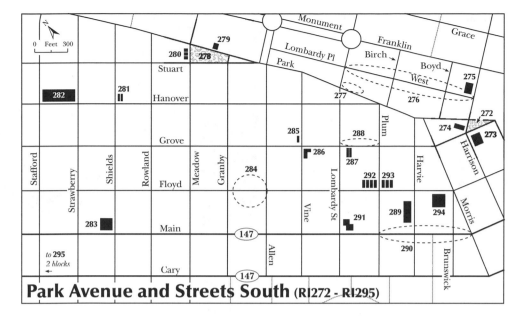

Park Avenue and Streets South (RI272 - RI295)

over the commercial space. The third floor contains a loggia. The tile roof is supported on a cornice of modillions.

RI275 **Apartment Building**

1892, Peter White. 318 N. Harrison St.

Although substantially altered, this relatively small structure was one of the early apartment buildings in the Fan area. Stylistically it might be called Queen Anne.

RI276 **West Avenue**

1900–1920

Although the structures on this short and narrow street were designed by a number of builders and architects, the streetscape is one of the most uniform in the Fan: two- and three-story town houses and row houses built with little or no setback. West Avenue is one of the most prestigious addressees in the Fan and has its own mayor.

RI277 **Houses**

1913–1915, W. Duncan Lee. 1500 block of Park Ave.

A nice group of Arts and Crafts houses can be found in this block. The architect W. Duncan Lee (1913–1915) designed the three houses at

1516, 1530, and 1534. The architecture firm of Asbury and Whitehurst (1914) designed those at 1514 and 1518. The Asbury and Whitehurst buildings are Georgian Revival structures with Arts and Crafts detailing. The Lee buildings are more directly influenced by English Arts and Crafts architecture. The properties are accentuated by staggered facades, created by shallower lots as they progress toward Harrison Street. It is surprising that such a unified group of facades was created by two different firms.

RI278 **Cutshaw Place** (Meadow Street Park)

c. 1900. Park Ave. at Meadow St.

This is the largest of the wedge-shaped parks along Park Avenue. It was renamed in 1909 in honor of city engineer Wilfred Emory Cutshaw, who, among other achievements, developed a tree-planting program for the Fan. At the eastern tip of the park is the 1st Virginia Regiment monument (c. 1920, Ferruccio Legnaioli), a tapered plinth with a solider on top.

RI279 **Sussex Apartments**

1912, W. Duncan Lee. 1816 Park Ave.

This three-story-tall block was an extremely influential apartment design for Richmond architects. Lee appears to have been heavily influenced in his early work by English Arts and

Crafts architects such as C. F. A. Voysey. The employment of steep tile roofs, contrasting brick and stucco, and groupings of windows are reminiscent of Voysey's work. The building dates from the beginning of a major period of apartment construction in the Fan and adjoining neighborhoods. Numerous successors indicate its influence, such as the Gloucester Apartments (1914, Asbury and Whitehurst), immediately to the west of the Sussex.

RI280 Row Houses

1908, Carl Ruehrmund. 400–414 N. Meadow St.

This row is representative of town houses in the Fan. The Georgian Revival facades are distinguished by alternating entrance porches, separated by brick piers, and unified by a strong common cornice line. At the north end of the buildings is a small corner store constructed as part of the development.

RI281 Row Houses

c. 1908, Albert F. Huntt. 2114–2116 Hanover Ave.

Another row of Georgian Revival town houses exhibits a different method of creating individuality. Huntt varied the brickwork, alternating between coursed and rusticated facades. Each of the houses has a strong entablature with brick panels, corner brackets, and modillions. Originally each building on this row had a one-bay entrance porch. Only one porch survives; denuding houses by removing porches was fashionable in the Fan in the 1950s, 1960s, and 1970s.

RI282 William Fox School

1911, c. 1920, east and west additions, Charles M. Robinson. 2300 Hanover Ave.

One of the finer designs by the architect of many of Richmond's schools, the William Fox School benefits from a relatively unconstricted block-long site. The horizontal emphasis created by a modestly pitched roof with wide overhanging eaves and banked windows recalls the midwestern Prairie School. Even the chimneys maintain a strong horizontality. The original structure was a five-part composition with a large central block with two connectors and two wings. This arrangement of projecting and receding planes enhanced the amount of avail-

RI279 Sussex Apartments

able window space. Robinson was greatly concerned with light and ventilation. Local legend has it that he sent his assistant to instruct teachers in the proper use of windows and blinds. The building has additions on the east and west ends that seamlessly follow the detailing of the original sections. The sole nod to Virginia historicism is the octagonal Tuscan cupola over the central section.

RI283 Morien House

1859. 2226 W. Main St.

This is the best preserved of the few antebellum suburban houses remaining in the Fan. The board-and-batten siding, portico, and bracketed cornice are Italianate, and the design probably owes a debt to the various publications of Andrew Jackson Downing or one of his contemporaries.

RI284 Houses

1919, Davis Brothers, architects and contractors. 1800–1814 and 1801–1815 Floyd Ave., 18–24 and 100–106 N. Allen Ave.

A large group of semidetached houses covers half a block on the north and south sides of Floyd Avenue and wraps around the Allen Avenue sides of these blocks. The houses display an interesting collection of Arts and Crafts motifs applied to otherwise identical buildings. Each of the units has stepped parapet end walls and maintains a uniform gabled roofline, though the projecting gables, porches, and wall surfaces vary.

RI285 House

1908, Albert F. Huntt. 1700 Grove Ave.

Huntt, one of the most sophisticated of Richmond's Colonial Revival architects, adopted the pedimented John Marshall House as the model for this house on a narrow Fan corner lot.

RI286 Columns on Grove (Mrs. Plyler's Home; Protestant Episcopal Church Home for Aged Women)

1908, Clinton and Russell. 1997, renovation, Robert P. Winthrop and Associates. 1617–1624 Grove Ave.

Clinton and Russell, architects from New York primarily known for their skyscrapers, created this impressive Beaux-Arts structure. The three-and-one-half-story elephantine Georgian Revival box looms above the two-story Corinthian portico. The structure extends the depth of the lot and has large three-story porches on the side and rear. The building, together with several adjoining town houses, has been adapted as senior housing.

RI287 Town Houses

1908, Carl Ruehrmund. 1525–1527 Grove Ave.

A pair of town houses illuminates another strain of the eclectic historicism of early twentieth-century architecture in the Fan, in this case a revival of the early sixteenth-century English Jacobean style. The houses have stepped gables that contrast with fanlights and Ionic-columned porches drawn from a century and a half later.

RI288 Old Dominion Row

1893, Poindexter and Bryant. 1500–1522 Grove Ave.

This is one of the finest speculative rows ever built in the city. The brick and brownstone buildings are an eclectic fusion of the Second Empire, Queen Anne, and Romanesque Revival styles. The height of the terraced lots on which the row sits makes it one of the most massive and impressive groupings in the Fan.

RI289 The Warsaw (Convent of the Little Sisters of the Poor)

1845. 1877, expanded. 1982, rehabilitation, SWA Architects. Harvie St. between Main St. and Floyd Ave.

This began as an antebellum country house situated on the highest piece of ground in the Fan—indicated today by its high retaining walls. The Catholic Diocese of Richmond acquired the residence after the Civil War and enlarged it, creating the Convent of the Little Sisters of the Poor. The main building of this complex is a massive Second Empire structure composed of three blocks and two connectors that face Harvie Street. After the church closed the convent, the structure was renovated as a condominium complex. The condominium successfully preserves one of the most important Victorian institutional buildings in Richmond and its setting.

RI290 Mid Town

c. 1900–c. 1920, c. 1980–c. 1990. 1300 and 1400 W. Main St.

The commercial area along West Main Street, known as Mid Town, is one of the more interesting commercial revitalization projects in Richmond. The area has been renovated with the application of Colonial Revival details and an eye-popping color scheme. One of the principal creators of the district was area businessman Edward Eck. Richmond wags have dubbed the project "Eck-a-tecture."

RI291 Stonewall Jackson School (West End School)

1886, Wilfred Emory Cutshaw, city engineer. 1980–1991, renovation. W. Main St. at Lombardy St.

The best-preserved and most spectacular of a series of schools by Cutshaw, this building has a lavish Italianate facade that displays a combination of cast iron, granite, and brick. The L-shaped plan of the building allowed for the maximum amount of light and air. A devastating fire destroyed much of the building in 1989. The reconstruction incorporates a restaurant in the raised basement level and offices above.

RI292 Town Houses

1889, John and Daniel Mahoney, developers; George Ryan, builder. 1500–1588 Floyd Ave.

This row of semidetached town houses on Floyd Avenue displays one of the largest groupings of cast iron porches in Richmond. The porches date from the pinnacle of the popularity of cast iron in the closing decades of the nineteenth century. Italianate row houses such as these were common throughout Richmond in the 1870s and 1880s. These are of interest because of the alternating receding and projecting facades.

RI293 Row Houses

1889, John and Daniel Mahoney, developers; George Ryan, builder. 1424–1432 Floyd Ave.

The Mahoneys were among Richmond's most prominent developers in the late nineteenth century, and Ryan ran one of the largest construction companies. This unusual grouping is unified by a continuous porch structure across the length of the row. The end buildings have false pedimented gables and the center units are articulated as one-and-one-half-story structures with a mansard roof.

RI294 Virginia Commonwealth University Dance Center (Sacred Heart School)

1917, Carneal and Johnston. c. 1970, renovation. Southwest corner of Floyd Ave. and Morris St.

The former Sacred Heart School resembles several other school buildings designed by Carneal and Johnston for the Catholic church

RI291 Stonewall Jackson School (West End School)

in Richmond. Large windows allow plenty of light and ventilation in this large, rectangular red brick box. Stylistically it is restrained Georgian Revival, the primary ornamentation being the Doric portico. The building is magnificently sited at a prominent bend in Floyd Avenue created by the original Sydney plan for the Fan.

RI295 Greater Richmond Transit Company Bus Depot (Virginia Railroad and Power Company Buildings)

c. 1900–c. 1930. Robinson and Cary sts.

This group of buildings represents one of Richmond's major claims to fame: the first successful electric streetcar system in the world. The system began as a series of competing companies that sprang up within a few years around 1890. Over time the Virginia Railway and Power Company acquired the separate lines and consolidated the system. The oldest building of the complex is Car Barn No. 1 (c. 1900), which has a large, gabled steel-truss roof. Car Barns No. 2 and No. 3 (c. 1920) are reinforced concrete fireproof structures divided into two separate bays. The rest of the complex consists of miscellaneous shops and an office building (1930) at Grayland and Davis avenues.

Monument Avenue   (RI296–RI304)

Monument Avenue extends the rich architectural heritage of Franklin Street into the twentieth century. A grand avenue in the tradition of earlier boulevards in Europe and America, the historic section of Monument Avenue stretches out from the old city limits for one and one-half miles. It was planned with a dual purpose. Proposed in 1887 to provide an appropriate setting for a major memorial to General Robert E. Lee, the avenue was also intended to encourage residential development west of the city. Ironically, Richmonders saw the combination of a memo-rial to the tragedy of the Lost Cause and a beautiful new boulevard as a means to establish themselves as leaders of the New South. In one grand gesture, they would leave behind the city's role as the capital of the Confederacy and develop a progressive civic space. The plan was laid out by a Richmond engineer, C. P. E. Burgwyn, who had studied at Harvard and was surely familiar with Boston's earlier grand boulevard, Commonwealth Avenue. The broad, tree-lined avenue inspired prominent citizens to erect a remarkably coherent collection of large town houses and apartment buildings, which are a catalog of early twentieth-century architectural styles. Although the avenue developed slowly and without consistent design covenants, a general compatibility in materials, cornices, rooflines, orientation, and setback helped link the blocks together. The western march of residential development was matched by a series of commemorative sculptures which, until 1996, all related to the Confederacy. It is this theme, creating a shrine to the Confederacy, that has bestowed fame on Monument Avenue and serves to remind visitors of Richmond's leading role in the Civil War.

The historic district reaches from St. James's Episcopal Church, one block from the end of Franklin Street, to the intersection of Roseneath Road, site of the most recent addition to the street's sculpture, the Arthur Ashe Monument. Moving westward from Stuart Circle, location of the easternmost statue, to Roseneath Road gives a sense of the chronological development of the street. Franklin Street traffic originally ran both ways, and the passage from the narrow, tree-darkened older street into the new, bright avenue must have been startling. Beginning at its eastern end, Monument Avenue was built up sporadically, but always reaching farther west. Residences in the first two blocks, which date from c. 1900, include some examples of the Queen Anne and Richardsonian Romanesque styles, but from the Lee Monument onward, the Colonial Revival style dominates the streetscape. Likewise, the street, which begins with a dense, vertical display of town houses, gradually includes mansions and then apartment buildings, and finally becomes more suburban in feeling, with more modest, horizontal houses set back farther from the street and from each other than the earlier buildings.

Note: There are no blocks numbered 1700, 1900, 2100, or 2400.

RI296 Stuart Circle

Intersection of Monument Ave. and Lombardy St.

Stuart Circle is named for the General J. E. B. Stuart Monument (RI296.1) (1907, Frederick Moynihan, sculptor), which shows the dashing cavalryman. It was unveiled at the largest Con-

RI296 Stuart Circle, J. E. B. Stuart Monument and Stuart Court Apartments

federate reunion ever held, seventeen years after the dedication of the Lee Monument. Frederick Moynihan, a New York sculptor who had worked locally as a studio assistant to Richmonder Edward Virginius Valentine, had won the commission. The sculpture's resemblance to an English monument in Calcutta and the awkward stance of the prancing horse created quite a stir at the time, but the main problem with the sculpture now is that it faces downtown, with its back to the flow of traffic.

Around Stuart Circle are the Stuart Circle Hospital (RI296.2) (1913–1914, Charles M. Robinson; later additions; 413 North Lombardy Street) and two towered Gothic Revival churches, St. John's United Church of Christ (RI296.3) (1921–1928, Carl Lindner; 503 North Lombardy Street) and First English Evangelical Lutheran Church (RI296.4) (1911, Charles M. Robinson; 1603 Monument Avenue), which balance each other across the circle. A third church, Grace Covenant Presbyterian Church (RI296.5) (1922, John Kevan Peebles; 1627 Monument Avenue) is on the south side of the first block of Monument Av-

RI297.1 R. E. Lee Monument

RI297.2 Jeffress House

enue. Last but not least is the massive Stuart Court Apartments (RI296.6) (1924, William Lawrence Bottomley; 1600 Monument Avenue), on the northwest corner of Lombardy Street, by a New York architect who became one of the most popular among wealthy Richmond patrons in the period 1918–1940. Although better known for his Colonial Revival and Georgian Revival designs, Bottomley had a facility with other styles, as demonstrated by Stuart Court, which is Mediterranean Revival. The roofline is ornamented by urns and fanciful structures, though the original cornice deteriorated and had to be removed.

RI297 Lee Monument Circle

Intersection of Monument and Allen aves.

The R. E. Lee Monument (RI297.1) (1886–1890, Jean Antonin Mercie, sculptor; Paul Pujot, designer of the base) was unveiled in 1890 at a Confederate reunion, eleven years before any buildings had been erected on Monument Avenue. First discussed days after Lee's death in 1870, the sculpture was not commissioned until 1887, because of years of infighting among competing committees. The sculpture was cast in France after a design by Mercie, one of the late nineteenth century's most famous sculptors. Shipped in pieces, the statue was pulled to the site by enthusiastic Richmonders. The financial panic of 1893 hit while the street was being graded, and the consequent

business downturn delayed residential construction almost a decade. The Lee Monument and Monument Avenue's intersection with Allen Avenue were the centerpieces of the original plan, which extended only two more blocks westward.

One of Bottomley's most celebrated Monument Avenue house designs, the Colonial Revival Jeffress House (RI297.2) (1929–1930; 1800 Monument Avenue), faces the Lee Monument from a northwest quadrant lot. The classical ornament, luxurious detail, and graceful handling of a potentially awkward lot all explain Bottomley's local popularity. He was also known for refined floor plans that allowed modern living and entertaining behind strict, symmetrical facades.

Adjacent to the Lee Monument are the Shenandoah Apartments (RI297.3) (1906, Carl Ruehrmund; 501 North Allen Avenue), built to provide luxury housing in the neighborhood. At the northwest intersection of West Grace Street and Allen Avenue stands the former home of the Jefferson Club (RI297.4) (1909, Marion J. Dimmock. 1800 West Grace Street), a prestigious men's club.

RI298 Monument Avenue: 2000, 2200, and 2300 Blocks

To many people these blocks represent the heart of Monument Avenue, for along this segment are some of the street's quintessential

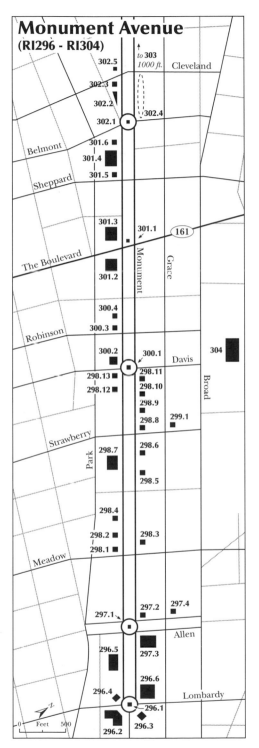

Monument Avenue
(RI296 - RI304)

to 303
1000 ft.

302.5

302.3

302.2

302.1 302.4

Cleveland

Belmont

301.6
301.4
301.5

Sheppard

301.3
301.1 161

The Boulevard

301.2

Monument

Grace

300.4
300.3

Robinson

300.2 300.1
Davis 304

290.13 298.11
298.12 298.10

298.9

298.8 299.1

Strawberry

Park

298.7 298.6

Broad

298.5

298.4

298.2 298.3
298.1

Meadow

297.2 297.4
297.1

Allen

296.5 297.3

296.6

296.4
Lombardy

296.1

296.2 296.3

0 Feet 500

Colonial Revival and Georgian Revival houses. The Bullock House (RI298.1) (1927, W. Duncan Lee; 2017–2019 Monument Avenue) was designed for use as a doctor's office and residence. The doctor's residential quarters above are elegantly indicated by a central Palladian window. Next door is the Johnson House (RI298.2) (1908, Claude K. Howell; 2023 Monument Avenue), a large house with unusual detailing, in the Tudor Revival mode though carried out in an American Stick Style aesthetic. The Chesterman House (RI298.3) (1905–1906, Noland and Baskervill; 2020 Monument Avenue) was the first three-story house on Monument, and is one of only a few with a limestone facade. A contractor named John Wilson built for himself a huge single-family dwelling, now known as the Wilson House (RI298.4) (1911; 2037 Monument Avenue), whose broad, Beaux-Arts facade looks institutional. Many realtors and leaders in building trades saw residences on Monument Avenue as a good advertisement for their firms and their own success and competed in building their own houses. A good example of this practice appears in the next block at the Harry S. Binswanger House (RI298.5) (1909, Claude K. Howell; 2220 Monument Avenue), designed for a local window manufacturer. The elaborate facade boasts different window types on each level. A few years later, the vice president of the same window company commissioned the Moses Bins-wanger House (RI298.6) (1913, D. Wiley Anderson; 2230 Monument Avenue).

Across the street, the Rixey Court Apartments (RI298.7) (1926, Bascom J. Rowlett; 2235 Monument Avenue) is one of the most glamorous apartment buildings on the street, obviously intended for an elegant clientele. Its lively facade includes Mediterranean Revival and Beaux-Arts classical elements.

The lots in the 2300 block are wider than those in the previous blocks, providing a spatial amplitude that complements the distinctive freestanding houses and mansions. And yet this block escapes the suburban feeling of some of the blocks farther west.

The Stuart McGuire House (RI298.8) (1924, Baskervill and Lambert; 2304 Monument Avenue) is based on Mompesson House in Salisbury, England. A later resident of the house recalled that when the architect asked Dr. Stuart McGuire, who had commissioned it, what type of house he would like, the doctor answered, "I never considered what kind of operation my patients would like; build me a house." The

RI300 Jefferson Davis Monument and John Kerr Branch House

huge Tudor Revival mansion, the Wallerstein House (RI298.9) (1915, Carneal and Johnston; 2312 Monument Avenue), was designed by a firm known for many Collegiate Gothic school and university buildings. Two houses with similar compositions but very different details sit next to each other: the Pollard House (RI298.10) (1915, W. Duncan Lee; 2314 Monument Avenue) and the Cary House (RI298.11) (1927, William Lawrence Bottomley; 2320 Monument Avenue). The later house is a Colonial Revival version of the Arts and Crafts house next door. A young family owned the earlier house, and the wife's mother admired the floor plan so much that she commissioned Bottomley to design a similar, though smaller, house on the adjacent lot. The red brick and slate give the facade of 2320 a more formal appearance.

An enormous Mediterranean villa on the south side of the street, the Jacquelin Taylor House (RI299.12) (1914, W. Duncan Lee; 2325 Monument Avenue) is still owned by the family that built it. At the corner in front of the Davis Monument is the Lewis H. Blair House (RI299.13) (1913, Walter D. Blair; 2327 Monument Avenue). It is the only Colonial Revival house on Monument with a freestanding monumental portico, the stereotypical southern architectural element probably most envisioned by visitors expecting hoop skirts and mint juleps.

RI299 Grace Street

Grace Street, the east-west street that separates Monument Avenue from Broad Street, was de-veloped slightly before Monument Avenue. A drive down Grace Street offers a glimpse of a street similar to Monument but without the median and the monuments. Some very large houses were built here, though fewer styles were explored. In the early nineteenth century, a few wealthy Richmonders suburban estates in the present-day Monument Avenue and Grace Street area, and several farmhouses were built as well. One of the latter, Talavera, survives (RI299.1 (1838; 2315 West Grace Street). It is known for Edgar Allan Poe's visits there to a young admirer, Susan Talley. Grace Street is experiencing a later, but just as welcome, rebirth due to the efforts of some determined homeowners.

RI300 Monument Avenue: Davis Monument and 2500–2600 Blocks

The Jefferson Davis Monument (RI300.1) (1904–1907, Edward V. Valentine, sculptor; William C. Noland, base and exedra; intersection of Davis and Monument avenues) dominates the next section of Monument Avenue. Unveiled five days after the Stuart Monument, it caused perhaps the most outrage among northerners, for it commemorated pure politics, not military exploits. The most elaborate composition on Monument Avenue, the Davis Monument is encircled by an exedra of thirteen Doric columns. Davis, the president of the Confederate States, is depicted as an orator standing on a pedestal at the base of a gargantuan Doric column sixty-five feet tall, topped by *Vindicatrix*, an allegorical figure representing the spirit of the South. Davis's words on leaving the United States Senate to serve the Confederacy ring the frieze around the exedra. Earlier plans included a domed temple and a triumphal arch, which were scrapped because of excessive costs.

Facing the Davis Monument on the south side of Monument Avenue is the John Kerr Branch House (RI300.2) (1913–1919, John Russell Pope; 2501 Monument Avenue; open on request), one of the largest single-family dwellings ever built in the city of Richmond. John Kerr Branch, a powerful local banker, bought the land from his father, one of the major landholders during the development of Monument Avenue. Branch was involved in the development of Union Station, two blocks to the north, and asked Pope to design a house for him. By this time Pope was an expert in designing Neo-Tudor houses, and legend has it that Otto Eggers, Pope's chief designer and later a partner in the successor firm of Eggers and Higgins, did the design. Branch family lore includes the story that Branch was always angry that Pope never came to Richmond to see the completed house. Much of the interior detailing was left to an Englishman named Spencer Guidael. As a prototype for the design, the Pope office turned to a well-known English country house of the Tudor period, Compton Wynyates. Compton's south elevation was adopted for the north facade of the Branch House. The large bay window on the south elevation of the Branch House came from the inner court at Compton Wynyates. A texture of age was imparted to the building through weathered exterior materials. Flemish bond brickwork, limestone window and door surrounds, and the clustered chimneys look many centuries old. Several inscriptions on the exterior related to the Branch family's arrival in Virginia in the seventeenth century. Stephen Bedford, who has written extensively on Pope, notes that the floor plan is H-shaped and conforms to Tudor plans with rooms opening onto each other. The floor levels were varied to indicate age. The interior decoration, which has mostly disappeared, included medieval, Georgian, and Adam Style rooms, again to give the impression that the house had grown over time. The 28,000-square-foot house sits on a landscaped lot. Branch evidently assumed that his sister would build a house on the other half of the block, but she never did.

Elsewhere in the 2500 and 2600 blocks a gradual encroachment of larger apartment buildings begins. The houses, which still dominate the streetscape, continue a pattern of mainly Colonial Revival styles with prominent cornices and one-story porches. The Jonathan Bryan House (RI300.3) (1923, W. Duncan Lee; 2605 Monument Avenue) illustrates the idiosyncratic character of the development in these blocks with a brick wall that blocks the view. The Cabell House (RI300.4) (1922–1924, William Lawrence Bottomley; 2601 Monument Avenue), at the corner of Robinson and Monument, is the second house based on Mompesson House. The thistle keystones denote the Scottish heritage of the original owners.

RI301 Monument Avenue: Jackson Monument and 2800–3000 Blocks

The Stonewall Jackson Monument (RI301.1) (1917–1919, F. William Sievers, sculptor) is jammed into the intersection of the Boulevard and Monument Avenue. A brilliant tactician and a deeply religious man, Jackson is portrayed sitting tranquilly on his mount, rising above the busy modern scene below. Squeezed by traffic on east and west, the sculpture faces north, reputedly because the old soldiers at the nearby home for Confederate veterans argued with the sculptor that Stonewall would never turn his back on a Yankee. Sievers, the sculptor, always regretted the orientation of the horse, which greets much of the automobile traffic with its rump.

RI301.1 Stonewall Jackson Monument

The southeast corner of Monument Avenue and the Boulevard is dominated by the First Baptist Church (RI301.2) (1927–1928, sanctuary, Herbert L. Cain with Joseph Hudnut, consulting architect; 1940–1941, sanctuary enlargement, W. Irving Dixon and Leonard Moore; 1948, east wing addition; 1996, infill) with its Doric distyle in antis portico. The existing complex was built piecemeal beginning in 1927, with care to break up the mass and to continue the architectural quality of the streetscape.

West of the Boulevard, the character of Monument Avenue changes dramatically. The first two blocks are dominated by apartment buildings much larger than those to the east. However, the landscaped median provides continuity, and mature trees help mask the scale of the buildings. The repetitive porches of the large apartment buildings contribute to the feeling of uniformity. Monument Avenue's apartment buildings were considered acceptable stylish alternatives for professionals who chose not to own houses. Colonial Revival, Craftsman, Classical Revival, and Mediterranean Revival styles are all represented. Notable buildings include the Anne-Frances Apartments (RI301.3) (1919–1920, Max Ruehrmund; 2805 Monument Avenue), the central porches of which form an elliptical bay over a rusticated arcade.

The south side of the 3000 block owes much of its interest to Max Ruehrmund. The Richmond architect and builder designed the Halifax Apartments (RI301.4) (1921, 3009 Monument Avenue), his own house, the Ruehrmund House (RI301.5) (1920, 3007 Monument Avenue), and the Kass House (RI301.6) (1921, 3015 Monument Avenue). The varied styles popular in Richmond during the 1920s are apparent in Ruehrmund's eclectic designs.

RI302 Monument Avenue: Maury Monument and 3100–3300 Blocks

The Matthew Fontaine Maury Monument (RI302.1) (1922–1929, F. William Sievers, sculptor; intersection of Belmont and Monument avenues) is the work of the Richmond-based sculptor who had completed the Jackson Monument a decade earlier. Maury represented the Confederate States diplomatically abroad and performed experiments on torpedoes for the Confederacy. However, the inspiration to include him on Monument Avenue also rose from Maury's international fame as an oceanographer and meteorologist. He is depicted as a man of ideas, seated beneath a globe, dramatically framed by two scenes, one of a shipwreck and the other of a storm on a farm. These illustrate Maury's concern for the impact that weather and the oceans can have on the peoples of the world. Details include salt- and freshwater creatures along the base and diagrams of the wind currents mapped by Maury.

A Beaux-Arts classical apartment building dominates the corner behind the Maury Monument, the Lord Fairfax (RI302.2) (1923, Lindner and Phillips; 3101–3115 Monument Avenue). Designed to fill a triangular lot, it contrasts in its understated detail with the row of urban cottages that completes the block, the Mayo Cottages (RI302.3) (1926, Carl M. Lindner; 3117–3133 Monument Avenue). Jeanette A. Mayo commissioned the entire row. Across the street is another block dominated by the designs of one architect, W. Duncan Lee (RI302.4). He designed four of the six houses—all of them Colonial Revival: the Raab House (1924, 3100 Monument Avenue), the Schwarzschild House (1927, 3114 Monument Avenue), the Lewis House (1923, 3142 Monument Avenue), and the Anderson House (1922, 3170 Monument Avenue). The north and south sides of the 3100 block combine all the elements that transform the rhythm of Monument after it crosses the Boulevard: a large apartment building, a row of cottages, and a block faced with luxurious houses of horizontal proportions on wide, irregular lots.

The north side of the street for the next two blocks is dominated by large houses, built in the 1920s and 1930s, on wider lots. The south side of the 3200 block begins with an oddly shaped house (RI302.5) (1910–1911, Carneal and Johnston; 3201 Monument Avenue), once the home of James Branch Cabell, a controversial early twentieth-century author. In 1910–1911 Carneal and Johnston designed the eclectic, eccentric house, which at the corner is only about 8 feet deep. That block is completed by another row of cottages in the form of a double house and three pairs of single-family houses constructed by Davis Brothers, all built between 1919 and 1923.

RI303 Ashe Monument

1993–1996, Paul DiPasquale, sculptor; Barry Starke, base. Intersection of Roseneath Rd. and Monument Ave.

RI304 Science Museum of Virginia (Broad Street Station)

The westernmost monument on the avenue faces west from the intersection at Roseneath Road. Paul DiPasquale, a Richmond sculptor, designed the statue, though the tennis player himself suggested the composition. The debate over the location, the artist, and the quality of the design rivaled the controversy over the Lee and Stuart monuments. The City Council gave final approval, indicating that many citizens believed that it was time to honor Ashe and that the appropriate spot was where Richmonders have honored so many of their heroes. The addition of the Ashe Monument has significantly altered the perception of Monument Avenue.

RI304 **Science Museum of Virginia** (Broad Street Station)

1913–1919, John Russell Pope; Warren Manning, landscape architect; U. Ricci, sculptor. 1954, dome renovation, Carneal and Johnston. 1976, Science Museum adaptation, Perry Dean Rogers; landscaping, James DiPasquale, Barry Starke. 1997–present, renovation, W. Kent Cooper. Broad St. at Robins St.

John Russell Pope's only railroad station has been a major landmark on West Broad Street since its construction. The structure was built on what was the western edge of the city to replace the outmoded facilities of the Richmond, Fredericksburg and Potomac and Atlantic Coastline railroads. Conspicuously absent from Pope's competition-winning 1913 design is the dome on the completed building. Construction on the project was delayed until 1917 because of opposition from downtown interests. When the project went ahead, the railroads requested a dome to distinguish the structure from recently completed facilities in other cities. Sited on a large artificial mound that screens the tracks, the station provides a grand processional approach from Broad Street. On the front, which is clad in Indiana limestone, is a portico modeled on the Doric order of St. Peter's Square in Rome. In the attic story is a large clock, flanked by the sculptural figures *Progress* and *Industry*. The dome rises on a polygonal drum pierced by lunettes modeled on those of the rotunda of Low Memorial Library at Columbia University. Originally covered with terra-cotta tiles, the present copper dome was completed in 1955. Flanking the central section behind simple piers were spaces for a variety of secondary functions, including the former "Negro Waiting Room" in the east wing. A loop of tracks brought all of the trains into the station from the same direction. Arriving passengers came up stairways on the west side of the building; departing passengers went down stairways on the east side. The cast iron train sheds can be seen on the exterior of the building.

The station closed in 1969, and the building was adapted for use by the Science Museum of Virginia in a sympathetic renovation that preserves its character. The domed portion of the building, which originally contained the ticket counters and main waiting room, now serves as the reception space of the museum. Beyond is the concourse, now the main exhibit area.

The Boulevard (RI305–RI313)

The cultural acropolis of Richmond, the Boulevard had its origins in the plan of the Fan district. In the 1880s the Commonwealth of Virginia acquired a tract of land for a Confederate veterans' home, to be known as the R. E. Lee Camp. In 1891 city engineer Wilfred Emory Cutshaw laid out a grand, 100-foot-wide boulevard that extended from West Broad Street on the north to the center of New Reservoir (now Byrd) Park on the south. Not until after 1910 did any appreciable building get underway. When it did begin, it took the form of speculative town houses, luxury apartment buildings, and cultural institutions. These structures went up a block at a time, and by 1930 the development was largely complete. The cottages of the veterans' home eventually gave way to institutions, including the Confederate Memorial Institute (now the Virginia Historical Society), the Virginia Museum of Fine Arts, and United Daughters of the Confederacy.

RI305 Sigma Phi Epsilon Fraternity (Henry Baskervill House)

1912, Noland and Baskervill. 310 S. Boulevard (at Idlewood Ave.)

Baskervill, presumably with his partner William Noland, who did most of the firm's design work, created this handsome, expansive Mediterranean Revival house before speculative town houses and apartment buildings came to dominate the streetscape of the Boulevard. Constructed of brick with a stucco exterior, the house has a recessed five-bay loggia, an element that later provided a motif for the firm's public buildings.

RI306 North Boulevard: 100 Block

1916, Davis Brothers

To a large extent Davis Brothers, architects and contractors, built the Boulevard, both houses and apartment buildings. Perhaps influenced by the nearly contemporaneous Panama Pacific Exhibition of 1915 in San Diego, Davis Brothers employed elements of the Mission Revival style, including porches, overhanging eaves, and tile roofs. As in this location, the firm generally built rows that followed a particular architectural theme or combination of themes, such as English Arts and Crafts or Georgian Revival.

RI305 Sigma Phi Epsilon Fraternity (Henry Baskervill House)

RI307 Virginia Museum of Fine Arts, original building, 1932–1936

RI307 Virginia Museum of Fine Arts

1932–1936, Peebles and Ferguson. 1954, 1970, additions. 1976, north wing, David Warren Harwicke Associates. 1982–1984, west wing, Hardy Holzman Pfeiffer Associates. 1976, sculpture court landscape design, Lawrence Halprin Associates. 2800 Grove Ave.

The Virginia Museum of Fine Arts, the nation's first state-supported art museum, opened in 1936. The building was funded in part as a Public Works Administration project. Although the original limestone-and-brick-faced Georgian Revival building faces the Boulevard, subsequent expansions and parking considerations have swung the building's orientation toward the inside of the block. The three-part core was

expanded to a five-part structure following Peebles and Ferguson's original design in 1954 and 1970. The expansion continued the tailored Flemish bond brickwork. The architects spelled out their original intention in a memorandum: "the design of the structure is that of the English Renaissance of the Wren period. . . . It is believed that this style is appropriate, that it is free from the coldness and the reserve of the severely Classic and the somewhat startling character of the so-called Modern." In 1976, however, the addition of a north wing marked a major departure stylistically. A new main entrance, auditorium, and additional galleries were contained in a Frank Lloyd Wright–influenced kidney-shaped addition that curators

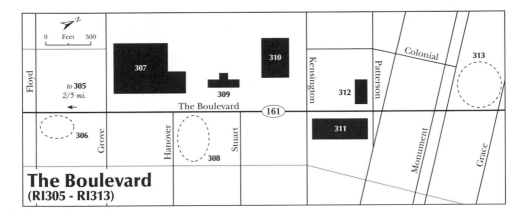

The Boulevard
(RI305 - RI313)

find a difficult space in which to display art. The sculpture court, built at the same time by Lawrence Halprin Associates, with its hard-edged, cubist foundation, has proven a more adaptable space for museum functions and concerts.

In 1984 the west wing was added, a gift of Mr. and Mrs. Paul Mellon and Sydney and Frances Lewis. While citing no specific sources, architect Malcolm Holzman suggested that H. H. Richardson's Allegheny County Courthouse in Pittsburgh may have inspired the use of the oversized granite blocks that create the rusticated base. Avowedly postmodernist in the contrast between the classical details employed on the stone podium and cornice and the glass-enclosed stairwells that abruptly emerge from the limestone-sheathed walls, the addition creates a dialogue with the original building. On the interior, two very separate galleries, one for small-

scale works donated by the Mellons, the other for large modern works donated by the Lewises, are tied together by a vast, corporate type of lobby. Upstairs in the Lewis side is an impressive collection of Art Nouveau, Arts and Crafts, and early modern furniture and decorative arts.

RI308 Apartment Buildings

1915–1920, Davis Brothers. 2706 Stuart Ave. (The Dorchester Apartments), 2716 Stuart Ave. (Wilmartin Apartments), 301 N. Boulevard (Wilson Apartments), 307 N. Boulevard (Sheppard Court Apartments), 313 N. Boulevard (Darlington Apartments), 319 N. Boulevard (Rosaleigh Apartments)

The Davis Brothers were just as prolific and innovative as architects and developers of apartment buildings as they were with town houses. The firm built a number of these buildings on the Boulevard and Monument Avenue and in neighborhoods west of the Boulevard. These blocks of Stuart Avenue and the Boulevard have one of the largest and most impressive groupings. The buildings are all basically the same structure, with variation in ornamentation expressed primarily through roofs and porches. Each of the buildings has two- or three-story porches, with either one porch extending the width of the building or two porches per building. The Dorchester is specifically neoclassical, while the Darlington is an elephantine Georgian Revival structure. The other buildings display an eclectic mix of classical and Arts and Crafts details.

RI308 Darlington Apartments

RI309 United Daughters of the Confederacy National Headquarters

1952, Ballou and Justice. 1996, renovation, Cox and Associates. 328 N. Boulevard

While decidedly modernist, this building uses a classical composition, a center block with lower flanking wings and a pyramidal roof. The large bronze doors and severe marble exterior give the effect of a mausoleum with a generally forbidding aspect.

RI310 Virginia Historical Society and Center for Virginia History (Battle Abbey–Confederate Memorial Institute)

1911–1921, Bissell and Sinkler; Warren A. Manning, landscape architect. 1960, building expansion, Carneal and Johnston. 1991, reading room auditorium, Glave, Newman, Anderson. 1997–1998, Center for Virginia History, James Glave and Associates. 428 N. Boulevard

The Confederate Memorial Institute held a national competition to create an archive for records associated with the Lost Cause and a structure to memorialize southern valor. Ironically, a northern firm won the competition. The building (subsequently named Battle Abbey) consisted of a classical temple set amid large formal gardens that extended from the Boulevard to Sheppard Street. Subsequent additions have all but obliterated the original landscaping. In the west wing of the building is a series of murals titled *The Four Seasons of the Confederacy*, one of the most important public art projects in the history of Richmond, executed by Charles Hoffbauer as a part of the original building design. In 1958 the merger of the Confederate Memorial Institute and the Virginia Historical Society resulted in three major expansions of the building. The most important of the society's expansions is the Center for Virginia History addition, which has nearly doubled the size of the building. The Boulevard facade of the addition partially extends the classical detailing of the Bissell and Sinkler facade. The Kensington Avenue face of the addition is a strong design presence.

RI311 Tuscan Villas

c. 1928. 500–513 N. Boulevard

The villas are one of the first and finest garden apartment enclaves in Richmond. Constructed of brick with stucco covering, they are crisply detailed in a Mediterranean Revival idiom, adorned with bas-relief panels, copper, iron balconies and grilles, and covered with tile roofs. The buildings lately have been converted to condominiums, and the condominium associations restored the original color scheme. The complex consists of five buildings. On the north and south ends, respectively, are the Pisa and the Lucca, and in the center, from north to south, three U-shaped courtyard buildings: the Florence, the Leghorn, and the Sienna. Two-story arcaded porches topped by towers provide an important visual terminus to each courtyard. The service entrances to the apartments are in the narrow passages between the buildings, screened by connecting walls.

RI312 St. Mark's Episcopal Church

1922–1926, Baskervill and Lambert. 1952, 1960, additions. 520 N. Boulevard

This brick building is the most sophisticated of three church buildings on the Boulevard. The steeple and portico of the Federal Revival structure were influenced by the work of James Gibbs and Charles Bulfinch and would not look out of place in New England. The pedimented Ionic-columned portico has a modillioned cornice. The tower rises in three stages with an octagonal cupola on top. The interior, with barrel-vaulted nave, recalls Peter Harrison's King's Chapel, Boston.

RI313 Row Houses

1921, attributed to W. Duncan Lee. 710–716 N. Boulevard and 2801 W. Grace St.

This ensemble, although nominally in what might be called a Colonial Revival idiom, is really more a sophisticated example of the Arts and Crafts movement. The attribution to Lee is based on his design of similar houses around Richmond. The building is red brick with half timbering. The massing of differently shaped facades and roofs—hipped, gable, jerkinhead—and the dormers create a lively and picturesque grouping.

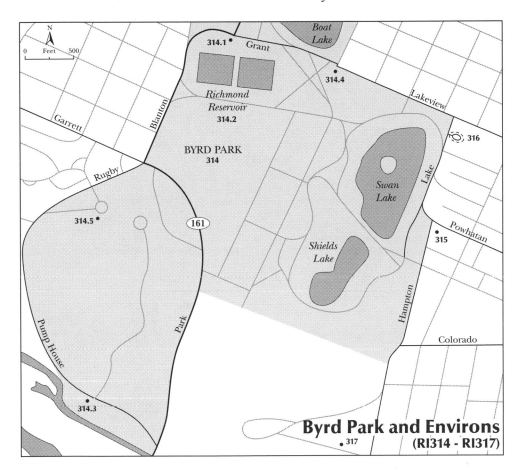

Byrd Park and Environs   (RI314–RI317)

Originally known as New Reservoir Park, this area developed as a complement and adjunct to the grand concourse of Monument Avenue and the Boulevard.

RI314 Byrd Park (New Reservoir Park)

1874–1906, Wilfred E. Cutshaw, city engineer. Boulevard at Grant St.

In 1873, city engineer Wilfred Cutshaw urged the city council to approve development of the site and "take such steps toward works of art, as we have means to devote to them." During his long tenure in his position (1873–1907) Cutshaw acquired eighteen parcels to form the present park. It embodies his talents, combining his technical abilities as an engineer with his aesthetic sensitivity as an architect and landscape designer. The popularity of the park, re-

named for the founder of Richmond, William Byrd, attracted builders and developers who constructed fashionable apartment buildings and homes on the perimeter of Cutshaw's "pleasure grounds."

In 1904, Cutshaw wrote: "Few persons are aware of the importance and purposes of the tree nurseries established . . . at New Reservoir Park." From this tree farm, thousands of saplings were transplanted to the streets and parks of Richmond, setting the precedent for the tree-shaded environment that Richmonders enjoy today. The oldest of the trees in the area south of the reservoir are said to be specimens from Cutshaw's nursery that grew too large to transplant. In addition to the nursery, the municipal stone quarry that became Shields Lake provided many of the curbstones that still border many city streets. Cutshaw employed the very fabric of the Byrd Park area to transform the cityscape at the turn of the century.

Cutshaw intended the Boulevard to be the principal approach to the park, in a sequence similar to the linked parks and avenues designed by Frederick Law Olmsted. The effect of a grand entrance to the precincts of Byrd Park was somewhat blurred by the intrusion in the 1970s of the Downtown Expressway, but once past the expressway overpass, the Columbus Memorial and city reservoir form the visual terminus that announces Byrd Park.

RI314.1 Columbus Memorial

1922, Ferruccio Legnaioli. Boulevard at Grant St.

The Richmond Italian community commissioned the memorial and its cascade backdrop from Florentine-born sculptor Legnaioli. Anti-Catholic and anti-immigrant Ku Klux Klan activity in Virginia was then at its height, and the prominent position of the statuary group is a powerful signal of the pride and determination of Richmond's Italians.

RI314.2 Richmond Reservoir

1874–1875, Wilfred E. Cutshaw. Boulevard at Grant St.

The cascading fountain backdrop behind the Columbus Memorial serves to conceal part of the pumping equipment for the reservoir. Remarkably, this containment of 40 million gallons of water has provided almost 125 years of service to the city of Richmond. In the 1960s a roof was constructed over the entire reservoir. On the opposite side of the reservoir, at 2700 Stafford Road, is a pumping station (c. 1920) that doubles as a classically detailed garden casino with arched openings, quoins, and cornice. Trefoil medallions decorate the facade, suggesting the turbines at the heart of the facility.

RI314.3 Pump House

1890, Marion J. Dimmock. Pump House Dr.

This granite Gothic Revival structure belongs to the wave of medieval-inspired public buildings influenced by the contemporary Richmond City Hall. The machinery was housed in the basement, and the main floor was used for dances. The building awaits a restoration appreciative of its charm and design. Beside it is a hydroelectric generating facility (c. 1910), a handsome representative of the rich ornament and stately designs that once characterized industrial architecture.

RI314.4 Byrd Park Clubhouse

1913, Carneal and Johnston. Westover Rd. at Lakeview Ave.

With its columned veranda and polygonal plan, this park house is a pleasing combination of Colonial Revival and Arts and Crafts elements. It is typical of the structures built in Richmond parks around the turn of the century, combining the functions of bandstand, restroom, tool house, and park keeper's office. It stands near the walled Shields and Robinson family cemetery, whose earliest interment dates from 1823. A small fountain in front of the clubhouse, erected by the local Women's Christian Temperance Union, commemorates an 1873 incident in the Ohio temperance movement.

RI314.5 Carillon Tower (Virginia War Memorial Tower)

1931–1932, Cram and Ferguson, and Carneal, Johnston and Wright. Byrd Park

A mania for memorials followed the conclusion of World War I, and Virginia was not immune. Philadelphia architect Paul P. Cret, in association with Marcellus E. Wright of Richmond, won the local competition 1925. Cret's design for a Moderne screen of columns met with some criticism, but construction started in 1926, only to be halted after three months. Instead, a citizens' committee started to raise funds for a carillon tower. Carillons became very popular in the 1920s, and a number were erected across the country. Discarding the original competition results and deciding against holding a new one, the War Memorial Commission chose Cram and Ferguson of Boston and local architects Carneal, Johnston and Wright to design a tall carillon. Cram, who was well known in Richmond for his work at the University of Richmond (see entry, below), took the

RI315 The Virginia Home (Virginia Home for the Incurables Building)

leading role in designing a 200-foot-tall carillon in a Georgian Revival idiom. A steel frame was encased in red brick with light-colored sandstone trim. At the base was a large plaza for public gatherings. The base itself was to house a museum of war relics. Promotional literature stressed that the bells could be heard for "400 square miles," and that they would play "the soldier's old songs . . . the National Anthem . . . the hymn General Lee liked." It was dedicated at a great ceremony in 1932.

The three-block area bordered by Byrd Park, Maymont, Westover, and Spottswood roads contains numerous examples of urban villas and speculative developments that rival those of Monument Avenue.

RI315 The Virginia Home (Virginia Home for the Incurables Building)

1930, Baskervill and Lambert. 1101 Hampton St.

The Art Deco style, or the idiom derived from the Paris Exposition of 1925, gained some following in Richmond, mainly for commercial structures. The state government only tentatively embraced it, for this large structure that might be mistaken for a hotel or an apartment building is actually part of the state's mental hospital system. The seven-story central pavilion is flanked by six-story wings, a treatment that recalls New York high-rise massing of the 1920s and 1930s. Height is emphasized by the vertical brick piers capped by cast stone floral ornament in the Parisian style of the period. A handsome Art Deco porte-cochere greets the visitor.

RI316 Byrd Park Court

c. 1920, Lindner and Phillips, Architects, and Crosby Builders. 705–733 Byrd Park Ct.

Few court groupings of this type can be found in Richmond. This is a charming solution to the challenge of placing large-scale houses in a very small but private urban setting. The variety of Tudor, colonial, and Spanish design influences in the homes clustered around a small fountain makes Byrd Park Court a virtual index of the revival styles of architecture.

RI317 Maymont

1890, Edgerton S. Rogers. 1903, farm buildings. 1907–1910, Italian gardens, Noland and Baskervill. 1911–1912, Japanese garden, "Mr. Muto." 1923, Dooley mausoleum, Baskervill and Lambert. 1700 Hampton St. Open to the public

Although very much in the spirit of the lavish and eclectic Edwardian mansions found along Richmond's Franklin Street, Maymont stands in solitary splendor on the site of what had been a rural dairy farm overlooking the James River. It was built by wealthy industrialist James H. Dooley for his wife, Sallie May, for whom the property was named. Dooley became prosperous in the years after the Civil War through speculation in railroads and real estate. He and his wife often traveled to Europe, returning to Richmond with works of art and exotic plants to embellish their estate on the fringes of the city. They chose as their architect Edgerton S. Rogers, the son of the sculptor Randolph Rogers. Edgerton Rogers, who died at the age of forty-one in 1901, also designed the Virginia

RI317 Maymont, Italian gardens

building for the World's Colombian Exposition of 1893.

Each facade of his design for Maymont presents different forms and profiles, combining round, polygonal, and square towers with narrow windows below smaller stained glass lights. Stylistically, Rogers combined elements of the Romanesque Revival and François Premier or Chateauesque styles in a house really more suited to a suburban than a solitary country site. Highly polished granite columns adorn the expansive porch on the west and south sides, providing a contrast to the rock-faced granite facade and the sandstone trim. A porte-cochere shelters the carriage entrance below a large stained glass window on the river side of the building. The interiors are largely intact and exhibit a contrasting variety of room sizes, styles, and motifs. The entrance hall off the porte-cochere is a two-story space with a vast fireplace and windows with glass in the American opalescent style. Mrs. Dooley's bedchamber on the second floor is furnished with a swan bed from the Dooleys' country house in the Blue Ridge, Swanannanoa. It demonstrates the appeal Richard Wagner's grand operas had for wealthy Americans at the turn of the twentieth century.

William Noland, of Noland and Baskervill, became Dooley's architect after Rogers's death and added the stable and farm building complex that resembles Philadelphia-area structures he might have observed while in the office of Cope and Stewardson. Below this service group on the hillside and along the former Kanawha Canal are a series of gardens that were a showcase for the Dooleys' taste in rare plant specimens and fine statuary. The stepped fountains of an Italian garden by Noland in turn feed the pools of a Japanese garden at the base of a rock face, designed by a Japanese gardener known as Mr. Muto, and then a grotto. Ornate gazebos dot the landscape below the mansion, inviting enjoyment of vistas of the house and gardens from the hillside.

Dooley and his wife made substantial bequests to the people of Richmond for the establishment of an orphanage, hospital, and public library. They also willed that, after their death, Maymont be maintained without fee as a park for the enjoyment of the citizens of the city. After a long decline in the years after World War II, Maymont and its grounds underwent extensive renovation. Dooley and his wife are buried near the mansion in a small, classical temple-form mausoleum.

West of the Boulevard   (RI318–RI335)

West of the Boulevard is a large, early twentieth-century residential neighborhood defined here as the blocks between Boulevard and Thompson and between Monument Avenue and Cary Street. Remarkably cohesive and well preserved, the West of the Boulevard area grew during a boom period in Richmond between about 1895 and 1940. Growth was boosted by the streetcars that served the area's main east-west arteries. Both detached residences and row houses line the shaded streets of the district, interspersed with many two- and three-story apartment buildings, several schools, and some churches. Development began at the eastern end of the neighborhood, continuing the grid pattern and density of the Fan.

RI318 Kensington Gardens Retirement Home (Johnston-Willis Hospital)

1923, Marcellus E. Wright. 1980, conversion. 2900 Kensington Ave.

This large, limestone-clad, classically detailed structure dominates this area of Kensington Avenue. Marcellus E. Wright, Sr., a native Virginian, had trained in Philadelphia and worked for Cope and Stewardson. Wright's firm became one of the largest in Richmond, specializing in institutional work of a high quality. His son, Marcellus E. Wright, Jr., joined the firm in the 1930s.

RI319 Houses

1917–1920, Muhleman and Kayhoe, builders. 3000 block Kensington Ave.

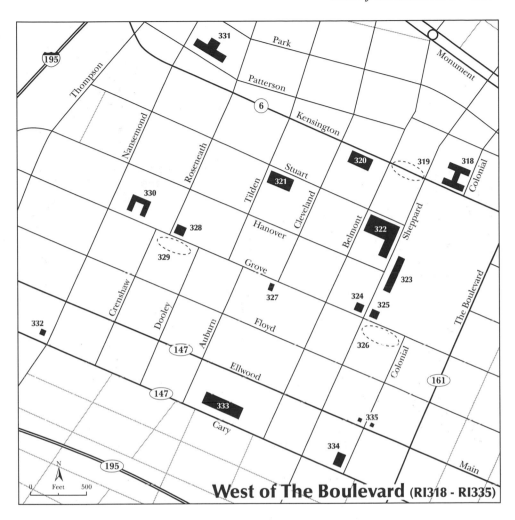

West of The Boulevard (RI318 - RI335)

On opposite sides of Kensington Avenue are two groups of residences built by one of Richmond's most prolific construction firms of the period 1910–1950. Muhleman and Kayhoe apparently had their own in-house designers who followed the broader national trends in housing and style. The row on the south side of the street is a mix of three-bay Renaissance Revival and Arts and Crafts houses unified by columned porches. On the north side the style is Tudor Revival, expressed in a profusion of differently shaped, steeply pitched roofs and some half timbering.

RI320 Robert E. Lee School

1919, Charles M. Robinson. 3101 Kensington Ave.

Richmond's impressive investment in public schools during the 1910s and 1920s is exemplified by this showy brick elementary school with a limestone base and trim. Suitably impressive to children would be the colossal engaged Corinthian colonnade and the wings with copper domes.

RI321 St. Gertrude's High School

1913, Maginnis and Walsh. 3215 Stuart Ave.

The Catholic church converted this former convent to a high school for girls in 1922. The architects, from Boston, were among the leading Catholic church designers of the first half of the twentieth century and had a nationwide practice. Charles Maginnis, the designing part-

RI320 Robert E. Lee School (right)

RI323 Virginia Museum of Fine Arts, Center for Education and Outreach (Home for Needy Confederate Women) (below, left)

RI325 Confederate Memorial Chapel (below, right)

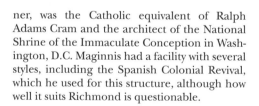

ner, was the Catholic equivalent of Ralph Adams Cram and the architect of the National Shrine of the Immaculate Conception in Washington, D.C. Maginnis had a facility with several styles, including the Spanish Colonial Revival, which he used for this structure, although how well it suits Richmond is questionable.

RI322 Benedictine High School

1911, Father Michael McInerney. 1986, renovations. 304 N. Sheppard St.

Designed by a Benedictine priest from Belmont Abbey in Belmont, North Carolina, this complex is in a refined Romanesque Revival idiom. Father McInerney also designed the priest's home (1924) and St. Benedict's Church (1929), which complement the school building. The church, with its deep central arch and wheel window, recalls northern Italian structures of the eleventh and twelfth centuries.

RI323 Virginia Museum of Fine Arts, Center for Education and Outreach
(Home for Needy Confederate Women)

1930–1932, Lee, Smith and Van Dervoort. 1994–1999, renovation and restoration, the Glave Firm. 301 N. Sheppard St.

Built as an annex of the R. E. Lee Confederate Veterans Camp, which originally stood on the site of the present-day Virginia Museum of Fine Arts, this building housed the wives and daughters of former Confederate soldiers. The seven remaining residents vacated the building in 1989, and the state legislature turned it over to the Virginia Museum. The Glave Firm has converted it into offices, reception, and classrooms for the museum. The original design architect, Merrill C. Lee, chose the north front of the White House as the motif for the central block. The replica, which has a limestone exterior, is scaled down; the portico is only one column deep and not as high as the original. To the eleven-bay central block, Lee attached hyphens and two flanking wings. On the interior the restorers attempted to maintain the 1930s Colonial Revival features and also added some new elements, such as a reproduction of Joseph Dufour's *Monument of Paris* wallpaper of 1815, which is in the dining room.

RI324 All Saints Reformed Presbyterian Church (First Congregational Church)

1922, Luther P. Hartsook, Richmond. 3000 Grove Ave.

This extremely ambitious church design by Hartsook, who maintained offices in Richmond and Ashland, drew upon McKim, Mead and White's Madison Square Presbyterian Church, New York (1906) for basic features such as the low, metal-clad dome and the tetrastyle Corinthian columned portico. He also employed a light-colored Roman brick, which the New York architects had helped to popularize. However, in contrast to the Early Christian character of the New York prototype, this church is more classical Roman in appearance.

RI325 Confederate Memorial Chapel

1887, Marion J. Dimmock. 2900 Grove Ave. Open by appointment

Across the street from All Saints Reformed is another remainder of the Confederate veterans' camp that used to occupy this site, a wistful Carpenter's Gothic structure. Dimmock, who was a veteran of Jeb Stuart's cavalry and liked to use the title "Captain," was the appropriate architect for the structure. Paid for by the veterans themselves, it served them until the last one died in 1941. The interior is simple but contains a nice set of stock painted Victorian glass.

RI326 Victorian Houses

c. 1895, attributed to D. Wiley Anderson. 1985, remodeling, Stanford Bond. 2911, 2915, 2919 Grove St.

On the opposite side of Grove are three granite Victorian houses adapted as offices and for other uses. They have the round, engaged towers and complicated rooflines of the Queen Anne style, but their ornamental porch detail looks as if it had been drawn from a pattern book of the 1870s. They complement each other with their lively rooflines and varied projections. Their distinctive pump houses are a rare survival.

RI327 Wendell Powell House

1911–1912, D. Wiley Anderson. 3201 Grove Ave.

This house is one of the largest in the neighborhood. Anderson's approach to the Colonial Revival, as in this design, was to greatly inflate the different elements and combine features from a number of different sources. On a two-and-one-half-story brick block, Anderson put a giant columnar portico, and then a second-floor balcony. On the ground floor, the portico is flanked by fanlighted windows, while above the windows are banked and capped with prominent keystones and lintels.

RI328 Temple Beth-El (Grove Avenue Presbyterian Church)

1923, Baskervill and Lambert. 1942–1949, conversion and addition, Alexander Sharove. 3330 Grove Ave.

This building began as a Colonial Revival church but in the 1940s was converted into the Temple Beth-El. The remodeled facade facing Grove Street appears as an abstracted or stripped Moderne–Colonial Revival composition with large pilasters.

RI329 Houses

1921, Davis Brothers, contractors. 3403–3411 Grove Ave.

This group of three-bay brick structures, built by one of the largest building contractors in the city, is in the American Foursquare idiom, popularized in publications on Arts and Crafts design and disseminated in building manuals of the period. This group, which is especially well designed, has details that might be called Arts and Crafts.

RI330 English Village

1927, Bascom J. Rowlett; Davis Brothers, contractors. 3418–3450 Grove Ave.

The name is appropriate for this experiment in speculative housing. Here Davis Brothers, as builders and real estate developers, teamed up with Rowlett, a local architect. These picturesque Tudor Revival town houses of brick, stone, and stucco with half timbering evoke English garden suburbs. The roofline is appropriately varied, and the clustered chimneys add charm. The U-shaped site plan, with houses around a public green, was common for such developments in these years. Many of these, however, were designed for workers and owned collectively. In Richmond a different mentality ruled: the development was aimed at upper-middle-class families, and owners individually held title to their units. Included in the original bylaws was a restriction on exterior changes, a factor crucial to maintaining the picturesque character of the village.

RI331 **Albert H. Hill School**

1926, Charles M. Robinson. 3400 Patterson Ave.

The Hill School illustrates Robinson's versatility and eclecticism. Best known as a Colonial Revival architect, he masterfully adopted a Mediterranean image for this large school, expressed in details that include thematic decorative tiles. As was typical of Robinson's school buildings, the emphasis is on well-lighted classrooms, and the window banks are especially striking.

At the southern edge of the West of the Boulevard area is a thriving, stylish retail district known as Carytown. Stretching from the Boulevard to Thompson, Carytown grew with the district. Originally there were only a few scattered groceries, laundries, and hardware stores. Many shopkeepers lived over their stores. As Cary Street established itself as the retail corridor, storefronts were added in front of the existing residences. Now the most trendy urban shopping area in Richmond, Carytown boasts a vital mix of up-to-the-minute clothing boutiques and holdovers from the earlier generation of mom-and-pop stores.

RI332 **Java Outpost** (Toll House)

c. 1804. Later remodelings and additions. 3500 W. Cary St.

This small two-story brick building with a steep double-pitched slate roof is a remarkable survival, a toll house remaining from the Westham Plank Road. Now it is attached on two sides to modern buildings but still visible from the parking lot between Cary and Ellwood.

RI333 **Cary Court**

1938, Henry Carl Messerschmidt. Later alterations. 3120–3158 W. Cary St.

RI330 English Village

One of the earliest architect-designed shopping centers within Richmond, Cary Court is composed of one-story glass-fronted structures and a two-story focal building. The brick and granite facades are in a very tame Moderne style. The important feature was the ample parking lot in front.

RI334 **Byrd Theater**

1928, Fred A. Bishop; decoration and artwork, Brounet Studios of New York; sculpture, Ferruccio Legnaioli. 2908 W. Cary St.

One of the focal points of Carytown is this theater, which epitomizes the grand movie palaces built in the 1920s and which captivated and distracted Depression-era audiences. Its two-story brick facade displays a wealth of terra-cotta in the Spanish Colonial and Mediterranean Revival idioms. The interior is still largely intact and continues the Spanish theme with plaster decoration and heavy metal fixtures. The auditorium still has an organ that rises to stage level as it is played and a glittering chandelier lit like a rainbow. Aside from the loss of its original marquee and signage, the Byrd has been lovingly maintained by private owners and has been in continuous use.

RI335 **Houses**

c. 1895, D. Wiley Anderson. 2818 and 2902 Ellwood Ave.

These two mirror-image brick Italianate villas, complete with towers, occupy opposite corners. Anderson was more comfortable with the highly picturesque nineteenth-century styles than with plainer ones, and the use of the Italianate in this case is unusual for its late date. Some of the details, such as the second-floor window in the tower, indicate the nascent Colonial Revival, but the major feature, the campanile, looks back to pattern books of the 1870s and even earlier.

Windsor Farms and Southwest   (RI336–RI340)

RI336 **Windsor Farms**

c. 1925 and later, John Nolen, planner, and others. Bounded on the south by the James River, on the north by Cary St., on the east by the Powhite Pkwy., and on the west by Lock Ln.

One of Richmond's distinguished residential addresses was developed by T. C. Williams, Jr., the owner of the original farm, a prominent Richmonder, and an ardent Anglophile. In the mid-1920s he hired Allen Saville, a local engineer, and John Nolen, a Boston-based landscape architect and planner, to recreate an English village in Virginia. Nolen's previous experience with subdivisions served him well, and the semicircular plan of intersecting streets is as charming as it is confusing to navigate. The early development team eventually included Henry Grant Morse, a New York architect who excelled at the details that articulated Williams's vision.

The plan included a village green and a few public buildings intended to create a sense of community. The land along the river was divided into larger lots than the rest of the tract, and these were developed early. Two of the first houses, Williams's Agecroft Hall and his next-door neighbors' Virginia House, were historic English houses that were purchased, dismantled into labeled parts, and shipped across the

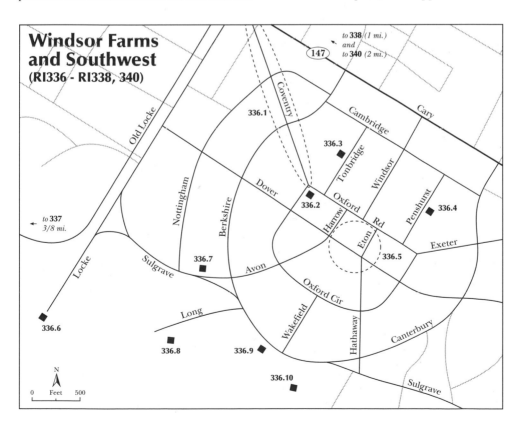

Windsor Farms and Southwest (RI336 - RI338, 340)

Atlantic for rebuilding in Virginia. Four of the other houses were designed by William Lawrence Bottomley.

Though Williams envisioned a village with English vernacular architecture, the Georgian image that the period conjured in the minds of the clients and the influence of Colonial Williamsburg overwhelmed Williams's ideas. The development today is dominated by Colonial Revival and Georgian Revival houses, although a scattering of the English vernacular architecture that Williams encouraged offers some variety. The neighborhood was carefully marketed, and many sales brochures extolled the natural beauty of the land and the artistic interpretation of the developers. The author of several early brochures and booklets almost comically embellished the historic importance of the land, at one point writing, "It is land whose every clod and stone could tell a story, if clods and stones could speak." The landscaping, lighting, brick sidewalks, public spaces, and winding roads were described poetically, and prospective buyers were reassured that a design review committee would rule out any inappropriate plans. The early vision included a tearoom on the village green, staffed by local socialites dressed in appropriate costumes; a small shop that sold crafts created or collected by locals (Morse's idea); and a charming firehouse. Williams sponsored a literary and social magazine, *The Black Swan*, which followed Richmond's latest fads. It included many essays on the romantic and scenic qualities of the growing community.

Williams's original farmhouse was demolished and replaced in the late 1940s with an uninspired Neo-Georgian house. Windsor Farms has remained the desirable address that Williams envisioned.

RI336.1 **Houses**

c. 1930, Eimer W. Cappelmann. 4600, 4503, and 4311 Coventry Rd.

By entering Windsor Farms almost at the western end of Coventry Road, visitors can see some of the earliest houses, including three designed in an English vernacular by an architect who designed many of the pre-1930 speculative houses in Windsor Farms. He subsequently moved to Washington, D.C., and had a long and successful career in that city. For these houses Cappelmann adopts the English Arts and Crafts idiom of high-pitched, spreading slate roofs covering a plain brick facade with windows arranged in banks.

RI336.2 **House**

1930, attributed to Eimer W. Cappelmann. 113 Oxford Circle

Traditionally associated with Cappelmann, this four-bay house is one of the earliest Colonial Revival designs in Windsor Farms.

RI336.3 **Anne Hathaway Cottage**

1927, Henry Grant Morse. 106 Tonbridge St.

On Tonbridge, Cambridge, and Penshurst streets are examples of the English vernacular T. C. Williams favored, as well as examples of the Colonial Revival houses that are more numerous in Windsor Farms. Williams commissioned this copy—loosely interpreted—of the famous cottage in Stratford-on-Avon to establish a historic English ambience. Of course, the half timbering is simulated and the roof is imitation thatch.

RI336.4 **House**

1929, Bascom Rowlett. 103 Penshurst St.

An elegant and rather convincing half-timbered companion to the Anne Hathaway Cottage, this house was also built on speculation for Williams.

RI336.5 **Village Green**

The village green is impressive for its space, but the architecture lacks distinction. The dominant feature is Grace Baptist Church (1949–1950) with its impressive spire. But the Colonial Revival building lacks inspiration. Also on the green at Dover Street are the half-timbered Community Building (1926, Henry Grant Morse), with diamond-paned casement windows, and the Georgian Revival Tuckahoe Women's Club (1954, C. W. Huff; 4215 Dover Street).

RI336.6 **Milburne**

1934–1935, William Lawrence Bottomley; Charles Gillette, landscape architect. 315 Lock Ln.

Milburne, commissioned by Ambassador Walter Robertson, is one of four Bottomley houses

RI336.5 Village Green, Community Building (above, left)

RI336.7 Ryland House (above, right)

RI336.8 Agecroft Hall (left)

in Windsor Farms and one of two that are visible from the street. It is sited to overlook the James River, with a gated entrance on axis with a pedimented central block flanked by hyphens and wings. As is typical of Bottomley's work, especially by the 1930s, when he had gained his stride, every detail is carefully studied, and all the proportions are correct. Commonly labeled as suburban James River Georgian Revival in style, the house is largely derived from Palladio. The interior, however, is more Adamesque or Federal Revival in character. The initial landscaping was by Gillette, but Arthur Shurcliff from Colonial Williamsburg worked on the river terrace. Umberto Innocenti of New York designed the wrought iron railing on the retaining wall for the river terrace. The walled garden on the east was the design of Alden Hopkins, also of Colonial Williamsburg.

RI336.7 Ryland House

1928, Luther Harsook. 4502 Sulgrave Rd.

Indicating the eclecticism of early Windsor Farms, this house, with a steep hipped roof, is French-influenced.

RI336.8 Agecroft Hall

1485–1650, various building campaigns. 1926, dismantling and reconstruction, Henry Grant Morse; Charles Gillette, landscape architect. 4305 Sulgrave Rd. Open to the public

Agecroft Hall is probably the best-known house in Windsor Farms. It is a half-timbered Tudor- and Stuart-era house that was dismantled, shipped from England, and reconstructed on this site. Although the house had deteriorated and vintage photographs show it in depressing surroundings of mines and railyards, there was a great protest in Britain when Williams bought the house. Morse was enlisted to adapt the original building to this site and to modern life. The huge house was placed down a winding drive, beyond the rolling lawn, on a tremendous lot overlooking the James River. Morse retained varied half-timbering motifs, accentuating sections of the facade and providing a jolt of pattern in the calm setting. A huge bay window with the original leaded glass is the focal point of the interior. The house is in no way an exact duplicate of the original house in England, but an American country-house adaptation with all the modern conveniences. The Williamses collected decorative arts of the Tudor and Stuart eras and set up a museum foundation to administer the house at their death. Consequently, Agecroft Hall is shown as a Tudor period house. The extensive formal garden is a great draw for the museum.

RI336.9 Virginia House

c. 1125, constructed as a monastery. c. 1530, conversion to a manor house. 1925–1926, dismantling and reconstruction, Henry Grant Morse; Charles Gillette, landscape architect. 1944–1946, loggia, William Lawrence Bottomley. 4301 Sulgrave Rd. Open to the public

Virginia House was actually begun before the Williamses purchased the house that would become Agecroft Hall. Ambassador Alexander Weddell and his wealthy wife, Virginia, were as avid about antiques and history as the Williamses. On a tour of England in 1925, they heard about a doomed twelfth-century priory. When Henry VIII dissolved the monasteries in the 1530s, Warwick Priory, as it was known, was converted into a manor house. By 1925 it had been engulfed in an industrial neighborhood, and the owners were forced to sell it. The Weddells immediately bought it from a contractor who was planning to use the building materials to erect a factory. Like the Williamses, the Weddells faced disapproval in England, and they had the further challenge of tracking down parts of the building that had already been dispersed.

Morse assisted in piecing together the elements in a way that made an elegant house out of a jumble of parts. The house is an impressive stone structure that is frankly a modern American country place. The Weddells had Morse design a wing as an exact reproduction of the south wing of Sulgrave Manor, the ancestral home of George Washington, as another visible connection between the old world and the new. (Mrs. Weddell falsely claimed a family connection to Washington.) The gardens, by Gillette, are spectacular and include several terraces that overlook the James River below. Virginia House

is also a museum, and the antiques, tapestries, and art the well-traveled Weddells collected enhance a fascinating setting. The most spectacular room is the vast second-floor library. The Weddells left Virginia House to the Virginia Historical Society, which administers it.

RI336.10 Williams House

1927, William Lawrence Bottomley; Charles Gillette, landscape architect. 4207 Sulgrave Rd. Not visible from the street

At the same time Virginia House and Agecroft were being reconstructed, Bottomley received a commission from E. Randolph Williams for this Georgian Revival house. The design is based on Westover, though Bottomley added and subtracted skillfully: it is five bays wide instead of seven, and recessed stucco panels on the entrance facade punctuate each bay. A stringcourse runs just below the second-story windows, and an elegantly designed door frame is derived from Palladio.

RI337 Rice House

1965, Richard Neutra; Thaddeus Longstreth, associate architect. 1000 Old Locke Ln. (on an island in the James River). Powhite Parkway south; first right exit onto Forest Hill Ave.; left onto Hathaway Dr.; left at intersection onto Scottview Dr., which becomes Riverside Dr. and proceeds to Pony Pasture Park. Visible from Riverside Dr. on the south side of the James, especially from Pony Pasture Park in the fall and winter months

Neutra's only known work in Virginia was commissioned by U.S. Ambassador (to Australia under the Nixon administration) and Mrs. Walter L. Rice. The house was a bold statement built within a stone's throw of the epitome of Colonial Revival suburbs, Windsor Farms. Neutra, an expatriate from Vienna, left the Berlin office of architect Erich Mendelsohn in 1924 and came to the United States, where he worked briefly with Frank Lloyd Wright and R. M. Schindler. He settled in Los Angeles and became one of the major exponents of the International Style in the 1920s and 1930s. The Rice House, built late in his career, echoes Wright's long horizontals. The island site is one of the most inspiring natural settings on the James River. According to Inger Rice, "Neutra fell in love with the site and even wanted to climb out on a cliff to look at the site. We tied a rope around him."

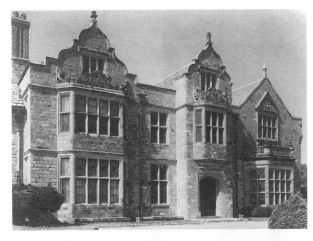

RI336.9 Virginia House
RI338 Wilton

The views of the river are spectacular from the floor-to-ceiling windows as well as a second-story deck that surrounds nearly half the house. The materials include Georgia marble (installed by three Georgians) and superbly fitted masonry throughout the overall light-colored form. The house also uses aluminum, which is appropriate for a Reynolds Metals vice president. The house has recently been given to the Science Museum of Virginia. The seventeen-acre island was once called Dead Man's Hill because two Civil War soldiers were buried there. The property also contains a mid-nineteenth-century Kanawha Canal lock and the remnants of a shot tower that was part of the Westham Foundry.

RI338 Wilton

1750–1753, attributed to Richard Taliaferro. 1933–1935, reconstruction, Claiborne and Taylor. 215 S. Wilton Rd. Open to the public

Originally built for William Randolph III on a riverside site fifteen miles away in eastern Henrico County, Wilton was one of the last of the great James River plantation houses. The house stood derelict for many years, until the 1930s, when it was threatened by demolition and the piecemeal sale of its fine paneled interior. Instead, the National Society of the Colonial Dames of America purchased Wilton, reassembled it on its present site overlooking the James River west of Richmond, and made it into a showplace of Georgian architecture and the decorative arts.

The plan is a straightforward central hall with rooms to either side. In contrast to the austere Georgian facade of the house, the interior decoration is astonishing. The entire interior, including the closets, is paneled from floor to ceiling. At the summit of the hierarchy of the interior decoration is the parlor. Here, rich carvings, arched recesses, and denticulated cornices complement the marble mantelpiece and

RI339.3 University of Richmond, North Court (right)

RI339.8 University of Richmond, Boatwright Library (below, left)

RI340 6426 Roselawn Road (below, right)

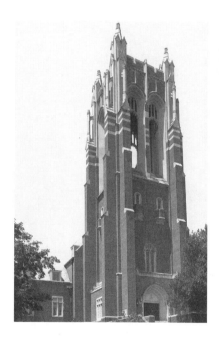

display the art of colonial wood crafting. Wilton docents claim the parlor to be one of the most beautiful rooms in America. Other rooms display the same high level of craftsmanship. The furnishings, while not original, are excellent examples of colonial and in particular Virginia decorative arts of the period.

RI339 University of Richmond

1910–1914, Cram, Goodhue and Ferguson; Warren Manning Associates, landscape architects, original campus plan and initial buildings. Many later additions. Towana Rd.

In 1910 Baptist-affiliated Richmond College moved its campus from downtown Richmond to a 200-acre tract in the western suburban area known as Westhampton. The college engaged the Boston firm of Cram, Goodhue and Ferguson to develop a campus plan. Ralph Adams Cram, a fervent high Episcopalian and internationally known as a fierce advocate of the

Gothic style, especially for religious and academic buildings, took charge. He was the architect of New York's Cathedral of St. John the Divine and many of the buildings at the U.S. Military Academy at West Point and Princeton University. For Richmond, Cram conceived a design that placed male students on the north side of a large existing lake and the female students on the other. He envisioned two respective tight-knit cloisters of buildings at the knolls of existing ridges that would interweave aspects of the Tudor, Gothic, and classical styles in their design.

The first buildings to be completed were Ryland Hall (RI339.1), which initially served as an administration building and library; the Refectory (RI339.2); North Court (RI339.3), a multipurpose building; a stadium; a power plant (RI339.4); and Thomas Hall (RI339.5) and Jetter Hall (RI339.6), both men's dormitories. Following World War I Cram designed the Milhiser Gymnasium (RI339.7) (c. 1920). Cram's idiom for all of these buildings was an adaptation of Tudor and Jacobean forms as found at Cambridge and Oxford. Red brick is the primary building material, and carved limestone details are generously used. Perhaps the most impressive is North Court, with its patterned brickwork and carved heads on the keystones, including one of Cram himself. Beginning in the 1920s the financially strapped university relied on Richmond architects for additional buildings. Many of Cram's successors respected his version of Collegiate Gothic by continuing the red brick trimmed in granite or precast stone. These architects included Charles M. Robinson, Merrill G. Lee, and the firm of Carneal and Johnston, the last of whom designed the landmark Boatwright Library (RI339.8) (1954), distinguished by its large Gothic tower. A major difference was that instead of designing attached structures that would have continued Cram's desired monastic, cloistered feeling, these later architects built freestanding buildings that began to dot the campus. Perhaps this change reflected the influence of Charles Gillette, whose firm, Warren Manning Associates, had been engaged to oversee the landscaping. Gillette, who would

stay in Richmond and continue to design major landscape projects for another half century, appears to have preferred a more picturesque placement of buildings in the wooded setting.

Following a period during the 1960s and 1970s when the campus acquired a number of Brutalist buildings, the university returned to a style closely approximating the Cram idiom. Recent buildings include the E. Claiborne Robins School of Business addition (RI339.9) (1982–1988, Marcellus Wright, Cox and Smith) and the George M. Modlin Center for the Arts (RI339.10) (1994–1997, Marcellus Wright, Cox and Smith). These are postmodern in that the details are frequently "funky," as described by lead designer Edward Smith, and the interiors "a surprise," with large atriums.

The Jepson Alumni Center (Wise-Hunton House) (RI339.11) (1915, William Lawrence Bottomley; 1997, Marcellus Wright, Cox and Smith; College Avenue) was originally not part of the campus, but stood nearby. It was the first commission of the New York–based architect Bottomley and began an architectural relationship with Richmond that set a standard for tra-

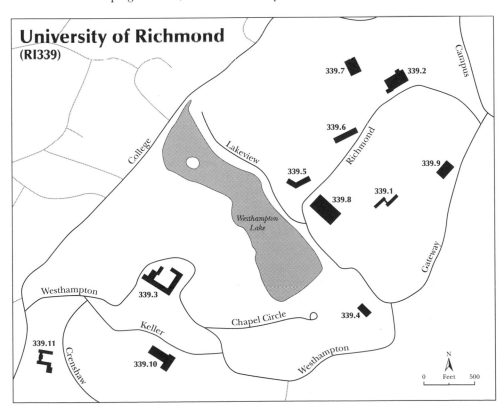

University of Richmond (RI339)

ditionalism and excellence in domestic design that still holds power today. This five-part Colonial Revival house for Jennings C. Wise originally stood across River Road. Unlike many of Bottomley's later designs in brick, the Wise House was finished in stucco and employed a wood frame. In 1997, after it was moved across River Road to its present site, the building was sensitively altered and enlarged with a one-story U-shaped addition to accommodate an alumni affairs office and conference center for the university. The house continues to present a domestic front on the street and provides a transition to the campus. A columned arcade faces the campus.

RI340 Residences

1925–1927, Ernest Flagg. 6300, 6302, and 6331 Ridgeway Rd.; 6426 Roselawn Rd. (south on Roselawn Rd. from Towana Rd.)

These four modest homes of rock-faced granite were designed by Ernest Flagg, a Beaux-Arts–trained New York architect, the designer of such landmark buildings as the Scribner Building in New York City, the Corcoran Museum of Art in Washington, D.C., and a number of major structures at the U.S. Naval Academy in Annapolis, Maryland. Toward the end of his career Flagg advocated the idea that every American should live in a stone house. In 1922 he published a book, *Small Houses: Their Economic Design and Construction.* These four Flagg-designed residences near the University of Richmond campus were built by a Richmond developer, and each reflects Flagg's interest in creating an original American domestic style by melding certain aspects of English and French vernacular architecture with early American architectural features.

Ginter Park and Virginia Union University
(RI341–RI353)

Ginter Park, bounded by Brook Road on the west, Moss Side Avenue on the east, North and Bellevue avenues on the north, and Brookland Park Boulevard on the south, is a turn-of-the-twentieth-century suburb that briefly became a separate town before it was annexed to Richmond in 1914. From before the Revolutionary War, Brook Road, a toll road, had served as the major link between Richmond and points north. During the Civil War the city's Confederate inner defenses crossed Brook Road at what is now Confederate Avenue, and its outer defenses crossed at a point just north of today's Azalea Avenue. By the late nineteenth century a number of Richmond's most prominent residents had established country estates along Brook Road. In 1893 Lewis Ginter and his associate, Joseph Bryan, began to acquire hundreds of acres in the area, creating the suburb of Ginter Park.

The streets of Ginter Park were paved with stone quarried from what is now Bryan Park. The first houses built were in the 3600 block of Hawthorne Avenue, the 1100 block of Westwood Avenue, and the 3400 block of Noble Avenue. Built for the families and the workmen who would construct the development's larger homes, these frame houses bear similarities to those published in period architectural pattern books. Bryan's children developed his estate, Laburnum, along Hermitage Road (an extension of the Boulevard) on the west to Brook Road on the east, and from Westwood Avenue on the south to Laburnum Avenue on the north.

RI341 House

c. 1893. 3601 Hawthorne Ave.

The largest of the workmen's homes is this frame Queen Anne house with a polychrome slate roof. The house was built for the supervisor of the land company. Many of these early cottages are painted in a lively palette of colors and are well maintained.

RI342 Lewis Ginter Community Building

c. 1895. 3421 Hawthorne Ave. (southeast corner of Hawthorne and Walton aves.)

This stucco and half-timbered building originally served as a school for the community. Today it is a neighborhood and recreation center and a private girls' school. The gymnasium wing was a gift in the 1920s of Grace E. Arents, a niece and heir of Lewis Ginter.

RI343 St. Thomas Episcopal Church

1911, Hill C. Linthicum, Jr. 1922, parish hall, Lee and Lee. 3602 Hawthorne Ave.

Diagonally across from the community building is this small rock-faced granite structure, which has the feel of an English country church. It was also a gift to the community from Grace Arents, a devoted Episcopalian. She and the architect wanted to emphasize the use of hand labor in the construction of the building, and hence many of the details are very much in the Arts and Crafts mode. Of special note is the small stained glass window over the main altar with a cross inside a Star of David. It was designed by Willoughby Ions, a prominent Richmond poet and artist who was a

longtime resident of Chamberlayne Avenue nearby.

RI344 Kline House

1895. 3601 Chamberlayne Ave. (U.S. 1)

This one-story turreted frame house with wraparound porch supported by Doric columns is one of the few surviving single residences on this major city thoroughfare. The avenue has lost most of its old homes to undistinguished low-rise apartment houses. In its heyday, however, this boulevard was Northside Richmond's equivalent to Monument Avenue and boasted some of the city's most impressive homes, all set behind uniform privet hedges. The construction of this house predates the establishment of Ginter Park. This was the longtime home of the Kline family, who moved here in 1911 when the Kline Motor Kar Corporation relocated from York, Pennsylvania. The company's Stanley Steamer and White Steamer models were the only automobiles ever manufactured in Richmond.

RI345 Neill Ray House

1899, attributed to D. Wiley Anderson. 3501 Seminary Ave.

This granite Colonial Revival house has no rival in the city when it comes to stone construction. Its four Tuscan Doric columns, supporting a hipped roof with exaggerated dormer windows on the third floor, are the largest granite columns in Richmond.

RI346 Gresham House

1899. 3500 Seminary Ave.

Like its neighbor across the street, this Queen Anne house is built of granite. It also shares the same basic floor plan. The builder, however, changed the exterior so that it presents a different face to the street. Houses alike in plan but with varied facades are common in Ginter Park.

RI347 Union Theological Seminary and Presbyterian School of Christian Education

1896 and later. 3401 Brock Rd.

Seminary Avenue, which runs north-south to Azalea Avenue, comes to an abrupt halt in the

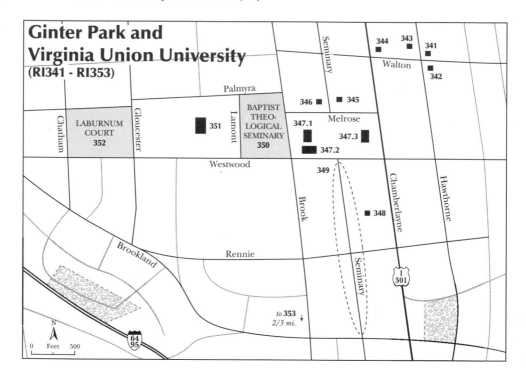

Ginter Park and Virginia Union University
(RI341 - RI353)

3400 block where it collides with the campus of Union Theological Seminary in Virginia and the Presbyterian School of Christian Education. In 1895 Lewis Ginter and associate Joseph Bryan invited the seminary to relocate to their envisioned suburb of Ginter Park from the Hampden-Sydney College campus near Farmville, Virginia. The Presbyterian seminary was given the development's choicest nine-acre tract.

RI347.1 Watts Hall

1896, Charles H. Read, Jr. 3401 Brook Rd.

This wildly exuberant Tudor pastiche in warm red brick with sandstone trim was designed by Charles H. Read, Jr., the son of a prominent local Presbyterian pastor and graduate of the University of Virginia. The influence of Jefferson's Lawn is evident in Read's placement of the institutional buildings: Watts Hall sits at the head of a grassy quadrangle, while faculty and student housing line the greensward. Read left the east end of the lawn open, just as Jefferson had done. (In both places, however, buildings would later enclose these spaces.) However, Read departed from Jefferson in a number of ways. He positioned his faculty

homes to look outward from the lawn to face the outside world, symbolic of Read's idea of how ministers should approach their work. He also separated the faculty homes, which face Westwood Avenue, from the student dormitories, such as Richmond Hall, on the other side of the campus.

RI347.1 Union Theological Seminary, Watts Hall

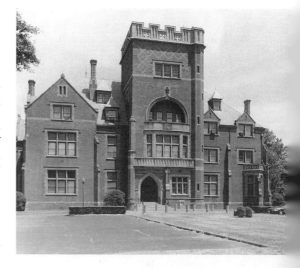

RI347.2 Old Library

1896, Charles H. Read, Jr. Brook Rd. at Westwood Ave.

Of special note on this Victorian-era building is the double-tiered cast iron porch on the campus entry to this building. The reading room, with its apse-like curve and balcony, is a handsome space.

RI347.3 William Morton Smith Library

1996, The Glave Firm (incorporating a 1922 chapel and classroom building by Baskervill and Son)

In its renovation of nearby Richmond Hall, a student dormitory that fronts the quadrangle, Glave reoriented the building to better address the heart of the campus. Similarly, in converting and enlarging a former chapel and classroom building for use as a new library, the architect placed the impressive building at the head of the quadrangle. Now a great tower entrance conducts an architectural conversation with the picturesque clock tower atop Watts Chapel at the opposite end of the campus. The building makes a strong case that historical styles (in this case Tudor) can be updated effectively for modern use. The interior atrium has soaring Gothic arches that lead the eye to a vaulted glass ceiling.

RI348 House

1782. c. 1820, alterations. 3207 Seminary Ave.

This weatherboarded frame farmhouse predates Seminary Avenue, so its driveway once wound to Brook Road. Today its setback from the street makes it a charming curiosity.

RI349 Houses

3000 and 3200 blocks of Seminary Ave.

These two blocks show the range of housing styles available to the upscale Richmond homeowner in the early decades of the twentieth century. The broad selection of designs includes Mediterranean and Colonial Revival, Arts and Crafts bungalows, and Foursquares.

RI350 Baptist Theological Seminary at Richmond

1922–1968, Baskervill and Son. Palmyra and Westwood aves. and Brook Rd. and Lamont Ave.

A school for training teachers of the Presbyterian faith was founded downtown in 1914 as the General Assembly School for Training. It soon outgrew its quarters and relocated near Union Theological Seminary. In 1921 the institution purchased its current grounds from the Joseph Bryan heirs, owners of nearby Laburnum. A campus of seven muscular, beautifully detailed Georgian Revival buildings was planned as an open-ended quadrangle, loosely based on the Lawn at the University of Virginia. The first two buildings were opened in early 1923. Four other buildings were added to the quadrangle over the next four decades, and five faculty and administrators' residences and a small residential quadrangle were built. The school was renamed the Presbyterian School of Christian Education. The southernmost building and property have recently been sold to the Baptist Theological Seminary, which plans to build on the site, possibly completing the south end of the quadrangle. The school is a radical contrast to the seminary across Brook Road, representing Virginia's shift in taste to the Colonial Revival style. The buildings are distinguished, detailed examples of the Georgian Revival style designed by the Baskervill firm over a period of forty years. The campus is oriented to Westwood Avenue, and because the proposed building at the corner of Brook Road was not built, it is difficult to appreciate the school without entering the quadrangle itself.

RI351 Richmond Memorial Hospital (Laburnum House)

1906–1908, Parish and Schroeder. 1957 and later additions, hospital complex, Baskervill and Son. 1300 Westwood Ave.

Laburnum, the enormous red brick Beaux-Arts mansion to which the hospital is attached, was built by Joseph Bryan, a prominent Richmond newspaper publisher, after an earlier house on the site burned. Laburnum originally included all the land between Brook and Hermitage roads and between Westwood and Laburnum avenues. The architects were from Philadelphia and freely mixed Virginia and Philadelphia elements. The major exterior feature was the gigantic hexastyle Corinthian portico, which, while recalling the popular vision of the Old South, gave the house an institutional feeling. Though Bryan died within a year of moving into the new house, his widow and one of their sons and his family continued to live in the sumptuously appointed house, entertaining such luminaries as Winston Churchill, Franklin Delano Roosevelt (then governor of New York), and Lady Nancy Astor. In 1949, the Bryans donated the house and the remaining part of the estate to Richmond Memorial Hospital, as a memorial to Richmonders who had died during World War II.

The construction of the seven-story hospital left the house mostly intact, adapting some of it for use as offices. The main hospital is a simple, modern building with a graceful curved canopy indicating the entrance. The lobby is a small, sleek space. The chapel is housed in a concrete extension to the brick body of the hospital above the entrance. It is ethereal, very compact in floor space, but five stories tall. Unfortunately, tall green Italian marble tablets engraved with the names of Richmond's World War II dead have been removed and replaced with an oversized American flag, which seems garish in the tight space. A medical office building was later added, and the hospital has grown with several additions. In 1965 Sheltering Arms Hospital moved from East Clay Street downtown to the Palmyra Avenue side of the site. Most of the Richmond Memorial's functions moved to a new location in Hanover County in 1998; current plans call for reuse of this building as a nursing home.

RI352 Laburnum Court

the houses support a modern lifestyle, with kitchens that were meant to be used by housewives instead of servants. They even included an early dishwasher that looked like a butter churn on its side. The name "court" refers to the private, commonly owned area in the center of the block. Garages are located on alleys, and the western end includes a central heating plant, an apartment for the "furnace man," and maids' rooms.

RI352 **Laburnum Court**

1919, Charles M. Robinson; Charles Gillette, landscape design. Bounded by Gloucester and Chatham roads and Westwood and Palmyra avenues

The twenty-four houses of Laburnum Court were designed when the Bryans decided to subdivide most of the Laburnum property. The larger neighborhood, known as Laburnum Park, was built mostly in the 1920s and early 1930s, with many homes designed by Charles M. Robinson. The block named Laburnum Court was an experiment in alternative housing. The twenty-four houses and lots were sold separately, but each owner became a shareholder in the corporation that owned and managed the common property in the center of the block, much like a modern condominium complex. The houses were built with only minor variations on the same floor plan and have five basic exterior elevations, which also vary slightly. The exteriors employ the popular styles of the period, including Mediterranean, Dutch Colonial, and Craftsman. The plans of

RI353 **Virginia Union University**

1897–present. Lombardy St. at Brook Rd.

From humble beginnings in a former slave jail in Richmond's Shockoe Bottom, Virginia Union University, formed by the merger of the Richmond Theological Society and the Wayland Seminary in the 1890s, has grown to occupy a sixty-five-acre site. Fueled by the efforts of northern philanthropists interested in providing an education for freed blacks, the school began an ambitious building campaign in 1897 that resulted in an outstanding collection of late Victorian collegiate architecture.

Their simultaneous construction between 1897 and 1901 and the use of identical rock-faced gray ashlar granite gave the Virginia Union buildings a consistent appearance, now blurred by later architecture. The designer of the original lecture hall, dormitory, dining hall, library, chapel, and residences for college officials was John H. Coxhead, a New Jersey native, who later designed hospitals and barracks for the army and air force between the world wars.

RI353.1 Virginia Union University Library

The stonework of the Coxhead buildings is of exceptional quality, expressing the solidity associated with the lasting benefits of higher learning. Among these structures are Martin E. Gray Hall (1897–1901, John H. Coxhead), whose boldly arched doorways are repeated in the fenestration. The interior of this building underwent extensive modification in the wake of a 1994 fire. Kingsley Hall (1897–1901, John H. Coxhead) is a large dormitory, consisting of a central pavilion flanked by towers. Now administration offices, the building known as the Old President's House (1897–1901, John H. Coxhead) has a semicircular porch and small, round attic windows in the corner tower, a design feature that appears on other buildings on the campus. The generous spacing of the buildings on the informally landscaped Virginia Union campus is representative of design during the era of the land grant universities.

Rising above this urban campus is the carillon of the most extraordinary structure of the Virginia Union buildings: the library (RI353.1) (1939, Victor Bourgeois, Leo Stijenen, and Henry Van de Velde; 1941, reconstruction, Hugo van Kuyck), which was built as the Belgian Pavilion for the 1939 New York World's Fair. Bourgeois and Stijenen designed the structure under the direction of Henry Van de Velde, an important early proponent of modernism and an early figure in the German Werkbund. The steel-frame building, designed on a U-shaped plan, was clad with brick, tiles, slate, and glass. It had elements of the International Style but with far more texture than is typical. The pavilion was originally intended to be moved to a university in Belgium after the fair, but this reuse was prevented by the outbreak of war in Europe. Instead, it was dismantled in New York and reassembled in Richmond (in a somewhat modified configuration) under the supervision of Hugo van Kuyck. The fabric of the building is symbolic of areas of Belgium: red tiles from Flanders, glass from Wallonia, and black slate from the Ardennes. Bas-relief panels by O. Jespers, H. Puvrez, and A. Dupagnes depicting culture and trade with the Belgian Congo and the international trade of Belgium serve as the principal decoration of this modernist structure.

The addition of the L. Douglas Wilder Library and Learning Resources Center (1994–1997, Livas Group) marks the return to the gabled and gray stone block flavor of the original Victorian structures at Virginia Union if not their elegance or significance. They are postmodern in style with large gable roofs, the stone only a thin veneer over a steel structural cage.

South of the James   (RI354–RI360)

Richmond south of the James River is both industrial and suburban. The area has been known by various names, including Manchester, a town annexed by the city in 1910. This part of Richmond is ignored by many visitors but is worthy of inspection.

RI354 **Philip Morris, Inc.**

1964, operations center, Ulrich Franzen and Associates. 1973, manufacturing center, Skidmore, Owings and Merrill. 4001 Commerce Rd. (Bells Rd. exit off I-95). Portions open to the public for tours

Philip Morris, Inc., conducts one of the world's largest cigarette research and manufacturing operations on this 200-acre site along I-95 in South Richmond. This campus of connected buildings also clearly demonstrates the company's corporate leadership in good architecture. Among them is a low-rise operations building by Ulrich Franzen Associates and the sprawling, 1.6 million-square-foot manufacturing center, designed by Gordon Bunshaft of Skidmore, Owings and Merrill. Stylistically the group of blocky forms arranged in an overlapping pattern might be called late International Style. Materials are the usual palette of brick, concrete, and glass. Of interest is the attempt at sun screens with pierced concrete panels. While the impact of the buildings has been subdued by the planting of large shade trees, a strikingly large information pylon graphically depicts the company's product logos. This feature was designed by the internationally known graphic design firm of Chermayeff and Geismar.

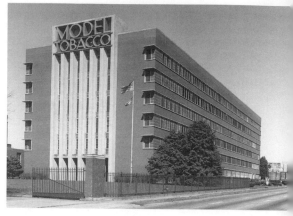

RI355 Model Tobacco

RI355 Model Tobacco

1938–1940, Schmidt, Garden, and Erikson. 11 Jefferson Davis Hwy. (U.S. 1)

Much of the industrial Southside, or the manufacturing area south of the James River, is unmemorable, but this building is one of the few exceptions. A significant piece of Streamline Moderne architecture, the Model Tobacco building also illuminates the new way in which buildings, formerly seen at pedestrian speed and close up, were experienced in the early automobile age. This powerful, boxy, six-story building looms above U.S. 1 as motorists approach at highway speeds. The horizontal ribbon windows on the street side of the brick structure only add to the streamlined sense of speed. At each end of the building, stylized engaged piers carry the eye to the words "Model Tobacco" in sans serif lettering embedded like graphic relief near the roofline. Designed by a well-known Chicago firm that participated in the commercial building revolution at the turn of the twentieth century, it brought to conservative Richmond a superb example of industrial architecture.

Southside Suburbs: Woodland Heights, Forest Hill Annex, Westover Hills (RI356–RI360)

These Southside suburbs form a necklace of distinct neighborhoods along Riverside Drive to the north, Semmes and Forest Hill avenues to the south, and Forest Hill Park in the center. During most of the nineteenth century, granite quarries and rugged woodland characterized the area. This all changed in 1888 when Richmond introduced the world's first successful electric streetcar system. In 1889 the Richmond and Southside Electric Railway Company and the Southside Land and Improvement Company founded the suburb of Woodland Heights and established the Forest Hill streetcar line. The line terminated at Forest Hill Park, which was developed as part of this venture.

The developers of Woodland Heights attempted to lure city dwellers with large lots, fresh spring water, and a clean rural environment, all of which was just a fifteen-minute streetcar ride from downtown. Unfortunately, the economic depression of the 1890s stunted development after it had barely begun. Only a few houses went up during this period. Development slowly returned after the turn of the century. In 1908 Forest Hill Annex was laid out to the west of Forest Hill Park along Forest Hill Avenue. Annexation in 1914 and the resulting improved city services spurred development in these areas.

By shortly after World War I, Woodland Heights and Forest Hill Annex were largely complete. Several real estate companies platted newer subdivisions to the west. The most substantial of these was Westover Hills, planned in 1928. These subdivisions were situated beyond the streetcar line and clearly oriented to automobile commuting. Amenities for the automotive suburbanite in-

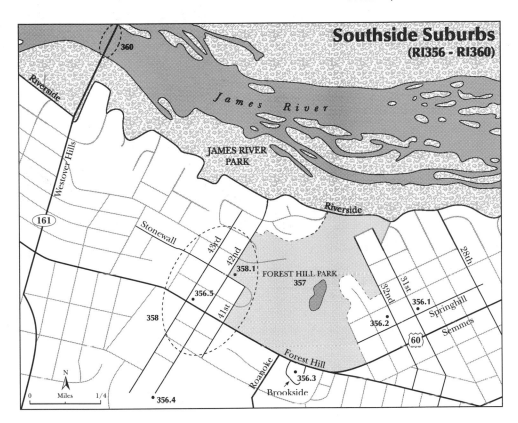

Southside Suburbs
(RI356 - RI360)

cluded a toll bridge (which in 1928 linked the area to the Byrd Park area on the north side of the river) and the development of Riverside Drive. By 1940, the city of Richmond had linked riverside streets in the various subdivisions into Riverside Drive, a single parkway from Cowardin Avenue on the east to Westover Hills on the west.

RI356 Woodland Heights

The Woodland Heights subdivision is situated on a large plateau above the James River. The neighborhood is characterized by blocks of long lots that face the north-south (numbered) streets. The median of Semmes Avenue, the main east-west thoroughfare of the neighborhood, denotes the former streetcar route, which extended down Semmes Avenue and out Forest Hill Avenue to the terminus at Forest Hill Park. The original (1889) street plan, laid out by civil engineer A. Langstaff Johnson, failed to take advantage of riverside views, an amenity provided in 1909 with the addition of Crestview and Ferncliff Avenues. The residential architecture of the neighborhood is characterized by a few Victorian homes and bungalows dispersed among a large num-

ber of Foursquare houses. The majority of the neighborhood buildings are simple frame houses constructed between 1910 and 1925. The 2700 block of Hillcrest Road was also added to Woodland Heights in 1909 to take advantage of the bluffs overlooking the James River. The substantial Georgian Revival homes on this street reflect the prominence of their riverfront location.

RI356.1 Woodland Heights Baptist Church

1916–1917, James M. McMichael. W. 31st St. and Springhill Ave.

This exuberant red brick Georgian Revival church with a full Ionic portico is one of the major landmarks of Woodland Heights. McMichael designed a number of Baptist churches in Virginia and North Carolina. As is typical of Baptist churches of the period, the interior is a large auditorium with a gallery in the rear.

RI356.2 Mann House

c. 1890. c. 1910, porch addition. 518 32nd St.

This impressive example of Queen Anne architecture was pictured in early promotional literature for Woodland Heights. Unfortunately, the economic depression of the 1890s put a stop to lavish architectural essays such as this. The design was probably taken from a pattern book such as those by George Barber. Constructed of wood with a corner tower, it displays a variety of ornamental details including half-timbering, scroll-sawn brackets, and turned spindle posts. The side bay with the second-floor loggia combines both Queen Anne and the earlier Eastlake motifs.

RI356.3 Brookside Avenue

1910–1920

A short street that loops through one of the more interesting subdivisions in the city, this mini-neighborhood possesses a coherent and impressive array of Tudor and Arts and Crafts houses, including several bungalows.

RI356.4 Norcroft Apartments Community Center

1911, Walter Dabney Blair. c. 1980, additions. 401 Norcroft Circle (at 42nd St.)

William Northrop, president of the Virginia Railway and Power Company (successor to the Richmond and Southside Electric Railway Company) built this frame Georgian Revival house to promote streetcar suburb living. The house was originally entered through the Forest Hill Annex neighborhood via 42nd Street and a private bridge (demolished) over Reedy Creek. The design derives from the south front of Mount Vernon. The architect purposely offset the entrance and employed a hipped roof with dormers and Chinese railings on the side porticoes. After being vacant for many years the property was acquired for apartment development. Plans originally called for leveling the mansion, but a public outcry caused the developer to reconsider. The result is that today the mansion serves as the community center for

the development. One-story apartment buildings now dot the grounds, their designs reflecting the original house.

RI356.5 Good Shepherd Episcopal Church

c. 1915. Forest Hill Ave. at 43rd St.

The modest brick Gothic Revival church reflects the inspiration of English country churches popularized by Ralph Adams Cram in his *Church Building* (1898). Cram's presence at the University of Richmond helped spark a wave of Neo-Gothic church building in the 1910s. The building also looks back to early Virginia Anglican churches such as St. Luke's, Isle of Wight County. The interior has wainscoting and stucco walls, and an open truss roof of wood and metal cables. The pews have tall endpieces containing trefoils.

RI357 Forest Hill Park

1889, A. Langstaff Johnston, civil engineer. 1934, public park improvements. James River on the north, Forest Hill and Semmes avenues on the south, and various streets on the east and west

Johnston laid out this park of approximately 100 acres concurrently with the Woodland Heights subdivision. In 1889, with the exception of some granite quarrying, the park was largely in a natural state, and the initial improvements consisted only of paths and bridges. The park was intended as an amenity for Woodland Heights residents and as a "Mecca of the lovers of nature," as promotional literature touted it. Apparently, nature was not a sufficient attraction, and after 1900 the Virginia Railway and Power Company constructed an amusement park to increase streetcar ridership. Closed during the Great Depression, the property was deeded to the city of Richmond in 1934. The city demolished the amusement park and built modest amenities such as picnic shelters.

RI358 Forest Hill Annex

The Forest Hill Land Company laid out this subdivision to the west and southwest of Forest Hill Park in 1906. The neighborhood is interesting because of the diversity of lot sizes and variety of architectural styles. Lots range from relatively compact properties along or near Forest Hill Avenue to virtual estates in the inte-

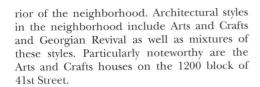

RI356.2 Mann House

RI356.3 Brookside Avenue

rior of the neighborhood. Architectural styles in the neighborhood include Arts and Crafts and Georgian Revival as well as mixtures of these styles. Particularly noteworthy are the Arts and Crafts houses on the 1200 block of 41st Street.

RI358.1 Holden Rhodes House (Old Stone House)

1836. 1936, renovation. West 41st St. at Stonewall St.

This vernacular stone cottage was constructed as the country house of a Manchester businessman. The building is an anomaly, one of the few stone buildings in the Richmond area built before the 1880s. The cottage has undergone some extensive porch modifications. Originally a simple entrance porch graced the structure. By 1900, when the building served as a trolley terminal, a veranda encircled it. In 1936 a local garden club restored the structure and added a replica of the Gothic porch of the river front at Gunston Hall in Fairfax County.

RI359 Westover Hills

The subdivision of Westover Hills, laid out in 1928 by James H. Saville, engineer, is distinguished by curvilinear streets near the river. Westover Hills Boulevard, which links the Boulevard Bridge on the north to Forest Hill Avenue, divides the neighborhood unevenly in two. Westover Hills has an impressive array of Georgian and other historical revival styles, and was one of the first distinctively automobile suburbs in the Richmond area.

RI360 Boulevard Bridge

1928. 1995, renovation

The developers of Westover Hills built this narrow truss bridge to provide a direct automobile connection to the near west end of Richmond. Renovation of the bridge replaced the decking and railing and reduced the sidewalks from two to one. Even though the toll now is 25 cents, Richmonders still euphemistically refer to it as the Nickel Bridge.

West of Richmond (RI361–RI373)

This tour includes the western section of Henrico County, from the western edge of Richmond west to Goochland County, with the James River on the south and U.S. 250 (Broad Street Road) on the north. The area, which was settled before Richmond was founded, is generally characterized as post–World War II suburbia. Its gently rolling hills and riverine val-

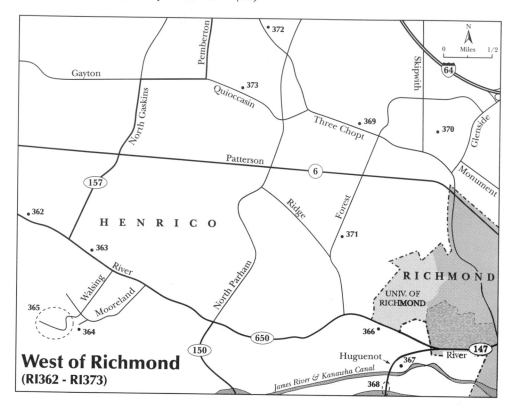

West of Richmond
(RI362 - RI373)

leys offered fertile lands for agriculture and, later, excellent opportunities for prime residential development. Remains of the plantation economy, such as Tuckahoe (just over the line in Goochland County and included in Piedmont section), still exist, as well as of coal mining, in traces of railroad beds in the Gayton Road area, from which coal was delivered along the Kanawha Canal. Vestiges of historic farms have survived in subdivision names: Westham, Windsor-on-the-James, Tuckahoe Place, Sleepy Hollow, Charter Oaks, Canterbury.

RI361 Reynolds Metals Company Executive Office Building

1953–1958, Skidmore, Owings and Merrill, Gordon Bunshaft, architect; Charles F. Gillette, landscape architect. 6601 W. Broad St. Lobby open to the public

Richard S. Reynolds, the founder of Reynolds Metals Company and a nephew of R. J. Reynolds, himself founder of the tobacco company, began in the soap business and wound up producing cigarette foil. In 1940 the corporate headquarters was relocated from New York to downtown Richmond. That same year the company became an aluminum producer. During World War II Reynolds Metals provided nearly a billion pounds of aluminum for use in mili-

tary equipment. Reynolds Wrap was introduced in 1947, and in 1963 the company produced the first all-aluminum twelve-ounce beverage can.

MIT-trained Gordon Bunshaft, head designer for Skidmore, Owings and Merrill's New York office, was also responsible for other nationally acclaimed corporate headquarters buildings, including Lever House, New York (1949–1952), and the Connecticut General Life Building, Bloomfield, Connecticut (1954–1957). The Reynolds headquarters showcases the company's major product: aluminum is employed as trim; for the sun louvers on the south, east, and west facades; on interior partitions; and for hardware, special file cabinets, furni-

RI361 Reynolds Metals Company Executive Office Building

RI362 Duval-Druin House

systems. A restrained complement to the rectilinear formality of the building is the interior court, a design incorporating gridded squares of grass and flowers, a magnolia tree, and a fountain, by Charles F. Gillette, the landscape architect for some of Richmond's finer "Banker's Georgian" houses. Positioned on a prominent rise, the building is an early corporate temple. Although he never admitted to the classical tendencies of the design, Bunshaft did remark: "This is how a temple should have been approached." Furnished with modern furniture, the building remains in pristine condition. It has been acquired by the University of Richmond for use as a conference center.

RI362 **Duval-Druin House**

c. 1760. c. 1880, front addition. 1994, restoration. 9904 River Rd. (corner of River Rd. and River Ct. Ln.; house is visible on the left)

The original house is believed to have been built for Samuel Druin, an English barber who worked for the Randolphs of Tuckahoe. The modest one-and-one-half-story hall-parlor dwelling was built on land near Tuckahoe plantation. The older section, now at the rear of the building and visible from the adjacent subdivision road, is identified by its large exterior chimneys with tiled shoulders. An 1880s Italianate addition, built by the Duval family, dominates the front. Possibly one of the oldest yeoman farmer's houses left in the county, the evolved Duval-Druin House was carefully rehabilitated in 1994.

RI363 **Whichello**

c. 1827. 9602 River Rd. (east of Gaskins Rd., next to Second Baptist Church)

Also known as the Tall House, Whichello is one the most visually prominent historic buildings on western River Road. It was built on land that was originally part of the Randolph family's Tuckahoe plantation for Catherine Woodward or for Richard Whichello, who ran a tavern here beginning in the late 1830s. Local lore recounts that Whichello was murdered by a cattle drover in a gambling dispute and was buried in the basement to prevent his slaves from mutilating his body. The tall frame building is set upon a slightly sunken English basement and rises to include a finished garret. The full-width porch and the unusual projecting eaves and

ture, and interior ductwork. Even the carpets were woven with aluminum fibers. The total weight of aluminum products used throughout the structure is 1,235,800 pounds. The sun louvers are controlled by an astronomical clock, which adjusts them according to the time of day. On overcast days, an electrical override allows them to stay open for maximum natural light. The second and third floors appear to hover upon a pedestal, and the aluminum-clad steel members lining the facades are reminiscent of the columnar divisions of a classical temple.

Completely symmetrical, with an open-air central court, the building features horizontal layering: base, piano nobile, and cornice, the composition common to the Italian palazzo tradition. The geometric lightness of the design is underscored by the reflecting pool (205,000 gallons) that fronts the entrance facade and serves as a reservoir for cooling and irrigation

cornice returns were probably later modifications. The property includes several outbuildings, extremely rare in this suburbanized area of the county.

RI364 Mooreland

1919, Henry Baskervill. 8901 Brennan Rd. (east on River Rd., right on South Mooreland Rd., .7 mile to Brennan Rd.)

The imposing Mediterranean Villa style house, behind a stucco wall and complete with red clay pantile roof, was designed by Richmond architect Henry Baskervill for Thomas L. Moore. The Moores operated a dairy farm, some of which was intact until the 1980s. With an imposing central tower, the tripartite fifteen-bay house is one of the largest mansions built in Richmond's western suburbs. The white, stucco-covered Mediterranean-inspired house contrasts sharply with the predominant Anglo-influenced brick buildings of the area.

RI365 Mooreland Landing

c. 1992. Mooreland Rd. (Mooreland Farms) (left on S. Mooreland Rd., left into Mooreland Landing through a brick gate)

One of the most recent "high end" subdivisions in western Henrico County, Mooreland Landing features some of the largest and most exaggerated postmodern colonial-style houses in the county; it is traditional Virginia on steroids.

RI366 Westham Plantation House

c. 1850. c. 1910–1920, additions. 6601 River Rd. (River Rd. east, left onto Highland Rd.; the house is on the right)

Believed to be the overseer's house for the 2,000-acre Westham Plantation, this antebellum building was updated with a rear two-story addition, Doric portico, and modillioned cornice sometime during the second decade of this century. The tall five-course brick bond chimneys are vestiges of the building's vernacular origins. Its present image falls into the familiar hybrid of Colonial Revival and Greek Revival styles popular in the first half of the twentieth century throughout this region. The formal classical front is enhanced by a deep front lawn that features specimen trees.

RI367 Virginia Eye Center

1990, Bond Comet Westmoreland and Hiner. Huguenot Bridge, north end (River Road Shopping Center, right toward the Huguenot Bridge, building is on the left)

This large building with complex, low-slung gables appears to float several feet above the floodplain. Obviously built with some care to accommodate the floodwaters of the James, it is one of the finer among the more recent office buildings in western Henrico County.

RI368 Huguenot Bridge and Kanawha Canal

1949, Huguenot Bridge. c. 1789, Kanawha Canal

An earlier metal truss bridge crossed the James River several hundred feet west of the present concrete and steel bridge. Old Bridge Lane, now a quiet suburban street, was the approach. The late 1940s replacement bridge has a delicate metal rail that allows views of the riverscape. Westham Station Road, which extends on the west side of the bridge, runs along one of the more intact sections of the Kanawha Canal. This is part of the first section completed between Richmond and the village of Westham. The Chesapeake and Ohio train tracks were laid in 1889 on the towpath, on the south side of the canal. George Washington's vision of a transportation route west was finally realized by rail, despite persistent efforts through the late 1870s to operate the canal.

RI369 Cheswick

c. 1830. 8106 Three Chopt Rd.

Cheswick was probably built for George G. Exall, who advertised his "Cheswick Classical & English School" in an 1857 edition of the *American Democrat* newspaper. The substantial tract, later referred to as Franklin Farm, survived through the post–World War II building boom, but in the early 1970s the Franklin family sold it to Koger Properties. The house was spared demolition when, to make way for the Koger Executive Center, the new owners moved it about 500 feet west. The one-and-one-half-story, heavy timber-frame house was set on an already existing raised English basement. The five-bay, center-hall plan has survived, as have the original exterior and interior trim. The exterior end chimneys are reconstructions.

RI370 **Skipwith Academy** (Bekeby)

1927. 7344 Townes Rd.

This well-designed Tudor–Jacobean Revival house, built in 1927 for Grey Skipwith, Sr., has outstanding brickwork and extensive decorative detail. The building that houses the garage and chauffeur's quarters, which now almost blends in with the surrounding brick tract houses, is sited behind Bekeby facing onto Harlow Road (drive south on Townes Road until it curves around into Harlow Road). Bekeby stands on a small part of the tract Grey Skipwith, Sr., divided between his sons, Grey, Jr., an admiral of the U.S. Navy, and Hugh, a tobacco industry executive. Bekeby features an irregular plan with a projecting stair tower on the rear. The brick exterior showcases cut stone, inlaid panels with the Skipwith crest, wrought

RI371 Paradise

RI373 Best Products Company Store (former)

iron Jacobean-style lamps, and false wooden timbering. The house is entered from a low-walled cobblestone court. The slate-roofed garage and servants' quarters are built of similar materials. Today Bekeby provides an unusual contrast to the small 1950s subdivision houses that surround it.

RI371 **Paradise and Tuckahoe School**

1825, Paradise. 821 Carrington Ct. 1949, Tuckahoe School. 700 block of Forest Ave., adjacent to Lindsay Dr. (Forest Ave., 1 mile to Lindsay Dr., school is visible from Lindsay)

Paradise, built for Dr. Thomas Patterson, is a two-story weatherboarded frame I-house surrounded by large subdivision houses that were built in the early 1990s. Several early outbuildings stand at the rear of the property. A former resident, Mrs. Tucker Carrington, taught first and second grade in the basement until Tuckahoe School was finished in the late 1940s. Tuckahoe School is a sharp contrast to the frame house. The two-tone yellow-tan brick school is one of the finest Moderne buildings in the county. The main entrance features a conical roof and a steel-rimmed covered entry with freestanding steel letters spelling out "Tuckahoe School."

RI372 **Blackburn**

c. 1830–1840. 9118 Three Chopt Rd. (on the right shortly after passing Dresden Rd.)

This traditional one-and-one-half-story I-house was probably built for Albert Blackburn sometime in the second quarter of the nineteenth century. The form of the house, with its steep roof, double-shouldered chimneys, and small garret windows, is typical of eastern Virginia farmhouses from the late eighteenth to the mid-nineteenth century. Although the front windows were enlarged sometime in the early twentieth century, Blackburn is the most intact example of an early nineteenth-century yeoman's farm in western Henrico County.

RI373 **Best Products Company Store** (former)

1978, James Wines and SITE. Quioccasin Rd. (across from Blue Jay Ln.)

Sydney and Frances Lewis founded Best Products in 1957. Their love for modern art and architecture overlapped with their vision of a corporate image. They commissioned James Wines and his firm, SITE, of New York City, to design a series of showrooms. Wines, trained as a sculptor, characterized his work as "de-architecture." The Quioccasin store was built to reflect the heavily wooded surroundings. A sliver of space planted with trees splits away the plain glass fa-

cade from the bulk of the showroom. Exotic landscaping in the parking lot and an unexpected green lobby prefaced a typical 1970s store interior. Best Products closed operations in 1997. In an unusual instance of adaptive reuse, the building was acquired by a Presbyterian church.

North of Richmond　(RI374–RI389)

Metropolitan Richmond in the northern part of Henrico County and the southern portion of Hanover County represents a sharp contrast between intense commercial and suburban development around U.S. 250, U.S. 1, I-95, and I-295 and adjacent rural areas. Once predominantly open farmland, this northern area has been transformed into a thriving commercial strip, beginning with the extension of Richmond's earlier automobile-related architecture. Willow Lawn, the area's oldest post–World War II shopping mall, opened in 1956, and the conversion from farm to automobile culture has occurred since then. Development continues to consume small crossroads communities like Short Pump. The following focuses on building adjacent to and north of U.S. 250.

RI374　Enterprise Center (Markel Building)

1966, Haig Jamgochian. 5310 Markel Dr. (W. Broad St. to Willow Lawn Dr., right on to Markel Dr.)

The Markel Corporation, an insurance company, set up business in downtown Richmond in the 1930s. When the company decided to move its business to the county, Richmond architect Haig Jamgochian was commissioned to design a unique building. Finished in 1966, the result is one of the most eye-catching, idiosyncratic modern buildings on all of Broad Street, and perhaps in all of the Richmond area. The Markel Building's shape may have been influenced by Frank Lloyd Wright's circular Guggenheim Museum in New York City. The steel and concrete structural system was clad in an aluminum skin, crinkled by rubber mallet–wielding workers. Today the building appears as a charismatic modern design from a period when architects were searching for innovative materials and shapes. A reaction to the strait-laced glass box, the Markel Building symbolized a departure from the somber, grid-clad conformity of the corporate world.

RI375　Lawrence Chrysler-Plymouth Dealership

c. 1965. 4808 W. Broad St. (northeast corner of W. Broad St. and Staples Mill Rd. intersection)

Current strip architecture is often insubstantial, built to last only a generation. The Lawrence Plymouth-Dodge dealership exudes the pride of the "jet age" 1960s. The round showroom with a white undulating concrete "parachute" roof captures the eye. The formal allusion here may be to the University of Virginia's U Hall, a large sports arena in Charlottesville. The U Hall roof was a symbol of architectural daring and progress in Richmond, where the architectural aesthetic favors gable and hipped roofs, even on commercial buildings. The striking design features original slant "7"-shaped lampposts.

RI376　Westland Shopping Center Sign

c. 1960. South side of 8000 block of W. Broad St.

Compared to its contemporary, Willow Lawn Shopping Center, this was truly in the "west lands" of Henrico County, so far west that a cactus was deemed appropriate for a logo. The sheet-metal box construction of the Westland Shopping Center sign is a rare survivor. Mod-

RI374 Enterprise Center (Markel Building)

RI376 Westland Shopping Center Sign

ern signs are built with lighter, less expensive materials—in most cases, plastics and plexiglass. The cactus sign incorporates neon lighting and is surrounded by a planting bed within a brick-walled base. Apparently the sign has received regular maintenance to keep it functional and brightly painted.

RI377 Lewis Ginter Botanical Gardens (Bloemendaal Farm) and Lakeside Area

c. 1880s–1930. Bloemendaal Farm, 1800 Lakeside Ave. (Lakeside Area starts at the county line on Lakeside Ave. at the south and continues past the Botanical Gardens to U.S. 1. Open to the public

The Bloemendaal Farm, a property that was once part of Patrick Henry's extensive holdings, was improved from a bicycle clubhouse to a comfortable estate at the turn of the twentieth century by Lewis Ginter's niece, Grace Arents. The rambling, Dutch Colonial–influenced mansion with its gambrel roof is complemented by a complex of outbuildings. The carriage house features a shingled tower, a creative solution to hide a utilitarian water tank. Part of the estate shared a large pond with Lakeside Park, an amusement park accessible from the city by streetcar. The pond survives, and the approach to the house now features one of the most elaborate gardens in the Richmond area. The Lewis Ginter Botanical Gardens have an ambitious master plan, and new parts of the complex are constructed every year. Lakeside Avenue, the main artery ap-

proaching the Botanical Gardens from the south, passes by neighborhoods of bungalows and Cape Cod colonial houses referred to collectively as Lakeside, one of the few Henrico County areas that has village characteristics.

RI378 Richmond, Fredericksburg, and Potomac Railroad Section Manager's House

c. 1900. 11010 Old Washington Hwy. (.75 mile from Mountain Rd., on the left)

This building is an unusual survivor. The Richmond, Fredericksburg and Potomac Railroad built section managers' houses at various points. Most were built from a common plan, and it seems likely that most of the materials, if not prefabricated sections of the buildings, were shipped to the site by rail. The board-and-batten siding gives the house a vaguely Gothic Revival look.

RI379 Meadow Farm Museum (at Crump Park)

c. 1800 and later. 3400 Mountain Rd. Open to the public

Here in 1800 two slaves informed Mosby Sheppard that Gabriel Prosser was organizing a slave rebellion. The miscreants were stopped and punished, and the event caused a series of reforms that diminished the rights of enslaved and freed blacks in Virginia.

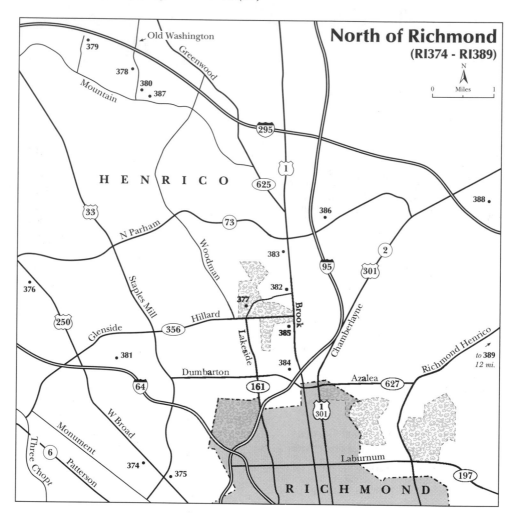

North of Richmond
(RI374 - RI389)

The property is now a Henrico County park comprising a series of buildings. The main structure is the Sheppard-Crump house (c. 1800, c. 1820, c. 1840, c. 1854; 1990, restoration), a one-and-one-half-story, five-bay, gable-roofed wooden I-house. It was built as a side-entrance, three-bay I-house; two bays were added to the west end for a parlor c. 1820. A shed-roofed porch, later enclosed, was added c. 1840, along with the Greek Revival entrance portico. Around 1854 a two-story wing with bracketed eaves was added to the rear, making a T-shaped plan. The house apparently remained unpainted until the 1930s. Restored to the period 1830–1860, it contains mostly original furnishings. Also on the property are outbuildings for animals and a blacksmith shed, both original and reconstructions that illus-

trate the farm life of a mid-nineteenth-century Virginia farm. The museum also owns a significant collection of Richmond-area folk art.

RI380 Henrico County Cultural Arts Center (Glen Allen School)

1911. 1914, 1919, 1926, additions. 1936, Auditorium Building. 1939, Home Economics Cottage. 1950s, rear addition. 1997–1999, conversion, W. Kent Cooper. 10771 Old Washington Hwy.

Glen Allen School was founded in 1886 by Elizabeth Jane Holladay, known locally as Miss Lizzie. She was thirty-eight years old when she began teaching children on the second floor of her simple frame home on Mountain Road. In 1899 a one-acre lot on the north side of Mountain Road was chosen as the site of a one-room schoolhouse, which was replaced by the present school in 1911. The oldest part of the complex is the two-story brick section with a bell tower containing a cast iron bell weighing more than 150 pounds. The additions built after 1919 were designed by the School Buildings Service of the Virginia Department of Education. Two attractive Colonial Revival buildings were constructed on the Glen Allen School grounds during the 1930s. The Depression-era auditorium (1936) and home economics cottage (1939) were probably funded by the Public Works Administration. The home economics cottage was basically a Cape Cod Colonial Revival house, the design probably supplied by the School Buildings Service. (Almost every high school in the county received exactly the same design.) The county has converted the school complex into a cultural arts center. The original front entry has been closed and a new, postmodern entry placed at the rear.

RI381 Penick House

c. 1815–1820. 4815 Belleglade Dr.

The Regency design work here compares to that of the Wickham-Valentine House in Richmond, making Penick House the most sophisticated antebellum house in Henrico County. The stucco exterior has recessed panels, and offset windows, also set in recessed panels, create a quirky fenestration pattern in the rear wall. The low hipped roof and rigid symmetry bespeak an architect's hand, but none has been identified. The house, once the center of a large farm, has been crowded in by 1950s subdivision houses.

RI382 Credit Car America (The Copa)

c. 1930. 7300 Brook Rd. (U.S. 1) (northwest corner of intersection of Brook Rd. and Lakeside Ave.)

The Spanish Colonial Revival references of this local landmark may have been drawn from St. Joseph's Villa (see below) about a half mile north of the Copa. The Copa has been well maintained, and it is an attractive commercial building in an area where the life span of commercial architecture is usually limited to a few decades. Directly across the street is a small tourist court, a rare survivor among the diners, tourist courts, and other roadside attractions that once occupied this stretch of U.S. 1.

RI382 Credit Car America (The Copa)

RI383 St. Joseph's Villa

1931, Carneal, Johnston and Wright. 8000 Brook Rd. (U.S. 1)

Father Timothy O'Brien founded an orphan asylum and school here in the 1830s. The collection of buildings now on the campus ranks among the most architecturally sophisticated ensembles in Henrico County. Carneal, Johnston and Wright drew upon a strain of Romanesque and Spanish Colonial Revival architecture that Charles D. Maginnis of Boston had promoted as suitable for Catholic churches and institutions. Maginnis was the Catholic architectural apostle and played a role similar to that of Ralph Adams Cram among Protestants. The Carneal architect obviously drew upon publications in designing the buildings. Constructed of yellow brick, the complex includes a towered chapel, large dormitories, and its own power plant. The chapel contains mosaics. The landscaping also bespeaks care in its strategically planted shade trees. A sunken area behind the campus marks the site of the Richmond-Ashland streetcar line. An early concrete pedestrian bridge still spans the sunken bed.

RI384 Emmanuel Episcopal Church

1859, Charles Hall. 1214 Wilmer Ave. (enter from Brook Rd. north of I-95)

Built for John Stewart of Brook Hill and designed by a Providence, Rhode Island, architect, this brick and stone church is one of the most sophisticated buildings in Henrico County for the period. It is Gothic Revival in

RI384 Emmanuel Episcopal Church

RI386 Best Corporation Headquarters

RI386 **Bank America Services** (Best Corporation Headquarters)

1981, Hardy Holzman Pfeiffer. c. 1989, Marcellus Wright, Cox and Smith. 1400 E. Parham Rd. (I-95 intersection with Parham Rd., east of I-95)

style, with a tower that shows the influence of William Butterfield and of English design on American architects in the 1850s. The Emmanuel Memorial Parish House (1910) stands nearby. Adjacent to the parklike setting of the church is the Wilmer Avenue Historic Area, which includes late nineteenth-century cottages associated with the Ginter estate (reputedly the gardeners' houses), along with later bungalows and Foursquare houses.

RI385 **North Run Bridge**

1938. U.S. 1, southbound lane only (.25 mile north of Brook Run Shopping Center)

The North Run Bridge serves U.S. 1. This interstate road was given its numerical designation by the federal government in 1925 to reflect its significance as the major highway from Maine to Florida, designed to tie together the major cities of the East Coast. When the North Run Bridge was built, the road was only two lanes wide in this vicinity. The bridge is of reinforced concrete construction, with three Gothic-arched spans. It rests on concrete abutments with span arches that repeat the Gothic motif. The North Run Bridge is a good example of a type of bridge that is becoming increasingly rare on Virginia's highways.

Best Corporation began in 1957, evolving from a family mail-order merchandising business. The company, run by Sydney and Frances Lewis, major patrons of the arts, commissioned several highly unusual showroom facades from James Wines and Robert Venturi. In 1981, with 100 showrooms and annual sales of more than $1 billion, the company moved its corporate headquarters from Ashland, in Hanover County, to this new building, designed in a postmodern style unexpected in a corporate headquarters. The building won an American Institute of Architects Honor Award for architectural excellence.

The primary facade is an aquamarine wall that sweeps in a broad curve across a site visible from Parham Road. It is composed of glass block with cut-stone molded trim lines. The glass block is a legacy of Art Deco and Moderne architectural detailing of the 1930s, 1940s, and 1950s, while the cut stone is perhaps a reference to the classical detailing often employed for federal government and bank buildings. A pool fronts the facade like a moat, and for artistic purposes, it reflects a wavering light across the glass brick. The entrance is formally introduced by two large sculptures of stone eagles topped by lanterns rescued from the demolition of New York City's old East Side Airlines Building (1939–1940), which stood opposite Grand Central Terminal. At their original site, the eagles perched on the roof of the terminal,

RI388 Richmond Times-Dispatch Newspapers Plant

several stories above a busy city street. Now these massive Moderne objects direct pedestrian circulation into the main entry. The addition, designed by Marcellus Wright, Cox and Smith, contrasts sharply with the original building in a fitting postmodern manner. The Best Company ceased operations in 1997, and other tenants now occupy the building.

RI387 Walkerton

c. 1825. 2892 Mountain Rd.

One of a few surviving tavern buildings in eastern Virginia, Walkerton, named for John Walker, who built it, may also rank as one of the largest. The four-chimney, five-bay brick structure rests on a high English basement. The first floor shows evidence of a "cage bar," and on the

second floor is an unusual hinged panel wall that folds in and out, originally to create private space for overnight lodgers. An early kitchen and laundry building stands to the rear, along with a smokehouse and the Hopkins family cemetery. The Hopkinses owned the house for more than 100 years, beginning in the 1830s. The property, recently restored, is now owned by the county and will be used as part of its history program.

RI388 Richmond Times-Dispatch Newspapers Plant

1990–1992, Baskervill and Son. Times-Dispatch Blvd. (I-295, exit 41, U.S. 301 north, .3 mile), Hanover County

A stunning high-tech newspaper printing plant, the sprawling 428,000-square-foot building is sheathed in aluminum panels of three different colors that delineate the different sections. Exposed structural steel is visible through clerestory window bands.

RI389 Immanuel Episcopal Church

1851–1853, 1879–1881, remodeling. 1916, 1967, interior refurbishing. VA 606 (Old Church Rd.; 1.7 miles east of U.S. 360, south side of the road), Mechanicsville

Quaintly "Hansel and Gretel" Gothic with its twin towers and elaborate window moldings, this church began as a simple rectangular box. A post–Civil War remodeling gave it the odd Gothic imagery of the tower, pinnacles, and windows. The interior has been refurbished several times.

East of Richmond (RI390–RI402)

The eastern end of Henrico County is often known by its historic name, Varina. The name originally denoted a strain of tobacco cultivated by Native Americans, which John Rolfe, a superb marketer, introduced in England. Varina contains some of the county's most significant historic sites. Here Nathaniel Bacon settled in the Curles Neck area, near the ancestral homes of the Cockes and Randolphs (Thomas Jefferson's ancestors were the Randolphs of Turkey Island). Below the James River fall line, generations of Native Americans enjoyed plentiful hunting and fishing. The site of Powhatan's village is thought to be in the floodplain vicinity of the historic Tree Hill Farm, a 1770s farmhouse barely visible from Virginia 5, just east of the Richmond city limits. Here, in the seventeenth century, Native Americans coexisted with the English, who lived on modest farmsteads. No architectural fabric survives

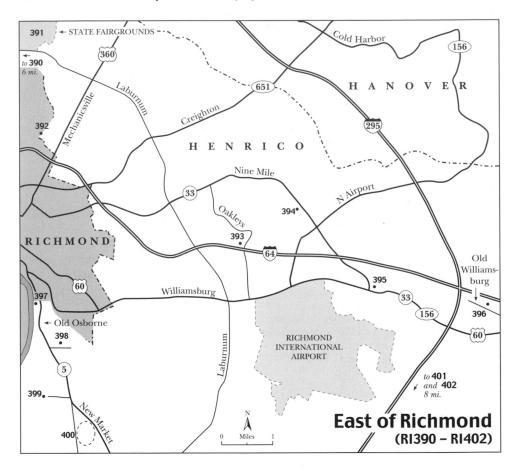

East of Richmond
(RI390 – RI402)

from the 1611 founders' period, and very little is left from the eighteenth century. Invasion of the area by Union troops twice during the Civil War, in 1862 and 1864, accounts for some architectural attrition. Three national cemeteries hold Union dead from battlefields at Fair Oaks, Seven Pines, Savage Station, New Market Heights, and Malvern Hill. The National Park Service has preserved some of the more intact trench lines and forts in its Richmond National Battlefield Park system. After the Civil War the agricultural community of Varina recovered, and demand for milk provided a market for major dairy operations in the early twentieth century. The city annexed the East Highland Park area, and, starting in the 1880s, trolley service—replaced later by large streetcars—was extended to the Seven Pines National Cemetery along what became Nine Mile Road. Henrico County's waterfront, adjacent to Richmond, became an extension of Richmond's late nineteenth-century industrial development. Here the Fulton rail yards became the focus of activity around which large factories were built. Sandston, one of the villages, started out as a military development around a World War I munitions plant and continued to thrive when Byrd Field evolved as a military facility. The military airfield later became Richmond International Airport. Although Varina has retained some of its rural character, the area has become ideal for industrial and suburban development.

RI390 Virginia Randolph–Mountain Road School Complex

1937. 2200 Mountain Rd. Open to the public

Virginia Randolph (1874–1958) began her teaching career in a small frame schoolhouse at this site. She kept an office in the one-and-one-half-story brick Colonial Revival Home Economics Cottage, which is now sited next to the Mountain Road School (c. 1935–1940), a Moderne structure. Randolph, recognized throughout the South as one of the most innovative among black educators, began her career in Henrico County in 1893. In 1903 she was selected to introduce a new form of teacher supervision throughout the county school system. She developed a method of teacher training that spread throughout the South and eventually to countries in Asia, Africa, and Latin America. Virginia Randolph died in 1958, after fifty-seven years of teaching. Her grave is at the school, in front of the Home Economics Cottage. The Home Economics Cottage was probably designed by the School Buildings Service of the Virginia Department of Education. The building and grave have been recognized as a National Historic Landmark.

RI391 Old Dominion Building, Virginia State Fairgrounds

1946, William Lawrence Bottomley, central fairgrounds area. Intersection of Laburnum Ave. and Richmond-Henrico Tpk.

The architect of this monumental, largely utilitarian building was better known for his academic Colonial Revival houses. The historic centerpiece of the present-day state fairgrounds, the Covered Ring, as Bottomley called

it, was designed and built in 1946 for the Atlantic Rural Exposition, Inc., for $116,000. The structure is of brick, with a two-story oval exhibition space capped by a hipped roof with twin ventilators. The directors of the Atlantic Rural Exposition named a committee to landscape the Covered Ring and appointed Bottomley as one of its members. Charles Gillette was asked to serve as the landscape architect, but he was allocated a minimal budget. One concept given consideration was to establish demonstration gardens at the exhibit grounds, to be titled Gardens on Parade. Whether this concept was carried out is not known, for the Covered Ring's landscaping does not survive. Today the building rises from an asphalt and gravel parking lot, the home of the Richmond area's NASCAR franchise.

RI392 Woodland Cemetery

Magnolia Rd.

Woodland Cemetery is one of the oldest black cemeteries in the Richmond area. It contains the graves of numerous prominent African Americans, including the notable Richmond minister John Jasper and the tennis star Arthur Ashe. Born in Richmond on July 10, 1943, Ashe was one of the great American tennis players. His professional accomplishments included championships at Wimbledon (1975), the Australian Open (1970), and the U.S. Open (1968). He also became known for his books, the three-volume series *A Hard Road to Glory: A History of the African American Athlete* (1988), and he collaborated with Arnold Rampersad on *Days of Grace: A Memoir* (1993). He died on February 6, 1993, in New York City after a prolonged battle against an HIV infection he acquired through blood transfusions. He is buried beside his mother. A wrought iron fence surrounds the site.

RI393 Mankin Mansion

c. 1921–1940, Edward Thurston Mankin. Oakleys Ln.

When Edward Thurston Mankin came to Richmond from Warren County he was a brickmason. By the mid-1920s he had become the operator of a factory that specialized in high-quality brick and special commissions. His products were used in buildings as far away as New York City, and he was the primary provider for Colonial Williamsburg and for Bottomley's Richmond-area houses. The massive beehive brick kilns that once sat adjacent to the Mankin House are now gone. Mankin built his quirky brick house near his plant in the early 1920s. A combination of Colonial Revival and Arts and Crafts idioms, the house and surrounding elements—brick paths, walls, and a strange pergola-like structure—were advertisements for his product. The rambling plan of the house gives the impression that the construction was additive; the different wings and chimneys appear to be demonstrations of construction experiments.

RI393 Mankin Mansion

RI394 Henrico Cinema

1940, Edward F. Sinnott. 300 block of E. Nine Mile Rd.

This is the most elaborate example of Moderne design still surviving in Henrico County. The monolithic stucco composition retains its original marquee and shiny metal hoods over the doors and windows. The name "Henrico" is proudly centered at the top of the tripartite front wall, above a clock. Henrico County has purchased the currently unusued structure and may locate a community hall here.

RI395 Seven Pines National Cemetery

c. 1866, Montgomery C. Meigs, quartermaster general, U.S. Army. Intersection of E. Nine Mile and Williamsburg rds.

Designs for the cemetery lodges at all of Virginia's national cemeteries came from the office of the quartermaster general of the army, engineer Montgomery Meigs, who also designed the monumental Pension Building in Washington, D.C. Although the building materials differed in some locations, all the lodges conformed to a standard type developed by the office, a single-story box with a mansard roof of slate. At Seven Pines, brick is the construction material for the walls above a rubble fieldstone base. The building has quoins at the corners and front and rear porches. Originally, the gravesites were marked with wooden headboards, most of which have been replaced with stones.

RI396 Cedar Knoll

c. 1820–1840. 3280 Old Williamsburg Rd.

Cedar Knoll survives on part of a stranded section of the old Williamsburg Road, which was replaced by U.S. 60 in the mid-twentieth century. The one-and-one-half-story I-house is frame with weatherboard and has a narrow east addition. It sits on a raised basement that helps give it a prominent image. Cedar Knoll is adjacent to the Savage Station Battlefield, and the house served as field hospital during the Civil War. The property also features a barn that may date from the nineteenth century.

RI397 Richmond Cedar Works

c. 1880. Old Osborne Tpk. (VA 5) (on the city-county border)

The Richmond Cedar Works comprises several large brick industrial buildings that sit at the border of the city of Richmond and Henrico County, where Virginia 5 leads into the county's Varina district. Cedar Works is one of few surviving factory buildings that once crowded this riverfront area, an extension of the Richmond seaport, called Rocketts. While the company is no longer in operation, at its peak in the twentieth century the Cedar Works employed 2,000 workers and produced washing machines, clothespins, churns, "ice cream freezers" (refrigerators), and tenners (barrels) for sauerkraut. During the same period the company owned 350,000 acres of land in Nansemond County's Great Dismal Swamp, a source of the plant's cedar supply. The size of the complex has been reduced in recent years.

RI398 Clarke-Palmore House (Marion Hill)

c. 1840. McCoul St. (west side of street at the top of the hill)

RI394 Henrico Cinema

The Clarke-Palmore House is part of an area known historically as Marion Hill. In contrast to the adjacent buildings, which are on small parcels of land, the house, a two-story, three-bay, side-hall-plan brick structure, still retains a moderately large plot. Also surviving are a brick smokehouse and a rare small brick barn. During the Civil War, Confederate defense Battery No. 7 stood several hundred yards south of the house. The hill area was used as a message station where coded messages were beamed by mirror from the roof of the state capitol to the upper floor of the Clarke-Palmore House, a distance of two miles. (Trees have since grown to obscure this view.) Henrico County recently purchased the property and is planning to preserve and interpret the building.

RI399 Tree Hill

c. 1780; later additions. Tree Hill Ln.–Private Dr. (off VA 5)

Most easily visible in the winter months when the trees that line the drive and provide a substantial surrounding canopy are bare, Tree Hill still lives up to its name. Built by Miles Selden, a delegate in Virginia's General Assembly, Tree Hill now displays its evolution through construction campaigns. Originally a moderately simple chimney-bracketed frame building, the house was updated c. 1808 with wings and front and rear porticoes. Several early outbuildings near the house include a smokehouse and kitchen. Selden's son-in-law, William Roane, who served in the U.S. Senate and House of Representatives, inherited the property in 1837. The Burlee family purchased

the property in 1910 and ran a successful dairy operation. Substantial early twentieth-century dairy buildings stand in the floodplain adjacent to the James River. Some of the most spectacular views of Tree Hill are from the James River, or from river vantage points along Richmond's eastern riverfront. Barely three miles away from the state capitol, Tree Hill's rural setting contrasts with the spectacular views of the modern Richmond skyline.

RI400 Capitol View–Antioch

c. 1890–1950. New Market Rd. (Virginia 5)

An African American community that had its start in the late nineteenth century, the Capitol View–Antioch area is a compact cluster of houses arranged around Henrico County's Virginia 5 corridor. In 1892, the Capitol View subdivision was laid out in lots along the west side of Virginia 5. Numbered avenues were arranged on a north-south axis, and present-day Herman Street ran east-west between New Market Road and Osborne Turnpike. Apparently Capitol View was an overly ambitious plan for the period, as the subdivision grid never filled out.

The oldest part of Capitol View is the Antioch Baptist Church area along Virginia 5. It includes the buildings that face the road on both sides from Herman to Loudoun Street. These include shotgun-plan, bungalow, and cottage dwellings; a former store; and a school. The buildings range in date from the 1890s through the 1960s. The Antioch Baptist Church (c. 1890, c. 1940) began as a wooden frame building. The present brick facade is a veneer over the original wooden structure. Stylistically, it is a combination of pointed windows and the earlier Greek Revival box of the Baptist church. To the rear of Antioch Church, not visible from the road, is the Chatsworth School, now vacant. This is one of a few surviving early twentieth-century school buildings in Henrico County.

RI401 Varina Plantation and Henrico Courthouse Site

c. 1855 (viewed from the east side of the Enon Bridge)

A large, late Greek Revival plantation house, Varina sits on land settled by John Rolfe in 1610. The site, still a substantial farm of 2,000 acres, was also the location of the county's earliest courthouse. The house is a substantial five-bay, two-story, hip-roofed structure with tall chimneys and a bracketed cornice. Attached at the east end are a single-story and a two-story wing. Originally a one-story tetrastyle portico with Ionic columns faced the riverfront. This has been partially reerected on the west facade. On the land approach was a similar portico, but it also has been replaced with a porch entirely different in design. In 1864, Union general Benjamin Butler made the house his headquarters. Scars in the exterior brick prove that it was in the line of fire from river gunboats during the Civil War.

RI402 **Varina-Enon Bridge**

1990, Figg Engineering Group. I-295, spanning the James River at the Henrico-Chesterfield county boundary (east on VA 5, just past the Varina School area, take the southbound entrance onto I-295 [toward Rockhill/Raleigh, N.C.]; the bridge is within 2 miles)

One of the most exciting recent bridge designs in Virginia, this graceful, minimalist silhouette sympathetically gestures to the natural and historic surroundings. (Varina Plantation stands within a quarter of a mile east of the bridge, clearly visible from the northbound lane.) The Varina-Enon was a first-of-a-kind construction. The bridge is a combination of stayed-cable technology and precast delta-frame truss construction that rises about 275 feet and spans 4,680 feet. The delta frame spans were made at the site and moved into place over the pier substructure. Two thin central pylons support gracefully splayed cables. The relatively flat landscape makes the effect even more dramatic. Although the stayed-cable design is traditionally reserved for center spans in excess of 800 feet, here the cable-suspended center is 630 feet. The Varina-Enon Bridge proved the efficiency of suspension construction for shorter spans. It is the only vehicular suspension bridge in the state. (There are some cable suspension pedestrian bridges in the western part of the state.)

Fredericksburg Metropolitan Area (FR)

L OCATED FIFTY MILES SOUTH OF WASHINGTON, D.C., ON THE FALL LINE OF
the Rappahannock River, Fredericksburg, since its establishment in the 1720s, has
been an important commercial junction for river traffic (steamboats lasted until the
1940s), turnpikes, railroads, and, more recently, the automobile. Originally laid out in a grid
pattern, with the streets named for the British royal family, it has considerably expanded. All
of the town's development until the early twentieth century took place with relation to the
Rappahannock River. Several prominent north-south streets, which parallel the river—Caroline (known as Main Street between c. 1880 and 1960), Princess Anne, Charles, and Washington)—became the principal sites for major buildings. The east-west streets, with a few significant exceptions (Hanover, William, and Amelia streets), received less impressive
structures. Originally, mills clustered at the north end of Fredericksburg along the river, but
little of significance remains. Numerous large houses survive, however, to testify to the town's
wealth in the eighteenth and nineteenth centuries. Because of its strategic location, Fredericksburg was frequently fought over during the Civil War, with several bloody encounters in
the town and the area.

In recent years Fredericksburg has become a suburb of Washington and northern Virginia,
with attendant development of sprawl, suburban tracts, and strips surrounding portions of
the city. However, the downtown still remains vital and provides an object lesson in planning
by its determined avoidance of the "olde towne" look. The older sections of town have a variety of important structures, and Mary Washington College displays impressive campus planning. The town's connections to George Washington and his family have meant considerable
focus on the early period in preservation efforts. Some of the APVA's earliest activity was here
(see entries on the Mary Washington House and Rising Sun Tavern, below), and another impetus came in the 1920s from a mother-daughter team, Vivian Minor Fleming and Annie
("Miss Annie") Fleming Smith. More recently, the Civil War legacy has meant several million
tourist dollars annually. Fredericksburg's 2000 population stood at 19,279; counts for the surrounding counties were far larger.

Downtown Fredericksburg (FR1–FR46)
(Map, p. 308)

This tour makes a large circle—with a few side excursions—through the downtown, examining the civic, religious, financial, and commercial core and the older residential sections. It begins and ends appropriately on Princess Anne Street, the principal civic-religious axis.

FR1 Fredericksburg Area Museum (City Hall and Market)

1814–1816. 907 Princess Anne St. Open to the public

Examples of this building type, combining civic and town market functions, could be found along the East Coast in the eighteenth and early nineteenth centuries. Fredericksburg's is a rare survivor. Located on a high spot in the downtown, the structure replaced an earlier building near this site. The Princess Anne Street elevation is the formal town face: a five-bay central pavilion with two lower flanking wings, constructed in brick with Federal-era details. Originally the first floor of the center was rented to businesses, the municipality occupied the wings, and the upper floor was used for civic functions such as meetings and entertainments. Lafayette was feted here in 1824. The market side to the rear, or east, has been altered and the ground-level arcade enclosed, though meat hooks are still mounted on the stone piers. The yard, surfaced with Belgian paving block, was originally larger, and temporary wooden stalls were set up. The building is now restored and converted into a museum.

FR2 St. George's Episcopal Church

1848–1849, attributed to Robert Cary Long and H. R. Reynold; later additions. 905 Princess Anne St.

Apparently the church held a competition or solicited designs for this building, since Rich-ard Upjohn submitted drawings. The building is also attributed to James Renwick and to Niernsee and Neilson of Baltimore, but the best evidence suggests that Baltimore architects Long and Reynold produced the design. Long and Reynold employed the round-arched Lombard-Romanesque idiom that Renwick and Upjohn used occasionally; however, the church lacks finesse in its proportions and details. The interior originally resembled a plain Protestant or "low" Episcopal box. There was no chancel, but a pulpit dead center on axis, with a large window

above. Although the arcade is original, the galleries and the lower capitals on the columns were installed after a fire in 1854. The pews appear to be original. The chancel is of a later date, as is the stained glass, which consists of three Tiffany windows, several examples of Colgate Art Glass, and work by Burnham of Boston. The city installed the steeple clock in 1850 and still provides maintenance. Unfortunately, the original brick exterior has been painted.

FR3 Princess Anne Building (Princess Anne Hotel)

1910, Philip N. Stern. c. 1980, remodeling. 904 Princess Anne St.

Stern, who had a major architectural practice in Fredericksburg from 1909 to the 1930s responded in the proportion and details of this design to Federal-era structures. The building has always been stuccoed, but the inappropriate windows are the result of remodeling.

FR4 National Bank of Fredericksburg (Farmers' Bank of Virginia)

1819–1820. 900 Princess Anne St.

A major example of a Federal-era commercial building designed in a temple format, the bank is of brick laid in a precise Flemish bond, with stone lintels and keystones. The ground floor originally served as the bank, and the cashier lived above, in quarters entered through the arched doorway on the side. The original interior woodwork survives, and a banking museum is located in the rear. Abraham Lincoln and Jefferson Davis appeared here at different times as part of their respective war efforts.

FR5 Presbyterian Church

1833, attributed to Malcolm B. Crawford and William B. Phillips. 1947, restoration, Courtney S. Welton. 300 George St.

FR1 Fredericksburg Area Museum (City Hall and Market) (top, left)

FR4 National Bank of Fredericksburg (Farmers' Bank of Virginia) (top, right)

FR5 Presbyterian Church (bottom, left)   FR6 Fredericksburg Courthouse (bottom, right)

The fine brickwork and details suggest that two of Jefferson's workmen may have provided the design and built the structure for this church, an exceptional example of the Jeffersonian Roman Revival. The Tuscan portico in antis is surmounted by a Doric entablature derived from the Baths of Diocletian. Four entrance doors provide access to the double aisles and the gallery. The interior is largely intact, though the pulpit is a Colonial Revival replacement. During the Civil War Clara Barton and Walt Whitman tended the wounded in this building.

FR6 Fredericksburg Courthouse

1851–1852, James Renwick. 1870, alterations, James Tingue. Later alterations. 815 Princess Anne St.

Unique in Virginia and significant nationally is this pre–Civil War Gothic Revival courthouse. Renwick had recently (1849) won the competition for the design of the Smithsonian Institution building (now the Smithsonian Castle) in Washington and had submitted an entry for the Washington Memorial competition in Richmond. The building was controversial with the citizenry because of a tax levy, and Renwick re-

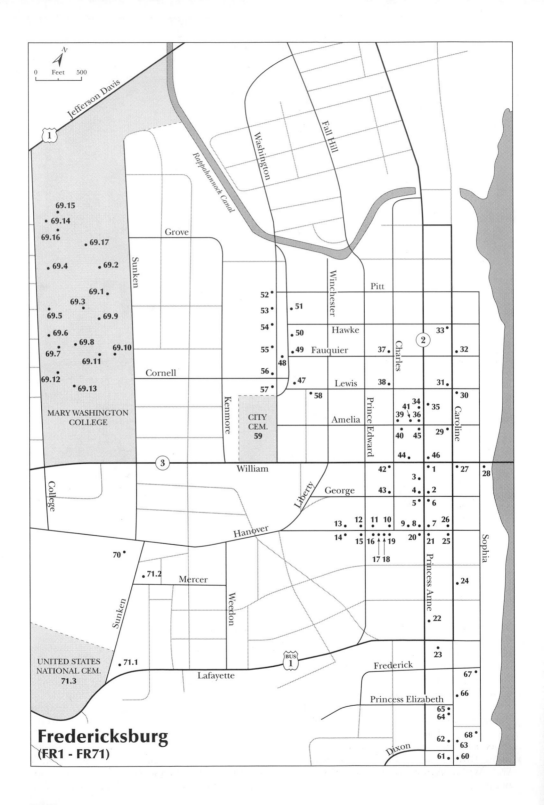

Fredericksburg
(FR1 - FR71)

sponded with a simplified and economical Gothic Revival design, on a plan in the form of an *E*. The entrance tower is the central feature. In the south wing at ground level the fire company had quarters; the arcades for firefighting equipment have been enclosed but remain visible. Constructed of brick, the building was originally covered with a light-colored stucco scored to resemble stone; a 1916 renovation installed the current rough pebble-dash stucco. Other alterations include the removal in 1870 of Renwick's raised parapets and steps on the gable ends and, later, the installation of a copper roof with extended eaves, which greatly changed the building's appearance. The tower also received alterations that changed the top and made it less phallic. On the north side is the former School Board Building (c. 1910; now a county building), a small Classical Revival structure which resembles Carnegie libraries of the period.

FR7 George Washington Masonic Museum

c. 1814; restored. 803 Princess Anne St.

The importance of the Masonic order in the early Republic socially, politically, and architecturally—through its symbolism as well as its buildings—cannot be underestimated. This fine Federal building is important historically because George Washington was inducted into the order through this lodge, though not in this building, which was constructed at least fifteen years after his death. Unfortunately, the restoration did not maintain the original quality of the brickwork. The museum contains some important artifacts, including a portrait of Washington by Gilbert Stuart and a bust of him by Jean Antoine Houdon. The lodge also commissioned from Hiram Powers in 1858 a statue of Washington which was sent to Richmond for safekeeping during the Civil War and was destroyed.

FR8 Tenement

c. 1830. 301–303 Hanover St.

Hanover Street is architecturally distinguished for its concentrated development between the 1780s and the early 1900s and its almost textbook examples of styles and house types. Among them are a number of "tenements" or,

to us today, double houses, such as these two three-bay structures with Flemish bond brickwork and sandstone sills. The detailing is Greek Revival.

FR9 Dr. James Carmichael House and Office

c. 1780, 1820. 307–309 Hanover St.

The five-bay wood-frame house, built first, follows the conventions of the colonial period with a hipped roof and entrance portico. Dr. Carmichael purchased the house in 1815 and a few years later erected the diminutive temple-form brick office and store. The trim boards of the eaves of the store mimic the moldings of the house.

FR10 Conway-Fitzhugh House

1851. 1902, enlargement. 401 Hanover St.

The original two-story house received a third floor and bay addition that continue its Italianate/classical detailing. The bases of the portico railings are console brackets enlarged to an almost gigantic scale, which replace conventional bases.

FR11 Robert C. Bruce Houses

1844; later wings. 407–409 Hanover St.

Bruce built these tenements as speculation. Number 407 is almost two feet wider than its neighbor. Both houses have side entrance halls and front and rear parlors. Detailing on both the exteriors and interiors is derived from Asher Benjamin's *The Practical House Carpenter* (1830) and survives essentially as built.

FR12 Lomax-Embrey House

c. 1819, c. 1902. 501 Hanover St.

John Tayloe Lomax, who owned Menokin in the Northern Neck (see the Peninsulas section), built a two-story brick house and taught law here until he accepted Thomas Jefferson's invitation to become the first professor of law at the new university in Charlottesville. Judge Alvin T. Embrey purchased the property in 1900 and, no doubt inspired and intimidated by the Greek Revival house across the street, proceeded to make it over in the Southern

Colonial mode with a giant-order columned portico and intersecting one-story porch. Also added were bay windows and a rear addition whose brick is thinner than that of the original house and laid up in American bond.

FR13 Fleming-Smith House

c. 1890. c. 1903, remodeling. 503 Hanover St.

Built as a simple five-bay house, the Fleming-Smith House received Victorian additions consisting of the angled corner tower, bays, a porch (now missing), and other trim after Vivian Minor Fleming acquired it around the turn of the twentieth century. She subsequently turned her architectural interests to preserving Kenmore (see entry, below), and this house became the center of Fredericksburg preservation efforts for decades. Her daughter, "Miss" Annie H. (Mrs. Horace) Smith inherited the house and lived here until 1952, raising over $750,000 for Kenmore. She became known for her motto: "Praise the Lord, work like the Devil, and love Kenmore." Much of the area beyond this house was destroyed during Civil War battles.

FR14 Federal Hill

c. 1792. 504 Hanover St.

The angular siting of this superb frame house, constructed before Hanover Street was laid out, took into account the view to the southwest. The five-bay west facade has a shallow pedimented central pavilion, while the east facade is plainer. The north end shows a local idiomatic expression, a flush chimney in which the outer brick surface, where it would be the hottest, is not enclosed by clapboards but exposed. The ornate exterior is complemented by an equally luxurious interior, especially the ballroom, which occupies the entire north end of the first floor and contains woodwork similar to that of Gadsby's Tavern in Alexandria. In the garden stands a rare early octagonal summerhouse with louvered sides and turreted, ogee-shaped roof.

FR15 Fredericksburg Pentecostal Church

1881. Southwest corner of Hanover and Prince Edward sts.

Built as Trinity Episcopal Church and designed in the vaguely English idiom then favored by Episcopalians in the North, this church, combining half timbering and shingles with a slate roof, displays an advanced architectural taste for Fredericksburg in the 1880s.

FR16 Green House

c. 1840. 408 Hanover St.

Fluted, giant-order Greek Doric columns, in place before 1862, rest on square plinths and are raised up on a high basement story, giving what is really a three-bay structure great presence on the street. One-story wings to each side add to the sense of height.

FR17 Hurkamp House

1853; later porch and additions. 406 Hanover St.

John G. Hurkamp, who owned an iron foundry in town, acquired the house in 1862 and added the iron fence, gate, and porch railings, which are marked with his foundry's name. The three-bay house with a side-hall entrance retains, as do all the other houses on this block, its original lot.

FR18 Carmichael-Chewning House

c. 1842. c. 1888, additions. 404 Hanover St.

Dr. George Chewning purchased the original three-bay house in 1888 and added a full porch. That addition is gone, but the original Greek Revival portico remains.

FR19 Dr. George Chewning House

1888. 402 Hanover St.

This Second Empire house with a mansard roof of patterned tin shingles continues Hanover Street's stylistic progression.

FR20 Fredericksburg United Methodist Church

1879–1882. 300 Hanover St.

Although the church is big and burly red brick Gothic Revival on the outside, the interior is surprisingly diminutive and more horizontal than vertical. Eastlake trusses support the roof

FR14 Federal Hill

over the nave. Perhaps because of the white color, the roof seems to press down on the interior space.

FR21 **City Hall** (U.S. Post Office)

1908–1911, James Knox Taylor, Supervising Architect, U.S. Treasury Department. 1937, extension. c. 1980, conversion. 715 Princess Anne St.

Taylor, a former partner of Cass Gilbert, fervently believed in classicism as the basis of an American national style. Nominally Georgian Revival in its red brick and limestone details, the former post office announces its importance with a trabeated portico of six Ionic columns and a broad platform of steps. The limestone came from Maine and the brick from local brickworks.

FR22 **Shiloh New Site Baptist Church**

1890; later additions. 525 Princess Anne St.

The designer of this prominent African American church looked back to church designs of the 1870s for this Italianate-looking structure, which contains a fine display of stained glass.

FR23 **Fredericksburg Train Station**

1910, 1927–1928, RF&P Engineering Department, J. E. Greiner, engineer and designer. South side of Lafayette Blvd. between Princess Anne and Caroline sts.

The Richmond, Fredericksburg and Potomac Railroad reached town in 1837. The present station closely followed the RF&P's turn-of-the-twentieth-century Georgian Revival mode, in red brick with white trim and a strong entrance pavilion. It resembles the Alexandria station, though here the entrance portico is more pinched. Although Amtrak and the commuter rail line to Washington still use the site, the station has been converted to a restaurant. Of more architectural interest is Greiner's raised platform to the south, built for tracks that had to be elevated for a new, higher bridge across the Rappahannock in 1927–1928. The design of the various ramps, stairs, and levels is truly distinguished.

Princess Anne Street south from this point contains a variety of house types worth a detour. In general the area has been well maintained.

FR24 **Le Lafayette Restaurant** (The Chimneys)

c. 1771. 623 Caroline St.

Caroline Street (known as Main Street from c. 1880 to c. 1960) from the 500 block through the 1000 block is a vital commercial street. As part of the city's enlightened planning, doctors' and lawyers' offices have not been allowed to congregate, and many buildings still have shops at street level and living quarters above.

The large five-bay house named for prominent chimneys that act as sculptural embellishments against the wooden clapboard was constructed for John Glassell, who returned to his native Scotland when the Revolution broke out. The interiors are impressive, especially the southwest parlor, where the woodwork includes carved swags and garlands on the chimneypiece and latticework friezes. The house was saved by the Historic Fredericksburg Foundation, which sold it with covenants to a restaurant.

FR25 **Exchange Hotel**

c. 1867. 200 Hanover St.

This multistory Italianate structure is of unusual bulk and presence for mid-nineteenth-century Fredericksburg. The Caroline Street elevation with its commercial level and cast iron balconies, lintels, and brackets maintains its original appearance.

FR26 Athens Hotel

c. 1910. 802 Caroline St.

The Athens Hotel is an impressive landmark that marks an important intersection. The designer obviously drew on Italian Renaissance palazzos to create an odd confection of parts. A heavy stone rusticated basement story features large windows; the brick upper floors have round arches that attempt to pull the composition together.

FR27 Colonial Theater

1929, Merrill C. Lee. 907 Caroline St.

A brick Colonial Revival theater that seated 1,300, the Colonial operated until 1989. Presently it is being converted into apartments. The facade follows a typical three-part format, with a high entrance pavilion in the center and lower wings.

FR28 Old Stone Warehouse

c. 1812. Sophia and William sts. Open to the public

What appears to be a low structure is actually three and one-half stories in height, but earth fill from the construction of the nearby bridge has partially buried it. The sandstone is laid without mortar. Over the years it has served as a smokehouse for fish, a fertilizer plant, a brewery, and, during the Civil War, a morgue.

FR29 Hugh Mercer's Apothecary Shop

c. 1780. 1929, restoration, Edward W. Donn, Jr. 1020 Caroline St. Open to the public

This one-and-one-half-story double cottage, combining an apothecary shop and a house, owes its survival to associations with George Washington: Washington called here, and Mercer served as a brigadier on his staff during the Revolution. Nearly demolished, it was saved by a group of Fredericksburg women and the APVA and restored by a leading Washington, D.C., architect.

FR30 Female Charity School

1835. 1902, addition. 1119 Caroline St.

This five-story, five-bay Federal building with Flemish bond brickwork proclaims its purpose

FR26 Athens Hotel

with inset plaques on the facade. It was part of a substantial charity operation created by St. George's Episcopal Church, which also had a male charity school nearby that has been demolished.

FR31 Fielding Lewis Store

c. 1792, c. 1807. 1200 Caroline St. (northwest side, near Lewis St.)

This brick store stands between Kenmore and the Rappahannock River, on land owned by Fielding Lewis before the Revolution. Although popularly associated with Lewis, it was probably built for William Stone soon after 1792, when it appeared on a tax list. Its brick walls with sandstone quoins seem to have been raised from one to two stories after an 1807 fire, and existing woodwork is in the neoclassical style of this later period. The shop at the front faced Caroline Street, and the office was at the rear, with its own exterior doorway. The building is owned by Historic Fredericksburg and awaits restoration.

FR32 Central Rappahannock Regional Library (Lafayette Elementary School)

1908, Philip N. Stern; E. G. Heflin and Company, builder. c. 1965, conversion. 1301 Caroline St. (at Lewis St.)

Although Stern moved toward the Colonial Revival in the design, the verticality, somewhat awkward massing, and patterned brickwork of this former school, more typical of the nine-

FR29 Hugh Mercer's Apothecary Shop
FR33 Rising Sun Tavern

teenth century than of the twentieth, indicate a lingering Victorian sensibility.

FR33 Rising Sun Tavern

c. 1760, 1792, 1907, 1982. 1306 Caroline St. Operated as a museum; open to the public

John Frazer converted a house built by Charles Washington, the president's younger brother, into the Golden Eagle tavern in 1792. The APVA acquired the structure in 1907 and restored it under the name of the Rising Sun Tavern on the basis of a sign; however, recent research indicates that the Rising Sun was located elsewhere in town. The long porch is a reconstruction, the result of recent archaeology.

FR34 John Allan House

c. 1742, c. 1800. 1106 Princess Anne St.

This and the house opposite (see next entry) are reputedly the two oldest in town. What at first glance appears to be a unified facade becomes under inspection an additive composition. The original house, recognizable as such by its trim and its smaller windows, is to the south. The north addition contains larger windows. The beaded clapboards are original, and ghosts of a porch can be seen.

FR35 Charles Dick House

c. 1740. 1796 and later, additions. 1107 Princess Anne St.

The Charles Dick House originally stood on the western edge of town and faced open land, siting still reflected in its large front yard. The dating of the Mount Vernon–style portico is controversial; some have claimed that it was added in the 1790s, but that is doubtful. It may be a very early imitation of Washington's home dating from the early nineteenth century.

FR36 Doswell House

c. 1820. 1108 Caroline St.

An extremely sophisticated example of the more urban tendencies of Federal-era designers, this suburban house could fit into a Washington or Richmond streetscape. The McDowell House has recessed arches that recall houses in Baltimore and Washington by such architects as Benjamin Henry Latrobe, Robert Mills, and George Hadfield and the Boston and Richmond work of Alexander Parris, who had worked for Charles Bulfinch. The tripartite or "modified Venetian" windows are impressive. The cast iron porch dates from the 1850s and may have come from a local foundry.

FR37 St. James House (James Mercer House)

c. 1760; later additions. 1300 Charles St.

James Mercer, who was Mary Ball Washington's attorney, built this house on a lot he purchased from her son, George Washington. A gambrel-

FR39 Smithsonia   FR44 Star Building

roofed cottage typical of upper-middle-class dwellings in pre-Revolutionary Virginia, it was later expanded. Restored in 1963, it is owned by the APVA but is not open to the public.

FR38 Mary Washington House

1750, 1772, c. 1800. Later additions and restoration. 1200 Charles St.

The fascination of Americans with George Washington and with his mother, who was notoriously difficult, is evidenced in the preservation of this house. Washington purchased the house so that his mother, Mary Ball Washington, could live near her daughter Betty Lewis (married to Fielding Lewis of Kenmore) and son Charles Washington. He added to it in 1770 and perhaps before her death in 1789. It passed through other hands and more additions were made. In 1890 the APVA, in one of its earliest endeavors, purchased the house to prevent its removal to Chicago for display at the World's Columbian Exposition.

The furnishings include some pieces that date from Mary Washington's occupancy. Architecturally the house is interesting for its various wings and additions and the garden porch. So deep that no sun could reach its inner recesses during a hot summer afternoon, it resembles porches on Tidewater houses. An exposed brick chimney breast can also be seen.

Mary Washington liked to garden, and the garden was restored by the Garden Club of Virginia in 1968. Although it contains some original boxwood, the design is Colonial Revival.

FR39 Smithsonia

1834; later additions. 307 Amelia St.

The southern affliction of "columnitis gigantis" appears in this house, which later generations tended to interpret as colonial rather than Greek Revival. Originally built as a Presbyterian girls' orphanage and school, it later became a residence. It is unusual in that the porch, with its massive brick and stucco columns, is cut into the bulk of the house, the roof forming a single, volumetric mass encompassing the portico.

FR40 W. M. Baggett House

c. 1851, attributed to James Renwick. 306 Amelia St.

This Gothic Revival brick cottage is a perfect foil to the overblown Greek Revival Smithsonia across the street. Baggett built the Fredericksburg Courthouse, which Renwick designed (see entry, above), and hence, at least locally, Renwick is thought to have designed Baggett's house. That much of the design is Renwick's is doubtful, since the house is somewhat tame by his standards.

FR41 Doggett House

c. 1820 (house and office); later additions. 303 Amelia St.

A wonderful ensemble of house, outbuildings, office, and gardens, this complex is also significant for two women who were connected with it. The famous photographer Frances Benjamin Johnston stayed here frequently; she was a friend of Kate Doggett Boggs, the owner, a noted authority on Virginia gardens and contributor to *The American Horticulturist.* Boggs began the Garden Club of Virginia's program

FR45 Fredericksburg Baptist Church

FR46 First Virginia Bank (Planters' Bank)

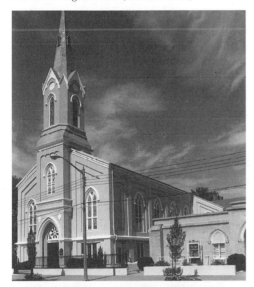

in restoration, and her first project was the creation of the gardens at Kenmore in 1929 (now destroyed).

FR42 James Monroe Museum and Library

c. 1815, 1850, 1960. 908 Charles St. Open to the public

Although earlier guides identify this as the office from which James Monroe practiced law beginning in 1786, that building is long gone; it stood on this site, but nearer to the corner of William Street. The three brick offices that make up the museum served local milling interests and stand on land Monroe owned. In addition to the library and archival materials, the museum contains numerous pieces of furniture Monroe purchased while he was in France as head of the American legation. Many of these pieces helped furnish the White House during his tenure as fifth president.

FR43 Masonic Cemetery

1784 and later. Charles St.

The importance of the Masons has been noted; this cemetery contains a number of early markers and tombs that display Masonic symbols as well as an early stone wall.

FR44 Star Building

1888, Mesker and Brothers. 303 William St.

Of the several commercial structures on William Street, this one, with a Queen Anne cast iron storefront in near-perfect condition, is easily the most impressive. The designers at the Mesker and Brothers foundry in St. Louis (whose identification appears on each pilaster's base and at the right side, first-floor level) had looked closely at recent English fashion as interpreted by New York architects.

FR45 Fredericksburg Baptist Church

1854–1855, James Renwick; later additions. 1019 Princess Anne St.

Architecturally far more sophisticated than the nearly contemporary St. George's Episcopal down Princess Anne Street (see entry, above), this church shows how quickly Protestant congregations accepted the Gothic image. Renwick's bulky forms, such as the engaged buttresses on the tower, combined with the stucco covering (over brick), produce wonderful shadows. The plan is typically Baptist, with the parish hall on the ground floor and a raised auditorium. Several of the stained glass windows are by Jakoby Art Glass of St. Louis.

FR46　First Virginia Bank (Planters' Bank)

1927, Frank Conger Baldwin. 1001 Princess Anne St.

Baldwin studied architecture at MIT and practiced in Detroit before moving in 1911 to Fredericksburg, where he maintained an office along with one in Washington, D.C. He became interested in Virginia "antiquities" and designed a room for the Metropolitan Museum's American Wing. This bank is one of the finest from the period in Virginia. It is Georgian Revival–Federal Revival in style, with a Regency delicacy in details such as the swags in the facade. The large windows create a spaciously open banking room.

Washington Avenue and Kenmore　(FR47–FR59)
(Map, p. 308)

The boulevard memorializes George Washington's mother, Mary Ball Washington; its original name was Mary Washington Avenue. When she died in 1789, she was buried at her request on Kenmore's grounds, on a site that would later be adjacent to Washington Avenue. Outcry over a proposed removal of her grave in 1889 led to the establishment of a memorial commission, which completed a monument in 1894. Contemporaneously, a development company purchased a large tract of land from the owners of Kenmore and subdivided it for houses. Together, the city, the memorial association, and the development company laid out a 150-foot-wide avenue with parallel roadways and center grass plots. It provided an entrance and protection for Kenmore, and Washington Avenue became Fredericksburg's answer to Monument Avenue in Richmond: the street of power, a center of conspicuous residential building, exhibiting a rich panoply of styles. The various monuments memorialize aspects of Virginia history.

FR47　Kenmore

1773–1775. 1929–1930, restorations; kitchen and office dependencies, Edward W. Donn, Jr., and Philip N. Stern. 1972, orientation building, Milton L. Grigg, 1201 Washington Ave. Open to the public

Built by George Washington's brother-in-law Fielding Lewis, Kenmore is among the most intact Georgian houses in the Chesapeake. Subsequent owners cultivated its appearance without substantially adjusting its form. As at Shirley, Menokin, and a number of Annapolis houses, the roadside doorway opens into a stair passage that extends only half the depth of the house, leading to a pair of entertaining rooms on the river or garden front. End doors provided service circulation through a secondary passage on the right (south) and through a closet linking the Lewises' "great room" and an elaborate first-floor bedchamber on the left.

The builders selected unglazed bricks for the facades and used a minimum of rubbed brick, an economy that created a stark appearance intended to be stylish. Successors to Lewis added a small Doric porch built of Aquia sandstone to the river side early in the nineteenth century, ornamenting an otherwise plain exterior. Mantels carved with swirling foliage, somewhat like those at Mount Vernon, were used in three first-floor rooms, with a more simply carved fireplace surround in a small, office-like space known from documents to have been occupied by a servant in 1782. An anonymous plasterer who worked at Mount Vernon ornamented the ceilings and overmantels in the Lewises' principal rooms in baroque and neoclassical manners not seen elsewhere in Virginia and one of the first examples in the colonies of certain neoclassical motifs. These were restored and expanded in 1882.

FR47 Kenmore

New houses were built on lots sold from the perimeter of the property early in this century, weaving Kenmore into a middle-class neighborhood developing west of the old town. The all-women Kenmore Association saved the property from further subdivision in 1922 and restored the house in 1929–1930. A concurrent garden restoration, planned by Charles F. Gillette and the first of many projects financed by the Garden Club of Virginia spring tours of historic sites, has been destroyed. Edward W. Donn, Jr., and Philip Stern collaborated in 1929–1930 on brick ancillary buildings, and a semisubterranean exhibit and orientation building designed by Milton Grigg was added in 1972.

FR48 Hugh Mercer Monument

1905, Edward V. Valentine, sculptor. Washington Ave.

An energetic composition by Virginia's leading sculptor of the period depicts a local apothecary who was also a brigadier on Washington's staff and lost his life at the Battle of Princeton.

FR49 W. T. Mills House

1896. 1303 Washington Ave.

This and the house next door at 1301, built by Mills, a local builder, were among the more modest houses constructed on Washington Avenue.

FR50 J. Conway Chichester House

1911, Philip N. Stern. 1307 Washington Ave.

The Arts and Crafts details of this house indicate that Stern had been looking at Stickley's *Craftsman Homes* (1909) or other similar publications. This and several other houses on the avenue designed by Stern evidence his adroitness in different idioms (see also the Shepard and Moon houses, also on Washington Avenue, below).

FR51 William Peden House

1909, Frank Stearns. 1411 Washington Ave.

This four-bay Queen Anne house has a four-stage corner tower that is rounded at the first level, becomes octagonal, and concludes with a bell shaped roof. Demi-octagonal bays and a full wrap-around porch break up the composition.

FR52 Mary Washington Monument

1889–1893, William J. Crawford. Adjacent to Washington Ave.

In 1833 President Andrew Jackson laid the cornerstone for a small obelisk memorial to George Washington's mother, but it was never completed. The partial monument was badly damaged in the Civil War, and relic hunters completed its destruction. Crawford designed a larger obelisk that was constructed out of granite and dedicated in 1894. Officiating at the dedication was President Grover Cleveland, accompanied by Vice President Adlai E. Stevenson. The monument's most interesting element, in addition to its shape and size, is the inscription, "Mary Mother of Washington." Also on the site is the caretaker's residence (c. 1894), built of local stone.

FR53 Sarah Cole House

1898, Frank Stearns. 1406 Washington Ave.

One of the earliest houses on the avenue, the Sarah Cole House is Queen Anne in detail, though the porch is a later replacement.

FR54 J. B. Rawlings House

1925, Frank Stearns. 1400 Washington Ave.

The Rawlings House is a five-bay Georgian Revival composition, very prim and proper amidst the display of other houses.

FR55 George W. Shepard House

1911–1912, Philip N. Stern. 1304 Washington Ave.

The Shepard House, of dark brick, is an earlier version of Georgian Revival, as revealed by the more elaborate lintels, columns, balustrade, and hipped roof.

FR56 E. J. Cartwright House

1906, Harry Heflin. 1206 Washington Ave.

Heflin, a contractor who also provided designs, here gives his interpretation of the French Chateauesque style with a square tower that makes it look as if it could have provided a model for Charles Addams's cartoons.

FR57 Victor Moon House

1916–1917, Philip N. Stern. 1200 Washington Ave.

Here Stern combined somewhat Oriental detailing in the brackets with a Spanish allusion in the roof tiles.

FR58 E. M. Curtis House

1928, Frank Stearns. 620 Lewis St.

Stearns employed a variety of window shapes in this three-bay stucco house with a hipped roof, which terminates Washington Avenue at its southern end.

FR59 City Cemetery–Confederate Cemetery

1844, 1867, and later. Northwest corner of Washington Ave. and William St.

The city established a cemetery here in 1844. It received many new occupants after the Battle of Fredericksburg, and in 1867 the Confederate name was added. The iron Confederate Cemetery gate (1870), manufactured by the Scott and Bowering Foundry, is ornate, round-arched, and French in feeling. On the inside are rows of plain Confederate grave markers, and in the middle is the monument *To the Confederate Dead* (1874, Charles Cassell). An early example of such monuments, it has a massive base and corner columns that recall the work of Frank Furness. The size of the base makes the bronze statue of a Confederate soldier (cast by the Monumental Bridge Company, Bridgeport, Connecticut) on top appear diminutive.

Lower Caroline Street–Sophia Street   (FR60–FR71)
(Map, p. 308)

This area lay outside the original city boundaries, and in 1749 Roger Dixon purchased the land and subdivided it. Dixon ran into financial problems and tried a lottery, as well as building at least one house on speculation. The site of a ferry landing, the area was built up over the next century, but it was heavily damaged during the Civil War by both Union and Confederate artillery. It is now a well-maintained neighborhood that presents a stunning group of restored houses.

FR60 The Sentry Box

1786 and later. 133 Caroline St.

Located at the southern end of Caroline Street near the former ferry landing and an old log wharf is this structure, built by Revolutionary War General George Weedon, who subsequently lived here. The house has been extensively restored, and the grounds contain a reproduction of a colonial icehouse and a kitchen.

FR61 Tenement Houses

c. 1855. 130, 132–134, 136–138 Caroline St.

Constructed as speculative housing by a later owner of the Sentry Box, these tenements are double houses. Number 130 is a half tenement; the construction of its other half may have been prevented by the Civil War. The porches are Greek Revival in style, while the bracketed eaves display Italianate ornateness. All of the houses have raised, or English, basements, side-hall entrances, and front and rear parlors.

FR62 **House**

c. 1890. 210 Caroline St.

This exuberant Stick Style dwelling probably derived from a design assembled by William Comstock, an author of popular pattern books in the 1880s.

FR63 **Dixon-Mortimer House**

1764. 213 Caroline St.

The oldest extant house on the street, this five-bay structure was constructed as speculation by John Dixon, the brother of Roger Dixon, who tried to develop the street. In 1772 Dr. Charles Mortimer, Mary Washington's physician, purchased it and later constructed other houses on the street. The Greek Revival portico is a twentieth-century addition; the iron fence dates from c. 1850. The house, with its gardens and outbuildings, retains its original relationship to the Rappahannock River.

FR64, FR65 **Dr. Charles Mortimer Houses**

c. 1780. 214 and 216 Caroline St.

Mortimer built these twin houses as speculation. Brick and five bays wide, they both were extensively altered in the late nineteenth century. Local architect Philip N. Stern "restored" number 214, adding a Georgian Revival pediment to replace a Victorian portico; the original survives at number 216.

FR66 **Judge Joseph Jones House**

1801. 303 Caroline St.

Land records indicate that a tenement for Jones's slaves stood on this site in 1797. In 1801 he constructed a small, gambrel-roofed house as rental property on this site.

FR67 **Commission House**

c. 1876. 100 Frederick St.

Sophia Street, east of Caroline Street, lies hard on the river and in the eighteenth and nineteenth centuries was lined with wharves, warehouses, and factories. This structure, the only remaining warehouse, was built by the A. K. Phillips Company, which ran an import-export business.

FR68 **Ferry Tollkeeper's House**

c. 1770. 208 Sophia St.

Although it is near the site of a ferry that once ran across the Rappahannock, the purpose of this simple brick structure with a raised basement is conjectural. From it one can see the RF&P Railroad bridge (1927, J. E. Grenier, engineer and designer), a concrete-arch structure.

Mary Washington College and Environs   (FR69–FR71)

(Map, p. 308)

FR69 **Mary Washington College**

1908–present. 1301 College Ave. (main entrance); bounded by U.S. 1, Sunken Rd., and VA 3 (William St.)

Founded in 1908 as Fredericksburg State Normal and Industrial School, the institution was renamed Fredericksburg State Teachers College, and then, in 1935, Mary Washington Col-

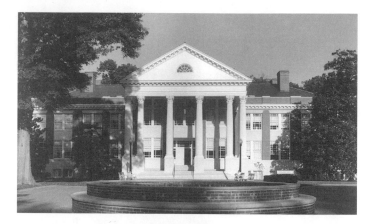

FR69.1 Monroe Hall
FR69.5 Chandler Hall

lege. From the late 1940s until 1972 it was the women's college branch of the University of Virginia; it became coeducational after it separated from the university. The campus is located west of downtown, along a ridge with numerous ravines, once the site of Civil War action. The college initially lacked an overall plan, but its first architect, Charles M. Robinson, initiated a scheme of clustering buildings around a green or circle that became the governing feature for future expansions, along with the Neo-Georgian architectural idiom of red brick and white trim. The consistency of the Georgian style with the siting and the preservation of the natural topography and the maintenance of indigenous trees—mature poplar, oak, beech, and hackberry—has resulted in a remarkably cohesive campus.

A campus tour logically begins in the front of the first building, Monroe Hall (FR69.1) (1909–1911, Charles M. Robinson, with Philip M. Stern and Charles K. Bryant), which housed all of the school's original academic activities. Behind the giant-order Ionic portico, the interior contains portions of a mural (c. 1920), reputedly painted by students, which illustrates Virginia history. Willard Hall (FR69.2) (1909–1911, Robinson, Stern and Bryant; 1911 addition, Robinson), to the north, was properly subservient and served as a dormitory. All evidence points to Robinson, who was the leading school architect in the state, as the principal designer for these buildings, since the next structure on the south side of Monroe, Virginia Hall (FR69.3) (1914, Robinson; 1934–1935, addition, John Binford Walford), is by him alone. Virginia Hall completed the third side of the enclosure, making a central green that is known as Normal Hill (the paving and fountain are 1980s additions). When Robinson's health failed, his associate John Binford Walford, took charge of the work; he remained as campus architect until his death in 1956. Seacobeck Dining Hall (FR69.4) (1928, Robinson

FR69.11 E. Lee Trinkle Library

FR69.17 Woodard Campus Center

and Walford; addition, 1950–1951, Walford and [D. Pendelton] Wright), is on axis with Monroe, but lower down the hill and connected by a bridge, completing the initial section. Particularly noteworthy are the retaining walls and terraces that handle the transition down the slope.

Chandler Hall (FR69.5) (1928, Robinson with Walford) began a new circle. Ball, Custis, and Madison halls (FR69.6, FR69.7, FR69.8) (1934–1935, Walford) and then, finally, Ann Carter Lee Hall (FR69.9) (1951–1953, Walford and Wright) completed this new cluster, named Ball Circle, albeit much more loosely grouped than the older one. The building on the top of the ridge, Lee Hall, the administrative and student services structure, received a more imposing facade; a broad podium supports eight Ionic columns in antis, and the wings are pushed forward. Tucked into a ravine behind Lee Hall is the Amphitheater (FR69.10) (1924, attributed to Robinson). The pattern of a ridgetop axis and a loosely defined circle continues with the next group to the south, E. Lee Trinkle Library (FR69.11) (1940–1942, Walford) (now a classroom building), with wings flanking a domed central section recalling the original University of Virginia library. Across and down the hill is Westmoreland Hall (FR69.12) (1938, Walford). The next structure, George Washington Hall (FR69.13) (1938–1939, Walford), the new administrative building, reverses the pattern by placing a dominant structure on the west side of the ridge; the reason is that Walford placed a new entrance drive from College Avenue to the immediate south of Washington Hall and designed the entrance

gates and brick walls which enclose the campus (1938).

At the opposite end, or north side of Normal Hill, the Fine Arts Center, comprising Jessie Ball du Pont, Pollard, and Melchers halls (FR69.14, FR69.15, FR69.16) (1951–1953, Walford and Wright) marks a shift, since the grand portico of du Pont Hall is oriented not to the center of the campus, but to College Avenue below. Later additions to the campus have maintained the red brick Georgian idiom and elements of Robinson and Walford's plan; one of the most recent, the Woodard Campus Center (FR69.17) (1986–1989, VMDO, Robert Vickery designer), has some postmodern elements. VMDO became the campus architects in the early 1980s and restored Robinson's vision by emphasizing the linear, pedestrian-oriented nature of the campus and creating a series of plazas.

FR70 **Brompton**

c. 1770, c. 1824, c. 1866, 1946. Northwest corner of Hanover St. and Sunken Rd.

Now the residence of the president of Mary Washington College, Brompton is sited prominently on what is known as Marye's Heights. The original house received extensive additions, including a dramatic Roman Revival flat-roofed Ionic portico, c. 1824, when a local businessman, John Lawrence Marye, purchased it. The portico received its pediment during repairs c. 1866, after the house was badly damaged by Civil War action. In 1946 the state purchased and restored the house.

FR71 Fredericksburg National Military Park

1936. 1013 Lafayette Blvd. (at Sunken Rd.)

The Fredericksburg National Military Park marks the site of some of the fiercest fighting of the Battle of Fredericksburg (1862) along Sunken Road.

FR71.1 Administration Building and Visitor Center

1937, National Park Service staff, Charles E. Peterson, architect

The Neo-Jeffersonian main structure, a two-story center block with lower wings, was designed by the architect who founded the Historic American Building Survey (HABS) in 1933–1934. Peterson went on to a noted career as a historian and preservationist. The CCC provided labor to construct the structure.

FR71.2 Kirkland Monument

1965, Felix de Weldon, sculptor

De Weldon, the sculptor of the Iwo Jima Memorial in Arlington, provided his usual spirited composition for *The Angel of Marye's Heights*, commemorating Sergeant Richard Kirkland of the 2nd South Carolina Volunteers, who carried water and nursed wounded Union troops.

FR71.3 United States National Cemetery

1866–1870 and later; Montgomery C. Meigs, Quartermaster General, U.S. Army

FR71.1 Fredericksburg National Military Park, Administration Building and Visitor Center

Laid out after the war on a portion of the former battlefield with a commanding view, the cemetery contains 6,603 graves of Union dead, of whom about half are unknown. The terracing apparently dates from Meigs's involvement in the 1860s, and his office—possibly with the participation of Alfred B. Mullett, then Supervising Architect of the Treasury—designed the stone, mansard-roofed superintendent's house. The cemetery contains several monuments of note, including the 38-foot-tall Doric column of the Butterfield 5th Corps Monument (1900, Hoffman and Prochzka of New York, contractors) and the bronze Humphreys Monument (1908, Herbert Adams), which stands atop a base of smooth pink granite from Stony Creek, Connecticut.

Stafford and Spotsylvania Counties   (FR72–FR81)

Around Fredericksburg and along the I-95 corridor has grown up a mini-metropolitan area in the counties of Stafford, across the Rappahannock River, and Spotsylvania, south of Fredericksburg. Although Stafford County in many ways retains a rural ambience, it is rapidly becoming part of the northern Virginia orbit, with many people commuting north on a daily basis. During the 1990s its population growth was nearly 60 percent. Spotsylvania County is also growing rapidly: it increased by an estimated 70 percent in the 1990s. Portions of this population commute south toward Richmond.

Falmouth   (FR72–FR76)

Falmouth is the principal settlement on the Rappahannock River above the falls from Fredericksburg. It has always been in the shadow of the larger city. Settled about 1727, it had several prosperous mills until the mid-nineteenth century, when the railroad bypassed the town to the south. Much of the old town has been destroyed, but it contains several items of interest.

FR72 **Chatham**

c. 1765, c. 1840. 1931, restoration, Merrill C. Lee. 120 Chatham Ln. Open to the public

On a hilltop with a view of Fredericksburg, Chatham is one of several spectacularly sited eighteenth- and early nineteenth-century houses in Falmouth, including Belmont (see entry, below) and Carlton (c. 1785; 501 Melchers Drive). The first owner of the seven-bay brick house was William Fitzhugh, the grandfather of Robert E. Lee. Chatham was the Union army headquarters during the Battle of Fredericksburg. Merrill Lee (not of the same family) extensively renovated and restored the house and removed the porches (c. 1840), which had been part of the house during the Union occupation. The interior has some fine detailing, such as the Doric pilasters on the chimney breast in the east room.

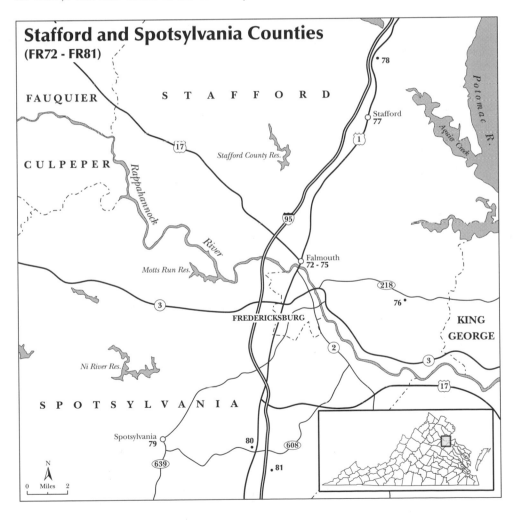

FR73 Vass-Moncure House

c. 1810. 305 River Rd.

This fine five-bay brick Federal house on the Rappahannock floodplain is a lonely survivor of a group that used to line the river. It is set on a high basement with the entrance in a semicircular raised brick archway.

FR74 Falmouth Downtown

In close proximity are several structures worth noting: the Temperance Tavern (1820–1821), originally a storehouse and dwelling; the former customhouse (c. 1800), one of the smallest in the country; and Union Church (c. 1850), on Carter Street. Only the facade remains of the church, which burned; it was saved as a civic landmark and nicely terminates the road axis. Next door is Master Hobby School (c. 1930, Edward W. Donn, Jr.), a reconstruction of the school George Washington supposedly attended, a log cabin with brick infill.

FR75 Belmont

c. 1790, c. 1850, c. 1918. 224 Washington St. Open to the public; marked with a sign

Sited above the Rappahannock River, this large white frame house with many additions passed through several hands before it became the home and studio of the American painter Gari Melchers and his wife, Corinne. Born in Detroit and trained in the European academic tradition, he achieved great popularity at the turn of the twentieth century, specializing in painting European peasantry, portraits, and murals (World's Columbian Exposition, Library of Congress). About 1900 he turned toward Impressionism and Symbolism. He maintained a studio in New York and used Belmont as his country house. Melchers and his wife made some additions to the house, including the sun porch at the south end, and filled it with a varied collection of antiques and art, which reflects their cosmopolitan tastes. They also landscaped the twenty-one acres, adding the terraces and gazebo. The stone studio (1923–1924, John Donaldson, with Philip Stern), in the French Provincial mode of the period, was designed by Melchers's Detroit architect friend, Donaldson, and overseen by local architect Stern. The stone came from bridges and mills that had been destroyed. Planned as a working studio with north light, it also served for receptions and as a gallery and a space where potential clients could see the painter at work. A large collection of Melchers's paintings are on display. Left by his widow to the state of Virginia, the property is now a historic house museum operated by Mary Washington College.

FR76 White Oak Primitive Baptist Church

c. 1789–c. 1835. 8 Caisson Rd. (intersection of VA 603 and VA 218)

This church illuminates one of the religious currents in Virginia in the late eighteenth, nineteenth, and twentieth centuries. The Primitive Baptist faith rests on the belief that doctrine originates in scripture, not in interpretation. Consequently, Primitive Baptist churches are exceedingly plain, without ornamentation, as well as nonhierarchical in interior arrangement. The exact date of this building remains unclear, although the later is the more probable. The building is largely unaltered, and the lean-to addition is of later date. The interior is one large room with pews, a wooden altar, and two cast iron stoves. The framing members are all pit sawn and hewn. The plaster walls and simple moldings date from 1867. Outbuildings consist of a woodshed and men's and women's outhouses. A graveyard is adjacent.

FR77 Stafford County Courthouse

1922, Philip N. Stern; later additions. U.S. 1, Stafford

Stafford has been the county seat since 1715, and the town still clusters around the courthouse, though growth is apparent. Stafford County needed a new courthouse when the old one was demolished for a widening of U.S. 1. Stern, of Fredericksburg, followed the Virginia tradition with a pedimented, hexastyle, Roman Doric temple front.

FR78 Aquia Church

1751–1754, 1755–1757, Mourning Richards and William Copein. 1915–1916 and 1958–1959, Milton L. Grigg. U.S. 1 at VA 610, 3 miles north of Stafford

One of the best preserved and most urbane of the early churches in Virginia, Aquia Church burned in 1755 just three days before its scheduled completion and was rebuilt by its original

FR78 Aquia Church

FR79.1 Spotswood Inn

undertaker, Richards, and its mason, Copein. The two-story church has a Greek cross plan, an unusual (for Virginia) central tower, and elaborate Aquia sandstone quoins and doorways. The brick walls of Flemish bond with glazed headers rest on a water table of common bond that was replaced in 1915–1916. All elevations but that on the east had pedimented and rusticated door frames of Aquia sandstone. The design for the doorways is similar to plate XXIX in Batty Langley's *Builder's and Workman's Treasury of Designs* (1750). The tower is brick on only one side and of frame construction on the others.

The interior is original, apart from the lowering of the height of the pews in the nineteenth century and reordering of the chancel in the twentieth. The three-tiered pulpit is unsurpassed. The pedimented Ionic altarpiece framing four tablets with arched tops is one of the few surviving architectural altarpieces in Virginia. The communion rail and other altar furniture are modern. According to James Scott Rawlings, the historian of eighteenth-century Virginia churches, "No other colonial gallery in Virginia even remotely approaches Aquia's west gallery." The cornice that serves as the rail of the gallery incorporates ovolo, fillet, cyma recta, cyma reversa, fascia, bead, soffit, and dentil moldings.

Abandoned during disestablishment, the church was unused for more than thirty years. By 1857 Bishop William Meade reported that he would "not have recognized the place or building." Occupying Union troops carved their names on the interior and exterior. Repairs took place at various times, and in the late 1950s Milton Grigg restored portions and designed the parish house down the hill.

The Aquia stone used in the church came from quarries at nearby Aquia Creek, the principal source for stone in the area. Aquia sandstone was used in Washington, for construction of the U.S. Capitol and the President's House, and elsewhere. Too soft and porous to withstand the elements, in most cases it has been replaced.

FR79 Spotsylvania

VA 208 and VA 613

A substantial ordinary has stood at this crossroads, on what was originally the major road between Richmond and Fredericksburg, since the late eighteenth century. The seat of Spotsylvania County had moved numerous times since its formation in 1722. In 1838 it was two miles from the present site, when a landowner donated to the justices of the county the "Tavern Tract," a ten-acre site adjacent to the tavern, in order to "procure the location of the seat." The Spotswood Inn (FR79.1) (c. 1800; later additions) dominates the crossroads with its two-story porch with crude Doric columns. Across the road and on its own shaded square is the Spotsylvania County Courthouse (1840, Malcolm F. Crawford; 1900, B[artholmew]. F. Smith Fireproof Construction Company of Alexandria; 1964, additions), initially designed and built by Crawford, who had worked for Jefferson at the University of Virginia. The design follows the Jeffersonian format of a Roman temple with widely spaced columns. The location also brought Lee and Grant together for eight days in May 1864, resulting in one of the bloodiest battles of the war, with 27,000 casualties. The courthouse suffered severe damage, but, except for temporary patches, little was done to repair it until 1900, when B. F. Smith virtually reconstructed the building using buff-colored fireproof brick, though reusing the original Tuscan columns. The fenestration pattern is Smith's, as is the interior trim. The sheriff's wing was a later addition. Also on the courthouse square are the usual adjacent structures, including the former county recorder's office and a late eighteenth-century former jail, moved from the earlier courthouse site.

Across from the courthouse on Virginia 208 stands the former Berea Christian Church (1856; Samuel Alsop, builder), now the Spotsylvania County Historical Museum, a tidy, temple-form brick structure with pointed-arched windows. Christ Episcopal Church (c. 1841) is an extremely modest brick structure on the east side of Virginia 208 adjacent to the courthouse. Both churches were heavily damaged during the Civil War fighting and served as shelters for the wounded. The former Spotsylvania High School (FR79.2) (c. 1925, School Buildings Service, Virginia Department of Education), .2 mile south of the Historical Museum on Virginia 208, is a grand Georgian Revival statement that stretches 100 yards. The Zion United Methodist Church (1859; Virginia 208), .1 mile farther south, is a typically modest twin-entrance brick structure.

North past the courthouse .2 mile, on the north side of Virginia 208, are the Dabney house and farm (c. 1840). The three-bay brick Federal house was the only residence in Spotsylvania to survive the fighting in 1864. Across from the farm on the south side of 208 is the access road to the Confederate Cemetery (1918), which covers a low rise. Some of the dead were brought from other sites; simple headstones radiate out from an obelisk surmounted by the statue of a soldier, erected by the United Daughters of the Confederacy. Stylistically, it looks back to the 1880s.

FR79.2 Spotsylvania High School (former)

FR81 Stirling Plantation

Three tall windows on each side admit plenty of light. A gallery supported by Tuscan columns runs around three sides. On the end elevation is the pulpit in front of a barrel-vaulted apse, which contains the baptism chamber. On the wall of the apse is a painting of a view down a river. The church was the scene of a council of war held by General Ulysses S. Grant and his staff on May 21, 1864, captured in a series of wet-plate negatives exposed by Timothy O. Sullivan.

FR80 Massaponax Baptist Church

1859. c. 1940 and 1961, additions. 5101 Massaponax Church Rd. (U.S. 1 and VA 608)

This restrained brick temple revival structure has a single front entrance and two side entrances which lead to a vestibule and then, through double doors, into the sanctuary, which has two aisles and three pew sections.

FR81 Stirling Plantation

1858–1860. 4911 Guinea Station Rd. (VA 607 and I-95), Massaponax

Easily visible from the road (and from I-95) is this large five-bay brick plantation house with exterior chimneys and outbuildings. Constructed for its owner, John Holladay, born in 1799, and his wife, Elizabeth Lewis Holladay, born in 1790, it is extremely conservative in form, essentially a continuation of Tidewater five-bay, double-pile brick main houses dating from the 1780s. Its details—cornice, porticoes, and interior trim—show an awareness of Greek Revival pattern books. Account books survive that show that by 1860 Holladay had paid $2,714.79 in cash for the construction. West of the main house stand the old kitchen and smokehouse, both of brick. Beyond these were the slave cabins; a chimney of one stands as a reminder.

The Peninsulas (PE)

T HE LAND LYING BETWEEN THE POTOMAC RIVER ON THE NORTH, CHESA-
peake Bay on the east, the James River on the south, and the fall line on the west is
generally known as the Peninsulas. The area includes the Northern Neck (or Northern, or Upper Peninsula), the Middle Peninsula, and the Lower (or Southern, or "The")
Peninsula. Although some of the geographic definitions have changed over time, in general
the Northern Peninsula encompasses the area between the Potomac and Rappahannock
rivers and includes King George, Westmoreland, Richmond, Northumberland, and Lancaster counties. The Middle Peninsula, defined as the area between the Rappahannock and
York rivers, includes Middlesex, Mathews, Gloucester, King and Queen, King William, Essex,
and Caroline counties. The Lower Peninsula, the land between the York and James rivers, includes the counties of New Kent and Charles City. (The eastern metropolitan area of the
Lower Peninsula, which includes Williamsburg, Jamestown, Yorktown, Newport News, and
Hampton cities, and James City and Yorktown counties, is covered in the Hampton Roads
section.)

English settlers found the tidal rivers separating the peninsulas easily navigable, as had Native Americans. As a result, some of the first English settlements occurred in this area, especially along the rivers. The Native Americans had farmed the rich land and engaged in maritime fishery, and the early English colonists followed this pattern, although at a much larger
scale. The settlers obliterated great portions of the peninsular forests to make way for crops,
including tobacco. Some of the greatest early Virginia fortunes were made through farming
and in land speculation. By 1756, a Board of Trade survey claimed 2,414 people in Northumberland County, 1,610 in Lancaster County, and 11,996 people in Richmond County. A range
of architectural accomplishments—such as Westover, Shirley, Mount Airy, Rosewell, and
Christ Church, Lancaster—along with many smaller but no less significant structures, reflect
this early prosperity.

By the early nineteenth century much of the land had lost its productivity because of the overcultivation of tobacco. An economic depression, still evident in many areas, set in. River commerce, which provided a livelihood for some, began to disappear with the arrival of the railroads and vanished in the twentieth century. Shellfishing still provides some with employment, but it has greatly diminished in recent years. Several large military installations in the area today provide jobs for others. Although farming continues, many of the former fields have been overwhelmed by second-, third-, and even fourth-growth forests. The timber industry is increasingly dominant.

Summer homes began to appear in the late nineteenth century. Today, along many of the rivers and on the bay, resorts, yacht clubs, and second homes abound. Although the inevitable suburban sprawl surrounds the metropolitan areas of Hampton Roads, Richmond, and Fredericksburg, great portions of the Peninsulas remain rural and retain a feeling of remoteness. Some of the towns still have the character of life in the nineteenth, if not the eighteenth, century. The isolated courthouse and church are still the centers of community life.

The following entries are arranged along the major travel routes of the region, by county, beginning on the Northern Peninsula, west to east; then the Middle Peninsula, east to west; and then the Lower Peninsula, through New Kent County and west to east in Charles City County, along the north side of the James. (From this point, the traveler can move on to the Hampton Roads section.)

King George County   (PE1–PE6)

PE1 **Lamb's Creek Church**

1769–1770, attributed to John Ariss. VA 3 and VA 694, Lamb's Creek area

One story in height, with seven bays, this building is notable for the quality of its colonial brickwork. The structure resembles a church that stood in Fairfax County (Payne's Church [1766–1768], demolished by Union troops) whose design is documented to Ariss. The fine, molded brick door pediments, rubbed brick dressings, and elegant round-headed windows recall similar details on buildings in the Williamsburg area. Ariss has been suggested as

the undertaker, or mason, if not the designer. The interior was gutted during the Civil War and has been restored.

PE2 **King George County Courthouse**

1923, E. G. Heflin. 1960, 1973, additions. VA 3, King George

King George County was formed in 1720, and this building is at least its third county courthouse. Designed by a Fredericksburg architect, the courthouse, with its pedimented portico and Roman Doric columns, follows the familiar

PE1 Lamb's Creek Church, south elevation

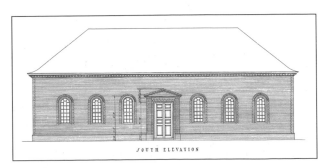

SOUTH ELEVATION

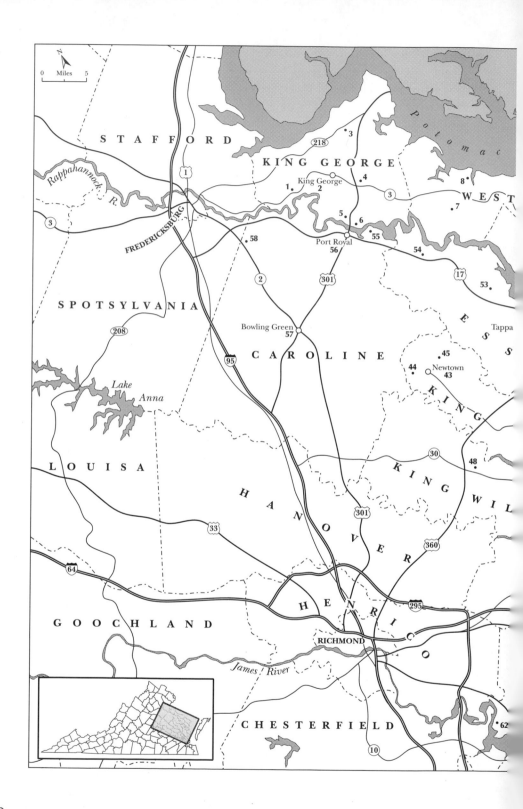

STAFFORD

KING GEORGE

218

• 3

King George
1   • •   • 4
•   2

1

Potomac

8•

WEST

• 7

5•   • 6
• 55

• 58

Port Royal
56

RAPPAHANNOCK R.

FREDERICKSBURG

54 •

17

53•

3

SPOTSYLVANIA

208

2

301

95

CAROLINE

Bowling Green
57

Tappa

45 •

44
•   Newtown
43

ESS

KING

Lake
Anna

LOUISA

HANOVER

30

48
•

KING   WIL

33

301

360

64

295

GOOCHLAND

HENRICO

62
•

RICHMOND

James River

CHESTERFIELD

10

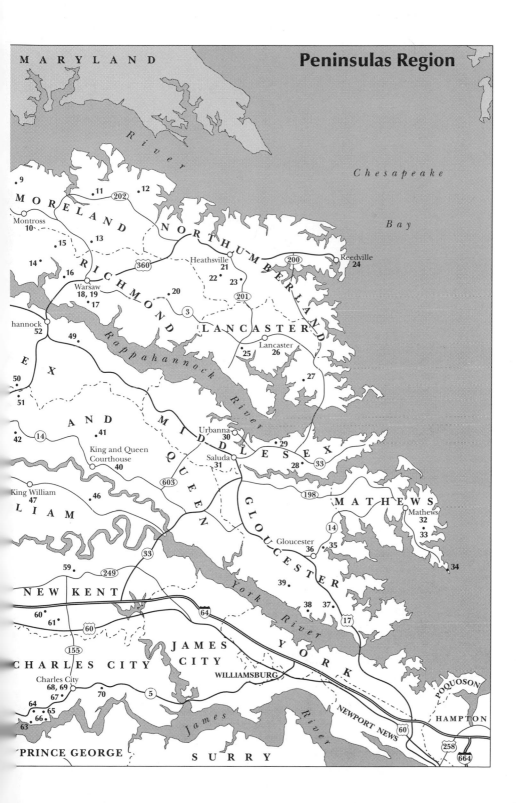

Peninsulas Region

MARYLAND

Chesapeake

Bay

MORELAND

NORTHUMBERLAND

RICHMOND

Montross
10

Heathsville
21

Warsaw
18, 19

Reedville
24

River

202

360

201

200

9

11

12

15

13

14

16

17

20

22

23

3

hannock
52

E X

50

51

42

A N D

41

14

King and Queen
Courthouse
40

King William
47

L I A M

46

LANCASTER

Lancaster
26

25

27

Rappahannock River

M
I
D
D
L
E
S
E
X

Urbanna
30

29

Saluda
31

28

33

603

198

MATHEWS

Mathews
32

33

34

Q
U
E
E
N

33

GLOUCESTER

Gloucester
36

35

39

14

59

249

60

38 37

NEW KENT

60

61

60

155

CHARLES CITY

Charles City
68, 69

67

64

65

66

63

PRINCE GEORGE

70

5

JAMES
CITY

WILLIAMSBURG

64

York

River

17

POQUOSON

NEWPORT NEWS

HAMPTON

60

258

664

James

River

S U R R Y

PE4 Office Hall Kitchen and Smokehouse

PE5 Emanuel Episcopal Church

Virginia temple-form pattern, which looks back to Jefferson. The large arched windows on either side of the entrance are the clues that it is a twentieth-century building. The surrounding town retains a nineteenth-century ambience as it spreads out along Virginia 3. Worthy of inspection are the small brick lawyer's office opposite the courthouse and the several churches, including St. John's Episcopal Church (c. 1843; c. 1880, additions).

PE3 St. Paul's Episcopal Church

c. 1766, c. 1830. VA 632 (south of VA 206/218), Bertaville (Owens)

In its two-story height and Greek cross plan, St. Paul's is comparable to Aquia Church in nearby Stafford County. Nonetheless, the exterior, remarkably austere despite its fine Flemish bond brickwork, has led historians to note the building's greater similarity to English Dissenter chapels than to more ornamented and richer Church of England structures. Abandoned during disestablishment, the structure was converted into a school in 1813. The entrances were altered by closing the north and west doorways and adding two doors on the south elevation. About 1830 restoration began. The interior woodwork largely dates from this period.

PE4 Office Hall Kitchen and Smokehouse

c. 1805–1820. U.S. 301 and VA 3 (north side), Office Hall

Originally these two brick structures served as a kitchen and smokehouse for Marengo (renamed Office Hall Plantation; destroyed). The kitchen, which is the larger of the two structures, is one of the few one-room, two-story brick kitchens known to have survived. Most kitchens were of wood and a single story. The construction of the smokehouse roof is unusual. The single cross beam and a king post eliminate the need for tie beams. At a later point, the structures were joined by a wooden connector. Reputedly John Wilkes Booth sought help in a nearby house during his flight south.

PE5 Emanuel Episcopal Church

c. 1850. VA 301 (.75 mile north), Port Conway

The employment of the fashionable Gothic Revival idiom in a remote rural area in Virginia is unusual for this date. The one-story brick structure, only two bays long, has prominent engaged buttresses. Nonetheless, it exerts a presence through the verticality of the tower, which, incongruously, has a prominent Italianate bracketed cornice.

PE6 Belle Grove

1794, attributed to Richard and Yelverton Stern. c. 1840, additions. VA 301 (left on private road .2 mile), Port Conway

Directly across from the village of Port Royal on the Rappahannock River, Belle Grove is typical of the many eighteenth-century wooden plantation houses that proliferated in the region. The structure, with a two-story clapboarded frame, was built by John Hipkins for his daughter Fannie, who had married William Bernard in 1789. The Sterns had constructed a similar house, with the wide elliptical arches on the interior and projecting entrance halls that are features of Belle Grove, in Caroline County. In the mid-nineteenth century Carolinus Turner purchased the house and added the wings and the two-story porticoes. On the river side is a two-tiered Roman Ionic over Greek Doric portico, and on the land side is a Doric portico. James Madison, fourth president of the United States, was born in a house that once stood on the property.

Westmoreland County (PE7–PE13)

PE7 Ingleside

1834; later alterations. VA 638 (2.6 miles south of VA 3, east side)

This building is a provincial interpretation of the Greek Revival. The columns sit on a high basement and are of an elongated Tuscan order, with capitals of three abacus courses in a descending order of circumference. The small lunette window in the pediment, the high basement, and the ascending central stairs recall the original configuration of James Madison's Montpelier, near Orange. Constructed as a private school, the Washington Academy—which accounts for its "public" appearance—became a residence ten years later and subsequently acquired the wings.

PE8 Wakefield (George Washington's Birthplace National Monument)

1930–1931, Edward W. Donn, Jr. VA 204

Washington's father purchased the land in 1718, and the future president was born here in 1732. Although the family moved when he was three, he returned at the age of eleven to study surveying with his half brother, Augustus, Jr., who inherited the property. Excavations in 1930 and 1936 indicated that the birthplace was a timber-frame, U-shaped house that burned in 1779. Next to the original house site is Memorial Hall, constructed by the Wakefield National Memorial Association in 1930–1931. The one-and-one-half-story brick structure with large exterior chimneys is a fanciful re-creation of a generic mid-sized Virginia plantation house of the period. Donn, a consummate colonial revivalist from Washington, D.C., tried not to reconstruct the past, but instead to provide a convincing impression of the period of Washington's birth. The property passed to the National Park Service in 1932 and today is maintained as a living history farm. The Washington family graveyard is nearby.

PE9 Stratford Hall

c. 1725–1738. 1929–1940, restoration, Fiske Kimball. VA 214. Open to the public

PE9 Stratford Hall

One of the best known of Virginia's houses, Stratford is important not only as the birthplace of Richard Henry Lee and Francis Lightfoot Lee, both signers of the Declaration of Independence, and of Robert E. Lee, but also for its architecture. Thomas Lee built the structure and named it after the ancestral home in East London of his grandfather, also Thomas Lee, who had emigrated to Virginia in the mid-1600s.

Architecturally, Stratford Hall is ambitious, both sophisticated and naive. It displays the wealth and aspirations of a mid-eighteenth-century Virginian. It also illustrates the problems of trying to build at such a scale in its time and place. Stratford Hall centers on a parterre. Four dependencies, one at each corner, contain an office and a kitchen-laundry on the south forecourt and other service functions in two smaller structures on the north forecourt. The H-plan house is composed of two three-bay hip-roofed end blocks, out of which rise two large clusters of chimney stacks joined with arches and rails. The piano nobile, unusual in Virginia houses, sits on a high basement. The floor levels are distinguished by brick of different colors and sizes laid in Flemish bond. Occupying the center of the house is the square "great hall," with elaborate bolection paneling, Corinthian pilasters, and an ogee-molded chair rail.

The precise sources for the design of Stratford Hall are unknown, and historians have had a field day identifying plates in Serlio, Gibbs, and Palladio and English precedents in the work of Lord Burlington and Vanbrugh. Whatever the source, Lee and his builders misjudged the proportional relationship of the chimneys, creating a sophisticated and yet provincial composition.

Stratford passed out of the Lee family's possession in 1828. In the 1920s the Robert E. Lee Memorial Association, established on the model of the Mount Vernon Ladies Association, purchased the property and employed Fiske Kimball, the scholar-architect, to direct the restoration. Kimball replaced most of the nineteenth-century window sash with sash based on more "correct" eighteenth-century models, repaneled several of the interior rooms with what he thought was more accurate woodwork, and designed exterior entrance stairs based on English precedent. For the association he also designed the nearby Regent's or Council House, a notable brick Colonial Revival structure.

PE10 Westmoreland County Courthouse

1900, B. F. Smith Fireproof Construction Company. 1930, alterations. Montross

Montross has been the county seat of Westmoreland County (created 1653) since the 1680s. The courthouse, which sits on a courthouse green with the inevitable Confederate monument (1876, Bevan and Sons), was designed and constructed by Smith, who made a career of designing modest courthouses on the Northern Neck and elsewhere in Virginia. Photographs show this building as originally a two-story, vaguely Italianate residential structure. In 1930, the Jeffersonian–Colonial Revival idiom arrived in town and the courthouse received its present Roman Doric portico. Adjacent is the old jail (1911, Pauly Jail Building Company). Now the headquarters of the Westmoreland Historical Society, it contains exhibits and collections, including a portrait of a toga-clad William Pitt by Charles Willson Peale.

PE11 Spring Grove

1834, VA 202 at VA 626, Machodoc

Essentially Federal in form, Spring Grove is a five-bay house with end chimneys and a dwarf Ionic portico. The interior woodwork and decorative plasterwork are derived from Asher Benjamin's pattern books. Built for a large landholder, Robert Murphy, the house is unusual for its material. Brick houses from this period are rare in the Northern Neck. They reflect the conservatism and the fleeting prosperity of the early nineteenth century in the region. Its rural setting remains unspoiled.

PE12 Yeocomico Church

1706. c. 1730, c. 1870, c. 1906, 1958–1959. VA 606 (.5 mile south of junction with VA 610), Tucker Hill

One of the oldest churches in Virginia, Yeocomico Church was built in 1706 to replace an earlier frame structure. Apparently some of the woodwork from the earlier church was reused. The south wall is the earliest, and the north wing, which gives Yeocomico its unique T shape, dates from c. 1730. The brickwork employs a number of different bonds and patterns. Carving, such as initials—at least eleven different sets—appears in a number of places. A Scottish thistle ornaments the main opening of the porch, which shelters the main entrance on the south. Of the three entrances, this one has been described by architect-historian James Scott Rawlings as "an extraordinary monument of our colonial heritage." An enormous Tudor battened door incorporating a wicket door is the only known surviving example of the type. The church was abandoned during disestablishment and not returned to service until the 1840s. Although the chancel remains in its original location, the pulpit has been moved. The paneling and most of the interior result from later renovations.

PE13 Rochester House

1746. VA 613 (1 mile north of VA 3 and VA 203), Lyells

This one-and-one-half-story yeoman's cottage is typical of dwellings that used to dot the Chesapeake landscape. The house, built by William Rochester, was in use until 1935. The building has an oak timber frame with mortise-and-tenon joints. The walls are timber and brick nogging covered with weatherboards, and the large T–end chimney is Flemish bond brick. The structure has a steep gable roof and a full brick basement, with English bond below grade and Flemish bond above and a single-room-hall plan. The interior walls were originally plastered. An enclosed stairway leads to the loft or attic level, which also originally was finely finished. Near the house are several surviving nineteenth-century farm structures, including a corncrib.

Richmond County (PE14–PE20)

PE14 Grove Mount

c. 1785; later additions. VA 635 (.4 mile north of VA 624)

Sited on a ridge, this timber-frame house commands a sweeping view of the Rappahannock River valley from its terraced south elevation. The approach to the house is from the north. The entrance axis continues into the hall and out to the south. The main facade of the north elevation contains four bays, with an ell making the fifth bay. Other later additions connect to this side. By contrast, the south elevation is rigidly symmetrical. Robert Mitchell built the house. His wife, Priscilla Carter Mitchell, was the daughter of the prominent Robert Carter III, one of the wealthiest men in the Northern Neck. The plan is conventional, organized around a central hall and passage with rooms dispersed to either side. West of the house stands a dairy (c. 1785), which is currently used as a smokehouse.

PE15 Menokin

1769–1775, William Buckland and William Wright. Southwest of VA 690, 3.75 miles north of intersection with U.S. 360. Open to the public

One of the great houses which survive from colonial Virginia's age of dominion by a landed elite, Menokin is the result of a unique collaboration between John Tayloe II of Mount Airy

and his new son-in-law, Francis Lightfoot Lee. Instead of the cash dowry he customarily bestowed, Tayloe gave Lee life interest in 1,000 acres of his vast Richmond County estate and agreed to build a gentleman's seat there. Tayloe and Lee selected a design by William Buckland, whose proposal represents the only presentation drawing known to exist for any colonial Virginia house. Working with local stonemason William Wright, Buckland also supervised construction at Menokin until 1771, when he left for more lucrative opportunities in Annapolis. By this time Menokin was complete enough to shelter Francis Lightfoot Lee and his young wife, but building on the site— including completion of the interior—continued for several years. The result is a house of remarkable qualities. Built of the same local iron-infused sandstone that distinguishes Mount Airy, Menokin's white-plastered elevations leave the dark brown stone exposed only where the masons shaped it into quoins, architrave, and belt courses. The effect is a visual inversion of Mount Airy's masonry color scheme, which underscores a complex parent-offspring relationship between these two grand houses.

Francis Lightfoot and Rebecca Tayloe Lee lived at Menokin for the rest of their lives. The house is notable as the dwelling of a founding father and signer of the Declaration of Independence. The Lees died in 1797, and Menokin reverted to the Tayloes and then passed out of the family. Menokin remained as a residence through the 1940s and thereafter stood vacant and untended. It was in a ruinous state by 1995 when the owners donated it to Menokin Foundation, a nonprofit organization devoted to its rescue and analysis.

PE16 Mount Airy

c. 1754–1764. VA 646 (.5 mile from VA 360, .3 mile on a private road). Open at selected times of the year (NHL)

Important socially and culturally as a "power house," Mount Airy is also one of the great Anglo-Palladian houses. English-born William was the first Tayloe to occupy the site, beginning in the 1680s. The Tayloes accumulated land and wealth, and in 1724 Catesby Cocke, a friend, wrote that the family "lived in a very genteel manner." John Tayloe II further enhanced the prestige of his family by constructing the present Mount Airy. Tayloe, who probably acted as the designer, although perhaps with some advice, turned to James Gibbs's *Book of Architecture* (1728), plate 58, for the south elevation, and plate 55 for the plan. While no proof exists that Tayloe owned Gibbs's publication, several copies are known to have existed in Virginia by the 1750s.

Sited along the north side of the Rappahannock River, Mount Airy consists of a central block flanked by two dependencies with connecting curved quadrants. The main block is two stories high and is set on a tall basement. Both of its principal facades are seven bays wide and have rusticated central pavilions of three bays. The windows of the remaining four bays are framed with stone architraves and sills. Rusticated quoins mark the corners, and a belt course encircles the facade. The arches contain heavy voussoirs and keystones. Local sandstone from Aquia in northern Virginia and a distinctive dark sandstone quarried on the property were the primary construction materials. Apparently Tayloe educated his slaves to execute the difficult and refined details apparent on the house. He employed William Buckland, who was working at Gunston Hall, to execute paneling and moldings for the interiors. Known to be elaborate, Buckland's interiors were lost in a fire in 1844 and rebuilt in a plain Greek Revival style.

The surrounding landscape bears traces of the plantation system and various outbuildings. Near the house on the land side is an informal park, and on the river frontage are broad for-

PE16 Mount Airy

mal terraces that contain remnants of colonial gardens.

PE17 Sabine Hall

1733–1742. 1760s, 1820s, and 1929, remodelings. VA 624 (end of the road, south of U.S. 360). Not visible

Sabine Hall, an important building of the colonial period, was built by the fourth son of Robert "King" Carter, Landon Carter, an innovative planter, politician, and patriot. As initially built, Sabine Hall was a typical large Georgian house, mathematically proportioned to be 60 by 40 by 30 feet below the eaves, symmetrical on all elevations, and crowned by a tall hipped roof with a pair of towering chimneys at either end. In the 1760s an early version of the east wing was built to connect the formerly detached kitchen to the main house. At the same time, a piazza (a covered walkway) was added to the river (south) facade. In the nineteenth century, the piazza was rebuilt as a veranda, the basic form of which survives today. In the 1820s the hipped roof and chimneys were lowered; the giant portico was constructed; a matching broad, classical pediment was added to the river facade; and the house was painted white.

The distinguishing feature of the original Sabine Hall facade is a narrow center pavilion of rusticated masonry. The pavilion appeared infrequently in the American colonies before mid-century, but it was known early in Virginia, from the reconstruction of the College of William and Mary after the fire of 1705. The Sabine Hall pavilion contains a "Rustic Door" below a "Rustic Window," as these details were described when published in architectural books of the period.

Carter's diary records examples of his hospitality, such as a "three day festival" at New Year's that was attended by five dozen guests. They could congregate in Carter's two great halls, each three bays wide, which bisect the house on both floors. In the manner of the European piano nobile, the upper hall is given prominence with a full entablature around its entire circumference.

The builder's grandson, Robert Wormeley Carter II, brought the house up to date stylistically in the 1820s. He added the Gothic Revival gate lodge. The form is probably based on William Strickland's Philadelphia Masonic Hall, which Carter thought "one of the most elegant buildings in America." The formal garden has always been planted, and it survives as one of the few eighteenth-century examples in Virginia. In the garden, flowers, vegetables, and fruits were grown on a series of terraces. The distinct form and gravel paths of the upper three terraces may reflect the layout of the originals.

PE18 Warsaw

U.S. 360 and VA 3

Warsaw has been the seat of Richmond County (formed 1692) since about 1730. The town's original name was Richmond County. The obvious confusion with the far larger city of Richmond led the citizens in 1845 to choose the unlikely name of Warsaw as an expression of their sympathy with the Polish fight for freedom from the Russians. A small courthouse and farming town, it remains oriented to the main highways, U.S. 360 and Virginia 3, which pass through it.

At the center of town on U.S. 360 is the third Richmond County Courthouse (1748–1750; restoration, 1877, T. Buckler Ghequiere; later additions). Landon Carter of Sabine Hall had it constructed on the site of a 1730 courthouse. Carter commissioned a rectangular structure with four bays of arcades on its two longer sides, which served as porches and gave access to the courtroom, oriented perpendicular to the entrance. Blind arches at the ends of the arcades gave the appearance of two additional bays to a side. In 1877 Baltimore architect T. Buckler Ghequiere remodeled the structure by enclosing the arcades and inserting an entrance at the north end. Ghequiere published a short article on the courthouse in *American Architect and Building News* (June 23, 1877), which is one of the first notices about Virginia's colonial past from an architectural point of view. The courthouse complex also includes the clerk's office (1816–1818) next door, which is now the county museum. This building was erected under the supervision of John Tayloe of Mount Airy. Like Mount Airy and Menokin, it is built of local sandstone and stuccoed above the water table. The stone base has galleted joints. The old jail (1872), a plain brick three-bay structure with two interior chimneys, has an attractive brick cornice. Across from the clerk's office stands a lawyer's office (c. 1800) that is unusual in its size—two stories—and in its three-bay facade.

The former post office, now the Northern Neck State Bank (c. 1937, Public Works Administration, Office of the Supervising Architect, U.S. Treasury Department, Louis A. Simon in charge; later alterations) is across U.S. 360 from the courthouse. It is classic Art Deco in style, with wonderful ornamental touches. Such fashionable architectural idioms are rare in the Northern Neck.

PE19 St. John's Episcopal Church

c. 1835; later additions. U.S. 360 (1 mile east of Warsaw)

The recessed triple-arched entrance is the dominant feature of this single-story, Flemish bond brick structure. The arcade may be a reference to the courthouse. The building initially served as a community church. Hence it has no central aisle and originally had no chancel. The chancel was added c. 1876 and then replaced c. 1929 as the church became more "ecclesiological." An interior rear gallery was also removed, and painted glass windows (c. 1920) were installed. The graveyard contains a large Beaux-Arts monument to Congressman William Atkinson Jones (1926, Don Mariano Benlliure, sculptor), given by the people of the Philippines, for whose independence he had been a fervent advocate.

PE20 Farnham Episcopal Church

c. 1737, 1834, 1873, 1921, 1959. VA 3, Farnham

Almost the only remaining eighteenth-century elements of this church are the brick walls, of

English bond below the water table and Flemish bond with glazed headers above. The walls have been repointed, and the gables are postcolonial. All three doorways are replacements, though the pedestals of the elaborate west doorway are original. Abandoned during disestablishment, it suffered various calamities, including bombing, use as a stable, and fire until its most recent exterior restoration in 1921. The interior dates from 1959.

Northumberland County   (PE21–PE24)

PE21 Heathsville

U.S. 360, Northumberland County

A principal Northern Neck farming town, Heathsville, originally named Court House, was established in 1681. The county dates back to c. 1645. The town clusters in a linear fashion along the highway, the center at the courthouse square and the Northumberland County Courthouse (PE21.1) (1900, B. [Bartholomew] F. Smith Fireproof Construction Company; later additions), which is dominated by the Confederate monument (1873) in front. Although the courthouse is reputed to date from 1851, it was designed and erected in 1900 by B. F. Smith of Alexandria, who specialized in modest courthouses. With three bays and a front porch, which has been altered, it could be mistaken for a residence. Wings have been added to the rear. The jail (1844), which originally had three cells per floor, now serves as a museum. Behind the courthouse is Rice's Hotel (Hughlett's Tavern) (PE21.1) (c. 1795 and later), the quintessential courthouse tavern, having grown in stages. A two-tier wooden piazza runs along a twelve-bay front. Currently it is undergoing restoration and stabilization. West .2 mile is St. Stephen's Church (PE21.2) (1881, T. Buckler Ghequiere), very much in the style of Richard Upjohn's *Upjohn's Rural Architecture* (1852). This small, board-and-batten Gothic Revival church has a diminutive freestanding bell cage at the back. Some of the fittings were sent from Baltimore, Ghequiere's home. Most of the stained glass windows and the paneling are later additions, some of which were executed by a parishioner, Clem Goodman. Springfield (1828, 1850; U.S. 360, north side, about .5 mile west from the center) is an impressive house set back from the road but fully visible. Built in 1828 in the Federal style by the merchant William Harding, the building was extended in 1850 with an addition that includes a two-story Classical Revival portico. The wings have un-

PE21.1 Rice's Hotel (Hughlett's Tavern)

PE21.2 St. Stephen's Church

usual stepped parapets, reminiscent of houses in southwestern Virginia.

PE22 Kirkland Campground

1892, William Dandridge Cockrell. VA 601 (south to VA 779), Heathsville vicinity

PE22 Kirkland Campground

PE24.1 Reedville, Albert Morris House

This unusually intact campground was once used by residents of the area who came during the summer to "tent" for a week of revival meetings. It contains three major original buildings, constructed of wood: the great Tabernacle, the Camper's Tent, and the Preacher's Tent. The lumber came from trees on the site. The Tabernacle, which measures 90 feet by 90 feet, reputedly follows dimensions given in the Old Testament. It is an impressive structure with its four-tiered roof and exposed wooden construction. It served as both an open-air house of worship and a dining area. Only one camper's tent survives, a two-story structure to the east, in poor condition. South of the Tabernacle is the Preacher's Tent, two stories with a second-story overhang. Also on the property are two modern concession stands, two large three-story hotels, and a few latter-day "tents" (two-story frame cottages). The complex is still used occasionally.

PE23 Howland Graded School and Teacher's Cottage

1867. VA 201 at the intersection of VA 642 (3.4 miles south of Heathsville)

The structure is a small one-room school, established by the local Baptist church after the Civil War to educate former slaves. It remains largely intact, although the board-and-batten siding has been replaced. The teacher's cottage stands on the property.

PE24 Reedville

VA 360 and VA 644 (Main St.)

Reedville was developed in the 1870s by a Maine sea captain, Elijah Reed, who established a fish-oil processing plant on the small peninsula. Reed came to the area in pursuit of a small, bony fish, the menhaden, which after the Civil War provided a replacement for whale oil. He and his family built a small town, based very much on a New England maritime model. It so prospered that by 1885 fifteen menhaden processing factories, now all destroyed, were located in the area. Hotels, a bank, and other structures joined the community. Reedville also attracted other industries and wealthy industrialists who constructed summer homes. These are clustered in a sort of "millionaires' row" near the apex of the point. George Reed, the son of Elijah, constructed his house (1897–1899; 77 Main Street), a large Queen Anne affair. Next door is the Gables, the Fisher house (1909; 76 Main Street), a brick Queen Anne. Opposite is Albert Morris's house (PE24.1) (1900; 62 Main Street), which resembles some of the designs promoted by George Barber of

Knoxville. Farther north is a row of earlier houses constructed by Elijah Reed (48–53 Main Street). The Bethany United Methodist Church (1899–1901, John Steelman; later alterations; 28 Main Street) is the product of a New Jersey contractor, in a Gothic idiom.

Lancaster County   (PE25–PE27)

PE25 St. Mary's Whitechapel

c. 1669, c. 1741, 1832; later alterations. VA 201 at VA 354 (3 miles south of Lively)

Named for the London suburb that had been home to some of its early communicants, this church may have begun as early as 1669. Originally a rectangular brick box, it was enlarged c. 1741 by the addition of transepts in a Flemish bond with glazed headers. Abandoned after disestablishment, the church fell into ruin. When it was reoccupied in 1832, the original nave and chancel were removed. The bricks were used to enclose the transept, which became the church. The round-headed windows date from the 1740s, but the doorways are from 1832. On the interior, the gallery, supported on Tuscan columns, is from the eighteenth century, but the remainder is post-1832. In the graveyard, a cast iron enclosure (c. 1875) contains a scene of lambs lying under weeping willows.

PE26 Lancaster

VA 3 and VA 600

This community is one of the best preserved of Virginia's rural courthouse towns. Although the county was formed in 1661, the county seat did not locate here until 1741. The village's focus remains the Lancaster County Courthouse (1860–1861, Edward O. Robinson, builder; 1937, addition; later modifications), which originally was a plain two-story brick structure resembling a meetinghouse. A narrow vestibule leads to a large courtroom. As did many Virginia courthouses during and after the Colonial–Jeffersonian Revival of the 1930s, the Lancaster courthouse received an elongated Roman Doric portico and a belfry. In front stands—reputedly—the earliest Confederate monument (not in a cemetery) in the state, erected by the Ladies Memorial Association in 1872. It is a marble obelisk, inscribed with names and bearing a small, sculpted plaque. Past the courthouse complex are the brick clerk's office (c. 1797) and the jail (c. 1870), which has been restored as a museum. For aficionados of Washington trivia, the Mary Ball Washington Museum (c. 1798) is across from the courthouse. Originally known as Lancaster House, this five-bay I-house dates from after the death of Washington's mother, who was born in the area. East .1 mile and across Virginia 3 is Trinity Episcopal Church (1884, V. Montgomery; 1954, 1970, additions), a board-and-batten rural Gothic structure, rather barnlike in appearance, erected by an architect-builder from Essex County. On the interior is an exposed X roof truss. Originally, the chancel had a stained glass window, which has been removed.

PE27 Christ Church, Lancaster

c. 1728–1732. VA 646 (.3 mile off VA 200), Irvington. NHL; open to the public

Photographs do little to prepare one for the size, scale, and impact of this building, one of the great landmarks of American architecture. Essentially intact, it is a remarkable survival. Historians have made claims for various designers for the edifice—among them Richard Taliaferro and Henry Cary Jr.—and the controversy continues. The design most likely resulted from a collaboration among the undertaker, the brickmasons, and the leading vestryman, Robert "King" Carter, who paid for its construction. Carter, who owned more than 300,000 acres of land and 1,000 slaves at his death in 1732, lived at Corotoman plantation (burned, 1729), a short distance away. Cruciform in plan with entrances in three of the wings, the church measures 70 feet square and about 48 feet in height. The walls are of Flemish bond brick with random glazed headers. The doorways, windows, and corners all have elaborate brick detailing. Perhaps the finest is the west doorway, which has a segmental pediment in a modified Doric order, 21 feet high. The overall impression, though, is of a certain austerity. The prominent roof with its flared surfaces gives an impression of a mausoleum-like building. The same austerity continues on the interior, which overwhelms with its height of 33 feet to the center of the plaster groin vaults, its Purbeck stone paving, tall pews—4 feet in height—and then plain plaster walls

above. Ornamentation is concentrated in the chancel, which contains a walnut reredos with a painted Decalogue of later date than the woodwork. An elaborate pulpit and sounding board are located at the corner of the nave and transept. Many of the remainder of the fittings, such as the communion table, date from c. 1732.

A brick wall encloses the churchyard. Although a replacement, it follows the original foundations. On the east side are a series of Carter family tombs from the eighteenth century that indicate the close attention paid to London fashions and various design books. Adjacent is the Carter Reception Center (1966–1976, Frederick D. Nichols and Carlo Pelliccia), an appropriately simple brick structure designed by two University of Virginia faculty members, which houses an exhibit related to Christ Church. The remarkable survival of Christ Church results largely from two facts: the Carter family owned the property until 1960, and no significant military action occurred in the area during the Civil War.

Middlesex County   (PE28–PE31)

PE28 **Methodist Lower Church** (Lower Chapel)

c. 1714–1717, 1857, 1912, 1946. VA 3 and VA 33 (south side, .1 mile on VA 649), Grafton area

Originally named the Lower Chapel, since it served the needs of the lower (more southern) section of Christ Church Parish, the church was considered a secondary structure. Hence the walls are of English bond brick. It lacks the rubbed and gauged trim work usual in churches of the period, although a few glazed bricks do appear. The distinguishing feature of the small rectangular building (34 by 56 feet) is the jerkinhead, or clipped gable, roof, which is original, though covered by later materials. It was abandoned at disestablishment, and the Methodist church took it over in 1857. None of the interior is original.

PE29 **Christ Church**

c. 1712–1714, c. 1717, 1843, 1900, 1931. VA 33, Christ Church

Standing on the site of an earlier church is the third of three churches to serve Christ Church Parish, considered because of its location to be the "middle" church. The outer walls of this rectangular structure, laid up in Flemish bond, were constructed, or superintended, by Alexander Graves. Although his name or initials do not appear, bricks in the west tympanum of the modern vestibule indicate that John Hipkins did the carpentry and the glazing. Other initials also appear. The brickwork has been much repaired. The south and west walls contain the most original fabric. Evidence suggests that the church had an altar screen and rich appointments, but all were destroyed during disestablishment. The church was revived in the 1840s, and the interior dates essentially from the twentieth century. The nearby Christ Church School (founded 1921), a boys' preparatory school, uses it as a chapel. The original churchyard was smaller. The present walls, a gift of the Garden Club of America, date from 1942. Some especially fine tombstones, such as those of the Wormeley family, survive from the colonial period.

PE30 Urbanna

Urbanna is a product of an act passed by the House of Burgesses in 1680 that encouraged the creation of port towns. Initially laid out in 1691, the town developed along Virginia Street, the main street. The location offered convenient access to the tobacco wharves along Urbanna Creek and the Rappahannock River. A resurvey of the town by Henry Towles in 1741 produced an irregular grid pattern that survives. In 1748, Urbanna became the county seat of Middlesex County and remained so until 1851, when the seat was moved to Saluda. When tobacco production declined, the town became a center for local commerce, including the shipment of farm produce by water. Later in the nineteenth century it became a resort town. A number of houses and churches date from this period. Oyster and crab harvesting also became an important part of the economy. Urbanna contains notable eighteenth- and nineteenth-century buildings.

PE30.1 Middleesex County Women's Club (Old Courthouse)

1744, c. 1850, c. 1948. Virginia St.

Converted into a church after the removal of the county seat, the building served as an interdenominational chapel. By 1907, it was an Episcopal church. When the Episcopalians left in 1948, the Women's Club took it over. The Gothic Revival cladding over the original brick dates from the 1850s. In addition to the wings and lancet windows, the building had decorative bargeboards, which have been removed.

PE30.2 Lansdowne

c. 1750, c. 1900. Virginia St. (west end, nearly opposite the Women's Club)

Built as a secondary residence for the large landowner Ralph Wormley IV and later owned by members of the Lee family, Lansdowne is a little known but fine mid-Georgian residence. Constructed of brick laid in Flemish bond with rubbed and gauged bricks, the building has an original two-story portico. Later additions to the rear and the interior have altered it, although the original paneling remains.

PE30.3 Van Wagenen House

c. 1900. Virginia St.

This house next door to Lansdowne presents a lively contrast. The design is probably derived from George Barber's pattern books (1898–1907). An aggressive Queen Anne pile, the structure contains a variety of projections, chimneys, and roofs. The large porch has Tuscan columns. Although Jefferson and his builders loved the Tuscan order, it is doubtful that this detail is an homage to him.

PE30.4 Wormeley Cottage

c. 1742. Virginia St.

A good surviving example of the typical eighteenth-century "middling class" house, this weatherboarded frame structure has a side-hall plan, a massive end chimney, and a steeply pitched roof with dormers.

PE30.5 Old Customs House (Little Sandwich)

c. 1805, 1934. Virginia St. (near the waterfront)

Although named for a royal customhouse that stood in Urbanna in the 1760s, this brick house appears to be of later date, although it may use materials from the earlier structure. A good surviving example of a vernacular house, the brick structure, laid in Flemish bond, has one exterior and one interior chimney.

PE30.6 Urbanna Public Library (Old Tobacco Warehouse)

c. 1760, c. 1938, 1969. Virginia St.

The library is a one-and-one-half-story brick structure which originally served as a storehouse for tobacco awaiting shipment. Constructed for factor James Mills, the building sits on a full basement and has large openings at each end, which facilitated the handling of tobacco. The long wooden porch is a reconstruction undertaken by the APVA after it purchased the property in 1938. Since 1969 the warehouse has served as the local library.

PE30.7 Urbanna Baptist Church

1896, Charles H. Palmer. 1903, 1954. Watling St. (north side)

Palmer, a local builder, spent seven years in New York as a carpenter and in 1874 returned to his

PE30.7 Urbanna Baptist Church

hometown, where he designed and erected many buildings until his death in 1904. The vibrant wood-frame church has pointed-arched windows, but references to Gothic are otherwise slim. Designed for the largest congregation in town, the structure openly announced the prominence of the Baptists. Directly across from it is the Palmer-Chowning house (1875, Charles H. Palmer; Watling Street, south side), which has a basic foursquare form and plan enlivened with a decorative porch.

PE30.8 Hewick Bed and Breakfast
(Hewick, or Hewrick, House)

c. 1750, c. 1810, c. 1849. VA 602, Urbanna. Identified with a sign

This house, approached by a long, tree-lined drive, illustrates the changing tastes of a Virginia family. The property has been owned by the politically important Robinson family and their heirs since the seventeenth century. It probably began as a single-story structure with a clipped gable roof. Early in the nineteenth century the roof forms were changed to gambrels,

one of which still remains on the ell. About mid-century the front section received a second floor and a Greek Revival gable roof. Tours are offered.

PE31 Middlesex County Courthouse

1851–1853, John P. Hill, builder. Additions. U.S. 17, Saluda

The county seat of Middlesex County (created c. 1669) moved here from Urbanna in 1851. The county justices selected a town hall–type plan that was then more than twenty years out of date. They paid $3,000 for the building. Recalling the courthouses of Jefferson's time and those of Fairfax (1799), Madison (c. 1830), and Caroline (c. 1830) counties, the structure has an arcade at ground level and jury rooms above the courtroom. The use of the Tuscan order for the cornice is a survival rather than a revival. Except for the thick treatment of the arches, the building looks like a work of 1820 rather than of the 1850s. An addition to the east (1966) mimics the original. The courthouse grounds contain the usual group of buildings, including the clerk's office (1875) and a Confederate monument (1910), put up by the United Daughters of the Confederacy.

Mathews County   (PE32–PE34)

PE32 Mathews

VA 14

The town grew up around a landing on the East River, and the buildings spread out along the main road (now Virginia 14). It became the county seat in 1790, when the area was split off from Gloucester County. The courthouse square is a modest but decorous group of structures, common in Virginia. The Mathews County Courthouse (c. 1830), a three-bay facade with a gable roof treated as a pediment, had been dated to 1795, but recent investigation indicates the later date. The courtroom is accessed through the central door. Offices originally occupied the flanking wings. Certainly the structure is conservative, no matter the date, and unique among Virginia's courthouses. Also on the square are the sheriff's office (c. 1795), the clerk's office (c. 1827), a Civil War monument (a sculpture entitled *Our Confederate Soldier* [1912]), and several lawyers' offices.

PE33 Methodist Tabernacle

1922. VA 611 at VA 644 (1.6 miles east of VA 14)

Most tabernacles used for revival meetings date from the nineteenth century. Thus this building is unusual both for its date and for its survival. The large, airy wooden structure is well preserved. The high monitor roof created a chimney effect on hot summer nights. All of the original fittings, including the speaker's platform, choir tiers, and "mourners' bench," remain. The structure is still in use.

PE34 New Point Comfort Lighthouse

1801–1805. Island at confluence of Chesapeake and Mobjack bays; visible from end of VA 600. Not accessible

Constructed of ashlar sandstone by a Mathews County resident, Elzy Burroughs, the lighthouse takes its tapering octagonal form from the Old Point Comfort Lighthouse. The federal government probably provided the design. The lighthouse remained in use until 1963, when the county took it over and restored it. The county continues to maintain the building.

Gloucester County   (PE35–PE39)

PE35 Ware Parish Church

c. 1710–1715. 1827, 1854, 1902, 1930. VA 3 and VA 14 (1.2 miles north of Gloucester)

This is the only surviving rectangular church in Virginia that still retains three entrances. The scale is impressive—80 feet, 9 inches on the long side and 40 feet, 9 inches on the shorter. The main entrance, a round-arched opening articulated by a primitive archivolt, pierces the tall, blank brick wall of the west facade. Above is a small circular window. The north and south facades are six bays in length with the entrance doors at the fifth bay. The windows are round-headed with gauged surrounds. The entrances have triangular pediments of gauged and rubbed brick. Like nearby Abingdon Church, Ware has exquisite Flemish bond brickwork. The rich red stretchers contrast with dark blue glazed headers that sparkle in sunlight. Abandoned at disestablishment, the church suffered. The Civil War and various modernization campaigns left their marks. Thus the interior is of only passing interest. The churchyard contains a number of colonial tombstones. Also of interest is the wall around the oldest part of the yard.

PE36 Gloucester County Courthouse

c. 1766. 1894–1895, 1907, 1956. U.S. 17, Gloucester Courthouse

Rural courthouse towns such as this, consisting of the courthouse, a few auxiliary buildings, and perhaps a tavern, are characteristic of eastern Virginia. Wealthy planters of the area formed Gloucester County in 1651 so they

PE35 Ware Parish Church (left)

PE37 Abingdon Church (above)

would not have to make the trip across the York River to attend court day. The courthouse square, which is actually an oval, is surrounded by a brick wall (1933) modeled after those of the Williamsburg restoration. (Courthouse grounds rarely were enclosed in the colonial period.) The Gloucester County Courthouse retains much of its original form and materials—a rectangular structure with round-headed windows, fine brickwork, and a modillioned cornice. The T-shaped plan is similar to that of the courthouse in Williamsburg. It originally had a central courtroom flanked by two heated jury rooms. In 1907 the plan was reoriented. The removal of the two partition walls allowed for the construction of a larger courtroom. Windows were added to the east and west ends of the building, and a new pedimented Ionic tetrastyle portico was added. Later more modifications and additions were made. Recently (1956, 1974) new and undistinguished courthouse annexes were erected nearby. Also on the square are the usual individual structures: the county clerk's office (now treasurer's office) (1822), in the fireproof materials of the time; debtors' jail (c. 1810); sheriff's office and jail (1873); clerk's office (1896); and Confederate memorial (1889). On the road surrounding the square stand several buildings of interest. To the east is the Gloucester County Office Building (Botetourt Hotel, or John New's Ordinary; c. 1770), a substantial two-story, six-bay brick structure of considerable refinement.

PE37 Abingdon Church

c. 1751–1755; later remodelings. U.S. 17, 1 mile south of White Marsh

One of the most sophisticated of mid-eighteenth-century Virginia churches, Abingdon should be compared to nearby Christ Church, Lancaster (see entry, above). The church has a Latin-cross plan, a form first used in Virginia at Bruton Parish church in Williamsburg in the 1710s and repeated in nearly a dozen other parishes over the next fifty years. The dimensions are extraordinarily large, 80.5 feet east to west and 75.5 feet north to south. All four arms have the same width, 35.5 feet on the outside, which on the interior helps to minimize the isolating effects possible with narrower wings. The walls are laid in a Flemish bond with glazed headers, and all three of the doorways exhibit high-quality molded and rubbed bricks. The west doorway, with its pilasters and segmental pediment, is frequently illustrated in publications. The three entrances retain their original, paneled folding doors. The window frames are decorated with fluted pilasters rather than the more typical molded architraves.

Closed with disestablishment, the building suffered. The church was reconstituted in 1826 and then damaged during the Civil War. Repairs were undertaken at various times. Hence the dating and originality of portions of the interior are controversial. The most notable early features include the galleries in the north and south arms and an enormous wooden reredos in the chancel in the east. The reredos may date from c. 1755, but its provenance is speculative; it may have come from another church. Originally it stood on the east wall. The large broken triangular pediment with a pineapple in the center, carried on a complicated entablature supported by two Corinthian columns, represents some of the finest colonial carving in Virginia. The pulpit originally stood in the southeast corner of the crossing. Repairs in 1897 changed the roof and ceiling form, and the reredos was reconfigured to form a small vesting room behind the chancel. The last major renovation occurred in 1986, when the floors were taken up and rebuilt and the sash repaired. The pews are more recent.

The churchyard walls on the east, west, and portions of the south date from the eighteenth century. The gates are new. Among the tombs are several eighteenth-century examples for the Burwell and Page families. Many of these were moved in the twentieth century from sites on local plantations, such as nearby Rosewell. Nearly all the gravestones were fabricated in England, since Virginia possessed neither the appropriate carving stone nor the carvers.

PE38 Rosewell

1726–1737. c. 1850, remodeling. 1916, burned. VA 644, White Marsh vicinity

Begun by Mann Page I in the 1720s and completed by 1737, Rosewell was probably the largest and most costly private house in the British American mainland colonies. It was remodeled with a plain Greek Revival interior in the mid-nineteenth century and burned in 1916. The remaining brick walls have been stabilized and are informative in spite of their fragmentary state.

Like the Governor's Palace in Williamsburg, the Nelson House in Yorktown, and Stratford Hall, Rosewell had a boastful form and bold silhouette. A pair of cupolas and four stone-capped chimneys rose above brick parapets over three-and-one-half-story walls. The masonry is the most refined in the Chesapeake. Gauged brick is used in the chimney stacks, skirts below windows, and richly detailed door surrounds. These surrounds, now largely lost, as well as Portland stone keystones and windowsills, closely relate Rosewell to Robert Carter's Christ Church, Lancaster (c. 1728–1732; see entry, above). Both also employed

PE39 Walter Reed Birthplace

fashionable London windows, with frames largely hidden behind brick jambs.

Sizable portions of the land (north) front and T-shaped end walls survive today. The latter provided additional space for closets and two richly worked stairs. The largest rose in an entrance hall at the front left (on the northeast), a grand reception space that occupied more than a quarter of the first floor. Superior chambers were on the west side of this story, and the small fireplaces that once heated the largest closets off both private rooms remain visible, as does the course of the main stair on the opposite end.

Archaeological investigation has recently revealed evidence of an extensive pre-1721 Page house complex with a different orientation on the same site. The test excavations have also confirmed that sizable brick ancillary buildings flanked a land-side courtyard but that their intended connections to the main house were never executed. Surviving end doorways were service entrances on the main floor. There was also direct access from this floor to cellar service and storage spaces, the most impressive being an extant vaulted room below part of the stair hall.

PE39 Walter Reed Birthplace

c. 1800. 1926, restoration. VA 616 at VA 614, Belroi. Open to the public

The house is a one-room, rural vernacular cottage, typical of the dwellings that used to dot the Chesapeake landscape. A frame building with brick nogging and weatherboard, it has two exterior chimneys, one for the main room and the other for the ell. Reed, who discovered the cause of and treatment for yellow fever, was born in the house in 1851, while his father, a Methodist minister, waited for completion of a nearby parsonage. Purchased and restored by the Medical Society of Virginia in 1926, it was transferred to the APVA, which manages the property.

King and Queen County   (PE40–PE45)

PE40 King and Queen Court House

VA 14

·Still a rural courthouse hamlet, the town, like the county, was named for William and Mary, who occupied the throne when the county was formed in 1691. The original King and Queen County Courthouse (c. 1750; 1828, rebuilding and addition. 1864, rebuilding. 1895, addition) is a mixed affair, with a small portion of original Flemish bond brickwork and glazed headers still visible beneath the later additions. A fire badly damaged the original T-shaped structure in 1828, and it was rebuilt and subsequently added to. Then Union raiders set it ablaze along with the adjacent clerk's office and jail. Rebuilt again in 1864, it received a further addition in 1895. The courthouse compound contains the usual Confederate monument (1913) and clerk's office and jail (c. 1870). The courthouse yard wall was constructed in the 1930s under WPA auspices. The new courthouse and county administration building (1997, Moseley, Harris, and McClintock) attempts to relate to the earlier courthouse through the colonnade, windows, cornice, and copper-clad arched roof. Adjacent is Fary Tavern (c. 1802). Immanuel Episcopal Church (1884) follows the Upjohn formula of board-and-batten siding, although the windows are round-headed rather than pointed. A sundial near the church door contains the mark of the maker, John Bowan, Bristol. It dates from 1715.

PE41 Mattapony (Mattaponi) Baptist Church

c. 1734. 1922, rebuilding. VA 14, Cumnor vicinity

The cruciform plan was reserved for the more important Anglican parishes. This building was originally the lower church of St. Stephen's parish. The exterior brickwork is a particularly fine Flemish bond with glazed headers. The pedimented doorways employ gauged and molded bricks. Abandoned during disestablishment, the church was taken over by a Baptist congregation in 1803. A fire in 1921 destroyed the interior. It has been rebuilt, although with alterations.

PE42 Bruington Baptist Church

c. 1790, c. 1845. VA 14 (north side) at VA 636, Bruington

Little is evident of the earlier structure on this site, for the building was vastly enlarged into its present two-story temple format around the middle of the nineteenth century. The size indicates the power the Baptists came to exercise in rural areas. The details, such as the modillion cornice and the doorway, are similar to illustrations in Minard Lafever's various books.

PE43 Newtown

VA 625 and VA 721

A rural crossroads town, Newtown began as a plantation that was sold in 1769. A settlement grew up on the Great Post Road from Williamsburg to Philadelphia. In the mid-nineteenth century, it was the largest town in King and Queen County and contained a number of academies. About ten older buildings survive. At the crossroads stands the post office and store (1923), a wooden vernacular structure. Adjacent to the crossroads on Virginia 721 is the most impressive survivor, the Lee Boulward house (c. 1823), a five-bay building with massive pillars supporting the portico. South of the store on Virginia 625 are the Richardson Lumpkin house (c. 1839), an eccentric four-bay wooden structure, and then The Hill (also known at Locust Hill; c. 1769; later additions), a three-bay farmhouse with a central entrance and a five-light transom. It is surrounded by several outbuildings.

PE44 Providence

1826. VA 627, King and Queen Courthouse vicinity

Built by Dr. William Dew, this tall, five-bay, single-pile brick house and its outbuildings make an impressive statement along the road. Dew apparently had his office in the basement, which perhaps accounts for its height.

PE45 Upper King and Queen Baptist Church

c. 1840. 1969, alterations. VA 635 (1 mile north of VA 623)

The Doric portico in antis is a significant departure from the plain Baptist churches of the period. The interior of the church was rebuilt after a tornado removed the roof.

King William County (PE46–PE48)

PE46 St. John's Episcopal Church

c. 1732, c. 1765. 1926, rose garden. VA 30 (north on VA 627, .1 mile)

An outstanding example of colonial masonry, the front section of St. John's was built first. The 1765 addition created the present T shape. A glistening Flemish bond appears above the water table and English bond below. The pedimented molded brick doorways are beautifully handled. The eight large windows, now lengthened, have semicircular arches with rubbed brick voussoirs. On the interior, the west and north galleries date from the enlargement. The reredos—13 feet, 3 inches wide—is the outstanding feature of the interior, but it probably is not original to the building since it does not fit into the space. Abandoned at disestablishment, the church was used by various groups. After the Civil War, the building was reconsecrated as an Episcopal church.

PE47 King William County Courthouse

c. 1725. c. 1810, c. 1920, 1983. VA 619 (.3 mile north of VA 30), King William

Although still seemingly isolated in a rural location, the building lies near the center of the county (formed in 1701). Activity revolved around court day and the courthouse, as it does today. This building may be the country's oldest public building still in use, although the date of construction is uncertain. Some historians have attempted to attribute its design to Richard Taliaferro, a brickmason from the Williamsburg area, but no evidence supports the claim. Probably the design came from justices in Williamsburg. The arcaded front created a civic presence and provided shelter. Its

immediate Virginia sources may be the Wren Building and the Capitol in Williamsburg.

The brickwork, Flemish bond with glazed headers and rubbed jack arches and corners, is characteristic of the second and third quarters of the eighteenth century. Like the Hanover, Charles City, and Isle of Wight county courthouses, the King William County Courthouse is T-shaped, with a central door opening off the entrance arcade into a courtroom. Flanking the courtroom are two small, heated jury rooms. In the early nineteenth century the building was altered. The courtroom was extended one bay in length to the north with a fireplace added at the end, the magistrates' platform was reconstructed, the jury room doors were moved, and two doors were inserted in the side walls to provide separate access to ancillary buildings for court officials. The building has undergone significant renovations in the twentieth century, first in the 1920s and then again in 1983, resulting in the removal or alteration of earlier fabric. The high, hipped roof was originally covered in shingles rather than in slate. The one-story clerk's office (1897) includes part of an old jail to the south, both incorporated beneath an arcade across the front added in 1928.

In front stands the inevitable Confederate monument (1901–1903). East of the courthouse stands a one-story brick jail (1890), which has been extended and modified (1970). The entire complex is surrounded by a late nineteenth-century brick wall. The entry is across a stile designed to keep cattle out of the grounds. Missing from this collection of public buildings are taverns and hotels, once an integral part of the scene on court day. Sites of at least three eighteenth- and nineteenth-century taverns are to the east, south, and west of the courthouse grounds

PE46 St. John's Episcopal Church

PE47 King William County Court-house

PE48 Fontainebleau-Robinson Sculpture Park

1934–1938, Hylah Edwards Robinson. VA 30 (1 mile east of U.S. 360), Central Garage vicinity. Open to the public

The park contains an amazing collection of sculpture by a self-taught artist who, to occupy her time after her children left home, began modeling a series of figures in cement. The subjects ranged from Adam and Eve to a reclining Greta Garbo. "Found" pieces of iron and other materials served as armatures for the figures. An automobile tire became the mold for the edges of birdbaths. Robinson also sculpted a self-portrait and those of several of her children and sculptures representing Pocahontas, Shirley Temple, and a variety of animals.

Essex County   (PE49–PE54)

PE49 Hundley Hall

1838. VA 1101, Dunnsville area

Illustrative of the conservatism of rural Virginia architecture on the Peninsulas, this prominent house is Georgian in form and Federal in details. Three bays across, it has a double-pile plan with a double parlor, balanced by a large dining room across the center hall.

PE50 St. Paul's Episcopal Church

1838–1840. c. 1859, c. 1890, alterations. U.S. 360, Miller's Tavern

Consecrated by Bishop Meade of Virginia in 1840, the building reflects the architectural conservatism of the Episcopal Church during the antebellum period. With its double doors and lack of a central aisle and an altar, it might be mistaken for a Baptist church. Exactly when the pointed-arched windows were installed is unclear, but it may have been before the Civil War.

PE51 Woodlawn

c. 1816. c. 1840, enlargement. 1997, restoration. U.S. 360 (south side), Miller's Tavern

Single-cell houses similar to this, with massive exterior chimneys, were a common sight in the landscape of the Virginia peninsulas in the eighteenth and nineteenth centuries. Woodlawn is well built and serviceable, with a gambrel roof that allowed for expansion. It stood vacant for many years before its recent restoration.

PE52 Tappahannock Historic District

Intersection of U.S. 17 and U.S. 360 (bounded by Rappahannock River, Queen Street, Church Lane, and Cross Street)

Originally known as Hobb's Hole, or Hobbs His Hole, Tappahannock received a formal charter in 1682. An important Rappahannock River port for the large plantations in the area, it became the seat of Essex County in 1692. The town prospered, became an international port, and grew so genteel in the eighteenth century that hogs were banned from the streets and wooden chimneys forbidden as fire hazards.

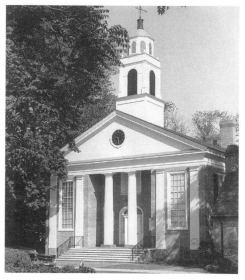

PE52.1 Essex County Courthouse

The British shelled the town in 1814. The tobacco on which Tappahannock's prosperity rested exhausted the surrounding soil. When the railroad replaced water transportation, the town became a backwater. The Downing Bridge (1927) across the river reinvigorated the town.

The Essex County Courthouse (PE52.1) (1848, 1926, 1965; 309 Prince Street), with its distyle in antis portico, dominated the center of town. It replaced an earlier courthouse. Although no architect has been identified, clearly someone with talent was involved. The white pilasters and Tuscan columns give an impression of a hexastyle portico. In the 1920s Jessie Ball du Pont, who lived in the area, financed a restoration and the addition of a clock tower. On the courthouse grounds are the usual outbuildings, including the clerk's office (c. 1800) and the debtors' prison (c. 1750). Also on the block is the Beale Memorial Baptist Church (c. 1855; additions), which contains walls of the 1728 courthouse.

The Ritchie House (1742; later additions and alterations; 227 Prince Street) was originally built as an inn and then used as a hotel. This one-and-one-half-story, Flemish bond brick structure was the home for many years of Thomas Ritchie, one of the group of political associates of Thomas Jefferson known as the

Virginia Junto. The customhouse (c. 1750; 109 Prince Street), despite its importance as a center for the town, is small and simple. The porch is an addition to this stucco-over-brick structure, which stands next to the river, where the wharves were located.

On Water Street, which crosses Prince, are many of the town's large houses. The Brockenborough House (c. 1780, later additions; Water Street on the campus of St. Margaret's School) is a frame house with elaborate interior paneling, cornices, and friezes. The black marble mantels may have been imported from Scotland. John Brockenborough, a banker, was a cousin of Ritchie and also a member of the Virginia Junto. Emerson's Ordinary (c. 1750; 314 Water Street) was apparently only an eating establishment and did not provide lodging. The frame one-and-one-half-story main building with prominent end chimneys has a gambrel-roofed rear wing.

The detailing of St. John's Episcopal Church (1849–1851; c. 1895; 1970–1973, restoration, Milton L. Grigg; Duke Street) resembles the wooden Gothic details illustrated in *Upjohn's Rural Church Architecture* (1852), although the book postdates the construction of the building. The minister of the parish, the Reverend John Peyton McGuire, had traveled widely and certainly knew of the Gothic revolution brewing in the North. McGuire was in charge of nearby St. Paul's, Millers Tavern, which is earlier and architecturally very conservative. The vestry minutes for June 5, 1849, noted communication with "skillful workmen in Baltimore," and the design may have come through that connection. St. John's is in Upjohn's rural Gothic mode, with pointed-arched openings, small finals, and board-and-batten siding. On the interior the pulpit stood in the center, indicating the evangelical orientation of mid-nineteenth-century Episcopalians in Virginia. A sac-

risty was added c. 1895 and the pulpit moved, but a restoration in the 1970s by Milton L. Grigg restored it to the center. Windows include one by Tiffany Studios, one by Lamb Studios, and two by Mayer of Munich.

PE53 **Blandfield**

1769–1774. Virginia 624 (.6 mile north from U.S. 17, private road, 2 miles). Visible from the Rappahannock River; sometimes open during Historic Garden Week

Blandfield, built by Robert Beverley II, is a five-part Palladian composition. The center sections are massive, pedimented pavilions. The floor plan owes a debt to James Gibbs's *Book of Architecture* (1728). Beverley spent twenty years extravagantly decorating and furnishing the interior. An 1844 remodeling removed some of the interior paneling, which a current restoration effort is attempting to replace.

PE54 **Vauter's (Vawter's) Church**

c. 1719, c. 1731, c. 1827. 1969, restoration, Milton L. Grigg. U.S. 17, Loretto

John Vauter built the rectangular section of this church first, and then Edward and Benjamin Vauter supervised the addition of the south wing, giving the structure a T shape. English bond was employed below the water table, Flemish bond with glazed headers above. High-quality brickwork is also observable in the rubbed corners, gauged arches, and molded and gauged pedimented doorways. Abandoned after disestablishment, the church was remodeled when services resumed in 1827. The pews were cut down, a two-story pulpit replaced the original three-story one, and the chancel was moved from the east to the north wall. Milton Grigg's restoration attempted to return the interior to its original condition.

Caroline County (PE55–PE58)

PE55 **Camden**

1859, Norris G. Starkwether. VA 686; .7 mile to a private road, then .8 mile; on Rappahannock River. Not visible (NHL)

Camden is one of the finest examples of the Italian Villa style in the state. William Carter

Pratt commissioned the house, which was to be constructed on the site of an earlier one that had been demolished. Starkwether, who had offices in Washington and Baltimore, produced a lavish design that had a large entrance tower (destroyed during the Civil War by Union gunboats). The house was advanced for the peninsula area in the period; its features included running water in every bedroom, central heating, gas lighting, and a conservatory. The house was constructed of wood with an exterior covering was flushboarded cypress, sanded and painted pale pink. The grounds were laid out in the Gardenesque manner, of which traces can still be seen.

PE56 Port Royal

The Virginia Council established Port Royal as a port on the Rappahannock River in 1744. Richard Taliaferro surveyed the town and laid it out on a grid with twelve square blocks that survive virtually intact. This small town was an international port for the tobacco trade and campaigned to become the national capital in the 1780s. Somnolence arrived when the railroads bypassed it. Architects for the Williamsburg restoration found it a particularly attractive source of precedents for their work in the colonial capital. The town retains an important concentration of more than thirty eighteenth- and early nineteenth-century buildings, in spite of substantial losses since the 1930s. King Street (U.S. 301) runs north-south and ends at the river, while Water Street parallels the river.

PE56.1 Brockenborough-Peyton-Hicks House

c. 1790. Southwest corner of Caroline and King sts.

This five-bay, two-story house with a hipped roof stands prominently as one of the largest in Port Royal. A portion of the original interior was removed in 1932 and is now in the Nelson Gallery of Art in Kansas City.

PE56.2 Caithness

1940, Thomas Tileston Waterman. King St. at the river

Waterman, an architect, architectural historian, and one of the original Colonial Williamsburg restorers, was sufficiently enamored of Port Royal to build his own house here, facing a garden and backing onto a lane that descends to the river. Its single-story height, U-shaped plan, and stucco finish appear to have been influenced by Waterman's vacations in the Caribbean. Details are rendered in a simple neoclassical manner with which he was very conv-ersant.

PE56.1 Brockenborough-Peyton-Hicks House

PE56.3 Farish Print Shop

c. 1790. East side of King St., between Middle and Caroline sts.

This unusually intact post-Revolutionary printing office was originally divided into a center sales room flanked by an office (with a glazed interior door) and storage room. Attic quarters were intended for the shopkeeper or his workers.

PE56.4 Fox's Tavern

c. 1750. East side of King Street between Water and Caroline streets)

The tavern was offered for rent in 1779 as the "much frequented house, formerly kept by Ann Fox and now by Mr. William Buckner." Originally five bays long, it has a peculiar arrangement of interior front and exterior rear chimneys, indicating the manipulation of room size in its Georgian plan to keep the rooms of a consistent size. English brown sandstone was used for mantels and exterior steps.

PE56.5 Holloway House

c. 1800. Southeast corner of King and Water sts.

This picturesque house began as one and one-half stories with its dining room connected to the rear by a short hyphen. Later in the nineteenth century it was raised to two stories, and an archaic-looking porch chamber was balanced on piers. A detached rear kitchen has riven clapboards as interior finish.

PE56.6 Masonic Hall

c. 1854. North side of King St. between Caroline and Water sts.

The gable-fronted building did double duty as Masonic hall and town hall, with shops (and once a post office) on the first floor. Chartered in 1755, Port Royal's is the second oldest Masonic lodge in Virginia. Two Greek Revival shop fronts survive in spite of the building's derelict state.

PE56.7 Townfield

c. 1854. North side of King Street between Caroline and Water sts.

The complex plan of Townfield developed from a simple center-passage house that was lengthened twice and connected to a two-story nineteenth-century wing set at a right angle. An enclosed projection facing the river was added to extend the original passage and provide windows on three sides. Thomas Waterman participated in the restoration when he resided in Port Royal.

PE56.8 St. Peter's Episcopal Church

c. 1830, 1849, 1868, and later. Northwest corner of Market and Water sts.

St. Peter's was originally built in the Greek Revival idiom with Doric columns in antis. A major fire in 1849 gutted the interior and led to a remodeling and the insertion of the pointed-arched windows. Then in 1868 lighting struck the steeple, causing another fire. Subsequently the vestry voted "no more steeples," and built a detached bell tower (1873) that recalls some of Richard Upjohn's work.

PE57 Bowling Green

Bowling Green is a county courthouse town that has grown following the traffic pattern along Main Street. The major interest is the Caroline County Courthouse (PE57.1) (c. 1830, attributed to William B. Phillips and Malcolm F. Crawford; 1907, addition, William C. West), a temple-form, arcaded courthouse that follows the Jeffersonian tradition. Caroline County was established in 1727, and this may be its sixth county courthouse. Although no records connect Jefferson's builders, Phillips and Crawford, with this building, it closely resembles their Madison County Courthouse. The proportions have been altered from those used at Madison: the space is cramped between the arches and the second-floor windows. The square latticework belfry is probably not original. The usual auxiliary buildings surround the courthouse. In front is a substantial Confederate monument (1906, J. Henry Brown). The town contains other nineteenth-century buildings, the most impressive being the Baptist Church (PE57.2) (1898–1899, D. Wiley Anderson; later additions) in the Baptist low Gothic mode, which would have appalled a proper gothicist like Ralph Adams Cram. It is extremely colorful with its polychromatic roof tiles, wide nave, and exuberant tower sporting an incongruous window.

PE58 Grace Episcopal Church

1834. VA 2 and VA 610, Corbin

Grace Episcopal is a plain, one-room brick structure in a Greek Revival temple form that reflects the influence of Baptist churches on Episcopalians. Except for its single entrance door, it might be mistaken for a Baptist-built structure. A slave gallery still exists on the interior. A painting of the Ascension by Arthur Pierson, placed above the altar in 1875, indicates the reorientation of Virginia Episcopalians toward more elaborate display.

New Kent County   (PE59–PE61)

PE59 St. Peter's Church

1701–1703, William Hughes, carpenter; Cornelius Hall, mason. 1739–1741, William Walker. 1872, 1950–1951, renovations. 1964–1965, restoration, J. Ambler Johnston and Harden deVoe Pratt. VA 642 (VA 106 north from I-64, VA 609 north from Talleysville 1 mile, right on VA 642 for .4 mile), Talleysville vicinity

One of the most celebrated and interpreted churches in Virginia, St. Peter's has been described as late Gothic, transitional to the classical, Jacobean, and baroque. Isolated and rural, it gives a sense of the opulence Virginia's colonial elite strove to attain. It is remarkable, but much has been reconstructed and is conjectural. Disestablishment and use as a stable during the Civil War destroyed great portions of the fabric. The main body of the church was constructed in the early eighteenth century to replace an earlier church at a different location. Investigations during the 1940s and early 1950s revealed that the Flemish gables had been reconstructed, but whether they are original is conjectural. They are of oversized brick laid up in an English bond, with molded elements that are particularly fine. The tower was added about 1740. It incorporates an amazing variety of elements: molded brick, cornices, massive corner pilasters, recessed panels, windows, and stuccoed urns, one of which serves as a chimney. The pyramidal roof and the dormer windows are conjectural reconstructions, possibly dating from the 1870s, though an early drawing does suggest them. The tower housed a vestry room, and apparently a stairway once led across the north archway giving access, though it may have been an early nineteenth-century addition. Original access is unclear. The Jacobean-style woodwork in the vestry room is recent. The internal door off the gallery probably dates from 1872. All of the interior is reconstruction except for the wainscoting in the chancel, which may date from the 1730s. The casement windows, although replacements, are confirmed as accurate by a 1704 order for glass, lead, and casements. A plaque on the north wall with an indistinct inscription commemorates the Reverend David Morsom, rector for four decades, who married George Washington and Martha Custis. She was a member of the parish during her youth. The graveyard contains pre-Revolutionary tombs.

PE59 St. Peter's Church

PE60 Emmaus Baptist Church

1852, c. 1960. VA 106 (.5 mile south of exit of I-64), Providence Forge vicinity

A product of the second "great awakening" of the mid-nineteenth century, this spartan Greek Revival brick box lacks a full portico. The church is quietly elegant with its twin doors and simple wooden entablature. The interior has a rear balcony and twin aisles leading to a raised dais that is a product of a 1960s renovation. The major feature of the interior is the bright luminosity provided by the large windows on three sides.

PE61 Olivet Presbyterian Church

1856. VA 618 (U.S. 60 west to VA 618, north 3.8 miles), Providence Forge vicinity

Buried deep in the woods in a rural landscape, this small temple-form church fronted by a tetrastyle portico with fluted Doric columns seems almost a garden folly. The building is a simple rectangle with twin entrance doors. The interior is largely original. A gallery is at the rear. The pews retain mahogany and bird's-eye maple graining. The pulpit is set off by marbleized steps. The congregation now resides in Providence Forge, and the church is open for memorial services.

Charles City County   (PE62–PE70)

PE62 Shirley Plantation

c. 1738, c. 1771. 501 Shirley Planation Rd. (off VA 5). Open to the public.

From either the water or the land approach, the buildings of Shirley Plantation are as handsome and imposing as any erected in the American colonies. They form an assemblage that is a model of control and order imposed upon a rural setting. In the eighteenth century this unique grouping of provincial Georgian structures must have seemed even more impressive, because it was larger then.

The surviving Shirley complex was begun by John Carter III (c. 1690–1743), the eldest son and principal heir of wealthy Robert "King" Carter of Lancaster County. In 1723 the younger Carter married Elizabeth Hill of Shirley, and when her brother died shortly thereafter, he inherited the Hill plantation. As late as 1738, a date suggested by both documentary evidence and the examination of builders' trenches, he initiated an ambitious building plan. He had the means to rebuild, for he owned property in nine counties and more cattle and slaves than any other Virginian of his era.

Carter constructed a massive house, flanked by dependencies almost as large. The mansion is three stories high, 48 feet square, and nearly a cube, an original design in the Anglo-Dutch style so prominently introduced in the colony

PE62 Shirley Plantation

at the Williamsburg Governor's Palace. The near dependencies, situated on the land side of the mansion and 36 feet distant, do not survive: the north one apparently burned in the early nineteenth century and the other was torn down in 1868. In 1979–1980 archaeologists identified those buildings as single-pile hall-parlor structures, embellished on the exterior with details of gauged brick and Portland sandstone. Their three-story elevations and hipped roofs are known from a pencil sketch drawn by landscapist Frederic Edwin Church in 1851 and still preserved at Shirley. The north dependency was a kitchen, and that on the south probably was an office. Each was 60 by 24 feet in size. These numbers are multiples of twelve, evidence that an imaginative mathematical scheme underlies Carter's plan. All three buildings apparently were roofed with reddish-orange ceramic tiles, large quantities of which were uncovered through archaeology.

Four additional dependencies, which survive and form a forecourt, were built later, possibly after 1771 when Charles Carter inherited the plantation from his father. These structures are linked to the earlier architecture, yet they are different in their design, execution, and placement. The buildings closest to the mansion apparently served as kitchen and office (thereby allowing for the eventual removal of the earlier dependencies). At the east end are two L-shaped buildings that have no fireplace and seem to have served as storehouses or granaries. The one at the north shelters an icehouse.

As to the mansion house itself, Charles Carter was responsible for major changes both outside and within. On the two principal facades, he replaced small brick porches with the Palladian double porticoes that survive today. These follow the fashion of the porticoes that had been added at mid-century to the Williamsburg Capitol. On the interior he replaced woodwork to bring fashion to an antiquated floor plan. With four corner rooms and neither a central passage nor a central hall, the house in plan perpetuates the informality of the hall-parlor tradition.

By its name, the Shirley plantation honors Cessayly Shirley, wife of a seventeenth-century governor, Thomas West, Lord De La Warr. The land holding known as Shirley Hundred had been patented in 1660 by Edward Hill, ancestor of the present owner. Charles Carter's daughter Ann Hill Carter, wife of Light Horse Harry Lee of Stratford and mother of Robert E. Lee, was born at Shirley in 1773.

PE63 Berkeley Plantation

c. 1726. 12602 Harrison Landing Rd. (VA 5). Open to the public

Berkeley is one of the earliest of the double-pile, two-story Georgian brick mansions of the colony. It was built by Benjamin Harrison IV, the husband of Robert "King" Carter's daughter Anne. The house is imposing from its sheer mass, regularity, and the bold lines of its tall ridge chimneys and distinctive pedimented roof. The well-crafted Flemish bond brickwork is original, but the doorway piers and pediments are modern. The plan is the center-hall, ridge-chimney type. The interior was extensively changed after 1800, when the original paneling was removed. An insurance policy of 1800 identifies two brick dependencies (20 feet by 45 feet) that flanked the house on the south side, toward the river; these were replaced in the mid-nineteenth century by the buildings that survive today.

Though the architecture of the house is significant, Berkeley Plantation is best known for a remarkable string of historical events associated with it. The site was settled early, in 1619, and there the first Thanksgiving in the colonies was offered, before the loss of the Berkeley Hundred landholding in the Indian massacre of 1622 resulted in its abandonment by English settlers. Berkeley was the birthplace of a signer of the Declaration of Independence (Benjamin Harrison V, son of the builder) and of the ninth president of the United States (William Henry Harrison, grandson of the builder). During the Revolutionary War, British troops under Benedict Arnold pillaged the house. After the Seven Days Battles of the Civil War, the Army of the Potomac under General George McClellan occupied the grounds, and there the bugle call *Taps* was composed and played for the first time. The house has been restored in recent years.

PE64 Westover Parish Church

c. 1731. c. 1867, rebuilding. 1956, 1969. John Taylor Hwy. (VA 5)

Westover Parish is very old, dating back to 1625. The church follows a form favored for smaller ecclesiastical buildings, a rectangle measuring about 62 feet by 30 feet. The jerkinhead roof form is original, though restored in 1969. Flemish bond is used above the beveled water table and English below. Rubbed brick with a yellowish cast delineates the four corners of the structure, as well as most of the window jambs (several of which have been rebuilt). The west doorway was renewed in 1956. The building was abandoned after 1805 for more than thirty years because of disestablishment and then returned to service only to be looted by Union troops; thus nothing of the colonial interior remains except the roof trusses. The church owns some early silver, and in the yard are the remains of early gravestones.

PE65 Westover

c. 1750, 1767, 1898. 7000 Westover Rd. (VA 5). Gardens open to the public

One of the best-known houses in the country, Westover is perhaps the quintessential James River planation house. It has long been associated with William Byrd II (1674–1744), but the present house was in fact built by his son, William Byrd III (1728–1777) shortly after a 1749 fire had destroyed the earlier dwelling. Westover's distinctive brickwork, with segmental window heads and ogee water table, was executed by the same bricklayer who later built the courthouse at Charles City, just a few miles away.

The outward symmetry of the dwelling masks an asymmetrical interior in which the two best rooms stand on the same side of the passage, with bedchambers opposite. The public rooms thus formed a coherent domain, drawing a clear line between the public and private ends of the house. The orientation of the stair, disposition of rooms, and detailing of the stone doorways leave no doubt that this house faced the river.

The original structure remains largely intact but incorporates changes made c. 1767, when William Byrd III returned from a long sojourn in Philadelphia. These include the Portland stone doorways and the rococo ceiling ornaments in the ground-floor passage. The ceiling ornaments in the southeast room are contemporary but were rearranged at the end of the nineteenth century.

In 1898, Clarice Sears Ramsay, then the

PE65 Westover

owner, embarked on far-reaching changes, with the assistance of New York architect William Howard Mesereau, who had earlier directed restorations at Fraunces Tavern and Washington Irving's Sunnyside. Mesereau reconstructed the previously destroyed east dependency, linked both flanking structures to the main house, and removed a longitudinal partition to create the present dining room. Upstairs, he installed a suite of sumptuously detailed mantels.

The chimneys of the west (kitchen) dependency predate the walls, which are laid to them. It is unclear whether this structure is an early dependency or a remnant of the house erected by William Byrd I in 1688. In either case, it was probably rebuilt in 1720, when Byrd II mentioned demolition of his "wash house" and the employment of a bricklayer. The present roof is one of only two known clasp-purlin examples in Virginia, the other being Pear Valley in Northampton County on the Eastern Shore.

At opposite extremities of the grounds stand single-bay wrought iron gates with the Byrd family arms in the overthrow, all dating from the lifetime of William Byrd II. North of the house is a contemporary double-bay gate with Byrd's cipher in the overthrow, made by the same shop that produced the other two examples. Paint studies revealed that all were once painted white, a common practice in the eighteenth century. North and west of the house is a garden, the enclosure of which seems to be relatively late, as it does not appear on a 1783 plan of the property. However, a significant vestige of the early garden survives in the tomb of William Byrd II, standing at the center of the present compound and marking the intersec-

tion of its principal axes. The monument is a limestone obelisk, known as the "pyramid," flanked by pedestals with flaming urns (the latter now turned upside down). Additional tombs stand at the former site of Westover church.

PE66 Evelynton

1936–1937, W. Duncan Lee. 6701 John Tyler Hwy. (VA 5). Open to the public

Evelynton is the paramount example of the twentieth-century revival of the James River plantation house. The house was commissioned by Mr. and Mrs. John Augustine Ruffin, Jr., for a site originally owned by the Byrd family of nearby Westover. Ruffin's family, which had owned the property since 1847, had fallen on hard times. He married a wealthy Richmond heiress, Mary Ball Saunders, who decided to replace an earlier house and hired Richmond architect W. Duncan Lee. In addition to designing many Richmond houses and buildings, Lee had directed the enlargement and restoration of Carter's Grove, had worked on Westover, and was a member of the architectural advisory board at Colonial Williamsburg. From these and other sources, such as Henry Chandler Forman's *Early Manor and Plantation Houses of Maryland* (1937), Lee concocted a formidable design.

The house is built of old brick laid in Flemish bond, the brickwork similar to that of the stable and caretaker's cottage at Carter's Grove. Located on Herring Creek, which empties into the James River, the house is on a north-south axis with the land approach from the north, down a tree-lined drive. This front is a five-part composition consisting of a central block of five bays (with a projecting pavilion of three bays), hyphens, and flanking pavilions. Following the eighteenth-century formula, the river, or south, approach is the more impressive, with a seven-bay central facade, hyphens, and flanking dependencies. Details are drawn from a variety of sources: the riverfront doorway resembles those at Westover and Wilton, the wide spacing of the chimneys comes from Gunston Hall, and the right-angled flanking pavilions were inspired by Woodlawn. Indeed, the entire house could inspire a session of the television show *Jeopardy*. The interior follows twentieth-century room arrangement and function, but with details drawn from the past. The influence of Carter's Grove is apparent in many details, including the large archway, but the entry sequence is shifted, with the staircase pulled off to the side, so that someone entering from the land (north) side has a clear view to the creek beyond. The other rooms are equally furnished.

PE67 Greenway

c. 1776 and later. John Tyler Hwy. (.6 mile west of intersection of VA 5 and VA 155)

Greenway is typical of lesser plantation houses of the late eighteenth century. It was built by Judge John Tyler, governor of Virginia and father of John Tyler, the tenth president of the United States, who was born here in 1790. Amid a cluster of outbuildings, the one-and-one-half-story frame structure with large exterior chimneys at either end sits on a brick basement, which exhibits two different types of bond (Flemish and English), probably indicating that the main portion of the house was enlarged at some point. An ell was added to the rear (c. 1800). Portions of the beaded clapboard are original. The interior contains some impressive carved woodwork, especially in the west room, which has a projecting, fully paneled chimney breast with fluted pilasters in double tiers.

PE68 Charles City County Courthouse

c. 1757; later alterations. 1880–1893, additions. John Tyler Hwy. (VA 5), Charles City Courthouse

Charles City County was formed in 1634 as one of Virginia's eight original shires. The present

Charles City County Courthouse was once very similar to surviving courthouses in Isle of Wight, King William, and Hanover counties. It was built between 1749, when Charles City justices finished raising money to finance the construction of a new building, and 1757, when they made a final payment to Colonel Richard Bland of neighboring Prince George County for completing the work. As originally built, the courthouse had a five-bay arcade, or piazza, fronting a central courtroom flanked by two jury rooms. In the early nineteenth century, a chimney was added in the south wall behind the magistrates' platform, a doorway was cut through one of the flanking courtroom windows to provide access to a small brick clerk's office erected to the west, and windows were punched into the south wall to provide better light for the bench.

Following heavy damage during the Civil War, most, but not all, of the sash were replaced (an original, wide-muntin sash window survives in the south wall window of the east jury room). Between 1880 and 1893 the courthouse was radically altered to provide more courtroom space. The orientation of the building was reversed. The chimney on the south end was removed, the flanking windows were blocked, and an entrance door was constructed. At the north end of the building, the wall dividing the courtroom from the arcade was removed, the arched openings of the piazza were enclosed, and the judge's bench and bar were erected in the former center bays of the piazza. The building has undergone a number of renovations over the past hundred years, including a major reworking following an arsonist's attempt to burn the courthouse down in 1989. The effort fell short, unlike many in the colonial days, when public buildings were all too often torched by rogues and disgruntled criminals.

PE69 Belle Air

c. 1700, c. 1800. 11800 John Tyler Hwy. (VA 5). Open by appointment

This frame and clapboard house built as a plantation house by a descendant of David Clarke, who purchased the property in 1662, is an example of an upper-middle-class dwelling of c. 1700. The exposed interior frame and the Jacobean stair railing are features of the seventeenth century; the symmetrical facade, originally five bays, and central-passage plan belong

PE70 Sherwood Forest

to the eighteenth. Later (c. 1800) three bays were added to the facade and a detached kitchen was built.

PE70 Sherwood Forest

c. 1780, c. 1845. 14501 John Tyler Hwy. (VA 5). Open to the public

John Tyler, born nearby at Greenway, the tenth U.S. president, former congressman, senator, governor, and, at his death in 1862, member of the Confederate Congress, purchased this house and attached farm in 1842, three years before leaving the presidency. To a simple three-bay frame house he made many additions, including a ballroom and an office, all one room deep, and built dependencies. Architectural historian Calder Loth believes that the result may, at 300 feet, be the longest domestic facade in the state. Remarkably unified in spite of its diversity, it is daunting. The interior details are based on Minard Lafever's publications. The wallpaper in the ballroom dates from 1844. The grounds immediately surrounding the house received a romantic treatment, and portions of that landscaping still survive.

Hampton Roads (HR)

Hampton Roads comprises the eastern end of the lower peninsula, including Williamsburg, Jamestown Island, Yorktown, Newport News, and Hampton and the counties of James River and Yorktown. The area is bounded by the James River on the south, the York River on the north, Chesapeake Bay and Hampton Roads on the east, and Charles City and New Kent counties on the west.

Historically, this part of Virginia is one of the most important areas in the country. Jamestown was the site of the first successful English settlement in North America, and Williamsburg served as the second capital of Virginia and is doubly important for its twentieth-century restoration. At Yorktown, Lord Cornwallis surrendered to George Washington, ensuring the establishment of the United States of America. Hampton University is among the oldest institutions of higher learning for African Americans. Many other buildings and sites are also significant.

The early landscape of the Native Americans and the English settlers has largely disappeared. It can be glimpsed in some places, such as Carter's Grove, and along certain stretches of the rivers, but overall the land has been dramatically transformed, largely in the last sixty years. Although shipbuilding and shipping clustered around Newport News and Hampton, much of the peninsula remained agricultural until c. 1940. World War II and the Cold War brought large permanent military installations to the area. Other industries and commerce arrived, with attendant growth and sprawl. The city of Hampton took over Elizabeth County in 1952, and the city of Newport News consolidated with Warwick County in 1958.

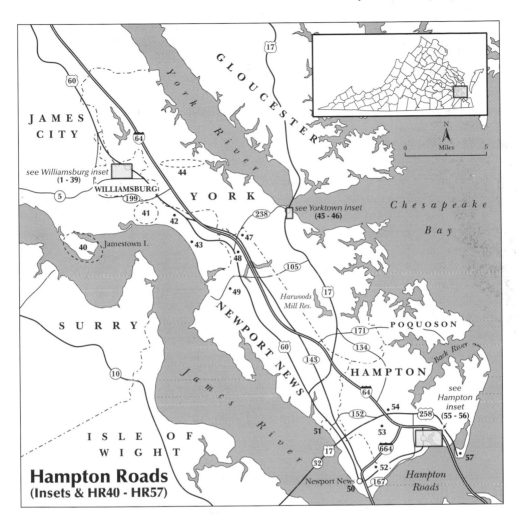

Hampton Roads
(Insets & HR40 - HR57)

Williamsburg

The double genesis of Williamsburg is a long-told tale. First, in 1699 Virginians abandoned the small, unhealthy old capital on marshy Jamestown Island to build a better-planned urban capital on the low ridge between the James and York rivers, a town that would be the scene of momentous decisions made by American citizens on the eve of the Revolution. After the seat of government moved to Richmond, the town lay dormant until the 1920s, when the Reverend W. A. R. Goodwin, rector of Williamsburg's Bruton Parish Church, convinced John D. Rockefeller, Jr., of the town's potential as a historic site and national shrine. Rockefeller began to purchase and subsequently restore and reconstruct what became the country's most substantial restoration effort. Both stories appealed to the progressive spirit of the 1930s as an American drama, not solely a regional or Virginia one.

Much of Williamsburg's appeal derives from the formality of its arrangement and the relative modesty of its buildings. The town plan is credibly attributed to Lieutenant Governor Francis Nicholson, then fresh from a capital-planning role in Annapolis. He laid out a wide main street, named for the Duke of Gloucester, stretching nearly a mile, from the College of William and Mary on the west to a site set aside for construction of a statehouse to the east. Nicholson named parallel streets for himself and planned a major cross axis that would focus on the governor's official residence. A large block near the center of town, bisected by Duke of Gloucester Street, was set aside for a market. Roads led from both ends of town to a port on tributaries of the James and York rivers.

Williamsburg reached the density of building now seen in the designated historic area in the third quarter of the eighteenth century. This museum zone represents perhaps 90 percent of the eighteenth-century town. Development along the main street was most congested west of the capitol, though a comparable mixture of taverns, shops, and dwellings extended its length. Most surviving buildings meet the size requirements and the consistent setback called for in the 1699 Town Act. Few of the buildings were attached to one another, however, and the town never had an urban appearance. Several of the most costly residences faced Palace Green, while other elite houses were built around the edges of the town, where estates resembling small plantations developed. Much of the housing was constructed for successful tradesmen in the 1760s and 1770s. Tenants resided in everything from small parts of houses and shops to lavish townsteads. Some of the most refined houses were, in fact, occupied by renters rather than property owners. Slaves lived in parts of virtually every kind of Williamsburg house and work building; very few buildings were constructed solely for the use of house workers.

Some eighteenth-century buildings were destroyed during the American Revolution and the following century, most notably the capitol, the Governor's Palace, and the public hospital, but other public edifices and numerous early houses survived into the twentieth century. Although removal of the state government and the absence of vigorous regional trade decreased development pressures, the town never really slumbered. Costly houses were built and remodeled in the nineteenth century, and both the college and a state mental hospital maintained an institutional life. White and black evangelical congregations built impressive masonry churches in the 1850s, many of which disappeared during the restoration. By the 1920s Duke of Gloucester Street and Williamsburg in general had taken on a look shared by thousands of American towns. Middle-class residential neighborhoods had begun to develop around the central core, and a sizable black community was centered on streets north of Richmond Road and west of Boundary Street. Rich and poor alike continued to occupy the peripheral eighteenth-century streets, and working-class houses were built along Penniman and Yorktown roads, both east of town.

The apparent erosion of old Williamsburg led Goodwin to propose the idea of a restored town. Goodwin and Rockefeller always conceived of Colonial Williamsburg as a portrait of a past community rather than a series of discrete house museums. But the restoration and reconstruction projects were widely dispersed across the city. The number of tourists visiting the town increased rapidly before the first projects were complete, but boundaries were not drawn to demarcate the historic area until 1949, and the streets lacked much sense of continuity until the 1950s.

Between 1928 and the 1960s, Williamsburg developed as a model town within a town. The Boston architecture firm of Perry, Shaw and Hepburn and later the Colonial Williamsburg Department of Architecture designed even the simplest of the museum buildings. First, Perry, Shaw and Hepburn designed Merchants Square (1928–1931), collecting many of the town's businesses into a block of witty historicist buildings at the west end of Duke of Gloucester Street. The style employed there—primarily drawn from American buildings of the early republic—had strong links to the older mode of the historic area but was sufficiently different to be perceptible to educated observers. Modernism came slowly to Williamsburg. Experimentation at the College of William and Mary in 1938–1939 came to naught, but the Rockefeller family's interest in modernism would lead to several post–World War II buildings such as the Visitor Center.

Museum acquisitions in the old part of town and the growth of both Colonial Williamsburg and the college encouraged suburban growth. Before succeeding Harry F. Byrd as governor in 1930, the progressive mayor John Garland Pollard began developing two garden suburb enclaves for college professors and other middle-class whites: Chandler Court and Pollard Park. Post–World War II Williamsburg expanded dramatically in response to a more mobile population, local and otherwise. The Colonial Williamsburg Foundation designed, built, and then sold Williamsburg Shopping Center (1955) on Richmond Road as locally oriented businesses moved away from the town center. Racial divisions tended to be more pronounced in the new development than they had been at the town center as late as the 1920s and 1930s. Suburban development has dramatically accelerated since the 1950s. The most orchestrated development has been at Busch Properties' Kingsmill, where land once cultivated by indentured workers and slaves is now the site of resort buildings and housing illustrative of evolution in middle-class American architectural taste since the mid-1970s. The associated Busch Gardens theme park has contributed to the growth of the strips on Virginia 60 east and west.

Colonial Williamsburg Historic Area (HR1–HR30)

HR1 **Capitol**

1701–1705, Henry Cary. 1931–1934, reconstruction, Perry, Shaw and Hepburn. East end of Duke of Gloucester St.

One of Virginia's most remarkable public buildings was the capitol constructed in 1701–1705, which stood at the east end of Duke of Gloucester Street until 1747. The House of Burgesses and committee rooms were housed in the east wing, and the General Court and Governor's Council in the west, connected by an arcaded piazza below a joint conference room. The masonry porch, as well as apses marking the superior south ends of both wings, became distinguishing features of Virginia's county courthouses over the next half-century. A west entrance with a semicircular porch seems to have spawned no copies. The building burned in 1747, and a replacement with a portico facing the main street and without the apses was constructed on the old foundations in 1751–1753. This later capitol, the scene of events leading to Virginia's entry into the American Revolution, was in turn lost to fire in 1832.

The first capitol was chosen for reconstruction in 1929 because of relatively extensive surviving specifications and a recent discovery, in the Bodleian Library at Oxford, of a copper engraving plate depicting the north elevation, as well as the perception that it was a more distinctive design. Nevertheless, architectural historian Carl Lounsbury has shown that their Beaux-Arts training misled Perry, Shaw and

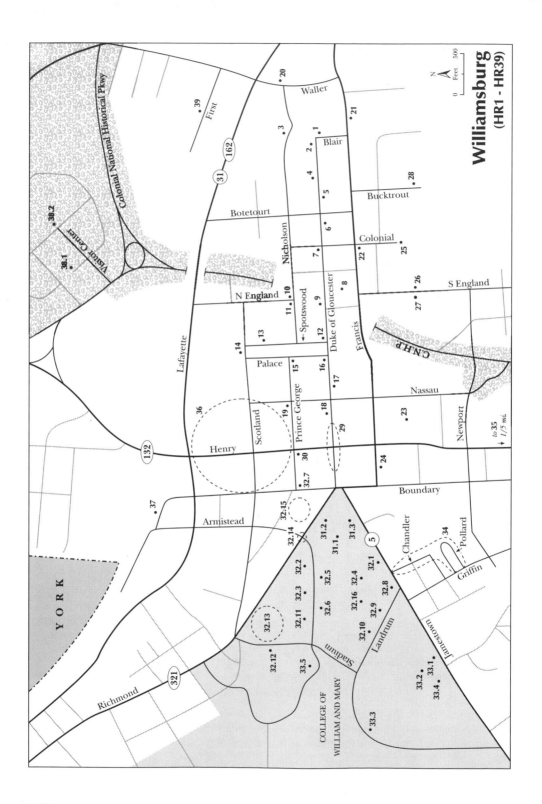

Williamsburg (HR1 - HR39)

HR1 Capitol

The group of buildings near the east end of eighteenth-century Williamsburg included the jail, where accused criminals awaited trial at the General Court and punishment, debtors were incarcerated, and runaway slaves and the insane were restrained. The initial construction, now the northeast section, included two first-floor cells to hold men and women, a chamber for petty offenders upstairs, modest housing for the jailer, and a walled exercise yard. Debtors' cells were added in 1711–1712 and improved keeper's quarters in 1722.

Hepburn, as well as the restoration Architects' Advisory Committee, in their interpretation of the evidence for circulation patterns, lateral fenestration, and the width of the arcade.

The interior finishes in the House of Burgesses, Council Chamber, General Court, and the stair passages are particularly interesting as 1930s interpretations of the 1705 burgesses' specifications, as well as of regional woodwork and painting.

HR2 Secretary's Office

1748. 1939–1940 and 1960, restoration. East end of Duke of Gloucester St.

Built after the fire that destroyed the capitol in 1747 to house the secretary of the colony and for "the Preservation of the Public Records and Papers," this brick building served as Virginia's clerical center. The colonial chief clerk trained all future county clerks here and maintained the official records of land grants. The building's quality and construction parallel those of Virginia courthouses and Anglican churches of the same era. Its refined brickwork is punctuated with a gauged brick frontispiece matching those at nearby Carter's Grove.

HR3 Public Gaol

1702–1703. 1711–1712 and 1722, additions. 1935–1936, restoration and reconstruction. Nicholson St. west of Waller St.

HR4 Raleigh Tavern

c. 1717. 1733–1735, c. 1749, and c. 1780, additions. 1930–1931, reconstruction, Perry, Shaw and Hepburn, Thomas Tileston Waterman, principal designer. Duke of Gloucester St. east of Botetourt St.

Among the largest taverns in eighteenth-century Virginia, the Raleigh is most famous as the site where burgesses met, in 1769 and 1774, after two successive governors dissolved what they perceived as rebellious general assemblies. Lafayette was feted with a banquet in the Apollo Room on his nostalgic return to America in 1824. These and other activities—Jefferson wrote of a "wretched" hangover after a night of dancing there—illustrate the Raleigh's role of providing entertainment and meeting space for hire. As such, the Apollo and Daphne rooms were the counterparts of private entertaining rooms like the ballroom and supper room at the Governor's Palace and the dining room at Peyton Randolph's house. Creation of such spaces was a chief reason for enlargement of the tavern, just as it was at the executive residence, Randolph's house, and other large houses and taverns.

The Raleigh was destroyed in 1859. The reconstructed tavern was the first building of the Williamsburg restoration, opened to the public in 1932. Perry, Shaw and Hepburn were able to base the form of the building and its room arrangements on the archaeological footprint and two 1848 engravings by Benson Lossing, but they drew most of the interior details from eighteenth-century Virginia houses. Woodwork was more richly applied here than in later reconstructions, relative to the rooms' functions, so the building has a freer Colonial Revival quality than later reconstructed buildings in the Williamsburg historic area.

HR5 Wetherburn's Tavern

c. 1742. c. 1751, addition. 1966–1967, restoration.
Duke of Gloucester St. east of Botetourt St.

Although Wetherburn's Tavern evolved in
somewhat the same manner as the Raleigh, its
survival gives it a greater sense of veracity than
its more famous competitor. It began in the
1740s as a five-bay house or tavern with a pair of
rooms on both sides of the stair passage. By
1751 Henry Wetherburn had added a large entertaining space, called the great room, at the
west end, embellished with a baroque marble
mantel and lighted by six closely spaced windows. A second front door afforded direct access to this, presumably the room in which the
tavernkeeper held a ball for a hundred ticket
purchasers in March 1752. Affluent Virginians
could rent the great room and two other first-
floor rooms for private parties, drink, eat, and
gamble there, and sleep in garret rooms above.
At least one of the upper rooms seems to have
been let to a full-time tenant when Wetherburn
died in 1760. The tavernkeeper's family occupied small rear chambers.

The building remained unrestored until
1966–1967, when Colonial Williamsburg architect Paul Buchanan led a restoration based on a
new, more rigorous approach to understanding
how the old structure evolved. In the same era,
archaeologist Ivor Noël Hume carried out a
thorough excavation of the site, providing evidence for the work buildings and the unrefined nature of the rear yard.

HR6 James Anderson House and Blacksmith Shop

HR8 Public Magazine

HR6 James Anderson House and Blacksmith Shop

c. 1770–1780. 1940, reconstruction, Department of
Architecture. 1985–1986, restoration, Dell Upton and
Department of Architectural Research, Colonial
Williamsburg. Duke of Gloucester St. west of Bote-
tourt St.

The house and large rear building are reconstructions of the blacksmith James Anderson's
house and shop, respectively. The house, a
small group of outbuildings, and a boxwood
garden were completed in 1940. Dramatic revi-
sions followed additional archaeological excavations in 1974–1976. A new and larger version
of Anderson's shop in its Revolutionary War
guise was recreated, reproducing cheaper construction techniques that received increased
scrutiny from a new generation of scholars in
the 1970s and 1980s. The new shop was in-

tended to represent both the extensive nature
of wartime ironworking in Williamsburg and
the character of relatively unrefined buildings
built in the eighteenth-century Chesapeake.

HR7 Prentis Store

1740. 1928–1931 and 1972, restoration. Duke of
Gloucester and Colonial sts.

Despite changes over the years and an unsym-
pathetic commercial interior, Prentis Store is
one of the best surviving pre-Revolutionary
stores in the Chesapeake. Its exterior is unusually costly for a commercial building of its time,
built of brick and finished with a modillion cornice and a pediment turned toward Duke of
Gloucester Street. The original plan is perceptible in the fenestration. The front door gave
public access to a sizable salesroom with shelves

running the length of the side walls. A rear door led to stairs and a small office lighted with side windows and heated with a small fireplace. Storage and perhaps workers' sleeping space in the attic was lighted by narrow dormers.

HR8　Public Magazine

1715, Alexander Spotswood. 1755, wall added. 1890, renovation. 1934–1935, restoration. Market Sq.

Sir William Keith wrote in his *History of the British Plantations in America* (1738) that Alexander Spotswood's skill as a mathematician was expressed in his design of the octagonal magazine built to house arms shipped by the crown to Virginia in 1715. Spotswood showed more interest in ornamenting the public square than in securing the arms. While magazines are often low, all-masonry buildings, this one has three floors, two of wood and one in the generous attic covered by a steeply pitched roof crowned by the remnants of an iron weather vane. This powder keg has stood in the middle of Market Square's southern half, untouched by lightning strikes, for nearly three centuries. Its most famous moment came in April 1775, when Lord Dunmore, the last royal governor, had gunpowder removed to a British naval vessel, precipitating a nearly flammable confrontation with Virginia separatists. The building was saved from dereliction by the Association for the Preservation of Virginia Antiquities in 1890 and restored by Colonial Williamsburg in 1934–1935.

HR9　Courthouse

1771. Late 1800s, remodeling. 1911–1912, 1932, and 1989–1991, restoration. Market Sq.

Ironically, eighteenth-century Williamsburg's most academic pediment lacks any apparent structural support. All but one nineteenth-century illustration show the porch unsupported, and in 1796 Benjamin Henry Latrobe commented on the absence of columns carrying the cantilevered structure. The pediment, an octagonal cupola, and round-headed windows emphasized the public function of the Williamsburg and James City Courthouse, built in 1771 to replace less generous quarters the Williamsburg court had occupied in the old Palace Street theater building since 1745 and in the James City County Courthouse at England and Francis streets. The porch also shel-

tered participants and onlookers on court days, as arcaded loggias did elsewhere in the colony. Inside the front door was sizable standing space for the public, flanked by a jury room, justices' chamber, and clerks' offices. Beyond, in the large central room, was an arrangement of sitting and standing spaces that embodied the Virginia leadership's sense of hierarchy, from the chief justice's cushioned ceremonial chair to the place where the accused stood beside the clerk's table. The interior, remodeled late in the nineteenth century, was lost in a 1911 fire, and the building has been restored three times, first to save and reuse the old walls and last to recreate the eighteenth-century fittings and their uses.

HR10　Peyton Randolph House

c. 1715–1718, c. 1752, c. 1850. 1939–1941, 1968, restorations. 1997–1999, reconstruction of outbuildings. Nicholson St. east of N. England St.

The Randolph House illustrates the development of an eighteenth-century property at the level of elite accommodation. William Robertson, clerk of the Governor's Council from 1698 until 1739, built the square house facing the side street in 1715–1718. It contained a small corner passage and three rooms on both floors. In 1754, Peyton Randolph, later Speaker of the House of Burgesses, transformed it into a seven-bay-long edifice facing Market Square, containing a grand new stair passage, dining room, and bedchamber with closets. Likewise, Randolph and his father transformed Robertson's motley collection of tenements in the rear yard into an impressive ensemble of service buildings used to support their household.

HR11　Grissell Hay Lodging House

c. 1760, c. 1840, addition. 1930–1931, restoration. Nicholson St. and N. England St.

In 1768, the widow Grissell Hay advertised this carefully ordered, frame Georgian-plan house facing Market Square as offering "very commodious lodgings to be let for a dozen gentlemen." Its size and regularity suggest a 1760s date, though both archaeological excavations and dendrochronology, or tree-ring dating, appear to support the long-held belief that it is an early eighteenth-century house. The porch is a Greek Revival addition, and the four rear outbuildings date from the late eighteenth and

HR14 Governor's Palace

early nineteenth centuries. These are the most recognized ancillary buildings in Williamsburg, largely because of the picturesque use of deep-coved eaves above the ventilation louvers on the dairy.

HR12 James Geddy House

1762. 1932 and 1968, restoration. Duke of Gloucester St. at Palace Green

Many of the Williamsburg houses that have become familiar images of early American life were built by successful artisans and retailers in the third quarter of the eighteenth century. A prominent example is that of silversmith James Geddy, Jr., who demolished his parents' old house and in 1762 replaced it with this two-story, center-passage house. An original ell contains Geddy's large reception room, which once opened directly onto Palace Green.

HR13 Brush-Everard House

c. 1719. c. 1721, addition. c. 1729–1742, remodeling. c. 1769–1773, renovation. 1949–1951 and 1993–1994, restoration. Palace Green north of Nicholson St.

Armorer John Brush built this as a center-passage house, ruder than the James Geddy House, about 1719 and added the left rear (northeast) wing one or two years later. Between 1729 and 1742 builder Henry Cary, Jr., remodeled it to make both the public and private spaces more refined. The stair, unusually rich for a Virginia house of this scale, dates

from Cary's refurbishing. The house reached its present appearance in the decade before the Revolution, when Mayor Thomas Everard added wainscoting, wallpaper, and at least eight different paint colors.

HR14 Governor's Palace

1706–1709, Henry Cary. c. 1710–1720, renovation, Alexander Spotswood. 1751–1752, addition, Richard Taliaferro. 1931–1934, reconstruction, Perry, Shaw and Hepburn, Thomas Tileston Waterman, principal designer; gardens by Arthur A. Shurcliff. 1980, alteration, departments of Architecture and Collections, Colonial Williamsburg. Palace Green

The Governor's Palace was a graphic expression of the crown's presence in the new capital. Its bold outline at the end of Palace Green punctuated Nicholson's town plan and inspired members of Virginia's elite to build the first generation of formal double-pile houses in the Chesapeake. Builder Henry Cary began the residence ten years after the capital's founding, and Lieutenant Governor Alexander Spotswood enriched the building and its gardens from 1710 until about 1720. By mid-century it was considered too small for the new mode of inviting large groups for dancing and eating, and a 75-foot-long wing was added to the rear.

The 1730s copperplate from the Bodleian Library supplied an elevation of the main building and a glimpse of its flankers and courtyard and the parterres immediately behind the main block as they looked before the mid-century changes. Re-creation of the palace buildings relied on this view, the only one that showed the building before its destruction by fire in 1781, as well as on later illustrations of the dependencies; Thomas Jefferson's measured plans of 1779–1781; the so-called Frenchman's Map, of about the same time; and a generous archaeological footprint. Landscape architect Arthur A. Shurcliff had some archaeological and topographic evidence as well, though his garden re-creation is considerably more hypothetical. Together, the palace buildings and gardens represent the largest element of the Williamsburg restoration.

HR15 George Wythe House

c. 1750, attributed to Richard Taliaferro. 1927, 1939–1940, and 1992–1993, restoration. Palace Green south of Prince George St.

A second five-bay brick house offers dramatic contrast to the nearby palace. While the palace is assertive, with an oversized cupola and a balustraded platform above a sharply pitched roof, the Wythe House, forty-some years younger, is calm and understated. The inside is as balanced as the repose of the exterior promises. Fireplaces are carefully worked into the transverse partition to serve a nearly identical pair of entertaining spaces at the front and private rooms at the rear upstairs, all reached by a central stair passage.

HR16 Bruton Parish Church

1711–1715, Alexander Spotswood. 1752, extension. 1752–1754, churchyard wall. 1769–1770, tower addition, Benjamin Powell. 1903–1907, restoration, Barney and Chapman. 1938–1942, restoration, Perry, Shaw and Hepburn. Duke of Gloucester St. at Palace Green

When Williamsburg was established, the existing (1683) church of Bruton Parish found itself in an angle at the intersection of Duke of Gloucester and Palace streets. The site was prominent but not dominant, lacking the drama of Francis Nicholson's Church Circle in Annapolis or the axial positions given to other institutional buildings here. For reasons of graveyard placement or Lockean ambivalence, the new church, designed in 1711 to serve the parish and the General Assembly, was built at the old location. Perhaps we again see Spotswood's imagination and assertiveness at work, as the church's scale and cruciform plan were then unprecedented in Virginia. The chancel

HR16 Bruton Parish Church

was extended 22 feet (beginning in 1752) and the present churchyard wall put up between 1752 and 1754. Williamsburg builder Benjamin Powell added the tower in 1769–1770.

The building was subdivided into a sanctuary and Sunday school room in 1840 and returned to its original interior and exterior configuration in 1903–1907, in a restoration led by W. A. R. Goodwin with direction from New York architect J. Stewart Barney. Inside, only the west gallery survives from the eighteenth century, most of the finish dating from a 1938–1942 restoration. The Beaux-Arts bronze lectern is attributed to Barney. The churchyard contains a fine collection of baroque monuments.

HR17 Bowden-Armistead House

1858. Duke of Gloucester St. east of Nassau St.

The best mid-nineteenth-century house built in Williamsburg is the only one of its date to survive largely intact. Mayor Lemuel J. Bowden purchased the lot from Bruton Parish Church and constructed his show house with machine-made face bricks and stylish Greek Revival woodwork at a time when most property owners satisfied the demands of current taste with a few mantels and a coat of red or white paint on the old brickwork.

HR18 John Blair House

1720–1723. c. 1750, addition. 1929, restoration. Duke of Gloucester St. west of Nassau St.

The Blair House evolved in a manner much like Wetherburn's Tavern, illustrating how close domestic and hostelry forms were in the eighteenth-century Chesapeake. This house began early in the century with two rooms flanking a stair passage, much like the Brush-Everard and Tucker houses. Around mid-century a superior entertaining room was added to the west (left), with independent outside access. Improvements in finish also transformed the house, from a building entirely covered with short, split clapboards to its present refined appearance, with shingles, planed weatherboards, and classically inspired moldings.

HR19 Timson House

1715, c. 1750, c. 1818, 1842, 1937. 1996, restoration. Prince George St. west of Nassau St.

Even small early houses generally have long histories of evolution. William Timson built this house with a single front room, entered from a central doorway between the present two principal windows, and a small rear space. Remodelings of the mid-eighteenth century, c. 1818, and 1842 created the present front appearance. The rear wing was added by the Reverend W. A. R. Goodwin, and a member of his family lived there until 1988.

HR20 Benjamin Powell House

c. 1750, 1763–1776. 1955–1956, restoration. Waller St. between Francis and Nicholson sts.

Builder Benjamin Powell was among the successful tradesmen who constructed houses for themselves in the Waller subdivision, east of the capitol. After buying his property in 1763, Powell built the wooden five-bay front section, incorporating an existing brick house as a rear wing. Behind the house are an early nineteenth-century kitchen, smokehouse, and dairy. The Powell property is part of the eastern neighborhood restored by Colonial Williamsburg in the decade after World War II.

HR21 William Finnie House

c. 1770–1780. 1932 and 1952, restoration. Francis St. west of Waller St.

HR20 Benjamin Powell House

The late eighteenth-century elite taste for geometric play in the planning of houses is expressed most often in Virginia in multipart houses, particularly those that follow the form of a two-story central block flanked by integral lower wings. Williamsburg's Finnie House is probably the earliest of these. Its principal pediment and a largely original porch emphasize that a more literal classicism traveled in company with compositional experimentation.

HR22 The Quarter

c. 1800. 1937, restoration. Francis St. west of Colonial St.

The most modest surviving early house in Williamsburg, the Quarter began with a single room on the opposite (east) side of the chimney. The present front room was constructed early in the nineteenth century, its frame exposed and whitewashed inside. The Quarter's character is sufficiently rough hewn to have made it the actor John Wayne's favorite residence whenever he stayed in Williamsburg.

HR23 Public Hospital and DeWitt Wallace Gallery

1770–1773. 1983–1985, reconstruction, Department of Architectural Research, Colonial Williamsburg, and Kevin Roche; garden, Peter Shepherd. Francis St. between Nassau and South Henry sts.

HR22 The Quarter

HR23 Public Hospital and DeWitt Wallace Gallery

The last public building constructed before the capital moved from Williamsburg was the first Anglo-American hospital established solely for the insane. Its designer was the Scotsman Robert Smith of Philadelphia, architect of Carpenter's Hall, the tower at Christ Church, and the Walnut Street Prison—all in Philadelphia—and Nassau Hall in Princeton. Outwardly, his design for the hospital was a rectangle with a pedimented pavilion at the front and a hipped roof with a cupola centered between internal chimneys. This was the same formula used in recasting the Wren Building of the College of William and Mary and employed for public edifices throughout much of the nineteenth century. Security was a principal concern, and

Smith provided specifications for window bars. By 1794 this conventional shell was framed by large, fenced yards where patients could exercise without danger of their escape. A central stair hall led to side corridors lined with cells, to a keeper's apartment on the first floor, and to a directors' meeting room above. The absence of space specifically for physicians and examination underscores the institution's role as a place of incarceration, although the act for its establishment specified that the hospital was intended only for curable patients.

The building was enlarged and transformed in the nineteenth-century era of expanding interest in the care of the mentally ill, and it burned in 1885. It was reconstructed to its early form in 1983–1985 and is used today both to house an exhibit on changing perceptions and treatments of mental illness and as an entrance to the DeWitt Wallace Gallery.

The Wallace Gallery provided Colonial Williamsburg with a generous space in which to show British and American decorative arts, liberating the historic buildings from the necessity to exhibit objects of fine quality that were not there in the eighteenth century. Kevin Roche designed the gallery to be semisubterranean, treated outside as an oversized garden or property wall. A tunnel connects the two buildings; its educational displays inform visitors about decorative arts while the tunnel delivers them to a stair hall exhibiting "masterworks." The classicized modernism of the hall sets the tone for a balanced arrangement of galleries, those on the east (left) circling an orchid-filled atrium and those on the west terminating in a walled garden by the British landscape architect Sir Peter Shepherd. Bronze furniture and stoneware pots by French sculptors Claude and François-Xavier LaLanne share space with exotic plants in both garden spaces, which repeat the building's classical structure.

HR24 William Byrd III House

c. 1770. c. 1900, remodeling. 410 Francis St., west of Henry St.

A costly remodeling around 1900 did relatively little to spoil the character of this, one of Williamsburg's best surviving eighteenth-century houses. It was owned by the wastrel William Byrd III from about 1770 to 1777, when his will referred to it as his town house. Like the earliest part of Wetherburn's Tavern, it has two rooms on both sides of a stair passage, with bedchambers in the upper half-story. Here both the plan and the finish are elaborated, with a bold arched entrance to a small side corridor off the passage, a large cupboard for the display of dinnerwares in the superior room (in the northwest or front right corner), and a large assortment of English sandstone mantels.

HR25 Williamsburg Inn

1936–1937, 1950 (east wing), Perry, Shaw and Hepburn. 1937, Craft House, Singleton Peabody Moorehead. 1954–1955, garden shop. 1972, Regency Dining Room, Department of Architecture, Colonial Williamsburg, and H. Chambers Company. Francis St. at Colonial St.

The inn was the first modern hotel in Williamsburg, and Rockefeller's architects designed it to be an elegant hostelry for refined guests. While it appears larger and more formal than buildings in Merchants Square, it is cast in a similar early nineteenth-century American guise, and a certain modesty was achieved by placing it back from Francis Street and on axis with a very minor cross street.

The scale has remained understated, with both original and subsequent wings built beyond the core, which focuses on a two-story Ionic portico above a loggia at the center of an H-shaped plan. Visually extending the loggia with blind arches below a second-floor promenade ensures that no sheer three-story walls are visible from the historic area. The rear is more freely handled, with a glazed three-story bow framed by shallow full-height pilasters. The public spaces inside are likewise finished in an urbane neoclassical style, less clearly American than the exterior. Extending west and then south from the 1937 lobby, these culminate in the Regency Dining Room, inspired by exotic fittings of the Royal Pavilion at Brighton. Added twelve years after Rockefeller's death in 1960, this principal dining room would never be mistaken for the hall of an old Virginia spa. The Washington, D.C., interior design firm H. Chambers Company collaborated with the Colonial Williamsburg Department of Architecture on the Regency-style fittings.

Though occupied by Winston Churchill and a long list of kings, presidents, and film stars, the guest rooms hold to a restrained neoclassical idiom. The simplest are the third-floor

HR25 Williamsburg Inn

HR29 Merchants Square

rooms, which Rockefeller took great interest in planning for chauffeurs and other workers traveling with inn guests.

In 1937 Singleton Peabody Moorehead designed the Craft House in a post-Revolutionary domestic style that, if not for its location just northwest of the inn, could seem part of the historic area. The present garden shop was added in 1954–1955 as a bicycle shed, its frame inspired by what then were thought to be typical seventeenth-century Virginia houses.

HR26 Abby Aldrich Rockefeller Folk Art Center

1956, Department of Architecture, Colonial Williamsburg. 1988–1991, renovation and addition, Kevin

Roche, John Dinkeloo and Associates. South of Francis St. and west of S. England St.

Foundation architect Ernest Frank created this reticent American neoclassical structure for Williamsburg's folk art collection. Abby Aldrich Rockefeller gave much of her collection to the museum in 1939. Her son David remarked much later that his father's gift of the building had personal rather than aesthetic motivation: "Father really disliked folk art, but he loved Mother." The large L-shaped wing designed by Kevin Roche provided flexible new gallery space but crouches less comfortably than the main block and ignores the subtlety of its details.

HR27 Williamsburg Lodge

1937–1938, Gilbert Stanley Underwood with Perry, Shaw and Hepburn. 1947 and 1957, Department of Architecture, Colonial Williamsburg. 1961–1963, Spencer and Lee. 1967, David Warren Hardwicke. 1985–1986, Juster, Pope, Frazier. 310 S. England St.

The lodge has had a varied and interesting ca reer as Colonial Williamsburg's largest hotel. Conceived as more affordable and less formal than the inn, it was given a name meant to evoke snug and informal accommodation associated with woodland parks. National Park Service head Horace Albright recommended Gilbert Stanley Underwood, known for his flamboyantly rustic Ahwahnee Lodge at Yosemite, to work with Perry, Shaw and Hepburn. Underwood's initial design is said to have resembled the Wren Building, so William Perry took over the exterior scheme, and the consultant was reduced to producing elegant neoclassical designs for bronze stair fittings and countless construction drawings. The collaboration produced a building that, in scale and materials, looks at home beside the historic area but incorporates details not found there, such as paired windows and quoins. Additions after World War II and in 1957 continued in this mode and in a more literal historicism.

Spencer and Lee of San Francisco, who had designed stylish hotel buildings for Jackson Hole, Wyoming, were hired in 1961 to plan expansion of the lodge into a conference center with additional rooms. Their work includes stylized references to eighteenth-century Virginia buildings—oversized brick arcades, large expanses of hardwood paneling, and chinoiserie frets—as well as an oversized Virginia Room,

lighted by a vast fixture resembling the *Starship Enterprise*. David Warren Hardwicke planned the auditorium in 1967. Eldridge T. Spencer also designed the west wing, visible from Colonial Parkway, as two curving blocks with an unusual skin of timber frame and gray weatherboards. Much less delicate are a sports center and group of three-story brick buildings to the south, with inset balconies, by Juster, Pope, Frazier.

HR28 Providence Hall Director's and Executive Wings

1971–1972, Phil Ives Associates; landscape by Peter G. Rolland. Bucktrout Ln.

This pair of elegantly detailed modernist hotel buildings, reminiscent of James Stirling's Ham Common (1957), was designed by New York architect Phil Ives for what had previously been an open pasture south of Francis Street. Tennis courts and a landscape by Peter G. Rolland create an environment entirely removed from the historic area.

HR29 Merchants Square

1928–1931, Perry, Shaw and Hepburn. 1939–1940 and 1961–1962, modifications and additions, Department of Architecture, Colonial Williamsburg. Duke of Gloucester St. between John Blair House and Boundary St., 110 N. Henry St., and 110 S. Henry St.

Before extensive restoration began in Williamsburg, Rockefeller and his planners struggled with where to locate private businesses. By 1928 they had settled on a block at the west end of Duke of Gloucester Street where most businesses were already clustered. This choice would eventually separate the College of William and Mary's old campus from the rest of the designated historic area. The planners made a useful decision to distinguish Merchants Square buildings from the original structures and reconstructions in that preserve. The designers' whimsy as well as their knowledge of early building grammar affected both, but they rendered these buildings for new functions with much more freedom and wit than they did the representations of older Williamsburg buildings. Varied setbacks likewise signaled that this was a different place. Some local businesses remained along the length of Duke of Gloucester Street, but in 1932 a grocery, drugstore, restaurant, and movie theater moved into this, one of the first comprehensively planned and themed American shopping districts.

Each Merchants Square element was given the same attention to design that had been lavished on the historic area buildings. Among the most interesting are the Craft House, inspired by University of Virginia pavilions and southern spas; the College Shop, with a frame upper story carried on a masonry story and a front colonnade drawn from Caribbean merchant buildings; R. Bryant, with shop windows behind engaged columns like those seen on a handful of eighteenth-century London shop windows; and a bank, composed of a square box with a peculiar pyramidal roof topped by a freely imagined cupola. The bank contains the best surviving interior on the block. Later additions include 110 North Henry Street, built as a post office in 1939–1940, and the much-remodeled 110 South Henry Street, built in 1961–1962, also as a post office.

HR30 Goodwin Building

1940, Department of Architecture, Colonial Williamsburg. 124 N. Henry St.

The administrative center of Colonial Williamsburg continues the design theme of Merchants Square, freely arranging details from post-Revolutionary American buildings. Here no less than nine units suggest separate buildings, all of comparable size (two stories, two to five bays), arranged in an H plan. Occasional shop windows suggest some of the promiscuous manner in which houses and shops were mixed in cities of the new republic but are here used entirely for ornamental effect. A wrought iron screen encloses a front courtyard treated as a garden. Brass doors with c. 1800 details open onto the courtyard and give access to corridors lined with offices. Light fixtures blur the line between neoclassical and Art Deco, and a fully paneled second-floor boardroom is hung with portraits of the museum's benefactor, designers, and presidents.

College of William and Mary in Virginia   (HR31–HR35)
(Map, p. 364)

William and Mary is the second-oldest institution of higher learning in the United States, chartered in 1693 by the reigning monarchs of England, for which it was named. It was controlled by Anglican clergy (as were all English colleges at the time). It opened in 1694, and its first building was completed in 1697. Many of the Virginia elite attended school there, including Thomas Jefferson, James Monroe, James Madison, and John Marshall. It closed during the Revolution, when troops occupied it; again during the Civil War; and, because of a shortage of funds, again in 1881–1888. Although Jefferson had considered making it a public institution, the college remained private and did not come under state control until 1906. In 1918 it became coeducational. Although most attention is justly focused on the Wren Building and eighteenth-century buildings, the campus has many other important structures.

The Colonial Revival at William and Mary College preceded Colonial Williamsburg. The first Taliaferro Hall (built 1894, demolished c. 1967) closely resembled the then 171-year-old Brafferton building, which stands in front of the Wren. Tucker Hall, originally the library (1908), was rendered with the details as well as the general aspect of an eighteenth-century Virginia courthouse. The state's most prolific school architect, Charles M. Robinson, began utilizing a Georgian Revival idiom for larger William and Mary buildings in 1920, and five years later he developed a master plan that was followed for a quarter-century. Williamsburg's one brush with modernism came in 1938–1939, when the American National Theater and Academy proposed William and Mary as the site for the first National Festival Theater. Eero Saarinen, Ralph Rapson, and Frederic James won the competition with an elegant design for the theater, and smaller pavilions to house architecture, sculpture, painting, and music that would be built around and over a small pond in a wooded ravine now called Crim Dell. The winning entry was thoroughly modern, as were those of all the principal competitors, but debate over the appropriateness of such untraditional designs, failure to raise significant funds, personal factors, and the approach of war sadly doomed the project.

HR31.1 Wren Building
HR31.2 The Brafferton

HR31 College of William and Mary, Old College Yard

West end of Duke of Gloucester St.

HR31.1 Wren Building

1695–1699. 1705–1715, rebuilding. 1729–1732, chapel, Henry Cary, Jr. 1859, rebuilding, Henry Exall and Eben Faxon. 1867–1869, rebuilding, Alfred L. Rives. 1928–1931, restoration, Perry, Shaw and Hepburn.

The first William and Mary building, still standing front and center after three fires (1705, 1859, and 1862), was begun in 1695, four years before establishment of the town. It faced down the ridge between the James and York river drainages and so became the western terminus of the town's main street. Hugh Jones wrote in *The Present State of Virginia* (1724) that the building was "first modeled by Sir Christopher Wren, adapted to the Nature of the Country by the Gentlemen there," creating a long-running debate about the origins of the design with little prospect of resolution. The initial in-

carnation was a full three and one-half stories above a relatively high cellar and thirteen bays long, with a sizable hall in a rear ell—a remarkable edifice almost certainly unequaled by any other seventeenth-century building in the still rough-and-tumble Chesapeake.

After the 1705 fire, the facade was reworked with only two and one-half stories and a cupola that was apparently lower than the original. But the rear, shown on the famous copperplate probably engraved for William Byrd's now lost history of Virginia, retained three full masonry stories, including a loggia. There is evidence that the building was intended to grow into a full quadrangle, and Lord Dunmore apparently asked Jefferson to produce a plan in 1771 or 1772. Construction began but soon ceased. Yet by 1729–1732, when the chapel had been added as a second rear wing, its end wall was expensively finished with good brickwork and round windows, and the corresponding wall of the hall was rebuilt in the same manner, suggesting little interest in further enclosure. Likewise, when the Brafferton building was constructed in 1723, followed by the President's House in 1732–1733, there was clearly an outward orientation, directing the college toward the town rather than in upon itself.

After the 1859 fire, architects Henry Exall and Eban Faxon redesigned the building in Italianate garb, adding a pair of three-story towers at the front and enclosing the loggia to house classrooms and a stair. Remarkably, the walls survived another fire sufficiently to be used in a more sober 1867–1869 rebuilding with a wider center pavilion, sans towers. Following considerable debate, this pavilion was removed and the surviving seventeenth- and eighteenth-century brickwork was incorporated into a restoration that returned the building to its second appearance, including the chapel. Much of the 1928–1931 Wren-ish chapel interior is by Thomas Tileston Waterman.

HR31.2 The Brafferton

1723. 1931–1932, restoration, Perry, Shaw and Hepburn

HR31.3 President's House

1732–1733, Henry Cary, Jr. 1786, restoration. 1931, restoration, Perry, Shaw and Hepburn

With construction of two houselike buildings flanking the main edifice, the college took on an aspect more resembling Georgian domestic ensembles than traditional English campuses. A plantation house analogy was strengthened, perhaps, by the formal arrangement of clipped hedges in a garden stretching toward Duke of Gloucester Street. The south flanker, the Brafferton, was built in 1723 from funds intended to support conversion of Native American children into literate Christian missionaries. Five-bay elevations masked an unbalanced first-floor plan with what was probably a single large classroom on the west and two rooms on the other side of a passage, one a cook room.

The President's House, to the north, was built with a similar outward form, including the dramatically steep hipped roof, but it was more vigorously formal inside, with four rooms on each floor, the larger spaces facing the college yard. Subtle manipulation of the window placement suggests further subdivision of the rear rooms. More early woodwork survives in the President's House than in the south building,

though apparently it dates from the restoration that followed a 1781 fire.

HR32 College of William and Mary, Old Campus

Between Richmond and Jamestown rds., east of Landrum Dr., west of Old College Yard

Much of the character of the main campus, immediately west of Old College Yard, is the work of Richmond architect Charles M. Robinson. Robinson led a tremendously productive team of school designers, which had demonstrated its reliability in a series of Richmond public schools and state normal (teachers) college buildings in Fredericksburg and Radford. Initially Robinson's firm designed Jefferson Hall (HR32.1) (1920–1924), as the first purpose-built women's dormitory, on Jamestown Road. Monroe Hall, for men (HR32.2) (1920–1924), occupied a similar position on Richmond Road. He also designed Blow Gymnasium (HR32.3) (1920–1924), as well as additions to the existing library. In 1925, energetic president Julian Chandler retained Robinson to produce a master plan for the college. The result was arguably Robinson's most successful work: the Sunken Garden, a large space inspired by the courtyard of Wren's Chelsea Hospital, used here as the organizing focus for a group of academic buildings, with dormitories along the edges of the campus. Streets set at oblique angles to the two public roads gave the campus a lozenge shape. Robinson designed most of the subsequent buildings on the main campus and set the tone for others. The idiom was a freer form of the Colonial Revival than that which the Colonial Williamsburg restoration would later spawn. Shallow neoclassical arcades and dormers are combined with bold classical stone and wood frontispieces, oversized modillion cornices, and distinctively pale pink brick with gray headers. The classroom buildings—Washington, Tyler, and Blair halls (HR32.4–HR32.6) (1925–1930, Robinson and Walford)—are tall, strait-laced, H-shaped edifices, the first two with entrances elevated halfway up the ground floors and stairs in paneled vestibules leading to lecture halls and offices off longitudinal corridors. The dorms—Barrett, Chandler, Brown, Landrum, and Old Dominion (HR32.7–HR32.11) (c. 1926–c. 1930)—designed by Robinson and his junior partner, John Binford Walford, are long slabs with central pavilions, entrances closer to grade, and connecting arcades that Robinson called cloisters. Robinson's declining health (and death in 1932) led Walford to take over as William and Mary's principal architect. He added Zable (formerly Cary) Stadium (HR32.12) (1935–1936) as a Public Works Administration–funded project and Brian dormitory complex (HR32.13) (1952–1953, 1959) in the same Colonial Revival style.

Colonial Revival gate piers (HR32.14) (1927–1929, Emil Siebern, sculptor) with lead statues of the royal namesakes were intended to provide a proper Ivy League entrance to the college at the end of Duke of Gloucester Street but fell prey to new standards for restoration of the Wren yard and were finally set up in 1932 at a lane northwest of the Wren Building. Across Richmond Road is Sorority Court, with five brick houses (HR32.15–HR32.19) (1929–1931, Robinson and Walford) facing an oval courtyard recessed behind similar houses at the street frontage.

The principal recent addition to Old Campus is McGlothin-Street (formerly Tercentenary) Hall (HR32.20) (1993–1995, Allan Greenberg in association with Rancorn, Wildman, Krause and Brezinski). It is larger and considerably more self-absorbed than its neighbors on the Sunken Garden, with a Hawksmoorian shell that houses an interior reminiscent of a budget motel. Greenberg, who claims to be a historical literalist, took his inspiration from Stratford Hall, Virginia's most mannered eighteenth-century building. The principal entry is through the rusticated ground floor, below an inaccessible balcony drawn from the Wren Building. Clustered chimneys and diagonal patterns of glazed brick are intended to emphasize the building's regional quality. The south (rear) wall is perhaps the most successful, with pedimented bays terminating a two-story range of pilasters planted on an otherwise flat wall.

A more lovable tricentennial monument in the same spirit is a statue of college founder James Blair (1993, Lewis Cohen), with overscaled proboscis and flowing robes, located between Tyler and Blair halls, opposite a distinctly fey statue of a college-age Jefferson. Students refer to the Blair statue as Darth Vader.

HR33 College of William and Mary, New Campus

West of Old Campus, between Jamestown Rd. and College Terrace

A new, if still conservative, architectural age opened at William and Mary with Phi Beta Kappa Hall (HR33.1) (1956, John Binford Walford and D. Pendelton Wright) on the south side of the New Campus. Built in pink brick with cast stone trim, it is a respectable member of the generation of theater–arts center complexes built for Virginia state colleges in the 1950s. It was followed ten years later by an arts classroom addition, Andrews Hall (HR33.2), and Swem Library (HR33.3) (both 1966, Wright, Jones and Wilkerson), which face one another across a square laced with diagonal walks. The axial orientation encouraged a formalized modernism, evident particularly in the ordering of the library's upper facades to suggest book stacks behind them. Swem Library was refronted with a mild postmodern facade (1986, Perry Dean Rogers) and given a larger wing (1998–1999, Shepley, Bulfinch, Richardson and Abbott). Inside the lower level at Swem can be found the English sculptor Richard Hayward's fine statue (1772) of the penultimate royal governor, Lord Botetourt, made for the loggia of Williamsburg's second capitol. Its plinth is among the earliest substantial expressions of neoclassicism in British America. Dropped less formally to the east and west of the composition are five classroom buildings, all designed by the same Richmond firm (1962 and 1974, Wright, Jones and Wilkerson).

The most imaginative and arresting element of the New Campus is a series of solar heat collectors filled with colored water along the side of the Muscarelle Museum of Art (HR33.4) (1982–1983, Carlton Abbott; 1986–1987, enlargement, Abbott). The museum has sharp angles reminiscent of I. M. Pei's East Building for the National Gallery of Art in Washington, D.C. (1976), though here the scale is small and the material is brown brick. The college employed Washington, D.C., artist Gene Davis to design a series of colors for the solar collectors, which are refilled periodically with a different ensemble of his colors.

The remainder of the New Campus was built between 1963 and 1978 after designs by Wright, Jones and Wilkerson. One major exception is University Center (HR33.5) (1991, The Architects Collaborative), facing Zable Stadium. The building, which incorporates deep-roofed pavilions and spaces with exposed trusses, makes literal references to eighteenth-century Virginia buildings, rendered in the college's traditional pink brick with gray headers.

HR34 Chandler Court and Pollard Park

1922–present, John Garland Pollard, Eimer Cappelmann, Thomas Tileston Waterman, Clarence Wright Huff, Jr., and others. South of Jamestown Rd., east of Griffin Ave.

Mayor, William and Mary professor, and later Virginia governor John Garland Pollard had design skills and money sufficient to create two of Williamsburg's most appealing twentieth-century neighborhoods. Chandler Court was laid out in 1922–1924 with two lanes meeting at a shared green. Its houses, including those at numbers 101, 116, and 119, occupied respectively by Pollard, history professor Richard L. Morton, and librarian E. G. Swem, are relatively free interpretations of colonial buildings.

Pollard Park followed in 1930, with a lane circling a wooded ravine. Most of the houses there are in a more literal eighteenth-century Chesapeake style, illustrating the influence of Colonial Williamsburg. Richmond architect Clarence Wright Huff, Jr., designed 604 and 608 Pollard Park; architect and architectural historian Thomas Tileston Waterman designed 601 Pollard Park and 140 Chandler Court (facing Ballard Lane). Eimer Cappelmann designed 600 Pollard Park in an earlier, more romantic English cottage style.

HR35 College of William and Mary, South Campus

South Henry St. south of Newport Ave.

Cramped for space on the old and new campuses, the college, in the mid-1970s, established what might be called a satellite campus about half a mile distant and transferred some functions there. The colonial idiom still reigns at the William and Mary Law School (1978–1979, Wright, Jones and Wilkerson). The Lettie Pate Whitehead Evans Graduate Student Housing (1990–1992, Hanbury Evans Newill Vlattas) is a courtyard of stylized interpretations of seventeenth-century English urban houses, and very appealing. The McCormack-Nagelson Tennis Center (1995, Worley Associates) is a hulking mass.

HR36 Peacock Hill

Bounded by Nassau St. on the east, North Boundary St. on the west, Prince George St. on the south, and Lafayette St. on the north

An area of scattered pre-Revolutionary town lots became an important middle-class neighborhood early in the twentieth century, before the creation of Colonial Williamsburg. The Cary Peyton Armistead House (c. 1890, 320 North Henry Street), which long remained an unexpected sight on Duke of Gloucester Street, was moved in 1995 to North Henry, an area that lost numerous turn-of-the-twentieth-century houses in the 1970s and 1980s. The oddest of the demolished houses was the home of Georgia O'Keeffe, built by her father with faux-stone concrete blocks. Town houses (1979–1981, Robert Magoon; 230 North Boundary Street) are consciously contextual, while their greater density and height give them the pleasing quality of a small urban enclave.

Less sympathetic was a plan prepared for Colonial Williamsburg by I. M. Pei in 1980–1981 that called for redeveloping half of Peacock Hill with stark, cubic town houses akin to Pei's 1960s attached residences in Society Hill, Philadelphia. Public opposition derailed the initial project, and subsequent efforts diminished its harshness. The east end of the neighborhood is anchored by the Colonial Revival Matthew Whaley School (1929, Charles M. Robinson; Scotland Street), built to replace a predecessor that stood briefly on Palace Green before reconstruction of the Governor's Palace.

HR37 Williamsburg Train Station

1935–1936. 468 North Boundary St.

The Chesapeake and Ohio station at the north end of Boundary Street combines colonial-style brickwork and a Beaux-Arts rendering of classical details in a collegiate manner that separates this from the far more literal designs for the Colonial Williamsburg Foundation and its associated entities. The yellow glazed brick interior respected Jim Crow restrictions. After purchasing tickets from the same window as whites, blacks were required to move into a much smaller waiting room on the east (right) with segregated toilets.

HR38 Colonial Williamsburg Visitor Center (Information Center)

The first experience of many visitors to Colonial Williamsburg, this area was developed in

to separate moviegoers in order to enhance the personal nature of their experience of Seaton's film.

HR38 Visitor Center (Information Center)

the 1950s in response to the growing numbers of visitors.

HR38.1 **Visitor Center** (Information Center)

1956–1957, Harrison and Abramovitz, and Benjamin Schlanger, Department of Architecture, Colonial Williamsburg. 1985, renovations, Cambridge Seven Associates. VA 132

Colonial Williamsburg's attention to recapturing eighteenth-century design has often cast it as a conservative force, but the foundation patronized substantial modernist work from the 1950s through the 1980s. Best known is the Visitor Center, designed by Max Abramovitz with the Williamsburg architectural staff in anticipation of the 350th anniversary of Virginia settlement.

Unlike Merchants Square and other historicist buildings immediately adjoining the historic area, Abramovitz's suburban building is sufficiently big and bold for its functions of selling tickets, orienting visitors, and sending them off to the historic area on a fleet of gray buses. Nevertheless, the eaves and entrances were kept low to maintain a reserved sense of scale. Visitors are prepared, both historically and emotionally, by the Paramount film *Williamsburg: The Story of a Patriot*, directed by George Seaton and shown continually since 1957 in two theaters specially planned by film theater architect Benjamin Schlanger. Although the main public hall was redesigned by Cambridge Seven in 1985, the theaters remain precisely as built, with experimental screens developed for wide-format film and pierced stainless steel covering every surface, including stanchions used

HR38.2 **Woodlands** (Motor House)

1956, Department of Architecture, Colonial Williamsburg. 1966–1967, Cascades Wings, David Warren Hardwicke Associates. 2001–2002, addition, Carlton Abbott. Visitor Center

Conceived as part of the Visitor Center complex, the Motor House was distinct in character from accommodations at the Williamsburg Inn and Williamsburg Lodge. While the prewar hotels emphasized old-fashioned comfort and relaxation, here even the name connoted rapid modern travel. Approached by car from the north, it has the appearance of a conventional motel, distinguished only by careful brickwork with eighteenth-century overtones and modernist gables reminiscent of Charles M. Goodman's work in the 1950s. A staggered site pattern created open-fronted courtyards and reduced the apparent scale of the complex. On the rear, large-mullioned windows looked onto wooded land and gave the rooms a modern residential quality. Rooms were originally furnished with Eero Saarinen furniture and Ansel Adams photographs.

Buildings added in the 1960s were conceived as a series of flat-roofed pavilions with double-loaded corridors on two floors. Richmond architect David Warren Hardwicke used gray wood siding applied vertically in a manner that allowed the walls to push out at the window bays, creating a columnar effect that stands comfortably in a mature pine grove. A portion of the 1956 woodlands is scheduled to be replaced by a multistory addition designed by Carlton Abbott.

HR39 **Colonial Williamsburg, Bruton Heights School Education Center**

1939–1940, Division of School Buildings, Virginia Department of Education. 1995–1996, remodeling and additions, Perry Dean Rogers; Juster, Pope, Frazier; and Department of Architecture, Colonial Williamsburg. 301, 309, and 313 First St.

John D. Rockefeller, Jr., and his wife, Abby Aldrich Rockefeller, contributed to a public school, north of the restored area, for black children. African American parents as well as Williamsburg's national visibility prodded the

HR40 Jamestown Island, Structure 17

HR40 Jamestown Island, Statehouse, reconstructed view by Cary Carson

school board to build a red brick, colonial-style school of unusual quality for a southern black community.

The school was abandoned in 1989 and was redeveloped by Colonial Williamsburg in 1995–1996 as a research center. The new campus is an eccentric mixture of styles. Colonial Williamsburg Foundation architects restored and extended the school in a monumental mode with oversized arcades mirroring the original auditorium windows. Juster, Pope, Frazier, from Shelburne Falls, Massachusetts, designed the modernist DeWitt Wallace Collections Building with deep embrasures and long weatherings that give a defensive quality to this container for Williamsburg's rare furnishings and their curators. Perry, Dean and Rogers' postmodern Rockefeller Library is a more playful presence, its collections sheltered by an airplane-hangar roof and fronted by a concave facade behind a paved piazza. Just inside this rather wacky shell is the best late twentieth-century public space in Williamsburg, a two-story hall with long and tight proportions reminiscent of Italian streets and courtyards.

John Page was among the landowners who held parts of the area known as Middle Plantation before Williamsburg's founding. Remains of his 1662 house were found at Bruton Heights in 1995, and its cross-shaped footprint can be seen just southeast of the school building.

(Note: For HR40–HR44, see Hampton Roads map, p. 361)

HR40 Jamestown Island

1607–present. East end of Colonial Pkwy., .3 mile south of James River ferry landing (VA 31)

Jamestown was England's seventeenth-century base camp on a faraway planet called Virginia. Like space stations today, the original (1607) fort and the settled town that it later became served as laboratories where colonists tested alternative strategies for making an alien environment safe and productive. Jamestown's manifest failures succeeded brilliantly in teaching Englishmen what not to expect from towns and cities in the southern American colonies.

No sooner had the colonial capital removed to Middle Plantation (renamed Williamsburg) in 1699 than Jamestown became a mecca for pilgrims. Its centennial and bicentennial were celebrated in 1707 and 1807, and since 1857 anniversaries have been observed every fifty years. These jubilees were mixed blessings. They attracted relic hunters who carried off genuine antiquities and ancestor worshippers who left behind dubious reliquaries. True preservation began only in 1893 when the Association for the Preservation of Virginia Antiquities acquired 22.5 acres at the western end of the island, including the churchyard and ruined bell tower of the former James City Parish Church (c. 1680), to which Boston architect Edward M. Wheelwright grafted a memorial church in 1907. The APVA added two statues, *Pocahontas* (1907, William Ordway Partridge) and *Captain John Smith* (1907, William Couper). The National Park Service rescued the rest of the island in

1934, combined it administratively with York-town battlefield to make Colonial National Historical Park in 1936, and launched a series of increasingly competent archaeological excavations leading up to the 350th anniversary in 1957.

Recently the island's two stewards have reevaluated and renewed that earlier work in preparation for the 400th anniversary observance in 2007. New Park Service scholarship and the unexpected discovery of the original fort site by William Kelso and APVA archaeologists (underneath the 1861 Confederate earthworks) have clarified Jamestown's role as an experimental station on the edge of England's Chesapeake empire. Archaeologists have identified four trial phases, each of which left its marks. (References are to various ruins, outlines, and other items on display on the site.)

Experiment 1: trading post. The expeditionary force that sailed up the James River in 1607 was searching for a place to build a trade castle, modeled after those run by the Portuguese in West Africa and Zanzibar. The first Englishmen came as middlemen, not settlers, counting on the Indians to supply them with riches from the interior just as Africans supplied the Portuguese with gold, slaves, and ivory. The triangular palisaded fort (rediscovered in 1994) enclosed warehouses, workshops, and barracks for the small staff of merchants, artisans, and soldiers needed to manage that trade.

Experiment 2: manufacturing center. The Algonquian Indians of the region disappointed those expectations. They had their own agenda, specifically, to tolerate the newcomers but subordinate them to the confederacy ruled by Chief Powhatan. Quickly perceiving their miscalculation, the directors of the Virginia Company set new goals. Henceforth the colony would pay back its investors by recruiting settlers and slaves to grow cash crops, notably tobacco after 1619, and by developing lucrative "projects," among them silk production and glassmaking (the 1608 glasshouse was reconstructed in 1957). Jamestown soon outgrew the fort, and entrepreneurs began to build warehouses (Structure 26) and numerous kilns (Structures 111 and 127), potteries (Structure 111), forges (Structure 24), and other heavy industries along the riverfront and adjoining Pit and Tar Swamp. Governors John Harvey and William Berkeley vigorously promoted the town as a port of entry and manufacturing center. Their ambitions were thwarted by English merchants and royal officials.

Experiment 3: speculative new town. England's commercial expansion after 1660 revived the idea of Jamestown as entrepôt. This time the Virginia Assembly authorized higher taxes and made sweetheart deals with private developers to encourage merchants and planters to build stores and brick town houses along the streets behind the waterfront. At least three row houses (Structures 17, 115, and Ludwell Statehouse Row) and a brick tavern (Structure 19) were built or enlarged in response to the 1662 Town Act. Their placement hints at a plan to create a large urban square. But the speculative bubble burst even before Nathaniel Bacon's rebel army sacked the town in 1676.

Experiment 4: seat of government. The flames devoured the speculators' dreams, but not the ruling gentry's determination to dignify the Jamestown capital. The courts, council, and assembly had always rented meeting rooms in taverns and private dwellings or gathered at the official residence—the "country's house"—of the governor. The term "statehouse" followed them wherever they sat. The General Assembly and the House of Burgesses began to meet in a purpose-built statehouse (refurbished Structure 112) only in the mid-1660s. But not for long. Bacon's insurgents burned it to the ground a decade later. Undaunted, the town fathers rebuilt it in 1684 as the centerpiece of their *civis urbis*. Alas, again not for long. An accidental fire destroyed the second and last formal statehouse in 1698 and, with it, all hopes for Jamestown as capital.

The spirit of experimentation survived, but not on Jamestown Island. Wealthy boosters at up-and-coming Middle Plantation played politics to move the capital—and the next attempt at town building—to Williamsburg.

HR41 **Kingsmill**

1969–present. U.S. 60 west of VA 199

Busch Properties purchased undeveloped woodlands and agricultural land between Colonial Williamsburg and Carter's Grove in 1969 and built a brewery, theme park, office park, and gated residential community, Kingsmill. By 1998, Kingsmill had grown to 5,000 people and 2,100 houses. Archaeologist William Kelso carried out excavations that for the first time revealed the broad spectrum of seventeenth- and eighteenth-century sites remaining on riverside Tidewater Virginia properties. Kelso's associated research contributed to the new residential identity of Kingsmill and influenced site planning and the names chosen for suburban enclaves. Sasaki Associates did initial planning, and, in 1974, the California firm of Callister, Payne and Bischoff designed the core site arrangement of sports facilities and enclaves of multifamily houses. All the multifamily complexes are the product of architectural offices, while most of the detached houses have been designed and built by contractors.

The first house designs, for an enclave called Winster Fox (1974, Fred Bainbridge), set the tone with attached versions of Charles Moore's work at Sea Ranch. Long, shingled roof slopes and rough-sawn vertical-board walls evoked old industrial buildings of the West, even though the architect was from Georgia and this was Virginia. The next enclave, Littletown Quarter (1975, Callister, Payne and Bischoff), designed by architects from California, followed with houses broken into much smaller parts. Virtually every room in these two- and three-bedroom houses has its own gable roof, creating a miniaturized quality that suggests unassuming vernacular farmsteads, crowded together as though land were limited by the oversettlement of a New England village. This woodsy idiom was continued in an expansion of Littletown Quarter (1977, Peckham and Guyton), designed by the St. Louis firm favored by Anheuser-Busch for its breweries and theme parks. The next enclave, Harrop's Glen (1977–1980, Carlton Abbott), designed by a Williamsburg architect, produced a distinctly personal rendition of the Sea Ranch look. The houses became pure form in Abbott's hands, with eaves reduced to a minimum and tiny private yards defended by high, unbroken fences.

A new, less ascetic age was announced at Archer's Mead (1980, Peckham and Guyton) where more than a hundred gray Mineshaft Modern houses were incongruously provided with big, round-headed church windows. At Moody's Run (1988, Bainbridge and Associates), Sea Ranch references receded in the presence of Reagan-Bush-era suburban historicism. Facade projections swelled into polygons, and the wood-sheathed chimneys morphed into Shavian brick stacks at Wareham's Point (1990, Bainbridge and Martin). The most recent unified housing, River's Edge (1994, Cline Davis) is a group of boastful historicist mansions, regrettably sited at the river. A second bold gesture to the James River is a suburb of large single-family houses in various styles, de-

signed by contractors at Burwell's Landing and located around the original pair of service buildings that flanked Lewis Burwell's mid-eighteenth-century Kingsmill mansion.

The centerpiece, the Golf Clubhouse and Restaurant (1974–1975, Callister, Payne and Bischoff; 1988, 1995–1996, remodeling and expansion, Bainbridge) was originally relatively restrained, but the remodeling and expansion in the style of an oversized railway station, with shingled walls and exaggerated tapered pergola piers locally referred to as the "Bainbridge Order," is cutesy postmodern. Bainbridge likewise designed large condominiums built around the new sports and conference center between 1988 and 1992. These combine vestiges of the architect's old Sea Ranch mode with wildly overscaled interpretations of the chimneys at Bacon's Castle, across the river.

HR42 Busch Gardens

1974–1975, Peckham and Guyton, and Peckham Guyton Albers and Viets. U.S. 60

At the other end of the entertainment spectrum from Colonial Williamsburg is this giant theme park. To talk about it as architecture is perhaps ludicrous, but it is designed by the St. Louis firm Anheuser-Busch has employed to design breweries, housing developments, and theme parks. Peckham and Guyton had confected the "Olde Country" for Busch Gardens beginning in 1974–1975, and the successor firm produced designs for its "Escape from Pompeii" water ride in 1994–1995 and its "Alpengeist" rollercoaster, which opened in 1997.

HR43 Carter's Grove

House: 1751–1755. 1928–1931, remodeling, W. Duncan Lee; stable and cottage by Lee; landscape by Arthur Shurcliff. Slave quarters: c. 1770–1780. 1987–1990, reconstruction, Department of Architectural Research, Colonial Williamsburg. Martin's Hundred–Wolstenholme Towne: 1984–1995, partial reconstruction, Ivor Noël Hume and the Department of Architectural Research. Winthrop Rockefeller Archaeology Museum: 1989–1991, Kevin Roche. Reception Center: 1984–1985, Carlton Abbott. Southwest of U.S. 60, southeast of Grove

The scenic Carter's Grove County Road links Colonial Williamsburg to Carter's Grove, a museum property used by Colonial Williamsburg to present elements of seventeenth-, eigh-

HR43 Carter's Grove, exterior (above), hall (below), and re-created slave quarters (right)

teenth-, and twentieth-century life in eastern Virginia. Architecturally the centerpiece is a Georgian house, built in 1751–1755 by Carter Burwell on land named and previously owned by his grandfather Robert "King" Carter. The plan of the house was extremely well resolved, with a T-shaped stair hall flanked by two entertaining rooms on the front and two private rooms on the rear. English carver and joiner Richard Bails produced virtuoso woodwork for the three public spaces, the most elaborate in the hall, where a full Ionic order and elliptical arch frame a richly detailed stair. Bails used a slightly simpler Doric order in the original parlor and dining room. The elevations respond to the plan, with seven bays on the river front and five on the rear. The brickwork, by mason-

builder David Minitree, is very refined, with extensive rubbing, a pair of brick door surrounds resembling that at the Secretary's Office in Williamsburg, and minimal use of glazed brick—contrasting with the heavily glazed walls of the two ancillary buildings, believed to be somewhat earlier.

The house remained in large part unchanged until 1928–1931, when Pittsburgh industrialist Archibald McCrea and his wife, Mollie Corling Dunlop, substantially and controversially remodeled it. Richmond architect W. Duncan Lee left the hall and front rooms virtually intact but redesigned the rear rooms and flankers and added hyphens to create a much larger circuit of spaces for entertaining. The roof was raised to provide additional bedrooms and to create the more assertive appearance the McCreas admired at Westover.

Colonial Williamsburg interprets the house as both eighteenth- and twentieth-century architecture, expressing the McCreas' social aspirations as well as Carter Burwell's. Boxwood plantings and the automobile approach date from the McCrea era, while the eight parterres of vegetables and ornamentals beyond the terraces are a 1970s re-creation of the Burwell landscape. The latter was the first in a series of big, paled, grid-pattern gardens, examples of which had recently been found by archaeologists at seventeenth- and eighteenth-century Tidewater plantations.

Nearby is a re-creation of the late colonial slave quarters: three houses, gardens, and a corncrib, based on extensive archaeological explorations here, at Kingsmill, and on other eighteenth-century quarters, as well as on a new generation of architectural fieldwork in the Chesapeake. The quarters offers a rare opportunity to see the sort of poor and relatively ephemeral accommodations much of Virginia's population occupied in the eighteenth century.

Excavations at Carter's Grove also brought to light remains of the Martin's Hundred settlement, established in 1619 and abandoned after it was attacked during the Powhatan Indian revolt of 1622. A schematic reconstruction outlines the fortified enclave and outlying sites. The story of Martin's Hundred and its discovery are chronicled in the Winthrop Rockefeller Archaeology Museum, another semisubterranean Colonial Williamsburg building designed by Kevin Roche. Entrance to the Carter's Grove property is by way of a visitor orientation building and bridge designed by Williamsburg architect Carlton Abbott.

HR44 Colonial National Historical Parkway

1938–1940, 1955–1957. National Park Service and Bureau of Public Roads staff, Stanley W. Abbott (Jamestown to Yorktown, through Williamsburg)

This wonderfully scenic thirty-mile drive links the three major colonial sites in Virginia, crossing from the James River to the York River. From open views of the rivers, the carefully maintained parkway passes through a rolling central section, a portion of which lies near various parks and military installations. The idea of such a roadway was initially broached early in the century, but not until 1930 did Congress, under the leadership of Representative Louis C. Cramton of Michigan, bring it into being. Abbott, who had worked on the Blue Ridge Parkway, was largely responsible for the design, which was built in several sections over nearly two decades. The parkway was essential for the success of the Williamsburg restoration, since it was submerged through the town and thus allowed traffic to bypass the historic core.

Yorktown   (HR45–HR46)

The village of Yorktown was established by the Virginia Port Act in 1691 and during the eighteenth century became one of the leading commercial centers in the American colonies. Located on the bluffs overlooking the York River, it possessed an excellent harbor, navigable by the largest ships of the period. Its population never exceeded 3,000. The Revolution was not kind to the town. A 1777 observer noted the "disorderly soldiers, and . . . Houses pulled down, others pulled to pieces for fuel, most of the Gardens thrown to the street. Everything in disorder." The 1781 battle (and ensuing surrender of Lord Charles Cornwallis to George Washington) caused additional damage; a fire in 1814 destroyed more buildings; and the town was the scene of minor Civil War action. Yorktown then lay dormant with little activity until its "rediscovery" in the 1920s. Today it spreads out along the York River; the points of interest are the historic center along Main Street and the waterfront, the monument, and the battlefield. The National Park Service owns and interprets several properties and operates the surrounding Colonial National Historical Park.

HR45 Main Street and Waterfront Area

HR45.1 Grace Church (York-Hampton Parish Church)

1687. 1848, 1871, 1931, rebuilding and other changes. Church St. (east side) at Main St.

The primary architectural interest of Grace Church is the original walls, of so-called Yorktown marl, cut slabs of shell deposits mixed with muck and clay from the nearby cliffs. It is the only known example of a colonial church built with this material. Originally rectangular in plan, the church later received a north wing. It was severely damaged during the Revolution (British General Cornwallis used it as a magazine). It burned in 1814, was not returned to service until 1848, and was again damaged during the Civil War. About the only remaining original features are the walls. The churchyard contains some early markers, including the Nelson family tombs. The churchyard wall dates from 1931.

HR45.2 Somerwell House

c. 1781. 1935–1936, restoration, National Park Service. Main St. at Church St. Open to the public

The original section of this T-shaped residence is now the rear wing. The larger section, to the street side, is an addition. The large-shouldered exterior brick chimneys give it great presence. Later it was used as a hotel.

HR45.3 Ambler's Storehouse (Customhouse, Peninsula Bank)

c. 1721. 1929–1930, restoration, W. Duncan Lee. Main St. at Read St. (southwest corner)

The impressive two-story store, with a prominent belt course and segmental arches over the doors and windows, is the only remaining element of successful merchant Richard Ambler's residential and commercial complex, begun about 1721. Ambler was customs collector, and the store has long been identified as the customhouse. It has the form of a conventional early Virginia store, with an unheated public room in front of a heated office. Emma Chenoweth led the local chapter of the Daughters of the American Revolution in restoring the building in 1929–1930 according to plans by Richmond architect W. Duncan Lee.

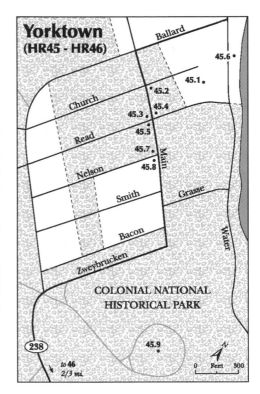

Yorktown
(HR45 - HR46)

COLONIAL NATIONAL
HISTORICAL PARK

to 46
2/3 mi.

HR45.4 Thomas Pate House

c. 1720–1740. 1924–1925, restoration, John Scarff. Main St. at Read St. (northwest corner)

Probably built as a merchant's residence about 1730, the three-room-plan building opposite Ambler's Storehouse had a high storage cellar entered from the rear, facing the river. Street filling in the nineteenth and early twentieth centuries has reduced its apparent height. John Scarff, from the Baltimore architecture firm of Wyatt and Nolting, planned the restoration in 1924–1925 for G. D. and Emma Chenoweth, with the intention of reversing nineteenth-century alterations to the fenestration and interior finish.

HR45.5 Poor Potter's Kiln

c. 1720–c. 1745, William Rogers. Read St., southwest of Main St. Open to the public

Lieutenant Governor Robert Dinwiddie assured the English Board of Trade that "the poor potter" of Yorktown produced wares insufficient to injure the mother country's trade, but archaeological excavations have revealed that William Rogers and, briefly, his heirs produced impressive quantities of stoneware and earthenware for the regional market for more than two decades. Two of Rogers's kilns and part of an associated work building were excavated in the 1970s. The exposed remains adjoin a stable (1916) designed by Griffin and Wynkoop for George P. Blow. A new visitor center has been designed by Carlton Abbott (1999–2000).

HR45.6 Archer Cottage

c. 1815. c. 1950, restoration. Waterfront

Rebuilt after the town fire of 1814, the small Archer Cottage is the sole above-ground remnant of Yorktown's lower town, a string of waterfront buildings built below the marl cliffs. It was substantially restored in the 1950s, but its ballast stone foundations survive from an earlier time.

HR45.7 Nelson House

c. 1730. c. 1920, renovation, George P. Blow with Percy Griffin; Charles Gillette, landscape architect. c. 1970, restoration, Lee Nelson and Robert Simmonds for the National Park Service. 508 Main St. (at Nelson St.). Open to the public

About 1730, Yorktown merchant Thomas Nelson erected the present dwelling on an urban estate that extended down to the water's edge. The house remains largely intact, despite serious damage sustained during the Revolution and the Civil War. With its two-story bulk and double-pile footprint, the Nelson House was an extraordinary creation for its time and place—one of the earliest realizations of the so-called Georgian plan in this region. In outward form and internal arrangement, it resembled Berkeley, seat of the Harrisons in Charles City County, with which it was nearly contemporary.

Thomas Nelson appears to have imported brick for his new house, as the chocolate-colored bricks with their yellow flashing resemble nothing made in the Virginia colony at the time. Together with the Portland stone elements and shiny rubbed bricks, they resemble materials employed in southern England and probably came from that region.

Owing to its early date, Nelson's house exhibited an unusual degree of ornamental vigor, inside and out. On the exterior, sandstone quoins define the corners while openings are picked out in bright red brick with Portland stone accents. The rubbed brick doorway is a characteristic and early example of the form. The full effect of the embellishments was reserved for the two street elevations; the plainer work, which now faces the garden, originally fronted on the kitchen or service yard. Inside, turnings and architectural orders in the public rooms were executed with license and imagination.

HR45.7 Nelson House

HR45.9 Yorktown Victory Monument

Early in the 1920s, George P. Blow of La Salle, Illinois, renovated the dwelling, assisted by New York architect Percy Griffin and Richmond landscape architect Charles Gillette. Griffin made extensive changes, adding dormers and areaways to maximize usable space in the attic and cellar. Early in the 1980s, York Hall, as it was then called, was acquired by the National Park Service and subsequently restored to its original appearance under the supervision of NPS architects Lee Nelson and Robert Simmonds.

HR45.8 **Sheild House** (Sessions-Sheild)

c. 1760. Later changes and rebuilding. 1931, restoration. Main St. (at Nelson St.). Open to the public

Two stories of brick with a jerkinhead roof, the Sheild House has been considerably rebuilt over time. The fine Flemish bond brickwork with glazed headers is fronted by a Doric portico added c. 1830. In 1935, while surveying Yorktown for the National Park Service, Charles Peterson described the house in what is probably the first historic structures report.

HR45.9 **Yorktown Victory Monument**

1880–1884, Richard Morris Hunt and Henry Van Brunt; John Quincy Adams Ward, sculptor. East of Main St. and Zweybrucken Rd.

The standard Trajan's Column format of a shaft with a crowning figure here receives further elaboration with a complex base composed of a pedimented podium and sculpted drum, a form based on several contemporary French monuments. In 1781 Congress ordered a marble column to be erected on the site to commemorate the victory over Cornwallis at Yorktown. Nothing was done, and in 1880 the secretary of war, Alexander Ramsey, created a commission and appointed Hunt, Van Brunt, and Ward to study the idea of a centennial monument. They in turn appointed themselves as the architects and sculptor, and Congress approved the design in March 1881. At the dedication in October 1881, President Chester A. Arthur spoke during elaborate ceremonies, but construction dragged on into 1884, when the crowning figure of Victory was finally hoisted into place.

HR46 **Moore House**

c. 1750, 1885, 1935–1936. VA 676. (1 mile east on Moore House St., then Washington Rd., or VA 238 from Yorktown). Open to the public

Famous as the site where Lord Cornwallis surrendered to General Washington, this two-story frame structure has been extensively rebuilt. The five-bay central section and the roof retain their original form.

Newport News (HR47–HR52)
(Hampton Roads map, p. 361)

HR47 **End View**

c. 1760–1775. 362 Yorktown Rd.

One of the relatively few pre-Revolutionary rural houses surviving south of Yorktown on the lower peninsula, this one was built with two rooms and a center passage on each of two floors. In its refined but modest details as well as its size, it closely resembles contemporary Williamsburg houses built for successful tradesmen. The house was owned and built by a member of the Harwood family who owned the surrounding land.

HR48 **Lee Hall**

1848–1859. Yorktown Rd. (VA 238, south of VA 143 near U.S. 60)

Lee Hall was built as a fashionable plantation house by Richard Decatur Lee. It was conceived as a two-and-one-half-story block, with accommodation for service in the relatively elevated ground floor. The roof was intentionally kept low, and understated grayish-brown brick was chosen to emphasize the Italianate porches and cornice, the latter with jigsawn brackets and turned pendants. Rooms flanking a central passage on all three floors are of a more consistent size and finish than those in eighteenth-century Virginia houses of this scale, illustrating the mid-nineteenth-century penchant for using Greek Revival and/or Italianate millwork with minimal hierarchical distinction among the spaces.

HR49 Matthew Jones House

c. 1720, 1727, 1729, 1892. Fort Eustis, Newport News. Open to the public

Merchant and planter Matthew Jones built a frame hall-chamber house with earth-fast posts and the present chimneys about 1720. He followed with a substantial kitchen in 1727, as evidenced by a brick with that date that was salvaged and used in the house during a remodeling in 1892. A guardian for Jones's son replaced the house walls with brick, added a two-story projection and a rear shed, and raised the chimneys in 1729. The walls were raised to a full two stories late in the nineteenth century, and most of the earlier interior was removed. The Jones House is now a museum focused on the physical evidence of its complex evolution.

HR50 Downtown Newport News

Although English settlers arrived early in the area, what we see today largely results from changes after 1879, when Colis P. Huntington, seeking an outlet for the shipment of coal from the west, located the eastern terminus of the Chesapeake and Ohio Railroad at the small fishing village of Newport News. By 1882 the line was complete, and the town became a major seaport. Huntington established the Chesapeake Dry Dock and Construction Company (now the Newport News Shipbuilding and Drydock Company), which, along with the Huntington Land Company, developed much of the town. The Spanish-American War saw the first major deployment of troops through the town, a pattern that would continue for over half a century. The Virginia Port Authority, which takes up the southwestern end of downtown, was established in 1926. In 1958 the city of Newport News absorbed the surrounding county of Warwick. Today the city spreads up the peninsula and represents, perhaps more urgently than any other Virginia city, the problems of suburban sprawl and misguided decisions on urban renewal of an old center city. The result is appalling urban decay.

  The significant structures can be found near the James River.

HR47 End View

HR50.1 Victory Arch

1919, 1962. West Ave. at 25th St.

Modeled after the Arch of Titus in Rome and constructed near the site of the embarkation of the American Expeditionary Force during World War I, the original arch was temporary and was reconstructed in 1962.

HR50.2 Warwick Hotel Annex

1927–1928, Peebles and Ferguson. 2410 West Ave.

The old Hotel Warwick was well known in the Hampton Roads area. The annex, in a 1920s version of Gothic Revival, was one of the tallest structures in town. It survived the fire that destroyed the original hotel and has been converted into apartments.

HR50.3 U.S. Post Office and Customhouse

1904, James Knox Taylor, Supervising Architect, U.S. Treasury Department. 1939–1940, addition, Federal Works Agency of the Public Buildings Administration. 101 25th St. and 102 26th St.

In its richly ornamented classicism, this building is an excellent example of the American Renaissance spirit. The building has entrances on either side of the block, one for the post office and the other for the custom house. Taylor loved elaborate Beaux-Arts-inspired compositions, and in the cornices here he outdid himself with the building up of layers of cavettos, modillions, and various cyma reversa moldings.

HR50.3 U.S. Post Office and Customhouse

HR50.5 Riverside Apartments

The addition maintains the same overall bay rhythm of the original, but the detailing is more austere. On the interior, the lobbies retain most of their original grandeur, with terrazzo floors and elaborate wall treatments. The post office lobby contains five bas-relief murals by Mary Fowler (1943) depicting scenes from local history. The building is a bright spot in the rather grim downtown.

HR50.4 First Baptist Church

1902–1903, Reuben Harrison Hunt. 1906–1907, rebuilding, Hunt. 29th St. at Washington Ave.

The former First Baptist Church is a substantial landmark with a tall tower and pink granite exterior. Hunt, from Chattanooga, Tennessee, where he was chairman of the board of deacons of the largest Baptist church, provided similar designs for other Baptist congregations in Virginia and throughout the South. Never a leader but a follower of popular architectural styles, Hunt chose the Richardsonian Romanesque, which by this time was well out of fashion in New York and Boston. Designed for a new minister whose sermons drew record crowds, the church is essentially a preaching church with a vast auditorium that seated 1,200 and was oriented on a diagonal. A fire in 1906 consumed the interior of the church, and it was rebuilt in the next year. The interior decoration is relatively sparse, in keeping with the focus on the spoken word. The congregation moved to more suburban quarters and the building is currently empty.

HR50.5 Riverside Apartments

1918, Francis Y. Joannes. 4500 Washington Ave. (at 45th St.)

Two large, U-shaped blocks of the original four remain of this significant attempt by the federal government to provide worker housing for the nearby Newport News Shipbuilding and Drydock Company. Commissioned by the U.S. Shipping Board Emergency Fleet Corporation, Joannes, who was also involved in nearby Hilton Village (see next entry), employed a New York open-stair tenement-type plan. The design incorporated the latest in construction techniques, with flat slab concrete floors for fire retardance and safety. The apartments were well lighted and ventilated.

HR51 Hilton Village

1918–1919, Henry Vincent Hubbard and Francis Y. Joannes. Warwick Blvd. to the James River, from Hopkins St. to Post St.

A significant development in the planning and design of middle-class housing in the United States, Hilton Village was constructed by the federal government in conjunction with the Newport News Shipbuilding and Dry Dock Company to house shipyard workers during World War I. Like the Riverside Apartments,

HR51 Hilton Village

the undertaking responded to an emergency need for permanent, good-quality housing for shipyard employees in a town overwhelmed by a wartime population boom. Hilton Village, however, was conceived on a larger scale, one among approximately two dozen emergency war towns erected with federal funds under the supervision of the Emergency Fleet Corporation. This sort of comprehensive plan, integrating living, working, and civic spaces, represented an innovative concept in housing design in the United States. Influenced by European, in particular English, precedents, American architects and planners took advantage of wartime housing shortages in shipbuilding towns along the Atlantic coast to apply their new convictions about housing design and planning.

Henry Vincent Hubbard, a noted town planner, and Francis Y. Joannes, a New York–based architect, conceived of Hilton Village as an integrated, self-sufficient community. They laid out a community of 473 English cottage–style single, double, and row houses on 95 acres adjacent to the James River. Following contemporary town planning initiatives of the day, Hubbard and Joannes employed a modified grid plan. A formal main street axis bisected the town, linking two pivotal public nodes, the community center and school and the village square. In addition, Hilton's careful layout employed a hierarchical arrangement of streets to control traffic flow and included public recreational, civic, and commercial spaces. The houses are typically one-and-one-half- and two-story frame buildings clad in combinations of weatherboard, stucco, and wood shingles. The distinctive steep, multigabled profiles of roofs clad in gray slate, along with the use of casement windows and asymmetrical massing, reflect the English heritage the architects drew upon.

HR52 Joseph Thomas Newsome House

1898. 1913, 1926, additions. 1989–1990, restoration, Roy Larson. 2803 Oak Ave. (northwest corner of Oak and 28th St.). Open to the public

Constructed as a rather plain rectangular building by an African American physician, Dr. William Granger, the house was purchased in 1906 by Newsome, a prominent African American lawyer, civil rights advocate, and newspaper editor. Newsome and his wife reoriented the entrance from Oak Street to 28th Street, and added the porch, turret, and Palladian window, making the house more Queen Anne in appearance. Another addition, consisting of the dining room–kitchen wing, came in 1926. In 1990 the house was restored on the exterior and converted into a museum on the interior.

Hampton   (HR53–HR56)

(Note: For HR53–HR54, see the Hampton Roads map, p. 361)

The English established a settlement along what is now Hampton (originally Southampton) River in 1610; the General Assembly designated it a port in 1708. Its strategic location required the construction of several forts, of which Fort Monroe is the most significant survivor. After the Civil War the town grew significantly, especially with the establishment of Hampton University. In 1952 the city of Hampton consolidated with Elizabeth City County, vastly enlarging its area.

HR53 Aberdeen Gardens

1934–1937, Hilyard Robinson and Lewis B. Walton. Area centered around Aberdeen Rd., Langston Blvd., Mary Peake Blvd., and Russell, Davis, Lewis, Weaver, and Walker rds.

Aberdeen Gardens comprises 158 single-family houses designed in a vaguely Colonial Revival idiom, on 110 acres laid out in a garden city–type site plan. The product of Franklin D. Roosevelt's Resettlement Administration, which attempted to improve housing conditions for the poor, this project was specifically aimed at the African American population. The intent was to create a model for other public and privately funded projects. Robinson, a noted African American architect and planner, was the senior architect for the Resettlement Administration and was well aware of contemporary ideas about the garden city. Each house stood on its own lot, which measured about 75 feet across and 220 to 290 feet deep, large by contemporary standards. Care was taken to preserve existing trees where possible, and the overall character was that of a large, shared open space. The lots were intended to be cultivated as kitchen and truck gardens, and chicken coops were provided along with 1,000 hens, 25,000 chicks, and 12 cows and mules. Fruit trees were supplied for the orchards. The houses were varied—some one and one-half stories, others two—and they offered a number of floor plans for four and five rooms. All houses had garages. A small Colonial Revival school building (destroyed) also functioned as a community center. Robinson foresaw that Aberdeen Road would become a major artery and hence placed no houses along it. The internal roads were named for prominent African Americans. On April 21, 1938, Eleanor Roosevelt toured the project. Although some of the lots have been subdivided, the project is well preserved.

HR54 Hampton Roads Coliseum

1968–1970, A. G. Odell, Jr., and Associates. 1000 Coliseum Dr.

Like a futuristic vision plucked from Frank Lloyd Wright's Broadacre City, the Hampton Roads Coliseum is designed to be viewed at high speed from a moving vehicle. Unlike the contemporaneous—and more expensive—Scope in Norfolk, the $8.5 million coliseum was intelligently situated outside downtown Hampton on a visually uninterrupted sweep of land and water on the north side of I-64; thus the straightforward radial design may be viewed from multiple angles across multiple terrains. The most distinctive exterior element is a repeated rhomboidal wall unit in precast concrete, intended to recall a ship's sail. The units are mounted on a reinforced concrete base, and they support a roofing system composed of a steel truss framework with suspension cables. On the interior are 7,336 permanent seats on two levels, with a maximum

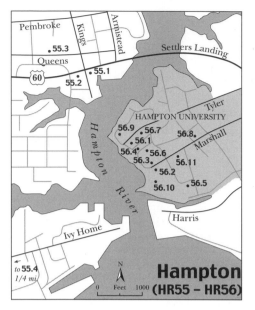

HR55.2 Virginia Air and Space Center and Hampton Roads History Center

1992, Rancorn, Wildman, Krause and Brezinski, with Mitchell/Giurgola. 600 Settlers Landing Rd.

The huge gull-like or airplane hangar–type wings that make up the main visual impression of this museum are clearly intended to symbolize the contents, both literally and metaphorically. The curved roofs, supported by banana-shaped trusses, contrast with the glazed infill and the lower red brick supporting structures, which have a more human scale along the major access road. Steven M. Goldberg of the New York office of Mitchell/Giurgola, who was the main designer, seems to have looked back to the German Expressionist designs of Erich Mendelsohn. The extruded tower on the east facade between the two hangars recall Mendelsohn's Schocken Department Store (1926) in Stuttgart. The exhibits include suspended aircraft and rockets and multiple levels of displays.

capacity of 11,027 seats. Southeast of the coliseum is a large spring-fed pond connected to the coliseum's cooling plant.

HR55 Hampton Downtown

Urban renewal and suburban flight have eroded much of the original downtown, leaving only a small portion on Queens Way (formerly Queen Street). The older residential areas close to downtown display a variety of housing types worthy of study.

HR55.1 Carousel

1920, Philadelphia Toboggan Company. 1991, restoration, R & F Designs. 610 Settlers Landing Rd.

Originally installed at nearby Buckroe Beach, which was a major amusement park and summer resort community, the carousel remained in operation until 1985. The city of Hampton purchased it and had it restored and relocated to its present location. It is one of the few still functional merry-go-rounds that survive of an estimated 6,000 wooden animal carousels that used to spin around the country. The forty-eight horses and two two-seat chariots were carved by Frank Carretta and Daniel C. Muller after pantographic carving machines allowed apprentices to rough out the bodies. The carousel, 45 feet in diameter, is a particularly fine example of the art form.

HR55.3 St. John's Episcopal Church

c. 1728, Henry Cary, Jr., builder. c. 1830, 1866, and later. 100 West Queens Way

St. John's status as an old and venerable parish is evident in the use of a Latin cross plan, usually reserved for larger, more urban congregations, as at Bruton Parish Church in Williamsburg. The brickwork—Flemish bond with glazed headers above the beveled water table and English bond below—is noteworthy. Some of the exterior windows have been enclosed. All three doorways apparently had brick pediments, which have been removed. The interior is all post–Civil War, since the town and the church were burned by retreating Confederate forces in 1861. Worthy of note is the silver communion service, which dates from c. 1619 and was made in London.

HR55.4 Little England Chapel

c. 1879. 4100 Kecoughtan Rd.

Tradition holds that this modest weatherboarded structure was constructed by Hampton Institute students under the sponsorship of the American Missionary Association. It was intended as a missionary chapel for the nearby heavily populated black area known as Cock's Newtown. The structure consists of a vestibule and a meeting room.

HR55.1 Carousel

HR55.4 Little England Chapel

HR56 Hampton University

1868; many additions. East Queen and Tyler sts.

The Hampton Normal and Agricultural Institute was founded in 1868 through the efforts of General Samuel C. Armstrong to provide education in manual skills and teaching for newly freed African Americans and for Native Americans. Armstrong, raised in the Hawaiian Islands, had observed missionaries working among the native tribes and conceived of duplicating these efforts in the American South. During the Civil War he commanded black troops in the Peninsular Campaign and later headed the Freedmen's Bureau in Virginia. The site he selected, fronting on Hampton Creek with a commanding view of Hampton Roads, was marked by a tree known as the Emancipation Oak Tree, which had been a gathering place for freedmen after the Civil War. An old plantation house, Mansion House (c. 1820), on the property near the waterfront, served and continues to serve as the President's House. Adjacent were a national soldiers' home and a national military cemetery.

Believing that environment played a role in education, General Armstrong selected his architects with care, a tradition that has continued. The initial architect for Hampton was a New Yorker, Richard Morris Hunt, who contributed three buildings, of which two remain. The selection of Hunt, the first American to attend the Ecole des Beaux-Arts and a leader of his profession, indicates the architectural aspirations of the school. Following Hunt came New Yorkers J. Cleveland Cady and the firm of Lud-

low and Peabody. In the 1940s Hilyard Robinson, a leading Washington-based African American architect, designed a number of structures that introduced International Style modernism to the campus. The initial buildings all fronted on the water, but Ludlow and Peabody, who became the campus architects in 1915, shifted the focus inland, away from the Hampton River, creating a series of loose quadrangles.

Virginia Hall (HR56.1) (1872–1879, 1885, Richard Morris Hunt) was Hunt's second building for the campus and by far his most commanding. A giant, bristling structure of red brick with tall mansard roofs, dormers on top of dormers, heavy buttresses, and elaborate wood bracing, it is difficult to define stylistically. Certainly it displays Hunt's French training—perhaps Néo-Grec would be the best term to apply—but it escapes those boundaries, for Virginia Hall is aggressively original and was part of Hunt's attempt in the 1860s and 1870s to create a new American architecture.

Second Academic Building (HR56.2) (1879–1881, Richard Morris Hunt) replaces Hunt's first building at the school, the First Academic Hall (1869–1870), which burned in 1879. Hunt's surviving drawings for this building (in the Prints and Drawings Collection, American Institute of Architects, Washington, D.C.) show a tower or campanile, which was eliminated during construction. Also, repainting over the years has diminished the original contrast between the revealed brick surrounds of the windows and the stucco infill panels. The large windows were a Hunt trademark derived from French studio buildings.

HR56.1 Hampton University, Virginia Hall
HR56.9 Hampton University, Davidson Hall

The Marquand Memorial Chapel (HR56.3) (1886, J. Cleveland Cady) was a gift of the New York financier and first president of the Metropolitan Museum of Art, Henry G. Marquand. For this large, assembly-hall type of structure, Cady, who ran a large New York firm, followed Hunt's lead by creating a landmark with a dominating campanile. Stylistically, Cady employed the fashionable Romanesque, though his treatment did not follow the Richardson lead as much as it provided a new interpretation. The ornament deserves attention, for heads of Native Americans and Africans are cast into the brick cornice.

Ogden Auditorium Hall (HR56.4) (1916, Ludlow and Peabody) is an impressive structure that illustrates a later stage of the Beaux-Arts in America, Hunt representing the earlier. Charles Peabody attended the Ecole des Beaux-Arts, and his New York firm was extremely prominent, both in the city and as university architects around the country. The entrance facade of Ogden Hall, with its paired Roman Doric columns, became the dominant element balancing the two Hunt buildings. The architects also attempted to mediate with a yellow-tan brick and Venetian red tile roof. Other Ludlow and Peabody buildings on the campus worthy of note and remarkably consistent in style, color, and form are James and Clarke halls (HR56.5) (1919), the Administration

HR57 Fort Monroe

Building (HR56.6) (1918), the Huntington Library (HR56.7) (1924), and the Science Building (HR56.8) (1928).

Davidson Hall (HR56.9) (1954–1956, Hilyard Robinson) marks the introduction of modernism at Hampton University. Designed as a women's dormitory and with a commanding view of the Hampton River, it is a taut, red-brick-veneered volume with a clear distinction between the commons area, the stair tower, and the dormitory wing. Robinson obtained the commission through William Henry Moses, who established an architecture department at Hampton in 1940 and took a great interest in expanding the campus in a contemporary mode and in engaging black architects to carry out the work. Very similar in style is the nearly contemporary Men's Dormitory (HR56.10) (1954, Hilyard Robinson).

Armstrong Hall (HR56.11) (1960–1962, Hilyard Robinson and William Henry Moses) is in the mode best known through Minoru Yamasaki's work of the period. A cast-concrete-block screen masks one elevation. The problems of designing a large container-type classroom building in a contemporary manner and fitting it into a Beaux-Arts campus are well illustrated.

HR57 Fort Monroe

1819–1834, Simon Bernard. Later additions and modifications. Chesapeake Bay at Hampton Roads (see Hampton Roads map, p. 361)

The nation's largest fortification in stone, Fort Monroe is a sublime marriage of engineering form and function, strategically sited where Hampton Roads meets Chesapeake Bay. The powerful massing of its walls reflected against the still waters of its perimeter moat testify to the clarity of vision, unencumbered by Romantic notions of ornament that prevailed in architectural circles in the early republic. Although it is no longer integral to the nation's defense, Fort Monroe remains the headquarters of the U.S. Army Training and Doctrine Command as well as an effective reminder of a site rich in military history.

Before landing at Jamestown in 1607, the first colonists stopped at the spit of land on the north shore of Hampton Roads, naming it Point Comfort in reference to their safe passage. The following year Captain John Smith surveyed the site for its defensive potential, finding it to be satisfactory. Fort Algernourne, an earthwork, was constructed in 1609, stockaded by 1611, and replaced in 1632. Fort George, the third on the site, was constructed of brick in 1728 but leveled by a hurricane twenty-one years later. Only a small battery stood on the site until the War of 1812, when it was briefly occupied by British troops, allowing for enemy incursions westward into the rivers beyond Hampton Roads and northward up the Chesapeake Bay as far as Washington and Baltimore. Alarmed by this breach of the nation's defenses, President James Madison ordered the construction of a series of forts along the Atlantic and Gulf coasts. In charge of the U.S. Army Board of Engineers undertaking the project was Brigadier General Simon Bernard, a French engineer who had previously served as aide-de-camp to Emperor Napoleon I.

Two forts were constructed flanking Hampton Roads. For the new fort at Point Comfort, named for President James Monroe, Bernard devised an irregular, seven-sided polygon, with two broad fronts facing Hampton Roads and polygonal bastions at each of the corners. A moat surrounds the entire fort so that it is accessible only via bridges that lead to narrow gates. The exterior walls are largely unornamented, save for the main sally port, executed in a severe Doric order reminiscent of the works of Claude-Nicolas Ledoux. Behind the segmental-arched embrasures in the walls are dozens of casemates—vaulted interior chambers—that are among the era's most sophisticated examples of masonry construction. Inverted arches beneath the floors distribute the heavy weight of the vaults evenly throughout the sandy soil. Most of the casemates were designed to house guns on swiveling carriages, but others were used as living quarters. Fort Wool (formerly Fort Calhoun), a much smaller, kidney-shaped fortification on the south side of Hampton Roads, was designed by the Board of Engineers to rest on the Rip Raps, a shoal enlarged with stones dumped into the channel to form an artificial island.

As an active defense post, Fort Monroe saw its most significant activity in the mid-nineteenth century. It is known principally as the backdrop for the Civil War's most famous naval engagement, the 1862 Battle of Hampton Roads, in which the former *U.S.S. Merrimac*, clad in iron and rechristened the *C.S.S. Virginia*, confronted the *U.S.S. Monitor*, a newly built ship that was also clad in iron. The battle ended in a draw, but it effectively altered the course of modern naval warfare. Throughout the war, the fort remained under Union control, and hundreds of slaves sought refuge behind its thick walls. Following the armistice, former Confederate President Jefferson Davis was imprisoned here for several months. His erstwhile cell forms the centerpiece of the Casemate Museum, which also includes informative exhibits on the fort's history, personnel, and artillery. Within the fort is the Protestant Chapel of the Centurion (1855–1858, after the designs of Richard Upjohn), a Carpenter's Gothic church with handsome stained glass windows, including three by Tiffany Studios (open to visitors).

On its exterior, the fort is surrounded by numerous historic buildings, of which the 1802 lighthouse is especially notable. Facing Hampton Roads is the imposing Georgian Revival Chamberlin Hotel (1926–1928, Marcellus Wright with Warren and Wetmore), a brick replacement for an earlier wooden hostelry (1890–1896, Smithmeyer and Pelz; 1893–1896, John Fraser), destroyed by fire in 1920. Fort Wool, across Hampton Roads, is accessible via an excursion boat from downtown Hampton.

Norfolk (NK)

LOCATED ON THE SOUTH SIDE OF HAMPTON ROADS, BORDERING THE Chesapeake Bay and the Elizabeth River, Norfolk is at the center of Virginia's principal port area and is home to the world's largest naval operation. The area was settled in the early seventeenth century, but not until 1680 was the town of Norfolk surveyed. Norfolk received the status of borough in 1736 and city in 1845. With its deep natural harbor, Norfolk quickly evolved into an international port whose strategic location made it particularly vulnerable in wartime. It was burned to the ground by its own fleeing residents during the Revolution, leaving only the walls of the borough church standing. During the Federal period, affluent merchants (including Moses Myers, whose elegant town house survives) slowly rebuilt Norfolk, only to see it suffer again during the maritime disruptions caused by the War of 1812. Another period of prosperity followed, as represented by a new city hall and courthouse, designed in part by Thomas U. Walter, and the growth of the Freemason neighborhood north of downtown. For most of the Civil War Norfolk was occupied by Union forces, who inflicted little damage. The city's economy recovered slowly during Reconstruction. By the end of the nineteenth century the BB&T Building, the city's first skyscraper, transformed the appearance of downtown; streetcar suburbs such as Ghent pushed the boundaries of the city even farther northward.

Norfolk remained a relatively small city until the early twentieth century, when two events catapulted it into national prominence. Thousands of tourists converged on the city and the adjacent region for the Jamestown Ter-Centennial Exposition (1907), a world's fair that celebrated the arrival of the English colonists in Virginia. The exposition simultaneously spurred downtown construction and outward residential expansion. Ten years later, when the United States entered World War I, the former fairgrounds were redeveloped as a naval base, which was greatly expanded during World War II and which has continued to grow in the post–Cold War era. The construction of new roads, bridges, and especially tunnels in the mid- to late twentieth century has linked Norfolk more effectively with the surrounding region while it has accelerated the abandonment of the city's retail district and neighborhoods

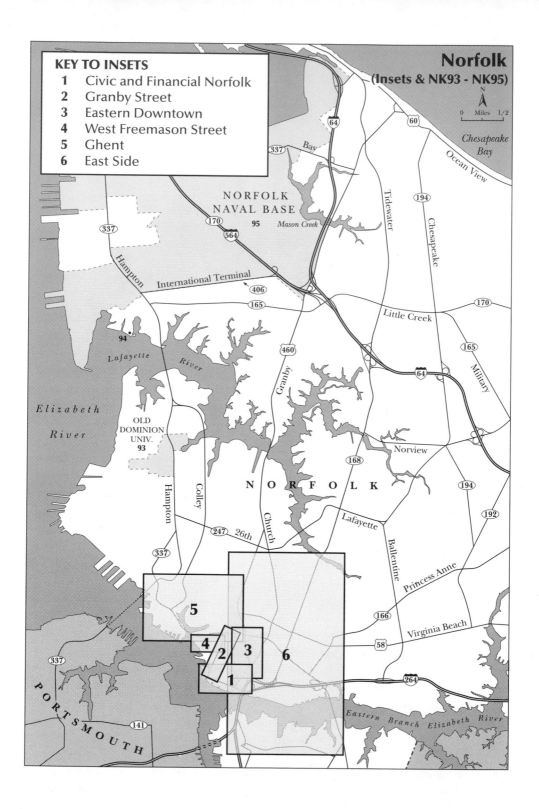

KEY TO INSETS

1. Civic and Financial Norfolk
2. Granby Street
3. Eastern Downtown
4. West Freemason Street
5. Ghent
6. East Side

Norfolk
(Insets & NK93 - NK95)

for the suburban areas of Virginia Beach, Chesapeake, Suffolk, and the Lower Peninsula. To fight this trend, Norfolk once again rebuilt itself, undertaking one of the nation's largest urban renewal programs, through which many important historic buildings were lost. The downtown waterfront was cleared of industrial warehouses, and the business district was rebuilt with modern and postmodern skyscrapers, such as the Bank of America Building. The intensity of this program has not abated, so some of the buildings from the initial period of redevelopment are already being demolished for new construction. Although for many years Virginia's largest city, Norfolk now trails Virginia Beach in population.

Civic and Financial Norfolk   (NK1–NK18)

This walking tour begins at the center of Norfolk's municipal government and moves eastward through the financial district along Main Street, one of the city's original seventeenth-century thoroughfares.

NK1 **Norfolk Civic Center**

1956–1965, Vincent G. Kling with Woodward, Oliver and Smith. 1967–1971, School Administration Building and Juvenile and Domestic Relations Court, Dudley, Morrisette, Cederquist and Associates; 1997–1998, renovation, Walker Woodward. 1994–1997, Public Safety Building addition, I.V. Harris and Associates. 810 Union St.

The award-winning Civic Center was the linchpin of Norfolk's postwar redevelopment effort and a potent symbol of its quest for modernity. Prewar Norfolk was characterized by narrow,

twisting streets and small-scale, eclectic architecture in drab colors. The new city, as represented by the Civic Center, would feature wide boulevards, open spaces, and bright, International Style skyscrapers. Vincent G. Kling, a Philadelphia architect, then at the beginning of a long and distinguished career, and Charles K. Agle, the designer of the city's 1956 master plan, were chiefly responsible for this remarkable transformation.

The increase in the city's population during World War II and the annexation of outlying territory had increased the size of the municipal government to a point where the old city hall had become hopelessly outmoded. Preliminary discussions for a new civic center began in 1953. Kling became a consultant in 1954, and Woodward, Oliver and Smith joined Kling as project architects the following year. The city council debated several downtown sites, and the waterfront location emerged as the front runner only after it was identified in Agle's master plan. The availability of the site, its proximity to the new Berkley Bridge, and its plentiful off-street parking ensured its selection.

Kling's site plan is asymmetrically balanced along a north-south axis. Each building is conceived as a rectangular unit within a regular grid, and exteriors are unified by a light-colored brick. Dominating the complex is the eleven-story City Hall, sheathed in glass with special *brise-soleil* of tinted glass that extend three feet from the inner curtain wall. The tower houses the municipal administration while its sprawling, one-story brick base con-

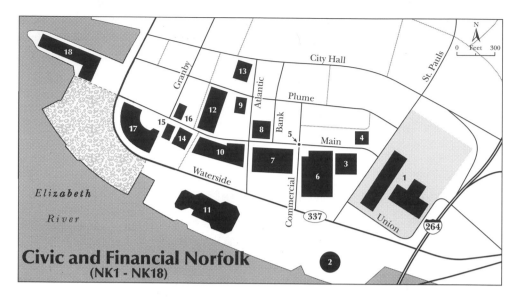

Civic and Financial Norfolk
(NK1 - NK18)

tains the city's public service departments. Immediately to the west of City Hall, facing St. Paul's Boulevard, is a two-story courthouse. These two buildings are separated from the Public Safety Building, at the northern edge of the site, by an open plaza with circular fountain. The narrow fenestration of the Public Safety Building identifies its function as the city jail, and this pattern is continued in the recent addition perpendicular to the original slab. Although considered a part of the Civic Center, the School Administration Building is visually and physically separated by City Hall Avenue. A Brutalist influence can be detected in its exposed concrete frame.

NK2 Dominion Tower

1984–1987, Harwood K. Smith and Partners. 999 Waterside Dr.

At twenty-six stories, Dominion Tower is the region's tallest skyscraper as well as its most vivid reminder of the fervid real estate speculation of the 1980s. Designed by a Dallas firm, the building has polished red granite walls and a postmodern crown that confirm its slick Sunbelt pedigree. Dominion Tower was intended to be the region's premier office building when it opened in the fall of 1987. Its opulent lobby is a showcase of imported marble and granite, and its cross-shaped plan increases the number of desirable corner offices on each floor with uninterrupted views of the Elizabeth River,

Norfolk, and Portsmouth. A glut of office space in the region coupled with an enormous debt load, however, nearly led to the property's foreclosure. A combination of new ownership and management reversed the building's fortunes.

Dominion Tower is best viewed from the Berkley Bridge, where its massive scale can be measured against the Norfolk skyline. From Waterside Drive the main, pseudo-Palladian entrance appears gargantuan and unapproachable. In 1993 the west wall of the adjacent parking garage was covered with a whaling mural by the artist Wyland. Next to Dominion Tower, even images of nature's largest mammals appear small.

NK3 First Virginia Bank (Bank of Virginia)

1973–1977, Dudley, Morrisette, Cedarquist and Associates. 555 E. Main St.

The seventeen-story headquarters for the Bank of Virginia is perhaps downtown Norfolk's most unattractive building, largely because of its bottom-heavy, fortresslike appearance. A five-level parking garage perches above the ground-floor lobby; its ribbed concrete walls and narrow ventilation slits are an excellent example of American Brutalism. Rising above the garage, the office tower is its visual opposite: narrow concrete piers juxtaposed with tinted glass curtain walls.

NK4 500 East Main Street

1966–1970, Vlastimil Koubek. 500 E. Main St.

The influence of German architect Ludwig Mies van der Rohe is readily apparent in this International Style bank building designed by a Washington-based architect. Rising eighteen stories without setbacks, the building's dark exterior is sheathed in anodized aluminum and tinted glass with I-beam mullions in the manner of Mies's Seagram Building (1956–1958) in New York City. The ground-level lobby is recessed behind the outermost piers and enclosed in glass. An unusual construction feature of the building is its Franki foundation, a Belgian technique for sinking concrete footings. Hollow metal tubes are hammered into the ground, and the bottom of each tube is filled with concrete to create a footing. A steel shell is inserted above the footing and filled with more concrete to form a pile, and the tube is then removed. About six footings per day were sunk in a process that is quieter than conventional pile driving.

NK5 Confederate Monument

1898–1907, William Couper. 1965, dismantled. 1971, rebuilt. Intersection of Commercial Pl. and E. Main St.

For most of the twentieth century, "Johnny Reb," the quintessential Confederate soldier, has stood watch 65 feet over the center of Norfolk, his gaze defiantly directed northward. The history of this impressive monument in many ways symbolizes the ambivalence with which this city views its past.

Union troops occupied Norfolk during most of the Civil War, and once they had departed, lingering resentment among the white population was channeled into the erection of a memorial to slain Confederate soldiers. Fund raising commenced in 1868 under the auspices of the Norfolk Monument Association, but not until the Pickett-Buchanan Camp of Confederate Veterans assumed control of the project in the 1890s did the city raise sufficient moneys and approve a site in the center of downtown.

The design, by sculptor William Couper, is essentially a smaller version of Richard Morris Hunt's Yorktown Victory Monument (1880–1884; see under Yorktown, in the Hampton Roads section). The dominant feature of the Confederate Monument is a colossal granite column cut with the mechanical precision typical of the era. Rising from a stepped base, its fluted and banded shaft is crowned by a stylized Ionic capital. Perched atop the column is a bronze statue of a Confederate soldier holding the army's standard in his left hand and a saber in his right. Bronze figures representing the Confederate army, navy, artillery, and infantry were intended for the base, but they were excluded from the final design because of insufficient funds, and granite cannonballs were substituted. With great fanfare, the monument's cornerstone was laid in 1899 and the column erected later that same year. The statue of Johnny Reb was not installed and unveiled until 1907, the year the city hosted the Jamestown Ter-Centennial Exposition.

Until World War II the monument stood at the very heart of Norfolk's bustling downtown near the point of departure for ferries across the Elizabeth River. Because of two construction projects—the bridge-tunnel to Berkley and Portsmouth in the early 1950s and later the nearby Virginia Bank Building—and the politics of the emerging civil rights movement, the Norfolk Redevelopment and Housing Authority dismantled and stored the monument. Although not perceived as especially controversial by the public, it remained something of an embarrassment to forward looking municipal officials. Finally, in 1971 the monument was rebuilt several feet to the east of its original location on a new axis created by the realignment of Commercial Place to the south and a park to the north that leads to the MacArthur Memorial.

NK6 Norfolk Southern Tower

1986–1988, Williams, Tazewell and Cooke and Associates. 3 Commercial Pl.

This sleek, twenty-story office tower serves as the headquarters for the Norfolk Southern Corporation, one of the nation's largest railroads. Rising from a trabeated base of polished marble, the polygonal tower is sheathed in reflective glass and set back in stages. The building appears particularly handsome at night when subtle floodlighting is directed at horizontal bands of reflective metal coping on the third, fourth, eighth, and fourteenth floors.

NK7 Bank of America Building (Virginia National Bank Building)

1965–1968, Skidmore, Owings and Merrill with Williams and Tazewell and Associates. 1 Commercial Pl.

This is Norfolk's finest modern skyscraper and a centerpiece of the city's early downtown rede-

NK7 Bank of America Building (Virginia National Bank Building)

NK9 Seaboard Center (U.S. Post Office and Federal Courts Building)

velopment efforts during the 1960s. The newly formed Virginia National Bank wanted to create a new headquarters that would symbolize its growth into a major statewide financial institution. To accomplish this task, the bank hired the New York office of Skidmore, Owings and Merrill, an architecture firm with an international reputation, along with Williams and Tazewell and Associates, a local firm. SOM produced a design that, while typical of the later International Style in its geometric exterior grid and flat roof, is distinguished by its three-dimensional modeling and careful attention to detail. The precast concrete frame was assembled from T-shaped units and finished in white quartz. It is fully exposed on the exterior, and the corners are cut away to reduce the building's bulk. A glass curtain wall is set several feet behind the frame so that the latter acts as a *brise-soleil*. The frame is in turn joined to the interior utility core to create virtually uninterrupted floor space. Across East Main Street is a six-and-one-half-story parking garage with a matching quartz finish, designed by SOM to serve the office building. The Virginia National Bank, the product of earlier bank absorptions, merged with the First and Merchants Bank to create Sovran Bank in 1983. Sovran Bank was absorbed by NationsBank in 1991, and Nations-Bank merged with the Bank of America in 1998. As a result of successive mergers in the

1980s and 1990s, the building is now occupied by Bank of America.

NK8 Main Street Tower

1988–1994, Burrell F. Saunders. 300 E. Main St.

With its minimalist exterior of blue reflective glass, Main Street Tower is a veritable cliché of corporate America during the early 1980s: big, slick, and attention-grabbing. What distinguishes this fourteen-story building is its tortured development history. Planned at the height of the real estate market, the project ran into financial difficulties two years into construction. The building stood as an embarrassing eyesore, half finished, for three years until a new owner resumed construction, opening it to tenants in 1994.

NK9 Seaboard Center (U.S. Post Office and Federal Courts Building)

1899–1900, Wyatt and Nolting with James K. Taylor, Supervising Architect, U.S. Treasury Department. 1984, restoration, OSC Associates. 235 E. Plume St. Lobby open to the public

A good example of Beaux-Arts urbanism, this former federal building nestles into an obliquely angled corner site in the heart of downtown. Wyatt and Nolting, a prominent Baltimore firm, chose a Neo-Palladian design that recalled the work of James Gibbs. The ground level is clad in rusticated limestone, while the piano nobile and attic levels are clad in brick with limestone ornamentation, including corner quoining and projecting window caps supported by consoles. The center of the main facade on Plume Street projects slightly and is distinguished on the upper levels by an engaged, three-bay Scamozzian Ionic portico with pediment and a central balcony over the main entrance. An interior court surrounded by early Renaissance arcades brings light into the center of the building. The post office once occupied the ground level, with the courtroom and auxiliary spaces on the upper levels.

The construction of a new U.S. post office and courthouse in the early 1930s on the northern edge of downtown made this building redundant. With only minor alterations, it was pressed into service as Norfolk's city hall (1938–1965), and the International Style Hipage Building, immediately adjacent (1954–1955, T. David Fitz-Gibbon; 227 East Plume Street) was constructed as a stopgap municipal annex during the protracted planning process for the new Norfolk Civic Center. Subsequently, with the completion of the Civic Center in the mid-1960s, it served other purposes and then was carefully restored by OSC Associates.

NK10 Norfolk Marriott Hotel and Convention Center

1989–1991, Cooper Carry and Associates. 235 E. Main St.

An excellent example of neotraditional urban planning, this design makes full use of a small (1.2-acre), irregular lot with a twenty-three-story hotel tower at the east end and a low-rise convention center at the west. The base of the complex, paneled in polished green granite, hugs a crook in the south side of East Main Street, its proportions mirroring those of older, neighboring buildings. Enormous plate glass windows open views of the interior to passersby, and a handsome canopy projects over the motor entrance. A high-rise parking garage with ground-level shops directly across from the hotel is connected to it by a slightly arched skywalk whose geometric framework links it visually to the entrance canopy beneath it. Overall, the $52 million complex has transformed East Main Street into a dense and lively urban corridor. The only discordant aspect of the design is the L-shaped postmodern hotel tower. Its precast synthetic stucco cladding, with horizontal seams that resemble rustication, fails to convince the viewer of its permanence, even at a distance.

NK11 Waterside Festival Marketplace

1981–1983, 1988–1990, Wallace, Robertson and Todd. 333 Waterside Dr.

During the 1970s and early 1980s James W. Rouse virtually reinvented the American downtown, developing a string of festival marketplaces that were modern-day versions of the Greek agora for cities along the eastern seaboard. What worked for Boston and Baltimore, however, failed in Norfolk's largely suburban metropolitan area. The $13.5 million Waterside never quite became an urban desti-

NK11 Waterside Festival Marketplace

nation in the mind of the public, and an $8.5 million expansion, finished in 1990, only exacerbated the marketplace's financial woes. But Waterside's fortunes improved later in the decade when the tenant mix was reshuffled in favor of large chain restaurants. Wallace, Robertson and Todd of Philadelphia essentially created an enlarged version of the ferry terminal that once stood at the foot of nearby Commercial Place, repeating the earlier building's graceful fanlights and hipped roof. Its polygonal glass curtain walls provide stunning views of the waterfront, Portsmouth, and downtown Norfolk. A riverfront esplanade connects the marketplace to Town Point Park and the Nauticus maritime center to the west and north and the Sheraton Hotel to the east. Unfortunately, the enormous width of Waterside Drive discourages pedestrians from exploring the downtown retail district, a situation reinforced by the skywalk connecting the marketplace to the parking garage directly opposite it.

NK12 Selden Arcade

1930–1931, Calrow, Browne and Fitz-Gibbon. 1965, renovation, Gideon Jeremitsky. 200 E. Main St.

NK13 Monticello Arcade

1906–1907, Neff and Thompson. 205–217 E. City Hall Ave.

Although common in Europe and found occasionally in the northeastern and midwestern United States, covered shopping arcades are rarer in the warmer climates of the American southeast. That Norfolk possesses two such buildings axially aligned on adjacent blocks is astonishing. Together they form a pleasant, if somewhat deserted, pedestrian spine that leads from Monticello Avenue and the center of downtown across East Plume Street to Martin's Lane and the waterfront.

The Monticello Arcade, the more distinguished of the pair, was constructed in anticipation of the surge in visitors to the city for the 1907 Jamestown Ter-Centennial Exposition. The local firm of Neff and Thompson designed a fireproof structure framed in reinforced concrete and clad in terra-cotta. The East City Hall Avenue and East Plume Street elevations are identical with engaged Ionic columns and split segmental pediments over centrally placed entrances. Inside, the well-proportioned, three-

NK13 Monticello Arcade

story atrium is illuminated by a gabled skylight. Galleries overlooking the main concourse at the upper levels are bounded by graceful iron railings. Although scaled for early twentieth-century commerce, the design of the Monticello Arcade is reminiscent of Warren and Bucklin's Greek Revival Providence (Rhode Island) Arcade (1828), America's first.

The success of the Monticello Arcade led to an attempt to extend southward, across Plume Street, a smaller, more modern arcade named after a prominent Norfolk family. The Selden Arcade is arranged on a single level with a concealed upper level at each end. Clerestory windows flood the main concourse with light. Only the south facade is original, and it is a handsome example of Art Deco design by a rather conservative Norfolk firm. A segmental arch with a chevron border spans the entrance portal, and stylized block letters announce the building's name to passing shoppers. To either side, abstracted fluted pilasters without capitals divide the facade into bays.

At one time both arcades were open to the street at each end. A Norfolk city ordinance requires that the owners of such buildings block public access to them annually for a brief period, lest they be declared public thoroughfares. At some point in the distant past, the owners of the Monticello Arcade evidently failed to comply with this ordinance, although it is unclear whether the city ever tested its authority in this matter. In any case, doors have since been added to both buildings. As with the rest of the downtown retail district, the arcades' fortunes declined after World War II with the development of outlying shopping centers. A misguided renovation in the mid-1960s stripped away the limestone from the north facade of the Selden Arcade and replaced it with an uninspired neoclassical design in white marble and black tile. In 1974 the Monticello Arcade was threatened with demolition when the city proposed extending Monticello Avenue to the waterfront. Quick action on the part of the local citizenry resulted in the building's nomination to the National Register of Historic Places the following year, and the city subsequently shelved its plans. Since then both arcades have undergone partial renovation.

NK14 BB&T Building

1897–1899, Charles E. Cassell. 1920, 1937, additions. 1990–1993, restoration, Cedarquist Rodriguez Ripley. 109 E. Main St.

For a brief period in the late 1980s Norfolkians, tired of the rampant demolition that had permanently scarred their downtown, rebelled. The building they rallied to preserve in many ways could not have been a more ironic choice. Constructed at the turn of the century for Citizens Bank, the seven-story building was the city's first skyscraper and a symbol of its long-sought recovery from the economic devastation of the Civil War. Moreover, it presaged the kind of large-scale redevelopment required for Norfolk's transformation from a sleepy seaport into a modern metropolis.

The restrained Renaissance Revival design by Charles E. Cassell combines handsomely detailed brickwork with elaborate terra-cotta ornamentation. The ground-level entrance on East Main Street is particularly imposing with round-arched openings framed by Corinthian pilasters and elegant, *rinceau*-filled spandrels. Sumptuous wreaths fill the tympana of the round-arched windows in the flanking bays. A series of attenuated pilasters links the ground level to the boldly projecting cornice that once terminated the facade; an eighth story, added in 1920, now peeks above the cornice. Because the building's western elevation serves as a backdrop to the adjacent customhouse, the articulation of the East Main Street facade is continued on this side; the east and south elevations, which were not meant to be seen from the surrounding streets, are strictly utilitarian in appearance. A respectful two-story annex was added to the east of the building in 1937. During its long history the building was occupied by a succession of banking institutions. It became fixed in the public imagination as the Wheat Building only after 1980, when Wheat First Securities became its principal tenant.

Like many other American cities, Norfolk participated enthusiastically in the real estate boom of the 1980s, a boom that accelerated the razing of the few historic buildings left standing after the urban renewal clearances of the previous two decades. A proposal to demolish the building led to a major public outcry. In the end, it was not public opposition but a faltering national economy that prevented its demolition. Careful restoration by Cedarquist Rodriguez Ripley returned the main banking hall to its former splendor. It is one of Norfolk's few preservation triumphs.

NK15 U.S. Customhouse and Post Office

1852–1859, Ammi Burnham Young. 1901, renovation, James K. Taylor, Supervising Architect, U.S. Treasury Department. 1999–2000, restoration, MMM Design. 101 E. Main St.

The U.S. Customhouse and Post Office is a rare example of an antebellum government building that has survived without significant interior or exterior alteration despite more than a century of continuous use. The city's first official customhouse was designed by Lovitt Fentress in 1819, but it had become outmoded by mid-century. In 1850 Congress passed an appropriation of $50,000 for a new building that would also include a post office, and it was completed in 1859 at a final cost of $204,000. Ammi Burnham Young, Supervising Architect of the Office of Construction of the U.S. Treasury Department, was responsible for the design; Captain Alexander H. Bowman was the engineer in charge of construction.

The building occupies a strategic site on Main Street with its rear facade oriented toward the waterfront. Its two distinct interior functions are made apparent on the granite exterior by raising the two levels comprising the customhouse offices above a high, rusticated basement containing the post office. As is often the case with Young's designs, the building combines elements of both Greek and Roman architecture. A two-story, pedimented portico with six Corinthian columns, reached by a flight of stairs from Main Street, projects from the principal facade. Corinthian pilasters articulate the sides and rear of the building. Both columns and pilasters have capitals of cast iron, an innovative material that Young used for the entablature as well. Although the exterior walls are built of load-bearing masonry, the interior, as engineered by Bowman, was designed with the latest fireproofing techniques, including iron doors and window shutters and cast and wrought iron framing members that support shallow masonry vaults. A curving, cantilevered double staircase, also constructed of iron, is located at the rear of the building. Some of the original black and white marble floor tiles still survive in places. The customhouse has recently been restored.

NK16 100 Main

1868–1869, attributed to George Edmund Lind. c. 1934, renovation. 1982, renovation, Oliver, Smith and Cooke. 100 E. Main St.

This Second Empire commercial building is an unusual survivor of the nineteenth century and the lone reminder of the time when Main Street was the city's retail center. Originally home to the S. A. Stevens Furniture Company, the building was later occupied by a succession of retail establishments. By the middle of the twentieth century it had been shorn of most of its exterior ornamentation. The building has been renovated and converted into offices.

NK17 World Trade Center

1981–1984, Skidmore, Owings and Merrill. 1985–1986, addition, Smallwood, Reynolds, Stewart, Stewart and Associates. Southeast corner of W. Main St. and Waterside Dr.

One of the few distinguished buildings to have emerged from the real estate boom of the 1980s, the World Trade Center bears the unmistakable modernist imprint of Skidmore, Owings and Merrill, the internationally renowned architectural firm.

Bruce Graham of SOM's Chicago office was the chief architect for the World Trade Center, and his restrained design looks to the future while acknowledging the past, all without lapsing into postmodern kitsch. From the waterfront, the aluminum facade of the nine-story building curves along the arc created by Waterside Drive, its tinted ribbon windows protected by *brise-soleil.* A handsome sculptural effect is created by the insertion of setbacks at the building's north end; from Main Street each level appears to be stacked and curved like a

NK18 Nauticus, The National Maritime Center

deck of cards. The design is somewhat reminiscent of Kohn Pedersen Fox's 333 West Wacker Drive in Chicago (1983), one of the most acclaimed skyscrapers of the early 1980s and, significantly, the occupant of a curved site on that city's riverfront. A more important precedent for the World Trade Center, however, was Erich Mendelsohn's Schocken Department Store in Chemnitz, Germany (1928–1929), whose curving facade was viewed as heretical by the early historians of modernism. In the context of Norfolk in the 1980s, its adaptation was a welcome antidote to the surrounding corporate postmodernism.

The entrance to the World Trade Center is behind a landscaped entrance court off West Main Street, the centerpiece of which is Bernar Venet's *Undetermined Line,* a large and controversial public sculpture. Constructed of painted steel that forms an irregular spiral, it harmonizes with the curving building behind it. A nine-story addition by an Atlanta firm extends the original design to the west, its upper levels boldly cantilevered in the direction of the customhouse.

NK18 Nauticus, The National Maritime Center

1991–1994, Centerbrook Architects with Shriver and Holland Associates. 1 Waterside Dr.

Never in Norfolk's history has a project failed on so many different levels: aesthetically, programmatically, and financially. In the early

1980s the city and the locally headquartered Cousteau Society discussed the creation of a facility that would focus on the work of renowned French oceanographer Jacques Cousteau. This idea faltered, and the city proposed Nauticus, a combined "infotainment" facility focusing on local maritime themes. The Hampton Roads Naval Museum joined it, creating a programmatic hodgepodge. The $52 million project opened in June of 1994 but lackluster attendance, caused partly by steep admission prices and lack of identity, caused the city to assume full control in January 1997.

Unfortunately, the center's many woes were compounded by its adventurous but ungainly design, one of the last works by noted American architect Charles Moore. Moore, in collaboration with Mark Simon of Centerbrook Architects, attempted to create a "duck," a build-ing that communicates its function through its very appearance. Responding to the waterfront location and multiple nautical themes, the architects designed an enormous gray superstructure above a pier perpendicular to the riverbank. There is a faint deconstructivist quality to the building's numerous curves and angles, as if a battleship had melted under nuclear attack. On the south side a bold diagonal element corresponds to an interior moving sidewalk connecting the different levels, while on the north side an A-4 jet appears lost amid the vast gray mass to which it is affixed. The interior resembles that of a suburban shopping mall. In December 2000 the U.S. Navy berthed the battleship *Wisconsin* on the north side of Nauticus, and subsequently the interior exhibits were reworked according to a more focused naval theme.

Granby Street   (NK19–NK33)

Granby Street, which after 1900 emerged as the city's principal retail corridor, leads northward from Main Street. During part of the 1970s and 1980s the street was closed to traffic and converted into a pedestrian mall; only forlorn vestiges of the pavement and street furniture now remain from that era.

NK19 Virginia Club

1908–1909, Wyatt and Nolting with Taylor and Hepburn. 101 Granby St.

Given the Virginia Club's seemingly impregnable appearance, it is not surprising that this limestone building was once the main branch of the Virginia Bank and Trust Company and, later, the Southern Bank of Norfolk. Three of the four architects associated with the building—Wyatt, Nolting, and Taylor—had earlier collaborated on the design of the old U.S. Post Office and Federal Courts Building on East Plume Street (see entry, above). For the bank project the architects drew upon motifs associated with ancient Greek treasuries, made popular at the turn of the century by the nationally renowned firm of McKim, Mead and White. Massive piers define the corners of the rectangular building, and fluted Ionic columns in antis stretch across the street facades and support a full entablature. A recessed grid of plate glass windows fills the space between the columns at the upper levels, but for security purposes the pedimented door and window frames at the ground level are small. The building ceased operating as a bank in the late 1970s, and the Virginia Club, one of Norfolk's oldest social organizations, moved into the building in 1997.

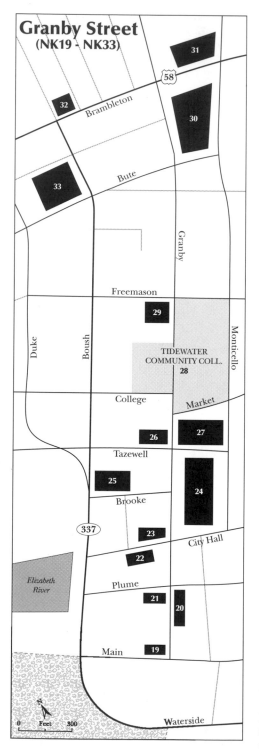

Granby Street
(NK19 - NK33)

31

58

32

Brambleton

30

33

Bute

Granby

Freemason

29

Duke

Boush

TIDEWATER
COMMUNITY COLL.
28

Monticello

College

Market

26

27

Tazewell

25

24

Brooke

337

23

City Hall

22

Elizabeth
River

Plume

21

20

Main   19

N

0   Feet   300

Waterside

NK20 Granby Row

North side of Granby St. between E. Main St. and E. Plume St.

Granby Row is one of the few blocks of low-rise commercial architecture in downtown Norfolk to have survived from the turn of the twentieth century. Its remarkable cohesion is due in part to the circumstances surrounding its construction. A major fire engulfed properties on both sides of the street in 1902, and the task of the reconstruction fell largely to the firm of Breese, Ferguson and Calrow. Over the years, the east side of the block evolved from a respectable row of small businesses into a disreputable row of sailors' bars. More recently, it has re-emerged as a vibrant row of small shops, galleries, and restaurants. The neoclassical Tradewinds Building (112–114 Granby Street; c. 1904–1905), the most elaborate of the group, may have been designed by architect James W. Lee, who maintained an office there. Above the ground-floor shop front is a mezzanine level ornamented with lions' heads, while the two upper levels are treated as a highly ornate Ionic temple front. The four adjacent buildings (116–118, 120–122, 126, and 128–130 Granby Street; 1902–1903) were built as a group in an *a-b-b-a* rhythm. They have been remodeled individually, but here and there remnants of the original Renaissance Revival ornament are visible and the overall design can be pieced together.

NK21 Helena Building

1902–1904, Kenneth M. Murchison, Jr. 1948, renovation. 1978–1980, renovation, Leavitt Associates. 131–133 Granby St.

The seven-story Helena Building is Norfolk's most lavishly ornamented Renaissance Revival skyscraper, resembling an overscaled Genoese palazzo. Much of the terra-cotta ornamentation has been removed from the ground level, but on the second floor, balconies supported by consoles and enclosed by balustrades project from windows with engaged Roman Doric columns and segmental pediments. Similar details appear on the fifth floor, but the cornice unfortunately has been removed.

The Helena Building was built as the clubhouse and office building for the Virginia Club, a social organization founded in 1873. The club's officers organized an architectural competition. Local entrants were John Kevan Peebles and the firm of Breese and Ferguson; at the national level, Frank E. Mead and Kenneth M. Murchison, Jr., both of New York City, submitted entries. Murchison, who was educated at Columbia University and the Ecole des Beaux-Arts in Paris, won the competition. Around World War I the Virginia Club moved to less expensive quarters. The clubhouse was converted entirely into offices and, in subsequent years, its exterior was remodeled and its top floor redesigned in the International Style as a sleek residential penthouse. A more recent renovation has further altered the appearance of the ground level and the penthouse.

NK22 **Fairfax Apartments** (Fairfax Hotel)

1905–1907, Mitchell and Breese. c. 1985–1986, renovation. 117 W. City Hall Ave.

Originally one of several medium-sized hotels erected around the time of the Jamestown Ter-Centennial Exposition, the Fairfax is designed in the Renaissance palazzo mode. The main entrance is particularly handsome with its round-arched portal flanked by similarly shaped windows and set beneath a balcony into which the name of the hotel is incised. The lower section of the building is rusticated, and quoins divide the upper street facades vertically into bays. Terra-cotta panels alternate with windows at the seventh story; a glimpse of the eighth story may be seen over the replacement cornice. Following a long decline, the hotel was renovated and converted into apartments in the mid-1980s. The main lobby has been partially restored.

NK23 **Royster Building**

1911–1912, Ferguson, Calrow and Taylor. 1997–1998, renovation, Glenn and Sadler and Canon Design. 201 Granby St. (northwest corner of Granby St. and W. City Hall Ave.)

Constructed as the headquarters of the Royster-Guano Fertilizer Company and now home to the Norfolk Redevelopment and Housing Authority, this building, at thirteen stories, was once Norfolk's tallest. The neoclassical design is divided into three parts: a limestone base articulated by Roman Doric pilasters and engaged columns, a brick shaft that is largely plain, and a bilevel attic elaborately decorated in terra-cotta with projecting consoles below lions'-head bosses. The cornice has recently been restored.

NK24 **Federal Building**

1977–1979, Vosbeck, Vosbeck, Kendrick and Redinger. 1993–1996, renovation, Steege, Crimm and Associates. 200 Granby St.

Never have the citizens of Norfolk so thoroughly scorned a work of architecture as they have the Federal Building. The need for such a building became apparent soon after World War II, when federal agencies began to outgrow the U.S. Post Office and Courthouse (now the Walter E. Hoffman Courthouse) several blocks north on Granby Street (see entry, below). It took nearly twenty years, however, for the plans to reach fruition and for the enabling legislation to be passed. To make way for the building, the Monticello Hotel (1899), a beloved city landmark, was razed, an act that proved ominous for the building's public reception.

As originally designed, the eight-story building was constructed of red brick with red mortar in the International Style. The main facade faced what was then known as Granby Mall, with a parking garage built into its base along Monticello Avenue to the rear of the site. A freestanding red steel arch—in reality two posts and a lintel—marked the main entrance on the mall side. Initial criticism focused on the red mortar, but soon the $14.5 million building exhibited other, more serious construction flaws. The windows leaked, and after several years, the brick cladding began to separate from the skeletal frame. In 1993–1996 the building was entirely reclad with white, cast concrete panels and reglazed at the additional cost of $6 million. Belt courses of thin aluminum were added to unify the exterior at the second-floor and roof levels, and the garage was screened with aluminum grates. To banish forever the taint associated with the building's red color, the "arch" was painted green. The Granby Street plaza contains an abstract sculpture by Athena Tacha, entitled *Ripples*.

NK25 **Union Mission (Navy YMCA)**

1906–1911, Louis Eugene Jallade. 130 Brooke Ave.

Somewhat forlorn looking at present, this Renaissance Revival building stands at what was once the center of Norfolk's bustling social scene. The building originally housed the Navy YMCA, providing sailors with offshore recreational opportunities and overnight accommodations. Funded by a $250,000 gift from John

D. Rockefeller, Sr., and designed by Louis Eugene Jallade, from New York, it proved to be a prescient undertaking. With the expansion of the navy in Hampton Roads during the world wars, the building assumed a key position in the social lives of unmarried men and women in Norfolk, many of whom were experiencing the lure of the city for the first time. A 1953 newspaper account claimed that foot traffic in and out of the arcaded entrance to the Navy Y was so heavy that the granite steps had been replaced seven times. In 1972, following the consolidation of the navy and civilian branches of the Y, the building was purchased by the Union Mission, a Protestant charitable organization. It now serves as a shelter.

NK26 Tazewell Hotel and Suites (Lorraine Hotel)

1905–1906, Ferguson and Calrow. c. 1910, 1940, renovations. 1999–2000, renovation, Burkhart Thomas. 245 Granby St.

Opened the year before the Jamestown Ter-Centennial Exposition amid the largest construction boom the city had yet witnessed, the Lorraine Hotel benefited from its location diagonally opposite the Monticello Hotel (demolished), then the city's premier hostelry. Rusticated brick covers the lower levels, and vertical tiers of bay windows, a Chicago innova-

tion, link the third through the fifth levels. The street elevations are terminated by a massive dentiled cornice, and Mannerist oversized keystones appear above the upper windows. The Lorraine Hotel stood adjacent to the Princess Hotel and Colonial Theater (1905, William Albert Swasey; demolished 1997), and for many years the buildings, which had a similar appearance and uniform cornice height, were managed together. Remodeled several times, in 1937 the Lorraine became the first hotel in Norfolk to be air conditioned. After another renovation in 1940, its name was changed to the Hotel Thomas Nelson. Despite these improvements, the hotel declined after World War II along with the Granby Street business district. It has recently been renovated and renamed. Its neoclassical lobby is particularly noteworthy.

NK27 Wells Theater

1912–1913, E. C. Horne and Sons. 1979–1980, renovation, Carter, Zinkl, Herman and Chapman. 1985–1987, restoration, Hanbury Evans Newill Vlattas and Company. 110 E. Tazewell St. Open for performances

The pinnacle of opulence when it opened in Norfolk in 1912, the Wells Theater was the flagship of a southern chain operated by Wells Amusement Enterprises. The theater hosted a variety of local and touring productions, and Will Rogers and Fred Astaire were among the many luminaries who performed on its stage. By the 1930s, however, legitimate theatrical productions at the Wells gave way to cinema, and by the 1960s the once-grand theater had become an X-rated movie house. Moreover, the proscenium was blocked and the stage and backstage were sublet to a disreputable nightclub. Like so many other downtown venues, the theater might have been demolished had some prescient preservationists not realized that its architectural fabric remained remarkably intact behind the garish placards. Restored as the home of the Virginia Stage Company during the 1980s, the Wells Theater has been returned to legitimate use once again.

As originally designed by E. C. Horne and Sons of New York, the exterior of the Wells Theater is composed of a relatively plain auditorium and fly loft set behind an elaborately decorated lobby tower and commercial wing. The building is framed in reinforced concrete, but its exterior is clad in brick, tile mosaic, and

NK27 Wells Theater

NK28.1 Alvah H. Martin Building, Tidewater Community College

terra-cotta in a manner that might best be characterized as Spanish Renaissance. The focal point is the three-story tower with its hipped, tiled roof supported by brackets, its lions' head ornaments, and its bow-shaped entrance. The theater's most stunning interior space is the outer lobby, where an oval dome carried on a high drum is ringed by stained glass windows. In a tour de force of Art Nouveau sculpture, graceful caryatids surround the treelike piers of the inner lobby. The auditorium once seated more than 1,000 spectators on three levels, but its capacity has been reduced to about 675 seats on two levels. Triple-tiered boxes flank the restored proscenium; above is a large mural depicting Apollo and the Muses.

NK28 Thomas W. Moss, Jr., Campus of Tidewater Community College

1994, master plan, UDA Architects with Williams, Tazewell and Associates. Vicinity of Granby St. and College Pl.

College Place was originally named after the Norfolk College for Young Ladies, a finishing school chartered in 1880 and housed in a substantial Second Empire building designed by James H. Calrow. The school graduated its last class in 1899, and the building, at the northwest corner of Granby Street and College Place,

went into a long decline before it was finally demolished in the 1980s. The site is now a park, but the street name is relevant once again, for College Place now leads to the Norfolk campus of Tidewater Community College, an amalgam of new and historic construction in the center of downtown.

The creation of the campus in the early to mid-1990s was part of a multipronged approach to rebuilding the business district, which had languished while the city's waterfront was being redeveloped during the previous decade. The centerpiece of the college, the Renaissance Revival Alvah H. Martin Building (NK28.1) (1912–1913, Lee and Diehl; c. 1917, remodeling; 300 Granby Street) had for many years been the flagship of the popular Smith and Welton Department Store. The building now serves as the college's library, housing offices and some classrooms. Across Granby Street stands the Mason C. Andrews Science Building (1994–1997, UDA Architects with Williams, Tazewell and Associates), an unobtrusive modern building, which opens to the aforementioned park. The Stanley C. Walker Technologies Building anchors the north end of the campus at the southeast corner of Granby Street and East Freemason Street. The Renaissance Revival building was originally built for the Norfolk YMCA (1908–1911, Rossell Edward Mitchell with Wood, Donn and

Deming); its present exterior appearance dates from about the mid-1930s, when the building was refaced in terra-cotta in the Art Deco manner for use as an F. W. Woolworth store. The former Loews Theater (1925, Thomas White Lamb; 334–344 Granby Street), a Renaissance Revival building adjacent to the Walker Building, contains additional classrooms, lecture halls, and a theater.

NK29 James Madison Hotel (Lynnhaven Hotel)

1906, John Kevan Peebles. 1981–1982, renovation, Morrisette Cederquist Bondurant and Associates. Southwest corner of W. Freemason St. and Granby St.

The Lynnhaven was one of several hotels built in downtown Norfolk just before the influx of visitors for the 1907 Jamestown Ter-Centennial Exposition. It conveys a sense of permanence and luxury through its Renaissance Revival brick exterior. The base is rusticated, and this treatment is continued as quoining framing the upper levels. A boldly detailed cornice of brick and terra-cotta caps the eight-story building. Over the years, the building underwent numerous renovations and changes of name, the most enduring of which was the Commodore Maury Hotel. The interior has been modernized, and unfortunately a motor entrance, constructed in the early 1980s, has superseded the main entrance on Granby Street.

NK30 Walter E. Hoffman Courthouse

1932–1934, Benjamin F. Mitchell with Rudolph, Cooke and Van Leewven. c. 1983, renovation, Williams and Tazewell and Associates. 600 Granby St. Lobby open to the public

Constructed during the Depression, this handsome edifice was Norfolk's second federal building, replacing a turn-of-the-twentieth-century facility on Plume Street. The building housed the U.S. post office, courthouse, and other federal offices. The two-part division of the building's principal functions is evident on the Granby Street facade, where a separate south entrance once led to the post office. Otherwise the exterior is symmetrical, with pavilions set back at the corners and a central projecting pavilion that marks the main entrance. The limestone exterior, in a stripped classical manner that was a popular choice for public buildings during the 1930s, has two three-story

NK32 Virginian-Pilot Building

Composite order columns in antis above the main entrance, but the remainder of the building, including the marble-paneled lobby, is ornamented in a less traditional Art Deco fashion. A frieze of triglyphs and stars punctuated by shields girdles the building between the first and second levels, and a simplified cornice crowns the main block and each of the pavilions. Following the construction of the new Federal Building on lower Granby Street (see entry, above) and a new post office headquarters east of downtown, the building was converted solely for use by the federal courts and named after Walter E. Hoffman, one of Norfolk's most distinguished jurists and a foe of segregation.

NK31 Greyhound Bus Terminal

1960–1961, Clarence W. Meakin. 701 Monticello Ave.

Built at a time when ridership was high and gasoline prices were low, the Greyhound Bus Terminal is a sleek monument to the open road. Its streamlined exterior of white glazed brick, with the rhythmically spaced letters of the Greyhound and Trailways signs as the only real decorative touch, lends an aura of cleanliness and respectability to an often-maligned form of travel. Standing free from the terminal at the corner of Granby Street and Monticello Avenue, an illuminated Greyhound logo perches atop a tapered column and umbrella-like canopy, a whimsical design reminiscent of the comparable supports used in Frank Lloyd Wright's Johnson Wax Building.

NK32 **Virginian-Pilot Building**

1936–1937, Finlay F. Ferguson, Sr. 150 W. Brambleton Ave.

An extreme example of the stripped classical mode made popular nationwide by Philadelphia architect Paul P. Cret, the building exudes authority as the headquarters of the local newspaper. The cubic massing of the limestone exterior is broken only by the slight projection of the central entrance pavilion on the Brambleton Avenue facade. Fluted pilasters without bases or capitals define the corners and divide the banks of tripled windows. A streamlined cornice terminates the design. The newspaper presses were once located in a low wing behind the main building.

NK33 **Wainwright Building** (Seaboard Air Line Railway)

1925–1926, Neff and Thompson. 229 W. Bute St.

Once defining the northern and western limits of downtown, this building originally served as headquarters of the Seaboard Air Line Railway and is the city's only Gothic-inspired skyscraper. The height of the building is emphasized by an alternating rhythm of solid piers and recessed window tiers that create the effect of a crenellated parapet at the top. Heraldic shields flank the entrance portal with its low, pointed arch and deeply recessed moldings. The lobby retains many of its original features, including Tudor-style plasterwork on the ceiling.

Eastern Downtown (NK34–NK47)

The eastern section of downtown Norfolk was the hardest hit during urban renewal, though a few significant structures were saved. This walking tour begins at the zero milepost in MacArthur Square and continues through the eastern part of downtown.

NK34 **General Douglas MacArthur Memorial** (Norfolk City Hall and Courthouse)

1847–1850, Thomas U. Walter and William R. Singleton. 1961–1963, renovation, Platt and Platt with Finlay F. Ferguson, Jr. MacArthur Sq. Open to the public

What Les Invalides is to Paris, the General Douglas MacArthur Memorial is to Norfolk: a

domed building designed for one purpose that was converted at a later date into a memorial and tomb for a military hero. Les Invalides (1678–1708) was designed by Jules-Hardouin Mansart as a military hospital chapel, and Napoleon's tomb is sunk into the floor directly beneath the majestic dome. In a similar fashion, the tomb of General Douglas MacArthur is recessed into the floor beneath the more modestly scaled dome of what was once Norfolk City Hall and Courthouse. Save for Ulysses S. Grant, Civil War general and U.S. president, no American military leader is so conspicuously enshrined for public viewing.

Even without the MacArthur connection, the Old City Hall, as it is still sometimes called, would be considered Norfolk's most important public building, and its design history is the most obscure. The decision to erect a new city hall to replace the postcolonial town hall was made in 1845, the year Norfolk was chartered as a city. The following year, the city council awarded the commission to William R. Singleton, a local architect with St. Louis connections. There must have been some dissatisfaction with the council's choice, however, since in 1847 Walter H. Taylor, a prominent local citizen, privately commissioned Thomas U. Walter of Philadelphia to provide another design. Taylor knew of Walter through Christopher Hall, chairman of the building committee of Norfolk Academy. Whether Walter was aware of Singleton's design is not known; Walter did not travel to Norfolk, and the two men presumably never met. The main block of the building has traditionally been assigned to Singleton and the cupola to Walter, but this division is by no means certain. Entries from Walter's diaries seem to indicate that his design superseded Singleton's original scheme.

As is typical of the American Greek Revival, the design freely combines Greek and Roman classical elements, and, as is typical of Walter's work, less expensive materials imitate more expensive ones. The two-story building is T-shaped with an entrance portico on the west facade. The portico, reached by a monumental staircase, is supported by six Tuscan columns with stucco-covered brick shafts and granite bases and capitals. Flanking the portico, the pilasters and intermediary panels of the end bays are faced in granite for maximum display; however, the segment of the west wall sheltered by the portico and the side and rear walls of the building are more economically finished. Pilasters and intermediary panels are constructed of brick and covered in stucco coursed to resemble ashlar in a manner similar to that employed at the Norfolk Academy. An entablature, partly constructed of granite, encircles the building, and the north and south gables are treated as pediments. The design culminates in a ribbed dome on a high drum ringed by Tuscan columns. Inside were once offices for the mayor and the city council and rooms for the U.S. District Court and the Circuit Court. Because of its marshy location at the head of what was once Back Creek and is now City Hall Avenue, Old City Hall was equipped with a 45,000-gallon cistern in its basement. Moreover, inverted arches of brick reinforce the granite basement walls on the north and east sides. The building ceased to house city offices in 1918, but it remained in use as a courthouse until 1960.

Long outmoded in a city that prided itself on its modernity, Old City Hall survived the rampant postwar demolition only through a fortuitous series of events. Early schemes for the new Civic Center involved razing the building. A significant public outcry eventually resulted in the choice of a less controversial and less expensive site several blocks to the southeast. As the new Civic Center took shape, finding a new use for

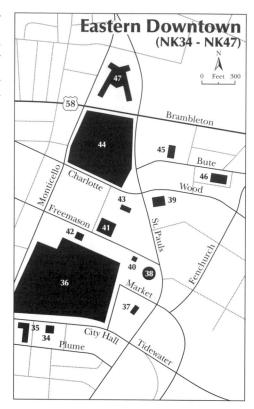

Eastern Downtown
(NK34 - NK47)

the building became more urgent. The solution proved to be as ingenious as it was controversial: a memorial to General Douglas MacArthur, the brilliant but contentious army commander. Mary Hardy MacArthur, the general's mother, had been a native of the city, and in 1951 a memorial to her was dedicated with great fanfare in the presence of the general.

NK36 MacArthur Center

Building on this connection, city leaders met with MacArthur in 1960, with the result that he agreed to donate his papers and memorabilia to Norfolk. The interior of Old City Hall was subsequently gutted, reinforced with steel, and reconfigured as a museum. Surprisingly, the wooden cupola, 32 feet in diameter and 52 feet high, survived the renovation largely intact. Shortly before his death in 1964, MacArthur agreed to be buried in the memorial. A statue of MacArthur (1968) by Walter Hancock keeps watch in front of the building.

NK35 Henry and Elizabeth Kirn Memorial Library

1959–1962, Lublin, McGaughy and Associates. 301 E. City Hall Ave.

A key part of downtown Norfolk's postwar redevelopment was the creation of a new central research library to replace the aging Carnegie library on Freemason Street. Although the Kirn is starkly modern in appearance and materials, its exterior is organized in a classicizing manner that harmonizes effectively with the MacArthur Memorial across the street and the nearby Monticello Arcade.

NK36 MacArthur Center

1993–1999, Hobbs and Black Associates, Inc. Northeast corner of E. City Hall Ave. and Monticello Ave.

Of all the scars inflicted by redevelopment of Norfolk's downtown in the 1950s and 1960s, the slowest to heal was the vast open tract east of Monticello Avenue and north of City Hall

NK37 St. Paul's Episcopal Church

Avenue that was created by the bulldozing of dozens of decayed but historic buildings. The site stood vacant for more than two decades, although several projects for it were floated, including a pleasure park modeled after Tivoli Gardens in Copenhagen.

The void has at last been filled by MacArthur Center, an ambitious three-level shopping mall anchored by two department stores and a multiplex cinema. The initial exterior design turned inward from the surrounding streets, but opposition by local members of the American Institute of Architects led to its redesign along postmodern lines. The most successful side of the mall fronts on Monticello Avenue, where diapered brickwork and cast concrete trim create an appealing and rhythmic facade. Geometric concrete screens give the two enormous parking garages flanking the mall an almost delicate appearance; a sloping concrete ramp along City Hall Avenue is a tour de force of retro highway design. The exterior classicizing details fail, however, to hide the bulky forms of the department stores. Inside, the design of the mall incorporates a variety of dynamic vistas.

NK37 St. Paul's Episcopal Church

c. 1736–1739. 1759, church walls begun. 1776, burned. 1785–1786, new roof. 1832, renovation, Levi Swain. 1865–1866, renovation. 1877, sacristy addition. c. 1877, slate roof and wooden cupola. 1901, tower addition. 1912–1913, restoration, Ferguson, Calrow and Taylor. 1998–1999, new roof. 1907–1909, parish house, Ferguson and Calrow. 201 St. Paul's Blvd.

St. Paul's is the only major structure to have survived the burning of the city at the beginning of the American Revolution. In addition to providing an important link to a distant past, the church and its churchyard form one of the few attractive green spaces left in all of downtown. St. Paul's was originally part of the Elizabeth River parish formed before 1641, and several structures predate the present building. In a somewhat unusual and flamboyant gesture, the date 1739 and the initials *SB* are crudely outlined in glazed headers flanking the entrance to the right transept. The initials may be those of Samuel Boush, mayor-elect of the then recently incorporated borough of Norfolk, or his son Samuel Boush, the owner of a nearby brickyard and possibly the gentleman-amateur in charge of the church's design. Cruciform in shape with an east-facing sanctuary, the church is essentially a provincial version of Williamsburg's Bruton Parish Church (1711–1715; see entry under Williamsburg in the Hampton Roads section). The brick walls are laid in Flemish bond with round-arched windows lining the nave and transepts and wheel windows above the three principal entrances. Construction began on the brick walls surrounding the churchyard in 1759. When the city was burned by retreating patriots on New Year's Day, 1776, only the walls of the church and the churchyard were left standing. Rebuilt with funds from a public lottery in 1785, the church suffered from religious friction that led to the periodic abandonment and reoccupation of the building by competing Protestant sects. Finally, in 1832, it became St. Paul's Episcopal Church. Further renovations were made to the building following its occupation by Union troops during the Civil War, and a sacristy was added to the northeast corner in 1877. About the same time, a polychrome slate roof (now removed) was installed, with a wooden cupola at the crossing. A crenellated tower was constructed to the west of the church in 1901, dramatically altering its exterior proportions. The 1907 Jamestown Ter-Centennial Exposition revived interest in the historic building, and its interior was heavily restored to its presumed colonial appearance in 1912–1913. Of the interior furnishings, only the reredos behind the altar dates from the eighteenth century; it was once located in St. John's Church, King William County. The numerous stained glass windows include one by Tiffany Studios, midway along the right side of the nave, and, directly opposite on the left side of the nave, a Tiffany-style window by the Hermann Company. The churchyard contains headstone carvings from the seventeenth through the nineteenth century.

NK38   Bank of Hampton Roads

1965–1966, Yates and Boggs. 415 St. Paul's Blvd.

Originally named the Rotunda, this is the area's only cylindrical office building and, because of its top-heavy appearance, one of the least attractive. The unusual shape of the building initially generated some interest from the public, but the circular floor plan proved confusing to tenants, and the experimental design was not repeated.

NK39   Fire Station One

1995–1997, TAF Group. Southeast corner of St. Paul's Blvd. and Wood St.

The horizontal neotraditional design of this fire station recalls the Prairie Style, made popular by Frank Lloyd Wright and his followers at the turn of the twentieth century. A low, hipped roof with deep eaves imparts a residential character to the building.

NK40   Willoughby-Baylor House

1794, William Willoughby. c. 1820, porch addition. 1968–1969, restoration. 601 E. Freemason St. Open to the public

One of Norfolk's most successful post-Revolutionary builders and the scion of a distinguished seventeenth-century family, William Willoughby designed and constructed his own house in 1794, after having purchased the site of the former Masonic lodge the previous year. Typical of Tidewater houses at the turn of the nineteenth century, the Willoughby-Baylor House has a side passage with entrances to the north and south and a double parlor to the east. Each parlor contains a hearth, allowing for a symmetrical arrangement of chimneys on the east wall. Apart from the Flemish bond brickwork used for the walls and the wooden cornice at the eaves, there is virtually no ornament on the exterior. The handsomely proportioned Greek Revival porch, with its sturdy, paired Doric columns, was probably added to the north entrance around 1820, not long after Willoughby's daughter, Mary, married William Sharp and took possession of the property. Ownership of the Willoughby-Baylor House passed out of the family in 1890, and the building eventually fell into disrepair along with the surrounding neighborhood. The Historic Norfolk Foundation rescued it from demolition when the immediate area was slated for redevelopment in the 1960s. The house was restored in 1968–1969, at which time a reproduction of the freestanding kitchen was constructed on the original foundations to the south of the main house. The interior contains period furnishings.

NK41   Freemason Street Baptist Church

1848–1850, Thomas U. Walter. 1893–1909, various additions. 1897, steeple replaced. 1915, education

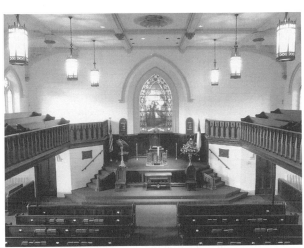

NK41 Freemason Street Baptist Church exteriot (left) and interior (below)

building, Louis R. Moss. 1941, 1970–1972, renovations. 1997–1999, restoration, Hanbury Evans Newill Vlattas and Company. 1956–1958, Melton Memorial Hall, Rudolph, Cooke and Van Leeuwen. Northeast corner of E. Freemason St. and Bank St.

Norfolk's earliest surviving Gothic Revival structure also represented a departure for Thomas U. Walter of Philadelphia. Walter preferred the Greek Revival mode, which he used in the design of the nearby Norfolk Academy and City Hall. The Gothic idiom may have represented a new beginning for the fledgling congregation of Freemason Street Baptist, which had split from the Cumberland Street Baptist Church in 1848. Thomas D. Toy, a leader of the new congregation, selected Walter on the basis of his reputation as a gifted architect and, perhaps more important, his personal reputation as a devout Baptist. Earlier in the decade Walter had designed the Second Baptist Church in Richmond (1840–1841). For the exterior of Freemason Street Baptist Church, Walter turned to the English Perpendicular as popularized by Richard Upjohn in his design for Trinity Church, New York City (1839–1846). The three-aisle basilica plan is unusual in that it is oriented south to north rather than west to east. An enormous tower, once the tallest structure in Norfolk, dominates the south facade; the steeple is a somewhat shorter steel replacement for the wooden original, which was top-

pled by a storm in 1879. The sides of the nave are rhythmically divided into bays by alternating pinnacled buttresses and lancet windows. A 1915 addition to the north, offset by doubled buttresses, follows the original design. Other additions to the east do not detract significantly from the nave. The exterior effect is convincing but at the same time deceptive. What appear to be smooth stone walls are in fact brick covered by stucco and coursed to resemble ashlar, and pinnacled buttresses soar but do not fly. On the interior, slim cast iron colonnettes substitute for stone piers, and above, instead of an open-truss wooden roof, is a flat plaster ceiling gridded and ornamented with pendants. The church has just undergone a major restoration, returning the exterior to its original warm brown color.

NK42 **Moses Myers House**

Before 1797. c. 1800, before 1815, additions. 1953, kitchen restoration. 1960–1962, restoration, Finlay F. Ferguson, Jr. South side of E. Freemason St. at Bank St. Open to the public

One of Virginia's finest Federal town houses was built for one of the city's most prominent merchants. The house set a new standard for urban sophistication in post-Revolutionary Norfolk, and its location beyond the limits of the old town presaged northward expansion. Moses Myers purchased the land in 1791 and erected the first phase of the two-and-one-half-story house before 1797. Constructed of brick laid in a Flemish bond with a limestone belt course, the house is distinguished by a pedimented upper gable with graceful fanlight. A central entrance on the first level of this facade opens laterally into a side passage, beyond which are a front and back parlor, each containing a hearth. Additional exterior doors at the north and south ends of the passage provide cross ventilation during the often sweltering Tidewater summers. A U-shaped staircase fills the south end of the passage, leading to an upper passage and three chambers. The original basement kitchen proved to be impractical because of the heat it generated in warm weather, and a freestanding kitchen with upper chamber was constructed c. 1800 and connected to the main house by a two-story hyphen. To accommodate the expanding family, a new wing, containing a dining room and two upper chambers and terminating in an elegant polygonal bay, was added to the west of the main house before 1818. This third phase may have been executed in imitation of Benjamin Henry Latrobe's design for the William Pennock House in Norfolk (c. 1796; demolished), which included a similar dining room window bay. The house underwent significant restoration around 1906, in time for the Jamestown Ter-Centennial Exposition.

As the city's first Jewish citizens, Moses and Eliza Myers encountered little prejudice from their Protestant neighbors, and they emerged as leading taste makers in Norfolk society. Their house was a showcase for the latest American, English, and French fashions, represented most notably by the Adamesque plaster ceiling in the passage. Some furniture was custom made for the house, including the sideboards in the dining room and the window seats in the front parlor. Portraits of Moses and Eliza by Gilbert Stuart hang in the latter room. The house remained in the possession of the Myers family until 1931, when it and its furnishings were sold to the Colonial House Corporation for conversion to a museum. The city assumed ownership of the property in 1951, and the house was restored to its late eighteenth-century appearance in 1960–1962. It is now operated as a historic house by the Chrysler Museum of Art.

NK43 Hampton Roads Chamber of Commerce (Norfolk Academy)

1840–1841, Thomas U. Walter. 1970–1972, renovation, Leavitt Associates. 420 Bank St.

The Norfolk Academy, founded in 1786, had by the early nineteenth century outgrown its original frame building on Church Street (now St. Paul's Boulevard). In 1840, the building committee, headed by Christopher Hall, commissioned Thomas U. Walter of Philadelphia to design a new building on land near the city's northern border. Although Walter never visited Norfolk, this was the first of several projects in the city to which he devoted his attention.

Walter preferred to design in the Greek Revival mode, and, given the classical foundations of American pedagogy in the nineteenth century, this style was considered to be especially appropriate for educational buildings. The building takes the form of a pseudo-peripteral Doric temple, with double-height porticoes at the east and west ends. Six unfluted columns support plain pediments, and an alternating rhythm of simple pilasters and recessed windows articulates the side walls. The brick construction is disguised by a stucco finish, coursed to resemble ashlar. In general, the building's early classical proportions recall the Temple of Hera II at Paestum (c. 450 B.C.), one of the best preserved of all ancient Greek temples.

The academy moved to a new campus in 1915, and for many years the building served the Norfolk Juvenile Court. A renovation in the early 1970s restored the exterior of the building to near its original appearance, but the interior was completely modernized.

NK44 Scope Cultural and Convention Center

1965–1972, Williams and Tazewell and Associates with Studio Nervi. Block bounded by E. Brambleton Avenue, St. Paul's Blvd., Charlotte St., and Monticello Ave.

The Scope Cultural and Convention Center is an example of a megastructure: an architectural complex consisting of one or more above-ground buildings linked by a subterranean structure impervious to the outdoor climate. Megastructures were enormously popular during the 1960s and 1970s, particularly in the business district of large cities in the northern United States and Canada, where cold winters make such expensive complexes economically

NK42 Moses Myers House

NK43 Hampton Roads Chamber of Commerce (Norfolk Academy)

viable. That Norfolk, with its moderate climate and relatively small downtown, has a megastructure thus reveals more about the politics of urban renewal than it does about the exigencies of entertaining the city's residents and visitors.

NK44 Scope Cultural and Convention Center

Before its construction, Norfolk's only major indoor recreational facility was the Arena Municipal Auditorium, adjoining the Center Theater. The need for a new facility became apparent by the mid-1960s, and clever maneuvering by Lawrence M. Cox, then the director of the Norfolk Redevelopment and Housing Authority, and the Virginia congressional delegation resulted in a multimillion-dollar appropriation for a new facility to combine sports, exhibits, and performing arts. Funded as part of the 1965 Housing Act, the appropriation was actually made in the form of credits to be used toward other urban renewal projects in the city, rather than a direct subsidy. Also, the new facility had to be built within an existing urban renewal zone, which was on East Brambleton Avenue. Astonishingly, these events transpired so rapidly that when the appropriation was passed the city had not yet chosen an architect for the facility, let alone a workable design.

Such a high-profile project required the services of a high-profile architect, at least in the eyes of Norfolk officials. Cox recommended that the city hire Pier Luigi Nervi, an Italian architect and world-renowned specialist in ferroconcrete (concrete reinforced with wire mesh). Nervi, who never traveled to Norfolk, submitted a design consisting of two chief components: a domed sports arena with exhibition areas beneath it, and a rectangular theater. For a variety of practical reasons, the details of the design had to be completely revamped by Williams and Tazewell and Associates, a local firm that subsequently took charge of the project, with Nervi acting as a consultant on the arena's dome. The new design retained Nervi's basic scheme while rearranging some of its elements and adding several new ones. A circular 11,500-seat arena fills the northwest corner of the site, and a rectangular 2,500-seat theater occupies the southeast corner behind a similarly shaped fountain. A 300-seat little theater occupies the lower level of the main theater building. Beneath the platform are parking for several hundred cars at the southwest corner and 75,000 square feet of meeting and exhibition space, opening directly into the lower lobby of the arena, at the northeast corner. Scope, an abbreviation of kaleidoscope, was the name chosen for the entire complex; it is now chiefly used in reference to the arena. Ground was broken in 1968, and the arena was completed in 1971. Chrysler Hall, the name given to the theater in honor of Norfolk benefactor Walter P. Chrysler, opened in 1972. Initially projected at $11 million, the final cost of the complex eventually mounted to $35 million, including an aboveground parking garage across Charlotte Street, which was not part of the original plan. Recently, the south end of the garage has been demolished to permit the reopening of East Freemason Street.

The most distinguished aspect of the design is Nervi's arena, with its ring of V-shaped concrete buttresses supporting the concrete saucer dome. It is strongly reminiscent of the architect's Palazzo dello Sport in Rome, built for the 1960 Olympic Games. Inside, the swirling coffers on the underside of the dome create a delicate, soaring effect that contrasts greatly with its smooth outer shell. The arena hosts a variety of sporting events, notably minor-league hockey. Not to be overlooked is the canopy to the east of the arena along St. Paul's Boulevard, which marks a seldom-used entrance to the subterranean meeting halls. Two tapered columns support ribbed panels in an umbrella-like fashion, a motif that Nervi had previously developed at the Turin Exhibition Hall (1962).

Chrysler Hall, by comparison, is less successful visually and functionally. Similar in appearance to Max Abramovitz's Avery Fisher Hall (1962) at New York City's Lincoln Center for the Performing Arts, Chrysler Hall is an equally dull essay in postwar neoclassicism. On the exterior, rhomboidal concrete columns surround the theater on three sides. Recessed behind the columns, the main and side facades are treated as glass curtain walls with the bilevel lobby visible behind them. Travertine panels clad the corners and the rear of the building. The interior, which was considered state of the art at the time it was designed, now seems hopelessly dated. The stage lacks a proscenium, and the continental seating plan without aisles makes

the task of finding one's seat unusually arduous. Two tiers of streamlined, reinforced concrete balconies appear to swoop down upon the orchestra seats in a way that is visually unsettling as well as jarring against the darker paneled walls

Scope is a megastructure in search of a densely developed city with the kind of recreational and cultural life that would justify it. Failing to connect with its surroundings, it is a monument to misguided urban renewal and bygone federal largesse.

NK45 First Baptist Church

1903–1906, Reuben H. Hunt. 1960, educational annex. 418 E. Bute St.

Well into the first decade of the twentieth century, the Romanesque Revival style remained popular with religious congregations because of the immense scale and metaphorical strength of its components. When First Baptist was built, Bute Street's urban character rendered all but the main facade of granite invisible to passersby. Large-scale urban renewal has left the church isolated, exposing its side and rear walls of brick. The church's overall massing is essentially square, but on the main facade its potentially boxy proportions are relieved by boldly projecting, asymmetrical towers. The turreted southeast tower is the facade's focal point, rising about twice the height of its truncated mate at the southwest corner. At the lower level, the towers are linked by a tripartite arcade supported by squat piers in the manner of Henry Hobson Richardson. The arcade creates an open narthex, the principal entrances to the sanctuary placed laterally at the base of each tower. A large, round-arched window is situated beneath the main gable at the center of the facade's upper level, and this motif is repeated at smaller scale in the various stages of the towers. The cavernous interior is covered by a handsome coffered ceiling and divided by a U-shaped gallery carried on cast iron supports.

Earlier Hunt had designed Baptist churches in Portsmouth and Newport News, and his selection as architect for the building was undoubtedly intended to reinforce the First Baptist Church's preeminent position among Norfolk's Baptist congregations at the turn of the twentieth century. In 1800, Norfolk Baptists had formed their own congregation and subsequently split and moved several times, finally arriving on Bute Street. The congregation was primarily African American, and the grandeur of First Baptist Church set a new standard for ecclesiastical design in the city and symbolized the prosperity of the congregation. An ambitious, block-long expansion of the church's community outreach facilities, designed by WTG Design Consultants, is planned.

NK46 St. John's African Methodist Episcopal Church

1887–1888, Charles M. Cassell. 1956, 1972, interior renovations. 1961–1963, exterior restoration. 1907, parsonage, John Anderson Lankford. 1961, new parsonage. 1989, educational annex. 539–545 E. Bute St.

In the latter part of the nineteenth century, the Romanesque Revival style in America was generally associated with the overscaled, massive forms of architect Henry Hobson Richardson. Cassell's Romanesque Revival design for this church is thus remarkable for its simplicity and restraint. The exterior is constructed of brick, with the exception of twin round-arched portals, executed in stone, that form the main entrance on the north facade. A tall, narrow round-arched window with elaborate plate tracery sits directly above the entrance, and to either side stand towers of unequal shape and height. Three levels of windows alternate with attached buttresses along the side walls, and

shed dormers break the slope of the handsomely patterned slate roof. The vast width of the interior is spanned by hammerbeam trusses reinforced by wrought iron tie rods. A U-shaped gallery supported on cast iron columns surrounds the side and rear walls. Installed around 1890 and substantially rebuilt and modernized over the ensuing years, St. John's pipe organ holds the distinction of being the first in an African American church in the city and, possibly, the commonwealth. The adjacent Colonial Revival parsonage was designed in 1907 by John Anderson Lankford, a pioneering African American architect who was closely associated with the African Methodist Episcopal Church.

NK47 Radisson Hotel (Golden Triangle Hotel)

1959–1961, Anthony F. Musolino and Morris Lapidus. 1971, renovation, Williams and Tazewell Partnership. 1997–1998, renovation. Triangular site bounded by E. Brambleton Ave., Monticello Ave., and St. Paul's Blvd.

When it opened in 1961, this building was an example of an exciting and innovative urban trend: the motor hotel. Built on restricted sites along congested downtown streets, older hotels could not keep pace with suburban motels in an age when travelers increasingly arrived by automobile rather than by railroad. Racially integrated from its opening, the Radisson Hotel also helped to close a tarnished chapter of the city's past.

The Radisson was originally known as the Golden Triangle Hotel because of its location on a wedge-shaped plot, formerly the site of one of the city's worst slums. The multi-use structure combines guest rooms, meeting facilities, offices, shops, and restaurants. As designed by Anthony F. Musolino, a long driveway, flanked by two curving ramps, leads to the motor entrance; there was once a circular fountain at its center. Glass curtain walls sheathe the thirteen-story V-shaped tower. Behind the tower, two motel-like wings stretch to the rear of the site with a pool at their center and parking spaces around their perimeter. In contrast to the relatively staid exterior, the hotel's interiors were the work of Morris Lapidus, the flamboyant designer of the Fontainebleau (1952) and Eden Roc (1954) hotels in Miami Beach. The guest rooms and the public areas projected an aura of sophistication and modernity that must have made Norfolk's other hotels look shabby and out of date. The Nations International Restaurant served cuisine from around the world. Each night of the week featured a menu from a different nation, and the staff's costumes and the room's accessories were changed accordingly. The Satellite Coffee House was designed around a futuristic theme. Subsequent renovations have unfortunately removed Lapidus's touches, save for the sweeping staircase in the trapezoidal lobby. Although across the street from the Scope Cultural and Convention Center, the Golden Triangle was too far removed from the heart of downtown to be profitable; consequently, it has undergone several changes of name and management. After a brush with demolition in early 1997, the hotel was acquired by new owners and renovated.

West Freemason Street   (NK48–NK62)

The West Freemason Street area was designated as the city's first historic district in 1971. One of the city's earliest elite residential areas, it has been successfully revitalized after a period of decline. In recent years the neighborhood has been a center for new residential construction, particularly around its once industrial fringes.

NK48 Epworth United Methodist Church

1893–1896, Carpenter and Peebles. 1915, 1917, additions, Mitchell and Wilcox. 1921, sanctuary remodeling. 1941, tower modification. 1953, educational annex and chapel, Vernon A. Moore. 124 W. Freemason St.

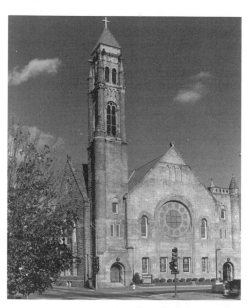

James E. R. Carpenter, the younger of the two partners responsible for the design of this church, had been trained in McKim, Mead and White's Boston office, close to many Richardsonian landmarks, including Trinity Church (1872–1876), a point of departure for this Romanesque Revival structure. Epworth's cross-in-square plan allowed the architects to make maximum use of a constricted but highly desirable corner lot. An enormous tower at the southwest corner (drawn from Richardson's Brattle Square Church, Boston, 1870–1872) breaks the cubic massing of the sanctuary and defines the main entrance at its base; truncated towers fill the other corners. Color, pattern, and texture are used to maximum effect on the exterior. Gray granite walls are juxtaposed with brownstone trim, and red tiles cover the cross-gabled roof. Rose windows with plate tracery pierce the north and south facades, while a triple lancet window fills the west facade. The present appearance of the interior dates from its remodeling in 1921. A low saucer dome carried on pendentives springs from the corner piers, and galleries surround the sanctuary on three sides. The stained glass windows, by the Masking Company of Rochester, are knockouts.

NK49 Freemason Abbey Restaurant
(Second Presbyterian Church)

1873, attributed to Charles Parker Breese. 1899, facade renovation, James E. R. Carpenter. c. 1943, 1988, renovations. 209 W. Freemason St.

An unusual adaptation, this structure was built for the Second Presbyterian Church as a brick box. In 1899, James Carpenter added the Gothic Revival granite and brownstone facade,

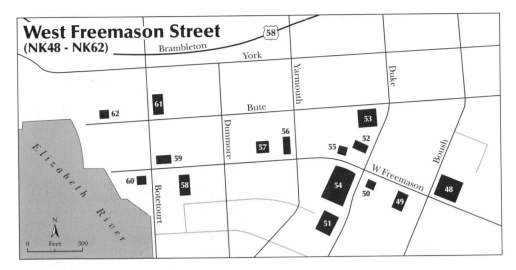

West Freemason Street
(NK48 - NK62)

Brambleton
York
Bute
Yarmouth
Duke
Dunmore
Boush
W Freemason
Botetourt
Elizabeth River

62
61
53
56
52
57
55
59
60
58
54
50
48
51
49

N
0 Feet 300

with its off-center tower, to provide contrast to the nearby Epworth United Methodist Church, which he had designed in part. Subsequently, the church building passed through other hands, and the rose window was filled with brick. Finally, in 1988, the building was transformed into a successful restaurant that trades upon its ecclesiastical past.

NK50 Taylor-Whittle House

c. 1791. c. 1880–1885, additions. 1972–1975, restoration, Spigel, Carter, Zinkl and Herman. 227 W. Freemason St.

The Taylor-Whittle House, like the Moses Myers House, is an elegant Federal town house that reflects the prosperity of Norfolk's post-Revolutionary merchant class. Its builder may have been either George Purdie, owner of the building lot after 1788, or John Cowper, who bought the property in 1802 while he was mayor of the city. Stylistically it is so similar to the Moses Myers House as to suggest that they were both designed by the same person. The main block of the house is two and one-half stories tall, with a pedimented gable and off-center entrance facing West Freemason Street; fanlights are inserted into the gable and, at smaller scale, over the front door. A limestone belt course divides the first two levels, and limestone lintels with oversized keystones cap the windows on the street facades. Later additions include the Doric entrance portico, the two-story Italianate porch on the east side, and the brick wing on the south side.

As evidenced by the internal positioning of

the twin chimneys, the plan of the house diverges considerably from the usual Tidewater arrangement of a side-passage entrance hall. Instead, a square entrance hall in the northwest corner features a graceful narrow staircase. A small chamber is located behind the entrance hall, and a double parlor fills the east portion of the house. The same four-part configuration is repeated on the upper level. Both upper and lower chambers are distinguished by finely detailed woodwork and Adamesque mantelpieces.

Richard Taylor purchased the house in late 1802, and descendants of the Taylor family later married into the Whittle family. A residence until the 1970s, the house was subsequently donated to the Historic Norfolk Foundation, restored, and acquired by the city. At present, it serves as the headquarters for the Junior League of Hampton Roads.

NK51 Allmand-Archer House

c. 1794. c. 1820, remodeling. 327 Duke St.

This house, now altered, originally resembled the Willoughby-Baylor House: a two-and-one-half-story brick Federal town house. It was probably built by Matthew Hervey, a Norfolk merchant who, in 1802, sold the house to Harrison Allmand, another well-to-do merchant. The plan is the standard side hall with double parlors. Sometime around 1820 the house received a Greek Revival facelift. The main facade was stuccoed and quoined, and stone lintels with Latrobe-inspired ornamented corner blocks and terminal bosses were installed over the windows. In addition, a new entrance was recessed into the wall plane with a flattened portico perched on a high podium. Its Roman Doric columns set in antis support an entablature and pediment. Remains of an earlier eighteenth-century structure are visible at the rear of the house.

Allmand's granddaughter married into the Archer family, and the house was occupied by her descendants until 1973. At present a fraternal organization uses the house for its offices.

NK52 Glisson House

c. 1840. c. 1870, remodeling. 405 Duke St.

The eclectic design of this house marries Greek Revival elements on the first three levels with an Italianate cornice and cupola. It was once the home of Commodore Oliver S. Glisson, who served as a Union officer during the Civil War.

NK53 Lekies House

c. 1850. 419 Duke St.

This is a symmetrical five-bay Italianate house with an entrance portico supported by Corinthian columns.

NK54 Khedive Temple

1938–1939, Rudolph, Cooke and Van Leeuwen. 243 W. Freemason St.

This fanciful building was formerly the local headquarters of the Shriners' fraternal organization. The choice of the Islamic Revival idiom was consistent with the organization's usurpation of many aspects of Muslim iconography. The deeply recessed entrance at the center of the building is framed by colonnettes supporting a Florentine arch and flanked by buttresses with domical caps. Whimsical horseshoe arches are sprinkled across the remainder of the main facade, which is stepped back symmetrically to either side of the entrance in a vaguely Art Deco manner.

NK55 Hunter House Victorian Museum

c. 1894, W. D. Wentworth. 1988, restoration, Reese Fowler. 240 W. Freemason St. Open to the public

NK55 Hunter House Victorian Museum

Boston architect W. D. Wentworth designed this combination of Richardsonian Romanesque and Queen Anne styles for a prominent local merchant. The tall, narrow proportions of the house point to the increasingly urban character of this end of Freemason Street at the turn of the century. The variety of door and window openings, multiple gables, polychromy, surface patterns, and textures create a virtual textbook of Victorian design. The house is restored and filled with period furniture.

NK56 Petty-Dickson House

c. 1852. c. 1870, remodeling and addition. 300 W. Freemason St.

What was once a Greek Revival residence was radically altered in the Second Empire mode by the addition of a third floor tucked beneath a mansard roof. The house is currently being used for offices.

NK57 Camp-Hubard House

c. 1850–1852. 308 W. Freemason St.

William S. Camp, a local banker, once owned this serene Greek Revival dwelling. Set behind an elaborate cast iron fence, the main facade is nearly devoid of ornament, with the notable exception of a boldly projecting entrance portico with fluted, paired Ionic columns.

NK58 Offices (Norfolk Public Library)

1903–1904, Hale and Morse. 1978, renovation. 345 W. Freemason St. Lobby open to the public

That this handsome brick and limestone building was once Norfolk's main library is not difficult to guess, given its encircling frieze containing the names of famous authors. The focal point of the Beaux-Arts classical design is the unpedimented entrance portico supported by paired, two-story Ionic columns. A bust of the goddess Athena Parthenos watches over the main doors. Along the sides of the building, elaborately framed windows alternate with pilasters.

The public library system in Norfolk began in 1870 with the founding of the Norfolk Library Association. A $50,000 donation from philanthropist Andrew Carnegie in 1901 spurred the construction of this building, which served the citizens of Norfolk from 1904 until the opening of the Kirn Library downtown in the early 1960s. Apparently it is the only Virginia work by Hale and Morse, an architecture firm active in the New England and Mid-Atlantic regions. The building has been converted to offices, but the lobby, with its grand staircase, coffered ceiling, and additional classical busts, remains.

NK59 Weston House

c. 1870. 358 W. Freemason St.

Now offices, this former residence is most notable for the delicate cast iron supports and lacelike bracketing of its wraparound porch. Because of its low mansard roof, the house might be deemed Second Empire, but its brick and terra-cotta exterior reveals the influence of the Néo-Grec style, particularly in the quirky handling of the doors and windows.

NK60 Selden's Point

c. 1807. 1858, 1869, additions, Edmund George Lind. 351 Botetourt St.

Dr. William Boswell Selden constructed this house on a site overlooking the Elizabeth River.

One of the oldest and largest houses in the West Freemason neighborhood, it was occupied by his descendants for most of the nineteenth century. Raised on a high English basement of brick, the two-and-one-half-story frame structure is five bays across and two rooms deep, with a central entrance and a symmetrical arrangement of side chimneys. In 1858 the Seldens hired Edmund George Lind for $1,600 to provide minor renovations to the house. Eleven years later Lind returned to renovate the house again at a cost of $10,000, undoubtedly to remove the stigma it carried following its occupation by Union officers during the Civil War. A porch with Roman Doric columns and turned balusters was added to the front along with polygonal dormers at the roofline. A brick service wing was constructed at the rear. To the left of the main house stands the Grandy House Kitchen, a small frame service building in the Second Empire style that was moved from the 300 block of West Freemason Street in 1978 and renovated as a residence.

NK61 Botetourt Apartments

1906, Breese and Mitchell. 1982, renovation, Shriver and Holland Associates. Northeast corner of Botetourt St. and W. Bute St.

This eight-story Renaissance Revival apartment building with stacked bay windows overlooking the Elizabeth River was constructed during the general real estate boom that accompanied the Jamestown Ter-Centennial. Originally designed as an apartment hotel, the building had a central kitchen with dumbwaiter service to individual apartments.

NK62 Kenmure

1845. c. 1870, remodeling. c. 1977, restoration, Carter Zinkl Herman. 420 W. Bute St.

Raised on a high or English basement, this Greek Revival house is nearly cubic in its proportions and relatively restrained in its ornamentation. A handsome Ionic portico shelters the main entrance, while an Italianate cupola crowns the roofline. Kenmure was originally the home of William W. Lamb, mayor of Norfolk during the Civil War, and the name derives from that of a family estate in Scotland.

Ghent   (NK63–NK78)

Ghent, the city's most fashionable streetcar suburb at the turn of the twentieth century, takes its name from a local farm, itself named for the Treaty of Ghent, the agreement that ended the War of 1812. The oldest section of the neighborhood dates from the 1890s, when Philadelphia engineer John Graham platted the subdivided farmland along the bent axis of Colonial Avenue. Now designated as the Ghent Historic District, this section is bounded by a semicircular inlet of the Elizabeth River known as the Hague (Smith's Creek) and West Olney Road. Substantial residential development continued north of West Olney Road well into the twentieth century. A second historic district has been created in the area bounded by West Olney Road, College Avenue, West Princess Anne Road, and the east side of Colonial Avenue. The former East Ghent, the area to the north of West Olney Road and east of Colonial Avenue, was razed during the 1970s to make way for new housing. It is now rebuilt as Ghent Square, a neotraditional neighborhood that covers 160 acres and combines single-family dwellings, town houses, condominiums, and apartments.

NK63 Fred Heutte Horticultural Center

1887. 1977, reconstruction. Botetourt Gardens at Raleigh Ave.

Although difficult to imagine in its present landscaped setting, the Heutte Horticultural Center was originally a bustling ferry terminal at the foot of Commercial Place, where it once met the Elizabeth River waterfront. Commuters bound for Berkley and Portsmouth swarmed under its broad, bracketed roof and graceful arched transoms, where virtually anything from newspapers to crabs could be purchased for the ride home. The opening of the Norfolk-Portsmouth Bridge-Tunnel in 1952 made ferry service redundant, and the building was abandoned.

The wholesale clearance of the waterfront in the 1960s almost claimed the terminal, but far-sighted officials at the Norfolk Redevelopment and Housing Authority acted—uncharacteristically—in time and dismantled the building. In 1977 it was restored as a horticultural center at a cost of $200,000 to be the centerpiece of Ghent Square. The outward appearance of the reconstructed terminal largely conforms to the original in all but one major respect: gray paint covers the exterior, which in its heyday had a red roof and orange walls to match the ferries.

Of the townhouses that suuround Ghent Square, the northwestern grouping, at 901–907 Botetourt Gardens, is a particularly handsome example of late modern contextual design,

by Barton Myers Associates (1977). Myers is a Norfolk native and a descendant of merchant Moses Myers.

NK64 Llewellyn-Omohundro House

c. 1830. 1980, renovation, Lewis A. Rightmier. 1010 Llewellyn Mews

This Greek Revival town house, with side passage and double internal chimney stacks, typifies the kind of modest dwelling once prevalent in East Ghent. It was moved to its present location in 1980 as part of the neighborhood's redevelopment.

NK63 Fred Heutte Horticultural Center

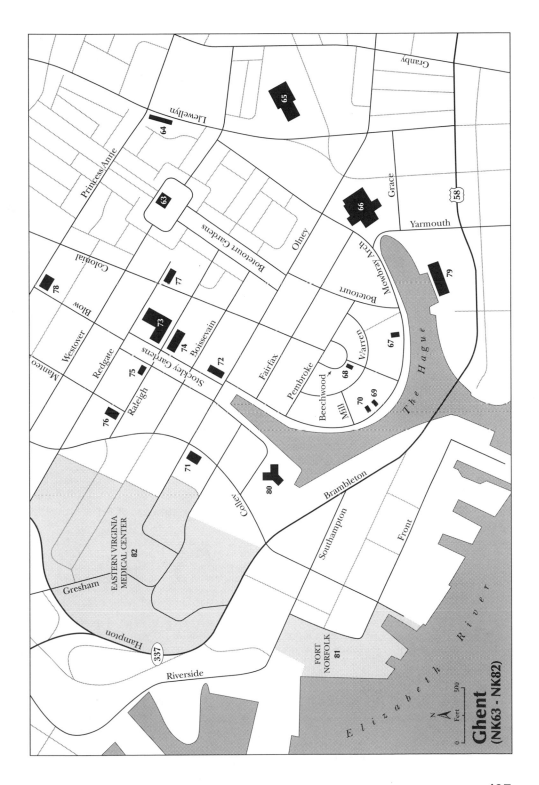

Ghent
(NK63 - NK82)

N

Feet 500

0

427

NK65 Harrison Opera House

1941–1943, Clarence A. Neff and T. David Fitz-Gibbon. 1990–1993, renovation and addition, Graham Gund Architects with Williams, Tazewell and Associates. Northeast corner of Virginia Beach Blvd. and Llewellyn Ave.

The Harrison Opera House was constructed during World War II as an entertainment complex for locally stationed troops who might otherwise have strayed to the bars and tattoo parlors farther downtown. Neff and Fitz-Gibbon's design combined two functions: an auditorium for stage shows and film screenings and an arena with bleacher seating for sporting events. The limestone exterior blended aspects of the Streamline Moderne and the International Style, including flat roofs, ribbon windows, and curving walls. It served as Norfolk's first real introduction to modern architecture. In the decades following the war, the Center Theater and the Arena Municipal Auditorium, as the two halves of the complex were once known, hosted virtually every major theatrical and sporting event held in the city. After the opening of Scope and Chrysler Hall in the 1970s, the complex stood dark much of the time.

What saved the Center Theater from almost certain demolition was its excellent acoustics. The building became the home of the newly formed Virginia Opera Company in the 1980s. As the company's reputation grew, so did the demands on its facility. In the early 1990s a $10 million renovation and enlargement was undertaken that both enhanced the theater's public areas and destroyed its historic character. A ponderous postmodern addition now envelops three sides of the old auditorium. Four massive towers with hipped roofs, intended to harmonize with the nearby Chrysler Museum of Art, mark the corners. The curve of the west facade echoes the curve of the old facade, which now defines the inner lobby. Inside the centerpiece of the addition is the upper-level lobby with its enormous plate glass windows and tiered chandeliers. Oval staircases within the towers link this level with the lower lobby. The auditorium is essentially unchanged save for the addition of box seating on either side of the proscenium. Because it was largely unaffected by the renovation, the east end of the building retains its historic appearance. This area is now used for storage and scenery construction.

NK65 Harrison Opera House, east facade

NK66 Chrysler Museum of Art

NK66 Chrysler Museum of Art

1928–1933, 1938–1939, Peebles and Ferguson with Calrow, Browne and Fitz-Gibbon. 1967, addition, William and Geoffrey Platt with Finlay F. Ferguson, Jr. 1974–1976, addition, Williams and Tazewell and Associates. 1985–1989, renovation and expansion, Hartman-Cox Architects. 1995–1997, addition, Pentecost, Deal and Associates. 245 W. Olney Rd.

Standing serenely at the end of the Hague, the Chrysler Museum of Art could have been depicted in a *veduta* by Canaletto; only the gondolas are missing. Although seemingly timeless, the view is in fact relatively recent. The unified appearance of the building and its many parts is the result one of the more felicitous episodes in recent postmodern architecture.

The establishment of an art museum in Norfolk was the direct result of the efforts of Irene Leache and her companion, Anna Cogswell

Wood, who in 1873 founded a women's seminary that bore their names. The arts were a central part of the curriculum, and upon the death of Leache, Wood established a small collection in her companion's memory, which eventually (around World War I) became the Norfolk Society of the Arts. Through the efforts of Florence Sloane, a site and operational funding were secured from the city, and the first wing of the Norfolk Museum of Arts and Sciences opened in 1933, at the height of the Great Depression.

Stylistically, the main limestone block of the museum resembles an early Italian Renaissance palazzo with its open arcade on the ground level and blind windows with pointed tracery on the upper level. The integrity of the design was compromised in the 1960s and 1970s by two major additions, however. Constructed of brick and outlined in limestone, the Houston Wing extended to the north and east of the main block, with a tower at the connection and a new entrance facing Olney Road away from the Hague. A second addition was built in the mid-1970s to accommodate the collection of Walter P. Chrysler, after whom the museum was renamed. Whereas the earlier addition attempted to blend somewhat with the earlier structure, this Brutalist addition, with its cantilevered northeast corner, seemed to stand defiantly apart from it. A major renovation and expansion in the 1980s by the Washington, D.C., firm of Hartman-Cox effectively masked these two modernist additions behind new construction that successfully harmonizes with the original block. A second tower was added to balance the first, and the entrance facing the Hague was restored. The open cloister at the center of the original block was covered with a skylight, supported by wooden trusses, to form a new inner lobby. The centerpiece of the expansion is a new north facade, early Florentine Renaissance in inspiration, that incorporates a blind arcade on the lower level with an open colonnade above it.

NK67 Tait House

1895. 436 Mowbray Arch

With the bulkheading of the Hague, Mowbray Arch became Norfolk's most desirable waterfront address, lined with large houses in a variety of revival styles. The design of the Tait House, probably by a local architect/builder,

derives from the Queen Anne–Shingle Style pattern books of the 1890s. Picturesque elements abound on the exterior, including asymmetrical gambrel gables, soaring chimney stack, and eyebrow dormer.

NK68 Royster House

1900, John Kevan Peebles. 303 Colonial Ave.

Colonial Avenue is Ghent's second most prestigious address, particularly the segment that widens to form the park known as Beechwood Place. Just south of the park is the Royster House, a handsome brick residence with stone and wood trim designed in the Colonial Revival style by one of Virginia's leading architects. With its Ionic pilasters, bow window bays, and hipped roof, the house exhibits a decidedly New England pedigree. Graceful porches, now removed, once spanned the east and south sides of the house. The house was built for Frank S. Royster of the Royster-Guano Fertilizer Company.

NK69 Robinson House

1905–1906, Gregory and Williamson, contractors. 570 Mowbray Arch

The roots of this Tudor Revival residence lie in the English Arts and Crafts movement of the nineteenth century. Balanced yet asymmetrically organized around a central exterior chimney, it displays a rich contrast of patterns and textures in terra-cotta, stucco, wood, and leaded glass.

NK70 Lewis House

1905–1906, Gregory and Williamson, contractors. 580 Mowbray Arch

Lewis was a partner of Robinson next door, and the same contractors were responsible for this dissimilar house, which is Colonial Revival with all of the pretensions of an antebellum plantation house. A two-story semicircular Ionic portico dominates the center of the facade while a graceful fanlight unfolds over the entrance. Mannerist keystones punctuate the lintels of the rectangular windows on both levels, providing a somewhat whimsical touch to an otherwise conservative design.

NK71 Central Baptist Church

1900–1904, Dwyer and Neff. 1921, Sunday school renovation, Herbert Levi Cain. 1962–1964, annex, A. Ray Pentecost, Jr. 1994–1996, restoration, José Francisco Soria. 701 W. Olney Rd.

The short-lived partnership of Dwyer and Neff designed this Gothic Revival church to serve the neighborhoods of Ghent and Atlantic City, which were rapidly developing at the turn of the twentieth century. A new congregation, only fifteen years old, commissioned a building to vie with those of older, more established congregations in Norfolk. The impressive edifice of textured gray brick has a cross-in-square plan with a prominent bell tower at the northeast corner, truncated towers at the other corners, and a classroom wing that extends to the south of the main block. The north facade is the most ornate with its projecting sanctuary bay and rose window. The interior is oriented south to north and is distinguished by an oak hammerbeam ceiling and vividly colored stained glass windows by the Colgate Art Glass Company of New York. In the early 1960s an incompatible modern office and classroom wing was added to the west of the church.

NK72 Christ and St. Luke's Episcopal Church

1909–1910, Watson and Huckle with Ferguson and Calrow. Northeast corner of W. Olney Rd. and Stockley Gardens

One of Norfolk's largest churches, Christ and St. Luke's demonstrates the return to academic principles in early twentieth-century Gothic Revival architecture, following the florid experimentation of the Victorian Gothic. The Christ Church congregation (formed 1800), originally located downtown, followed the migration to the developing residential suburb of Ghent. Watson and Huckle of Philadelphia, with the assistance of Ferguson and Calrow, a local firm, designed the granite and limestone building in the English Perpendicular manner, effectively combining academic materials and details with picturesque massing. The enormous scale of the church proved fortuitous, for in 1935 Christ Church merged with St. Luke's, a nearby Episcopal parish founded in 1873.

Taking maximum advantage of the waterfront location, the architects placed a 130-foot tower at the southwest corner of the building, with the main entrance at its base. The nave is oriented from south to north with a false transept, invisible from the interior, near the northwest corner. Attached buttresses and lancet windows articulate the aisle walls with corresponding lancet windows at the clerestory level. Enormous lancet windows with Perpendicular tracery terminate the nave at each end. An enclosed garden to the east of the church is reached by a handsome lych gate. Since there is no narthex, the interior of the church is revealed slowly; only after the worshiper has entered and turned through the vestibule of the southwest tower are the full 55-foot height and 150-foot length of the nave apparent. Dark oak ceiling beams contrast with gray limestone walls, and outside light is diffused through the many stained glass windows by Mayer and Company of Munich. A pale Caen stone was used for the elaborate reredos that decorates the rear wall beneath the north window of the raised sanctuary. The whole effect is remarkably true to the spirit of fifteenth-century English craftsmanship.

NK73 Temple Ohef Shalom

1916–1918, Ferguson, Calrow and Wrenn. 1965, Kaufman Hall, Brundage, Cohen, Kraskin. Northeast corner of Stockley Gardens and Raleigh Ave.

NK74 Ghent United Methodist Church

1919–1922, 1924, Peebles and Ferguson. 1961, renovation and steeple replacement, Lublin, McGaughy

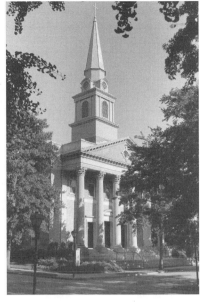

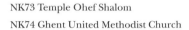

NK73 Temple Ohef Shalom
NK74 Ghent United Methodist Church

and Associates. Southeast corner of Stockley Gardens and Raleigh Ave.

Stockley Gardens is a formal greenway that extends the open vista created by the western boundary of the Hague several blocks northward into the heart of north Ghent. The gardens are divided into northern and southern sections, each extending for several blocks, and they are joined along the axis formed by Blow Street. The northern section is predominantly residential. The southern section is home to several of Norfolk's most prominent religious institutions, and it is also the setting for the city's finest essay in City Beautiful planning.

The pairing of Temple Ohef Shalom and its neighbor, Ghent United Methodist Church, is a potent symbol of Jewish-Christian ecumenism in a city of long-standing religious tolerance. The design of each building speaks of the infinite adaptability of classicism to varying symbolic and functional needs. The continuity of design is no doubt due to the involvement of Finlay F. Ferguson, Sr., who left one partnership to form another in the years that intervened between the two commissions.

Following the 1916 fire that destroyed the Palladian Revival sanctuary of Temple Ohef Shalom (1902, John Kevan Peebles) in downtown Norfolk, the temple moved to the quieter surroundings of Ghent. The design of the new Temple Ohef Shalom is an adaptation of a Roman temple to suit the liturgical needs of a Reform congregation. A hexastyle limestone portico with fluted Ionic columns and pediment dominates the west facade of the building. Three entrances lead into the sanctuary at the lower level, and five windows covered by grilles are visible between the columns at the upper level. The walls of the building are constructed of tan brick with limestone detailing. Along each side the sanctuary windows, filled with translucent slag glass panels, extend to nearly the full height of the building.

The Ghent United Methodist congregation, founded in 1902 and temporarily housed in a Victorian Gothic building, decided in 1918 that it needed a new church. The model for the resulting building is more specific than that of its neighbor: James Gibbs's St. Martin-in-the-Fields, London (1721–1726), one of the most widely copied churches in Christendom. The building materials and the proportions of the church and its attached portico are nearly identical to those of Temple Ohef Shalom, but the details vary considerably. The columns are unfluted Corinthian, and the tower and a steeple atop the portico clearly identify the ecclesiastical function of the building. Along the sides of the building are two levels of windows, which indicate the presence of interior galleries. The church was extensively renovated in 1961, at which time the green aluminum steeple, similar in form to the original copper structure, was installed.

NK75 Henke House

1909, Lee and Diehl. 801 Stockley Gardens

For evidence that eclecticism in American residential architecture survived well into the first decade of the twentieth century, one need only look at the design of this rather curious house. With its hipped roof, angled bays, and broad porch, the exterior reveals an informal Craftsman touch, even as its crenellated parapets and clustered porch piers hint at manorial aspirations.

NK76 Raleigh Square

1904, John Kevan Peebles. 1975–1976, renovation. 700 Raleigh Ave.

This delightful group of town houses recalls an English mews in its U-shaped plan, central garden, and picturesque details. The lower sections are covered with rough-cast stucco while the upper levels are shingled.

NK77 First Presbyterian Church

1910–1912, Ferguson, Calrow and Taylor. 1971, education building, Oliver and Smith. 1989, preschool building, Hanbury Evans Newill Vlattas and Company. Southeast corner of Colonial Ave. and Redgate Ave.

A Scottish church purportedly inspired the design, but Norfolk's First Presbyterian Church more closely resembles a suburban English parish church of the Edwardian era. This likeness is due largely to the Perpendicular Gothic treatment of its exterior, which is executed in brick with limestone trim. The focal point of the cruciform church is the blocky western tower with the main entrance at its base. An alternating rhythm of small windows and simple buttresses along the side aisles contrasts effectively with the enormous traceried windows that punctuate the clerestory level. The three-aisle interior is restrained, save for the extraordinary stained glass windows by J. and R. Lamb Studios of New York and Willet Stained Glass Studios of Philadelphia. The architect, Finlay F. Ferguson, Sr., was a member of the congregation.

NK78 Roman Catholic Church of the Sacred Heart

1924–1925, Peebles and Ferguson. 1957, renovation. 1988, renovation and addition, Design Collaborative. Southeast corner of W. Princess Anne Rd. and Blow St.

Alone among the numerous churches of Ghent, the Roman Catholic Church of the Sacred Heart reflects in its design the increased interest in Italo-Byzantine architecture in the years following World War I. Based loosely on the fifth-century Church of Sant'Apollinare Nuovo in Ravenna, Sacred Heart is a three-aisle basilica terminated by a triple apse at its east end. With its simple round-arched windows, brick walls, and tile roof, the church appears unusually restrained when viewed from the sides and rear. Only the west facade is highly ornamented, in terra-cotta and marble. The three entrances are framed by a triple arcade supported by engaged Corinthian columns that flank the center opening and corbeled Corinthian capitals that terminate each end. Above the entrances, the tympana of the arcade are filled with polychrome reliefs in the style of the della Robbia workshops of Florence. A majestic wheel window dominates the upper level of the facade. To the right of the church, a sympathetic addition of the 1980s now provides the primary access to the church while linking it to the Italianate rectory on Graydon Avenue.

The interior of Sacred Heart is light and airy, primarily because of the translucent glazing of the clerestory level and the white stuccoed wall surfaces. Marble Corinthian columns with stylized, gilded capitals line the nave, leading to the principal and subsidiary apses. The stained glass windows along the aisle walls were designed by Mayer and Company of Munich. Both aisles and nave are covered by open-truss ceilings of wood, subtly painted in geometric patterns.

NK79 Hague Towers

1963–1965, W. L. Mayne and Associates. 330 W. Brambleton Ave.

NK80 Pembroke Towers

1960–1962, Paul and Jarmul with Leavitt and Associates. 601 Pembroke Ave.

These two buildings initiated a brief craze in the early 1960s for high-rise apartment living that threatened to transform Norfolk into a small-scale copy of Arlington, Virginia. They are situated at opposite ends of the south bank of the Hague, a small, curving inlet of the Elizabeth River, and they stand like sentinels in front of the low-scale, historic neighborhood of Ghent to the north. Pembroke Towers, a single building with a plural name, is a thirteen-story, Y-shaped skyscraper designed in the International Style. The exterior is clad in a buff-colored brick, and the underlying concrete frame is revealed at each level by boldly cantilevered balconies. Hague Towers is also saddled with a plural name, but in this case it refers to a second tower that was never built; by the late 1960s, the high-rise residential real estate market had softened. At twenty stories, it was the tallest apartment building in Virginia when it opened its doors in 1965. The International Style design assumes a slab shape, with the reinforced concrete frame fully exposed. The shorter ends of the slab are sheathed in brick, and the longer sides are enlivened by cantilevered balconies, ribbon windows, and brick panels.

NK81 Fort Norfolk

c. 1810, rebuilding. c. 1850–1855, additions. c. 1920–1923, c. 1943–1947, renovations. 1991–1998, restoration, Hanbury Evans Newill Vlattas, and Joseph D. Lahendro. 803 Front St. Open to the public

Norfolk's strategic location near the mouth of the Chesapeake Bay situated it ideally for regional and national commerce but at the same time made it especially vulnerable to attack. Sometime during the eighteenth century two earthworks, Fort Norfolk and Fort Nelson, were constructed along the Elizabeth River's north and south banks, respectively. Although well situated, the two forts were severely damaged during the Revolutionary War; their reconstruction under the direction of John Jacob Ulrich Rivardi did not commence until 1794. A view of Norfolk and Portsmouth drawn by Benjamin Henry Latrobe around 1796 depicts Fort Norfolk as having a polygonal berm. Unfortunately for the city's defense, Latrobe's 1798 proposals to redesign Forts Norfolk and Nelson seem to have been scuttled for political reasons. In 1807 the *Leopard,* a British frigate, attacked the American vessel *Chesapeake* near Cape Henry. Many of the latter's crew members were killed or wounded and several were captured and impressed. The incident rattled the citizenry and led to the reinforcement of Fort Norfolk. The result must have proved insufficient, since the fort was almost completely rebuilt around 1810, perhaps incorporating portions of the earlier earthwork. Fort Nelson was destroyed to

make way for the U.S. Naval Hospital in Portsmouth during the 1820s.

The present appearance of Fort Norfolk is the result of two major building campaigns. The irregularly shaped perimeter walls and earthen ramparts, the main gate, and three major interior buildings can be assigned to the first campaign, which was completed just before the War of 1812. Except for a missing section of hornwork that would have protected an exposed building on the east side of the fort, the brick walls survive in excellent condition; an arcing section facing the harbor is particularly noteworthy. Visitors pass through the original wooden gates and beneath a guardhouse. A vaulted chamber, immediately adjacent to the gate at the right, is popularly known as the dungeon but was more likely a storeroom. To the left is a one-and-one-half-story building formerly used as a barracks. A parade ground extends northward from the gate, and the east side is lined with two Federal buildings: a small storehouse that has been restored as the headquarters of the Norfolk Historical Society, and a larger officers' quarters. Ironically, the reconstructed fort was never tested by military action. A hastily constructed fort downriver at Craney Island repelled advancing British forces in 1813, and the erection of Fort Monroe and Fort Wool at Hampton Roads following the Treaty of Ghent (1814) rendered Fort Norfolk redundant.

The second building campaign at Fort Norfolk dates to around 1850–1855, when the U.S. Navy assumed control of the property from the U.S. Army and converted it into a navy magazine, demolishing some older buildings in the process. A large magazine was constructed on the west side of the parade ground with numerous fireproofing safeguards, including brick walls with granite trim, interior vaults of brick, and copper-lined wooden shutters and doors. A wooden canopy with delicate cast iron supports links the magazine to the officers' quarters, which was extensively remodeled into a facility for the assembly and storage of ordnance. This building contains one of the fort's most unusual attractions. Around 1864, following a tumultuous wartime interlude when control of the fort shifted from the Union to the Confederacy and back again to the Union, a group of captive blockade runners scrawled humorous and somewhat obscene graffiti in a second-floor chamber to while away their time. After the Civil War, concern about safety led to the removal of the naval magazine to a location well beyond the growing city and the abandonment of the fort about 1880. In 1923, the U.S. Army Corps of Engineers renovated the fort for its district headquarters, which has since been moved to a modern office building outside the perimeter walls.

NK82 Eastern Virginia Medical Center

1966, master plan, Vincent Kling and Associates. Site bounded by Colley Ave., Brambleton Ave., and Redgate Ave.

Norfolk's attempt to refashion itself as a modern city in the decades following World War II included a state-of-the-art medical center. Not until construction of the Norfolk Civic Center was underway in the early 1960s did the city turn its attention to the southwest corner of Ghent, where it adjoined Atlantic City, a rundown residential neighborhood slated for demolition. Norfolk General Hospital and the Children's Hospital of the King's Daughters already occupied the site, but the most ambitious part of the proposal, the creation of a new medical school to serve southeastern Virginia, was a political and economic undertaking virtually without precedent. The city commissioned Vincent Kling, who was designing the Norfolk Civic Center, to devise a master plan for the medical center that would coordinate with redevelopment efforts underway in Ghent. Kling devised

a 51-acre campus that accommodated the two hospitals and future expansion, a new city public health center, an existing medical tower Kling had designed in 1961, a campus for the proposed medical school, and the realignment of Colley Avenue, a major north-south thoroughfare. Kling's plan took shape gradually over the next decade as the city demolished dozens of buildings and reconfigured the surrounding streets. The need for surface parking has prevented the campus from developing a central focus thus far. Political wrangling between state and city officials delayed the opening of the medical school until 1973. Kling designed Lewis Hall (1975–1978), the school's first building, and the adjacent Jones Institute for Fertility Research (1990–1992). The former is a rather straightforward International Style building, while the latter has a more boldly expressionistic curving glass facade. Abutting Lewis Hall to the north and west, the Edward E. Brickell Medical Sciences Library (1998–2000, Tymoff and Moss), with its *tholos*-like entrance, represents a postmodern departure for the campus. By contrast, Hofheimer Hall (1981–1985, Hellmuth, Obata and Kassabaum) is a rather sedate essay in late modernism. What was once a redevelopment gamble has proven to be a financial success, with new construction underway to expand the medical center across Brambleton Avenue to the south.

East Side (NK83–NK92)

NK83 Doumar's Cones and Barbecue

1934. Northeast corner of 20th St. and Monticello Ave.

As recognized by the Smithsonian Institution, the founder of this popular drive-in restaurant was also the inventor of the ice cream cone. Abe Doumar devised the familiar confection while selling souvenirs near a waffle vendor at the 1904 Louisiana Purchase Exposition in St. Louis. This much remodeled Populuxe-Redux drive-in is the successor to the ice cream stand that Doumar opened at Ocean View Amusement Park after a successful stint at the 1907 Jamestown Ter-Centennial Exposition. In fair weather customers can still watch batter being formed into cones by a vintage machine in front of the restaurant. Curb service is avail-

NK83 Doumar's Cones and Barbecue

able to customers who choose to remain in their cars.

NK84 Coca-Cola Bottling Plant

1958, A. Ray Pentecost, Jr. Southeast corner of Monticello Ave. and 21st St.

By the middle of the twentieth century many of the city's leading food and beverage companies had forsaken downtown for the light industrial and commercial zone that straddles Monticello Avenue to the north. Of those that remain, the International Style Coca-Cola Bottling Plant is the most distinguished. Each area of the building is articulated as a separate box grouped around an off-center fire tower that also supports the company's signage. Brick is used on the building's exterior except at its southwest corner, where creamy marble panels attached by silver rivets create a decorative grid that draws attention to the glass-enclosed entrance below. The adjacent tower is clad in dark green marble with a vertical ribbon window. Plate glass windows along Monticello Avenue once afforded passersby a view of the bottling machinery. These have been sealed for security reasons, but their protective *brise-soleil* of metal slats remains.

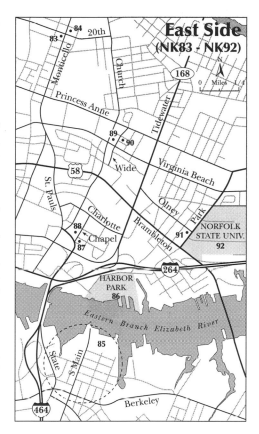

East Side
(NK83 - NK92)

NK85 Berkley Neighborhood Historic District

East of I-464, north of Berkley Ave., west of Pescara Creek, and south of the Eastern Branch of the Elizabeth River

The Berkley Historic District encompasses only a small part of a larger neighborhood whose historic character has been mostly lost through urban renewal. Because of its location at the confluence of the eastern and southern branches of the Elizabeth River, Berkley has been a center for shipping and shipbuilding since the colonial period. From 1789 until the mid-nineteenth century, it was the Norfolk County seat, but the area beyond the waterfront village remained rural until immediately after the Civil War, when Lycurgus Berkley, a local landowner, subdivided his property and established the eponymous town. Norfolk annexed Berkley in 1906. Ferries and the South Main Street drawbridge knit the two halves of the city together until the opening of the Norfolk-Portsmouth Bridge-Tunnel in the early 1950s. As with many older Norfolk neighbor-

hoods, Berkley went into slow decline after World War II as many of its religious institutions and retail establishments relocated to the suburbs.

This tour covers only the northern section of the neighborhood. The southern section, Bell-Diamond Manor, was successfully redeveloped on a suburban model in the late 1960s and 1970s; the eastern and oldest section was eradicated during the construction of I-464 during the 1980s.

Several of Berkley's most impressive public buildings line the northern side of Berkley Avenue. At the intersection of Dinwiddie Street is the Antioch Baptist Church (Memorial Methodist Episcopal Church) (1899–1900, James E. R. Carpenter with Charles J. Calrow; 1928–1929, annexes, attributed to Diehl and Land; 1982, renovation), a cruciform Gothic Revival design. The Tabernacle of God Holiness Church of Divine Healing (Berkley Avenue Baptist Church) (1885–1888, L. B. Volk; 1890, 1908–1909, additions), near the intersection of State Street and visible from I-464, is a picturesque Victorian Gothic church by a New York architect. Directly adjacent is the former Merchants and Planters Bank (1909, Lee and Diehl) with a neoclassical facade. The Queen Anne Norfleet House (c. 1900, northwest corner of South Main Street and Indian River Road) is the neighborhood's finest and most elaborate, with its turreted corner and wraparound porch.

The residential section north of Berkley Avenue and east of South Main Street was developed primarily between 1890 and 1930 on the grounds of Riveredge, a Greek Revival house that was home to generations of the Hardy family, including, briefly, its most famous member, General Douglas MacArthur. Riveredge fell into disrepair in the early twentieth century, burned in 1949, and was demolished two years later. One of Norfolk's most curious landmarks, the Mary Hardy MacArthur Memorial (1951, Finlay F. Ferguson, Jr.), is near the northeast corner of South Main Street and Bellamy Avenue, not far from the erstwhile site of Riveredge: a small, walled garden dedicated to the general's mother and constructed of materials salvaged from the ruins of the house. Neighborhood residents still refer to this section of the neighborhood as Hardyfields, and it is characterized by modest Colonial Revival and Queen Anne houses, American Foursquares, and bungalows.

NK86 Harbor Park

1991–1993, Hellmuth, Obata and Kassabaum. I-264 at Bessie's Place

Home to the minor-league Norfolk Tides, Harbor Park is a neotraditional baseball stadium designed by a nationally acclaimed Kansas City firm that specializes in large-scale facilities, including sporting arenas. The stadium is a smaller version of the firm's successful design for the Baltimore Orioles at Camden Yards, combining diapered brickwork with cast concrete ornament in a rhythmic arrangement of arches and piers. Beyond the grandly scaled entrance at the northwest corner, the field is oriented to give fans a sweeping view of the Elizabeth River beyond second base. For the players on the field, the city's skyline provides an impressive backdrop to the stands.

NK87 Roman Catholic Basilica of St. Mary of the Immaculate Conception

1857–1858, Patrick Charles Keely. 1983–1989, renovation. 1996–1999, renovation, Baldridge Architects and Engineers, Inc. 1963–1964, school, McElroy and Baldwin. 232 Chapel St.

A few Catholics lived in the Hampton Roads area in the seventeenth century, but the major influx came with the arrival of French immigrants to Norfolk in 1791. On the site of the present church a small wooden chapel was built, and then replaced in 1842 by a Greek Revival structure that burned December 8, 1856. In 1991 Pope John Paul II designated St. Mary's a "minor basilica" in recognition of its special significance as the city's oldest Roman Catholic church. Currently the church is home to the area's largest African American Roman Catholic congregation.

St. Mary's, although sometimes attributed to James Renwick, is the work of Patrick Charles Keely, an Irish-born architect who built extensively for the Catholic Church in the United States. Like Renwick's design for St. Patrick's Cathedral, New York (1853–1858), however, St. Mary's draws upon French Gothic models. The focal point of the three-aisle basilica is its western tower and highly decorated steeple that soars 240 feet above the ground. Although the view of the west facade is partially obstructed by an on-ramp to I-264, the view of the nave and its spectacularly patterned slate roof from the elevated interstate is unsurpassed. Originally exposed, the brick walls of the exterior were stuccoed in the 1920s. The interior of St. Mary's was extensively modernized during the 1980s, but the architectonic progression of the clustered piers leading to the polygonal apse at the east end remains undisturbed. Above the low clerestory, the elaborate lierne vaulting, executed in plaster, is especially noteworthy. The stained glass windows were designed by Mayer and Company of Munich, and the organ was made by Ferris and Stuart of New York.

NK88 St. Mary's Home for Disabled

1963–1964, McElroy and Baldwin. 317 Chapel St.

Starkly juxtaposed with the church is this medical facility, formerly affiliated with the parish. The parabolic entrance pavilion of its International Style exterior is strongly reminiscent of Oscar Niemeyer's Church of St. Francis of Assisi at Pampulha, Brazil (1943).

NK89 Attucks Theater

1919, Harvey N. Johnson, Sr., with Charles T. Russell.
1008–1012 Church St. Open occasionally for tours

Church Street was once the commercial and cultural heart of Norfolk's African American community, its sidewalks lined with shops, restaurants, and a variety of other establishments. It was also the city's major north-south thoroughfare, taking its name from historic St. Paul's Church (see entry, above). The postwar redevelopment of downtown and the creation of St. Paul's Boulevard, however, resulted in the truncation of Church Street's southern end and a major drop in its pedestrian and motor traffic. Moreover, with the end of racial segregation, the street lost most of its vitality as blacks went elsewhere in search of shopping and entertainment. The subsequent widening of the street into a suburban-style parkway during the 1980s and 1990s has resulted in the wholesale demolition of the historic business district and its replacement with strip shopping centers. Only the Attucks Theater survives as a forlorn reminder of the street's heyday between the 1920s and 1940s.

With its densely packed urban context now destroyed, the Attucks Theater now has a somewhat awkward appearance. Only the lobby facade was meant to be seen from the street, since the massive brick auditorium would have once been separated from neighboring buildings only by narrow alleys. Missing its decorative marquee, the facade is a sober exercise in

the Renaissance Revival. Terra-cotta pilasters divide the brick facade into three bays with wide tripartite windows; the name plate below the cornice and the date plate above it provide a modicum of ornament.

The lobby has been remodeled beyond recognition, but the basic contours of the 600-seat auditorium remain. A graceful balcony curves around the rear of the theater while box seats flank the square proscenium. The theater's most unusual interior feature—and the one that holds the key to its unusual name—is the asbestos fire curtain over the stage. On it the New York–based Lee Lash Studios painted a stirring representation of the Boston Massacre. Crispus Attucks, an African American man believed to have been the first victim of the American Revolution, is the figure sprawled face down in the front of the scene. Upstairs over the lobby were offices once rented to black professionals.

The Attucks is purported to be the nation's oldest theater designed, developed, and financed by African Americans under the auspices of the Twin Cities Amusement Corporation. Harvey Johnson, the theater's designer, was a prominent Norfolk architect who later entered the ministry. The theater began its life as a cinema and vaudeville house with performers such as Ethel Waters and Cab Calloway. In 1933 it was renovated and renamed the Booker T. Theater. The theater was closed in 1955 and the lobby converted to retail use. At present the building is vacant and awaiting restoration by the city as the Crispus Attucks Cultural Center.

NK90 First Calvary Baptist Church

1915–1916, Mitchell and Wilcox. 1968–1969, educational annex, McGaughy, Marshall, and McMillan. 1979, interior renovation. 1036–1040 Wide St.

From the exterior one might easily mistake First Calvary Baptist Church for a town hall or lyceum; only the bell tower at the northwest corner provides a reassuring ecclesiastical touch. The Georgian Revival exterior is constructed of brick with nearly identical, double-stacked Corinthian porticoes, executed in terra-cotta, on the north and west facades. Perched above the second of two full entablatures, a terra-cotta balustrade with decorative finials conceals the roof, a motif reminiscent of the work of James Gibbs (1682–1754). When it was completed in 1916, the church signaled architecturally the maturation of a relatively young African American congregation, which, after its founding in 1880, had met in a small commercial building on nearby Church Street.

NK91 Shiloh Baptist Church

1895–1896, Carpenter and Peebles. 1970–1971, interior renovation. Southwest corner of Park Ave. N. and Highland Ave.

At the turn of the twentieth century, Park Avenue was the most fashionable street in the rapidly developing Brambleton neighborhood. That the rugged Richardson Romanesque Shiloh Baptist Church closely resembles Epworth Methodist Church across town was no accident, for the same architecture firm designed both buildings at about the same time. Originally called the Park Avenue Baptist Church, the building is constructed of gray granite with brownstone trim. An enormous tower at the northeast corner dominates the exterior, but unlike Epworth, the church is longitudinally oriented east to west. The east facade is dominated by a circular stained glass window with plate tracery, and the north and south sides appear unusually low beneath the broad sweep of the roof. Small clerestory windows are located close together in a ribbonlike fashion. Wooden piers joined by wooden arches support a stately hammerbeam ceiling on the interior.

NK92 Norfolk State University

1965, master plan, Shriver and Holland. 2401 Corprew Ave.

That Norfolk has two major universities is a major source of civic pride, but it is also a pointed reminder of the commonwealth's segregated past. The origins of Norfolk State University, the commonwealth's largest historically black institution of higher education, can be traced to 1935, when Virginia Union University opened a Norfolk unit. It was renamed Norfolk Polytechnic College in 1942 to reflect the school's vocational and technical orientation. In 1944 the school became affiliated with Virginia State College, and several years later the city conveyed the old Memorial Park Golf Course to the school for its present campus. Not until 1969 did the school become independent under the name Norfolk State College; university status was granted in 1979.

NK91 Shiloh Baptist Church

NK92.1 Phyllis Wheatley Residence Hall, Norfolk State University

The development of the campus has followed a master plan created by Shriver and Holland in 1965, with most growth concentrated to the east of Park Avenue and north of Brambleton Avenue. Shriver and Holland have also designed many of the campus's buildings in a harmonious blend of modern idioms. An exception is the Phyllis Wheatley Residence Hall (NK92.1) (Mary F. Ballentine Home for the Aged) (1893–1894, Bradford Lee Gilbert), a Romanesque Revival building later used as a branch of the YWCA on the west side of Park Avenue. This is evidently the only work in Virginia by the New York architect Gilbert. The university is seeking to expand southward across Brambleton Avenue.

Norfolk Area (NK93–NK95)
(Map, p. 398)

NK93 **Old Dominion University**

1956, 1963, master plans, Oliver and Smith. 1966, McGaughy, Marshall and McMillan. 1973, 1977, Williams and Tazewell and Associates with Sasaki, Dawson, Demay Associates. 1993–1994, Ayers Saint Gross. Site bounded roughly by W. 43rd St., the Elizabeth River, 49th St., Bluestone Ave., Bolling Ave., and Hampton Blvd.

Until the Great Depression only the well-to-do in Norfolk sent their sons and daughters to college, preferably to Williamsburg, Charlottesville, or Lexington. With the city's dramatic population increase in the years following World War I, however, the need for a local institution of higher education could no longer be ignored. In 1930 the Norfolk Division of the College of William and Mary opened its doors in an abandoned elementary school on Hampton Boulevard with technical courses offered by an extension of the Virginia Polytechnic Institute. Although it took thirty-two years for the division to be granted independent status under the name Old Dominion College, growth during the mid-1960s was rapid enough to warrant the change to Old Dominion University by 1969.

The original section of the campus is north of 49th Street along Hampton Boulevard. Georgian Revival buildings are set behind a curving brick wall that recalls the mother campus in Williamsburg. Rollins Hall (1935, Clarence A. Neff) echoes the rear elevation of William and Mary's Wren Building, which had just been reconstructed, although its details are

actually Federal in style. The end pavilions in particular mimic the facade of the Taylor-Whittle House downtown. Neff also designed the adjacent Foreman Field (1935) and the encircling wall at about the same time. Spong Hall (1953–1955, Walford and Wright, with T. David Fitz-Gibbon) continues the Williamsburg motif, although on a stripped-down scale. Across Bolling Avenue a soccer field marks the location of the elementary school that served as the university's first classroom building.

South of 49th Street, the main campus's modern look appears to renounce the Williamsburg connection completely. The centerpiece, Kaufman Mall, laid out perpendicular to Hampton Boulevard, is lined for the most part with International Style buildings. The oldest of the group, Hughes Hall (1955–1959, Oliver and Smith, Edward Durrell Stone, and Walter H. Kilham, Jr., consultants), at the southwest corner of 49th Street and Hampton Boulevard, once housed the university's library. Very much in Stone's idiom of the 1950s, it is completely encased in a *brise-soleil* of perforated ceramic blocks broken only at the entrances. The mall is anchored at the west by Webb Student Center (NK93.1) (1962–1966, Lublin McGaughy and Associates; 1991–1993, additions, Odell Associates), whose vaguely neoclassical appearance recalls Stone's U.S. Embassy in New Delhi (1957–1959). South of the mall at the northwest corner of 43rd Street and Hampton Boulevard, the nine-story Batten Arts and Letters Building (1968–1972, Williams and Tazewell

NK93.1 Webb Student Center, Old Dominion University

and Associates), a Brutalist building completely out of scale with its neighbors, creates a fortresslike impression. Of the recent additions to the campus, the most distinguished is the Oceanography and Physical Science Building (1995–1997, Perkins and Will with Rancorn Wildman Associates) near the northeast corner of West 43rd Street and Elkhorn Avenue. Its glazed eastern exposure is vaguely reminiscent of Gropius and Meyer's Fagus Factory (1911) in Alfeld, Germany, an early icon of modernism. Plans call for a major expansion of the university eastward across Hampton Boulevard.

NK94 Hermitage Foundation Museum

1906–1946, Charles J. Woodsend and Michael F. McCarthy. 7637 N. Shore Rd. Open to the public

The Arts and Crafts movement's best showcase in Norfolk is this sprawling, Tudor Revival–Shingle Style residence in the city's Lochhaven neighborhood. Originally intended as a summer residence for William Sloane and his wife Florence, it evolved into a year-round and lifelong project that combined art collecting with architectural patronage in the peculiarly American tradition spearheaded by Isabella Stewart Gardner of Boston. Florence Sloane helped establish the Norfolk Museum (now the Chrysler Museum). The Sloanes' private domain opened to the public in 1942 with the establishment of the Hermitage Foundation Museum.

The Hermitage is the collaborative design of a patron and a master craftsman, with Florence Sloane in the role of the former and Charles J. Woodsend, an architect and woodcarver, in the role of the latter. Michael F. McCarthy replaced Woodsend after his death in the 1920s, supervising the numerous craftsmen at work on the house at any given time. Norfolk architect Wickham C. Taylor may have been associated with the design as well. The exterior is constructed on a brick foundation with naturally stained wooden shingles covering most surfaces. A variety of leaded glass windows, some from European sources, provided striking views of the surrounding gardens and the Lafayette River to the south. A picturesque combination of chimneys and gables with elaborate vergeboards completes the design, which appears to have evolved over centuries rather than decades. A variety of outbuildings continues the illusion of an English country estate.

On the interior, the plan is predictably irregular, with public rooms located to the west side

NK94 Hermitage Foundation Museum

of the house and private apartments to the east. Many of the rooms are richly paneled in traditional English patterns, including the linenfold design. The art collection is informally arranged as it was when the Sloanes lived there, and, although it ranges widely over time and geography, it is particularly strong in Asian art. Perhaps the most whimsical touch in this unusual dwelling is the motto carved in the main hall: "This is the house that Jack built," which refers both to the nursery rhyme and to Florence Sloane, whose nickname was Jack.

NK95 Norfolk Naval Base

1917, Neff and Thompson. Main gate, intersection of Hampton Blvd. and Taussig Blvd.

Norfolk might have remained a sleepy southern town until late in the twentieth century had the U.S. Navy not established a base within its borders at the outset of World War I. Home to the Atlantic Fleet, the North American headquarters of the North Atlantic Treaty Organization (NATO), and thousands of military and civilian personnel, the Norfolk Naval Base is reputedly the world's largest, a sprawling compound that includes many sites of architectural and historic interest.

The genesis of the base can be traced to 1907, the year Norfolk hosted the Jamestown Ter-Centennial Exposition in honor of the 300th anniversary of Virginia. In preparation for the event, several hundred acres of wetlands were cleared and drained north of the city overlooking Hampton Roads, the shipping channel that links the Chesapeake Bay with the Elizabeth and James rivers. An architectural team led by John Kevan Peebles modeled the fairgrounds after the 1893 World's Columbian Exposition in Chicago. The principal axis extended northward into Hampton Roads, where jetties created a protected lagoon. The three-part domed Administration Group at the southern end of the axis was designed in a Beaux-Arts, Palladian Revival idiom in homage to Thomas Jefferson. Although the lagoon was filled long ago, many of the original exposition buildings remain. Admiral's Row (Dillingham Boulevard between Bacon Street and Moffett Avenue) consists of more than a dozen buildings that were formerly pavilions built by individual states for the exposition. The most curious is the Pennsylvania Building (1907, Brockie and Hastings), a replica of Independence Hall at one-third scale. Most of the others are also executed in colonial or Federal dress, but they are more domestic in appearance. The grandest of these is the Virginia Building (1907, Breese and Mitchell), a free interpretation of a colonial house that now serves as the residence of the Atlantic Fleet's commander in chief.

Although the exposition lost money, it was an economic boon to the city as a whole. When it closed in the fall of 1907, some farsighted citizens began lobbying Congress for the establishment of a naval base on the former fairgrounds. President Theodore Roosevelt's Great White Fleet had called at the exposition, proving the suitability of the site for harboring oceangoing vessels. Not until the United States entered World War I, however, did Congress authorize the new base. Construction began in the summer of 1917 under the supervision of Neff and Thompson, a Norfolk firm. Many of the exposition buildings were retained but converted to military use. The former History Building was made into a gymnasium (1907, Gilbert Street, N-24), while the east and west wings of the former Administration Group (Gilbert Street, N-21 and N-23) were rebuilt as part of the Naval Command Headquarters. The central, domed building of the Administration Group was destroyed by fire in 1941, and its stripped classical replacement (1942, Giffles and Vallet, N-26) has Art Deco touches. The base grew by leaps and bounds before, during, and after World War II, and it has continued to expand even during the military retrenchment of the post–Cold War era. The Naval Base Norfolk 2010 Land Use Plan (EDAW, Inc., with Patton, Harris, Rust, and Associates and Shriver and Holland Associates) will guide redevelopment into the twenty-first century.

Portsmouth (PO)

C OLONEL WILLIAM CRAWFORD FOUNDED PORTSMOUTH IN 1752 THROUGH the subdivision of his land on the south side of the Elizabeth River across from Norfolk. The village was platted on a regular grid with High Street as its principal east-west axis. It developed as a seaport, and the U.S. Navy located a shipyard and other facilities here in the 1790s. Portsmouth became a city in 1858 and was a principal port for the Confederate navy. Because it escaped some of the worst ravages of both war and urban renewal, a greater concentration of historic architecture remains here than in the other cities of southeastern Virginia. Economically, the city's fortunes have been closely tied to shipping, shipbuilding, and railroads. The 2000 population was 100,565.

Downtown Portsmouth   (PO1–PO14)

This walking tour of the downtown connects many of the city's public buildings.

PO1 Seaboard Building

c. 1894, Seaboard and Roanoke Railroad architecture staff. 1908, renovation, Edward Overman. 1914–1915, addition. c. 1985, renovation. 1 High St.

Originally constructed as the passenger terminal and offices of the Seaboard and Roanoke Railroad, this building was prominently situated on the waterfront to ensure easy connections to Norfolk and Berkley via ferryboat as well as to offer convenient proximity to the railroad's warehouses. The Renaissance Revival design is distinguished by a semicircular bay supported by a ground-level arcade facing High Street. A two-story addition to the top of

the building was constructed in 1914–1915. Following the removal of the Seaboard headquarters to Richmond in the late 1950s, the building was converted for use as Portsmouth City Hall (1958–1980). Subsequently it was renovated as a mixed-use residential and office building.

PO2 Portsmouth Civic Center

1966–1970, Yates and Boggs. 601 Crawford St.

Like larger cities across Virginia in the postwar period, Portsmouth erected a new civic center both to cope with an expanding municipal bu-

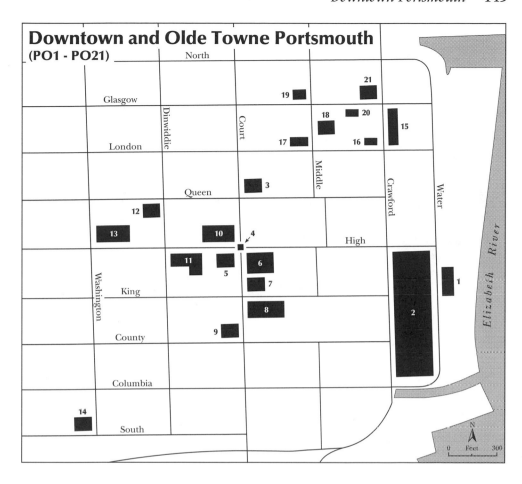

Downtown and Olde Towne Portsmouth
(PO1 - PO21)

North

Glasgow

London

Queen

High

King

County

Columbia

South

Dinwiddie

Court

Middle

Crawford

Water

Washington

Elizabeth River

19

21

18   20

17   16

15

3

12

13   10   4

11   5   6

7

8

9

1

2

14

0   Feet   300

reaucracy and to assert its aspirations to modernity. Semi-Brutalist design in brick and precast concrete unites the various elements of the

PO1 Seaboard Building

Civic Center, including two courthouses, the jail, and the police headquarters. The nearby International Style City Hall (1977–1980, Thomas F. Marshall; 801 Crawford Street) was privately financed and leased to the city, an unusual arrangement at the time that has since become commonplace.

PO3 Court Street Baptist Church

1901–1903, Reuben H. Hunt. 1888, Sunday school. 1911, renovation and enlargement, M. L. Parker. 1957, Sunday school addition. 447 Court St.

The visual impact of this massive building symbolizes the Baptist ascendancy in the city at the turn of the twentieth century. Court Street Baptist is the oldest Baptist congregation in southeastern Virginia, tracing its roots to 1789, when the Portsmouth and Norfolk Baptist Church was established in Portsmouth. As with

PO3 Court Street Baptist Church

Hunt's other Baptist churches in Norfolk and Newport News, the Richardsonian Romanesque is transformed into a highly idiosyncratic design. The exterior is constructed of pink rusticated rock-faced granite with limestone trim. Two towers flank a recessed porch formed by immense arches on the west facade. Although at six stories the right tower is twice the height of the left, the latter terminates in a fanciful cylindrical cupola. Both are capped by somewhat Byzantine-looking onion roofs.

PO4 Confederate Memorial

1875–1893, Charles E. Cassell. Center of Court St. north of High St.

Located to one side of the city's main intersection, the Confederate monument is a prominent reminder of Portsmouth's involvement in the Civil War. Sponsored by the Ladies Memorial Aid Association and designed by a Baltimore architect originally from Portsmouth, the monument consists of a 35-foot granite obelisk on a 20-foot pedimented base, guarded by bronze statues of four men representing (clockwise from the south elevation) the Confederate infantry, cavalry, artillery, and navy. Significantly, the sailor's headband is inscribed *Merrimac*, a reference to the Confederate ironclad, fashioned in nearby Norfolk Naval Shipyard.

PO5 Trinity Episcopal Church

1828–1830. 1884, renovation. 1893, annex and tower addition, W. D. Wentworth. 1961–1962, renovation, Williams and Tazewell. 1954–1956, parish house, Williams, Coile and Blanchard. 500 Court St.

Trinity Episcopal, the city's oldest religious congregation, was formed from the subdivision of the Elizabeth River Parish in 1761. The first church was constructed of brick the following year. Although the parish survived disestablishment, it became inactive between 1809 and 1820. During an attempted enlargement in 1828 the parish leaders determined that the building's fabric had deteriorated to such an extent that they decided to construct an entirely new church instead. Rectangular in shape, the stucco-over-brick church is oriented east-west, with a small, enclosed portico on Court Street to define the main entrance and an apse projecting from the west wall. The new structure retained eighteenth-century-style round-arched windows combined with a Greek Revival wooden Doric entablature below the eaves and a pedimented gable facing Court Street. A small belfry once crowned the gable over the main facade. The church's picturesque appearance dates from the 1890s, when the quasi-Romanesque tower and annex were added to the south side of the building and the belfry was removed. Several of the stained glass windows were designed by Henry Sharp of New York and installed in 1859. An 1868 stained glass window is the city's first Confederate memorial. The controversy that followed its installation—close on the heels of the Civil War—resulted in its removal for two years while a more acceptable inscription was composed. Three later windows are by Tiffany Studios.

PO6 Bangel Law Building

1878. 1948–1949, remodeling. 505 Court St.

This Second Empire building served as Portsmouth's city hall and fire department headquarters during the late nineteenth and early twentieth centuries. Before its conversion to an office building, large openings on the ground level contained the storage bays for fire engines. Segmental-arched windows on the upper levels identified the office portion of the building. The mansard roof with clock tower now seems fussy in comparison to the stripped classical appearance of the limestone facade.

PO7 First Presbyterian Church

1877. 1997, renovation. 1972, Sunday school addition. 515 Court St.

The mid-nineteenth-century phase of the Romanesque Revival, popularized by Richard Upjohn's work, lacks the weight and strength of H. H. Richardson's architecture. This is apparent in First Presbyterian Church, with its corner tower and steeple, round-arched windows, and attached wall buttresses. The congregation was established in Portsmouth in 1822, and the present church replaces one destroyed by fire in 1877.

PO8 Portsmouth Public Library (U.S. Post Office)

1907–1909, James K. Taylor, Supervising Architect, U.S. Treasury Department. 1931, annex, James Alphonso Wetmore, Supervising Architect, U.S. Treasury Department. 1963–1964, renovation, Yates and Boggs. 601 Court St.

Taylor transformed the architectural idiom of the U.S. Treasury Department from Victorian to classical, as exemplified in this very French Beaux-Arts building, originally the city's main post office. The brick and limestone exterior has a hexastyle, Scamozzian Ionic entrance portico on the west facade. A 1931 annex continued the Beaux-Arts idiom eastward. The post office vacated the building in 1961 and the city acquired it for use as a public library shortly thereafter.

PO9 Pythian Castle

1897–1898, Edward Overman. c. 1908, addition. 1983–1984, renovation, Hanbury and Company. 610–612 Court St.

The Knights of Pythias, a secret fraternal order founded in the mid-nineteenth century, commissioned local architect and builder Edward Overman to design this extravagantly appointed meeting hall. The Romanesque Revival style selected for the exterior is consistent with the organization's medieval pretensions. The main facade is richly polychromed and ornamented with rusticated end pavilions and corner entrances treated as baldachins. The ground level was rented to commercial tenants, while the upper levels contained meeting rooms for the Knights. At present the building houses the southeastern regional office of the Virginia Department of Historic Resources.

PO10 The Arts Center of the Portsmouth Museums

1845–1846, William R. Singleton. c. 1867, remodeling. c. 1978–1982, renovation, Hanbury and Company. 420 High St. Open to the public

This impressive brick Greek Revival building was formerly the Norfolk County Courthouse, built to replace one in Berkley. Designed by William R. Singleton, who may have had some involvement with the Norfolk City Hall, the building is raised on a high basement with a tetrastyle Tuscan portico facing High Street. The columns are composed of granite bases, brick shafts, and sandstone capitals. Similarly arranged pilasters articulate all but the rear wall of the building. A flight of stairs once led to an entrance in antis on Court Street, but the entrance was moved to the High Street portico when the courthouse was remodeled to accommodate municipal courts after the city's incorporation in 1858. The pediment of the portico and the cylindrical Ionic cupola that crowns the roofline were recreated as part of the restoration of the building in the early 1980s, following the departure of the county and municipal courts. The building currently serves as the Arts Center of the Portsmouth Museums.

PO11 Commodore Theater

1945, John J. Zink. 1987–1989, renovation. 421 High St.

An excellent example of the Streamline Moderne style of the 1940s, the Commodore Theater is downtown Portsmouth's last active motion picture theater. Designed by a Baltimore architect who designed theaters for the Wilder chain, the Commodore has a limestone and brick facade resembling that of Norfolk's Arena Municipal Auditorium, especially in the use of vertically slit windows of glass block. Most of the exterior details survive intact, including the marquee, the illuminated poster cases, and the curving ticket booth. The interior was renovated in the late 1980s to accommodate nightclub-style seating in the orchestra, although theater seats were retained in the balcony. At the same time, side murals depicting local and national progress painted by R.

PO6 Bangel Law Building

PO9 Pythian Castle

PO11 Commodore Theater

S. Tanek of the Paramount Decorating Company, also of Baltimore, were cleaned, restored, and embellished by artist James Nelson Johnson.

PO12 Monumental United Methodist Church

1873–1876, Albert L. West. 1954–1955, chapel and education building. 450 Dinwiddie St.

Methodism was first established in southeastern Virginia in 1772 under the auspices of the Methodist Society in the Norfolk-Portsmouth circuit. The church occupied two other sites in Portsmouth before the current location was purchased in 1831. A brick church, housing both white and black congregations, was erected two years later, but in 1856–1857 the latter group built its own house of worship, eventually affiliating with the African Methodist Episcopal Church. The present building was erected in 1873–1876 to the designs of Albert L. West, a practicing Methodist who received numerous commissions from congregations throughout Virginia and North Carolina. West's Gothic structure looks back to the decades of the 1840s and 1850s and specifically to Thomas U. Walter's Gothic Revival Freemason Street Baptist Church in Norfolk. The stucco-over-brick church is oriented east to west with a central tower and steeple facing Dinwiddie Street. Attached buttresses alternate with lancet windows along the nave.

PO13 St. Paul's Roman Catholic Church

1897, Carpenter and Peebles. 1913, rectory, J. F. Donohoe. 518 High St.

The area's most elaborate Roman Catholic Church indicates the financial strength of Portsmouth's Catholic population at the turn of the twentieth century. Designed in the Ralph Adams Cram–inspired academic Gothic manner that eventually supplanted the earlier and more experimental Victorian Gothic style, the rock-faced granite and limestone church is essentially a small version of a medieval cathedral. The focal point of the main facade is an enormous southwest tower whose steeple is supported by flying buttresses. A single flying buttress continues the line of the main gable to the left aisle at the northwest corner. At the center of the facade is a deep portal framed by colonnettes and surmounted by a carved tympanum that depicts the Agony in the Garden. A rhythmic progression of clerestory and aisle windows articulates the nave, and polygonal bays terminate the transept arms and apse.

PO14 Central Methodist Church

c. 1901–1903, attributed to James E. R. Carpenter. 1914, Sunday school addition, Benjamin F. Mitchell. Northwest corner of South and Washington sts.

A comparison between this church and St. Paul's reveals the enormous divergence in ecclesiastical taste that occurred at the turn of the twentieth century. Whereas St. Paul's is monochromatic with academic detailing in the latest fashion, this eclectic Victorian Gothic-Romanesque church is polychromed and inventively detailed, but somewhat old fashioned for the time. Florentine arches with exaggerated voussoirs are used around the exterior, while the checkered patterns of brownstone and granite in the tower and gables are especially vivid. Originally built for the congregation of Central Methodist Church, in its cross-in-square plan with corner tower the building closely follows Carpenter and Peebles's design for Epworth United Methodist Church in Norfolk.

Olde Towne Portsmouth (PO15–PO21)
(Map, p. 443)

This residential neighborhood of about twenty blocks on the north side of downtown contains many fine examples of eighteenth-, nineteenth-, and twentieth-century architecture. The federally assisted Olde Towne Conservation Project, initiated in 1968, prevented the widespread demolition of housing that took place on the south side of Portsmouth's downtown.

PO15 Benthall Brooks Row

c. 1840–1850. 415–421 Crawford St.

These three brick Greek Revival town houses were built as a group by an early real estate speculator, a Captain Brooks. Because of the site's high water table, each house is raised on a high basement. The upper floors follow a traditional side-passage plan. Doric porticos shield the front entrances.

PO16 Pass House

c. 1841–1842. 422 Crawford St.

Similar to the houses of Benthall Brooks Row, the Pass House is a two-and-one-half-story brick Greek Revival town house raised on a high basement with a side-passage plan. The corner house has two Doric porticoes on the first level: one on the left side of the Crawford Street elevation and one in the center of the London Street elevation. The staircase is visible just a few inches behind the sashes of the left windows on the London Street side. "Pass" is not a former occupant's name—the original owner was James Murdough, an attorney—but a nickname from the Civil War, when the house was occupied by the federal adjutant general's office and residents were required to secure passes for movement in and out of the city.

PO17 Olde Towne Inn

c. 1885. c. 1985–1990, restoration and porch addition. 420 Middle St.

The asymmetrical front elevation of this two-story brick Italianate town house balances the main entrance to the right, behind an ornate wooden portico, with a two-story polygonal window bay to the left. Elegant brackets punctuate the cornice. The side elevation facing London Street has a particularly handsome cast and wrought iron porch on the ground level. The second porch level, constructed of wood, is a later addition. Built for Joseph Bourke, a prominent Portsmouth resident, it has been converted to a bed-and-breakfast inn.

PO18 Nivison-Ball House

c. 1780. 1869, relocation. 417 Middle St.

Originally constructed at Crawford and Glasgow Street, this wood-frame late Georgian house was sold to John Nivison in 1784. It was moved one block to its present location in 1869, after which it was occupied by the Ball family. The symmetrical facade is five bays across with a central entrance behind a simple portico on the first level. The second level is tucked beneath a gambrel roof with a dentiled cornice along the eaves.

PO19 Nash-Gill House

c. 1885. 370 Middle St.

Exuberantly Victorian, this house combines a variety of idioms. The focal point is a tower whose base forms the front entrance and whose top is crowned by a mansard roof. Although the remaining elements of the east elevation are arranged symmetrically around the tower, the picturesque view from the southeast includes a two-story, polygonal window bay and decorative millwork at the apex of the principal gable. The front porch is particularly elaborate: chamfered posts sprout millwork along the top, and quatrefoil railings lend an ecclesiastical touch.

PO20 Hill House Museum

c. 1807. c. 1820–1830, portico addition. c. 1850, hyphen and interior remodeling. c. 1900–1910, dormers and rear porch. 1974, restoration. 221 North St. Open to the public

The rapid shifts in nineteenth-century architectural taste are well represented in the Hill House Museum. Built for Colonel John Thompson and later the home of his adopted son, John Thompson Hill, and his descendants, this was initially a two-and-one-half-story, side-passage Federal town house on a high base-

PO16 Pass House

PO19 Nash-Gill House

ment with a freestanding two-story kitchen at the rear. A Greek Revival portico was added to the main entrance around 1820. The interior of the house was remodeled in the Italianate mode at mid-century with elaborate plasterwork and mantelpieces. The staircase layout was retained in the remodeling, but ornate balusters and wide railings were installed. One section of the delicate Federal railing remains near the top, providing a rather vivid contrast. Probably at mid-century the main house and the kitchen were joined at the first level above the basement. Finally, around 1900, dormers were added to the roof to give the house a quasi-colonial appearance. Converted to a museum under the auspices of the Portsmouth

Historical Association, it is presented as a mid-twentieth-century house representing the period when the last members of the Hill family lived there.

PO21 Grice-Neely House

c. 1820. c. 1968, restoration. 202 North St.

Raised on a high basement, the Grice-Neely House is unusual in that its principal entrance is on the east side of the house, away from North Street. The entrance is sheltered by a Doric portico and reached by a flight of stone stairs. The relatively plain exterior of the main facade is relieved by an elegant cast and wrought iron balcony, with a pattern of stylized lilies, on the first level above the basement.

Naval Portsmouth   (PO22–PO24)

PO22 U.S. Naval Hospital

1826–1828, John Haviland. c. 1898, south wing addition. 1906–1910, renovation and additions, Wood, Donn and Deming. 1999, restoration in progress, Shriver, Holland, and Associates. Naval Medical Center, Hospital Point

The navy has maintained a continuous presence in Portsmouth since the eighteenth century. Built when the bureaucracy of the federal government was just beginning to expand, the original building of the U.S. Naval Hospital at Portsmouth has proven its adaptability through more than 170 years of continuous service. The Greek Revival hospital occupies the former site of Fort Nelson, an eighteenth-century stronghold across the Elizabeth River from Fort Norfolk. As the only institutional building of its era to take advantage of the riverfront, the hospital serves as a monumental gateway to the cities of Portsmouth and Norfolk.

The origins of the hospital date to the turn of the nineteenth century. In 1798 the U.S. Congress established the Marine Hospital Service in preparation for the construction of a hospital near the Norfolk Naval Shipyard. The hospital was originally located in Berkley, across the south branch of the Elizabeth River. When the site of Fort Nelson became available following the construction of Forts Monroe and Wool downriver at Hampton Roads (see entry on Fort Monroe in the Hampton Roads section), a decision was made to build a new hospital at Portsmouth. John Haviland, a well-established British-born Philadelphia architect with significant experience in the design of institutional buildings, received the commission. Although well versed in more picturesque and romantic idioms, Haviland selected an archaic Doric mode for the hospital. The main facade is distinguished by an unusually wide decastyle pedimented portico with unfluted columns of Virginia freestone. The sides and rear of the building once enclosed a courtyard. The state-of-the-art design included such features as exterior wooden galleries for maximum ventilation and interior chambers spanned by fireproof brick vaults. During the Civil War the Confederates captured the hospital and briefly held it, renaming it Fort Nelson. When the Union recaptured it in 1863, it was pressed into service as a U.S. Army field hospital before being returned to the navy. At the turn of the twentieth century the hospital underwent major reconstruction, beginning with the addition of a south wing. The rear of the building was subsequently reconfigured, and a shallow dome on an octagonal drum was added to the portico. A new seventeen-story hospital was erected to the south between 1955 and 1960 (Skidmore, Owings and Merrill with Hayes, Seay, Mattern and Mattern).

Its crisp International Style profile of perpendicular slabs harmonizes surprisingly well with the original building. A postmodern addition to the new hospital, the Charette Health Care Center (1989–1999, HDR Architects), now provides a rather unfortunate interruption between the two older buildings. Haviland also designed a neoclassical funerary monument in front of the hospital (1828) over the grave of Major John Saunders, who once commanded both Fort Nelson and Fort Norfolk.

PO23 Norfolk Naval Shipyard

1767–. Lincoln and 1st sts.

The Norfolk Naval Shipyard is the nation's oldest and most venerable facility for shipbuilding and repair. Established under King George III in 1767 as the Gosport Shipyard, Virginia usurped it during the American Revolution. It was leased to the U.S. Navy in 1794, purchased outright in 1801, and enlarged in the decades following the War of 1812. The shipyard was burned twice during the Civil War: first by fleeing Union troops and then by fleeing Confederate troops. Between the two conflagrations, Confederate shipbuilders covered the charred remnants of the frigate *U.S.S. Merrimac* with iron plates and rechristened it the *C.S.S. Virginia*, a bold maneuver that, however briefly, provided the South with an unrivaled naval advantage. In the years since the Civil War the shipyard has been expanded and modernized continuously and is still in active service.

Only Trophy Park, a greensward filled with military hardware on the north side of the shipyard, is open regularly to the public via trolley tours that leave from the Portsmouth Visitor Information Center (High Street Landing). Visible on the perimeter of the park are Quarters A, B, and C (c. 1837–1842), Greek Revival houses adapted from Asher Benjamin's *Practical House Carpenter* (1830). Quarters A still serves as the residence of the shipyard commandant. This section of the shipyard is surrounded by a brick wall designed by John Haviland in 1831; closed Confederate embrasures may be seen on its exterior. Unfortunately, Dry Dock 1 (1827–1834), the oldest dry dock in the western hemisphere, is not open to the public because it is still in active use. Historic and didactic exhibits related to the shipyard and a restored lightship may be found at the Naval Shipyard Museum (2 High Street).

PO24 Cradock Historic District and Truxtun Historic District

Cradock: 1918, George B. Post and Sons. Site bounded by George Washington Hwy., Victory Blvd., and Paradise Creek.

Truxtun: 1918, Rossell Edward Mitchell. Vicinity of Portsmouth Blvd. and Deep Creek Blvd., including Manly St., Hobson St., and Dewey St.

Designed under the auspices of the U.S. Housing Corporation, Cradock and Truxtun were among the numerous planned communities built along the East Coast to house shipyard workers and their families during World War I (see Hilton Village, Newport News, in the Hampton Roads section). As such they represented the federal government's initial foray into public housing and community design, incorporating some of the most advanced garden

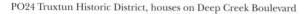
PO24 Truxtun Historic District, houses on Deep Creek Boulevard

city principles imported from Great Britain. All of the communities were transferred to private ownership by the early 1920s.

Both Cradock and Truxtun are within a short drive of the Norfolk Naval Shipyard along routes once served by streetcars. The former is named for British Rear Admiral Sir Christopher G. F. W. Cradock, a World War I naval hero, and the latter for Thomas Truxtun, an American naval officer at the turn of the nineteenth century. Although one large community probably would have sufficed, federal policy required that separate residential areas be constructed for white and for black workers.

Cradock, the white community, has a more elaborate plan, more spacious houses, and more institutional and commercial amenities. The centerpiece of the design is Afton Parkway, a greensward perpendicular to George Washington Highway and flanked symmetrically by substantial houses, churches, and schools. Afton Parkway leads to a public square with a quaint wooden bandstand at its center and a perimeter lined with shops and a movie theater. The style of the commercial buildings and the residences is Colonial Revival, but with enough picturesque touches to create varied streetscapes, many of them curved. While single-family frame houses predominate, there are terrace blocks along many of the side streets. Portsmouth annexed Cradock in 1960.

Truxtun was the only one of the U.S. Housing Corporation's communities to be designed expressly for black shipyard workers. Although its largely rectangular plan covers one-third the area of Cradock's and lacks many of the amenities of the latter community, its architecture is no less distinguished. Single- and two-family Craftsman houses, with a variety of porch and roof treatments that include triangular and jerkinhead gables, create a pleasant rhythmic effect down the long blocks.

Virginia Beach (VB)

T HE COMMONWEALTH'S LARGEST CITY (2000 POPULATION, 425,257), VIRginia Beach was formed in 1963 from the merger of the then smaller city of Virginia Beach with the surrounding county of Princess Anne. What had been a summer resort strip along the Atlantic Ocean with farmland to the west has become a sprawling, yearround Edge City with its own recreational, residential, retail, military, and service sector nodes, but as yet no downtown to give it a truly urban identity. The southern half of the city, bordering North Carolina, remains agricultural.

The entries begin in the populous northern section of the city, move eastward to Cape Henry, then continue through the densely developed resort strip along the oceanfront, and terminate in the rural section to the south.

VB1 Francis Land House Historic Site and Garden

c. 1780–1810. c. 1912, roof raised. c. 1920–1930, window alteration and rear porch addition. c. 1954, entrance hood addition and interior renovation. 1986–present, restoration. 3131 Virginia Beach Blvd. Open to the public

Until the mid-twentieth century, this late Georgian house was at the center of an active farm. Now it is a house museum completely surrounded by commercial and residential development. Built in the late eighteenth century for either Francis Land V or Francis Land VI, planters from a well-established Princess Anne County family, the house is five bays across with a center-passage plan. The walls are constructed of Flemish bond brick without a water table. Around 1912 the gambrel roof was raised

to its present height; during the 1920s, the window openings were widened on the main facade, and a wooden porch was added to the rear. The pedimented hood over the front entrance dates from the mid-twentieth century, when the house was converted to a dress shop. Some original paneling survives on the interior, most notably in the dining room. The house is gradually being restored and furnished.

VB2 Old Donation Episcopal Church

1736. 1822–1824, renovation. 1913–1916, restoration and additions, James W. Lee. 1966, restoration, Milton Grigg with Oliver and Smith. 4449 N. Witchduck Rd.

The unusual name of this colonial church stems from the donation of land to the parish

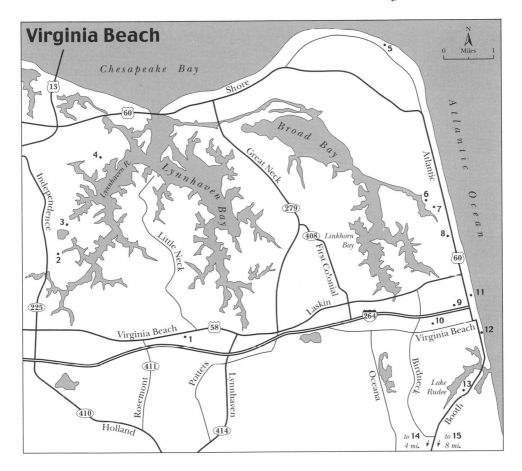

Virginia Beach

by Reverend Robert Dickson, a former rector. Built in 1736, the present building is the third church of the Lynnhaven Parish, which was established before 1640. With several modifications, the eighteenth-century church served its parishioners through disestablishment and, following repairs in 1822–1824, until 1843, when it was abandoned. An 1882 fire gutted the structure, leaving only the Flemish bond brick walls standing. Popular interest in the ruined church grew steadily, and in the second decade of the twentieth century, it was restored to its present exterior appearance.

The plan of the church is a simple rectangle oriented west to east. The entrance has been altered by the addition of an enclosed porch and the southeast corner by a small sacristy, but the other walls and wall openings are original. The fenestration of the side walls is particularly interesting, for it reveals, in addition to the usual round-arched windows, odd-sized rectangular openings near the eaves that indicate the placement of long-vanished galleries. The heavily restored, early twentieth-century interior incorporates a reredos, an altar, a pulpit, a lectern, and a communion rail taken from St. Paul's Episcopal Church in Norfolk (see entry), then undergoing its own restoration. The interior was restored again in the 1960s when the current pews were installed.

VB3 Lynnhaven House

1724–1725. 1971–1976, restoration. 4405 Wishart Rd. Open to the public

Built for Francis Thelabell III and his wife Abigail in the early eighteenth century, the Lynnhaven House is a remarkably well-preserved farmer's dwelling. Its vernacular late medieval design seems to indicate resistance in the lower Tidewater to the academic Georgian manner then emerging in other parts of the colony. The one-and-one-half-story house derives its current name from a nearby branch of the Lynnhaven River. Its construction date has been confirmed by dendrochronological analysis. The house exterior is constructed of brick laid in an English bond with a water table a few feet above ground level and massive end chimneys that rise in several stages. Near symmetry characterizes the southwest or principal elevation. Three bays wide, it has a central door flanked by windows on the first level; however, the three dormer windows in the gabled roof do not align with the openings below them. The northeast, or rear, elevation is asymmetrically balanced, with two dormer windows in the roof and a door and a window unevenly spaced on the first level; the rear door once led to an attached buttery that has been demolished. The conformity of the exterior in virtually every respect to sixteenth- and seventeenth-century English prototypes guided the restoration during the 1970s of the shake roof, the diamond-paned windows, and the wooden exterior stairs.

The interior follows a hall-and-parlor arrangement, with the parlor in the larger of the two spaces. The main entrance opens directly into the parlor, which is lit by front and rear windows and heated by a large hearth. Joiners' chalk marks are still visible in the exposed wooden ceiling, while an L-shaped, closed-string staircase, with most of its original components intact, fills the north corner. On the other side of the first-floor partition, the hall is conveniently ventilated by a window and a door flanking the expansive cooking hearth, a window at the front, and the door to the parlor. Two partitions on the upper level separate the end chambers from the staircase between them.

Just enough of the surrounding forest and open fields of the former Thelabell estate survives to suggest the once-rustic setting. The house is maintained by the APVA and is furnished with period pieces and reproductions.

VB4　Adam Thoroughgood House

c. 1680. c. 1720, interior renovation. 1922–1926, window alterations, front and rear steps. 1957–1960, restoration, Finlay F. Ferguson, Jr. 1636 Parish Rd. Open to the public

Long assigned a construction date of 1636 that ranked it among America's oldest colonial residences, the Thoroughgood House is now thought to have been built about fifty years later and to have undergone significant interior renovations in the first quarter of the eigh-

teenth century. The complex fabric of the house, altered further during the course of two twentieth-century restorations, has yet to be fully deciphered, and its changing interpretation reflects ongoing research into early colonial architecture.

From the exterior, the one-and-one-half-story house is slightly larger than, but remarkably similar in appearance to, the Lynnhaven House, which at one time would have been considered a close neighbor to the south along the Western Branch of the Lynnhaven River. The construction of the former, however, incorporates several subtleties lacking in the latter. The west, or land, facade of the Thoroughgood House is constructed of brick laid in Flemish bond, while the remaining walls are laid in English bond; a water table surrounds the house a few feet above ground level. Both the west and east facades are nearly symmetrical, each with a center door flanked by windows. The north chimney is contained within its end wall, but the south chimney projects boldly, rising in several stages. Dormer windows once punctuated the gable roof, but they were removed in a 1950s restoration. The sash windows from a previous Colonial Revival remodeling were also removed at this time and replaced by diamond-paned casements, and an exterior door in the southeast corner next to the chimney was converted to a window.

The interior was initially organized according to a hall-and-chamber plan, with both east and west entrances opening into the larger space of the hall. Traces of the original partition may be seen on the ceiling above the west entrance. An enclosed staircase probably occupied the northeast corner of the parlor. A staircase was inserted into a newly built center passage around 1720. This alteration involved reducing the size of the hall by erecting a south partition and moving the old partition northward by about a foot. Structural damage visible in the joists at the west eaves may have resulted from the shift in what must have been a load-bearing wall. The paneling in the center passage and the parlor may date from this renovation as well. A single partition divides the upper level.

The purported date of 1636 was attached to the house in the early twentieth century, when it was thought to have been the residence of Adam Thoroughgood, a planter and burgess who had purchased the surrounding tract the previous year and named the nearby river after his birthplace, King's Lynn, Norfolk County,

VB4 Adam Thoroughgood House

VB5 Old Cape Henry Lighthouse

England. The house may actually have been built by his grandson, who was also named Adam. Restored in 1957–1960 by the Adam Thoroughgood Foundation, the house was donated to the city of Norfolk in 1961 and is currently administered by the Virginia Beach Department of Tourism and the Chrysler Museum of Art. High-style period furnishings are displayed in the rooms. The formal garden on the east side of the house is based on seventeenth-century English models and was planted by the Garden Club of Virginia.

VB5 Old Cape Henry Lighthouse

1791–1792, John McComb, Jr. 1841, lantern reconstruction. 1857, lens replacement. 1867, brick shaft lining and iron staircase. 1881, decommissioned. Fort Story, Cape Henry Dr. and Atlantic Ave. (enter at east gate, 89th St. and Atlantic Ave.). Open to the public

The first colonists landed at Cape Henry in 1607, but it would be more than 180 years before a permanent lighthouse was erected to guide ships safely into the mouth of the Chesapeake Bay. Governor Alexander Spotswood was the first to recommend construction of a lighthouse on the site. In 1789 the First Congress of the United States enacted legislation that created the lighthouse service and gave the Cape Henry project priority status. Virginia conveyed the two-acre site to the federal government later that year, and in the spring of 1791, John Mc-

Comb, Jr., best known as one of the architects of New York's City Hall (1802–1811), was awarded a contract to build the lighthouse. Based on Delaware's Cape Henlopen Lighthouse (1767; destroyed 1924), the Cape Henry Lighthouse consists of a tapered octagonal shaft of dressed stone with east- and west-facing windows. Like its predecessor in Delaware, the lighthouse was situated atop a large dune for greater visibility. McComb's contract also called for the erection of a wooden keeper's cottage and an underground oil storage vault. Despite the necessity of sinking the foundations of the lighthouse deeper than expected, work proceeded quickly, and the 92-foot-high landmark was operational by October 1792. After visiting the lighthouse in 1798, Benjamin Henry Latrobe described it as "solid," but criticized its interior wooden staircase as a potential fire hazard.

The lighthouse guided ships past Cape Henry through most of the nineteenth century, aided by several modifications, including its lantern, lens, and a new tower shaft. Concerns first expressed in an 1872 inspection about its stability eventually led to its replacement. Between 1875 and 1881, a new 157-foot lighthouse of cast and wrought iron, containing more powerful lamps, was constructed 350 feet southeast of the original structure. Access to the old lighthouse was given to the APVA, which placed a tablet commemorating the landing of the first colonists at is base in 1896; it was deeded to the association in 1930.

VB6 Greystone Manor

1906–1908, Arnold E. Eberhard. 515 Wilder Point

Constructed at a time when Virginia Beach was a small coastal resort, Greystone Manor initiated the fashion for large, upper-class summer residences in the area. The house was built for John W. Miller-Masury, heir to a paint manufacturing fortune, and named Lakeside. During the mid-1930s it was leased to the Crystal Club, one of the Beach's most popular entertainment venues. The house was returned to residential use in 1942, when it was purchased by William S. Wilder, the owner of a local theater chain (see Commodore Theater, Portsmouth), who renamed it Greystone Manor. The Queen Anne design of the L-shaped house creates a multitude of picturesque perspectives from land and from Crystal Lake, an inlet to the west. Slate wall shingles and masonry are skillfully juxtaposed with a variety of chimneys, gables, door and window openings, and porches, while a three-story castellated tower creates a focal point on the waterfront.

VB7 Cooke House

1951–1960, Frank Lloyd Wright. c. 1985, restoration. 320 51st St.

The Cooke House is one of only three houses designed by Frank Lloyd Wright in the commonwealth and the least known of the group. Dr. Andrew B. Cooke, a dentist, and his wife, Maude, commissioned a house from Wright in 1951; however, construction did not begin until just before the architect's death in 1959. Although Wright evidently never visited the site, the resulting design demonstrates his trademark balance between natural and built environments. The house is perched on a small bluff overlooking Crystal Lake, its public areas taking full advantage of its southwestern exposure. From the driveway, the northeast side of the house, mostly tan brick, ensures its inhabitants' privacy.

A Usonian design from the end of Wright's lengthy career, the house incorporates such familiar elements as radiant-slab heating, built-in furniture, clerestory windows, a hipped roof, and a carport. What distinguishes this house from other Usonian examples is its unusual plan, which, quixotically, forms a question mark. It is oriented so that the indoor living-dining area and the outdoor patio together form a quadrant; French doors give a sense of unbro-

VB8 Cavalier Hotel

ken space between the two. Although never built, a spectacular circular plunge pool was intended for the focal point of the quadrant, with cascades of water overflowing to Crystal Lake. Sleeping areas are located in the plan's "stem," and a servant's room, separated by an angular carport, fills the "period" at the plan's bottom. On a formal level, the house—contemporaneous with the Guggenheim Museum (1943–1959)—indicates Wright's fascination with interlocking geometric shapes, in particular the circle with its many cosmic implications. On a conceptual level, the house is an enduring monument to the interrogative process out of which all architecture is created. The Cooke House remains a private residence, and it is screened from the street by thick vegetation.

VB8 Cavalier Hotel

1925–1927, Neff and Thompson. 1976 to present, renovation. 42nd St. and Atlantic Ave.

The seven-story Cavalier Hotel is Virginia Beach's most prominent landmark and an opulent reminder of luxury travel in the first half of the twentieth century. Constructed during the boom years of the 1920s with funds raised by public subscription, the hotel was evidently positioned to compete with other, more established resorts in the commonwealth and along the Atlantic Seaboard. What set the Cavalier Hotel apart from its competitors was the distinct beauty of its oceanfront setting, which at the time of its construction was sparsely developed. Even today the hotel maintains a commanding, isolated position on a large, beauti-

VB11 Old Coast Guard Station

A serene East Asian feeling pervades the design of this templelike building dedicated to contemporary art. White brick with granite accents is used for the exterior wall surfaces, and dark-stained wood surrounds the doors and windows. An extended, hip-roofed entrance canopy draws the visitor toward the generously proportioned interior spaces, including offices, galleries, an auditorium, and a central, two-story enclosed court.

VB10 Pavilion Convention Center

1975–1981, Walshe and Ashe with Odell Associates, Inc. 1000 19th St.

The Pavilion Convention Center was conceived during the 1970s as part of a strategy to develop a year-round market for Virginia Beach's many oceanfront hotel rooms. Positioned prominently at the end of the Virginia Beach–Norfolk Expressway, the building was also intended to serve as a kind of monumental gateway to the resort strip. The resulting design is a highly serviceable if somewhat uninspired reworking of Louis Kahn's Kimbell Art Museum (1966–1972) in Forth Worth, Texas. Ten white, steel-framed barrel vaults with end walls of dark-tinted glass unfurl rhythmically along the south side of the highway, effectively screening the rectangular exhibition halls and 1,000-seat theater from view. The main entrance faces the parking lot on the rear elevation. From this perspective, the unfenestrated walls of precast concrete panels appear particularly dreary.

VB11 Old Coast Guard Station

1903, George R. Tolman. 1933, renovation and expansion.1979, reorientation. 1980–1981, restoration, Melvin M. Spence and Associates. 24th St. and the Oceanfront. Open to the public

Following the Civil War an increase in shipping accidents along the nation's coastal and inland waterways prompted the federal government to establish the U.S. Lifesaving Service. Of the many stations erected along the Virginia coast, this building, formerly known as the Seatack Lifesaving Station, is one of the few that survives. "Seatack" is a slang contraction used locally to refer to the British "sea attack" during the War of 1812. Architect George L. Tolman developed the prototype design for the station—dubbed "the Quonochontaug" after a Rhode Island beach—in 1891, and it was used

fully landscaped hill that slopes gently down to the beach across Atlantic Avenue. Designed by the Norfolk firm of Neff and Thompson, the building is distinguished by the use of Jeffersonian details on its exterior, tying it visually to some of Virginia's most esteemed architectural landmarks. The approach to the hotel's northern entrance is framed by serpentine walls that mimic the enclosed gardens of the University of Virginia, and the entrance pavilion is a variation on the east portico of Monticello. The three wings of the Y-shaped building, crowned at their juncture by an ornamental cupola, provide guest rooms with maximum exposure to the ocean. Among the generously appointed public spaces are an oval, Adamesque outer lobby; an indoor swimming pool; and long sun porches.

Until the end of World War II the Cavalier Hotel was Virginia Beach's premier hostelry, attracting such luminaries as Zelda and Scott Fitzgerald, Mary Pickford, and Will Rogers. After the war, however, competition from motels that catered more effectively to middle-class families diminished the business of older hotels. In response, a modern hotel, the Cavalier Oceanfront (1974, Shriver and Holland and Associates), was constructed across Atlantic Avenue, next to the site of the hotel's beach club, and the old building was closed for several seasons. The historic structure has since reopened, and renovations are ongoing.

VB9 Contemporary Art Center of Virginia

1983–1989, E. Verner Johnson and Associates. 2200 Parks Ave. Open to the public

for more than twenty stations erected for the Lifesaving Service around the country. The Shingle Style building once contained offices and storage for rescue boats on the ground level and dormitory space on the upper level, beneath the gently sloping roof with dormer windows. A four-story lookout tower, added in 1933, forms the focal point of the asymmetrical main facade. Prior to the station's refurbishment as a museum in 1981, it was moved about 100 feet and reoriented 90 degrees to allow construction of an adjacent hotel.

VB12 Atlantic Wildfowl Heritage Museum

1895. 1990–1995, restoration. 12th St. and the Oceanfront. Open to the public

This simple Foursquare house with some Queen Anne details is the sole remaining oceanfront residence in the heavily developed southern section of the resort strip. Constructed of brick with wooden trim, the house is wrapped on three sides by porches supported by bracketed posts, and it is crowned by an open belvedere. Built in 1895 for Bernard Peabody Holland, Virginia Beach's first mayor, it was purchased after the turn of the twentieth century by the de Witt family, who lived there until 1988. The house has been converted to a museum with exhibits on wildfowl and wildfowl art.

VB13 Virginia Marine Science Museum

1982–1986, Shriver and Holland with E. Verner Johnson Associates. 1994–1996, remodeling and expansion, E. Verner Johnson and Associates. 717 General Booth Blvd.

The short-lived deconstructivist movement of the early 1990s inspired the exterior of this delightfully sculptural building. Positioned on a narrow strip of land between General Booth Boulevard and Owl Creek, the museum resembles a large and colorful container ship pulling into dock. The focal point of the entrance driveway is a dramatically suspended steel canopy that shields a swimming pool for seals, giving the visitor a glimpse of the many live exhibits within the building. Splashing fountains line the entrance walk to the right; to the left, the enormous concrete bulk of the museum's theater is relieved by brightly colored, corrugated metal panels and stainless steel buttresses that support a six-story IMAX projection screen. Together, the combination of colors and shapes communicates abstractly the excitement of scientific discovery. Although a relatively young institution, the museum is already one of the commonwealth's most popular tourist attractions. Another major expansion is in the planning stage.

VB14 Nimmo United Methodist Church

1864. 1893–1894, steeple. c. 1945–1965, c. 1990, additions. 2200 Princess Anne Rd.

This Italianate church was built on the foundations of its late eighteenth-century predecessor, which had burned. Despite later additions that have cluttered the exterior, the main body of the wood-frame church is still visible. A projecting western tower and steeple are joined to a rectangular nave with bracketed cornices. The church is named for Anne Nimmo, who deeded the property to the church in 1791.

VB15 Pleasant Ridge Elementary School

c. 1880–1890. 1918, division and relocation. 1990–1996, renovation. 1392 Princess Anne Rd.

Before World War II most of Princess Anne County resembled the rural enclave of Pleasant Ridge, which surrounds this vernacular one-room schoolhouse. Built at the end of the nineteenth century as a two-room school for white children in another part of the county, it was divided around World War I so that the larger of the two rooms could be moved to Pleasant Ridge for the education of the area's African American children. The school closed in 1956. Although the building is not generally open to the public, the simple interior may be viewed easily through its multipaned windows.

Southern Tidewater (ST)

THE AREA SOUTH OF THE JAMES RIVER, SOMETIMES CALLED THE SOUTHern Tidewater, includes the cities of Chesapeake and Suffolk and the counties of Isle of Wight, Southampton, Surry, and Prince George. The cities of Chesapeake and Suffolk are really municipal counties covering large land areas. The City of Chesapeake, formed in 1963, takes in the former Norfolk County and city of South Norfolk. The City of Suffolk, created in 1974, takes in the former Nansemond County.

The terrain is very flat and is drained by many rivers, lakes, and inlets. Part of both Suffolk and Chesapeake are covered by the Great Dismal Swamp, 200,000 acres of forested peat, a western portion of which in 1974 became the 107,000-acre Great Dismal Swamp National Wildlife Refuge. The English settled the area early. Some of Virginia's most important and venerable buildings of the seventeenth century are here, including Bacon's Castle and St. Luke's Church. By the late eighteenth and the nineteenth century, the soil was exhausted, and many families left. In the late nineteenth century new crops and enterprises appeared: peanuts, timber, and pig farming. Along the James at Hopewell, another industry, munitions, became a staple in the early twentieth century. This development has led to some rejuvenation, but great portions of the area remain rural and agricultural. They retain an air of time passed by. At the east, extensive suburban development, a spillover from Virginia Beach, is taking place in Chesapeake.

City of Chesapeake   (ST1–ST6)

ST1 Chesapeake (South Norfolk) Historic District

Bounded by the Norfolk and Western tracks on the east, Lakeside Park and Truitt Junior High School on the south, Bainbridge Blvd. on the west, and an irregular edge from Poindexter St. to 16th St. on the north

South Norfolk originated as a streetcar suburb of Norfolk, became an independent town in 1919, and then in 1963 joined Norfolk County in forming the City of Chesapeake. South Norfolk became known as Chesapeake. This area contains the highest concentration of historic structures in the City of Chesapeake and retains a distinct identity. The residential neighborhoods along Chesapeake, Rogers, and D streets are characterized by single-family dwellings uniformly set back from the street on well-shaded lots that were originally 25 feet in width. Houses represent the usual variety of pattern-book styles from 1880–1920. An exuberant example of the Queen Anne style can be seen in the two-and-one-half-story Rogers-Cuthrell House (ST1.1) (c. 1900; 1146 Rogers Street), which utilizes concrete block on the first story. The source for the design may be Knoxville, Tennessee, architect George P. Barber's various publications. The usual tower is attached, while at ground level, the porch is supported by classically inspired tapered columns.

The Dorothy Truitt Junior High School (South Norfolk High School) (1929, Benjamin F. Mitchell and Randolph, Cooke and Van Leeuwen; 1100 Holly Street, corner of Holly and Rogers streets) is a tame neoclassical design, of brick with almost flush cast stone details: water table, wall niches, pilasters, and entrance surrounds.

ST2 Portlock Public School (C. C. Walton School)

c. 1908, Ferguson and Calrow; 1995, remodeling, Hanbury Evans Newill Vlattas. 3815 Bainbridge Blvd. Open to the public

A modest example of Colonial Revival public schools built in Virginia during the early twentieth century, the single-story, two-classroom building gains distinction from its pedimented portico, supported by paired Tuscan columns. It now serves as a local museum and visitor center.

ST1.1 Rogers-Cuthrell House

ST2 Portlock Public School (C. C. Walton School)

ST3 Albemarle and Chesapeake Canal

1855–1859, 1873, 1932, 1973. From the Southern Branch of the Elizabeth River at Great Bridge to the North Landing River at the Chesapeake–Virginia Beach city limits. Canal and locks visible from Great Bridge Locks Park, west end of Locks Rd.

Built in competition with the Dismal Swamp Canal (see next entry), the 8-mile long, 12-foot deep, 90-foot wide Albemarle and Chesapeake Canal connects the Southern Branch of the Elizabeth River to the North Landing River in Virginia and ultimately to Albemarle Sound in North Carolina. The canal is an important part of the Atlantic Intracoastal Waterway (AIW).

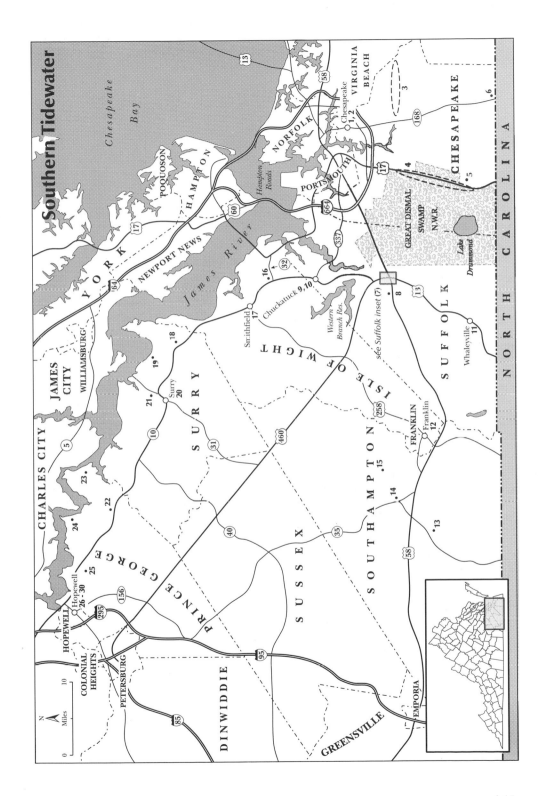

Southern Tidewater

Chesapeake Bay

Hampton Roads

James River

YORK

CHARLES CITY

JAMES CITY

WILLIAMSBURG

POQUOSON

HAMPTON

NEWPORT NEWS

SURRY

Surry
20

Smithfield
17

Chuckatuck **9,10**

Western Branch Res.

ISLE OF WIGHT

see Suffolk inset (7)

NORFOLK

PORTSMOUTH

Chesapeake
1,2

VIRGINIA BEACH

CHESAPEAKE

GREAT DISMAL SWAMP N.W.R.

Lake Drummond

SUFFOLK

Whaleville
11

Franklin
12

SOUTHAMPTON

SUSSEX

PRINCE GEORGE

Hopewell
26–30

COLONIAL HEIGHTS

PETERSBURG

DINWIDDIE

GREENSVILLE

EMPORIA

NORTH CAROLINA

• 16
• 18
• 19
21. •
• 23.
24. •
• 22
25. •
• 13
• 14
.15
258
• 3
4
• 5
.6
8   13
32
5
10
31
40
460
35
58
85
95
295
156
13
58
168
117
17
664
337
60
64
7
17

N
Miles
0   10

461

The canal, completed in 1859 by a private company, runs west to east. Since the Albemarle and Chesapeake Canal is wider and deeper than the Dismal Swamp Canal, it carries almost all commercial traffic along the AIW as well as recreational craft that are too large for the other canal. A survey for the canal was authorized by the Virginia legislature in 1772, and within two years Isaac Hildrith had drawn up plans for a canal, lock, and drawbridge; but it was not until 1850 and after more surveys that construction began with John Lathrop as the chief engineer. At the time of its completion in 1859, the Great Lock, measuring 220 feet long and 40 feet wide, was the largest lock on the Atlantic coast, superseded only by the lock between Lake Superior and Lake Huron in Sault Sainte Marie. The original walls of the lock were constructed of Maryland granite shipped to the site via the Chesapeake Bay. Union forces used the canal during the war. Since 1912, it has been operated by the U.S. Army Corps of Engineers. Because the Elizabeth River is subject to tidal change from the Chesapeake Bay, a 600-foot-long, 75-foot-wide tidal guard located at Great Bridge in Chesapeake was constructed in 1932.

ST4   Dismal Swamp Canal

1793–1805, 1812, 1829, 1896–1899, 1933, 1940, 1963. Deep Creek, Virginia to South Mills, N.C.

The Dismal Swamp Canal, the oldest operating canal in the country, is a 22-mile-long manmade waterway that runs north to south through the Great Dismal Swamp. Lake Drummond, one of only two natural lakes in Virginia, is located approximately in the center of the swamp. A series of locks controls the water level in the canal and the release of water from the lake. The Dismal Swamp Canal is one of two alternate routes along the Atlantic Intracoastal Waterway. The construction of the canal, authorized by the Virginia legislature in 1787 and ratified by North Carolina in 1790, began at both ends in 1793 and was completed in 1805. The canal was the key transportation artery and inland link between southeast Virginia and northeast North Carolina. The feeder ditch from Lake Drummond was cut in 1812, and three of four locks were constructed. Between 1827 and 1829 the canal was widened and deepened. The canal suffered severe damage during the Civil War, as it was heavily used by occupying Union forces. During the late 1890s substantial improvements were made to the waterway. In 1929 the U.S. Army Corps of Engineers took over the operation.

ST5   Beechwood

1850. 3728 Belle Haven St. Not open to the public

Some of the original rural isolation of the area can be grasped from Beechwood, one of the best surviving plantation houses in Chesapeake. Built by William Charles Stewart and his wife Catherine, the I-house has two rear single-story projecting wings, creating a U-type plan. The minimal exterior details are Italianate, while the interior has Greek Revival features.

ST6   Sanderson-Hathaway House

c. 1790s. 4676 Battlefield Blvd. Not open to the public

An excellent example of the most characteristic type of late eighteenth-century Tidewater domestic architecture is this three-bay frame gambrel-roofed house on a raised basement, built by Edward Doughty, a local merchant. Many comparable examples, built as homes in small villages and as farmhouses, can be found scattered throughout southern Chesapeake. Such houses had either single or, as in this case, double-pile plans. These houses attest to the conservative nature of late eighteenth-century Virginia society. An original one-story lean-to addition is on the north side, and the house has three exterior chimneys. A raised stoop leads to the principal entrance, which is topped by a five-light transom and opens directly into a large hall. The main floor of the interior is divided into four other spaces: kitchen, chamber, chamber-parlor, and a small closet.

City of Suffolk   (ST7–ST11)

ST7 Suffolk Downtown

Now the urban center of the City of Suffolk, Suffolk dates from a charter from the Virginia General Assembly in 1742 and was for years the seat of Nansemond County, formed in 1636. In 1974 the entire county became the City of Suffolk. Situated along the Nansemond River, the community was a trading port. In 1779 the British destroyed what little existed of the town. The original section was rebuilt after the war and became known as Old Town. Concentrated at the intersection of U.S. 58 and U.S. Business 460, or Main Street, it contains government functions. The area south along Main Street was developed as the business-residential center and became known as Up Town. The railroad arrived in 1834, and a conflagration consumed most of the town in 1837. During the Civil War, Union troops occupied Suffolk for four years and caused much destruction. Economic prosperity returned after the war, first with oyster packing, then as Suffolk became a center for the processing

and shipping of lumber by the Seaboard and Roanoke and the Norfolk and Western railroads. Peanuts became the new growth industry at the end of the century. The first successful peanut processing plant in Suffolk was established in 1898 by John Beauregard Pinner and John King. Planters Peanuts, founded by Italian immigrant Amadeo Obici in Wilkes-Barre, Pennsylvania, moved its main processing plant to Suffolk in 1912. The economic activity brought real estate speculation and a new section of town, known as New Town. Still an important rail and peanut center, Suffolk, as have many Virginia cities, has suffered from strip developments and the abandonment of the central city. The town contains a variety of buildings, of which some are noted below; additionally, several areas close to the downtown contain a wide variety of housing types. The tour begins near the river on North Main Street in Old Town and proceeds south.

ST7.1 City of Suffolk Courthouse
(Nansemond County Courthouse)

1838, 1909, John Kevan Peebles. 1913, Finlay F. Ferguson, Sr.; 1958, Paul D. Woodward and Shriver and Holland. 524 North Main St. (corner of Main St. and Constance Rd.)

This building replaced a courthouse burned in the fire of 1837. A temple-form structure that bespeaks Thomas Jefferson's influence, it is crude in its details: the Tuscan columns are too elongated, and the pediment's pitch is too shallow. Unlike other courthouses of the period, the courtroom was located on the second floor. Both Peebles and Ferguson provided modest additions, all evidence of which is blurred by the 1958 remodeling, which totally obliterated the original interior and added the vintage aluminum panel annex. With the construction of the new courthouse (see below) the building will be redundant, and new uses are sought.

ST7.2 John Riddick House

1837. 510 North Main St. Open to the public

Put up after the 1837 fire, this is the most prominent of Suffolk's early houses: a sub-

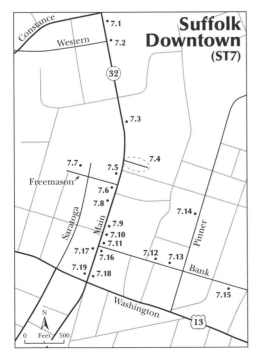

ST7.2 John Riddick House

tailed houses have the usual low-lying aspect, with extended eaves, brackets, beveled glass door panes, and a variety of porch columns and posts, some with an Oriental cast to them. The enclave is slated for restoration.

ST7.5 Richard Seth Eley House

1878. 251 N. Main St.

This house prominently displays the new wealth of the end of Reconstruction in a virtual pile of all the Second Empire features found in pattern books such as those by Samuel Sloan and E. C. Hussey. The mansard roof is multicolored and slate-covered, prominent brackets are below, the windows have pedimented hoods, and multiple verandas open out at ground level.

ST7.6 John Granberry House

c. 1795; later additions. 227 N. Main St.

The former home of the large landowner who subdivided his land for the section of Suffolk known as Up Town, this weatherboarded frame house is one of the few early buildings to survive. Federal in style with a Tidewater type of three-bay, side-passage plan, the building sits on a raised basement. A kitchen ell is on the south side. The portico is well executed with fluted Doric columns and pilasters protecting a simple fanlight entrance.

stantial Greek Revival design, five bays with finely jointed brickwork and a prominent side porch. The interior spaces on the ground floor are large and contain heavy Greek Revival molding.

ST7.3 Seaboard and Roanoke Railroad Station

1885. 326 North Main St.

The station, probably designed by the railroad's staff architects, is essentially a Queen Anne house turned into a station. The brick base supports broad, sheltering roofs and shingled gables. The porch becomes a waiting platform, and the ubiquitous tower of Queen Anne dwellings actually has a purpose as the signalman's perch.

ST7.4 College Court

1914–1920. East side of Main St.

An ornamental iron gate mounted on molded brick piers serves as pedestrian access to six bungalows surrounding a grassy common. Typical of Southern California and of Pasadena in particular, bungalow courts are relatively uncommon in Virginia. The designer of College Court likely had seen Gustav Stickley's various publications or perhaps Henry Wilson's *The Bungalow Magazine*, for the individually de-

ST7.7 Suffolk School Buildings

1911, 1922, Charles M. Robinson. 301 N. Saratoga St.

Robinson, the favorite school architect of Virginia, designed Suffolk's education center. The former Suffolk High School (1922) shows his ability to create impressive facades with great economy. The building is raised on a high basement, windows are grouped for effect and light, and a great flight of steps leads up to a portico in antis. Double-height Ionic columns support an entablature with a frieze that runs around the structure. Just behind the high school is the Jefferson School (1911), a slightly earlier effort by Robinson, very much in the same idiom.

ST7.8 St. Paul's Episcopal Church

1892, Bernard J. Black. Later alterations, 207 N. Main St.

ST7.9 Suffolk Christian Church

to medieval design, this church is a somber English Gothic affair, more academically correct than Suffolk Christian Church.

ST7.11 U.S. Post Office (former)

1911–1913, James Knox Taylor, Supervising Architect, U.S. Treasury Department. 200 N. Main St.

The federal government had a presence on Suffolk's Main Street, though the former post office, now attorneys' offices, might be mistaken for a bank with its dressed limestone exterior and large side windows. Taylor, Supervising Architect of the U.S. Department of the Treasury from 1897 to 1912, had previously been a partner of Cass Gilbert and strongly believed in an American Renaissance: for him, classicism formed the basis of an American style.

ST7.12 George W. Truitt House

1909. 204 Bank St.

Bank Street, along with Franklin, Holladay, and Pinner streets, was developed in the elite residential section of New Town by land speculator John Franklin Pinner. Turn-of-the-twentieth-century prosperity is obvious in this example of the Southern Colonial Revival, with its giant Temple of the Winds Corinthian columns. Truitt, a local lumber magnate, wanted to impress and hired an artist (reputedly from New York) to paint murals above the fireplaces. The house has 24-inch steel beams and 18-inch-thick brick walls.

Part of a religious enclave created by the grouping of several churches of various styles, the Episcopal church is exuberantly High Victorian with the polychrome contrast of red brick and white trim, while a massive corner tower dominates one end. The interior is typically Virginia "low church" of the period, with a wide nave. A signed Tiffany window is in the north wall. Several other windows are by lesser American opalescent glass studios. The altar was remodeled c. 1920.

ST7.9 Suffolk Christian Church

1891–1892, Charles E. Cassell. 1927, alterations, Herbert Levi Cain. 214 N. Main St.

Cassell, a Baltimore-based architect who did extensive work in Virginia, designed a Romanesque-inspired structure that looks not to H. H. Richardson but to the earlier (1850s) Romanesque-Norman revival work of architects such as Thomas Tefft and James Renwick. In 1927 the towers were raised, the vestibule roof was added, and the nave roof was heightened.

ST7.10 Main Street Methodist Episcopal Church

1914, Neff and Thompson. 204 North Main St.

Reflecting its later date and the impact of Ralph Adams Cram's more scholarly approach

ST7.13 Holland House Apartments (Colonel Edward E. Holland House)

c. 1885, c. 1930. 216 Bank St.

This more modest version of the Eley house on Main Street was originally the residence of Colonel Edward E. Holland, an important local politician. The house has three bays with a side-hall plan and a veranda that is a virtuoso display of ornamental forms.

ST7.14 John Beauregard Pinner House

c. 1930. 227 Pinner St.

Built by the son of the developer of the area, the Pinner House combines Tudor and Craftsman idioms. Next door is John Pinner's father's house (c. 1870, c. 1920; 231 Pinner Street), which has been much altered.

ST7.15 Norfolk and Western Railroad Depot

1909, Charles S. Churchill. Bank St. at railroad tracks

This standard-issue railroad depot combines freight and passenger facilities in the same structure.

ST7.16 Suffolk Courts Complex

1996–1998, Moseley McClintock Group. 180 N. Main St. (southeast corner of Bank and Main sts.)

Designed by a firm that has specialized in Virginia court complexes, the building adds an impressive note to the street with an entrance pavilion that picks up on the design of the former Post Office. Overall, though, the postmodern overscaled moldings and trim seem jarring.

ST7.17 Suffolk Towers (Elliott Hotel)

1925, Peebles and Ferguson. 181 N. Main St.

Dominating the street and an Up Town landmark, this building was one of Suffolk's entries in the skyscraper sweepstakes of the 1920s. An eight-story tower rises out of a two-story base that extends along the street front. The base contained commercial spaces and the hotel's

dining room and ballroom. The idiom, as might be expected from the Peebles office, is Colonial-Georgian Revival and very well carried out.

ST7.18 Professional Building

1919. 100 N. Main St. (northeast corner of N. Main and Washington sts.)

This tame three-bay structure is one of three high rises that mark the center of Up Town.

ST7.19 American Bank of Suffolk (former)

1916, John Kevan Peebles. 101 North Main St.

Suffolk's third impressive skyscraper is again by Peebles. In his use of the overhanging cornice, the overall massing, and very New Yorkish design, Peebles shows his admiration for the works of McKim, Mead and White. The high limestone base is ornamented with gold coin medallions.

ST8 T. J. Lipton Factory

c. 1955. .7 mile west of Suffolk on U.S. Business 58

One of the most attractive modern factories in the commonwealth retains a 1950s verve in its painted metal exterior. An entrance pavilion with a large red square is joined to a white office and factory block that has yellow structural supports.

ST9 Chuckatuck Historic District

Intersection of VA 10 (Godwin Blvd.) and VA 125 (King's Hwy.)

Chuckatuck is a good example of a southern Tidewater village on a deepwater river (Chuckatuck Creek) which provided transportation for the agricultural economy of the surrounding area. A crossroads settlement was formed here by 1672. It escaped destruction during the Revolution and the Civil War. Farming remains its primary support.

One of the town's most prominent architectural landmarks is the Godwin-Knight House (ST9.1) (1856, 1900; 140 King's Highway), originally constructed as a two-and-one-half-story dwelling with a side-hall plan. It underwent a significant remodeling in 1900, when Queen Anne features—a wraparound porch, a

ST9.1 Godwin-Knight House

ST9.2 Lafayette Gwaltney Store

ST10 St. John's Church (Chuckatuck Church)

corner tower, shingles, and a third floor balcony—were added. The remodeling demonstrates the persistence of the Queen Anne style

in provincial areas of Virginia. The source was possibly one of George Barber's publications. Visible from the road are outbuildings dating from c. 1880–c. 1920: chicken houses, a smokehouse, a garage, a summer kitchen, and a Delco generator house. The house was the home of a two-term Virginia governor, Mills E. Godwin, Jr. The house across the road is virtually identical.

A group of bungalows (c. 1915–1930; 153, 256, 260, 264, and 282 King's Highway) were constructed for workers of the Lone Star Cement Company, which located near here; they demonstrate a range of "bungaloid" variations in siting and porches.

A village needs a general store, and the Lafayette Gwaltney Store (ST9.2) (c. 1840, c. 1890; 5996 Godwin Boulevard, corner of King's Highway), located prominently at the crossroads, is the only survivor of the three that provided supplies for local farmers and town residents. It was originally built as a residence, but George Britten converted the downstairs into a store c. 1890 by installing large storefront windows and a shed-roofed porch supported by square posts with scalloped trim.

ST10 St. John's Church (Chuckatuck Church)

1755, 1826, 1888, William Whitney. North side of VA 125, 2 miles east of Chuckatuck

A modest, rectangular Anglican church oriented to the northeast, St. John's was originally named Chuckatuck Church after the parish it served. Abandoned during disestablishment, it returned to service and in 1828 was renamed St. John's. During the Civil War federal forces used it as a stable, damaging the building. Whitney carried out a restoration in 1888. The one-story church has 27-inch-thick brick walls, laid in Flemish bond with glazed headers above a beveled water table. Rubbed bricks appear at the building's corners and along all door and window jambs. The original door with a brick pediment was at the southwest window. Rubbed brick pilasters remain. The original clipped gable roof has been replaced by a steep pitched gable roof and the gable ends enfilade with light-colored brick. The large, round-arched windows, four in the side walls and one in the end wall, create a luminous interior. The tongue-and-grove, herringbone-pattern paneling dates from 1888. The pink sandstone in the nave may be original.

ST11 Whaleyville Historic District

Intersection of U.S. 13 (Whaleyville Blvd.) and VA 616 (Mineral Spring Rd.)

Located in the southern portion of the City of Suffolk (or the former Nansemond County), Whaleyville was established in 1877 around a sawmill. The Norfolk and Carolina Railroad, later the Atlantic Coast Line, arrived in 1884, and the Jackson Timber Company established a modern lumber mill and brought workers to the area. Although the Jackson Company left in 1919, the town remained a lumber processing as well as an agricultural center. Its rural and isolated location has meant the preservation of much of its historic character as a small, turn-of-the-twentieth-century industrial community. Most of Whaleyville's residences date from c. 1884–c. 1910 and are frame, one-and-one-half or two-story structures with front porches and modest millwork exterior detailing: turned or classical columns on porches and bracketed eaves. Roofs include gable and hipped forms and are usually covered with standing-seam metal. Decorative windows, such as side lights, transoms, and diamond-shaped windows, are also common features on these houses. The sources appear to be various pattern books adapted to local building practices. A variation on the American Foursquare is at 6411 Whaleyville Boulevard. An I-house is at 6413 Whaleyville Boulevard, and a variation on the bungalow is at 6313 Whaleyville Boulevard. The Bank of Whaleyville (c. 1900), 6431 Whaleyville Boulevard, a single-story brick structure, served as one of the town's centers, for in addition to banking, it was used for weekly court sessions.

Southampton County (ST12–ST15)

ST12 Franklin

A small industrial city dominated since the late nineteenth century by the Union Camp Corporation, one of the world's largest wood products companies, Franklin also owes its prosperity to peanut processing. The town was founded in 1835 with the arrival of the Portsmouth and Roanoke Railroad. Its location on the Blackwater River allowed the transfer of goods between rail and steamship and transport into North Carolina. It also became a major shipment point for the agricultural products of Southampton County, including cotton, tobacco, and livestock. Originally known as Blackwater Depot, the town was laid out on a grid with two major axes: the railroad and First Avenue create an east-west axis, while Main Street, which parallels the river, runs north-south. The Civil War ruined the economy, but the architecture is reflective of the economic resurgence Franklin experienced during the late nineteenth century. A fire destroyed the downtown commercial area in 1881, and the town council adopted an ordinance requiring all new commercial structures to be constructed of brick or stone. In recent years Franklin has been a Main Street community under the program developed by the National Trust for Historic Preservation, and the downtown has experienced a rejuvenation. Hurricane Floyd caused severe flooding to downtown Franklin in 1999; recovery is underway.

Structures of interest can be found along Main Street. The residential areas of Franklin—located to the west of downtown along High, Clay, Lee, and Norfleet streets and West First and West Second avenues—contain a variety of Italianate, Queen Anne, Colonial Revival, Foursquare, and bungalow examples, as well as other residential types, along with churches, all worthy of inspection.

ST12.1 Lyons State Theater

1937. 221 South Main St.

Art Deco with fluted stone bands and panels that contrast with recessed brick panels, this is the only modernist intrusion into downtown.

ST12.2 James River Bank (W. T. Pace Hardware Store)

1902. 200 N. Main St.

This three-story building, standing above the surrounding one- and two-story structures, marks the center of town. It is designed in the

ST12.3 Franklin Post Office (former)

commercial Italianate idiom with corbeled brick or terra-cotta cornices and segmental arches over the upper-story windows. Neighboring one-story brick buildings (c. 1900) have corner pilasters and decorative parapet attics. In this case Doric pilasters, classical entablature, and simple brick parapet wall are used. The base has been altered.

ST12.3 **Franklin Post Office (former)**

1916–1917, James A. Wetmore, architect in charge; Louis A. Simon, Supervising Architect of the U.S. Treasury Department. 301 N. Main St. (northwest corner of N. Main St. and W. 3rd Ave.)

The gem of downtown is now business offices. A typically excellent government-issue design, its facade recalls McKim, Mead and White's Pierpont Morgan Library (1906) in New York, though here the materials relate to colonial and Georgian architecture.

ST12.4 **Rhodes Building**

c. 1916. 300 N. Main St.

The other standout on the street is this Colonial Revival building with a crenellated parapet.

ST12.5 **Emmanuel Episcopal Church**

1913, Ferguson, Calrow and Taylor. 400 N. High St. (northeast corner of W. 4th and N. High sts.)

This small Arts and Crafts structure that combines half timbering and Gothic detailing has a particularly fine interior.

ST12.6 **Franklin Congregational Christian Church**

1915, William Newton Diehl. 412 N. High St.

Diehl specialized in creating aggressive brick piles. Franklin Congregational Christian Church, nominally Romanesque Revival in style, has a prominent stone belt course and castellated parapet that help it stand out over its more modest Episcopalian neighbor.

ST12.7 **The Elms** (Paul D. Camp House)

1889; later alterations. 717 Clay St.

Of Franklin's houses easily the most prosperous and well set back on its own large plot is this one, built by the founder of the Union Camp Corporation. The brick walls, based on designs in Queen Anne pattern books, were later stuccoed. The house still has broad verandas and tall brick chimneys with corbeled caps. Decorative iron cresting tops the large hipped roof.

ST13 **Sunnyside**

c. 1810, 1847, 1870. VA 673 near intersection with VA 703

The early nineteenth-century plantation known as Sunnyside consists of a main residence, which evolved throughout the nineteenth century, and a fine complex of domestic and farm outbuildings which date from the mid- to late nineteenth century. Sunnyside is surrounded by a rural countryside that looks much as it did when the house was built. The two-story frame residence was built in three stages. A one-room structure built c. 1810 for Joseph Pope was doubled in 1847 by Pope's son, Harrison. Profiting from the sale of contraband provisions in 1870, Harrison Pope achieved a prosperity rare in rural Virginia and constructed a two-story Doric portico with fluted columns. The domestic outbuildings date from the third quarter of the nineteenth century, while the farm buildings date from 1870 and later. The outbuildings at Sunnyside include a schoolhouse, schoolmaster's house, dairy, milk house, tenant's house, privy, pump house, sheds, peanut barn, tall smokehouse, kitchen-laundry, and garage. The outbuildings, like the main house, are covered with weatherboard. The outbuildings are formally arranged in relation to the main house. The yard of the main house is enclosed by a picket fence, and the outbuildings are separated from the pastures and fields by a rail fence.

ST14   Southampton County Courthouse

1834. 1924, Clement Rochelle and Jeremiah Cobb; 1960, addition, Shriver and Holland, U.S. Business 58, Courtland

Formed in 1749, Southampton County remains largely rural, with peanuts, tobacco, cotton, and lumber its major products. The slave insurrection of 1831, led by Nat Turner, is the most significant event in the county's history. Turner was hanged in front of the Southampton courthouse on November 11, 1831. When that courthouse was constructed in 1798, the town was named Jerusalem; the name was changed to Courtland in 1888. It remains a small town. The present Southampton County Courthouse was originally an austere, two-story, brick temple-form building with a pedimented gable, simple entablature, and lunette window. In 1924 it received a tetrastyle Tuscan portico, pilasters, full entablature, and circular window, which gave the building an 1820s Greco-Roman or Jeffersonian appearance. The 1960 addition is awful. Across the street from the courthouse is the former Mahone Tavern (c. 1820), a two-story clapboard structure.

ST15   Beechwood (Jericho; Denson-Pretlow-Darden House)

c. 1790. 19th century, additions. 19636 Governor Darden Rd. (VA 643 near intersection with VA 646)

Jordan Denson, a planter who owned about 200 acres in rural eighteenth-century Southampton County, erected the first sections of Beechwood, a two-story frame house that evolved from a one-room, one-story dwelling constructed in the late eighteenth century. The house is typical of the spacious but unpretentious type favored by southeastern Virginia planters in the early nineteenth century. Today it consists of a two-story, three-bay main block (the earliest section) with a small, one-bay wing at the east end and a two-bay, one-cell wing at the west. To the south of the west wing is a two-story, two-room ell. The main block of the house has a side-hall, double-

ST14 Southampton County Courthouse

ST15 Beechwood (Jericho; Denson-Pretlow-Darden House)

pile room arrangement that began as a single, square, one-story cell. Numerous additions took place during the last part of the eighteenth century and throughout the nineteenth century. Two rooms were added to the rear of the original room as well as a side passage, a full second story on the main block, a two-story, one-cell addition to the southwest corner and a two-room rear wing. The main block of the house is clad with beaded weatherboards with a modillion cornice, which gives it a unified appearance.

Isle of Wight County (ST16–ST21)

ST16 **St. Luke's Church** (Newport Parish Church, Old Brick Church)

1632–1685, 1890, 1950–1957. VA 10, .1 mile northwest of junction with VA 32, Benns Church. Open to the public

Probably Virginia's most famous church, St. Luke's Church, as it became known in the nineteenth century, is easily the oldest surviving Anglican parish church in Virginia. It represents the transfer of some elements of English medieval church design to the New World. The date assigned to its construction is controversial, ranging from 1632 to 1685. The 1632 date is plainly too early for a building of this size and construction and incorporating so many classical features (the round-arched tower entrance opening and the artisan mannerist pedimented frontispiece, for example) that did not appear in English parish church architecture until the middle of the century. A more likely date is perhaps some fifty years later, in the 1680s, which would tie this building to two other churches (the firmly dated first Bruton Parish Church and the Jamestown church) which featured similar plans and details. All three churches were nearly twice as long as they were broad and each had a chancel door on the south side and buttresses on the side walls between apertures. The latest scholarly consensus is that St. Luke's plan, the lancet and tracery windows, and the buttresses date from the original construction, and that the crow-step gable, corner

quoins, and a pedimented entrance were added soon after completion. A two-story tower was part of the church's original design; a third story was added later in the seventeenth century. The 2-foot-thick brick walls are laid in Flemish bond and include a double, molded water table and molded brick tracery. Unlike many English parish churches, whose principal entrances were on the south wall near the west end, St. Luke's is entered through the arched entry of the west tower. Abandoned after the American Revolution, it suffered structural damage in the 1880s when a storm caused part of the roof and the east end to collapse. First restored in the 1890s, it was again restored in 1950–1957 by a team headed by Robert I. Powell, of Chapman, Evans and Delahanty.

Like all Anglican churches in Virginia, St. Luke's is oriented with its altar in the east end and lit by a large brick mullion window, four lights wide and divided into three tiers by tracery. This massive east-end window was characteristic of church architecture in Virginia until the second quarter of the eighteenth century, when builders began to de-emphasize the east end of the church in favor of windows indistinguishable in size and shape from others in the building. Evidence exists that a chancel screen once existed. The pulpit, benches, and altar rails are loosely based on seventeenth-century English examples. The church also possesses many of its original seventeenth-century furnishings, including the English box organ, communion silver, textiles, and candlesticks. The stained glass windows, replacing what originally must have been diamond-paned windows, were installed during the 1890 restoration. The window at the east end and the pair of windows on the side walls nearest that end are reputedly antique windows from Munich, Germany. Other windows bear representations of John Smith, John Rolfe, Pocahontas, George Washington, Robert E. Lee, Joseph Bridger (the church's senior warden during the late 1670s), and the Reverend William Hubbard (the last colonial rector). Some windows are dedicated to local families, including the Parkers, Jordans, and Thomases. The elliptical openings in the entry porch formerly held stained glass windows depicting the colonial seal of Virginia and the seal of the Episcopal Church.

ST17.1 Old Isle of Wight County Courthouse as restored (left) and before restoration

ST17 Smithfield

In 1779, the E. M. Todd Company opened the first meat packing operation in the country and began producing the traditional local specialty, Smithfield hams. Smithfield was established in 1749 as a port on the Pagan River and platted as a town of small farmsteads, on part of the plantation owned by Arthur Smith. The Isle of Wight County Court moved here in 1752. As the county's port, Smithfield had a large export trade with England and the West Indies. The peanut industry has also been a mainstay of the Smithfield economy since the late nineteenth century. The merchants who made their money in these industries built some of Smithfield's most opulent houses. In 1921 a disastrous fire swept along the wharf, wiping out many local businesses and older commercial structures. The buildings of major interest are located along Main Street, perpendicular to Church Street, which parallels the river.

ST17.1 Old Isle of Wight County Courthouse

1752, William Rand. 1810s. 1960, restoration, A. Lawrence Kocher. 130 Main St. (corner of Main and Church sts.). Open to the public

Because there were few concentrated centers of population in the plantation economy, many counties found it simply uneconomical to construct permanent brick courthouses, and the courts met in makeshift quarters. For nearly a century after its establishment, this was the case with the county of Isle of Wright. Finally, in 1749 Colonel Arthur Smith donated land for the new town of Smithfield and provided lots within the town to build a new courthouse. In 1749 the court ordered the new courthouse and further stipulated that "John Willis and William Hodseden, gentlemen apply to some undertaker to Prepare a Plan for the said building." William Rand was the builder, or undertaker.

A T-shaped brick structure with a five-bay front arcade and a rear apse, the Isle of Wight courthouse is one of about a half dozen courthouses built in eighteenth-century Virginia to have such features. The brickwork is fine, with rubbed bricks for the arcade and Flemish bond above the English bond water table. Both the arcade, or "piazza," as it is also called, and the apse can be traced as public building design elements to the first capitol in Williamsburg. Both features also have an earlier history in English public buildings—in town halls and market houses erected in the century following the Restoration. In Virginia the arcade served as a place for court participants and spectators to gather before entering directly into the courtroom and provided a symbolic face to what would otherwise have been a very domestic-looking structure. The center arch is larger than the flanking arches. At the back of the courtroom stood a raised magistrates' platform very similar to the one in the Williamsburg courthouse. So that the magistrates could communicate with one another the bench curved in a semicircle. In a feature absent from the Williamsburg courthouse but evident in the capitol, this curved bench is expressed on the exterior in the shape of the apse. Off to the side were two jury rooms. The ecclesiastical references are clear. The justices sat within the apse, with the contesting parties in front; a turned-baluster railing separated the court functions from the onlookers. A courthouse, jail, and clerk's office were erected and are extant, although modified. Two lots to the east of the courthouse stands a two-story tavern now known as the Smithfield Inn (c. 1752), which was also built by William Rand. The county seat was moved again around 1800, to a more centrally located site, and the old courthouse converted into a residence. The arcade was filled in, and dormers were added. The local branch of the APVA purchased the building in 1938 and in 1960 restored it to its present use as a county museum. For this work the APVA hired A. Lawrence Kocher, an architect who had worked for Colonial Williamsburg but had also designed modernist buildings at Black Mountain College in western North Carolina. The fittings that Kocher designed for the interior do not necessarily reflect an accurate interpretation of such features.

ST17.2 Wentworth-Barrett House

c. 1752. 117 S. Church St.

The Wentworth-Barrett House was one of the first to be erected in the newly established town. Built for Captain Samuel Wentworth, it was restored in the 1950s. One and one-half stories in height and of Flemish bond brick construction, the house is flanked by two end chimneys. The east chimney is T shaped. The central front door is accessed by a brick stairway that arches over the entrance to the English basement below.

ST17.3 The Cottage (Boynkin House)

c. 1879. 201 S. Church St.

As an example of the generally conservative nature of Virginia architecture, the design origins of this cottage probably lie in A. J. Downing's books, originally published before the Civil War. Downing's designs, however, were intended for a rural setting rather than for an urban center. The two-story house is of board-and-batten frame construction with a gable

ST17.6 Todd House (Nicholas Parker House)

roof. Bargeboards decorate the gable, and railings and latticed columns detail the porch.

ST17.4 Pembroke Decatur Gwaltney House

1877. 226 South Church St.

Far more adventurous and fashionable than the Boynkin House and reflective of new wealth is this house, built by one of the founders of the Gwaltney-Bunkley Peanut Company, originally of Smithfield and after 1921 of Suffolk. Later Gwaltney established the meat curing and packing company that bears his name today. Wooden and three stories in height, it was designed from one of the pattern books produced by George E. Woodward or George and Charles Palliser. Stylistically the house is in the then new Queen Anne mode, its tall, conical-roofed tower balanced (unevenly) by a prominent gable with heavy cornice. Decorative shingles, brackets, and a Palladian window help to create visual interest. The porch, composed of several juxtaposed forms, is supported by fluted Ionic columns on tall pedestals.

ST17.5 The Grove (Thomas Pierce House)

c. 1790, 1956. 220 Grace Street (corner of Grace and Mason sts.)

Federal in style, this square, two-and-one-half-story brick house with front and side entrance porticoes stands prominently at a major corner.

The house resembles the Moses Myers house in nearby Norfolk. The major entrance, on Grace Street, is distinguished by the portico's shallow barrel vault and two fluted Doric columns. By comparison the side entrance, which contains a fanlight, is covered by a flat-roofed portico. Brick jack arches are employed over the first-story windows, and the second-story windows have stone lintels with keystones.

ST17.6 Todd House (Nicholas Parker House)

1752, c. 1780. Late 1980s, restoration. 30 Main St.

One of the most impressive buildings on Main Street, the Todd House was constructed in 1752 by Nicholas Parker, a local cabinetmaker. Captain Mallory Todd, a native of Bermuda who in 1779 founded the first ham curing and packing company in the town, purchased the house in the 1770s. The two-and-one-half-story house is wood frame on a brick basement. The heavy wooden cornices and elaborate exterior detailing and porches reflect the expertise of the original owner. Interior details such as wainscoting and paneled mantelpieces also show the hand of a master cabinetmaker. The two-leaf entrance is surrounded by a thirteen-star and wine cup doorway motif. Vacant for many years, the house underwent extensive restorations during the mid- to late 1980s that maintained the historic integrity of the structure.

Surry County (ST18–ST21)

ST18 Bacon's Castle (Arthur Allen House)

c. 1665, c. 1740, c. 1850. 1995, restoration. .5 mile east of the junction of VA 10 and VA 617. Open to the public seasonally

Often cited as one of the earliest surviving brick houses in America, Bacon's Castle certainly is one of the country's finest extant examples of seventeenth-century domestic architecture. The house known as Bacon's Castle was constructed c. 1665 for English immigrant Arthur Allen on the 200 acres he had patented in 1649. In 1676 the followers of Nathaniel Bacon, who organized a revolt against Governor William Berkeley, occupied the house after burning Jamestown. Bacon probably never visited the Allen House, but his name has been attached to it for over 300 years. In 1973 the APVA purchased the house and undertook preservation and stabilization. The house is presented as an example of 300 years of change.

At the time of its construction, the house was considered to be quite large and elaborate, especially in comparison to the prevailing frame houses. Bacon's Castle reflects the wealth of Virginia's tobacco economy and points the way toward the grand and refined brick plantation houses that would be built in the eighteenth century. The architectural style of the house also shows that Allen, a justice of the peace and successful merchant who was aware of the houses of the English gentry, attempted to du-

ST18 Bacon's Castle (Arthur Allen House)

plicate the English standard of living on the colonial frontier.

Bacon's Castle is a two-and-one-half-story brick structure with a molded brick water table. The steeply pitched gable roof, now covered with wood shakes, at first had sandstone tiles. The many window openings originally held diamond-paned casement windows. The exterior window surrounds are of raised and plastered (pargeted) brick. The brick of the walls is laid in English bond, and a plastered stringcourse surrounds the house at the second-floor level. A projecting, two-story entrance tower once on the front of the house was balanced by a projecting stair tower on the rear. The house exhibits several features typically identified as Jacobean, Tudor, or Stuart in style, including curved and stepped gable ends, clustered chimney stacks set at a diagonal to the main house, and a chamber above an entrance porch.

The cruciform plan of the house is an early example of the form. On the first floor the entrance porch (or vestibule) gives access to the hall, which is on the east side and contains closets that flank the central fireplace. A parlor-chamber takes up the west half of the first floor. A staircase occupied the rear porch area. The second floor contained two large rooms and small rooms in the tower. A garret was under the steep roof. The basement originally contained the kitchen and service areas. A detached, or summer, kitchen was constructed behind the house sometime before the turn of the eighteenth century.

Later alterations visible from the exterior include the 1850s replacement of casement windows with sash windows, the removal of the plastered surrounds from the first-floor windows, and the conversion of the original brick pedimented doorway into a window. A frame addition originally on the east side of the house was relocated to the rear (where it stands today as the caretaker's house), and a hyphen and a two-story brick east wing with Greek Revival features were built. The floor plan was altered c. 1740 to create a central passage through the first floor, a change that reflects the increasing importance of domestic privacy for elite Virginians in those years. Paneling was installed c. 1740 in the first-floor rooms. The hall has been restored to its Jacobean character with diamond-paned windows, open-timber ceiling, and oversized hearth, while the parlor exhibits the paneling and well-appointed interiors enjoyed by the family 100 years later.

Allen's one-and-one-half-acre garden (c. 1680) has been restored on the basis of evidence gained from an archaeological investigation (1984–1991) funded by the Garden Club of Virginia. Packed white sand paths divide the rectangular grid into six areas planted with herbs, vegetables, and flowers. Evidence suggests that brick garden buildings stood at some of the corners. The archaeological investigations also indicated that four outbuildings constructed in the seventeenth and early eigh-

teenth centuries stood in the front yard. The earliest still extant outbuilding at Bacon's Castle is the Allen Smokehouse (c. 1750; c. 1830, wings), formed of a central bay and flanking wing additions and covered in weatherboarding. Other outbuildings to the rear include, in addition to the aforementioned caretaker's house (c. 1700; removed from the main house in 1854), a smokehouse (c. 1850), a raised barn, and slave quarters (c. 1825), as well as a few twentieth-century structures.

ST19 Chippokes Plantation State Park

1616, c. 1830, c. 1854. VA 634, northeast of VA 10, between Smithfield and Surry. Open to the public

Chippokes Plantation, located on the south side of the James River just opposite Jamestown Island, is one of the oldest continuously farmed plantations in the country, a producer of tobacco, corn, wheat, apples, and livestock. In 1616 the land was patented to Captain William Powell, a shareholder in the Virginia Company of 1609. The plantation was named for Choupocke, a friendly Native American chief in whose domain the property was located. The land passed from the Powell family to Governor William Berkeley and then to the Ludwell family, who owned it until 1837. The 1,403-acre plantation was given to the commonwealth of Virginia in 1967, a gift of Mrs. Victor Stewart, who, together with her husband, had purchased the property in 1917. Operated by the Chippokes Plantation Farm Foundation, it houses permanent and special exhibits on the history of Virginia agriculture. Two houses and a variety of outbuildings, including slave quarters, early twentieth-century farm buildings, and sharecroppers' dwellings, are on the plantation. The earlier of the houses (c. 1830), a one-and-one-half-story vernacular frame dwelling with a raised brick basement and four tall brick exterior end chimneys, can only be viewed only on the exterior. The other house (c. 1854) is two stories, of brick with Greek Revival detailing, and is filled with period antiques.

ST20 Surry Courthouse Complex

1923, George R. Berryman. VA 10, Surry

Surry County was formed in 1652, and the county seat moved frequently. This is the seventh county courthouse and the fourth to be located at the crossroads town of Surry, originally known as Scuffletown. The architect, George R. Berryman, a Surry native and graduate of George Washington University's School of Architecture, had a practice in Wilson, North Carolina. He had designed the predecessor (1907) courthouse, which burned, and this is a near duplicate except for the deletion of the cupola. Stylistically it is Jeffersonian Revival: red brick with white trim and a giant Ionic portico and full entablature recalling Pavilion V at the University of Virginia. The interior of the main courtroom, unchanged since the 1920s, includes the original judge's bench, placed within a recessed arch that constitutes the bar, and jury seating. Also on the courthouse grounds are an 1825 clerk's office, a 1909 Confederate memorial, and general district court building.

ST21 Smith's Fort Plantation

c. 1605, c. 1750. VA 31, south side of the James River opposite Jamestown Island, 3 miles south of the ferry landing. Open to the public in season

Smith's Fort Plantation consists of an eighteenth-century brick house and the remnants of an earthwork constructed in the seventeenth century by John Smith as a refuge for the Jamestown settlers in case of an enemy attack.

The fort, begun in 1606, was only half finished when the settlers abandoned the project because they found their supplies at the fort ravaged by rot and rats. Remnants of Smith's earthworks are in the woods behind the house. Archaeological investigations conducted in 1981 indicated that the fort was a simple earth construction, without palisades.

In 1614 Chief Powhatan gave the land to John Rolfe, husband of Pocahontas, but Rolfe probably never settled on the land. Eventually (c. 1680) the site of the fort was incorporated into the plantation of Thomas Warren. From this succession of owners the house on the property became known as the Rolfe-Warren House, but architectural evidence indicates its date as 1750–1775, with an addition built c. 1790 when it was the home of Jacob Faulcon. The house will be familiar to visitors, since its form has inspired numerous "colonial" reproductions. The five-bay brick house has a raised basement level with access through a bulkhead entrance. Three dormers were added later to light the attic space. There are two interior end chimneys with stepped brick copings. The Williamsburg Holding Company, John D. Rockefeller's forerunner to the Colonial Williamsburg Foundation, purchased the property in 1928 and in 1934 gave it to the APVA, which has restored the house. The Garden Club of Virginia replanted the gardens.

Prince George County   (ST22–ST25)

ST22 Martin's Brandon Church

1857, Niernsee and Neilson. 1962, renovation. VA 10 (James River Dr.) at junction with VA 1201, Burrowsville

The fourth church for this parish was the last colonial-era church, built around 1723 and destroyed sometime after disestablishment. Its site lies across Virginia 10 from the present church, an Italianate structure of brick with scored stucco, designed by a Baltimore firm. A tower with a pyramidal roof adds an appropriate picturesque touch. Several of the windows are attributed to Tiffany Studios. Some original elements, such as the roof trusses, remain, but a 1960s renovation removed a great deal of the early fabric.

ST23 Brandon Plantation

c. 1765. Brandon Rd. (VA 611). Privately owned; open in April during Historic Garden Week and at other times by appointment

One of the best known of Virginia houses, Brandon reflects the impact of Palladio. The property on which Brandon stands was patented in 1616 and subsequently farmed. It passed into the Harrison family in 1720, but a house was not constructed until c. 1765, when Nathaniel Harrison II built Brandon as a wedding present for his son, Benjamin. Robert Morris's *Select Architecture* (1755) probably inspired the plan and the facades. Since Thomas Jefferson, a close friend to Harrison, owned a copy of Morris's book, Brandon has often been attributed to Jefferson. Jefferson's involvement is doubtful since he would have been only twenty-two years old

ST22 Martin's Brandon Church

and his ownership of Morris's work cannot be confirmed as earlier than 1770.

Brandon is a seven-part structure: a two-story central section with a pyramidal roof flanked by one-story wings with half-hipped roofs and two-story terminal wings with hipped roofs, set perpendicular to the house and attached by low, one-story hyphens. The terminal wings, originally one and one-half stories, were the first structures built, apparently intended to be incorporated into a larger house. The exterior of the house is a uniform brick, simply detailed, with a scrolled and carved modillion cornice along the eaves of the central section and uncarved modillions on the wings. A carved pineapple finial sits at the apex of the roof of the center section. The east wing originally served as a kitchen, which has since been moved to the basement. The west wing con-

tains four paneled rooms similar to those found in the center section of the house. The center hall of the west wing is detailed with a full Doric entablature and an elaborate Chinese trellis stair rail.

The house has undergone several alterations since its construction, including the replacement of all windows, the replacement of one-story pedimented porticos on the center section by one-story Corinthian porticoes with balconies, the addition of bathrooms, and some interior trim alterations. The interior paneling had to be replaced after the Civil War because of damage inflicted by occupying troops. Brandon also boasts large gardens, both formal and informal.

ST24 Flowerdew Hundred Plantation

1619. About 5 miles east of the Benjamin Harrison Bridge, north of VA 10. Open to the public April to November (except Mondays)

One of the earliest English settlements in the New World, Flowerdew Hundred was established in 1619 by Governor George Yeardly on a peninsula at a bend in the James River and was probably named for Yeardly's bride, Temperance Flowerdew. The 1,400 acres now encompassed in the plantation are part of the original fortified settlement, which contained almost a dozen individual dwellings. Occupied through the eighteenth century, it disappeared c. 1800, but the property continued as a plantation until 1971, when David A. Harrison III set up the Flowerdew Hundred Foundation and began extensive archaeological investigations. These have yielded information about the Native American inhabitants of the area as well as about the colonial settlers. The site is inter-

ST23 Brandon Plantation

preted through a variety of exhibits and reconstructions of historic buildings. America's first
windmill was erected here in 1621; on the site is
a reconstructed seventeenth-century-style windmill erected in 1975.

ST25 Merchant's Hope Episcopal Church

c. 1725. VA 641, .5 mile south of VA 10

The date of Merchant's Hope Church, named
for a seventeenth-century ship and nearby plantation, is in dispute. The traditional date has
been given as 1657, which is too early. In plan
and appearance this brick church is very similar to other Anglican parish churches built at
the beginning of the second quarter of the
eighteenth century. The pattern of the Flemish
bond brick with its glazed headers, the round-
arched windows, raised-panel doors, two east
windows, and window architraves resemble
those of nearby Westover, Blandford, and Fork
churches, all of which were built in the 1730s.
The original king-post roof truss is also a form
that did not appear in Virginia before the first
quarter of the century.

Growing out of an older English tradition
and nourished by nearly a century of local
building practices, the plan of Merchant's
Hope Church is an elongated rectangle, measuring more than twice as long as it is wide (29
by 64 feet). Most Anglican churches in the
neighboring colonies, such as Maryland and
South Carolina, had configurations which were
squarer, following the shape of the auditory
preaching boxes recommended by Christopher
Wren. By contrast colonial Virginia churches
retained their link to an earlier tradition of
elongated proportions, a characteristic also

ST25 Merchant's Hope Episcopal Church

of the eighteenth-century Anglican churches of
Bermuda. The principal entrance into Merchant's Hope Church was through a pair of
raised-panel doors in the west end. Just inside
the doorway a staircase rose to a west gallery, a
place often reserved for less important members of the church (though rarely given over
solely to slaves). A center aisle, laid with limestone pavers imported from England, was
flanked in the colonial period by tall box pews.
These have long since been swept away in one
of the periods when the church fell on hard
times. The pulpit was probably located on the
north wall near the east end of the building (or
possibly against the south wall near the chancel
door). As with Newport Parish Church (St.
Luke's), a south chancel door near the altarpiece provided a secondary entrance. This
door was given up in the design of later colonial churches in favor of a centrally located
doorway placed in the middle of the south wall.

City of Hopewell (ST26–ST31)

Located at the junction of the Appomattox and James rivers, Hopewell dates from 1613,
when it was established as Bermuda City. In 1622 a colony-wide attack by Native Americans
wiped out the settlement. The town was reestablished in the 1630s but grew very slowly into
the mid-nineteenth century. During the Civil War it was a strategic center of activity, and the
population boomed. After the war the town returned to its former small size until 1913,
when E. I. du Pont established a munitions factory. During World War I the town grew almost
overnight to nearly 40,000. Some of the housing in the town came from the Aladdin Company of Bay City, Michigan, which supplied about 165 individual homes and a variety of other
accommodations, delivered in fifty boxcars. After the war the population again plummeted,

but since World War II it has become a center of synthetic textile and nitrogen production. The town has grown to a 2000 population of 22,354.

ST26 Hopewell Downtown

ST26.1 Hopewell Municipal Building (Hopewell Civic Center)

1924–1925, Fred A. Bishop; additions. 300 Main St.

Striving to attract new industries to Hopewell, the city fathers commissioned Petersburg architect Fred A. Bishop to design an urban landmark and paid the Miller Engineering Company of Norfolk $46,500 to erect it. A standard Beaux-Arts rectangular box, the structure is distinguished by a two-story Ionic portico in antis. On the interior is a 1989 mural by Jay Bohannon depicting the story of Hopewell, a well-done reprise of WPA work.

ST26.2 Hopewell Courts Building

1994, Moseley McClintock Group, 1 E. Broadway

Across the street from the Municipal Building is an example of the "new" Virginia civic image, postmodern with thin walls and lots of glass.

ST27 Hopewell City Point Historic District

Northeast of downtown, bounded by the Appomattox and James rivers on the west, north and east, and on the south by an irregular line from Francis St. to Water St.

ST26.1 Hopewell Municipal Building (Hopewell Civic Center)

The site of a 1613 settlement of which little remains, this area became the Union army headquarters during the sieges of Petersburg and Richmond. Over 100,000 Union troops passed through the town, and it was the site of a vast supply depot. During World War I, as the location of the army's Camp Lee, Hopewell became a major embarkation point for troops bound for Europe. The City Point Historic District contains approximately seven blocks of tree-lined streets, with buildings that date largely from the nineteenth century and exhibiting a variety of styles.

ST27.1 St. John's Episcopal Church

1840, 1894. 505 Cedar Ln.

Although built in 1840, St. John's was dramatically transformed from its original Greek Revival idiom with the addition of transepts to the nave and Gothic details in 1894. The interior has big, energetic Gothic trusses. A small cemetery is attached. The parish house dates from 1933.

ST27.2 Appomattox Manor

c. 1763 and later. End of Cedar Ln. Open to the public

The view from this point of land between the Appomattox and James rivers is overwhelming. Francis Epees received the property in 1635, and it remained in the family for over 300 years, until sold to the National Park Service in 1979. The house is a large, rambling, U-shaped structure. A small entry porch with Tuscan Doric columns is at the front, and large porches wrap around other sides. The original portion of the house is the central one-and-one-half-story wood-frame section with a traditional double-pile plan. An east wing in the Downing mode which contained another parlor and a library was added c. 1840. In 1850 another addition was built, this time to the west. In the early twentieth century more changes were made. Two rooms restored to c. 1850 can be toured. On the grounds of the main house are several nineteenth-century frame outbuildings: two smokehouses, a dairy, and a kitchen–wash house.

Between June 1864 and April 1865 General U. S. Grant had his tent and later his cabin on the

ST27.2 Appomattox Manor

ST30 Crescent Hills Subdivision, 102 Crescent Avenue (below, left) and 202 Crescent Avenue (below, right)

east grounds of the manor. Lincoln visited and used Appomattox Manor as an office. Grant's headquarters cabin, constructed in November 1864, still stands to the east of the house but is mostly rebuilt. Shown at the 1876 Philadelphia Centennial, it remained in Fairmont Park until 1981, when the National Park Service returned it to the site. The vertical timber construction was a common Civil War framing method.

ST27.3 City Point History Museum at St. Dennis Chapel

1887. Brown Ave. Open to the public

Constructed by the U.S. Navy, which maintained a base in City Point, this small vertical board-and-batten chapel has been converted into a museum.

ST27.4 Bonnaccord

1842–1845, 1916. 1015 Pecan Ave. (north side of the street)

The structure began as a Greek Revival house, but in 1916 it received a Colonial Revival porch with Tuscan columns. Originally constructed as the first rectory for St. John's Episcopal Church on Cedar Lane, it was named in 1862 by the owner at the time, Elizabeth Cocke. The Epees family, owners of Appomattox Manor, purchased it in 1902.

ST28 City Point National Cemetery

1866. 10th Ave. and Davis St.

Authorized as part of the National Cemetery System (1862), the City Point National Cemetery, along with twenty others, was established in April 1866 through a later joint resolution of Congress. Military in form, the rectangular 7.5-acre cemetery has a semicircular entrance with a wrought iron gate and stone piers. A 4-foot wall of uncoursed fieldstone surrounds the cemetery. At the center a roadway encircles a flagpole and a monument dedicated to the memory of the dead of the Army of the James.

An 1868 stone lodge constructed as a residence and office for the superintendent of the cemetery was demolished in 1928 and replaced by the present one-and-one-half-story brick and stucco building with a gambrel roof. The lodge is based on a prototypical plan designed by Quartermaster General Montgomery C. Meigs c. 1865. The more than 5,100 interments of Civil War soldiers and sailors at City Point include approximately 1,400 unknown soldiers and 118 Confederate soldiers.

ST29 Weston Manor

c. 1789. Weston Ln. and 21st Ave. Open to the public

A wood-frame structure covered in original beaded weatherboard, this double-pile, five-bay plantation house is one of the best preserved in Virginia. Semi-isolated on the Appomattox River, Weston (originally "Western") Manor has the traditional river and land entrances, a hipped roof, and four end chimneys with corbeled caps, the very essence of the formal Tidewater plantation house. Most of the interior woodwork is original. The plan is traditional, featuring a long central hall with a central arch and a spiral staircase to one side.

ST30 Crescent Hills Subdivision

1926–1937, M. T. Broyhill, developer, and Sears, Roebuck and Company. Oakwood Ave., Prince George Ave., and Crescent Ave., bounded by City Point Rd. and Broadway

Developed as a "strictly high class" enclave for middle management personnel connected with the new industries in Hopewell, Crescent Hills contains forty-four Sears, Roebuck and Company "Honor Bilt" prefabricated houses erected over a ten-year period. Part of its attraction was the financing plans Sears offered, along with the chance to modify or customize to individual preferences. The following mentions houses for which specific models can be identified in Sears catalogs published in the years indicated.

Oakwood Avenue: At 102 Oakwood Avenue is the Oakdale (model 3314, 1925–1937). At 104 Oakwood is the Rochelle (1929–1933) but with a projecting gabled entrance and stucco covering. Number 106 is the Oakdale, but with a screened porch and altered entrance. Sears described what was built at 202 Oakwood Avenue as the "Americanized English." Number 205 is the Lexington (model 3255, 1921–1933). Number 208 is the Oak Park model, but with a brick exterior and without the side lights flanking the doorway; it appeared in the catalog 1926–1933. Number 209 is the Cambridge model (1926–1929), but with a brick peaked gable; the wing is a later addition. Number 211 is the Lexington again, but with an entrance porch and doorway from the Magnolia model.

Prince George Avenue: Number 102 is the Maplewood model, which appeared in the catalog 1932–1933; a later addition is to the right. Number 104 is the Rochelle, but with a different entrance. Number 106 is the Bellewood model, which appeared in the catalog 1931–1933. Number 107 is the Alhambra model, influenced by the Spanish mission craze. Number 109 is the Rochelle model again, but with a different entrance. Number 200 is the Belmont (1932–1933), but with a brick exterior and a reversed floor plan. Number 201 is the Van Jean model (1928–1929), but with a different doorway and windows. Number 206 is the Hawthorne (1931–1933). Finally, number 210 is the Oak Park.

Crescent Avenue: Number 101 is the Branford model (1937), originally built without the wings shown in the catalog, which were later added. Number 102 (ST30.1) is the Rochelle, but with a different entrance. Number 104 is the Belmont model, almost identical to 200 Prince George Avenue. Number 106 is the Newbury model (1934–1939), but with a different roof treatment. Number 108 is the Mansfield model (1932–1933), but with different roof treatment. Number 201 is the Lexington, but with added dormers. Number 202 (ST30.2) is the Colchester (1932–1933), but with added half timbering.

City Point Road: Number 2603 is the original model for Crescent Hills and M. T. Broyhill's home. It is based on the Lexington but with modified window treatment. Number 2705 is the Rochelle model.

Eastern Shore (ES)

THE EASTERN SHORE HAS SINCE THE MID-SEVENTEENTH CENTURY COM-prised two counties: Accomack County, the northernmost, named for the Native American tribe that originally inhabited the area, and Northampton County, named for the English shire. Patterns of development in the area can be read in the landscape. Initial settlement followed the shoreline and extended to the offshore islands on the seaside. Agriculture, fishing, timber, and shipping were primary activities. By the late seventeenth century some inland development had occurred, such as that at Pear Valley, a unique survivor, but large houses remained closer to the shore. Through the eighteenth and mid-nineteenth centuries this pattern continued, though a few small inland towns grew up along the stagecoach roads. The bayside developments had commercial ties to Baltimore and Norfolk, while the seaside looked northward to Philadelphia, New York, and New England. Union forces under General Henry Lockwood occupied the peninsula during the Civil War, and he directed that no buildings be destroyed. A shift toward developing the middle of the peninsula came in 1884 when the New York, Philadelphia and Norfolk Railroad ran its tracks down the center of the peninsula, creating a series of railroad towns. Automobiles continued the reorientation; U.S. 13 came up the center in the 1920s, and the completion of the Chesapeake Bay Bridge and Tunnel in 1964 intensified automobile-related development. Refrigeration brought a boom in commercial fishing for much of the twentieth century, although today that industry is in decline. Although strip commercialism has crept in along U.S. 13, much of the landscape beyond this narrow band is maintained for farming and fishing, still primary occupations for this largely rural area, along with tourism. The terrain has a quiet, lonely, haunting quality, the flat fields bordered by trees or running into marshes. The town of Accomac has the finest collection of eighteenth- and early nineteenth-century structures, Onancock the best for late nineteenth-century buildings, and Cape Charles for the early twentieth century. However, many other towns are worth a visit, as are various independent structures that display the unique Eastern Shore form of "big house," "little house," colonnade, and kitchen. The driving tour is arranged south to north and oriented to U.S. 13.

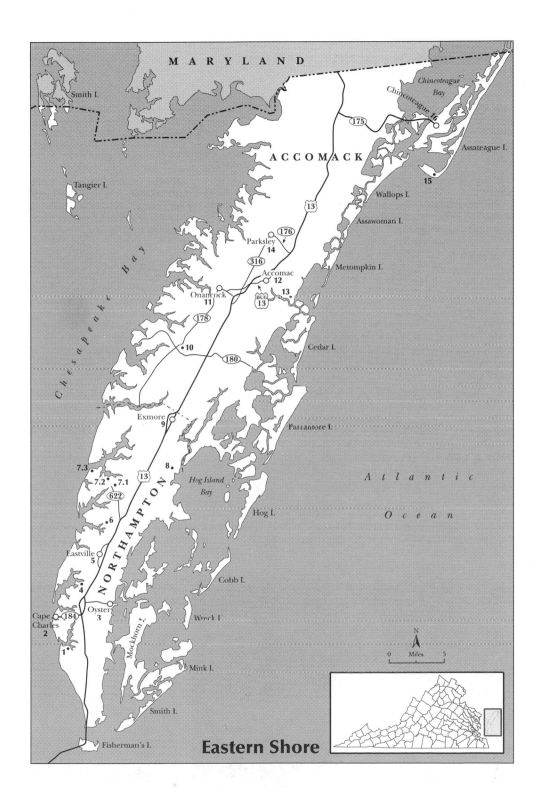

Eastern Shore

MARYLAND

Smith I.

Chincoteague Bay

Chincoteague 16

ACCOMACK

Tangier I.

Assateague I.

175

15

Wallops I.

13

Assawoman I.

176

Parksley

14

Metompkin I.

316

Accomac

12

Onancock

11

13

BUS 13

178

Cedar I.

10

180

Exmore

9

Parramore I.

7.3

8

7.2 7.1

13

Hog Island Bay

622

Hog I.

6

Eastville

5

Cobb I.

4

Oyster

3

Wreck I.

Cape Charles

2

184

Mockhorn I.

Mink I.

1

Smith I.

Fisherman's I.

Atlantic

Ocean

Chesapeake Bay

NORTHAMPTON

N

0 Miles 5

483

Northampton County   (ES1–ES9)

ES1 Custis Tombs

c. 1750. VA 644, 2.1 miles west from U.S. 13

One of the most important examples of colonial funerary art, the site is owned by the APVA. The carving on the tomb of John Custis IV, including the family coat of arms, drapery, and a skull, was executed in London by one William Colley of Fenn Church Street. The tombs are near the site of the Custis family home, Arlington, after which George Washington named a plantation he owned in Fairfax County, which later became the site of Arlington House and Arlington Cemetery.

ES2 Cape Charles

Cape Charles was created in 1884 as the southern terminus of the Eastern Shore's first railroad, the New York, Philadelphia and Norfolk (NYP&N), owned by William Lawrence Scott and Alexander Cassatt (later president of the Pennsylvania Railroad). From Cape Charles, barges would carry railroad cars across the Chesapeake Bay to Norfolk. The harbor was dredged and the town laid out. Civil engineer William Bauman planned the town on a grid pattern with twenty-seven rectangular and square blocks formed by six north-south streets named for fruits and seven east-west streets named for Virginia statesmen. In the center of the grid is a park (now fenced). The main business street, Mason Avenue, is at the southern edge, fronting on the railroad, barge yards, and waterfront. Rail and barge traffic began to decline after World War II, and today service is limited. The town retains much of its earlier character.

The main architectural landmark of Cape Charles is the Water Tower (c. 1985), which imitates a large lighthouse. At the corner of Mason Avenue and Fig Street is an amazing survivor, the Jacobean Revival Kellogg Building (ES2.1) (c. 1926), a former automobile dealership and attached gas station constructed of tan and brown brick. You fill your car with gas in front of gables remindful of Bacon's Castle. Farther down Mason Avenue, at the corner of Peach Street, is another survivor of the hundreds of Pure Oil service stations that used to dot the East Coast (1930, Carl A. Peterson). (A Pure Oil in ruins is on Virginia 184.) Designed in the English "cottage style," they were built in the 1920s and 1930s and were instantly recognizable by their blue tile roofs and trim. Peach Street, a boulevard, is the town's north-south axis. Two banks occupy the next corner, at Mason Avenue and Pine Street. The town's largest and most impressive building is the Sovran Bank (formerly the Northampton County Trust Bank) (ES2.2) (1921, Wyatt and Nolting), a Neoclassical Revival building with engaged in antis colonnade in a colossal Ionic order and full entablature. On the opposite corner is the Colonial Revival Mumford Bank (ES2.3) (1895, W. H. Lambertson), in tan brick

ES1 Custis Tombs, with detail of carving

ES2.1 Kellogg Building

ES2.2 Sovran Bank (Northampton County Trust Bank)

ES2.3 Mumford Bank

with classical details. The U.S. Post Office (1932, Louis A. Simon, Supervising Architect of the Treasury) at Randolph Avenue and Strawberry Street, is the usual government-issue Colonial Revival.

The residential area to the north of Mason Avenue dates from 1884 to 1920 and is composed of a variety of Queen Anne, Colonial Revival, bungaloid, and Foursquare houses. The area is a historic district, and many houses display plaques with dates. Reputedly many of the houses are Sears, Roebuck mail order, but this origin has not been confirmed. Bay Avenue, at the end of Mason Avenue and fronting on the bay, was the elite address and has the most impressive houses. The A. L. Detwiler House (1919, Charles Weber Bolton of Philadelphia), 212 Bay Avenue, is a large Colonial Revival house. The Jack V. Moore House (1909, William Newton Diehl of Norfolk), 306 Bay Avenue, is in the Southern Colonial Revival mode, with a giant portico. The Pavilion (1923), on Bay Avenue opposite the termination of Randolph Avenue, is a simple octagonal frame gazebo, built by a local contractor, Conrad Grimmer.

ES3 Oyster

VA 639

A poignant reminder of the fishing industry, Oyster has escaped modernization and remains almost untouched. Home to about 250 people, it dates from c. 1900 and is composed of about fifty buildings, including the usual house types, a dock, B. L. Bell and Son Packing House (currently not in use), other smaller packing sheds, and a small Methodist church (Travis Chapel By-the-Sea). Some of the houses and the post office were ferried over from barrier island communities when they were abandoned c. 1900. The process continues; in May 1998 an abandoned U.S. Coast Guard Lifeboat Station (1936) from Cobb Island, weighing 200 tons, was ferried over by the Nature Conservancy to be used as a tourist lodge. The town of Willis Wharf (Virginia 639), also on the ocean side of

ES4 Eyre Hall

the Eastern Shore and about twenty-nine miles north, is similar, though more altered.

ES4 Eyre Hall

1735, 1750, 1796. Eyre Hall Rd., 1 mile west from U.S. 13, Chesapeake vicinity. Gardens open to the public

A spectacular approach down a tree-lined drive leads to an archetypal Eastern Shore house arrangement of "big house," "little house," colonnade, kitchen. Here the silhouette helps tell the story. The initial structure was the two-story clapboard wing, c. 1735, followed by the kitchen, added a few years later. The large, gambrel-roofed addition came in 1796, and about the same time the colonnade was added, uniting the group. Fine woodwork and French scenic wallpaper by Dufour, c. 1816, embellish the interior of the addition. The grounds contain a group of original outbuildings, and behind the house is a formal garden dating from c. 1800.

ES5 Eastville

U.S. Business 13

The county seat of Northampton County since 1677, this small town centers on a complex of buildings on the courthouse green, several of which are maintained by the APVA and serve as museums. On the north side of the green is the former Northampton County Courthouse (ES5.1) (1731), a pretty brick structure with an entrance on the gable end, erected by John Marshall, a local builder. It served as a court-house until 1795 and then passed through many uses. In 1913 it was moved to its present location so that a Confederate monument could be erected. The entrance front—Federal in style—dates from this "restoration." Next door to the west are the former county clerk's office (c. 1725–1750) and the debtors' prison (c. 1814). Along the south side of the green are a row of four frame law offices and a two-story brick store. The "new" Northampton County Courthouse (1899, B. [Bartholomew] F. Smith Fireproof Construction Company), which replaced an "old and dilapidated" 1795 structure, was constructed by an Alexandria firm. It is not imposing and retains the residential scale of the earlier structures. Originally a balcony was over the entrance; the present porch is a later addition which lends a Colonial Revival character. Across from the courthouse complex is the Eastville Inn (c. 1780, 1928), a rambling frame structure with an impressive porch which for years served as the social hub of the town. Plans are currently underway to rehabilitate the inn as a Heritage Trail Center. Eastville has a number of other structures of importance. U.S. Business 13 (Court House Road) bisects the town; on the south side of town on Court House Road stands Cessford, a large, five-bay brick house (1832) built for John Kerr, a relative of the family that built Kerr Place in Onancock. In spite of its date, Cessford is largely Federal in style, indicating the conservatism of the Eastern Shore in the mid-nineteenth century. North about 400 yards from the courthouse green is Christ Episcopal Church (1828), brick, with a substantial Greek Revival portico; the steeple is a later addition, and the chancel has been extended.

ES5.1 Northampton County Courthouse (former)

ES6 **Pear Valley**

c. 1740. Pear Valley Ln. (VA 689), Shadyside vicinity (west on VA 628 [Wilson Neck Dr.] .7 mile from U.S. 13; right on VA 689). Open to the public by appointment

Described by historians as an important survivor of eighteenth-century Virginia building, this cottage provides a rare glimpse of the smaller houses that once dotted the Chesapeake. The house stands about 200 feet on the east near a barn. A one-room-and-loft frame house with an elaborate brick end, it dates, according to the most recent research and dendrochronolgy, from 1740; earlier literature dated it much earlier. Handsome craftsmanship is displayed in the chamfering of the ceiling joists and other exposed structural posts. The tilted "false

plates" that support the rafters are visibly pegged through round-ended ceiling joists, and glassed headers in the brick end-wall form decorative patterns. This clasp-purlin type of roof is one of the two known examples in Virginia. The wood lath in the loft has feathered and lapped ends, thus requiring only one nail for fastening. The property is owned by the APVA. A modest restoration is underway, and the local APVA chapter installed a tin roof and wood siding to shield the building from the elements.

ES7 **Hungar's Episcopal Church and Glebe**

1742–1751, 1850. Church Neck Rd. (VA 619), Bridgetown vicinity (west 1 mile from U.S. 13; north 2.7 miles on VA 622 [Glebe Rd.]; right on VA 619, 1 mile). Marked with a sign

Abandoned after disestablishment, this church was restored to use in 1819. Originally over 90 feet in length, the church was shortened in 1850 by about 20 feet because the west wall had deteriorated. The brickwork and especially the arches and keystones illuminate the talent of the builders. Although it appears isolated, the church served as the center of a small settlement. Across the field to the west can be glimpsed Chatham (1818), a substantial brick house. East 1.4 miles on Virginia 622 is Hungar's Glebe (c. 1745), the former rectory, whose date is controversial but which, in spite of a claim to c. 1643, probably dates from c. 1745. A nice example of a single-story, three-bay brick dwelling with glazed headers, it has an evocative setting on the marshes.

ES7 Hungar's Glebe

ES8 Brownsville

1806, 1809. Virginia 608 (Brownsville Rd.), Nassawadox vicinity (east VA 606 from U.S. 13; north on VA 600 [Seaside Rd.]; east on VA 608 1.8 miles). Open to the public upon request

Spectacular in its lonely setting facing the Atlantic Ocean, Brownsville is currently owned by the Nature Conservancy and serves as its Eastern Shore headquarters. Originally built for John Upshur, whose ancestor John Browne patented the land there in 1652, the three-bay "big house" of Flemish bond brick has an impressive set of attached buildings in the Eastern Shore manner. In addition to the usual sequence, Upshur added a long wing in 1809 to house numerous relatives. The overall quality of the Federal structure is high, and the detailing, such as the Doric entrance portico with Chinese Chippendale railings, is rare on the Eastern Shore. The interior woodwork is sophisticated: a wide, carved arch divides the cross hall, and the parlor has seventeen different patterns worked into wood and plaster.

ES9 Exmore

An important crossroads town, Exmore was established in 1884 and named for the fact that it was the tenth NYP&N station (X-more) south of Delaware. A commercial center that the highway has bypassed, the town had substantial canning operations and retains a group of well-kept brick and frame houses. On U.S. Business 13 on the south side of Exmore is the Exmore Diner (ES9.1) (c. 1940, Silk City of Paterson, New Jersey). Preston Kellam, owner of a produce trucking company, spied the diner in New Jersey in 1953 and wired home for $5,000 to purchase it as an addition to a truck stop. It is virtually intact, the only modification being the roadside sign. The monitor-style roof, suggesting that of a railroad car, is a feature that disap-

ES8 Brownsville

ES9.1 Exmore Diner

peared in the 1950s from diners made by Silk City. The stainless steel and porcelain enamel exterior panels are complemented by the neon-lit clock. The interior is well preserved down to the tile on the floor, the stainless steel back bar, and the high-back oak booths.

Accomack County ES10–ES16)

ES10 St. George's Episcopal Church

1763, 1885. VA 178, Pungoteague vicinity

Known as Pungoteague Church until 1800, when its name became St. George's, it was built in 1763 by Severn Guttridge on a Latin cross plan with a rounded apse. Abandoned in 1812 after disestablishment of the Anglican church, the building was later returned to use but then, in one of the rare such occurrences on the Eastern Shore, severely mutilated by Union troops. A substantial rebuilding in 1885 elimi-

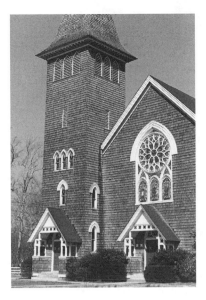

ES11.1 Market Street
United Methodist Church

ES11.2 Kerr Place, detail
of chair molding

nated the nave and apse and transformed the transepts into the church, with the south wall serving as the entrance facade. The Flemish bond brickwork, its dark red stretchers contrasting with the clear-blue-glazed headers, is some of the finest colonial brickwork in the state.

ES11 Onancock

Onancock, on the bay side of the Eastern Shore, was settled in the 1680s. The town had several periods of growth: the 1780s, the 1820s, and then after the Civil War, when it became a stop for steamboats ferrying passengers and freight on Chesapeake Bay. With an orientation north to Baltimore and south to Norfolk, it became one of the hubs of the Eastern Shore, with buildings that reflected its prosperity. Steamboats stopped running in the mid-1930s; the town has developed little since then and is particularly pretty and well-preserved.

The major architectural sites are along and just off Market Street, which terminates at the harbor and curves around into King Street. Beginning at the east end of Market Street, as one enters town, the first is Naomi Makemie Presbyterian Church (1895), at 89 Market Street, a simple wooden Gothic Revival building named for the wife of Francis Makemie, one of the founders of American Presbyterianism. The Market Street United Methodist Church (ES11.1) (1882; 1898, remodeling, Benjamin

B. Owens of Baltimore), a large, shingled building at 75 Market Street, is the more impressive church with its dominant tower at the west and a smaller octagonal tower at the east. The interior contains an important set of stained glass windows by William A. Heffernan of Washington, D.C.

On College Street, which intersects Market Street, is the former Onancock High School (1921, Carneal and Johnston), which is white-trimmed red brick Colonial Revival (what else?), elegantly carried out, with an impressive, though shallow, pedimented entrance porch. Although Carneal and Johnston are the architects of record for this single-story, hip-roofed school, buildings virtually identical to it except in detail were constructed across the commonwealth, indicating that the School Buildings Service of the Virginia Department of Education provided the plans.

At 69 Market Street is the most impressive Eastern Shore house open to the public, Kerr Place (ES11.2) (1799–1806; marked with a sign). Owned by the Eastern Shore Historical Society, it is in a continual process of restoration. Local lore holds that an emigré English architect designed the house for the local merchant John Stephen Ker (later Kerr). Surviving accounts show that Ker paid John Rouse as a supervisor of seven workmen: the brickmason was Cyrus Sharp, who was paid 94 pounds and used slave labor, and Isaac Gibbons received $370 for carpentry. Constructed of brick laid up in Flemish bond, the kitchen, to the west, was incorporated as a wing c. 1900. The entrance porch is not original. On the interior is an impressive set of high-ceilinged (13 feet) rooms where paint research has revealed extensive marbleizing. The designer obviously had access to books by Robert Adam or a follower. The applied composition or gesso ornament may have been made by a craftsman from Baltimore or Washington, D.C. Although no original furnishings are displayed, the collection contains excellent examples of Eastern Shore cabinetry.

The Frank A. Slocomb House (1890), 68 Market Street, now the rectory for the church next door, has a mansard roof—indicating how late the Second Empire style lasted—and elaborate gingerbread trim. Holy Trinity Episcopal Church (1884–1886, Charles E. Cassell of Baltimore), 66 Market Street, is a nice wooden Gothic Revival structure with an elaborate hammer-beam truss roof on the interior. Originally it had an entrance tower with a spire, but that has been removed. Onancock Baptist Church (1891, front section, John A. and William T. Wilson of Baltimore; 1855, rear section), 60 Market Street, illustrates how buildings change. The rear section, originally located elsewhere in town, was moved to the site and the front half added. The more recent facade is modest with a small tower and trefoil-arched stained glass windows.

A fire destroyed part of Onancock's commercial area in 1899, and some buildings are early twentieth-century replacements. More recent is the Roseland Theater (c. 1940), 54 Market Street, a tame Art Deco structure with Carrara glass panels, streamlined metal bands, and a neon marquee. The First Virginia (National) Bank (1894, S. S. and William T. Wilson; 1921, remodeling, attributed to Carneal and Johnston), 52 Market Street, began as a Romanesque Revival structure but fell prey to the galloping "colonialism" of the 1920s. The Fosque House (1882), 16 Market Street, has—for the Eastern Shore—impressive gingerbread decoration. The Scott House (1778; addition, c. 1920), 12 Market Street, is reputedly the oldest building in Onancock. The original portion is to the rear; a Scott family cemetery is located to the side. The Hopkins House (c. 1860), 8 Market Street, with Federal and Greek Revival features, was built near the family store.

Market Street ends at the town wharf (which has been on this site for more than 300 years). Next door is the Hopkins and Brothers Store (ES11.3) (c. 1842, c. 1880), a two-story frame commercial structure that originally stood a

short distance from its present site on Onancock Creek. It remained in family hands until 1965 and was moved in 1970; it is owned and leased out by the APVA. The earliest section is the ell; the front, with pilasters, bracketed cornice, and Gothic window, is later. The store retains most of its nineteenth-century fittings, including cases, and is a good example of a small maritime shop. Next door is the Eastern Shore Steamship Company's former ticket office (1906), a small, rectangular building with bracketed eaves.

ES12 Accomac

Slightly inland from the Atlantic and at the head of Folly Inlet, Accomac, established in 1690 as the county seat, is the most intact and in many ways the most interesting architecturally of the Eastern Shore towns. It offers a wealth of buildings from the 1700s to the early 1900s. The present street pattern dates to 1786. Although fires destroyed some of the downtown in the 1860s and 1920s, the railroad bypassed it, helping to preserve its character. A general lack of affluence has allowed property owners to improve their buildings only gradually, rather than wholesale. In 1830 Accomac had a population of 240; in 2000 the number of inhabitants stood at 547. Bisected by U.S. Business 13, or Front Street, the town was initially known as Metompkin, then Drummondtown, and finally acquired its present name c. 1890. The Virginia General Assembly mandated the difference in spelling between Accomack County and the county seat in 1940.

ES11.3 Hopkins and Brothers Store

At the center of the town are the courthouse green and the Accomack County Courthouse (1899, B. [Bartholomew] F. Smith Fireproof Construction Company). Although a tame composition in comparison to other Victorian courthouses in Virginia, this one, with its tower and round-arched windows, is livelier than Smith's contemporary design in nearby Northampton County. It was intended to be prominent, since Accomac had just staved off a referendum moving the county seat to Parksley, and Smith gave it more emphasis by adding a tower. The overall form, with the gables on the long side, recalls late eighteenth- and early nineteenth-century buildings such as nearby Kerr Place in Onancock; but the round-arched openings and prominent brick belt courses recall Richardsonian Romanesque. Next door is the county clerk's office (1889, W. F. Weber), a lively Romanesque Revival affair with a jerkinhead roof. The remaining buildings of the courthouse green are law offices and include a mansarded structure from c. 1900, one from c. 1850, and a third, built in 1954.

Across Cross Street (Virginia 764) is the Old Mercantile Building (c. 1819), a stuccofronted, two-story brick structure with a fine cornice, a rare example of Federal commercial architecture. Down the street and marked with a sign is the Debtors' Prison (1783), originally erected as the jailer's residence and converted into a jail in 1824. The APVA has restored it and opens it to the public.

Back on Front Street, the large (empty as of this writing) brick structure across from the courthouse green (with the Virginia Landmark sign noting it as the birth site of Governor Wise) is the former Drummondtown Tavern, later Accomac Hotel (1921–1922, Robert Gardner). An imposing landmark with its two-story portico, it is a New York architect's idea of "Southern Colonial" and obviously has little reference to Eastern Shore building traditions.

West, on the south side of Front Street, is the imposing Seymour House (1791–1815), which well illustrates the Eastern Shore building form. The sequence began with the old kitchen (to the far west), followed in the late eighteenth century by the colonnade, which served as a doctor's office, then by the little house and half of the big house, and finally the last two (east) bays of the big house. The interior has fine carved woodwork in the Federal idiom.

Left on Virginia 605 (Drummondtown Road) sits St. James Episcopal Church (1838). An imposing edifice with its Greek Doric portico and later Gothic Revival spire, the structure is brick covered with scored stucco resembling sandstone. An itinerant artist, Jean G. Potts, decorated the interior c. 1860 with a trompe l'oeil fresco incorporating a receding arch intended to lengthen the chancel visually. The interior and the fresco have recently been restored.

The next cross street, Back Street (paralleling Front Street), contains an impressive group of buildings ranging from the late eighteenth to the early twentieth century. At the corner of Back Street and Drummondtown Road is Bloodworth Cottage (c. 1776; 1966–1975, restored). Farther down Back Street, on the southwest corner of Cross Street, is the Greek Revival Makemie Presbyterian Church (1837), with unfluted wood Doric columns. The cupola dates from 1889. On its grounds stands a copy of A. Stirling Calder's Francis Makemie Memorial. On the northeast corner is Seven Gables (c. 1788 and later), a house with seven dormers whose odd shape results from the Eastern Shore penchant for additions. On the southeast corner is Drummond House (ES12.1) (c. 1817), more formal in its main block but with the usual additions. Many of the other houses on Back Street are identified by historic markers and should be examined.

ES13 **Bowman's Folly**

c. 1815. 1988, restoration, J. Floyd Nock III. Bowman's Folly Dr. (north from Accomac .5 mile on U.S. Business 13, right on VA 652 [Joynes Neck Rd.] 2.5 miles, right on Bowman's Folly Dr. .4 mile)

This private house on an imposing site on Foley Inlet can be examined from the road. Constructed by a Revolutionary War general and politician, John Cropper, Jr., it is one of the most substantial houses on the Eastern Shore. The wood-frame central section with Palladian windows has brick ends. As is typical, a set of outbuildings trails off on one side and includes, in addition to the usual forms, a dovecote and a privy with raised paneling on the interior.

ES14 **Parksley**

More Victorian in character than most of the towns on the Eastern Shore, Parksley resulted from the railroad's drive down the peninsula in 1884. Henry R. Bennett, a traveling salesman, conceived of a model town and, with friends, purchased 160 acres and laid out a gridiron on either side of the tracks. At the center lay the town square, occupied by the railroad station and a rail siding; the commercial area surrounded it. Bennett set aside land for churches, schools, and parks and banned liquor. Streets are named for Bennett family members, notables such as William Lloyd Garrison, and railroad executives such as Alexander Cassatt. The too-pretty railroad station sitting in the center is not original but came from the town of Hopeton about three miles up the tracks; it was moved and restored in 1988. It houses the Eastern Shore of Virginia Railroad Museum. Unfortunately much of the downtown has been modernized. The best row of Victorian-era houses is on Mary Street, on the east side of the tracks.

ES15 Chincoteague

The Indian meaning of the name is "beautiful land across the water," and Chincoteague Island from a distance presents this aspect. On closer view, however, the town of Chincoteague displays all the problems of a too-popular summer resort. Today it is the Eastern Shore's largest town. Settled c. 1700 and known in lore as the lair of pirates, the town grew slowly and was extremely isolated until the 1870s, when the railroad arrived, and then 1922, when an automobile causeway opened to the mainland. Fires, overbuilding, and intense development have destroyed many notable buildings. The older section of downtown, and especially Main Street, has an assemblage of turn-of-the-twenti-eth-century structures of some interest. Among new buildings, the most significant is the U.S. Coast Guard Berthing Facility (1997, Hanbury Evans Newill Vlattas). Lighthouse shapes serve as stair towers, and the overall blocky form takes its cue from earlier Coast Guard stations.

ES16 Assateague Island

Assateague Island is flat and low, with a memorable landscape of pine woods, marshes, and sand, partially shaped by man, in that a settlement of nearly 200 people and their livestock lived here until the 1920s. It is the outermost part of the better-known Chincoteague barrier island chain popularized by Marguerite Henry's *Misty of Chincoteague* (1947) and the later film (1960). The island as a whole is a wildlife refuge and a National Seashore operated by the commonwealth of Virginia and the National Park Service.

ES16.1 Assateague Lighthouse

1866–1867. Assateague Island. Open to the public

The Coast Guard operates the lighthouse, which replaced an 1831 structure. Standing 142 feet high and built of brick, it is one of the last operating lighthouses on the East Coast. Adjacent is the former U.S. Coast Guard Station (1922), which served until after World War II as a life-saving station. The complex includes a quarters for personnel, a boathouse, a lookout tower, and launches for boats.

Selected Bibliography

Abbott, Carl. "Norfolk in the New Century: The Jamestown Exposition and Urban Boosterism." *Virginia Magazine of History and Biography* 85 (January 1977): 86–96.

Allen, William Charles. "Hawkswood: A Country House in the Tuscan Villa Style." Master's thesis, University of Virginia, 1974.

American Architects Dictionary. Edited by George S. Koyl. New York: R. R. Bowker Co., 1955, 1962.

Anderson, D. Wiley. *Short Reviews, A Few Recent Designs.* Photocopy on deposit at the Virginia Department of Historic Resources. c. 1904.

———. *Specifications for Fireproofing and Additions to the Virginia State Capitol.* N.p., n.d.

Andrews, Wayne. *Pride of the South.* New York: Atheneum, 1979.

Archer, John. *The Literature of British Domestic Architecture, 1715–1842.* Cambridge: MIT Press, 1985.

Architect's Emergency Committee. *Great Georgian Houses of America.* Vol. 1, New York: The Kalkhoff Press, 1933. Vol. 2, New York: Scribner Press, 1937. Reprint, New York: Dover, 1970.

"Architects Form an Association." *The Concrete Age* 15 (October 1911): 26.

"The Army's Pentagon Building." *Architectural Record* 93 (January 1943): 63.

Art of Architecture in Downtown Richmond, 1789–1989. Exhibition catalog. Richmond: Second Presbyterian Church, 1989.

Askins, Norman Davenport. "A Treatise on the Paneling at Wilton with Notes on the Randolph Family and Georgian Architecture in Virginia." Master's thesis, University of Virginia, 1968.

Axelrod, Alan, ed. *The Colonial Revival in America.* New York: W. W. Norton, 1985.

Badger, Curtis J. *Virginia's Eastern Shore: A Pictorial History.* Norfolk: Donning Co., c. 1983.

Bailey, James Henry. *History of St. Peter's Church, Richmond, Virginia, 125 Years 1834–1959.* Richmond: Lewis Printing, 1959.

Baldwin, Charles. *Stanford White.* New York: Dodd, Mead, 1931.

Barber, George Franklin. *Modern American Homes.* Knoxville: Gaut-Ogden Co., 1903–1907.

———. *Modern Dwellings.* Knoxville, Tenn.: S. B. Newman and Co., 1898–1907.

Beckerdite, Luke. "William Buckland and William Bernard Sears: The Designer and the Carver." *Journal of Early Southern Decorative Arts* 8 (November 1982): 6–41.

Beiswanger, William L. "Thomas Jefferson's Designs for Garden Structures at Monticello." Master's thesis, University of Virginia, 1977.

Bell, Alison, and James Deetz. "Folk Housing Revisited." *Louisia County Historical Magazine* 26 (1996): 59–71.

Benjamin, Asher. *The Architect, or Practical House Carpenter.* 1830. Reprint, New York: Dover Publications, 1988.

———. *Practice of Architecture and The Builder's Guide: Two Pattern Books of American Classical Architecture in the United States of America.* 1839, 1845. Reprint, New York: Da Capo Press, 1994.

Benjamin, Asher, and Daniel Raynerd. *The American Builder's Companion: or, A New System of Architecture, particularly Adapted to the Present Style of Building in the United States of America.* 1806. 6th ed., 1827. Reprint, with introduction by William Morgan, New York: Dover Publications, 1969. Reprint, New York: Da Capo Press, 1972.

Ray H. Bennett Lumber Co., Inc. *Bennett's Small House Catalog, 1920.* New York: Dover Publications, 1993. Reprint of *Bennett Homes: Better-Built Ready-Cut,* catalog no. 18. 1920.

Bibb, A. Burnley. "Old Colonial Work of Virginia and Maryland." *American Architect and Building News*, 15 June 1889, 279–81. Reprinted in *The Georgian Period*. New York: American Architect and Building News, 1898–1901.

A. J. Bicknell & Co. *Bicknell's Victorian Buildings*. New York: Dover Publications, 1979. Reprint of *Bicknell's Village Builder and Supplement*. 1878.

———. *Bicknell's Village Builder*. Watkins Glen, N.Y.: American Life Foundation and Study Institute, 1976 [1872].

Binney, Marcus. "An English Garden Suburb on the James." *Country Life*, 4 April 1985, 912–14. *The Black Swan*

Boggs, Kate Doggett. *Once a Village: Fredericksburg, Virginia*. N.p., c. 1944.

———. *Prints and Plants of Old Gardens*. Richmond: Garrett and Massie, [c. 1932].

Bossom, Alfred Charles. *Building to the Skies: The Romance of the Skyscraper*. London and New York: The Studio Ltd., 1934.

Boyd, John Taylor, Jr. "The Country House and the Developed Landscape: William Lawrence Bottomley Expresses His Point of View about the Relation of the Country House to Its Environment in an Interview." *Arts and Decoration* 31 (November 1929): 100.

Boyd, Sterling M. "The Adam Style in America, 1770–1820." Ph.D. diss., Princeton University, 1966. Published in *Outstanding Dissertations in the Fine Arts*. New York: Garland Publishing, 1985.

Brock, Henry Irving. *Colonial Churches in Virginia*. Richmond: Dale Press, 1930.

Brown, Glenn. "Old Colonial Work in Virginia and Maryland." *American Architect and Building News*, 22 October, 19 November, 26 November 1887. Reprinted in *The Georgian Period*. Parts 1–2. New York: American Architect and Building News, 1898–1901.

Brown, Thelma Robbins. "Memorial Chapel: The Culmination of the Development of the Campus of Hampton Institute, Hampton, Virginia, 1867–1887." Master's thesis, University of Virginia, 1971.

Brownell, Charles E., Calder Loth, William M. S. Rasmussen, and Richard Guy Wilson. *The Making of Virginia Architecture*. Richmond: Virginia Museum of Fine Arts; Charlottesville: University Press of Virginia, 1992.

Bruce, Philip Alexander. *History of the University of Virginia, 1819–1919: The Lengthened Shadow of One Man*. 5 vols. New York: Macmillan Company, 1920–22.

Bruder, Anne Elizabeth. "The Evangelical Architecture of the Protestant Episcopal Church in Virginia." Master's thesis, University of Virginia, 1996.

Bryant, H. Stafford, Jr. "Two Twentieth-Century Domestic Architects in the South: Neel Reid and William L. Bottomley." *Classic America* 1, no. 2 (1972): 30–36.

———. "Classical Ensemble." *Arts in Virginia* 11 (winter 1971): 118–24.

Butt, Marshall W. *Portsmouth Under Four Flags: 1752–1970*. Portsmouth: Portsmouth Historical Association and the Friends of the Portsmouth Naval Shipyard Museum, 1971.

Caldwell, John Edwards. *A Tour through Part of Virginia, in the Summer of 1808 [with] an Account of . . . Monticello. . . .* New York, 1809.

Campbell, Colen et al. *Vitruvius Britannicus, or The British Architect*. 5 vols, 1715–1808. Reprint, New York: Benjamin Blom, 1972.

Campbell, Edward D. C., Jr., and Kym S. Rice, eds. *Before Freedom Came: African-American Life in the Antebellum South*. Richmond: Museum of the Confederacy, 1991.

Campbell, Fay. "Thomas Tileston Waterman: Student of American Colonial Architecture." *Winterthur Portfolio* 20 (summer–autumn 1985): 103–47.

Carmichael, Virginia. *Porches and Portals of Old Fredericksburg, Virginia*. Richmond: Old Dominion Press, 1929.

Carneal, Drew St. J. *Richmond's Fan District*. Richmond: Historic Richmond Foundation, 1996.

Carson, Cary, Norman F. Barka, William M. Kelso, Garry Wheeler Stone, and Dell Upton. "Impermanent Architecture in the Southern American Colonies." *Winterthur Portfolio* 17 (summer–autumn 1982): 95–119; and 16 (summer–autumn 1981): 135–96.

Cawthon, Richard James. "The Anglican Church and Churchyard in Colonial Virginia: A Study in Building-Site Relationships." Master's thesis, University of Virginia, 1983.

Chambers, Sir William. *A Treatise on the Decorative Part of Civil Architecture*. London, 1791. Reprint, with introduction by John Harris, New York: Benjamin Blom, 1968.

Chapin, J. R. "The Westover Estate." *Harper's* 42 (1871): 801–10.

Chappell, Edward A. "Architects of Colonial Williamsburg." In *Encyclopedia of Southern Culture*. Edited by C. R. Wilson and W. Ferris. Chapel Hill: University of North Carolina Press, 1989.

———. "Architectural Recording and the Open-Air Museum: A View from the Field." *Perspectives in Vernacular Architecture*, 2. Columbia: University of Missouri Press, 1986.

———. *John A. Barrows and the Rediscovery of Early Virginia Architecture*. Williamsburg: Colonial Williamsburg Foundation, 1991.

Cheek, Richard, and John G. Zehmer. *Old Richmond Today*. Richmond: The Council of Historic Richmond Foundation, 1988.

Chesson, Michael B., *Richmond After the War, 1865–1890*. Richmond: State Library and Archives, 1981.

Christian, Frances Archer, and Susanne Williams Massie, eds. *Homes and Gardens in Old Virginia*. Richmond: Garrett and Massie, 1931.

Christian, W. Asbury. *Richmond: Her Past and Present.* Richmond: H. L. Jenkins, 1912.

Claflin, Mary Anne, and Elizabeth Guy Richardson. *Bon Air: A History.* Richmond: Hale Publishing, [1977].

Clérisseau, Charles Louis. *Antiquités de la France.* Paris, 1778.

Coffin, Lewis A., Jr., and Arthur C. Holden. *Brick Architecture of the Colonial Period in Maryland and Virginia.* 1919. Reprint, New York: Dover, 1970.

Comstock, William T. *Turn-of-the-Century House Designs.* New York: Dover, 1994. Reprint of *Suburban and Country Homes.* 1893.

Conner, Michael F. "Antebellum Urban Environmental Reform: Richmond, Virginia, 1847–1861." Master's thesis, University of Virginia, 1980.

Corrigan, Michael Patrick. "Puritans in Priestly Garb: The 'Gothic Taste' in Antebellum Virginia Church Architecture." Master's thesis, Virginia Commonwealth University, 1988.

Cote, Richard Charles. "The Architectural Workmen of Thomas Jefferson in Virginia." 2 vols. Ph.D. diss., Boston University, 1986.

Cox, James A. D. "Frank Lloyd Wright and His Houses in Virginia." *Arts in Virginia* 13 (1972): 10–17.

Cram, Ralph Adams. *American Churches.* Vol. 1. New York: The American Architect, 1915.

———. *My Life in Architecture.* Boston: Little, Brown, 1936.

Crumley, Marguerite, and John G. Zehmer. *Church Hill: The St. John's Church Historic District.* Richmond: Historic Richmond Foundation, 1991.

Cummings, M. F., and C. C. Miller. *Designs for Street Fronts, Suburban Houses and Cottages.* 1865. Reprint, New York: Dover Publications, 1997.

Curran, Kathleen. "The German Rundbogenstil and Reflections on the American Round-Arch Style." *Journal of the Society of Architectural Historians* 47 (December 1988): 351–73.

Daniel, Ann Milner. "The Early Architecture of Ralph Adams Cram, 1889–1902." Ph.D. diss., University of North Carolina at Chapel Hill, 1978.

Dashiell, David A. "Between Earthly Wisdom and Heavenly Truth: The Effort to Build a Chapel at the University of Virginia, 1835–1890." Master's thesis, University of Virginia, 1992.

Davis, Vernon Perdue, and James Scott Rawlings. *Virginia's Ante-Bellum Churches: An Introduction with Particular Attention to Their Furnishings.* Richmond: Dietz Press, 1978.

Divine, John E. *When Waterford and I Were Young.* Waterford: Historic Waterford Foundation, 1997.

Downing, A. J. *The Architecture of Country Houses; Including . . . Cottages, Farm Houses, and Villas, . . . Interiors, Furniture, and . . . Warming and Ventilating.* 1850. Reprint, New York: Da Capo Press, 1968.

———. *Victorian Cottage Residences.* Preface by Adolf K. Placzek. New York: Dover Publications, 1981. Reprint of *Cottage Residences, or, A Series of Designs for Rural Cottages and Cottage Villas, and Their . . . Grounds, Adapted to North America. . . .* Edited by George E. Harney. 1842, 1873.

Dozier, Richard K. "The Black Architectural Experience in America." *AIA Journal* 65 (July 1976): 162–68.

Driggs, Sarah Shields. "Otis Mansion and Neoclassicism in Central Virginia." Master's thesis, University of Virginia, 1988.

Driggs, Sarah Shields, and John L. Orrock. *Save Outdoor Sculpture! A Survey of Sculpture in Virginia.* Richmond: Department of Historic Resources, 1996.

Driggs, Sarah Shields, Richard Guy Wilson, and Robert P. Winthrop. *Richmond's Monument Avenue.* Photographs by John O. Peters. Chapel Hill: University of North Carolina Press, 2001.

Dulaney, Paul. *The Architecture of Historic Richmond.* Charlottesville: University Press of Virginia, 1968.

Durilin, Tatiana S. "Bremo Recess: A Colonial Jacobean Revival." Master's thesis, University of Virginia, 1990.

Edwards, Kathy, Esme Howard, and Toni Prawl. *Monument Avenue: History and Architecture.* Washington, D.C.: Historic American Buildings Survey, 1992.

Eggleston, Edward. "Social Conditions in the Colonies." *Century* 28 (October 1884): 848–71.

Fahlman, Betsy L. et al. *A Tricentennial Celebration: Norfolk, 1682–1982.* Norfolk: Chrysler Museum, 1982.

Ford, Katherine Morrow, and Thomas H. Creighton. *The American House Today.* New York: Reinhold, 1951.

Forman, Henry Chandlee. "A New Story about the Old Adam Thoroughgood House." *Norfolk Museum Bulletin* 12 (January 1962): n.p.

Forman, Henry Chandlee. *The Virginia Eastern Shore and Its British Origins: History, Gardens and Antiquities.* Easton, Md.: Eastern Shore Publisher's Associates, c. 1975.

Foster, Gaines M. *Ghosts of the Confederacy: Defeat, the Lost Cause, and the Emergence of the New South, 1865 to 1913.* New York: Oxford University Press, 1987.

Frazier, William T. "T. J. Collins: A Local Virginia Architect and His Practice at the Turn of the Century." Master's thesis, University of Virginia, 1976.

Fréat, Roland, Sieur de Chambray. *A Parallel of the Ancient Architecture with the Modern, In a Collection of Ten Principal Authors who have written upon the Five Orders. . . [with] an Account of Architects and Architecture, in an . . . Explanation of certain Tearms. . . . With Leon Baptista Alberti's Treatise of Statues.* 1664. Compiled and translated by John Evelyn. Reprint, Farnborough, England: Gregg International Publishers, 1970.

Garreau, Joel. *Edge City: Life on the New Frontier.* New York: Doubleday, 1991.

Gettings, Kathryn Ann. " 'An Environment Worthy of Our Civilization': Hilton Village, Virginia and the Government's Model Town Experiments of the First World War." Master's thesis, University of Virginia, 1996.

Gibbs, James. *A Book of Architecture Containing Designs of Buildings and Ornaments.* London, 1728. Reprint, New York: Benjamin Blom, 1968.

Giles, Leslie A. "Decorative Painting at the Wickham House, Richmond, Virginia: Their Sources, Their Author, and Decor." Master's thesis, University of Virginia, 1990.

Glassie, Henry. *Pattern in the Material Folk Culture of the Eastern United States.* Philadelphia: University of Pennsylvania Press, 1968.

———. *Folk Housing in Middle Virginia.* Knoxville: University of Tennessee Press, 1975.

Goeldner, Paul. "Elijah E. Myers: Politics, Patronage and Professionalism." Master's thesis, University of Virginia, 1976.

Gordon-Van Tine Co. 117 House Designs of the Twenties. New York: Dover Publications, 1992. Reprint of *Gordon-Van Tine Homes.* 1923.

Goyert, Philip Renner. "Reston, Virginia: An Architectural History." Master's thesis, University of Virginia, 1970.

Grady, Henry. *The New South, Writings and Speeches of Henry Grady.* Savannah: Beehive Press, 1971.

Graham, John Paul. "Carrère and Hastings and the American Renaissance in Richmond, Virginia." Master's thesis, University of Virginia, 1988.

Green, Bryan Clark. "The Market House in Virginia, 1736–ca. 1860." Master's thesis, University of Virginia, 1991.

Green, Bryan Clark, Calder Loth, and William M. S. Rasmussen. *Lost Virginia: Vanished Architecture of the Old Dominion.* Charlottesville: Howell Press, 2001.

Haley, Drucilla Gatewood. "Redlands: The Documentation of a Carter Plantation, Albemarle County, Virginia." Master's thesis, University of Virginia, 1977.

Hall, James Anthony. "William Buckland's Anglo-Palladian Interior Ornament at Gunston Hall." Master's thesis, University of Virginia, 1989.

Hall, Virginius Cornick. "The Virginia Historical Society: An Anniversary Narrative of Its First Century and a Half." *Virginia Magazine of History and Biography* 90 (January 1982): 100–05.

Hamlin, Talbot. *Benjamin Henry Latrobe.* New York: Oxford University Press, 1955.

———. *Greek Revival Architecture in America: Being an Account of Important Trends in . . . Architecture and . . . Life Prior to the War between the States.* 1944. Reprint, New York: Dover Publications, 1964.

Handlin, David P. *American Architecture.* New York: Thames and Hudson, 1985.

Harnsberger, Douglas James. "In Delorme's Manner . . . : A Study of the Applications of Philibert Delorme's Dome Construction Method in Early 19th Century American Architecture." Master's thesis, University of Virginia, 1981.

Heck, Marlene Elizabeth. "Palladian Architecture and Social Change in Post-Revolutionary Virginia." Ph.D. diss., University of Pennsylvania, 1988.

Henley, Julia Todd. "The Eighteenth-Century Dwelling-Houses of King William County, Virginia." Master's thesis, University of Virginia, 1979.

Hewitt, Mark Alan. *The Architect and the American Country House.* New Haven: Yale University Press, 1990.

Historical Negro Biographies. New York: Historical Negro Biographies, 1967.

Historic American Buildings Survey. *Virginia Catalogue.* Compiled by the Virginia Historic Landmarks Commission. Charlottesville: University Press of Virginia, 1976.

Hitchcock, Henry-Russell. *American Architectural Books: A List of Books, Portfolios, and Pamphlets on Architecture and Related Subjects Published in America before 1895.* 1962. Reprint, New York: Da Capo Press, 1976.

Hitchcock, Henry-Russell, and William Seale. *Temples of Democracy: The State Capitols of the U.S.A.* New York: Harcourt Brace Jovanovich, 1976.

Hodson, Peter. "The Design and Building of Bremo: 1815–1820." Master's thesis, University of Virginia, 1967.

Holly, Henry Hudson. *Holly's Picturesque Country Seats: A Complete Reprint of the 1863 Classic.* New York: Dover Publications, 1993. Reprint of *Holly's Country Seats: Containing Lithographic Designs for Cottages, Villas, Mansions . . ., With Their Accompanying Outbuildings; Railway Stations. . . .* 1863.

———. *Modern Dwellings in Town and Country.* New York: Harper and Brothers, 1878.

Holmes, David L. *Brief History of the Episcopal Church.* Valley Forge, Pa.: Trinity Press International, 1993

Hood, Davyd Foard. "William Lawrence Bottomley in Virginia: The 'Neo-Georgian' House in Richmond." Master's thesis, University of Virginia, 1975.

———. "Georgian Revival Architecture." In *Encyclopedia of Southern Culture.* Edited by C. R. Wilson and W. Ferris. Chapel Hill: University of North Carolina Press, 1989.

Hosmer, Charles B., Jr. *Preservation Comes of Age: From Williamsburg to the National Trust, 1926–1949.* 2 vols. Charlottesville: University Press of Virginia, 1981.

———. *Presence of the Past.* New York: G. P. Putnam's Sons, 1965.

Hotchkiss, J., ed. "Virginia: New Ways in the Old Dominion." *Scribner's* 5 (December 1872): 137–60.

Howell, Herbert H. "Washington International Airport: A Model for the Jet Age." *Civil Engineering* 29 (May 1959): 42–45.

Hudnut, Joseph. "Washington National Airport." *Architectural Forum* 75 (September 1941): 169–76.

Huiner, Majorie Joan. "The Domestic Architecture of Eugene Bradbury in Charlottesville, Virginia, 1907–1927." Master's thesis, University of Virginia, 1986.

Hussey, E. C. *Cottage Architecture of Victorian America*. New York: Dover Publications, 1988. Reprint of *National Cottage Architecture: or, Homes for Every One. . . .* 1874.

Illustrated History of the Jamestown Exposition. Norfolk: Hampton Roads Naval Museum, n.d.

Isaac, Rhys. *The Transformation of Virginia, 1740–1790*. Chapel Hill: University of North Carolina Press, for the Institute of Early American History and Culture, 1982.

Jamestown Exposition Illustrated. Norfolk: Jamestown Official Photographic Corp., 1907.

Janney, Werner, and Asa Moore Janney. *Ye Meetg Hous Smal: A Short Account of Friends in Loudoun County, Virginia*. Elkton, Va.: X-High Graphic Arts, 1994.

Jefferson, Thomas. *The Papers of Thomas Jefferson*. Edited by Julian P. Boyd et al. 23 vols. to date. Princeton: Princeton University Press, 1950–.

———. *The Writings of Thomas Jefferson*. Compiled and edited by Paul Leicester Ford. 10 vols. New York: G. P. Putnam's Sons, 1892–99.

———. *The Writings of Thomas Jefferson*. Edited by Andrew A. Lipscomb and Albert Ellery Bergh. 20 vols. Washington, D.C.: Thomas Jefferson Memorial Association, 1903–04.

Johnston, Frances Benjamin. *Albemarle County Photos by Francis [sic] B. Johnston: Series 2-V in the Fiske Kimball Library: A Guide to the Copy Negatives and Proofs in the Manuscripts Division*. Charlottesville: Rare Books and Manuscripts, Alderman Library, University of Virginia, [1990].

———. *The Hampton Album: 44 Photographs from an Album of Hampton Institute*. New York: Museum of Modern Art, 1966.

———. *Historic Houses of Virginia and Charleston, S.C., Photographed by Frances Benjamin Johnston*. N.p., 193–.

Jolley, Harley E. *Painting with a Comet's Tail*. Boone, N.C.: Appalachian Consortium, 1987.

———. *The Blue Ridge Parkway*. Knoxville: University of Tennessee Press, 1969.

Jones, Hugh. *The Present State of Virginia*. Edited by Richard L. Morton. Chapel Hill: University of North Carolina Press, 1966.

Jordan, James M., IV, and Frederick S. Jordan, *Virginia Beach: A Pictorial History*. Richmond: T. F. Hale, 1974.

Kalbian, Maral S. "The Ionic Order and the Progression of the Orders in American Palladianism before 1812." Master's thesis, University of Virginia, 1988.

Kaye, Ruth Lincoln. *The Rebuilding of Captain's Row, 100 Block Prince Street, Alexandria, Virginia, After the Great Fire of 1827*. Privately printed, October 1994.

Keller, Genevieve Pace. "Designating Local Landmarks: Town Imagery in Culpeper, Virginia." Master's thesis, University of Virginia, 1975.

Kent, William, ed. *The Designs of Inigo Jones, Consisting of Plans and Elevations for Public and Private Buildings. . . .* 2 vols. in 1. [London], 1727. Reprint, Farnborough, England: Gregg International Publishers, 1966.

Kern, Susan A. "Virginia's World War I Memorial: Government versus Public Opinion." Master's thesis, University of Virginia, 1990.

Kimball, Gregg D. *American City, Southern Place: A Cultural History of Antebellum Richmond*. Athens: University of Georgia Press, 2000.

Kimball, Sidney Fiske. *Domestic Architecture of the Colonies and the Early Republic*. New York: Charles Scribner's Sons, 1922.

———. *Thomas Jefferson, Architect: Original Designs in the Collection of Thomas Jefferson Coolidge, Junior*. 1916. Reprint, with introduction by Frederick Doveton Nichols, New York: Da Capo Press, 1968.

———. "Thomas Tileston Waterman." *AIA* 15 (May 1951).

King, Edward. "The Great South: A Ramble in Scribner's Virginia." *Scribner's* 7 (April 1874): 645–74.

Kinnard, Wade Tyree. *Wilton*. Richmond: The Colonial Dames of America in the Commonwealth of Virginia, 1994.

Kitchen, Judith L. "Revivalism versus Eclecticism: A Re-examination of Architectural Stylistic Movements During the Period 1820–1860 in the United States, Illustrated by a Study of Richmond, Virginia." Master's thesis, University of Virginia, 1969.

Kocher, A. Lawrence. "The American Country House." *Architectural Record* 58 (November 1925): 402–43.

Kornwolf, James D. *"So Good a Design," The Colonial Campus of William and Mary: Its History, Background, and Legacy*. Exhibition catalog. Williamsburg: Joseph and Margaret Muscarelle Museum of Art, College of William and Mary, 1989.

Kummer, Karen Lang. "The Evolution of the Virginia State Capitol, 1779–1965." Master's thesis, University of Virginia, 1981.

Kuranda, Kathryn. "A Study of Port Royal, Virginia, 1740–1840." Master's thesis, University of Virginia, 1984.

Kyle, Louisa Venable. *The History of Eastern Shore Chapel and Lynnhaven Parish, 1642–1969*. Norfolk: N.p., 1969.

Lafever, Minard. *The Beauties of American Architecture*. Woodbridge, Conn.: Research Publications, 1973.

———. *The Modern Builder's Guide*. New York: H. C. Sleight, Collins & Hannay, 1833.

Lahendro, Joseph Dye. "Fiske Kimball: American Renaissance Historian." Master's thesis, University of Virginia, 1982.

Lane, Mills. *Architecture of the Old South: Virginia*. Savannah: Beehive Press, 1987.

Landford, Sarah Drummond. "Ralph Adams Cram as College Architect." Master's thesis, University of Virginia, 1981.

Langhorne, Elizabeth, K. Edward Lay, and William D. Rieley. *A Virginia Family and Its Plantation Houses.* Charlottesville: University Press of Virginia, 1987.

Langley, Batty. *The City and Country Builder's and Workman's Treasury of Designs: Or the Art of Drawing and Working the Ornamental Parts of Architecture. . . .* 1750. Reprint, New York: Benjamin Blom, 1967.

Lankford, John A. *Artistic Designs.* Washington, D.C.: Self-published, 1916.

Lasala, Joseph Michael. "Thomas Jefferson's Designs for the University of Virginia." Master's thesis, University of Virginia, 1992.

Latrobe, Benjamin Henry. *The Architectural Drawings of Benjamin Henry Latrobe.* Edited by Jeffrey A. Cohen and Charles E. Brownell. 2 vols. Series 2, Architectural and Engineering Drawings, of *The Papers of Benjamin Henry Latrobe.* New Haven: Yale University Press, 1994.

———. *The Correspondence and Miscellaneous Papers of Benjamin Henry Latrobe.* Edited by John C. Van Horne et al. 3 vols. Series 4, Correspondence and Miscellaneous Papers, of *The Papers of Benjamin Henry Latrobe.* New Haven: Yale University Press, 1984–88.

———. *Latrobe's View of America, 1795–1820.* Edited by Edward C. Carter II et al. Series 3, Sketchbooks and Miscellaneous Drawings, of *The Papers of Benjamin Henry Latrobe.* New Haven: Yale University Press, 1985.

———. *The Papers of Benjamin Henry Latrobe.* Edited by Thomas E. Jeffery. Clifton, N.J.: James T. White and Company, 1976. Microfiche.

———. *The Virginia Journals of Benjamin Henry Latrobe, 1795–1798.* Edited by Edward C. Carter II et al. 2 vols. Series 1, Journals, of *The Papers of Benjamin Henry Latrobe.* New Haven: Yale University Press, 1977.

Lay, K. Edward. "The American Renaissance at U.Va.: A Walking Tour of Buildings Jefferson Did Not Design." *University of Virginia Alumni News* 82 (November–December 1993): 16–21.

———. *The Architecture of Jefferson Country: Charlottesville and Albemarle County, Virginia.* Charlottesville: University Press of Virginia, 2000.

———. "Charlottesville's Architectural Legacy." *The Magazine of Albemarle County History* 46 (1988): 29+.

Lay, K. Edward, and Martha Tuzson Stockton. "Castle Hill: The Walker Family Estate." *Magazine of Albemarle County History* 52 (1994): 38–64.

Leach, Sara Amy. "The Detached Kitchen in Context: Architectural and Social Significance in Eighteenth-Century Tidewater, Virginia." Master's thesis, University of Virginia, 1987.

Lee, Anne Carter. "Architectural Ironwork on Main Street, Richmond, VA." Master's thesis, University of Virginia, 1970.

Lee, W. Duncan. "The Renascence of Carter's Grove." *Architecture* 67 (April 1933): 185–95.

Lindgren, James M. *Preserving the Old Dominion: Historic Preservation and Virginia Traditionalism.* Charlottesville: University Press of Virginia, 1993.

Little, Lewis Peyton. *History of the First Baptist Church of Newport News, Virginia, from 1883 to 1933.* Newport News: Franklin Printing Company, 1936.

Lossing, Benson J. *Mount Vernon.* New York, 1859.

Lord, Jill Marie. "Educating an American Architect: Robert Mills, Thomas Jefferson, and Benjamin Henry Latrobe." Master's thesis, University of Virginia, 1996.

Loth, Calder. "Notes on the Evolution of Virginia Brickwork from the Seventeenth Century." *Association for Preservation Technology Bulletin* 6, no. 2 (1974): 82–120.

Loth, Calder, ed. *The Virginia Landmarks Register.* 3d ed. Charlottesville: University Press of Virginia, for the Historic Landmarks Board, 1986.

Loth, Calder, ed. *The Virginia Landmarks Register.* 4th ed. Charlottesville: University Press of Virginia, for the Virginia Department of Historic Resources, 1999.

Loth, Calder, and Julius Trousdale Sadler. *The Only Proper Style: Gothic Architecture in America.* Boston: New York Graphic Society, 1975.

Lounsbury, Carl R. "Beaux-Arts Ideals and Colonial Reality: The Reconstruction of Williamsburg's Capitol, 1928–1934." *Journal of the Society of Architectural Historians* 49 (December 1990): 373–89.

———. " 'An Elegant and Commodius Building': William Buckland and the Design of the Prince William County Courthouse." *Journal of the Society of Architectural Historians* 46 (September 1987): 228–40.

Lounsbury, Carl R., ed. *An Illustrated Glossary of Early Southern Architecture and Landscape.* New York: Oxford University Press, 1994.

Lounsbury, Carl R. "The Structures of Justice: The Courthouses of Colonial Virginia." In *Perspectives in Vernacular Architecture*, 3. Edited by Thomas Carter and Bernard L. Herman. Columbia: University of Missouri Press, 1989.

Lucas, Ann M. "Ordering His Environment: Thomas Jefferson's Architecture from Monticello to the University of Virginia." Master's thesis, University of Virginia, 1989.

Lyne, Cassie Moncure. "Historic Homes in Virginia Owned by the duPonts. . . ." *Richmond Magazine* 14 (November 1927): 19+.

Maccubbin, Robert P., and Peter Martin, eds. *British and American Gardens in the Eighteenth Century.* Williamsburg: Colonial Williamsburg Foundation, 1984.

MacDougal, Bruce. "The Architecture of the Farmer's Bank of Virginia, Seen through its Fredericksburg's Branch." Master's thesis, University of Virginia, 1972.

Macmillan Encyclopedia of Architects. Edited by Adolph K. Placzek. 4 vols. New York: Free Press, 1982.

Maley, M. Bridget. "A Very Genteel Manner: Virginia Architecture and the Tayloe Family." Master's thesis, University of Virginia, 1993.

Manning, Warren H. "Jamestown Exposition." *Transactions of the American Society of Landscape Architects, 1899–1908.* Vol. 1, 1910.

Mariner, Kirk. *Off 13: The Eastern Shore of Virginia Guidebook.* New Church, Va.: Miona Publishing, 1987.

Martin, Joseph, ed. *A New and Comprehensive Gazetteer of Virginia and the District of Columbia.* Charlottesville, 1835.

Massie, Mrs. William R., and Mrs. Andrew H. Christian, comps. *Descriptive Guide Book of Virginia's Old Gardens.* Richmond: Garden Club of Virginia, 1929.

McDonald, Travis C., Jr. *The Art of Architecture in Downtown Richmond, 1789–1989.* Exhibition catalog. Richmond: Second Presbyterian Church, 1989.

McElroy, Margaret Randolph Williams. "Memories of Windsor Farms." *Richmond Quarterly* 2, no. 2 (fall 1988): 33–39.

McGee, Carden C. "The Planning, Sculpture, and Architecture of Monument Avenue, Richmond, Virginia." Master's thesis, University of Virginia, 1980.

McHugh, Kevin. "Form and Fitness: John Rochester Thomas and Brooks Museum at the University of Virginia." Master's thesis, University of Virginia, 1987.

McLean, Ann Hunter. "Unveiling the Lost Cause: A Study of Monuments to the Civil War Memory in Richmond, Virginia and Vicinity." Ph.D. diss., University of Virginia, 1998.

McVarish, Douglas, with K. Edward Lay and Boyd Coons. "Architectural Education at the University of Virginia." *Colonnade* 3 (summer 1988); 4 (winter 1989); 4 (summer–autumn 1989).

Meade, Bishop William. *Old Churches, Ministers, and Families of Virginia.* 2 vols. Philadelphia: J. B. Lippincott, 1857.

Men of Mark in Virginia. Ideals of American Life. A Collection of Biographies and Autobiographies of the Leading Men in the State. Washington, D.C.: Men of Mark Publishing Co., 1906.

Mencken, H. L. "The Sahara of the Bozart." In *Prejudices: Second Series.* New York: Alfred A. Knopf, 1920.

Millburg, Steve. "Waterford: The Past Today" *Southern Living,* January 1993, 62–65.

Miller, Ann Louise Brush. " 'Buildings, Works and Improvements': Early Patent Structures in Spotsylvania County, Virginia, 1721–1735." Master's thesis, University of Virginia, 1989.

Mills, Donna Rachal. "An Architectural and Social Analysis of Beverley Manor, Virginia (1745–1770)." Master's thesis, University of Virginia, 1990.

Mitchell, Mary H. *Hollywood Cemetery: The History of a Southern Shrine.* Richmond: Virginia State Library, 1985.

Mooney, Barbara B. " 'True Worth Is Highly Shown in Living Well': Architectural Patronage in Eighteenth-Century Virginia." Ph.D. diss., University of Illinois at Urbana-Champaign, 1991.

Mordecai, Samuel. *Virginia, Especially Richmond, in By-Gone Days; with a Glance at the Present: Being Reminiscences and Last Words of a Old Citizen.* 2d ed. Richmond: West and Johnston, 1860.

Morgan, Philip D. *Slave Counterpoint: Black Culture in the Eighteenth-Century Chesapeake and Lowcountry.* Chapel Hill: University of North Carolina Press, 1998.

Morrill, Penny. *Who Built Alexandria? Architects in Alexandria, 1750–1900.* Exhibition catalog. Alexandria: Carlyle House Historic Park, 1979.

Morris, Robert. *Select Architecture, Being Regular Designs of Plans and Elevations Well Suited to both Town and Country.* 2d ed., 1757. Reprint, with foreword by Adolf K. Placzek, New York: Da Capo Press, 1973.

Netherton, Ross, and Nan Netherton. *Fairfax County in Virginia: A Pictorial History.* Norfolk: Donning Co., 1986.

———. *Fairfax County: A Contemporary Portrait.* Norfolk: Donning Co., 1992.

Nichols, Frederick Doveton. *Architecture in Virginia, 1776–1958: The Old Dominion's Twelve Best Buildings.* Richmond: Virginia Museum of Fine Arts, 1958.

———. *Early Charlottesville Architecture.* N.p., 1953.

———. *Monticello.* Monticello, Va.: Thomas Jefferson Memorial Foundation, 1967.

———. *Notes on Some Virginia Houses.* Portland, Me.: Walpole Society, 1960.

———. *Thomas Jefferson's Architectural Drawings . . . with Commentary and a Check List.* 5th ed. Boston: Massachusetts Historical Society, 1984.

———. *Thomas Jefferson, Landscape Architect.* Charlottesville: University Press of Virginia, 1978.

Nicholson, Peter. *The New Practical Builder, and Workman's Companion . . . and the Theory and Practice of the Five Orders.* London, 1823–[25?].

Nock, Anne B. *Child of the Bay: Past, Present, and Future.* Norfolk: Hampton Roads Publishing Co., 1992.

Nock, L. Floyd, III. *Drummondtown: A One Horse Town.* Accomack Court House, Va.: McClure Press, 1976.

———. *Walking Tours of Accomac.* Richmond: Dietz Press, 1986.

———. *What "The Saturday Evening Post" Missed.* Accomac, Va.: Privately printed, 1986.

Novelli, Christopher Vincent. "William Noland and Residential Design on Richmond's Franklin Street." Master's thesis, University of Virginia, 1996.

"Observations in Several Voyages and Travels in America in the Year 1736." *The London Magazine.* July 1746.

O'Dell, Jeffrey M. *Chesterfield County: Early Architecture and Historic Sites.* Chesterfield, Va.: Chesterfield County Planning Dept., 1983.

O'Dell, Jeffrey M. *Inventory of Early Architecture and Historic Sites, County of Henrico, Virginia.* Rev. ed. Richmond: County of Henrico, 1978.

The Official Blue Book of the Jamestown TerCentennial Exposition. Norfolk: Colonial Publishing Co., 1907.

"The Old State-House at Richmond, Virginia." *Architectural Record* 88 (December 1940): 16–18.

Old Towne Walking Tour, Smithfield, Virginia. Isle of Wight: Smithfield Chamber of Commerce, 1990.

O'Neal, William Bainter. *Architectural Drawing in Virginia, 1819–1969.* Exhibition catalog. Charlottesville: School of Architecture, University of Virginia; Richmond: Virginia Museum of Fine Arts, 1969.

———. *Architecture in Virginia: An Official Guide to Four Centuries of Building in the Old Dominion.* New York: Walker and Company, for the Virginia Museum, 1968.

———. *Jefferson's Buildings at the University of Virginia.* Charlottesville: University Press of Virginia, 1960.

———. *Jefferson's Fine Arts Library: His Selections for the University of Virginia, together with His Own Architectural Books.* Charlottesville: University Press of Virginia, 1976.

———. *Pictorial History of the University of Virginia.* Charlottesville: University Press of Virginia, 1976.

O'Neal, William Bainter, and Christopher Weeks. *The Work of William Lawrence Bottomley in Richmond.* Charlottesville: University Press of Virginia, 1985.

Owen, Scott Campbell. "George Washington's Mount Vernon as British Palladian Architecture." Master's thesis, University of Virginia, 1991.

Packer, Nancy Elizabeth. *White Gloves and Red Bricks: APVA 1889–1989.* Exhibition catalog. Richmond: Association for the Preservation of Virginia Antiquities, 1989.

Page, Thomas Nelson. "Old Yorktown." *Century* 22 (October 1881).

———. *The Old South.* New York: Scribner's, 1893.

———. *In Ole Virginia.* New York: Scribner's, 1897.

———. *The Old Dominion.* New York: Scribner's, 1908.

Palladio, Andrea. *The Architecture of A. Palladio; in Four Books.* Translated by Nichcolas Dubois; edited by Giacomo Leoni. 2d ed. 2 vols. London, 1721.

———. *Quattro Libri dell'Architettura di Andrea Palladio.* 1570. Reprint with Ottavio Cabiati, "Nota al Palladio." 1945. Milan: Ulrico Hoepli, 1968.

———. *The Four Books of Andrea Palladio's Architecture.* Translated by Isaac Ware and Richard Boyle, Third Earl of Burlington. 1738. Reprint, with introduction by Adolf K. Placzek, New York: Dover Publications, 1965.

Palliser's Model Homes. Bridgeport, Conn.: Palliser and Palliser, 1878; 2d ed., rev., 1878.

Palliser's New Cottage Homes and Details. 1887. Reprint, New York: Da Capo Press, 1975.

Parramore, Thomas C. et al. *Norfolk: The First Four Centuries.* Charlottesville: University Press of Virginia, 1994.

Paulson, Darryl. "Masters of It All: Black Builders in This Century." *Southern Exposure* 8 (spring 1980): 3–13.

Peebles, John Kevan. "Thos. Jefferson, Architect." *Alumni Bulletin* [University of Virginia] 1 (November 1894): 68–74. Reprinted as "Thomas Jefferson, Architect," *American Architect and Building News*, 19 January 1895, 29–30.

Perry, William G. "Notes on the Architecture" and "Restoration of Colonial Williamsburg." *Architectural Record* 78 (December 1935): 373.

Persichetty, Elizabeth Teresa. "Alexander Spotswood's Probate Inventory: Documentary Evidence and the Recovery of Historical Architecture." Master's thesis, University of Virginia, 1996.

Peters, John O., and Margaret T. Peters. *Virginia's Historic Courthouses.* Charlottesville: University Press of Virginia, 1995.

Peterson, Charles E. "Thomas T. Waterman (1900–1951)." *Journal of the Society of Architectural Historians* 102 (1951): 25.

Poffenberger, Brien J. "Jefferson's Design of the Capitol of Virginia." Master's thesis, University of Virginia, 1991.

Pope, Loren. "The Love Affair of a Man and His House." *House Beautiful*, August 1948, 34.

———. "Five Decades Later." In *Frank Lloyd Wright Remembered.* Edited by P. Meehan. Washington, D.C.: Preservation Press, 1991.

Preddy, Jane. *Palaces of Dreams: The Movie Theaters of John Eberson.* Exhibition catalog. San Antonio: McNay Art Museum, 1991.

———. *Glamour, Glitz and Sparkle: The Deco Theaters of John Eberson.* Chicago: Theater Historical Society of America, 1989.

Prothro, Kimberly. "Monticello: A Roman Villa?" Master's thesis, University of Virginia, 1988.

Quenroe, Elroy E. "John Eberson in Richmond, Virginia—Architect for the Twenties." Master's thesis, University of Virginia, 1975.

———. "Movie House Architecture, Twenties Style." *Arts in Virginia* 16 (fall 1976): 22–31.

Rasmussen, William M. S. "Designers, Builders, and Architectural Traditions in Colonial Virginia." *Virginia Magazine of History and Biography* 90 (April 1982): 198–212.

———. "For Profit and Pleasure: The Art of Gardening in Colonial Virginia—Landon Carter's Sabine Hall." *Arts in Virginia* 21 (fall 1980): 18–27.

———. "Palladio in Tidewater Virginia: Mount Airy and Blandfield." In *Building by the Book.* Edited by Mario di Valmarana. Charlottesville: University Press of Virginia, 1984.

———. "Sabine Hall: A Classic Villa in Virginia." *Journal of the Society of Architectural Historians* 39 (December 1980): 286–96.

Rawlings, James Scott. *Virginia's Colonial Churches: An Architectural Guide.* Richmond: Garrett and Massie, 1963.

Reed, Helen Scott Townsend. "Agecroft Hall, Richmond, Virginia." *The Magazine Antiques* 123 (February 1983): 392–98.

———. "Jefferson's Observation Tower Projects for Montalto and the University of Virginia." Master's thesis, University of Virginia, 1991.

Reid, Robert A., ed. *The Jamestown Exposition Beautifully Illustrated.* New York: Jamestown Official Photograph Corp., 1907.

Reiff, Daniel D. *Small Georgian Houses in England and Virginia: Origins and Development through the 1750s.* Newark, Del.: University of Delaware Press, 1986.

Reps, John W. *Tidewater Towns: City Planning in Colonial Virginia and Maryland.* Williamsburg: Colonial Williamsburg Foundation, 1972.

"Restoration of Colonial Williamsburg." *Architectural Record* 78 (December 1935).

Rhinehart, Theodore R., ed. *The Architecture of Shirley Plantation.* Charlottesville: University Press of Virginia, 1984.

Richardson, Selden. " 'Architect of the City': Wilfred Emory Cutshaw (1838–1907) and Municipal Architecture in Richmond." Master's thesis, Virginia Commonwealth University, 1996.

Riddick, Susan C. "The Influence of B. H. Latrobe on Jefferson's Design for the University of Virginia." Master's thesis, University of Virginia, 1988.

Rueda, Luis R., ed. *Robert A. M. Stern: Buildings and Projects, 1981–1985.* New York: Rizzoli, 1986.

Saarinen, Eero. "Dulles International Airport." *Architectural Record* 134 (July 1963): 109.

St. Amant, Sue Bratt. *St. John's Church, Henrico Parish, Richmond Virginia: A Pictorial History.* Richmond: St. John's Foundation, 1996.

Salmon, Emily J. *A Hornbook of Virginia History.* 4th ed. Richmond: Virginia State Library, 1994.

Sanborn Map Company. *Insurance Maps of Richmond Virginia.* Vol. 2. New York: Sanborn Map Company, 1925 (updated 1951).

Saylor, Henry H. "James River Colonial—Historic American Style." *House and Garden,* January 1935.

Scheel, Eugene M. *The Guide to Loudoun: A Survey of the Architecture and History of a Virginia County.* Leesburg: Potomac Press, 1975.

Schimmleman, Janice G. "Architectural Treatises and Building Handbooks Available in American Libraries and Bookstores through 1800." *Proceedings of the American Antiquarian Society.* Vol. 95, pt. 2 (October 1985): 317–500.

Scott, Mary Wingfield. *Houses of Old Richmond.* 1941. Reprint, New York: Bonanza Books, n.d.

———. *Old Richmond Neighborhoods.* 1950. Reprint, Richmond: Valentine Museum, 1984.

Scully, Vincent, Jr. *The Shingle Style.* New Haven: Yale University Press, 1955.

Sears, Roebuck & Co. *Sears, Roebuck Catalog of Houses.* New York: Dover Publications, 1991. Reprint of *Honor Bilt Modern Homes.* 1926.

———. *Sears, Roebuck Home Builder's Catalog: The Complete Illustrated 1910 Edition.* New York: Dover Publications, 1990. Reprint of *Our Special Catalog for Home Builders.* 1910.

Severens, Kenneth. *Southern Architecture.* New York: E. P. Dutton, 1981.

Sharp, Dennis, with Peter Wylde and Martha B. Caldwell. *Alfred C. Bossom's American Architecture, 1903–1926.* London: Book Art, 1984.

Shaw, Edward. *Civil Architecture; or a complete theoretical and practical system of building; . . . [with] a great variety of examples selected from Vitruvius, Stuart, Chambers and Nicholson.* 3d ed., rev., 1832. Reprint, Woodbridge, Conn.: Research Publications, 1973.

———. *The Modern Architect: A Classic Victorian Stylebook and Carpenter's Manual.* Introduction by Earle G. Shettleworth, Jr. New York: Dover Publications, 1996. Reprint of *The Modern Architect; or, Every Carpenter His Own Master.* 1854.

———. *Rural Architecture; consisting of classic dwellings, Doric, Ionic, Corinthian and Gothic, and details connected with each of the orders; . . . designed for the United States of America.* Reprint, New Haven: Research Publications, 1972.

Shoppell, R. W. et al. *Turn-of-the-Century Houses, Cottages and Villas.* New York: Dover, 1983. Reprint of *Shoppell's Modern Houses, Building Designs.*

Silverman, Richard. "Latrobe's Design for the Virginia Penitentiary." Master's thesis, University of Virginia, 1992.

Sloan, Samuel. *Sloan's Victorian Buildings: Illustrations and Floor Plans for 56 Residences and Other Structures.* New York: Dover Publications, 1980. Reprint of *The Model Architect.* 2 vols. 1852.

Smith, Darrell Hevenor. *The Office of the Supervising Architect of the Treasury: Its History, Activities, and Organization.* Baltimore: Johns Hopkins Press, 1923.

Smith, Sallie Arlyn. "Chesapeake Diaries: A Prototypical Outbuilding Study of Southampton County, Virginia." Master's thesis, University of Virginia, 1982.

Sobel, Mechal. *The World They Made Together: Black and White Values in Eighteenth-Century Virginia.* Princeton: Princeton University Press, 1987.

Southern Architecture Illustrated. Atlanta: Harman Publishing Company, 1931.

Stanard, Mary Newton. *Windsor Farms, Hauntingly Reminiscent of Old England.* Richmond: Windsor Farms, Inc., 1926

Stapleford, Richard, and Jane Preddy. *Temples of Illusion: The Atmospheric Theaters of John Eberson.* Exhibition catalog. New York: Bertha and Karl Leubsdorf Art Gallery, Hunter College, 1988.

"The State Capitol of Virginia." *American Architect and Building News* 22 (November 1887): 235.

Stephenson, Mary A. *Carter's Grove Plantation: A History.* Sealantic Fund, 1964.

Stickley, Gustav. *Craftsman Homes: Architecture and Furnishings of the American Arts and Crafts Movement.* 1909. Reprint, New York: Dover Publications, 1979.

Stiverson, Cynthia Zignego. *Architecture and the Decorative Arts: The A. Lawrence Kocher Collection of Books at the Colonial Williamsburg Foundation.* Introduction by Lawrence Wodehouse; foreword by Albert Frey. West Cornwall, Conn.: Locust Hill Press, 1989.

Stockton, Frank B. "The Later Years of Monticello." *Century* 34 (September 1887): 642+.

Stuart, James, with Nicholas Revett et al. *The Antiquities of Athens.* 3 vols. 1763–95. Reprint, New York: Arno Press, 1980.

Stuntz, Connie Pendelton, and Mary Sturdevant Stuntz. *This Was Tysons Corner, Virginia.* Vienna, Va.: Stuntz, 1990.

Swan, Abraham. *The British Architect: or, The Builder's Treasury of Stair-Cases.* New ed., 1758. Reprint, New York: Da Capo Press, 1967.

Swofford, Donald Anthony. "The William Walker House, Warren, Virginia: A Study for Adaptive Restoration." Master's thesis, University of Virginia, 1976.

Tatman, Sandra L., and Roger W. Moss. *Biographical Dictionary of Philadelphia Architects: 1700–1930.* Boston: G. K. Hall and Co., 1985.

Taylor, Thomas H., Jr. "The Williamsburg Restoration and Its Reception by the American Public: 1926–1942." Ph.D. diss., George Washington University, 1989.

———. "Exeter: An 18th Century Plantation in Loudoun County, Virginia." Master's thesis, University of Virginia, 1973.

Taylor, Yardley. *Memoir of Loudoun County, Virginia: To Accompany the Map of Loudoun County.* Leesburg: T. Reynolds; Philadelphia: R. P. Smith, 1853.

Templeman, Eleanor Lee, and Nan Netherton. *Northern Virginia Heritage.* Privately published, 1966.

Townsend, Gavin. "The Tudor House in America: 1890–1930." Ph.D. diss., University of California at Santa Barbara, 1986.

Tucker, Lisa Marie. "Samuel Dobie's Design for the U.S. Capitol and Architectural Literature in Virginia circa 1790." Master's thesis, University of Virginia, 1990.

Tyler-McGraw, Marie, *At the Falls: Richmond, Virginia, and Its People.* Chapel Hill: University of North Carolina Press, 1994

U.S. Congress. Senate. *Report of the Arlington Memorial Bridge Commission.* 68th Congress, 1st sess., 1924. Doc. 95. Washington, D.C.: Government Printing Office.

Updike, Elizabeth Drake. "Henry Eugene Baskerville and William Churchill Noland: Richmond's Response to the American Renaissance." Master's thesis, University of Virginia, 1987.

Upjohn, Richard. *Upjohn's Rural Architecture.* New York: G. P. Putman, 1852.

Upton, Dell. *Holy Things and Profane: Anglican Parish Churches in Colonial Virginia.* New York: Architectural History Foundation, 1986.

———. "Vernacular Domestic Architecture in Eighteenth-Century Virginia." *Winterthur Portfolio* 17 (summer–autumn 1982): 95–119. Reprinted in *Common Places: Readings in American Vernacular Architecture.* Edited by Dell Upton and John Michael Vlach. Athens: University of Georgia Press, 1986.

———. "New Views of the Virginia Landscape." *Virginia Magazine of History and Biography* 96 (October 1988): 403–70.

Van Derpoole, James Grote. "The Restoration of St. Luke's, Smithfield, Virginia." *Journal of the Society of Architectural Historians* 27 (January 1958): 12–18.

"The Virginia Chapter, AIA: A History." *Virginia Architect's Handbook.* Richmond: Virginia AIA, 1968.

Vaux, Calvert. *Villas and Cottages: A Series of Designs Prepared for Execution in the United States.* 1857. Reprint, with a new introduction by Henry Hope Reed, New York: Da Capo Press, 1968.

Walker, Carroll. *Norfolk: A Pictorial History.* Virginia Beach: Donning Company, 1975.

Ware, Isaac. *A Complete Body of Architecture Adorned with Plans and Elevations, from Original Designs. In Which Are Interspersed Some Designs of Inigo Jones, Never before Published.* 2d ed. 2 vols., [1767]–1768. Reprint, Farnborough, England: Gregg International Publishers, 1971.

Ware, William R. *American Vignola.* Part 1, 1902; part 2, 1906. Reprint, New York: W. W. Norton Co., 1977.

Ware, William Rotch, and Charles S. Keefe, eds. *The Georgian Period: Being Photographs and Measured Drawings of Colonial Work with Text.* Rev. ed. 3 vols. New York: U. P. C. Book Company, 1923.

Waterman, Thomas Tileston. *The Mansions of Virginia, 1706–1776.* 1946. Reprint, New York: Bonanza Books, 1965.

Waterman, Thomas Tileston, and John Barrows. *Domestic Colonial Architecture of Tidewater Virginia.* 1932. Reprint, New York: Dover Publications, 1969.

Watt, Dan, ed. *Reston: The First Twenty Years.* Reston: Reston Publishing Co., 1985.

Wells, Camille. "The Eighteenth-Century Landscape of Virginia's Northern Neck." *Northern Neck of Virginia Historical Magazine* 37 (December 1987): 4217–255.

———. "Kingsmill Plantation: A Cultural Analysis." Master's thesis, University of Virginia, 1976.

———. "New Light on Sunnyside: Architectural and Documentary Testaments of an Early Virginia House." *Bulletin of the Northumberland County Historical Society* 32 (1995): 3–26.

———. "Old Claims and New Demands: Vernacular Architecture Today." *Perspectives in Vernacular Architecture,* 2. Columbia: University of Missouri Press, 1986.

———. "The Planter's Prospect: Houses, Outbuildings, and Rural Landscapes in Eighteenth-Century Virginia." *Winterthur Portfolio* 28, no. 1 (spring 1993): [1]–31.

———. "Social and Economic Aspect of 18th-Century Housing on Virginia's Northern Neck." Ph.D. diss., College of William and Mary, 1994.

Wells, John E., and Robert E. Dalton. *The Virginia Architects, 1835–1955.* Richmond: New South Architectural Press, 1997.

Wenger, Mark James. "Architecture of West Feliciana, 1767–1820: Its Beginnings and Its Sources." Master's thesis, University of Virginia, 1978.

Wenger, Mark R. "Reconstruction of the Governor's Palace in Williamsburg, Virginia." Colonial Williamsburg Foundation Library Research Report Series. Williamsburg: Colonial Williamsburg Foundation Library, March 1980.

———. "Westover: William Byrd's Mansion Reconsidered." Master's thesis, University of Virginia, 1981.

———. "The Central Passage in Virginia: Evolution of an Eighteenth-Century Living Space." In *Perspectives in Vernacular Architecture*, 2. Edited by C. Wells. Columbia: University of Missouri Press, 1986.

———. "The Dining Room in Early Virginia." In *Perspectives in Vernacular Architecture*, 3. Edited by Thomas Carter and Bernard L. Herman. Columbia: University of Missouri Press, 1989.

Wentz, Robert W., Jr. *Portsmouth: A Pictorial History.* Virginia Beach: Donning Co., 1975.

Wertenbaker, Thomas J., and Marvin W. Schlegel. *Norfolk: Historic Southern Port.* 2d ed. Durham: Duke University Press, 1962.

Whiffen, Marcus. "The Early County Courthouses of Virginia." *Journal of the Society of Architectural Historians* 18 (March 1959): 2–10.

———. *The Eighteenth-Century Houses of Williamsburg: A Study of Architecture and Building in the Colonial Capital of Virginia.* Williamsburg Architectural Studies. Williamsburg: Colonial Williamsburg Foundation, 1960. Revised, 1984.

———. *The Public Buildings of Williamsburg, Colonial Capital of Virginia: An Architectural History.* Vol. 1 of Williamsburg Architectural Studies. Williamsburg: Colonial Williamsburg Foundation, 1958.

Whiffen, Marcus, and Frederick Koeper. *American Architecture, 1607–1976.* Cambridge: MIT Press, 1981.

Whitelaw, Ralph T. *Virginia's Eastern Shores.* 2 vols. Gloucester, Mass.: Peter Smith, 1968.

The White Pine Series of Architectural Monographs. 26 vols. in 21. New York, 1915–40.

Wigren, Christopher. "Thomas Jefferson's Chinese Designs." Master's thesis, University of Virginia, 1989.

Williamson, Margareta E. "Renwick's Virginia Courthouse: A Product of Patriotism." Master's thesis, University of Virginia, 1987.

Wilson, Richard Guy. "Monument Avenue, Richmond." In *The Grand American Avenue, 1850–1920.* Edited by Jan Cigliano and Sarah Bradford Landau. San Francisco: Pomegranate Artbooks, for The Octagon, the Museum of the American Architectural Foundation, 1994.

———. *McKim, Mead & White, Architects.* New York: Rizzoli, 1983.

Wilson, Richard Guy, ed. *The Architecture of McKim, Mead & White.* New York: Dover, 1990. Reprint of *A Monograph of the Works of McKim, Mead & White 1879–1915.* New York: Architectural Book Pub. Co., 1915–20.

———. *Thomas Jefferson's Academical Village: The Creation of an Architectural Masterpiece.* Charlottesville: Bayly Art Museum of the University of Virginia and University Press of Virginia, 1993.

Wilson, Richard Guy, Dianne Pilgrim, and Richard Murray. *The American Renaissance, 1876–1917.* Brooklyn and New York: The Brooklyn Museum and Pantheon Books, 1979.

Winthrop, Robert P. *Architecture in Downtown Richmond.* Edited by Virginius Dabney. Richmond: Junior Board of Historic Richmond Foundation, 1982.

———. *Cast and Wrought: Iron Architecture in Richmond, Virginia.* Richmond: Historic Richmond Foundation 1982.

———. *The Jackson Ward Historic District.* Richmond: City of Richmond, 1980.

Wittkofski, J. Mark. *Theses and Dissertations Relevant to Virginia Archaeology, Architecture, and Material Culture.* Bibliography Series, No. 3 (revised). Richmond: Virginia Department of Historic Resources, 1991.

Withey, Henry F., and Elsie Rathburn Withey. *Biographical Dictionary of American Architects (Deceased).* Los Angeles: Hennessey and Ingalls, Inc., 1970.

Wood, Peter H. "Whetting, Setting and Laying Timbers, Black Builders in the Early South." *Southern Exposure* 8 (spring 1980): 3–13.

Woodward, C. Vann. *Origins of the New South.* Baton Rouge: Louisiana State University, 1951.

Woodward, George Everton. *Rural church architecture: comprising a series of designs for churches, exemplified in plans, elevations, sections, and details by Upjohn, Renwick, Wheeler, Wells, Austin, Stone, Cleveland, Backus, Reeve, &c. . . .* New Haven: Research Publications, 1972.

———. *Victorian City and Country Houses: Plans and Details.* New York: Dover Publications, 1996. Reprint of *Woodward's National Architect, Vol. II, Containing Original Designs, Plans and Details, To Working Scale, for City and Country Houses.* 1877.

Woodward, George Everton, and Edward G. Thompson. *A Victorian Housebuilder's Guide: "Woodward's National Architect" of 1869.* New York: Dover Publications, 1988. Reprint of *Woodward's National Architect.* 1869.

"The Works of Carrère & Hastings." *Architectural Record* 27 (January 1910): 1–120.

Worsham, John Gibson, Jr. "Carrère and Hastings' Jefferson Hotel." Master's thesis, University of Virginia, 1996.

Yetter, George Humphrey. *Willamsburg Before and After: The Rebirth of Virginia's Capital.* Williamsburg: Colonial Williamsburg Foundation, 1988.

———. "Stanford White at the University of Virginia: The New Buildings on the South Lawn and the Reconstruction of the Rotunda in 1896." Master's thesis, University of Virginia, 1980.

———. "Stanford White at the University of Virginia: Some New Light on an Old Question." *Journal of the Society of Architectural Historians* 40 (December 1981): 320–25.

Young, Dwight. "The Building of the Richmond City Hall, 1870–1894." Master's thesis, University of Virginia, 1976.

Zimmer, Edward Francis, and Pamela Scott. "Alexander Parris, B. Henry Latrobe, and the John Wickham House in Richmond, Virginia." *Journal of the Society of Architectural Historians* 41 (October 1982): 202–11.

Glossary

AIA See *American Institute of Architects.*

abacus The top member of a column capital. In the Doric order, it is a flat block, square in plan, between the echinus of the capital and the architrave of the entablature above.

Academic Gothic See *Collegiate Gothic.*

acroterium, acroterion (plural: acroteria) **1** A pedestal for a statue or similar decorative feature at the apex or at the lower corners of a pediment. **2** Any ornamental feature at these locations.

Adamesque A mode of architectural design, with emphasis on interiors, reminiscent of the work of the Scottish architects Robert Adam (1728–1792) and his brother James (1732–1794). It is characterized by attenuated proportions, bright color, and elegant linear detailing. Adamesque interiors, as one aspect of the broader Neoclassical movement, became popular in the late eighteenth century in Britain, Russia, and elsewhere in northern Europe. Simplified versions of these interiors began to be seen in the United States around the year 1800 in the work of Charles Bulfinch (1763–1844) and Samuel McIntire (1757–1811). Adamesque interiors, often emulating original Adam designs, were again popular in the 1920s. See also the related term *Federal.*

aedicule, aedicular An exterior niche, door, or window, framed by columns or pilasters and topped by an entablature and pediment. Meaning has been extended to a smaller-scale representation of a temple front on an interior wall. Distinguished from a tabernacle (definition 1), which usually occurs on an interior wall. See also the related term *niche.*

Aesthetic movement A late nineteenth-century movement in interior design and the decorative arts, emphasizing the application of artistic principles in the production of objects and the creation of interior ensembles. Aesthetic movement works are characterized by a broad eclecticism of materials and styles (especially the exotic) and by a preference for "conventionalized" (i.e., stylized) ornament, rather than naturalistic. The movement flourished in Britain from the 1850s through the 1870s and in the United States from the 1870s through the 1880s. Designers associated with the movement include William Morris (1834–1896) in England and Herter Brothers (1865–1905) in America. The Aesthetic movement evolved into and overlapped with the Art Nouveau and Arts and Crafts movements. See also the related term *Queen Anne* (definition 4).

ambulatory A passageway around the apse of a church, allowing for circulation behind the sanctuary.

American Adam Style See *Federal.*

American bond See *common bond.*

American Foursquare See *foursquare house.*

American Institute of Architects (AIA) The national professional organization of architects, established in New York in 1857. The first national convention was held in New York in 1867, and at that meeting, provision was made for the creation of local chapters. In 1889, the American Institute of Architects absorbed the independent Chicago-based Western Association of Architects (established 1884). The headquarters of the national organization moved from New York to Washington in 1898.

American Renaissance Term applied to classically inspired architecture, sculpture, decorative arts,

505

and painting from the 1880s to the 1930s. See also *Beaux-Arts classicism, Colonial Revival.*

Anglo-Palladianism, Anglo-Palladian An architectural movement in England motivated by a reaction against the English Baroque and by a rediscovery of the work of the English Renaissance architect Inigo Jones (1573–1652) and the Italian Renaissance architect Andrea Palladio (1508–1580). Anglo-Palladianism flourished in England (c. 1710–1760s) and in the British North American colonies (c. 1740–1790s). Key figures in the Anglo-Palladian movement were Colen Campbell (1676–1729) and Richard Boyle, Lord Burlington (1694–1753). Sometimes called Burlingtonian, Palladian Revival. See also the more general term *Palladianism* and the related terms *Georgian period, Jeffersonian.*

antefix. In classical architecture, a small upright decoration at the eaves of a roof, originally devised to hide the ends of the roof tiles. Also, a similar ornament along the ridge of the roof.

anthemion (plural: anthemions) A Greek ornamental motif based upon the honeysuckle or palmette. It may appear as a single element on an antefix or as a running ornament on a frieze or other banded feature.

antiquity The broad epoch of Western history preceding the Middle Ages and including such ancient civilizations as Egyptian, Greek, and Roman.

apse, apsidal A semicircular or polygonal feature projecting as a major element from an important interior space, especially at the chancel end of a church. Distinguished from an exedra, which is a semicircular or polygonal space, usually containing a bench, in the wall of a garden or nonreligious building. A substantial apse in a church, containing an ambulatory and radiating chapels, is called a chevet. The terms apse and chevet are used to describe the *form* of the end of the church containing the altar, while the terms chancel, choir, and sanctuary are used to describe the liturgical *function* of this end of the church and the spaces within it. Less substantial projections in nonreligious buildings are called bays if polygonal or bowfronts if curved.

arbor 1 An openwork structure covered with climbing plants. Distinguished from a trellis, which is generally a simpler, more two-dimensional structure, often attached to a wall. Distinguished from a pergola, which is an openwork structure supported by a colonnade, creating a shaded walk. 2 A grouping of closely planted trees or shrubs, trained together and self-supporting.

arcade 1 A series of arches, carried on columns or piers or other supports. 2 A covered walkway, one side of which is part of a building, while the other is open, as a series of arches, to the exterior. 3 In the nineteenth and early twentieth centuries, an interior street or other extensive space lined with shops and stores.

arch A curved construction that spans an opening. (Some arches may be flat or triangular, and many have a complex or compound curvature.) A masonry arch consists of a series of wedge-shaped parts (voussoirs) that press together toward the center while being restrained from spreading outward by the surrounding wall or the adjacent arch.

architrave 1 The lowest member of a classical entablature. 2 The moldings on the face of a wall around a doorway or other opening. Sometimes called the casing. Distinguished from the jambs, which are the vertical linings perpendicular to the wall planes at the sides of an opening. Distinguished from surround, a term usually applied to the entire door or window frame considered as a unit.

archivolt The group of moldings following the shape of an arched opening.

arcuation, arcuated Construction using arches.

Art Deco A modernistic style of the 1920s and 1930s characterized by sharp angular and curvilinear forms, by richness of materials (including polished metal, stone, and exotic woods), and by an overall sleekness of design. The term was first used in 1961 to refer to the Exposition Internationale des Arts Décoratifs et Industriels Modernes, held in Paris in 1925. The style was often used in the commercial and residential architecture of the 1930s (e.g., skyscrapers, hotels, apartment buildings). Sometimes called Art Deco Moderne, Deco, Jazz Moderne, Zigzag Moderne, Zigzag Modernistic. See also the more general term *Moderne* and the related terms *Mayan Revival, PWA Moderne, Streamline Moderne.*

Art Moderne See *Moderne.*

Art Nouveau A style in architecture, interior design, and the decorative arts that flourished principally in France and Belgium in the 1890s. The Art Nouveau is characterized by undulating and whiplash lines and by sensuous organic forms. The Art Nouveau in Britain and the United States evolved from and overlapped with the Aesthetic movement.

Arts and Crafts A late nineteenth- and early twentieth-century movement in interior design and the decorative arts, emphasizing the importance of hand crafting for everyday objects. Arts and Crafts works are characterized by rectilinear geometries and high contrasts between figure and ground, and the furniture often features expressed construction. The term originated with the Arts and Crafts Exhibition Society, founded in England in 1888. Designers associated with the movement include C. F. A. Voysey (1857–1941) in England and the brothers Charles S. Greene (1868–1957) and Henry M. Greene (1870–1954) in America. The Arts and Crafts movement evolved from and overlapped with the Aesthetic movement. For a more specific term, used in the United States after 1900, see also *Craftsman.*

ashlar Squared blocks of stone that fit tightly against one another.

atelier 1 A studio where the fine arts, including architecture, are taught. Applied particularly to the offices of prominent architects in Paris who provided design training to students enrolled in or informally attached to the Ecole des Beaux-Arts. By extension, any working office where some organized teaching is done. **2** A place where artworks or handicrafts are produced by skilled workers. **3** An artist's studio or workshop.

attic 1 The area beneath the roof and above the main stories (or story) of a building. Sometimes called a garret. **2** A low story above the entablature, often a blocklike mass that caps the building.

axis An imaginary center line to which are referred the parts of a building or the relations of a number of buildings to one another.

axonometric drawing A pictorial drawing using axonometric projection, in which horizontal lines that are perpendicular in an object, building, or space are drawn as perpendicular (usually at two 45-degree angles from the vertical, or at complementary angles of 30 and 60 degrees). Consequently, all angular and dimensional relationships in plan remain the same in the drawing as in the thing depicted. Sometimes called an axon or an axonometric. See also the related terms *isometric drawing, perspective drawing.*

balloon-frame construction A system of light frame construction in which single studs extend the full height of the frame (commonly two stories), from the foundation to the roof. Floor joists are fastened to the sides of the studs. Structural members are usually sawn lumber, ranging from two-by-fours to two-by-tens, and are fastened with nails. Sometimes called balloon framing. The technique, developed in Chicago and other boomtowns of the 1830s, has been largely replaced in the twentieth century by platform frame construction.

baluster One of a series of short vertical members, often vase-shaped in profile, used to support a handrail for a stair or a railing. Balusters that are thinner and simpler in profile are sometimes called banisters.

balustrade A series of balusters or posts supporting a rail or coping across the top (and sometimes resting on a lower rail). Balustrades are often found on stairs, balconies, parapets, and terraces.

band course Ambiguous term. See instead *band molding* or *stringcourse.*

band molding In masonry or frame construction, any horizontal flat member or molding or group of moldings projecting slightly from a wall and marking a division in the wall. Not properly a synonym for band course. Simpler

horizontal bands in masonry are generally called stringcourses.

bandstand A small pavilion, usually polygonal or circular in plan, designed to shelter bands during public concerts in a garden, park, green, or square. See also the related terms *gazebo, kiosk.*

banister 1 Corrupted spelling of baluster, in use since about the seventeenth century. Now occasionally used for balusters that are thinner and simpler in profile than classical vase-shaped balusters. **2** Improperly used to mean the handrail of a stair.

bargeboard An ornate fascia board that is attached to the sloping edges (verges) of a roof, covering the ends of the horizontal roof timbers (purlins). Bargeboards are usually ornamented with carved, turned, or jigsawn forms. Sometimes called gableboards, vergeboards. Less ornate boards along the verges of a roof are simply called fascia boards.

Baroque A style of art and architecture that flourished in Europe and colonial North America during the seventeenth and eighteenth centuries. Although based on the architecture of the Renaissance, Baroque architecture was more dynamic, with circles frequently giving way to ovals, flat walls to curved or undulating ones, and separate elements to interlocking forms. It was a monumental and richly three-dimensional style with elaborate systems of ornamental and figural sculpture. See also the related terms *Renaissance, Rococo.*

Baroque Revival See *Neo-Baroque.*

barrel vault A vaulted roof or ceiling of semicircular or semielliptical cross section, forming a tunnellike enclosure over an apartment, corridor, or similar space.

basement 1 The lowest story of a building, either partly or entirely below grade. **2** The lower part of the walls of any building, usually articulated distinctly from the upper part of the walls.

batten 1 A narrow strip of wood applied to cover a joint along the edges of two parallel boards in the same plane. **2** A strip of wood fastened across two or more parallel boards to hold them together. Sometimes called a cross batten. See also the related term *board-and-batten siding.*

battered (adjective). Inclined from the vertical. A wall is said to be battered or to have a batter when it recedes as it rises.

battlement, battlemented See *crenellation.*

Bauhaus 1 Work in any of the visual arts by the faculty and students of the Bauhaus, the innovative design school founded by Walter Gropius (1883–1969) and an active force in German modernism from 1919 until 1933. **2** Work in any of the visual arts by the former faculty and students of the Bauhaus, or by individuals influenced by them. See also the related terms *International Style, Miesian.*

bay 1 The interval between two recurring members. A facade is frequently measured by window bays, a skeletal frame by structural bays. **2** A polygonal or curved unit of one or more stories, projecting from the wall and usually containing grouped windows (bay windows) on each story. See also the more specific term *bowfront.*

bay window The horizontally grouped windows in a projecting bay (definition 2), or the projecting bay itself, if it is not more than one story. Distinguished from an oriel, which does not rise from the foundation and has a suspended rather than rooted appearance. A semicircular or semielliptical bay window is called a bow window. A bay window with a central section of plate glass in a late nineteenth-century commercial building is called a Chicago window.

beam A structural spanning member of stone, wood, iron, steel, or reinforced concrete. See also the more specific terms *girder, I-beam, joist.*

bearing wall A wall that is fully structural, carrying the load of the floors and roof all the way to the foundation. Sometimes called a supporting wall. Distinguished from curtain wall. See also the related term *load-bearing.*

Beaux-Arts Design on a monumental scale, as taught at the Ecole des Beaux-Arts in Paris throughout the nineteenth century and early twentieth century. The term Beaux-Arts is generally applied to an eclectic Roman-Renaissance-Baroque architecture of the 1850s through the 1920s, disseminated internationally by students and followers of the Ecole des Beaux-Arts. As a general style term Beaux-Arts connotes an academically grounded discipline for historical eclecticism, rather than one single style, as well as the disciplined development of a *parti* into a fully visualized design. More specific style terms include Néo-Grec (1840–1870s) and Beaux-Arts classicism (1870–1930s). See also the related terms *Neoclassicism,* for describing Ecole-related work from the 1790s to the 1840s, and *Second Empire,* for describing the work from the 1850s to the 1880s.

Beaux-Arts classicism, Beaux-Arts classical Term applied to eclectic Roman-Renaissance-Baroque architecture and urbanism after the Néo-Grec and Second Empire phases, i.e., from the 1870s through the 1930s. Sometimes called Classic Revival, Classical Revival, McKim classicism, Neoclassical Revival. See also the more general term *Beaux-Arts* and the related terms *City Beautiful movement, PWA Moderne.*

belfry A cupola, turret, or room in a tower where a bell is housed.

bell cote A small gabled structure astride the ridge of a roof, which shelters a bell. It is usually close to the front wall plane of the building.

belt course See *stringcourse.*

belvedere **1** Any building, especially a pavilion or shelter, that is located to take advantage of a view. See also the related term *gazebo.* **2** See *cupola* (definition 2).

blind (adjective) Term applied to the surface use

of elements that would otherwise articulate an opening but where no opening exists. Used in such combinations as blind arcade, blind arch, blind door, blind window.

board-and-batten siding A type of siding for wood-frame buildings, consisting of wide vertical boards with narrow strips of wood (battens) covering the joints. (In rare instances, the battens may be fastened behind the joints. If the gaps between boards are wide and the back battens approach the width of the outer boards, the siding is called board-on-board.) See also the related term *batten.*

board-on-board siding A type of siding for wood-frame buildings, consisting of two layers of vertical boards, with the outer layer of boards covering the wide gaps between the boards of the inner layer.

bowfront A semicircular or semielliptical bay (definition 2).

bow window A semicircular or semielliptical bay window.

brace A single wooden or metal member placed diagonally within a framework or truss or beneath an overhang. Distinguished from a bracket, which is a more substantial triangular feature, and from a strut, which is essentially a post set in a diagonal position.

braced-frame construction A combination of heavy and light timber-frame construction, in which the principal vertical and horizontal framing members (posts and girts) are fastened by mortise and tenon joints, while the one-story-high studs are nailed to the heavy timber frame. The overall frame is made more rigid by diagonal braces. Sometimes called braced framing.

bracket Any solid, pierced, or built-up triangular feature projecting from the face of a wall to support a projecting element, like the top member of a cornice or the verges or eaves of a roof. Brackets are frequently used for ornamental as well as structural purposes. Distinguished from a brace, which is a simple barlike structural member. Distinguished from the more specific term console, which has a height greater than its projection from the wall. See also the related term *corbel.*

Bracketed Style A nineteenth-century term for Italianate.

brick bonds, brickwork See the more specific terms *common bond, English bond, Flemish bond, running bond.*

British colonial A term applied to buildings, towns, landscapes, and other artifacts from the period of actual British colonial occupation of large parts of eastern North America (c. 1607–1781 for the United States; c. 1750–1867 for much of Canada). The British colonial period saw the introduction into the New World of various regional strains of English and Scotch-Irish folk culture, as well as high-style Anglo-European Renaissance, Baroque, and Neoclassical design. Sometimes called English colonial. Loosely called colonial or Early American. See also the related term *Georgian period*.

Brutalism An architectural style of the 1950s through 1970s, characterized by complex massing and by a frank expression of structural members, elements of building systems, and materials (especially concrete). Some of the work of Paul Rudolph (born 1918) is associated with this style. Sometimes called New Brutalism.

bungalow A low one- or one-and-one-half-story house of modest pretensions with a low-pitched gable or hipped roof, a conspicuous porch, and projecting eaves. This house type was a popular builders' type from around 1900 to 1930. The term bungalow was also loosely applied to any vernacular building of a semirustic nature, including vacation cottages and lodges.

Burlingtonian See *Anglo-Palladianism*.

buttress An exterior mass of masonry bonded into a wall that it strengthens or supports. Buttresses often absorb lateral thrusts from roofs or vaults.

Byzantine Term applied to the art and architecture of the Eastern Roman Empire centered at Byzantium (i.e., Constantinople, Istanbul) from the early 500s to the mid–1400s. Byzantine architecture is characterized by massive domes, round arches, richly carved capitals, and the extensive use of mosaic.

Byzantine Revival See *Neo-Byzantine*.

campanile In Italian, a bell tower. While usually freestanding in medieval and Renaissance architecture, it was often incorporated as a prominent unit in the massing of picturesque nineteenth-century buildings.

cantilever A beam, girder, slab, truss, or other structural member that projects beyond its supporting wall or column.

cap A canopy, ledge, molding, or pediment over a window. Sometimes called a window cap. Distinguished from a hood, which is a similar feature over a door. See also the related term *head molding*.

capital The moldings and carved enrichment at the top of a column, pilaster, pier, or pedestal.

Carpenter's Gothic Term applied to a version of the Gothic Revival (c. 1840–1870s), in which Gothic motifs are adapted to the kind of wooden details that can be produced by lathes, jigsaws, and molding machines. Sometimes called Carpenter Gothic, Gingerbread Style, Steamboat Gothic. See also the more general term *Gothic Revival*.

carriage porch See *porte-cochere*.

casement window A window that opens from the side on hinges, like a door, out from the plane of the wall. Distinguished from a double-hung window.

casing See *architrave* (definition 2).

cast iron Iron shaped by a molding process, generally strong in compression but brittle in tension.

Distinguished from wrought iron, which has been forged to increase its tensile properties.

cast iron front An architectural facade made of prefabricated molded iron parts, often markedly skeletal in appearance with extensive glass infilling. Prevalent from the late 1840s to the early 1870s.

castellated Having the elements of a medieval castle, such as crenellation and turrets.

cavetto cornice See *coved cornice*.

cement A mixture of burnt lime and clay with water, which hardens permanently when dry. When a fine aggregate of sand is added, the cement may be used as a mortar for masonry construction or as a plaster or stucco coating. When a coarser aggregate of gravel or crushed stone is added, along with sand, the mixture is called concrete.

chamfer The oblique surface formed by cutting off a square edge at an equal angle to each face.

chancel 1 The end of a church containing the altar and set apart for the clergy and choir by a screen, rail, or steps. Usually the entire eastern end of a church beyond the crossing. In churches that have a long chancel space, the part of the chancel between the crossing and the apse, where the singers participate in the service, is called the choir. The innermost part of the chancel, containing the principal altar, is called the sanctuary. **2** In less extensive churches, the terms chancel and choir are often used interchangeably to mean the entire eastern arm of the church.

Chateauesque A term applied to masonry buildings from the 1870s through the 1920s in which stylistic references are derived from early French Renaissance chateaux, from the reign of Francis I (1515–1547) or even earlier. Sometimes called Chateau Style, Chateauesque Revival, Francis I Style, François Premier.

chevet In large churches, particularly those based upon French Gothic precedents, a substantial apse surrounded by an ambulatory and often containing radiating chapels.

Chicago School A diverse group of architects associated with the development of the tall (i.e., six- to twenty-story), usually metal-frame commercial building in Chicago during the 1880s and 1890s. William Le Baron Jenney, Burnham and Root, and Adler and Sullivan are identified with this group. Sometimes called Chicago Commercial Style, Commercial Style. See also the related term *Prairie School*.

Chicago window A tripartite oblong window in which a large fixed center pane is placed between two narrow sash windows. Popularized in Chicago commercial buildings of the 1880–1890s. See also *bay window*.

chimney girt In timber-frame construction, a major wooden beam that passes across the breast of the central chimney. It is supported at its ends by the longitudinal girts of the building and sometimes carries one end of the summer beam.

choir 1 The part of a church where the singers participate in the service. Usually the space within the chancel arm of the church, situated between the crossing to the west and the sanctuary to the east. **2** In less extensive churches, the terms choir and chancel are often used interchangeably to mean the entire eastern arm of the church.

Churrigueresque Term applied to Spanish and Spanish colonial Baroque architecture resembling the work of the Spanish architect José Benito de Churriguera (1665–1725) and his brothers. The style is characterized by a freely interpreted assemblage of such elements as twisted columns, broken pediments, and scroll brackets. See also the related term *Spanish colonial.*

cinquefoil A type of Gothic tracery having five parts (lobes or foils) separated by pointed elements (cusps).

City Beautiful movement A movement in architecture, landscape architecture, and planning in the United States from the 1890s through the 1920s, advocating the beautification of cities in the image of some of the most urbane places of the time: the world's fairs. City Beautiful schemes emphasized civic centers, boulevards, and waterfront improvements, and sometimes included comprehensive metropolitan plans for parks, parkways, and transportation facilities. See also the related term *Beaux-Arts classicism.*

clapboard A tapered board that is thinner along the top edge and thicker along the bottom edge, applied horizontally with edges overlapping to provide weathertight siding on a building of wood construction. Early clapboards were split (rived, riven) and were used for barrel staves and for wainscoting. The term now applies to any beveled siding board, whether split or sawn, rabbeted or not, regardless of length or width. (The term is sometimes applied only to a form of bevel siding used in New England, about four feet long and quarter-sawn.) Sometimes called weatherboards.

classical orders See *order.*

classical rectangle See *golden section.*

Classical Revival Term applied to (1) Neoclassical design of the late eighteenth and early nineteenth centuries, including the Greek Revival; or (2) Beaux-Arts classical design of the late nineteenth and early twentieth centuries. Sometimes called Classic Revival. See also *Beaux-Arts classicism, Greek Revival, Neoclassicism.*

classicism, classical, classicizing Terms describing the application of principles or elements derived from the visual arts of the Greco-Roman era (seventh century B.C. through fourth century A.D.) at any subsequent period of Western civilization, but particularly since the Renaissance. More a descriptive term for an approach to design and for a general cultural sensibility than for any particular style. See also the related term *Neoclassicism.*

clerestory A part of a building that rises above the roof of another part and has windows in its walls.

clipped gable roof See *jerkinhead roof.*

coffer A recessed panel, usually square or octagonal, in a ceiling. Such panels are also found on the inner surfaces of domes and vaults.

collar beam A horizontal tension member in a pitched roof connecting opposite rafters, generally halfway up or higher. Its function is to tie the angular members together and prevent them from spreading.

Collegiate Gothic 1 Originally, a secular version of English Gothic architecture, characteristic of the older colleges of Oxford and Cambridge. **2** A secular version of Late Gothic Revival architecture, which became a popular style for North American colleges and universities from the 1890s through the 1920s. Sometimes called Academic Gothic.

colonial 1 Not strictly a style term, but a term for the entire period during which a particular European country held political dominion over a part of the Western Hemisphere, Africa, Asia, Australia, or Oceania. See also the more specific terms *British colonial, Dutch colonial, French colonial, Spanish colonial.* **2** Loosely used to mean the British colonial period in North America (c. 1607–1781 for the United States; c. 1750–1867 for much of Canada).

Colonial Revival Generally understood to mean the revival of forms from British colonial design. Instances of the revival of colonial forms can be found as early as the 1820s, though as a sustained public movement that produced substantial numbers of buildings drawing upon the early American past, it dates from the 1870s. See also the more specific term *Georgian Revival* and the related terms *Federal Revival, Shingle Style.*

colonnade A series of freestanding or engaged columns supporting an entablature or simple beam.

colonnette A diminutive, often attenuated, column.

colossal order See *giant order.*

column 1 A vertical supporting element, usually cylindrical and slightly tapering, consisting of a base (except in the Greek Doric order), shaft, and capital. See also the related terms *entablature, entasis, order.* **2** Any vertical supporting element in a skeletal frame.

Commercial Style Applied in general to commercial buildings with large areas of glazing and minimal trim. The term is sometimes used interchangeably with Chciago School, but the style can be found anywhere.

common bond A pattern of brickwork in which every fifth or sixth course consists of all headers, the other courses being all stretchers. Sometimes called American bond. Distinguished from running bond, in which no headers appear.

Composite order An ensemble of classical column and entablature elements, particularly characterized by large Ionic volutes and Corinthian acanthus leaves in the capital of the column. See also the more general term *order*.

concrete An artificial stone made by mixing cement, water, sand, and a coarse aggregate (such as gravel or crushed stone) in specified proportions. The mix is shaped in molds called forms. Distinguished from cement, which is the binder without the aggregate.

console A type of bracket with a scroll-shaped or S-curve profile and a height greater than its projection from the wall. Distinguished from the more general term bracket, which is usually applied to supports whose projection and height are nearly equal. Distinguished from a modillion, which usually is smaller, has a projection greater than its height (or thickness), and appears in a series, as in a classical cornice.

coping The cap or top course of a wall, parapet, balustrade, or chimney, usually designed to shed water.

corbel A projecting stone that supports a superincumbent weight. In medieval architecture and its derivatives, a support for such major features as vaulting shafts, vaulting ribs, or oriels. See also the related term *bracket*.

corbeled construction Masonry that is built outward beyond the vertical by letting successive courses project beyond those below. Sometimes called corbeling.

corbeled cornice A cornice made up of courses of projecting masonry, each of which extends farther outward than the one below.

Corinthian order An ensemble of classical column and entablature elements, particularly characterized by acanthus leaves and small volutes in the capital of the column. See also the more general term *order*.

cornice The crowning member of a wall or entablature.

Corporate International Style A term used for curtain wall commercial, institutional, and governmental buildings built since the Second World War which represent a widespread adoption of selected International Style ideas from the 1920s. See also the more general term *International Style*.

Corporate Style An architectural style developed in the early industrial communities of New England during the first half of the nineteenth century. This austere but graceful mode of construction was derived from the red-brick Federal architecture of the early nineteenth century and is characterized by the same elegant proportions, cleanly cut openings, and simple refined detailing. The term was coined by William

Pierson in the 1970s. Not to be confused with Corporate International Style.

cottage 1 A relatively modest rural or suburban dwelling. Distinguished from a villa, which is a more substantial and often more elaborate dwelling. **2** A seasonal dwelling, regardless of size, especially one located in a resort community.

cottage orné A rustic building in the romantic, picturesque tradition, noted for such features as bay windows, oriels, ornamented gables, and clustered chimneys.

course A layer of building blocks, such as bricks or stones, extending the full length and thickness of a wall.

coved ceiling A ceiling in which the transition between wall and ceiling is formed by a large concave panel or molding. Sometimes called a cove ceiling.

coved cornice A cornice with a concave profile. Sometimes called a cavetto cornice.

Craftsman A style of furniture and interior design belonging to the Arts and Crafts movement in the United States, and specifically related to *The Craftsman* magazine (1901–1916), published by Gustav Stickley (1858–1942). Some entire houses known to be derived from this publication can be called Craftsman houses. See also the more general term *Arts and Crafts*.

crenellation, crenellated A form of embellishment on a parapet consisting of indentations (crenels or embrasures) alternating with solid blocks of wall (merlons). Virtually synonymous with battlement, battlemented; embattlement, embattled.

cresting An ornamental strip or fencelike feature, usually of metal or tile, along the ridgeline or summit of a roof.

crocket In Gothic architecture, a small ornament resembling bunched foliage, placed at intervals on the sloping edges of gables, pinnacles, or spires.

crossing In a church with a cruciform plan, the area where the arms of the cross intersect; specifically, the space where the transept crosses the nave and chancel.

cross rib See *lierne*.

cross section See *section*.

crown The central, or highest, part of an arch or vault.

crown molding The highest in a series of moldings.

crowstep Any one of the progressions in a gable that ascends in steps rather than in a continuous slope.

cruciform In the shape of a cross. Usually used to describe the ground plans of buildings. See also the more specific terms *Greek cross, Latin cross*.

cupola 1 A small domed structure on top of a belfry, steeple, or tower. **2** A lantern, square or polygonal in plan, with windows or vents, which is located at the summit of a roof. Sometimes called a belvedere. Distinguished from a skylight, which is a lesser feature located on the slope of a roof. **3** In historic English usage, synonymous with dome. A dome is now understood to be a more substantial feature.

curtain wall In skeleton frame or reinforced concrete construction, a thin nonstructural cladding of stone, brick, terra cotta, glass, or metal veneer. Distinguished from bearing wall. See also the related term *load-bearing.*

cusp. The pointed, roughly triangular intersection of the arcs of lobes or foils in the tracery of windows, screens, or panels.

dado A broad decorative band around the lower portion of an interior wall, between the baseboard and dado rail or cap molding. (The term is often applied to this entire zone, including baseboard and dado rail.) The dado may be painted, papered, or covered with some other material, so as to have a different treatment from the upper zone of the wall. Dado connotes any continuous lower zone in a room, equivalent to a pedestal. A wood-paneled dado is called a wainscot.

Deco. See *Art Deco.*

dentil, denticulated A small ornamental block forming one of a series set in a row. A dentil molding is composed of such a series.

dependency A building, wing, or room, subordinate to or serving as an adjunct to a main building. A dependency may be attached to or detached from a main building. Distinguished from an outbuilding, which is always detached.

diaper An overall repetitive pattern on a flat surface, especially a pattern of geometric or representational forms arranged in a diamond-shaped or checkerboard grid. Sometimes called diaper work.

discharging arch See *relieving arch.*

dome A major hemispherical or curved roof feature rising from a circular, polygonal, or square base. Distinguished from a cupola, which is a smaller, usually subordinate, domical element.

Doric order An ensemble of classical column and entablature elements, particularly characterized by the use of triglyphs and metopes in the frieze of the entablature. See also the more general term *order.*

dormer A roof-sheltered window (or vent), usually with vertical sides and front, set into a sloping roof. Sometimes called a dormer window.

dosseret See *impost block.*

double-hung window A window consisting of a pair of frames, or sashes, one above the other, arranged to slide up and down. Their movement is sometimes stabilized by a system of cords and counterbalancing weights contained in narrow boxing at each side of the window frame. Sometimes called guillotine sash.

double-pen In vernacular architecture, particularly houses, a term applied to a plan consisting of two rooms side by side or separated by a hallway.

double-pile In vernacular architecture, particularly houses, a term applied to a plan that is two rooms deep and any number of rooms wide.

drip molding See *head molding.*

drum **1** A cylindrical or polygonal wall zone upon which a dome rests. **2** One of the cylinders of stone that form the shaft of a column.

Dutch colonial A term applied to buildings, towns, landscapes, and other artifacts from the period of actual Dutch colonial occupation of the Hudson River valley and adjacent areas (c. 1614–1664). Meaning has been extended to apply to the artifacts of Dutch ethnic groups and their descendants, even into the early nineteenth century. It is associated specifically with the gambrel roof form.

Dutch Colonial Revival The revival of forms from design in the Dutch tradition.

ear A slight projection just below the upper corners of a door or window architrave or casing. Sometimes called a shouldered architrave.

Early American See *British colonial.*

Early Christian A style of art and architecture in the Mediterranean world that was developed by the early Christians before the fall of the Western Roman Empire, derived from late Roman art and architecture and leading to the Romanesque (early fourth to early sixth century).

Early Georgian period Not strictly a style term, but a term for a period in British and British colonial history approximately coinciding with the reigns of George I (1714–1727) and George II (1727–1760). See also the related term *Late Georgian period.*

Early Gothic Revival A term for the Gothic Revival work of the late eighteenth to the mid-nineteenth century. See also the related term *Late Gothic Revival.*

Eastlake A decorative arts and interior design term of the 1860s and 1880s sometimes applied to architecture. Named after Charles Locke Eastlake (1836–1906), an English advocate of the application of Gothic principles of construction and design, rather than mere Gothic elements. Characterized by simplicity and solidity of forms, which are sometimes embellished with chamfered, turned, or incised details. Sometimes called Eastlake Gothic, Modern Gothic. See also the related term *Queen Anne.*

eaves The horizontal lower edges of a roof plane, usually projecting beyond the wall below. Distinguished from verges, which are the sloping edges of a roof plane.

echinus A heavy molding with a curved profile placed immediately below the abacus, or top member, of a classical capital. Particularly prominent in the Doric and Tuscan orders.

eclecticism, eclectic A sensibility in design, prevalent since the eighteenth century, involving the selection of elements from a variety of sources, including historical periods of high-style design (Western and non-Western), vernacular design

(Western and non-Western), and (in the twentieth century) contemporary industrial design. Distinguished from historicism and revivalism by drawing upon a wider range of sources than the historical periods of high-style design.

Ecole, Ecole des Beaux-Arts See *Beaux-Arts.*

Egyptian Revival Term applied to eclectic works or elements of those works that emulate forms in the visual arts of ancient Egyptian civilization.

elevation A drawing (in orthographic projection) of an upright, planar aspect of an object or building. The vertical complement of a plan. Sometimes loosely used in the sense of a facade view or any frontal representation of a wall, whether photograph or drawing, whether measured to scale or not.

Elizabethan Manor Style See *Neo-Tudor.*

Elizabethan period A term for a period in English history coinciding with the reign of Elizabeth I (1558–1603). See also the more general term *Tudor period* and the related term *Jacobean period* for the succeeding period.

embattlement, embattled See *crenellation.*

encaustic tile A tile decorated by a polychrome glazed or ceramic inlay pattern.

engaged column A half-round column attached to a wall. Distinguished from a free-standing column by seeming to be built into the wall. Distinguished from a pilaster, which is a flattened column. Distinguished from a recessed column, which is a fully round column set into a niche-like space.

English bond A pattern of brickwork in which the bricks are set in alternating courses of stretchers and headers.

English colonial See *British colonial.*

English Half-timber Style See *Neo-Tudor.*

entablature In a classical order, a richly detailed horizontal member resting on columns or pilasters. It is divided horizontally into three main parts. The lowest is the architrave (definition 1), the structural part, and is generally an unornamented continuous beam or series of beams. The middle part is the frieze (definition 1), which is generally the most freely ornamented part. The uppermost is the cornice. Composed of a sequence of moldings, the cornice overhangs the frieze and architrave and serves as a crown to the whole. Each part has the moldings and decorative treatment that are characteristic of the particular order, but modern adaptations often alter canonical details. See also the related terms *column, order.*

entablature block A block bearing the canonical elements of a classical entablature on three or all four sides, placed between a column capital and a feature above, such as a balcony or ceiling. Distinguished from an impost block, which has the form of an inverted truncated pyramid and detailing typical of medieval architecture.

entasis The slight convex curving of the vertical profile of a tapered column.

exedra A semicircular or polygonal space usually containing a bench, in the wall of a garden or a building other than a church. Distinguished from a niche, which is usually a smaller feature higher in a wall, and from an apse, which is usually identified with churches.

exotic revivals A term occasionally used to suggest a distinction between revivals of European styles (e.g., Greek, Gothic Revivals) and non-European styles (e.g., Egyptian, Moorish Revivals). See also the more specific terms *Egyptian Revival, Mayan Revival, Moorish Revival.*

extrados The outer curve or outside surface of an arch. See also the related term *intrados.*

eyebrow dormer A low dormer with a small segmental window or vent but no sides. The roofing warps or bows over the window or vent in a wavy line.

facade An exterior face of a building, especially the principal or entrance front. Distinguished from an elevation, which is an orthographic drawing of a building face.

Fachwerk A form of half-timber construction introduced by German-speaking immigrants.

false half-timbering A surface treatment that simulates half-timber construction, consisting of a lattice of broad boards and stucco applied as an exterior veneer on a building of masonry or wood-frame construction. Most commonly seen in domestic architecture from the late nineteenth century onward.

fanlight A semicircular or semielliptical window over a door, with radiating mullions in the form of an open fan. Sometimes called a sunburst light. See also the more general term *transom* (definition 1) and the related term *side light.*

fan vault A type of Gothic vault in which the primary ribs all have the same curvature and radiate in a half circle around the springing point.

fascia 1 A plain, molded, or ornamented board that covers the horizontal edges (eaves) or sloping edges (verges) of a roof. Distinguished from the more specific term bargeboards, which are ornate fascia boards attached to the sloping edges of a roof. Distinguished from a frieze (definition 2), which is located at the top of a wall. **2** One of the broad continuous bands that make up the architrave of the Ionic, Corinthian, or Composite order.

Federal A version of Neoclassical architecture in the United States popular from New England to Virginia, and in other regions influenced by the Northeast. It flourished from the 1790s through the 1820s and is found in some regions as late as the 1840s. Sometimes called American Adam Style. Not to be confused with Federalist. See also the related terms *Jeffersonian, Roman Revival.*

Federal Revival Term applied to eclectic works (c. 1890–1930s) or elements of those works that emulate forms in the visual arts of the Federal period. Sometimes called Neo-Federal.

See also the related terms *Colonial Revival, Georgian Revival.*

Federalist Name of an American political party and the era it dominated (c. 1787–1820). Not to be confused with Federal.

fenestration Window treatment: arrangement and proportioning.

festoon A motif representing entwined leaves, flowers, or fruits, hung in a catenary curve from two points. Distinguished from a swag, which is a motif representing a fold of drapery hung in a similar curve. See also the more general term *garland.*

fillet 1 A relatively narrow flat molding. **2** Any thin band.

finial A vertical ornament placed upon the apex of an architectural feature, such as a gable, turret, or canopy. Distinguished from a pinnacle, which is a larger feature, usually associated with Gothic architecture.

fireproofing In metal skeletal framing, the wrapping of structural members in terra-cotta tile or other fire-resistant material.

flashing A strip of metal, plastic, or various flexible compositional materials used at roof valleys and ridges and at chimney corners to keep water out. Any similar material used to protect door and window heads and sills.

Flemish bond A pattern of brickwork in which the stretchers and headers alternate in the same row and are staggered from one row to the next. Because this creates a more animated texture than English bond, Flemish bond was favored for front facades and more elegant buildings.

Flemish gable A gable whose upper slopes ascend in steps rather than in a straight line. These steps may be rectilinear or curved, or a combination of both.

fluting, fluted A series of parallel grooves or channels (flutes), usually semicircular or semielliptical in plan, that accentuate the verticality of the shaft of a column or pilaster.

flying buttress In Gothic architecture a spanning member, usually in the form of an arch, that reaches across the open space from an exterior buttress pier to that point on the wall of the building where the thrusts of the interior vaults are concentrated. Because of its arched construction, a flying buttress exerts a counterthrust against the pressure of the vaults contained by the vertical strength of the buttress pier.

foliated (adjective). In the form of leaves or leaflike shapes.

folk Not a style term in itself, but a descriptive term, applicable to all the visual arts and all styles and periods. Applied to (1) a regional, often ethnic, tradition in which continuities through the years in the overall appearance of artifacts (including buildings) are more important than changes in stylistic embellishment; (2) the work of individual artists and artisans unexposed to or uninterested in prevailing or avant-garde ideals of form and technique. Approximate synonyms include anonymous, naive, primitive, traditional. For architecture, see also the more general term *vernacular* and the related term *popular.*

four-part vault See *quadripartite vault.*

foursquare house A hip-roofed, two-story house with four principal rooms on each floor and a symmetrical facade. It usually has a front porch across the full width of the house and one or more large dormers on the roof. A common suburban house type from the 1890s to the 1920s. Sometimes called American Foursquare, Prairie Box.

frame construction, frame Ambiguous terms. See instead *braced frame construction, light frame construction (balloon frame construction, platform frame construction), skeleton construction, timber-frame construction.* Not properly synonymous with wood construction, wood-clad, or wooden.

Francis I Style See *Chateauesque.*

François Premier See *Chateauesque.*

French colonial A term applied to buildings, towns, landscapes, and other artifacts from the period of actual French colonial occupation of large parts of eastern North America (c. 1605–1763). The term is extended to apply to the artifacts of French ethnic groups and their descendants well into the nineteenth century.

French Norman A style associated since the 1920s with residential architecture based on rural houses of the French provinces of Normandy and Brittany. While not a major revival style, it is characterized by asymmetrical plans, round stair towers with conical roofs, stucco walls, and steep hipped roofs. Sometimes called Norman French.

fret An ornament, usually in series, as a band or field, consisting of a latticelike interlocking of right-angled linear elements.

frieze 1 The broad horizontal band that forms the central part of a classical entablature. **2** Any long horizontal band or zone, especially one that has a chiefly decorative purpose, located at the top of a wall. Distinguished from a fascia, which is attached to the horizontal edge of a roof.

front gabled Term applied to a building whose principal gable end faces the front of the lot or some feature like a street or open space. Sometimes called gable front. Distinguished from side gabled.

gable The wall area immediately below the end of a gable, gambrel, or jerkinhead roof.

gableboard See *bargeboard.*

gable front See *front gabled.*

gable roof A roof in which the two planes slope equally toward each other to a common ridge. Sometimes called a pitched roof.

galerie In French colonial domestic architecture, a porch or veranda, usually sheltered by an extension of the hipped roof of the house.

gambrel roof A roof that has a single ridgepole but a double pitch. The lower plane, which rises from the eaves, is rather steep. The upper plane, which extends from the lower plane to the ridgeline, has a flatter pitch.

garland A motif representing a rope of entwined leaves, flowers, ribbons, or drapery, regardless of its shape or position. It may be formed into a wreath, festoon, or swag, or follow the outline of a rectilinear architectural element.

garret See *attic* (definition 1).

gauged brick A brick that has been cut or rubbed to a uniform size and shape.

gazebo A small pavilion, usually polygonal or circular in plan and serving as a garden or park shelter. Distinguished from a kiosk, which generally has some commercial or public function. See also the related terms *bandstand, belvedere* (definition 1).

General Grant Style See *Second Empire*.

Georgian period A term for a period in British and British colonial history, frequently applied to architecture and the other visual arts dating from this time. The Georgian period begins with the coronation of George I in 1714 and extends until about 1781 in the area that became the United States (and in Britain, until the death of George IV in 1830). See also the related terms *Anglo-Palladianism, British colonial*.

Georgian plan See *double-pile* plus *double-pen* (i.e., a four-room plan with central hallway).

Georgian Revival A revival of Georgian period forms—in England, from the 1860s to the present, and in the United States, from the 1880s to the present. Sometimes called Neo-Georgian. See also the more general term *Colonial Revival* and the related term *Federal Revival*.

giant order A composition involving any one of the five principal classical orders, in which the columns or pilasters are nearly as tall as the height of the entire building. Sometimes called a colossal order. See also the more general term *order*.

Gingerbread Style See *Carpenter's Gothic*.

girder A major horizontal spanning member, comparable in function to a beam, but larger and often built up of a number of parts. It usually runs at right angles to the beams and serves as their principal means of support.

girt In timber-frame construction, a horizontal beam at intermediate (e.g., second-floor) level, spanning between posts.

glazing bar See *muntin*.

golden section Any line divided into two parts so that the ratio of the longer part to the shorter part equals the ratio of the length of the whole line to the longer part: $a/b - (a+b)/a$. This ratio is approximately 1.618:1. A golden rectangle, or classical rectangle, is a rectangle whose long side is related to the short side in the same ratio as the golden section. It is proportioned so that neither the long nor the short side seems to dominate. In a Fibonacci series (i.e., 1, 2, 3, 5, 8, 13, . . .), the sum of the two preceding terms gives the next. The higher one goes in such a series, the closer the ratio of two sequential terms approaches the golden section.

Gothic An architectural style prevalent in Europe from the twelfth century into the fifteenth in Italy (and into the sixteenth century in the rest of Europe). It is characterized by pointed arches and ribbed vaults and by the dominance of openings over masonry mass in the wall. The Gothic was preceded by the Romanesque and followed by the Renaissance.

Gothic Revival A movement in Europe and North America devoted to reviving the forms and the spirit of Gothic architecture and the allied arts. It originated in the mid-eighteenth century. Sometimes called the Pointed Style in the nineteenth century, and sometimes called Neo-Gothic. See also the more specific terms *Carpenter's Gothic, Collegiate Gothic, Early Gothic Revival, High Victorian Gothic, Late Gothic Revival*.

Grecian A nineteenth-century term for Greek Revival.

Greek cross A cross with four equal arms. Usually used to describe the ground plan of a building. See also the more general term *cruciform*.

Greek Revival A movement in Europe and North America devoted to reviving the forms and the spirit of classical Greek architecture, sculpture, and decorative arts. It originated in the mid-eighteenth century, culminated in the 1830s, and continued into the 1860s. Sometimes called Grecian in the nineteenth century. See also the more general term *Neoclassical*.

groin The curved edge formed by the intersection of two vaults.

guillotine sash See *double-hung window*.

HABS See *Historic American Buildings Survey*.

HAER See *Historic American Engineering Record*.

half-timber construction A variety of timber-frame construction in which the framing members are exposed on the exterior of the wall, with the spaces between timbers being filled with wattle-and-daub (i.e., woven lath and plaster) or masonry materials, such as brick or stone. These masonry materials may also be covered with stucco. Sometimes called half-timbered construction.

hall-and-parlor house, hall-and-parlor plan A double-pen house (i.e., a house that is one room deep and two rooms wide). Usually applied to houses without a central through-passage, to distinguish from hall-passage-parlor houses.

hall-passage-parlor house, hall-passage-parlor plan A two-room house with a central through-passage or hallway.

hammer beam A short horizontal beam projecting inward from the foot of the principal rafter and supported below by a diagonal brace tied into a vertical wall post. The hammer beams carry much of the load of the roof trussing above. Hammer beam trusses, which could be assembled using a series of smaller timbers, were often used in late medieval England instead of conventional trusses, which required long horizontal tie beams extending across an entire interior space.

haunch The part of the arch between the crown or keystone and the springing.

header A brick laid across the thickness of a wall, so that the short end of the brick shows on the exterior.

head molding A molding or set of moldings designed to shelter and embellish the top of a door or window. Sometimes called a drip molding. See also the related terms *cap* (for windows) and *hood* (for doors).

heavy timber construction See *timber-frame construction*.

high style or high-style (adjective) Not a style term in itself, but a descriptive term, applicable to all the visual arts and all styles and periods. Applied to the works of the masters and their schools and disciples, usually reflecting a cosmopolitan awareness of traditions beyond a particular place or time. Usually contrasted with vernacular (including the folk and popular traditions).

high tech Term applied to architecture in which building materials and elements of building systems are used to celebrate contemporary technology. Elemental geometric forms, primary colors, and metallic finishes are used to heighten the technological imagery.

High Victorian Gothic A version of the Gothic Revival that originated in England in the 1850s and spread to North America in the 1860s. Characterized by polychromatic exteriors inspired by the medieval Gothic architecture of northern Italy. Sometimes called Ruskin Gothic, Ruskinian Gothic, Venetian Gothic, Victorian Gothic. See also the more general term *Gothic Revival*.

hipped gable roof See *jerkinhead roof*.

hipped roof A roof that pitches inward from all four sides. The edge where any two planes meet is called the hip.

Historic American Buildings Survey (HABS) A branch of the National Park Service of the United States Department of the Interior, established in 1933 to produce detailed documentation of American architecture. HABS documentation typically includes historical and architectural data, photographs, and measured drawings, and is deposited in the Prints and Photographs Division of the Library of Congress. See also the related term *Historic American Engineering Record*.

Historic American Engineering Record (HAER) A branch of the National Park Service of the United States Department of the Interior, established in 1969 to produce detailed documentation of sites and structures associated with industry, transportation, and other areas of technology. See also the related term *Historic American Buildings Survey*.

historicism, historicist, historicizing A type of eclecticism prevalent since the eighteenth century, involving the use of forms from historical periods of high-style design (usually in the Western tradition) and, occasionally, from favored traditions of vernacular design (such as the various colonial traditions in the United States). Historicist influences are designated by the use of the prefix Neo- with a previous historical style (e.g., Neo-Baroque). Distinguished from the more general term eclecticism, which draws upon a wider range of sources in addition to the historical. See also the more specific term *revivalism*.

hollow building tile A hollow terra-cotta building block used for constructing exterior bearing walls of buildings up to about three stories, as well as interior walls and partitions.

hood A canopy, ledge, molding, or pediment over a door. Distinguished from a cap, which is a similar feature over a window. Sometimes called a hood molding. See also the related term *head molding*.

horizontal plank frame construction A system of wood construction in which horizontal planks are set or nailed into the corner posts of a timber-frame building. There are, however, no studs or intermediate posts connecting the sill and the plate. See also the related term *vertical plank frame construction*.

hung ceiling See *suspended ceiling*.

hyphen A subsidiary building unit, often one story, connecting the central block and the wings or dependencies.

I-beam The most common profile in steel structural shapes (although it also appears in cast iron and in reinforced concrete). Used especially for spanning elements, it is shaped like the capital letter *I* to make the most efficient use of the material consistent with a shape that permits easy assemblage. The vertical face of the *I* is the web. The horizontal faces are the flanges. Other standard shapes for steel framing elements are *H*s, *T*s, *Z*s, *L*s (known as angles), and square-cornered *U*s (channels).

I-house A two-story house, one room deep and two rooms wide, usually with a central hallway. The I-house is a nineteenth-century descendant of the hall-and-parlor houses of the colonial period. The term is commonly applied to the end-chimney houses of the southern and mid-Atlantic traditions. The term most likely derives from the resemblance between the tall, narrow end walls of these houses and the capital letter *I*.

impost The top part of a pier or wall, upon which rests the springer or lowest voussoir of an arch.

impost block A block, often in the form of an inverted truncated pyramid, placed between a column capital and the lowest voussoirs of an arch above. Distinguished from an entablature block, which has the details found in a classical entablature. Sometimes called a dosseret or supercapital.

in antis Columns in antis are placed between two projecting sections of wall, in an imaginary plane connecting the ends of the two wall elements.

intermediate rib See *tierceron.*

International Style A style that originated in the 1920s and flourished into the 1970s, characterized by the expression of volume and surface and by the suppression of historicist ornament and axial symmetry. The term was originally applied by Henry-Russell Hitchcock and Philip Johnson to the new, nontraditional, mostly European, architecture of the 1920s in their 1932 exhibition at the Museum of Modern Art and in their accompanying book, *The International Style.* Also called International, International Modern. See also the more specific term *Corporate International Style* and the related terms *Bauhaus, Miesian, Second Chicago School.*

intrados The inner curve or underside (soffit) of an arch. See also the related term *extrados.*

Ionic order An ensemble of classical column and entablature elements, particularly characterized by the use of large volutes in the capital of the column. See also the more general term *order.*

isometric drawing A pictorial drawing using isometric projection, in which all horizontal lines that are perpendicular in an object, building, or space are drawn at 60-degree angles from the vertical. Consequently, a single scale can be used for all three dimensions. Sometimes called an isometric. See also the related terms *axonometric drawing, perspective drawing.*

Italianate 1 A general term for an eclectic Neo-Renaissance and Neo-Romanesque style, originating in England and Germany in the early nineteenth century and prevalent in the United States between the 1840s and 1880s, not only in houses but also in Main Street commercial buildings. The Italianate is characterized by prominent window heads and bracketed cornices. Called the Bracketed Style in the nineteenth century. See also the more specific term *Italian Villa Style,* and the related terms *Renaissance Revival, Round Arch mode, Second Empire.* **2** A specific term for Italianate buildings that are predominantly symmetrical in plan and elevation. Distinguished from Barryesque, which is applied to more formal institutional and governmental buildings.

Italian Villa Style A subtype of the Italianate style (definition 1), originating in England and Germany in the early nineteenth century and prevalent in the United States between the 1840s and 1870s, mostly in houses, but also churches and other public buildings. The style is characterized by asymmetrical plans and elevations, irregular blocklike massing, round arch arcades and

openings, and northern Italian Romanesque detailing. Larger Italian Villa buildings often had a campanile-like tower. Distinguished from the more symmetrical Italianate style (definition 2) by having the northern Italian rural vernacular villa as prototype.

Jacobean period A term for a period in British history coinciding with the rule of James I (1603–1625). See also the related term *Elizabethan* for the immediately preceding period, which itself is part of the Tudor period.

Jacobethan Revival See *Neo-Tudor.*

jamb The vertical side face of a door or window opening, amounting to the full thickness of the wall, and usually enriched with paneling, moldings, or jamb shafts (which are engaged columns set into a splayed, or angled, jamb). In an opening containing a door or window, the jamb is distinguished from the reveal, which is the portion of wall thickness between the door or window frame and the outer surface of the wall. (In an opening without a door or window, the terms jamb and reveal are used interchangeably.) Also distinguished from an architrave (definition 2), which consists of the moldings on the face of a wall around the opening.

Jazz Moderne See *Art Deco.*

Jeffersonian A personal style of Neoclassicism identified with the architecture of Thomas Jefferson (1743–1826), derived in part from Palladian ideas and in part from Imperial Roman prototypes. The style had an impact in the Piedmont of Virginia, the upper deep South (northern Georgia, Alabama, South Carolina), and across the Appalachians into the Ohio River valley. Sometimes called Jeffersonian Classicism. See also the related terms *Anglo-Palladianism, Federal, Roman Revival.*

jerkinhead roof A gable roof in which the upper portion of the gable end is hipped, or inclined inward along the ridgeline, forming a small triangle of roof surface. Sometimes called a clipped gable roof or hipped gable roof.

joist One of a series of small horizontal beams that support a floor or ceiling.

keystone The central wedge-shaped stone at the crown of an arch.

king post In a truss, the vertical suspension member that connects the tie beam with the apex of opposing principal rafters.

kiosk Originally, a Turkish summer palace. Since the nineteenth century, the term has been applied to any small pavilion or stand, usually found in public gardens, parks, streets, and malls, where it serves some commercial or public function. Distinguished from a gazebo, which may be found in public or private gardens or parks, but which usually serves as a sheltered resting place. See also the related term *bandstand.*

label 1 A drip molding, over a square-headed door or window, which extends for a short distance down each side of the opening. **2** A similar vertical downward extension of a drip molding over an arch of any form. Sometimes called a label molding.

label stop **1** An L-shaped termination at the lower ends of a label. **2** Any decorative boss or other termination of a label.

lancet arch An arch generally tall and sharply pointed, whose centers are farther apart than the width or span of the arch.

lantern **1** The uppermost stage of a dome, containing windows or arcaded openings. **2** Any feature, square or polygonal in plan and usually containing windows, rising above the roof of a building. The square structures that serve as skylights on the roofs of nineteenth-century buildings—particularly houses—were also called lantern lights, and, in Italianate and Second Empire buildings, came to be called cupolas.

Late Georgian period Not strictly a style term, but a term for a period in British and British colonial history approximately coinciding with the reigns of George III (1760–1820) and George IV (1820–1830). In the United States, the Late Georgian period is now understood to end sometime during the Revolutionary War (1775–1781) and to be followed by the Federal period (c. 1787–1820). In Britain, the Late Georgian period includes the Regency period (1811–1820s). See also the related term *Early Georgian period.*

Late Gothic Revival A term for the Gothic Revival work of the late nineteenth and early twentieth centuries. See also the more specific term *Collegiate Gothic* (definition 2) and the related term *Early Gothic Revival.*

lath A latticelike, continuous surface of small wooden strips or metal mesh nailed to walls or partitions to hold plaster.

Latin cross A cross with one long and three short arms. Usually used to describe the ground plans of Roman Catholic and Protestant churches. See also the more general term *cruciform.*

leaded glass Panes of glass held in place by lead strips, or cames. The panes, clear or stained, may be of any shape.

lean-to roof. See *shed roof.*

lierne In a Gothic vault, a short ornamental rib connecting the major transverse ribs and the secondary tiercerons. Sometimes called a cross rib or tertiary rib.

light frame construction A type of wood-frame construction in which relatively light structural members (usually sawn lumber, ranging from two-by-fours to two-by-tens) are fastened with nails. Distinguished from timber-frame construction, in which relatively heavy structural members (hewn or sawn timbers, measuring six by six and larger) are fastened with mortise-and-tenon joints. See the more specific terms *balloon-frame construction, platform frame construction.*

lintel A horizontal structural member that supports the wall over an opening or spans between two adjacent piers or columns.

living hall In Queen Anne, Shingle Style, and Colonial Revival houses, an extensive room, often containing the entry, the main staircase, a fireplace, and an inglenook.

load-bearing Term applied to a wall, column, pier, or any vertical supporting member, constructed so that all loads are carried to the ground through the wall, column, or pier. See also the related terms *bearing wall, curtain wall.*

loggia **1** A porch or open-air room, particularly one set within the body of a building. **2** An arcaded or colonnaded structure, open on one or more sides, sometimes with an upper story. **3** An eighteenth- and nineteenth-century term for a porch or veranda.

Lombard A style term applied in the United States in the mid-nineteenth century to buildings derived from the Romanesque architecture of northern Italy (especially Lombardy) and the earlier nineteenth-century architecture of southern Germany. Characterized by the use of brick for both structural and ornamental purposes. Also called Lombardic. See also the related term *Round Arch mode.*

lunette **1** A semicircular area, especially one that contains some decorative treatment or a mural painting. **2** A semicircular window in such an area.

Mannerism, Mannerist **1** A phase of Renaissance art and architecture in the mid-sixteenth century, characterized by distortions, contortions, inversions, odd juxtapositions, and other departures from High Renaissance canons of design. **2** (Not capitalized) A sensibility in design, regardless of style or period, characterized by a knowledgeable violation of rules and intended as a comment on the very nature of convention.

mansard roof A hipped roof with double pitch. The upper slope may approach flatness, while the lower slope has a very steep pitch, sometimes flaring in a concave curve (or swelling in a convex curve) as it comes to the eaves. This lower slope usually has windows, and the area under the roof often amounts to a full story. The name is a corruption of that of François Mansart (1598–1666), who designed roofs of this type, which was revived in Paris during the Second Empire period.

Mansard Style, Mansardic See *Second Empire.*

masonry Construction using stone, brick, block, or some other hard and durable material laid up in units and usually bonded by mortar.

massing The grouping or arrangement of the primary volumetric components of a building.

Mayan Revival Term applied to eclectic works or elements of those works that emulate forms in the visual arts of the Maya civilization of Central America. See also the related term *Art Deco.*

McKim classicism, McKim classical Architecture of, or in the manner of, the firm of McKim,

Mead and White, 1890–1920s. See *Beaux-Arts classicism.*

medieval Term applied to the Middle Ages in European civilization between the age of antiquity and the age of the Renaissance (i.e., mid-400s to mid–1400s in Italy; mid-400s to late 1500s in England). In architecture and the other visual arts, the medieval period included the end of the Early Christian period, then the Byzantine, the Romanesque, and the Gothic styles or periods.

Mediterranean Revival A style generally associated since the early twentieth century with residential architecture based on Italian villas of the sixteenth century. While not a major revival style, it is characterized by symmetrical arrangements, stucco walls, and low-pitch tile roofs. Sometimes called Mediterranean Villa, Neo-Mediterranean. See also the related term *Spanish Colonial Revival.*

metope In a Doric entablature, that part of the frieze which falls between two triglyphs. In the Greek Doric order the metopes often contain small sculptural reliefs.

Middle Ages See *medieval.*

Miesian Term applied to work showing the influence of the German-American architect Ludwig Mies van der Rohe (1886–1969). See also the related terms *Bauhaus, International Style, Second Chicago School.*

Mission Revival A style originating in the 1890s, and making use of forms and materials from the Spanish and Mexican mission architecture of the eighteenth and early nineteenth centuries. Not to be confused with Mission furniture of the Arts and Crafts movement. See also the more general term *Spanish Colonial Revival.*

modern Term applied in various ways during the past century to the history of the visual arts and world history generally: (1) from the 1910s to the present (see also the more specific terms *Bauhaus, International Style*); (2) from the 1860s, 1870s, 1880s, or 1890s to the present; (3) from the Enlightenment or the advent of Neoclassicism or the industrial revolution, c. 1750, to the present; (4) from the Renaissance in Italy, c. 1450, to the present.

Modern Gothic See *Eastlake.*

Moderne A term applied to a wide range of design work from the 1920s through the 1940s, in which aspects of traditionalism and modernism coexist and in which eclecticism (from a historical, exotic, or machine aesthetic) is inseparable from the urge for stylization. Sometimes called Art Moderne, Modernistic. See also the more specific terms *Art Deco, PWA Moderne, Streamline Moderne.*

modillion One of a series of small, thin scroll brackets under the projecting crown molding of a classical cornice. It is found in the Corinthian and Composite orders. Distinguished from a console, which usually is larger and has a height greater than its projection from the wall.

molding A running surface composed of parallel and continuous sections of simple or compound curves and flat areas.

monitor An extensive shed-roofed feature on a roof, containing a band of windows or vents. It may be located along one of the roof slopes (a trap-door monitor) or along the ridgeline (a clerestory monitor), and it usually runs the entire length of the roof. Distinguished from a skylight, which is a low-profile or flush-mounted feature in the plane of the roof.

Moorish Revival Term applied to eclectic works or elements of those works that emulate forms in the visual arts of those parts of North Africa and Spain under Muslim domination from the seventh through the fifteenth century. See also the related term *Oriental Revival.*

mortar A mixture of cement or lime with water and a fine aggregate of sand used to secure bricks or stones in masonry construction.

mortise-and-tenon joint A timber framing joint that is made by one member having its end shaped into a projecting piece (tenon) that fits exactly into a hole (mortise) in the other member. Once joined, the pieces are held together by a peg that passes through the tenon.

mullion 1 A post or similar vertical member dividing a window into two or more units, or lights, each of which may be further subdivided (by muntins) into panes. **2** A post or similar vertical member dividing a wall opening into two or more contiguous windows.

muntin One of the small vertical or horizontal members that hold panes of glass within a window or glazed door. Distinguished from a mullion, which is a heavier vertical member separating paired or grouped windows. Sometimes called a glazing bar, sash bar, or window bar.

mushroom column A reinforced concrete column that flares at the top in order to counteract shear stresses in the vicinity of the column.

National Register of Historic Places A branch of the National Park Service of the United States Department of the Interior, established by the National Historic Preservation Act of 1966, to maintain files of documentation on districts, sites, buildings, structures, and objects of national, state, or local significance. Properties listed on the National Register are afforded administrative—and, ultimately, judicial—review in instances where projects funded or assisted by federal agencies might have an impact on the historic property. Properties listed on the register may also be eligible for certain tax benefits.

nave 1 The entire body of a church between the entrance and the crossing. **2** The central space of a church, between the side aisles, extending from the entrance end to the crossing.

Neo-Baroque Term applied to eclectic works or elements of those works that emulate forms in the visual arts of the Baroque style or period. Sometimes called Baroque Revival.

Neo-Byzantine Term applied to eclectic works or elements of those works that emulate forms in the visual arts of the Byzantine style or period. Sometimes called Byzantine Revival.

Neoclassical Revival See *Beaux-Arts classicism.*

neoclassicism, neoclassical A broad movement in the visual arts which drew its inspiration from ancient Greece and Rome. It began in the mid-eighteenth century with the advent of the science of archaeology and extended into the mid-nineteenth century (in some Beaux-Arts work, into the 1930s; in some postmodern work, even into the present). See also the related terms *Beaux-Arts, Beaux-Arts classicism, classicism,* and the more specific terms *Greek Revival, Roman Revival.*

Neo-Colonial See *Colonial Revival.*

Neo-Federal See *Federal Revival.*

Neo-Georgian See *Georgian Revival.*

Neo-Gothic Term applied to eclectic works or elements of those works that emulate forms in the visual arts of the Gothic style or period. The cultural movement that produced so many such works in the eighteenth, nineteenth, and twentieth centuries is called the Gothic Revival, though that term covers a wide range of work.

Néo-Grec An architectural style developed in connection with the Ecole des Beaux-Arts in Paris during the 1840s and characterized by the use of stylized Greek elements, often in conjunction with cast iron or brick construction. See also the more general term *Beaux-Arts.*

Neo-Hispanic See *Spanish Colonial Revival.*

Neo-Mediterranean See *Mediterranean Revival.*

Neo-Norman Term applied to eclectic works or elements of those works that emulate forms in the visual arts of the eleventh- and twelfth-century Romanesque of Norman France and Britain.

Neo-Palladian See *Palladianism.*

Neo-Renaissance Term applied to eclectic works or elements of those works that emulate forms in the visual arts of the Renaissance style or period. The mid- to late nineteenth-century cultural movement that produced so many such works is called the Renaissance Revival, though that term covers a wide range of work.

Neo-Romanesque Term applied to eclectic works or elements of those works that emulate forms in the visual arts of the Romanesque style or period. The mid-nineteenth-century cultural movement that produced so many such works is called the Romanesque Revival, though that term covers a wide range of work.

Neo-Tudor Term applied to eclectic works or elements of those works that emulate forms in the visual arts of the Tudor period. Sometimes loosely called Elizabethan Manor Style, English Half-timber Style, Jacobethan Revival, Tudor Revival.

New Brutalism See *Brutalism.*

New Formalism A style prevalent since the 1960s, characterized by symmetrical arrangements, rich materials (marble cladding, metal grillework), and stylized classical (even Gothic) detailing. Architects associated with this style include Philip Johnson (born 1906), Edward Durell Stone (1902–1978), and Minoru Yamasaki (born 1912).

newel post A post at the head or foot of a flight of stairs, to which the handrail is fastened. Newel posts occur in a variety of shapes, in profile and cross section, and are generally more substantial elements than the individual balusters that support the handrail.

niche A recess in a wall, usually designed to contain sculpture or an urn. A niche is often semicircular in plan and surmounted by a half dome or shell form. See also the related terms *aedicule, tabernacle* (definition 1).

nogging Brickwork that fills the spaces between members of a timber-frame wall or partition.

Norman French See *French Norman.*

octagon house A rare house type of the 1850s, based on the ideas of Orson Squire Fowler (1809–1887), who argued for the efficiencies of an octagonal floor plan. Sometimes called octagon mode.

oculus A circular opening in a ceiling or wall or at the top of a dome.

ogee arch A pointed arch formed by a pair of opposing S-shaped curves.

order The most important constituents of classical architecture are the orders, first developed as a structural-aesthetic system by the ancient Greeks. An order has two major components. A column with its capital is the main vertical supporting member. The principal horizontal member is the entablature. The Greeks developed three different types of order, the Doric, Ionic, and Corinthian, each distinguishable by its own decorative system and proportions. All three were taken over and modified by the Romans, who added two orders of their own, the Tuscan, which is a simplified form of the Doric, and the Composite, which is made up of elements of both the Ionic and the Corinthian. The Romans often used the orders as a structural system in the same manner as the Greeks. Unlike the Greeks, however, they also applied them as decoration to the surfaces of walls that were supported by other means. Sometimes called classical orders. See also the related terms *column, entablature, giant order, superposition* (definition 1).

oriel A projecting polygonal or curved window unit of one or more stories, supported on brackets or corbels. Sometimes called an oriel window. Distinguished from a bay window, which rises from the foundation and has a rooted rather than a suspended appearance. However, a multistory projection in a tall building, whether cantilevered out or built from the foundation, is called a projecting bay or a unit of bay windows.

Oriental Revival Ambiguous term, suggesting eclectic influences from any period in any culture in the "Orient," or Asia, including Turkish, Persian, Indian, Chinese, and Japanese, as well as Arabic (even the Moorish of North Africa and Spain). Sometimes called Oriental style. See also the related term *Moorish Revival.*

orthographic projection A system of visual representation in which all details on or near some principal plane, object, building, or space are projected, to scale, onto the parallel plane of the drawing. Orthographic projection thus flattens all forms into a single two-dimensional picture plane and allows for an exact scaling of every feature in that plane. Distinguished from pictorial projection, which creates the illusion of three-dimensional depth. See also the more specific terms *elevation, plan, section.*

outbuilding A building subsidiary to and completely detached from another building. Distinguished from a dependency, which may be attached or detached.

overhang The projection of part of a structure beyond the portion below.

PWA Moderne A synthesis of the Moderne (i.e., Art Deco or Streamline Moderne) with an austere late type of Beaux-Arts classicism, often associated with federal government buildings of the 1930s and 1940s during the Public Works Administration. See also the more general term *Moderne* and the related terms *Art Deco, Beaux-Arts classicism, Streamline Moderne.*

Palladianism, Palladian Work influenced by the Italian Renaissance architect Andrea Palladio (1508–1580), particularly by means of his treatise, *I Quattro Libri dell'Architettura* (*The Four Books of Architecture*, originally published in 1570 and disseminated throughout Europe in numerous translations and editions until the mid-eighteenth century). The most significant flourishing of Palladianism was in England, from the 1710s to the 1760s, and in the British North American colonies, from the 1740s to the 1790s. Sometimes called Neo-Palladian, Palladian classical. See also the more specific term *Anglo-Palladianism.*

Palladian motif A three-part composition for a door or window, in which a round-headed opening is flanked by lower flat-headed openings and separated from them by columns, pilasters, or mullions. The flanking sections, and sometimes the entire unit, may be blind (i.e., not open).

Palladian Revival See *Anglo-Palladianism.*

Palladian window A window subdivided as in the Palladian motif.

parapet A low wall at the edge of a roof, balcony, or terrace, sometimes formed by the upward extension of the wall below.

pargeting Elaborate stucco or plasterwork, especially an ornamental finish for exterior plaster walls, sometimes decorated with figures in low relief or indented. Found in late medieval, Queen Anne, and period revival buildings. Sometimes called parging, pargework. See also the more general term *stucco.*

parquet Inlaid wood flooring, usually set in simple geometric patterns.

parti The essential solution to an architectural program or problem; the basic concept for the arrangement of spaces, before the development and elaboration of the design.

patera (plural: paterae) A circular or oval panel or plaque decorated with stylized flower petals or radiating linear motifs. Distinguished from a roundel, which is always circular.

pavilion 1 A central or corner unit that projects from a larger architectural mass and is usually accented by a special treatment of the wall or roof. **2** A detached or semidetached structure used for specialized activities, as at a hospital. **3** In a garden or fairground, a temporary structure or tent, usually ornamented.

pediment 1 In classical architecture, the low triangular gable end of the roof, framed by raking cornices along the inclined edges of the roof and by a horizontal cornice below. **2** In Renaissance and Baroque and later classically derived architecture, the triangular or curvilinear culmination of a prominent part of a facade. **3** A similar but smaller-scale feature over a door or window. It may be triangular or curvilinear.

pendentive A concave surface in the form of a spherical triangle that forms the structural transition from the square plan of a crossing to the circular plan of a dome.

pergola A structure with an open wood-framed roof, often latticed, and supported by a colonnade. It is usually covered by climbing plants, such as vines or roses, and provides shade for a garden walk or a passageway to a building. Distinguished from arbors or trellises, which are less extensive accessory structures lacking the colonnade.

period house Term applied to suburban and country houses in which period revival styles are dominant.

period revival Term applied to eclectic works—particularly suburban and country houses—of the first three decades of the twentieth century, in which a particular historical or regional style is dominant. See also the more specific terms *Colonial Revival, Dutch Colonial Revival, Georgian Revival, Neo-Tudor, Spanish Colonial Revival.*

peripteral (adjective) Surrounded by a single row of columns.

peristyle A range of columns surrounding a building or an open court.

perspective drawing A pictorial drawing representing an object, building, or space, as if seen from a single vantage point. The illusion of three dimensions is created by using a system based on the optical laws of converging lines and vanishing points. See also the related terms *axonometric drawing, isometric drawing.*

piano nobile (plural: piani nobili) In Renaissance and later architecture, a floor with formal reception, living, and dining rooms. The principal and often tallest story in a building, usually one level above the ground level.

piazza 1 A plaza or square. **2** An eighteenth- and nineteenth-century term for a porch or veranda.

pictorial projection A system of visual representation in which an object, building, or space is projected onto the picture plane in such a way that the illusion of three-dimensional depth is created. Distinguished from orthographic projection, in which the dimension of depth is excluded. See also the more specific terms *axonometric drawing, isometric drawing, perspective drawing.*

picturesque An aesthetic category in architecture and landscape architecture in the late eighteenth and early nineteenth centuries. It is characterized by relationships among buildings and landscape features that evoke the qualities of landscape paintings, in which the eye is led past a variety of forms and spaces into the distance and the mind is led to contemplate a sense of age (by means of ruins, fallen trees, weathered rocks, and mossy surfaces on all of these). In actual settings, asymmetrical and eclectic buildings, indirect approaches, and contrasting clusters of plantings heighten the experience of the picturesque.

pier 1 A freestanding mass, supporting a concentrated load from an arch, a beam, a truss, or a girder. While generally rectilinear in plan, piers in buildings based upon medieval precedents are often curvilinear in plan. **2** An upright portion of a wall that performs a columnar function. The pier may be continuous with the plane of the wall, or it may be distinguished from the plane of the wall to give it a columnlike independence.

pier and spandrel. A type of skeletal wall organization in which the vertical metal columns (and their square-cornered cladding) project in front of the plane of windows and their spandrel panels. The spandrel panels may be exposed structural spanning members. More often they provide decorative covering for the structure.

pilaster 1 A flattened column, with or without fluting, that is attached to a wall. It is usually finished with the same capital and base as a freestanding column. **2** Any narrow, vertical strip attached to a wall. Distinguished from an engaged column, which has a convex curvature.

pillar Ambiguous term, often used interchangeably with column, pier, or post. See instead one of those terms. (Although the term pillar is sometimes applied to columns that are square in plan, the term pier is preferable.)

pinnacle In Gothic architecture, a small spirelike element providing an ornamental finish to the highest part of a buttress or roof. It has a slender pyramidal or conical form and is often articulated with crockets or ribs and is topped by a finial. Distinguished from a finial, which is a smaller feature appearing by itself.

pitched roof See *gable roof.*

plan A drawing (in orthographic projection) representing all or part of an object, building, or space, as if viewed from directly above. A floor plan is a drawing of a horizontal cut through a building, usually at the level of the windows, showing the configuration of walls and openings. Other types of plans may illustrate ceilings, roofs, structural elements, and mechanical systems.

plank construction General term. See instead the more specific terms *horizontal plank frame construction, vertical plank construction.*

plate 1 In timber-frame construction, the topmost horizontal structural member of a wall, to which the roof rafters are fastened. **2** In platform and balloon-frame construction, the horizontal members to which the tops and bottoms of studs are nailed. The bottom plate is sometimes called the sill plate or sole plate.

Plateresque Term applied to Spanish and Spanish colonial Renaissance architecture from the early sixteenth century onward, in which the delicate, finely sculptured detail resembles the work of a silversmith (*platero*). See also the related term *Spanish colonial.*

platform frame construction A system of light frame construction in which each story is built as an independent unit and the studs are only one story high. The floor joists of each story rest on the top plates of the story below, and the bearing walls or partitions rest on the subfloor of each floor unit or platform. Platform framing is easier to construct and more rigid than balloon framing and has become the common framing method in the twentieth century. Structural members are usually sawn lumber, ranging from two-by-fours to two-by-tens, and are fastened with nails. Sometimes called platform framing, western frame, western framing.

plinth The base block of a column, pilaster, pedestal, dado, or door architrave.

Pointed Style A nineteenth-century term for Gothic Revival.

polychromy, polychromatic, polychrome A many-colored treatment, especially the combination of materials in various colors or the application of surface color, to articulate wall and roof planes and to highlight structure.

popular A term applied to vernacular architecture influenced by such publications as books of the orders, builders' guides, style books, pattern books, mail-order catalogs, architectural periodicals, and household magazines. Architecture in the popular tradition may be built according to commercially available plans or from widely distributed components; or it may be built by local practitioners (architects, builders, contractors) emulating buildings that are represented in publications. The distinction between popular architecture and high-style architecture by lesser-known architects depends on one's point of view with regard to the division between vernacular and high-style. See also the more general term *vernacular* and the related term *folk*.

porch A structure attached to a building to shelter an entrance or to serve as a semienclosed sitting, working, or sleeping space. Distinguished from a portico, which is either a pedimented feature at least one story in height supported by classical columns or a more extensive colonnaded feature.

porte-cochere A porch projecting over a driveway and providing shelter to people leaving a vehicle and entering a building, or vice versa. Also called a carriage porch.

portico 1 A porch at least one story in height consisting of a low-pitched roof supported on classical columns and finished in front with an entablature and pediment. 2 An extensive porch supported by a colonnade.

post A vertical supporting element, either square or circular in plan. Posts are the integral vertical members of a frame or truss, whether of wood or metal. Posts may also carry fences or gates, or may serve as freestanding markers (e.g., mileposts).

post-and-beam construction A structural system in which the main support is provided by vertical members (posts) carrying horizontal members (beams or lintels). Sometimes called post-and-girt construction, post-and-lintel construction, trabeation, trabeated construction.

postmodernism, postmodern A term applied to work that involves a reaction against the ideas and works of various twentieth-century modern movements, particularly the Bauhaus and the International Style. Postmodern work makes use of historicism, yet the traditional elements are often merely applied to buildings that, in every other respect, are products of modern movement design. The term is also applied to works that are attempting to demonstrate an extension of the principles of various modern movements.

Prairie Box See *foursquare house*.

Prairie School, Prairie Style A diverse group of architects working in Chicago and throughout the Midwest from the 1890s to the 1920s, strongly influenced by Frank Lloyd Wright and to a lesser degree by Louis Sullivan. The term is applied mainly to domestic architecture. An architect is said to belong to the Prairie School; a work of architecture is said to be in the Prairie Style. Sometimes called Prairie, for short. See also the related terms *Chicago School, Wrightian*.

pre-Columbian Term applied to the major cultures of Latin American (e.g., Aztec, Maya,

Inca) that flourished prior to the discovery of the New World by Columbus in 1492 and the Spanish conquests of the sixteenth century. Distinguished from North American Indian, which is generally applied to indigenous cultures within the area that would become the United States and Canada.

pressed metal Thin sheets of metal (usually galvanized or tin-plated iron) stamped into patterned panels for covering ceilings and exterior and interior walls or into molding profiles and other details for assembly into exterior and interior cornices. Loosely called pressed tin or stamped metal. Prevalent from the 1870s through the 1920s.

program The list of functional, spatial, and other requirements that guides an architect in developing a design.

proscenium In a recessed stage, the area between the orchestra and the curtain.

proscenium arch In a recessed stage, the enframement of the opening.

prostyle Having a columnar portico in front, but not on the sides and rear.

provincialism, provincial Term applied to work in an isolated area (such as a province of a cosmopolitan center or a colony of a mother country), where traditional practices persist, with some awareness of what is being done in the cosmopolitan center or the homeland.

purlin In roof construction, a structural member laid across the principal rafters and parallel to the wall plate and the ridge beam. The light common rafters to which the roofing surface is attached are fastened across the purlins. See also the related term *rafter*.

pylon 1 Originally, the gateway facade of an Egyptian temple complex, consisting of a truncated broad pyramidal form with battered (inclined) wall surfaces on all four sides, or two truncated pyramidal towers flanking an entrance portal. 2 Any towerlike structure from which bridge cables or utility lines are suspended.

quadripartite vault A vault divided into four triangular sections by a pair of diagonal ribs. Sometimes called a four-part vault.

quarry-faced See *rock-faced*.

quatrefoil A type of Gothic tracery having four parts (lobes or foils) separated by pointed elements (cusps).

Queen Anne 1 In architecture, the Queen Anne Style is an eclectic style of the 1860s through 1910s in England and the United States, characterized by the incorporation of forms from postmedieval vernacular architecture and the architecture of the Georgian period. Sometimes called Queen Anne Revival. See also the more specific term *Shingle Style* and the related terms *Eastlake, Stick Style*. 2 In architecture, the original Queen Anne period extends from the late seventeenth into the early eighteenth century. 3 In the decorative arts, the Queen Anne Style and period properly refer to work of the early eighteenth century during the reign of Queen Anne (1702–1714), i.e., after William and Mary and before Georgian). **4** In the decorative arts, eclectic work of the 1860s to 1880s is properly referred to as Queen Anne Revival. See also the related term *Aesthetic movement.*

quoin One of the bricks or stones laid in alternating directions, which bond and form the exterior corner of a building. Sometimes simulated in wood or stucco.

rafter One of the inclined structural members of a roof. Principal rafters are primary supporting elements spanning between the walls and the apex of the roof and carrying the longitudinal purlins. Common rafters are secondary supporting elements fastened onto purlins to carry the roof surfacing. See also the related term *purlin.*

raking cornice A cornice that finishes the sloping edges of a gable roof, such as the inclined sides of a triangular pediment.

random ashlar A type of masonry in which squared and dressed blocks are laid in a random pattern rather than in straight horizontal courses.

recessed column A fully round column set into a nichelike space only slightly larger than the column. Distinguished from an engaged column, which appears to be built into the wall.

reentrant angle An acute angle created by the juncture of two planes, such as walls.

refectory A dining hall, especially in medieval architecture.

regionalism 1 The sum of cultural characteristics (including material culture, language) that define a geographic region, usually extending beyond a single state or province and coinciding with one or more large physiographic areas. **2** The conscious use, within a region, of forms and materials identified with that region, creating an architecture that is in keeping with the historical architecture of the region, and even a distinctive new regional style.

register A horizontal zone of a wall, altarpiece, or other vertical feature. Usually synonymous with story, but more inclusive, allowing for the description of zones with no corresponding interior spaces.

relieving arch An arch, usually of masonry, built over the lintel of an opening to carry the load of the wall above and relieve the lintel of carrying such load. Sometimes called a discharging arch or safety arch.

Renaissance The period in European civilization identified with a rediscovery or rebirth (*rinascimento*) of classical Roman (and to a lesser extent, Greek) learning, art, and architecture. Renaissance architecture began in Italy in the mid–1400s (Early Renaissance) and reached a peak in the early to mid–1500s (High Renais-

sance). In England, Renaissance architecture did not begin until the late 1500s or early 1600s. The Renaissance in art and architecture was preceded by the Gothic and followed by the Baroque.

Renaissance Revival 1 In architecture, an ambiguous term, applied to *(a)* Italianate work of the 1840s through 1880s and *(b)* Beaux-Arts classical work of the 1880s through 1920s. **2** In the decorative arts, an eclectic furniture style incorporating a variety of Renaissance, Baroque, and Néo-Grec architectural motifs and utilizing wood marquetry, incised lines (often gilded), and ormolu and porcelain ornaments. Sometimes called Neo-Renaissance.

rendering Any drawing, whether orthographic (plan, elevation, section) or pictorial (perspective), in which shades and shadows are represented.

reredos A screen or wall at the back of an altar, usually with architectural and figural decoration.

return The continuation of a molding, cornice, or other projecting member, in a different direction, as in the horizontal cornice returns at the base of the raking cornices of a triangular pediment.

reveal 1 The portion of wall thickness between a door or window frame and the outer face of the wall. **2** Same as jamb, but only in an opening without a door or window.

revival, revivalism A type of historicism prevalent since the eighteenth century, involving the adaptation of historical forms to contemporary functions. Distinguished from a more pervasive historicism by an ideological conviction that sought to rationalize the choice of a historical style according to the values of the historical period that produced it. (The Gothic Revival, for instance, was associated with the Christianity of the Middle Ages.) Revival works, therefore, tend to invoke a single historical style. More hybrid works are manifestations of a less dogmatic historicism or eclecticism. See also the more general terms *historicism, eclecticism.*

rib The projecting linear element that separates the curved planar cells (or webs) of vaulting. Originally these were the supporting members for the vaulting, but they may also be purely decorative.

Richardsonian Term applied to any work showing the influence of the American architect Henry Hobson Richardson (1838–1886). See the note under the more limiting term *Richardsonian Romanesque.*

Richardsonian Romanesque Term applied to Neo-Romanesque work showing the influence of the American architect Henry Hobson Richardson (1838–1886). While many of Richardson's works make eclectic use of round arches and Romanesque details, many of his works show a creative eclecticism that transcends any particular historical style. The term Richardsonian, therefore, is a more inclusive term for the work of his followers than Richardsonian Romanesque—a term that continues to be widely used. Sometimes called Richardson Romanesque, Richardsonian Romanesque Revival.

ridgepole The horizontal beam or board at the apex of a roof, to which the upper ends of the rafters are fastened. Sometimes called a ridge beam, ridgeboard, ridge piece.

rinceau An ornamental device consisting of a sinuous and branching scroll elaborated with leaves and other natural forms.

rock-faced Term applied to the rough, unfinished face of a stone used in building. Sometimes called quarry-faced.

Rococo. A late phase of the Baroque, marked by elegant reverse-curve ornament, light scale, and delicate color. See also the related term *Baroque.*

Romanesque A medieval architectural style which reached its height in the eleventh and twelfth centuries. It is characterized by round arched construction and massive masonry walls. The Romanesque was preceded by the Early Christian and Byzantine periods in the eastern Mediterranean world and by a variety of localized styles and periods in northern and western Europe; it was followed throughout Europe by the Gothic.

Romanesque Revival Term applied to (1) Rundbogenstil and Round Arch work in the United States as early as the 1840s and (2) Richardsonian Romanesque work into the 1890s. Sometimes called Neo-Romanesque.

Roman Revival A term, not widely accepted, for a version of Neoclassicism involving the use of forms from the visual arts of the Imperial Roman period. Applied to various works in Italy, England, and the United States, where it is most clearly visible in the architecture of Thomas Jefferson. See also the related terms *Federal, Jeffersonian, Neoclassicism.*

rood screen An ornamental screen that serves as a partition between the crossing and the chancel or choir of a church.

rosette A circular floral ornament similar to an open rose.

rotunda **1** A circular hall in a large building, especially an area beneath a dome or cupola. **2** A building round both inside and outside, usually domed.

Round Arch mode The American counterpart of the German Rundbogenstil, characterized by the predominance of round arches, whether these are accentuated by Romanesque or Renaissance detailing or left as simple unadorned openings. See also the related terms *Italianate, Lombard, Rundbogenstil.*

roundel. A circular panel or plaque. Distinguished from a patera, which is oval shaped.

rubble masonry A type of masonry utilizing uncut or roughly shaped stone, such as fieldstone or boulders.

Rundbogenstil Literally, "round arch style," a historicist style originating in Germany in the 1820s and spreading to Britain and the United States from the 1840s through the 1860s. It is characterized by an eclectic combination of Romanesque and Renaissance elements. See also the related term *Round Arch mode.*

running bond A pattern of brickwork in which only stretchers appear, with the vertical joints of one course falling halfway between the vertical joints of adjacent courses. Sometimes called stretcher bond. Distinguished from common bond, in which every fifth or sixth course consists of all headers.

Ruskin Gothic, Ruskinian Gothic. See *High Victorian Gothic.*

rustication, rusticated Masonry in which the joints are emphasized by narrow recessed channels or grooves outlining each block. Sometimes simulated in wood or stucco.

sacristy A room in a church where liturgical vessels and vestments are kept.

safety arch See *relieving arch.*

sanctuary **1** The part of a church that contains the principal altar. Usually the innermost space within the chancel arm of the church, situated to the east of the choir. **2** Loosely used to mean a place of worship, a sacred place.

sash Any framework of a window. It may be movable or fixed. It may slide in a vertical plane (as in a double-hung window) or may be pivoted (as in a casement window).

sash bar See *muntin.*

Secession movement The refined classicist Austrian (Viennese) version of the Art Nouveau style, so named because the artists and architects involved seceded from the official Academy in 1897. Josef Hoffmann (1870–1956) is the architect most frequently mentioned in association with this movement.

Second Chicago School A term sometimes applied to the International Style in Chicago from the 1940s to the 1970s, particularly the work of Mies van der Rohe. See also the related terms *International Style, Miesian.*

Second Empire Not strictly a style term but a term for a period in French history coinciding with the rule of Napoleon III (1852–1870). Generally applied in the United States, however, to a phase of Beaux-Arts governmental and institutional architecture (1850–1880s) as well as to countless hybrids of Beaux-Arts and Italianate forms in residential, commercial, and industrial architecture (1850–1880s). Sometimes called General Grant Style, Mansard Style, Mansardic. See also the related terms *Beaux-Arts, Italianate* (definition 1).

section A drawing (in orthographic projection) representing a vertical cut through an object, building, or space. An architectural section shows interior relationships of space and structure and may also include mechanical systems. Sometimes called a cross section.

segmental arch An arch formed on a segmental curve. Its center lies below the springing line.

segmental curve A curve that is a segment (i.e., less than half the circumference) of a circle or an ellipse. The baseline of the curve is a chord measuring less than the diameter of the larger circle from which the segment is taken.

segmental pediment A pediment whose top is a segmental curve.

segmental vault A vault whose cross section is a segmental curve. A dome built on segmental curves is called a saucer dome.

setback 1 In architecture, particularly in the design of tall buildings, a series of upper stories that are stepped back to allow more sunlight to reach the streets. 2 In planning, the amount of space between the lot line and the perimeter of a building.

shaft The tall part of a column between the base and the capital.

shed roof A roof having only one sloping plane. Sometimes called a lean-to roof.

Shingle Style A term applied primarily to American domestic architecture of the 1870s through the 1890s, in which broad expanses of wood shingles dominate the exterior roof and wall planes. Rooms open widely into one another and to the outdoors, and the ample living hall or stair hall is often the dominant feature of the interior. The term was coined in the 1940s by Vincent Scully for a series of seaside and suburban houses of the northeastern United States. The Shingle Style is a version of the Anglo-American Queen Anne Style. See also the related terms *Colonial Revival, Stick Style.*

shouldered architrave See *ear.*

side gabled Term applied to a building whose gable ends face the sides of a lot. Distinguished from front gabled.

side light A framed area of fixed glass alongside a door or window. See also the related term *fanlight.*

sill course In masonry, a stringcourse set at windowsill level, usually differentiated from the wall by its greater projection, its finish, or its thickness. Not applicable to frame construction.

sill plate See *plate* (definition 2).

skeleton construction, skeleton frame A system of construction in which all loads are carried to the ground through a rigid framework of iron, steel, or reinforced concrete. The exterior walls are curtain walls (i.e., not load-bearing).

skylight A window in a roof, specifically one that is flush with the roof plane or only slightly protruding. Distinguished from a cupola (definition 2), which is a major centralized feature at the summit of a roof. Distinguished from a monitor, which is an extensive roof feature containing a band of windows or vents.

soffit The exposed underside of any overhead component, such as an arch, beam, cornice, or lintel. See also the related term *intrados.*

sole plate See *plate* (definition 2).

space frame A series of trusses placed side by side and joined to one another by triangulated rods, tubes, or beams, so that the individual planar trusses are united into a three-dimensional structural framework. Often used in roof structures requiring long spans.

spandrel 1 The quasi-triangular space between two adjoining arches and a line connecting their crowns, or between an arch and the columns and entablature that frame it. 2 In skeletal construction, the wall area between the top of a window and the sill of the window in the story above. Sometimes called a spandrel panel.

Spanish colonial A term applied to buildings, towns, landscapes, and other artifacts from the various periods of actual Spanish colonial occupation in North America (c. 1565–1821 in Florida; c. 1763–1800 in Louisiana and the Lower Mississippi valley; c. 1590–1821 in Texas and the southwestern United States; c. 1769–1821 in California). The term is extended to apply to the artifacts of Hispanic ethnic groups (e.g., Mexicans, Puerto Ricans, Cubans) and their descendants, even into the early twentieth century. See also the related terms *Churrigueresque, Plateresque.*

Spanish Colonial Revival The revival of forms from Spanish colonial and provincial Mexican design. The Spanish Colonial Revival began in Florida and California in the 1880s and continues nationwide into the present. Sometimes called Neo-Hispanic, Spanish Eclectic, Spanish Revival. See also the more specific term *Mission Revival* and the related term *Mediterranean Revival.*

spindle A turned wooden element, thicker toward the middle and thinner at either end, found in arch screens, porch trim, and other ornamental assemblages. Banisters (i.e., thin, simple balusters) may be spindle-shaped, but the term spindle, when used alone, usually connotes shorter elements.

spire A slender pointed element surmounting a building. A tall, attenuated pyramidal form with any number of thin triangular faces that are unbroken or articulated only with crockets, pinnacles, or small dormers. Distinguished from a steeple, which is divided into stages and which may be topped with a spire.

splay The slanting surface formed by cutting off a right-angle corner at an oblique angle to one face. A reveal at an oblique angle to the exterior face of the wall.

springing, springing line, springing point The line or point where an arch or vault rises from its supports and begins to curve. Usually the juncture between the impost of the support below and the springer, or first voussoir, of the arch above.

squinch An arch, lintel, or corbeling, built across the interior corner of two walls to form one side of an octagonal base for a dome. This octagonal base serves as the structural transition from a square interior crossing space to an octagonal or round dome.

stair A series of steps, or flights of steps connected by landings, which connects two or more levels or floors.

staircase The ensemble of a stair and its enclosing walls. Sometimes called a stairway.

stair tower A projecting tower or other building block that contains a stair.

stamped metal See *pressed metal.*

Steamboat Gothic See *Carpenter's Gothic.*

steeple 1 A tall structure rising from a tower, consisting of a series of superimposed stages diminishing in plan, and usually topped by a spire or small cupola. Distinguished from a spire, which is not divided into stages. 2 Less commonly used to mean the whole of the tower, from the ground to the top of the spire or cupola.

stepped gable A gable in which the wall rises in a series of steps above the planes of the roof.

stereotomy The science of cutting three-dimensional shapes from stone, such as the units that make up a carefully fitted masonry vault.

Stick Style A term applied primarily to American domestic architecture of the 1850s through the 1870s, in which exterior wall planes are subdivided into bays and stories outlined by narrow boards called "stickwork." The term was coined by Vincent Scully in the 1940s for a series of houses with clearly articulated wall panels and sticklike porch supports and eaves brackets. Sources include the English and German picturesque traditions, as well as the French rationalist tradition. See also the related terms *Queen Anne, Shingle Style.*

story (plural: stories). The space in a building between floor levels. British spelling is storey, storeys. Sometimes called a register, a more inclusive term applied to horizontal zones on a vertical plane that do not correspond to actual floor levels.

Streamline Moderne A later phase of the Moderne, popular in the 1930s and 1940s and characterized by stucco surfaces with rounded corners, by horizontal banding, overhangs, and window groupings, and by other details suggestive of modern Machine Age aerodynamic forms. Sometimes called Streamline Modern, Streamline Modernistic. See also the more general term *Moderne* and the related terms *Art Deco* and *PWA Moderne.*

stretcher A brick laid the length of a wall, so that the long side of the brick shows on the exterior.

stretcher bond See *running bond.*

string In a stair, an inclined board that supports the ends of the steps. Sometimes called a stringer.

stringcourse In masonry, a horizontal band, generally narrower than other courses, extending across the facade of a building and in some instances encircling such features as pillars or columns. It may be flush or projecting; of identical or contrasting material; flat, molded, or richly carved. Not applicable to frame construction. Sometimes called a band course or belt course. More elaborate horizontal bands in masonry or frame construction are generally called band moldings.

strut A column, post, or pole that is set in a diagonal position and thus serves as a stiffener by triangulation. Distinguished from a brace, which is usually a shorter bracketlike member.

stucco 1 An exterior plaster finish, usually textured, composed of portland cement, lime, and sand, which are mixed with water. 2 A fine plaster used for decorative work or moldings. See also the more specific term *pargeting.*

stud One of the vertical supporting elements in a wall, especially in balloon- and platform frame construction. Studs are relatively lightweight members (usually two-by-fours).

Sullivanesque Term applied to work showing the influence of the American architect Louis Henry Sullivan (1856–1924).

sunburst light See *fanlight.*

supercapital See *impost block.*

supercolumniation See *superposition* (definition 1).

superimposition, superimposed See *superposition.*

superposition, superposed 1 The use of an ensemble of the classical orders, one above the other, as the major elements articulating a facade. When this is done, the Doric, considered the simplest order, is used on or near the ground story. The Ionic, considered more complex, comes next; and the Corinthian, considered the most complex, is used at the top. Sometimes the Tuscan order or rusticated masonry may be used for the ground story beneath the Doric order, and the Composite order may be used above the Corinthian order. Sometimes called supercolumniation, superimposition. See also the related term *order.* 2 Less commonly, any vertical relationship of architectural elements (e.g., windows, piers, colonnettes) in any style or period.

superstructure A structure raised upon another structure, as a building upon a foundation, basement, or substructure.

Supervising Architect The Supervising Architect of the United States Treasury Department, whose office was responsible for the design and construction of all major federal government buildings (such as courthouses, customhouses, and post offices) from the 1850s through the 1930s. The Office of the Supervising Architect was formally established by Congress in 1864 and lasted until 1939, when its functions were absorbed into the Public Buildings Administration (and in 1949, into the General Services Administration).

supporting wall See *bearing wall.*

surround An encircling border or decorative frame around a door or window. Distinguished from architrave (definition 2), a term usually applied to the frame around an opening when considered as a series of relatively flat face moldings.

suspended ceiling A ceiling suspended from rod-like hangers below the level of the floor above. The interval between the floor slab above and the suspended ceiling often serves as a space for ducts, utilities, and air circulation. Sometimes called a hung ceiling.

swag A motif representing a suspended fold of drapery hanging in a catenary curve from two points. Distinguished from a festoon, which is a motif representing entwined leaves, flowers, or fruits, hung in a similar curve. See also the more general term *garland.*

tabernacle 1 A niche or recess, usually on an interior wall, framed by columns or pilasters and topped by an entablature and pediment. Distinguished from an aedicule, which more often occurs on an exterior wall. See also the related term *niche.* 2 In the Jewish religion, a portable sanctuary. 3 In Protestant denominations, a large auditorium church.

terra cotta A hard ceramic material used for (1) fireproofing, especially as a fitted cladding around metal skeletal construction; or (2) an exterior or interior wall cladding, which is often glazed and multicolored.

tertiary rib See *lierne.*

thermal window A large lunette window similar to those found in ancient Roman baths (*thermae*). The window is subdivided into three to five parts by vertical mullions. Sometimes called a *thermae* window.

three-hinged arch An arch in two major segments anchored with cylindrical "hinge" pins at either end and at the crown. Movement within the arch, caused by temperature changes, the torsion of wind movements, or other forces, can be absorbed by the movement of the arch around the pins, thereby avoiding stresses that would occur in the structural frame if the arches were fixed.

tie beam A horizontal tension member that ties together the opposing angular members of a truss and prevents them from spreading.

tier A group of stories or any zone of architectural elements arranged horizontally.

tierceron In a Gothic vault, a secondary rib that rises from the springing to an intermediate position on either side of the diagonal ribs. Sometimes called an intermediate rib.

tie rod A metal rod that spans the distance between two structural members and, by its tensile strength, restrains them against tendencies to collapse outward.

timber-frame construction, timber framing A type of wood-frame construction in which heavy timber posts and beams (six-by-sixes and larger) are fastened using mortise and tenon joints. Sometimes called heavy timber construction. Distinguished from light frame construction, in which relatively light structural members (two-by-fours to two-by-tens) are fastened with nails.

trabeation, trabeated construction. See *post-and-beam construction.*

tracery Decoration within an arch or other opening, made up of narrow curvilinear bands or more elaborately molded strips. In Gothic architecture, the curved interlocking stone bars that contain the leaded stained glass.

transept The lateral arm of a cross-shaped church, usually between the nave (the area for the congregation) and the chancel (the area for the altar, clergy, and choir).

transom 1 A narrow horizontal window unit, either fixed or movable, over a door. Sometimes called a transom light. See also the more specific term *fanlight.* 2 A horizontal bar, as distinguished from a vertical mullion, especially one crossing a door or window opening near the top.

transverse rib In a Gothic vault, a rib at right angles to the ridge rib.

trefoil A type of Gothic tracery having three parts (lobes or foils) separated by pointed elements (cusps).

trellis Any open latticework made of strips of wood or metal crossing one another, usually supporting climbing plants. Distinguished from an arbor, which is generally a more substantial yet compact three-dimensional structure, and from a pergola, which is a more extensive colonnaded structure.

triforium In a Gothic church, an arcade in the wall above the arches of the nave, choir, or transept and below the clerestory window.

triglyph One of the slightly raised blocks in a Doric frieze. It consists of three narrow vertical bands separated by two V-shaped grooves.

triumphal arch 1 A freestanding arch erected for a victory procession. It usually consists of a broad central arched opening, flanked by two smaller bays (usually with open or blind arches). The bays are usually articulated by classical columns supporting an entablature and a high attic. 2 A similar configuration applied to a facade to denote a monumental entryway.

truss A rigid triangular framework made up of beams, posts, braces, struts, and ties and used for the spanning of large spaces. The major horizontal or inclined members are called chords. The connecting vertical and diagonal elements are called the web members.

Tudor arch A low-profile arch characterized by two pairs of arcs, one pair of tight arcs at the springing, another pair of broad (nearly flat) arcs at the apex or crown.

Tudor period A term for a period in English history coinciding with the rule of monarchs of the house of Tudor (1485–1603). Tudor period architecture is Late Gothic, with only hints of the Renaissance. See also the more specific term *Elizabethan period* for the end of this period, and the related term *Jacobean period* for the succeeding period.

Tudor Revival See *Neo-Tudor*.

turret A small towerlike structure, often circular in plan, built against the side or at an exterior or interior corner of a building.

Tuscan order An ensemble of classical column and entablature elements, similar to the Roman Doric order, but without triglyphs in the frieze and without mutules (domino-like blocks) in the cornice of the entablature. See also the more general term *order*.

tympanum (plural: tympana) **1** The triangular or segmental area enclosed by the cornice moldings of a pediment, frequently ornamented with sculpture. **2** Any space similarly delineated or bounded, as between the lintel of a door or window and the arch above.

umbrage A term used by Alexander Jackson Davis (1803–1892) as a synonym for veranda, the implication being a shadowed area.

vault An arched roof or ceiling, usually constructed in brick or stone, but also in tile, metal, or concrete. A nonstructural plaster ceiling that simulates a masonry vault.

Venetian Gothic See *High Victorian Gothic*.

veranda A nineteenth-century term for porch. Sometimes spelled verandah.

vergeboard See *bargeboard*.

verges The sloping edges of a gable, gambrel, or lean-to roof, usually projecting beyond the wall below. Distinguished from eaves, which are the horizontal lower edges of a roof plane.

vernacular Not a style in itself, but a descriptive term, applicable primarily to architecture, covering the vast range of ordinary buildings that are produced outside the high-style tradition of well-known architects. The vernacular tradition includes the folk tradition of regional and ethnic buildings whose forms (plan and massing) remain relatively constant through the years, in spite of stylistic embellishments. The term vernacular architecture is often used as if it meant only folk architecture. However, the vernacular tradition in architecture also includes the popular tradition of buildings whose design was influenced by such publications as books of the orders, builders' guides, style books, pattern books, mail-order catalogs, architectural periodicals, and household magazines. Usually contrasted with high-style. See also the more specific terms *folk, popular*.

vertical plank construction A system of wood construction in which vertical planks are set or nailed into heavy timber horizontal sills and plates. A building so constructed has no corner posts and no studs. Two-story vertical plank buildings have planks extending the full height of the building, with no girt between the two stories. Second-floor joists are merely mortised into the planks. Distinguished from the more specific term vertical plank frame construction, in which there are corner posts.

vertical plank frame construction A type of vertical plank construction, in which heavy timber corner posts are introduced to provide support for the plate, to which the tops of the planks are fastened. See also the related term *horizontal plank frame construction*.

vestibule A small entry hall between the outer door and the main hallway of a building.

Victorian Gothic See *High Victorian Gothic*.

Victorian period A term for a period in British, British colonial, and Anglo-American history, and not, in architecture or the other visual arts, a sufficiently specific style term. The Victorian period extended across eight decades, from the coronation of Queen Victoria in 1837 to her death in 1901. See instead *Eastlake, Gothic Revival, Greek Revival, Queen Anne, Shingle Style, Stick Style*, and other specific style terms.

Victorian Romanesque See *Richardsonian Romanesque, Romanesque Revival, Round Arch mode*.

villa. 1 In the Roman and Renaissance periods, a suburban or rural residential complex, often quite elaborate, consisting of a house, dependencies, and gardens. **2** Since the eighteenth century, any detached suburban or rural house of picturesque character and some pretension. Distinguished from the more modest house form known as a cottage.

volute 1 A spiral scroll, especially the one that is a distinctive feature of the Ionic capital. **2** A large scroll-shaped buttress on a facade or dome.

voussoir A wedge-shaped stone or brick used in the construction of an arch. Its tapering sides coincide with radii of the arch.

wainscot A decorative or protective facing, usually of wood paneling, applied to the lower portion of an interior partition or wall. Distinguished from a dado, which is the zone at the base of a wall, regardless of the material used to cover it. Wainscot properly connotes woodwork. Sometimes called wainscoting.

water table 1 In masonry, a course of molded bricks or stones set forward several inches near the base of a wall and serving as the cap of the basement courses. **2** In frame construction, a ledge or projecting molding just above the foundation to protect it from rainwater. **3** In masonry or frame construction, any horizontal exterior ledge on a wall, pier, or buttress. Often sloped and provided with a drip molding to prevent water from running down the face of the wall below.

weatherboard See *clapboard*.

weathering The inclination given to the upper surface of any element so that it will shed water.

web 1 The relatively thin shell of masonry between the ribs of a ribbed vault. **2** The portion of a truss between the chords, or the portion of a girder or I-beam between the flanges.

western frame, western framing See *platform frame construction.*

winder A step, more or less wedge-shaped, with its tread wider at one end than the other.

window bar See *muntin.*

window cap See *cap.*

window head A head molding or pedimented feature over a window.

Wrightian Term applied to work showing the influence of the American architect Frank Lloyd Wright (1867–1959). See also the related term *Prairie School.*

wrought iron Iron shaped by a hammering process to improve the tensile properties of the metal. Distinguished from cast iron, a brittle material, which is formed in molds.

Zigzag Moderne, Zigzag Modernistic See *Art Deco.*

Illustration Credits

INTRODUCTION

Page 4, *Richmond Times-Dispatch*, photograph Special Collections Department, University of Virginia Library; **p. 9,** LVA; **p. 11,** VMFA; **p. 12,** Maryland Historical Society (bottom); **p. 14,** Colonial Williamsburg Foundation; **p. 16,** Special Collections Department, University of Virginia Library; **p. 21,** LVA; **p. 22,** Maryland Historical Society; **p. 24,** Thomas Jefferson Memorial Foundation (© 1993 Robert C. Lautman/Monticello); **pp. 27, 28, 30** Valentine Museum, Richmond; **p. 32,** Special Collections Department, Manuscripts Division, Cocke Papers, University of Virginia Library (top); Mount Vernon Ladies Association (bottom); **p. 34,** Library of Congress; **p. 39,** George Mason University Libraries

NORTHERN VIRGINIA

NV1 VDHR; NV3.1 Bill Sublette; NV6, NV8, NV12 Bill Sublette; NV14.2 VMFA; NV14.3, NV14.4, NV14.6 Bill Sublette; NV15, NV17 VDHR; NV18.1, NV18.2 Bill Sublette; NV19 VDHR; NV23 Bill Sublette; NV27 VDHR; NV30, NV33, NV35 Bill Sublette; NV37, NV38, NV40.1, NV40.10, NV40.16 VDHR; NV41 Bill Sublette; NV42.1 VDHR; NV46 Bill Sublette; NV47 HABS; NV51 VDHR; NV53 HABS (photos by Jack Boucher); NV55 Bill Sublette

ALEXANDRIA

AL1, AL2 VDHR; AL6, AL12 HABS AL19, AL22 VDHR; AL26 LVA; AL29 VDHR; AL36, AL38 VDHR; AL41, AL49 VDHR; AL50 LVA; AL51 Bill Sublette; AL54 VDHR

NORTHERN PIEDMONT

All VDHR

PIEDMONT

All VDHR except the following: PI10.1 VDHR; PI15 LVA; PI23 APVA (photo by Katherine Stetson); PI33.1, PI40 Special Collections Department, University of Virginia Library; PI43 VMFA

CHARLOTTESVILLE METROPOLITAN AREA

CH2, CH4, VDHR; CH14, p. 148 (unnumbered), Bill Sublette; CH26 VDHR; CH28, CH28.1, Bill Sublette; CH28.2 Special Collections Department, University of Virginia Library; CH28.9 VDHR; CH28.14, CH29.18 Hartman-Cox Architects; CH29.4, CH31.1 VDHR; CH32.5 Bill Sublette; CH37 VDHR; CH38 VMFA; CH44 Special Collections Department, University of Virginia Library (photo by Atcheson L. Hench)

RICHMOND METROPOLITAN AREA

RI1 HABS (photo by Jack Boucher); RI2 VMFA; RI5 VDHR; RI6 Pierre Courtois; RI10 VDHR; RI13 VMFA; RI17, RI20 VDHR; RI21 VMFA; RI22 VDHR; RI23 VMFA; RI27 VDHR; RI28 Pierre Courtois; RI30 LVA; RI31 VDHR; RI34, RI39, RI43, RI49 Pierre Courtois; RI64 LVA; RI66 VDHR; RI69 Pierre Courtois; RI77 VDHR; RI80 Pierre Courtois; RI88 VDHR; RI93 Pierre Courtois; RI96, RI106 VDHR; RI108 Pierre Courtois; RI109 VDHR; RI111 Pierre Courtois; RI122, RI124, RI128, RI129 VDHR; RI132 Pierre Courtois; RI135, RI136 VDHR; RI143 Valentine Museum, Richmond; RI144, RI150, RI152, RI153, RI158, RI160 VDHR; RI163 HABS (photo by Jack Boucher); RI173 Pierre Courtois; RI177, RI178, RI181, RI182, RI185, RI189, RI190, RI194 VDHR; RI207 VMFA; RI212, RI213, RI225, RI227, RI228, RI235, RI245 VDHR; RI246 Pierre Courtois; RI251 VDHR (photo), VMFA (drawing); RI252 LVA; RI256 Pierre Courtois; RI257, RI260, RI262, RI266, RI279 VDHR; RI286 Pierre Courtois; RI291 VDHR; RI296 HABS (photo by Jack Boucher); RI297.1 Valentine Museum, Richmond; RI297.2 VDHR; RI300, RI301.1 HABS (photos by Jack Boucher); RI302.1 LVA; RI304, RI307, RI308 VDHR; RI315 Pierre Courtois; RI317 Maymont Foundation (photo by Jay Paul); RI320, RI323, RI325, RI330 VDHR; RI336.5, RI335.7 Pierre Courtois; RI336.8 VMFA; RI336.9 Virginia Historical Society; RI338 HABS; RI339.3, RI339.8, RI340 Pierre Coutois; RI342, RI347.1 VDHR; RI352 Pierre Courtois; RI353.1 VDHR; University Library; RI355 VMFA;

RI356.2, RI356.3 Pierre Courtois; **RI361** Reynolds Metals Company; **RI362, RI371** VDHR; **RI373** VMFA; **RI374, RI375, RI382** Pierre Courtois; **RI384** VDHR; **RI386, RI399** Pierre Courtois; **RI390, RI393** VDHR; **RI394** Pierre Courtois

FREDERICKSBURG METROPOLITAN AREA

FR1, FR4 VDHR; **FR5** Pierre Courtois; **FR6, FR14** VDHR; **FR26, FR29** Pierre Courtois; **FR33** APVA; **FR39, FR44, FR45, FR46** Pierre Courtois; **FR47** VDHR; **FR62** Pierre Courtois; **FR69.1** Pierre Courtois; **FR69.5** VDHR; **FR69.11, FR69.17, FR71.1** Pierre Courtois; **FR78** VDHR; **FR79.1, FR79.2, FR81** VDHR

THE PENINSULAS

All VDHR except the following: **PE1** HABS (drawing by Albert P. Erb); **PE9** HABS (photo by Jack Boucher); **PE39** APVA; **PE65** HABS (photo by Ronald Jennings)

HAMPTON ROADS

HR1-HR38 Colonial Williamsburg Foundation; **HR40** VMFA (photo); Cary Carson (drawing); **HR43** Colonial Williamsburg Foundation (all); **HR45.7** LVA; **HR45.9** VMFA; **HR47** VDHR; **HR50.3** Jason R. Waicunas; **HR50.5** VDHR; **HR51, HR53** Jason R. Waicunas; **HR55.1, HR55.4** VDHR; **HR56.1, HR56.9** Jason R. Waicunas; **HR57** VDHR

NORFOLK

NK1 Jason R. Waicunas; **NK9** VDHR; **NK11** Jason R. Waicunas; **NK13** VDHR; **NK18** Jason R. Waicunas; **NK19, NK26** VDHR; **NK27, NK28.1, NK32** Jason R. Waicunas; **NK34** HABS (photo by Charles Ansell); **NK36** Jason R. Waicunas; **NK37, NK41** VDHR; **NK41** VDHR (exterior), Jason R. Waicunas (interior); **NK42, NK43** VDHR; **NK44** Jason R. Waicunas; **NK45, NK48** VDHR; **NK55, NK63, NK65, NK66** Jason R. Waicunas; **NK72** VMFA; **NK73** VDHR; **NK74, NK83** Jason R. Waicunas; **NK91** VDHR; **NK92.1, NK93.1** Jason R. Waicunas; **NK94** VDHR

PORTSMOUTH

All by Jason R. Waicunas except the following: **PO3, PO9, PO11** VDHR

VIRGINIA BEACH

VB4, VB5 VMFA; **VB8, VB9** Jason R. Waicunas; **VB11** VDHR; **VB13** Jason R. Waicunas

SOUTHERN TIDEWATER

ST1.1, ST2 Jason R. Waicunas; **ST7.2, ST7.9, ST7.17, ST9.1, ST9.2, ST10,** VDHR; **ST12.3** Jason R. Waicunas; **ST14, ST15,** VDHR; **ST16** HABS; **ST17.1** APVA (both); **ST17.6** VDHR; **ST18,** APVA; **ST22, ST23** VDHR; **ST25** HABS; **ST26.1** VDHR; **ST27.2** Jason R. Waicunas; **ST29** VDHR; **ST30** Jason R. Waicunas (both)

EASTERN SHORE

All VDHR except the following: **ES1** APVA (photo, left, by Virginia Stetson); **ES9.1** LVA

Index

Page numbers in **boldface** refer to illustrations.